The Dev

"Dennis Wheatley's novels were enor~~mo~~...
difficult to see why. He provided clear conflicts of Goo~~d~~ ...
had a talent for nailing archetypes, coupled with a simple determinati~~on~~
to entertain . . . Wheatley is almost forgotten today . . . and one might
wonder if there is a case for 609 pages about him. In fact Phil Baker,
critically sifting the evidence and placing Wheatley with perfect accuracy
in the English class system, makes his case admirably. He provides us with
a good story, well told, and plenty of jokes. Wheatley would have been
delighted."   S.E.G. Hopkin in *The Spectator*

"It is lively and full of period evocation. Baker takes an amused,
pin-pricking but affectionate stance towards his subject."
                                                     Peter Lewis in *The Daily Mail*

"Phil Baker's *The Devil Is a Gentleman* recounts the extraordinary life of
Britain's most prolific occultist, Dennis Wheatley."
                        Rowan Pelling in Books of the Year in *The Daily Telegraph*

"A fantastically entertaining biography of one of the most popular
writers of the twentieth-century whose work is still part of the public
imagination."   James Doyle in *Book Munch*

"Wheatley, unusual, overripe and positively fruity by the end, cries out
for contextualization. This is provided by an elegant and skilful writer,
possessed of an excellent wit which he uses sparingly and only ever to
precise effect. Highly sensitive to period, Baker deals with areas such as
appeasement and anti-Semitism (not a Wheatley failing) with much
more intelligence than is usually encountered."
                        H.E. Taylor in *The Anthony Powell Society Newsletter*

"He, of all people, deserves to come back from the dead and win a new
following of thrill-starved souls in thrall to his dark magic."   *The Oldie*

"Wheatley took up writing when the family wine business failed, and his
mixture of sex, sadism, snobbery and Satanism proved irresistible to the
reading public."   Stephen Holden in *The Chap*

"Here is a masterful account of a writer's internal and external selves, revealing the degree to which any creative author's life must necessarily be a work of fiction. Baker as a biographer, frankly, is some kind of God-damned life-archaeologist, approaching the famed occult novelist as a real, seriocomic man who was far more than the sum of his parts. It is difficult to imagine a more sensitive and knowledgeable investigation. Black magic stories? That was the least of it: the reader is left far more astonished by the magic Wheatley wove around his own life, as revealed by Baker. Superb, concise, insightful and sublime."

Jay Rath in *The Fortean Times*

"Phil Baker . . . recounts some wonderfully funny moments. A plethora of witty asides, and a cast of nutters beyond anything Wheatley ever invented, add up to a very entertaining read."

Mick Herron in *The Bookdealer*

"Like Maugham, Greene and Le Carré, Wheatley's career was influenced by his intelligence contacts, as was that of another writer whose debt to him is nearly always overlooked. Ian Fleming stripped down Wheatley's model to three essentials identified by Cyril Connolly as the winning formula for the Bond series: sex, snobbery and sadism."

Chris Petit in *The Guardian*

"Phil Baker's knockout *The Devil Is A Gentleman* gives us the biography of Dennis Wheatley, war propagandist and author of Satanic novels read by millions but loathed by critics." Christopher Fowler

"The war was the high point of Wheatley's life; it's also the high point of Baker's biography." Robert Hanks in *The London Review of Books*

". . . it's lively, racy reading throughout. An enjoyable read, especially for those of us who remember all those occult novels as a guilty adolescent pleasure. As David Blundy of *The Observer* once wrote: 'Wheatley has been grappling with the Devil for over thirty years now, and frankly, the Devil's been pretty decent about it'."

David Langford in *Murky Depths*

Phil Baker

The Devil is a Gentleman

The Life and Times of Dennis Wheatley

Dedalus

Published in the UK by Dedalus Limited,
24–26, St Judith's Lane, Sawtry, Cambs, PE28 5XE
Email: info@dedalusbooks.com
www.dedalusbooks.com

ISBN   printed book 978 1 907650 32 1
ISBN   e-book 978 1 907650 50 5

Dedalus is distributed in the USA and Canada by SCB Distributors,
15608 South New Century Drive, Gardena, CA 90248
email: info@scbdistributors.com   web: www.scbdistributors.com

Dedalus is distributed in Australia by Peribo Pty Ltd.
58, Beaumont Road, Mount Kuring-gai N.S.W. 2080
email: info@peribo.com.au

Publishing History
First published by Dedalus in hardcover in 2009
First paperback edition 2011
First e-book edition 2011

Printed in Finland by Bookwell
Typeset by RefineCatch Limited, Bungay, Suffolk

Contents

*Wheatley's bookplate, showing Wheatley with Eric Gordon Tombe
as a satyr.*

For N.C.

INTRODUCTION

The Devil is a Gentleman

". . . the fruits of a good library, a well–stocked cellar,
rosy twilight on the skulls of stone demons."
– Iain Sinclair

Dennis Wheatley held twentieth–century Britain spellbound.
Loathed by the critics, his total sales nevertheless reached
around fifty million, spearheaded by his immensely popular
Black Magic titles. In the early Seventies his distinctive
paperbacks were everywhere, part of the zeitgeist. Wheatley
virtually invented the public image of Satanism, and he made
it seem strangely seductive. If the appeal of black magic in the
popular culture of the time was ultimately erotic, it was
largely due to Wheatley.

More than just salacious, his books were the absolute
incarnation of what has been nicely called "the luxury tradition of cheap fiction." His Duke de Richleau series presents
a world of pentagrams in country house libraries, a place
where rare tomes and old brandies meet the Prince of
Darkness. People who remember Wheatley still laugh with
nostalgic glee at the very mention of *Imperial Tokay* wine and
Hoyo de Monterrey cigars.

Like Sax Rohmer and John Buchan, Wheatley has moved
from being merely dated to positively vintage. He was criticised in the Thirties for being dangerously American, but
modern readers are more likely to be struck by the British-
ness of his books. When a criminal mastermind threatens to
send a young duchess down in a submarine with a time
bomb, another character blurts out "God man! You're English! You couldn't do it!" And when Simon Aron brings
trouble on his friends in *The Devil Rides Out*, despite Richard
Eaton's assurance that he doesn't blame anyone ("That's

decent of you, Richard," says the Duke de Richleau; "Damned decent," says Simon) Aron knows exactly what he has to do. The loyal band of chums find him gone in the morning, having slipped away before dawn to face the Satanists alone. It is one of the most decent exits since Captain Oates left the tent.

It has been said that to study Wheatley is to study British popular taste. More than that, it is to study the shadowier side of recent British history. Wheatley was as interested in politics as he was in magic, and he was close to the intelligence community and the secret establishment. This fed into his work, from his inside knowledge of MI5's investigation of Dartington Hall School (which inspired *The Haunting of Toby Jugg*) to his Fifties involvement in a British scheme to engineer a revival of Islam, writing a propaganda novel for the Arab market.

Even for the home audience, Wheatley's books are almost unparalleled in their calculated propaganda content, from his classic *The Devil Rides Out* (in its original 1934 context an early Appeasement novel, with a message of peace with Nazi Germany) to his late novel *Gateway to Hell*, with its fears of ethnic conflict and the Black Power movement in America. Between the two came a series of occult thrillers addressing the Communist menace, the need for Britain to have nuclear armaments, and even the spectre of Satanic Trade Unionism.

Wheatley was a frankly reactionary writer, appalled by the passing of time and the slippages of history. "The ideology which shows through is indescribably ripe," says one of his best commentators, Maurice Richardson: "Perhaps it appeals to some subterranean Edwardian current that still trickles through the minds of a wide range of age-groups." Wheatley saw existence as a Manichaean conflict between the forces of light and darkness, with the forces of darkness threatening to come out on top as the century staggered onwards. The identity that Wheatley carved out for himself as the smoking-jacketed connoisseur with his cellar and his library was inseparable from a strong dose of cultural pessimism, and a sense that living well is the best revenge.

Unlike many purveyors of luxury pulp fiction, Wheatley knew what he was talking about. He was originally a Mayfair wine merchant, and he wrote himself out of bankruptcy when his business was caught in the Depression. If the wine trade was one half of his education, the other half came from his involvement with a man named Eric Gordon Tombe, a fraudster and gentleman criminal whom Wheatley came to know in the First War when they were young officers together. Wheatley was fascinated by Tombe, who introduced him to paganism and decadence and led him to read widely, from Oscar Wilde to Lao Tzu. Tombe's disappearance in the Twenties was one of the most painful episodes of Wheatley's life, recorded blow by blow in an unpublished memoir.

Having begun to write, Wheatley never looked back, from being "Public Thriller Writer No.1" in the Thirties and "Prince of Thriller Writers" in the Forties to becoming Britain's occult uncle in the Sixties and Seventies. Together with Edgar Wallace and Agatha Christie, Wheatley towered over the century's popular fiction, with an output that included historical romances, highly innovative "Crime Dossiers," and even board games. His books also have far more love interest than those of most thriller writers, and a large female readership was one of the secrets of his success.

Wheatley was much loved but never quite respectable (even in 1994 a librarian in Montana lost her job for lending students a copy of *The Devil And All His Works*). Wickedness aside, critics hated him for his poor prose style: Wheatley "pads like a truss-stuffer" said one, while another described his prose as a "lumbering, stilted, cliché-infested" hybrid of "pompous bank manager" and "romantic lady novelist." For all his bad style, Wheatley was a writer who knew exactly what he was doing. His friend Anthony Powell asked his advice on plotting *A Dance to the Music of Time* (and there is a larger significance in the fact that a character based on Wheatley is the central figure of Powell's final novel, *The Fisher King*.)

"Sex, Jingoism and Black Magic" is how one commentator

sums up Wheatley's work. Although his black magic books were only a small part of his overall output, they are the part he is likely to be remembered for – often with a touch of affectionate bathos. Many occultists began with reading Dennis Wheatley, although they might not always admit it. Initiated into a black magical group in Robert Irwin's comic novel, *Satan Wants Me*, the young hero is lectured by the Master of the Lodge over his magical diary:

> . . . he went on about how my stuff resembled pulp fiction by the hands of someone like Dennis Wheatley. Not only that, but my fantasies of what I was going to do with Maud resembled the nefarious thoughts of a preposterous, lip-smacking villain in a Wheatley novel. But I was thinking, if Felton despises Wheatley's novels as much as he says he does, how come he is so familiar with their contents?

Indeed. Felton has no doubt been drawn in, like millions of other readers, by the curiously charming ambience of the Wheatley world. Whatever Wheatley professed to think about Satanism – that it was a cover for Communism, for example, and vice versa – he wrote about it like a man who was oddly on home ground, infusing it with something of his own sense of luxury and *snobisme*. In turn it made his fortune. Noting in a 1970 profile that Wheatley lived in "some splendour," journalist David Blundy observed "Wheatley's been grappling with the Devil for over thirty years now, and frankly, the Devil's been pretty decent about it."

CHAPTER ONE

Family Romances

One night in the middle of the nineteenth century, two twelve year old boys entered the darkness of Bruton Place, a quiet mews running into Berkeley Square, and climbed furtively into a bread van to sleep. They had walked sixty miles to seek their fortunes, and now they had arrived in the big city.

One of the boys was Dennis Wheatley: not the writer but his grandfather, a farm boy from Bluntisham-cum-Earith in Huntingdonshire, where his widowed mother worked in a bakery, and the other was his friend Charlie. Climbing out of the van in the early morning, they set off in opposite directions to look for work. Charlie went along Oxford Street and found a safe harbour at D.H.Evans, where by years of hard work he eventually became a director, while young Wheatley walked a few yards to what was then the celebrated grocery and poultry emporium of Cadbury and Pratt, Cheese-mongers and Poulterers to Her Majesty, at number 24–25 New Bond Street. He started as an errand boy, became a delivery roundsman, and rapidly rose in the firm.

The story of these two boys is just the kind of narrative the Victorians enjoyed: it is like something out of Samuel Smiles's secular bible of 1859, *Self Help*. But although the tale of Wheatley's grandfather might be the sort of story the Victorians liked, it is not the sort they loved best of all, which would involve self-sacrifice, sentiment, and charity to others. There is precious little of those things in the story of "Ready Money Wheatley," as he would later be known. As well as an extraordinary ability for business, he had more than a grain of mercantile brutishness in his character. Where Oliver Twist asked for more, Ready Money Wheatley would have schemed to corner the gruel market.

Wheatley the writer tells the tale of his grandfather in his charming but not entirely reliable autobiography. There are some inconsistencies – for one thing D.H.Evans wasn't founded until 1879, a couple of decades later – but the overall picture is clear enough, and by the 1970s Wheatley must have thought the story was not only a perfect cornerstone to his own existence, but a good example to the young. He liked to put messages in his books, as we shall see.

★

Ready Money met a girl named Sarah Hart, probably a cook in one of the households Cadbury and Pratt catered to, and decided to marry her. As Wheatley tells it, his employers proposed giving him a pay rise, but to their surprise it wasn't enough. Wheatley wanted double wages, or he would quit. Cadbury and Pratt were reluctant to let him go, and he reminded them that if he left he would take many of their best customers with him. Unless they agreed to double his wages he was going to open up in business himself, competing with Cadbury and Pratt, and this is what he finally did.

In 1867 Ready Money married Sarah Hart, but in 1871 he was still a "journeyman" cheesemonger, not self-employed but paid wages by the day. Aged twenty four, he was living at Whitaker Street, in what were then mean and shabby streets behind Sloane Square, with his thirty year old wife and their children, Elena aged two and Jesse, still not one, followed by Bert, the novelist's father, born in 1871. They lodged there with a builder's clerk and his wife, and shared the house with another lodger, a journeyman fishmonger.

It is not clear how Ready Money financed the leap to shopkeeping in Mayfair on his own account, but somehow he did. He worked hard for virtually all his waking hours, never taking holidays, going to market before it was light, opening the shop at eight, and doing his accounts until midnight. On Sunday mornings he would do an early delivery round before his obligatory attendance at church, to worship "the Great God Respectability".

Pork unsold on Saturday would spoil before Monday, so Ready Money and his children would set up trestles and sell pork scraps on the pavement until midnight. Very different from Wheatley's household trade, the clientele for the pavement meat were the crowds of poorer people who lived in the meaner streets on the Northern side of the Oxford Street divide, who would come down and haggle over their pickings.

One way and another Wheatley's fortunes consolidated and he became known as "Ready Money Wheatley" because it was his practice to take a bag of gold sovereigns with him when he went to market. Getting up at five, he would drive his horse and van to Leadenhall in the City, and use his gold as an incentive to get the lowest prices for poultry. At some point he stopped handling his own cash and had a bagman who walked behind him, dispensing the ready money. He became a major player at Leadenhall Market, to the extent that the best goods were reserved for his first choice. Street trading with the poor was now behind him.

★

Looking back on his paternal grandfather, Wheatley thought of the old proverb, "Better to be born lucky than rich," and he felt this luck was something they had in common.

The family moved to St.John's Wood, while the shop moved to Mount Street, just off Park Lane. The family began to play croquet, but "Ready Money" was not a croquet enthusiast. He could exercise his competitive instincts in the real world, and he now began to enjoy an extraordinary run of luck, in which wine vintages behaved like stocks and shares. The great clarets of the 1870s were, as Wheatley the writer (henceforth just "Wheatley") remembered them, "not only the vintage of a generation, they were the vintage of a lifetime . . . but when they were young those '70s were the very devil."

Wine merchants invested in them heavily, even selling off their vintage port to raise the money, but then something went wrong. They failed to develop in the bottles, and after ten years – with increasingly anxious tasting as time went by – they remained full of tannin. Some wine merchants lost heart, and began offloading them at the price of *vin ordinaire*. It was like an investment in Chinese Railway Bonds.

One of the businesses who burnt their fingers was Barrett and Clay (Wheatley remembers them as Davey and Pain) at 16a South Audley Street. They also had the misfortune to owe money to Wheatley's grandfather, which they couldn't pay back because they had sunk it into the claret. Ready Money called in his debts, and they were ruined. Like a country house changing hands in an eighteenth century gambling hell, their shop became his, with the claret still in the cellars. And then suddenly the claret bounced back. To the amazement of the wine trade, it finally started to 'go right' in the bottles, and its value rocketed.

Ready Money was no longer just a grocer: a Mayfair wine merchants had fallen into his grip. Now, when the Grosvenor Estate embarked on a redevelopment of South Audley Street, Ready Money bagged himself a further prime site on the corner next to Grosvenor Chapel. He was allowed to build a shop at 26 South Audley Street with three residential floors above it and a single storey cellar below, and when the builders began to dig they struck silver sand (which was valuable, hence the Victorian expression "happy as a sandboy").

Ready Money was on a winning streak, and he excavated deeper without permission. He had doubled his cellarage as well as selling the sand, and the building further paid for itself when he let the upper floors. He continued to prosper, acquiring further shops, but the decisive twist for our unborn novelist was the split in the business between poultry and wine (there was a law forbidding shops to sell game alongside wines and spirits, originally to prevent poachers swapping dead birds for drink). The new shop at number 26 sold only drink, and the groceries moved to another branch across the road.

A nineteenth century psychiatrist once complained that the business of "lunatic-keeping" was like the wine trade: they were both jobs for a man who had failed at something else. But in this story, the wine trade has a more positive aspect. It is not as socially limiting as the unmistakably déclassé business – however much money it might make – of grocery and poultry. The calling of wine merchant is almost gentlemanly in comparison, like the upper reaches of the antiquarian book trade.

It was lucky that Ready Money took Wheatley's father Bert to be his lieutenant in the drink business, while his brother Jess, Wheatley's uncle, was innocently condemned to the purveying of poultry over the road. The cards had now fallen in such a way that Wheatley in turn would become a wine merchant, with a business that would one day pride itself on supplying wine to "three kings, twenty-one princes, and many millionaires."

★

We have seen a classic rags-to-riches story and we are about to see another, on the maternal side of the family. But at this point another narrative appears, an old tale which has been known since Freud as the "family romance"; the childhood fantasy that one's apparent parents are not the real ones, and that one is actually of noble or even royal birth.

Wheatley's maternal grandfather, William Yeats Baker, was made of altogether finer stuff than Ready Money Wheatley. Despite being born in humble circumstances in what was then the village of Wandsworth, he would sometimes show his grandson Dennis a crested envelope with a bear holding a staff, telling him that it was the crest of the Earls of Warwick and that they were descended from this family.

Wheatley wanted to believe it, and in later life he tried to rationalise it: perhaps William Yeats Baker's mother was the mistress of an aristocrat, and WYB (as he became known) was his illegitimate son. Certainly his father was never mentioned in the family. Further, WYB's mother kept her infant son clean, and supplied him with fresh laundry every day, which pointed in Wheatley's mind to a certain gentility.

Baker had slender, "beautifully modelled" hands, and small feet, which Wheatley himself was proud to have in turn, and which he felt – somewhat oddly – were an aristocratic trait. More than that, Baker was pleasantly spoken, naturally courteous, and had a feeling for "things old, rare or beautiful."

Wheatley believed that such qualities were unlikely in a man of low birth, "however rich he may become"; they had to be, as we might say today, genetic.

Or perhaps not. At any rate, when he was about twelve William Yeats Baker became an office boy in Blackfriars, earning six shillings a week at the Thamesbank Iron Company. In order to save on the extravagance of fares he left Wandsworth every morning at 6.30, carrying a sandwich, walked five miles to work, and every evening walked the five miles back again.

Baker married a woman with the potentially more distinguished surname of Herbert, but she was no more than lower-middle class, if that: her intensely class-conscious grandson knew this because her sister, his Aunt Betsy, was for many years a housekeeper, and she dropped her aitches.

Baker slowly became a central figure in the company, and at the age of 30 he was made a partner. Then comes another of those strange leaps, like Ready Money's leap to his first shop. In his thirties, as a partner, WYB somehow found the capital to buy out his fellow directors and become the sole owner of the company.

WYB became a rich Victorian iron-master, building gasometers all over the country, and he now travelled in a horse-drawn Brougham carriage. He lived in a mansion at the top of Brixton Hill named Aspen House, where he enjoyed pottering among his orchids and collecting art.

*

WYB's wife died young, leaving him to bring up their teenage daughter Dolly. She seems to have been spoiled for this reason, and because she had a long period of childhood invalidism. She was well enough to be sent to a boarding school, Rokesley School at Brighton (Wheatley describes it as the forerunner of Roedean, which is untrue but for the fact that they are both in Brighton).

WYB was not pleased when Bert Wheatley – very much 'in trade', working in a shop – arrived to court his daughter. He feared Bert might be a fortune hunter, and in any case

Dolly should have done better: an aristocrat would have been perfect, crowning the trajectory accomplished so far, or at least a gentleman. And this Bert Wheatley was not, although (as Wheatley says) he was probably the most gentlemanly of the four brothers and at least had no cockney in his accent.

With its objets d'art and its leisured inhabitants Aspen House must have seemed extraordinarily gracious to Bert, and Dolly must have seemed like the inhabitant of a higher plane. Despite having a squint and few social graces, Bert succeeded in winning her affections.

WYB seems to have been a generous individual and he doted on his only daughter, so it is some indication of his feelings that he threatened to stop paying her allowance if she married Bert Wheatley. But Bert and Dolly insisted, and in 1896 they were married at Christ Church Brixton, Dolly wearing a heavy satin dress with a ten-foot train and an almost unbelievable sixteen inch waist, found in a trunk after her death.

*

There was to be another variant of the "family romance" with Dolly and Bert, neatly completing its operation on both sides of the family and capping both 'rags-to-riches' stories. One day in the 1920s they were motoring near Eastbourne when they stopped to look at a church at Pevensey. There they found the alabaster monument of an Elizabethan gentleman lying on his side, wearing a ruff round his neck and bearing the name of John Wheatley.

Wheatley's father asked the vicar about this Wheatley, and he was told John Wheatley had helped Queen Elizabeth fund the fleet that sank the Armada. He had no known descendants, and Bert Wheatley at once claimed him as an ancestor. As Wheatley writes, "the fact that there was not a single link to connect the sixteenth-century courtier with the twentieth-century wine merchant troubled my father not at all". It is well known that you can never be too careful when it comes to choosing your parents, and now the

Wheatleys had done the next best thing. They had adopted some ancestors.

★

Recalling Wheatley in his later life, people tend to agree he was a snob. But when we consider Wheatley's background as a high-class tradesman, it is almost impossible that he would not have become acutely class-conscious. If some measure of snobbery was a given for Wheatley, it is more surprising how humane and down to earth he could be about social class, as well as having far less rosy-tinted nostalgia for the Victorians than one might expect.

Wheatley was aware that the lower orders had to work appalling hours. More than that, "the appalling conditions imposed for gain upon the poorer classes" – in addition to Victorian sexual morality and hypocrisy, which Wheatley particularly hated, and which would incline him to paganism – "makes the upper- and middle-class Victorians . . . the most sanctimonious and truly immoral generations of which we have any record."

As for the Wheatleys' Elizabethan ancestry, it was just possible that he was descended from John Wheatley, but after sixteen generations, "a simple calculation shows that no fewer than 65,532 other people have since contributed to my blood – which clearly demonstrates how pointless such claims really are." He may be slightly out with his arithmetic[1] but the point remains, and it is not a point we would expect him to make.

And yet. It is not a point we would expect if it was purely about breeding, but there is another animus at work. Wheatley could afford to mock the Wheatleys' pretensions to gentility while safely enjoying his second wife's Norman forebears and aristocratic credentials. Similarly, he pours no scorn on the idea that the Baker side of the family was linked to the Earls of Warwick, and Warwick the Kingmaker.

Wheatley's debunking of John Wheatley fits into a lifelong

---

[1] I am told it should be 65,536.

pattern of doing down the Wheatley side of his family. Wheatley was not illegitimate, he tells us, so he is at least entitled to bear the Wheatley name, "*for what it is worth*" [my emphasis]. Compared to Ready Money Wheatley, William Yeats Baker "started life under no less difficult circumstances, made a much larger fortune, and possessed *qualities which lifted him far above the level of a successful tradesman*" [my emphasis: and for Wheatley's generation the word tradesman had a particularly poisonous ring to it.] Again, "My mother detested the Wheatleys and, as far as my grandmother was concerned, *I don't blame her.*"

Having grown up disliking his paternal grandfather and father, in due course Wheatley would come to dislike his mother too, bludgeoning her in the head and drowning her in his first mature novel. But this is to get ahead of the story. On the evening of Friday 8th January 1897 – the year of Queen Victoria's Diamond Jubilee, with the British Empire dominating the globe – Dennis Yeats Wheatley was born.

CHAPTER TWO

The Lost Land

Wheatley was an infant during the Boer War, an ugly war which killed over twenty thousand British soldiers and began to break the Victorians' faith in the Empire. The major event in the public mind was the siege of Mafeking, where an outnumbered and under-equipped British garrison of soldiers and trapped civilians held out from October 1899 to May 1900, eating their horses and printing their own currency and stamps. They were shelled by Boer artillery every day except Sundays, when they listened to their military band and played cricket.

The conflict was keenly followed in Britain, and when Mafeking was saved there was jubilation on the streets of London. "Mafficking" (to celebrate wildly) became a verb of the time, and The Relief of Mafeking was the only day that Wheatley's father ever came home drunk. The walls of Wheatley's nursery were papered in a pattern of khaki on white, and showed scenes from the Boer War. Wheatley always remembered a British soldier walking forwards under a white flag of truce, but being gunned down regardless by the dishonourable foreign Boer. This was the wallpaper of Wheatley's earliest years.

*

Wheatley's parents had a second boy when Wheatley was less than two, but he died while Wheatley was still too young to remember him, choked by a whooping cough that his parents believed he caught from Dennis.

Wheatley took better care of his doll, a little man called Charlie who wore a blue velvet suit. Long before the characters of his fiction – novelistic dolls and puppets of whom an interviewer noted that he talked about them "in such affectionate, avuncular terms that one almost expects that at any moment they will be shown into his study" – Wheatley had a vivid imaginative relationship with Charlie. When the family were about to set off on holiday, and their trunks were loaded onto the horse-carriage that was taking them to the railway station, Wheatley suddenly needed to know where Charlie was, and began to scream that Charlie would suffocate, until the trunks were unpacked and Charlie was rescued. Charlie spent the rest of the journey in Wheatley's overcoat pocket, with his head sticking out so he could breathe.

Wheatley was a wilful child, capable of shouting, repeating a request endlessly, or even lying flat on his back and screaming until he got his own way. Had his father been anything like the ogre that Wheatley imagined, this behaviour might have been knocked out of him, but it never was. Wheatley's inability to like this well-meaning man is the saddest aspect of his childhood. As he grew up he found his father boring, business-obsessed, humourless, and unread, but almost from the beginning he found him frightening.

His father's eyes were round, bland and inscrutable, so it was impossible for Wheatley to tell what he was thinking. His expressionless stare would terrify Wheatley, who feared that he had been found out doing something wrong. Wheatley even wondered if his father's strange, implacable eyes had hypnotised his mother into marrying him.

Not that his father always helped his own cause. Before Wheatley could read, he took immense pleasure in being read to by his mother or his nanny. His pocket money was a penny a week, which he generally spent on sweets, but one day when he went to the shop with his nanny, his attention was caught by the boy's paper *Chums*. As Wheatley remembered it, the characteristically thrilling cover picture showed a Red Indian sneaking up on an unwary cowboy. The urge to hear the story behind this anxious scenario, and to know what happened, was so strong that it won out over Wheatley's liking for sweets, and he invested the whole of his penny in that week's copy of *Chums*.

Wholesome, patriotic and deliberately "decent", *Chums* was widely regarded as the best of the boys' papers at the time. It was packed with outdoor adventure, cliff-hanging action, and plucky ruses for outwitting malevolent natives. It also carried educational features on music and industry, and it had a social conscience, with photo-illustrated pieces on the education of poorer chums in the East End (all boys were generically 'chums' as far as *Chums* was concerned, so a socially aware piece on Jewish boys in Britain, for example, was about "Jewish chums").

A hundred years on, it is still striking what a quality paper *Chums* was, with articles like 'A Visit to Admiral Markham' (in the series 'Notable Men with Private Museums: and Stories of How They Founded Them'). Self-improvement was the order of the day, whether 'From Street Arab to Author' or 'From Pit to Parliament', but it was never easy, as in 'The Struggles of a Great Violinist: Mr. Tivadar Nachez's Rise to Fame'.

A typical *Chums* feature might be 'Queen Victoria's Life in Stamps: Portraits from all Parts of the Empire' (something Wheatley collected in later life, displayed under glass), and the paper was interspersed with cartoons, perhaps featuring visual puns, or talking oysters. Other pictures almost defy parody, like 'The Joy of Life', in which a female elephant, wearing a spotty dress, is jumping up and down while waving a Union Jack in her trunk. And above all, *Chums* carried cliff-hanging stories, like the irresistibly titled 'Above The Clouds With A Madman: Professor Gasley's Weird Voyage.'

The covers were even more cliff-hanging than the contents. "Percy . . . hung and swayed over an abyss of death" is the picture on one, while on another "The Gorilla was now less than six feet away," or "Shielding the Young Trooper's Body With His Own, He Turned to Face the Savages." It was all-important to stick together, like the two Englishmen who stand back to back with a gun and sword as a crowd of armed Chinese attacks them, and it was hardly less important to do the decent thing, like giving water to a wounded Boer ('An Enemy in Need').

Wheatley never found out what happened to the unwary cowboy. When he got home, his father caught sight of the comic and made a terrible error of judgement. Bearing down with his frightening eyes, he snatched it away, gave the nanny a dressing down for letting him buy it, and put it on the living room fire, where little Dennis had to watch it burn.

Wheatley's father must have thought it was a "penny dreadful", like the lurid vampire and Ripper shockers from a few years earlier, but it was as unjust as if a 1950s father had snatched and burned a copy of *The Eagle*. It seems to have been the injustice that shocked young Wheatley as much as anything else. He intuited *Chums* was "good" (the pictures, for one thing, were like his stirring nursery wall-paper) and he knew a wrong had been done, but he was too young to put it into words, and in any case he was powerless. And that was it between Wheatley and his father: "this sudden harsh and unjustifiable punishment started a festering sore that was not to be healed finally for nearly a quarter of a century."

When he grew a little older, the *Chums* annual was Wheatley's favourite Christmas present, year after year. Seventy years later he was still defending it: "I can recall no story in it which did not encourage in young readers an admiration for courage, audacity, loyalty and mercy in the hour of victory."

One of the most arresting aspects of *Chums* is its small adverts. The firm of Gamages, for example – the once great Holborn department store – seems to have appointed itself as armourer to the nation's youth. It offered the 'Son of a Gun' water pistol which "protects bicyclists against vicious dogs and footpads; travellers against robbers and roughs; houses against thieves and tramps" (possibly it had to be filled with ammonia; whatever the secret was, "full directions will be found on the inside of the box.") Still in keeping with the hazardous, conflict-ridden nature of the *Chums* world, Gamages also offered an alarming range of swordsticks. "Strong bamboo, stout blade" could belong to any reader for 1/6d including postage, while "Choice bamboo, mounted nickel silver, stout square blade, 26in. long (a very neat stick)" was 2/3d. Wheatley grew up with a liking for swordsticks, and owned several as an adult.

★

Wheatley's father was not a reader and he considered fiction, in particular, to be a waste of time. In contrast, his more cultivated mother was an avid reader, so the realm of books and stories was more maternal in its early associations, and belonged to the Baker rather than Wheatley side of his family.

Wheatley regarded his mother as a great beauty when he was a child. He grew less fond of her as he grew up, and his opinion of her features changed accordingly ("I now know that her features, though regular, were too coarse for her ever to have been really lovely"). As an adult, he looked back on her as snobbish and lazy, although he remembered her lively mind and sense of humour, and he conceded that her charm led people to think of her as a socially distinguished woman – "other than the few who were capable of detecting her occasional middle-class lapses".

There is probably more tender-hearted romance in Wheatley's novels than there is in the work of any comparable male thriller writer, and the fact that they appealed to women as well as men would increase the immense readership for his work. As a small boy Wheatley was very close to his mother, who would let him help her choose her clothes and make decisions at the dressmaker. In turn, he seems to have known how to get round her: she gave him his first piano lessons, and one day when he was playing badly, she tapped him on the fingers with a pencil, at which he began to sob and howl. "Come, darling, come," she said, hugging him, "I couldn't possibly have hurt you." "No," said Wheatley, "but you *hurt my little feelings.*"

Wheatley had a little sister, Muriel, who was plain but had an abundance of golden hair: Wheatley's father, in an affectionate and playful mood, would pretend to lose gold sovereigns in it. Rather than little sisters, Wheatley had a lifelong liking for girls on the 'big sister' model, the first of

26

Wheatley and his mother.

Resolute little chap: Wheatley circa 1900.

Bric-a-brac: the interior of Aspen House.

Wheatley as a cadet on HMS Worcester.

whom was a neighbouring girl named Dorothy Sharp, five years older than Wheatley – nine to his four – who lived nearby. Wheatley's mother enrolled him in a kindergarten where Dorothy was also a pupil, and it was arranged that she would call for him every morning and escort him there. "I became very fond of her", writes Wheatley, "in the way that one is of an elder sister."

It was at the kindergarten that romantic love first struck for Wheatley, with unhappy results. He became aware of two much older sisters, Janie and Honor, and he thought Honor was lovely, indeed "the most lovely person I had ever seen." Still barely more than a toddler, Wheatley had romantic fantasies about Honor, in which he would rescue her from terrible *Chums*-style perils such as burglars and Red Indians.

Dorothy Sharp took Wheatley to the kindergarten, but it was his nanny who had to collect him and take him home again. One day his nanny was late, and Wheatley sat there miserably waiting for her: he had his overcoat and hat on, but he had not yet mastered the art of tying his bootlaces, which his nanny had to do. When Honor – entirely unaware of the role she played in Wheatley's fantasy life – happened to come by and see this poor little mite sitting there so miserably, she asked what was wrong, and without any fuss she did his boots up for him. They had never spoken before and now Wheatley was confused, dumbstruck and generally mortified with "wonder, embarrassment, and shame". It took him days to recover from this "shattering experience" – even as an old man he still remembered it with some intensity.

★

Wheatley had a strong sense of the two sides of his family as separate. His Wheatley grandmother Sarah was grim, ignorant, Low Church, strait-laced, and mean, but life was very different at Aspen House, where Grandfather Baker lived with his pictures and his orchids, along with four full-time gardeners. When he called on friends he would take orchids for their wives, bowing and producing them like a conjurer out of his bowler hat. On Sundays in the late summer and autumn he would invite twenty or thirty friends round to drink champagne, after which he would give away the produce of his garden.

Living nearby, the Wheatleys would go up to Aspen house two or three days a week. Wheatley always remembered the food: Grandfather Baker would have a steak or a Dover sole for his breakfast, and there would be high teas with eggs, kippers, or crab, followed by generous quantities ("masses", writes Wheatley excitedly) of strawberries or raspberries with cream. Weekday dinners and Sunday lunches meant duck, salmon, pheasants, chickens and lobsters, ending with fruit and nuts after "rich puddings."

Aspen house was filled with artworks and china, including a tea service that was said to have belonged to Lord Byron, a smoking outfit belonging to Napoleon, and the once famous mechanical singing bullfinch from the 1851 Exhibition, as well as a painting which had a working clock in it. The walls were completely covered with pictures, frame-to-frame. The overall effect was intensely cluttered and somewhat Continental in taste, with ormolu-mounted Buhl cabinets, endless vases and vessels, Dresden china groups, and glass display cabinets full of china and figurines.

Quite unlike the so-called country-house look, it must have been like living in a high-class department store, and it took twenty-one days of auctions to disperse Grandfather Baker's collection when he died, beginning with a sale of pictures at Christie's. Wheatley always looked back on him as the source of his own love of the finer things in life.

★

Things were less grand, but still comfortable, further down Brixton Hill at Wheatley's parents house in Raleigh Gardens, towards Streatham, a large suburban semi-detached bought for them by Grandfather Baker, who had since relented about Dolly's allowance.

At first the Wheatleys had only one servant, a girl of 20 named Kate. Wheatley's mother could barely boil a kettle and never cooked, so Kate was up at six for cleaning, scrubbing and laundering. In the afternoon she was in her best outfit to attend on callers, before cooking the dinner, serving it, and washing up. She was paid a pound a month (about £60 now), and as a Christmas present she would be given material to make herself a new uniform.

Kate was a 'general', which is to say she did everything, until after Wheatley's birth the family also took on her younger sister, which freed Kate for helping with Wheatley. Most local families had servants, and Wheatley felt sorry for the family of his friend Dorothy Sharp, who seemed to have trouble making ends meet and had only one servant, a slovenly teenage girl from Kent.

The Wheatleys were lucky in their neighbours. Next door lived the Kellys, and Wheatley thought of Charlie Kelly as a painter, which brought him into WYB's circle, but this seems to have been a sideline; he was principally a toy importer. Kelly was a dwarfish man with a high voice and what Wheatley thought of as negroid features, and at Christmas he would sing "Negro ditties". His little daughter was Wheatley's first playmate, but unfortunately "ugly and stupid into the bargain." On the other side was a widow, Mrs. Mills, who bought Wheatley toys, including a set of knights in armour. Looking back on them late in life, Wheatley characteristically adds "if such a set were procurable today I doubt its price would be less than £300."

WYB's household also included a housekeeper, Nelly Mackie, who may have been a relative; she always called WYB "Uncle", and her son Laurence was thought of as a kind of cousin. She was an attractively plump woman in her thirties, and Wheatley came to think she may have been there primarily as company, and perhaps more, for WYB: "One of his dictums was that a girl should be 'as fresh as a peach and as plump as a partridge', and if that was his taste then the young Nellie Mackie may well have been a great source of pleasure to him."

Laurence ("Laurie", or "Cousin Los") became like a much-loved elder brother to Wheatley, and when he was back from his boarding school, he would play with him in the

31

garden – with what Wheatley later realised was kindness and patience, given their five year age difference – and tell him stories about the little people who lived in the rockery.

★

WYB's garden – a small remnant of the much larger Roupell Park – came from the Elizabethan period. His mulberry trees were said to have been planted by Elizabeth, although Wheatley thought it was more likely they were from the reign of James I, who encouraged the planting of mulberries to build up a native silkworm industry. WYB's garden seemed enormous to Wheatley. Beyond the lawn with the mulberry trees lay the peach house, the tomato house, two orchid houses and a couple of other hot houses. Further on were the orchards, the summer house, an archery target and a swing, and a walled kitchen garden. "What a feast of joys it was for any small boy to roam in on long summer afternoons!"

This sense of a lost Edwardian wonderland is pervasive in the early parts of Wheatley's autobiography, inseparable from the Edwardian nostalgia just under the surface of his fiction. He remembers cakes from the once famous Buszards on Oxford Street, and magic lantern shows at parties.

There were rockpools to explore at the seaside, and he particularly remembered the Surrey countryside around Churt, where his father rented a cottage. It was still "entirely unspoilt" and "within the range of a morning's walk there were not more than half a dozen modern houses". Wheatley saw a profusion of wild flowers, which he was fond of as a child, coloured dragon flies hovering above bulrushes, and small waterfalls in a woodland stream. "For me the most lovely thing in nature is a woodland glade", Wheatley thought, and despite his later travelling around the world "I still have no memories . . . which exceed in beauty those of the Surrey woods."

The nostalgic tone continues when Wheatley talks about Brixton. It was still quite green in those days, although it also had Electric Avenue – the first street in Britain to be lit by electricity – and a couple of modern department stores, where customers' money was spirited around the shop by a Heath Robinson arrangement of pulleys and wires: a container would rocket away and disappear into unknown regions, zooming back a few minutes later with the receipt and the change.

Wheatley's doting parents often took him to a Mr. Treble's photography studio, and in one of Wheatley's favourite photos of himself he was posed in an eighteenth-century style three-cornered hat, of the kind worn by pantomime leads and Toby jugs; Wheatley thought of it as a "highwayman's hat." The past always seemed more picturesque.

★

Streatham was not a smart address. Journalist Olga Franklin wrote of a man she knew, "who had a dreadful secret . . . He was quite tormented by it. He roamed the world, living in Malaya, India, Japan, America . . . only not to be at home face to face with The Secret. One day the ugly truth came out. He had been born and brought up in Streatham."

Bert Wheatley was working hard at the wine business, and in 1904 he was able to move his family to a less suburban house, still in Streatham but in a better neighbourhood. This was Wootton Lodge, which had a central building, two wings on either side, and a curving drive. Wheatley's father modernised it and installed speaking tubes, so that servants in the basement could be spoken to without having to summon them by ringing.

All this social mobility had to be paid for, and Wheatley's father was surviving far better than some of his uncles. Ne'er-do-well Uncle Johnny Baker wore loud check suits with extravagant flowers in his buttonhole and spent too much time at the races or entertaining chorus girls, and then let the side down by marrying a barmaid, who divorced him for philandering. WYB grew similarly tired of his dissipation, and pensioned him off on the condition he lived abroad.

One unfortunate incident involving Johnny was no fault of his own. At Aspen House was a large bulldog which was extremely fond of young Wheatley. One day Wheatley ran towards Uncle Johnny, and his expansive uncle snatched him off the ground and swung him up in the air. Springing to defend the child, the dog jumped at Johnny and sank its teeth in his chin: "as bulldogs are renowned for refusing to leave go," says Wheatley, "the horrible scene that followed can be imagined." Wheatley had no conscious recollection of this, but he became afraid of dogs and was never again comfortable with them. It seems to have become one of those things that we never remember and never forget.

Uncle Jess was harder working but came to a spectacular downfall. He was in charge of the shop at 65 South Audley Street, where his particular problem was the system of routine fraud and embezzlement, whereby chefs and other powerful servants would take a commission on everything that was supplied. If tradesmen refused to play, then the chefs and butlers could guide their masters' accounts elsewhere, if necessary by serving bad goods and blaming the suppliers. Charging for goods not supplied was another long established custom, and chefs could insist on tradesmen adding a fraudulent ten or twenty pounds a month to their bills and splitting it with them. The strain of all this drove Uncle Jess to drink.

People are sometimes said, figuratively, to swing on the chandelier. One night Uncle Jess was literally swinging on the chandelier when he and it came crashing down on to the table below. That was the end; Ready Money sacked him from South Audley Street. He and his wife Emily were exiled to run a small grocery at St.Margaret's Bay, near Dover.

One day in the 1920s, Wheatley himself was working in the South Audley Street shop, when a woman came in asking for his father; "a woman who would neither state her business nor go away." Wheatley was called from his office, and saw "a small, faded, seedily dressed woman", to whom he explained that his father really was out. Could he be of assistance? "Oh, Dennis," she said, "don't you know me? I'm your Aunt Emily." A few years later she was dead.

★

Young Wheatley's life continued happily at Wootton Lodge,

untroubled by the business realities that kept it going. It had a bigger garden than their previous address, a summer house with coloured-glass windows and a greenhouse where orange trees grew.

The garden was the special domain of Mr. Gunn the gardener, "the ruler of this small boy's paradise." He found time to make Wheatley toy swords, and bows and arrows, and he was also a keen amateur "naturalist," which in those days was a collecting activity. Gunn showed Wheatley how to catch and preserve butterflies, and he was sometimes allowed to go to Gunn's house for tea, where he saw the birds that Gunn had stuffed and mounted, and his butterfly and beetle collections. Wheatley treasured the two glass cases of butterflies that Gunn gave him as Christmas presents.

But a shadow was soon to fall across this small boy's paradise, and Wheatley would soon have tribulations of his own to deal with. The time had come for him to go away to boarding school.

CHAPTER THREE

Telling Tales

Wheatley's parents were concerned that he was delicate and the family doctor thought sea air would do him good, so he was sent to Skelsmergh, a school at Margate. Shortly after his eighth birthday in 1905 a train already full of boys, having begun its journey at Victoria, pulled in at Herne Hill Station, and Wheatley's mother put him on board.

Margate was famed for its 'air', and it was about as cold as the south of England gets (like Skegness, Margate was thought to be "bracing"). In winter the boys had to break the ice on their wash basins. But as *Historic Margate* puts it, "A healthy mind requires a healthy body, and both could be developed in Margate."

Wheatley was not a natural for school life, but he survived. He loathed team games, and he was already a fussy eater. He was also unable to eat butter, which made him sick, and at home he was always given beef dripping instead.

There was little bullying at Skelsmergh, and instead the primate savagery of boys confined together found its outlet in a ritualised activity known as "mobbing". This would settle on a victim at random, when a rumour would spread through the school that such-and-such a boy was going to be "mobbed." As Wheatley says, "It can be likened only to an impulse running through a herd". It could fall on anybody, popular or unpopular, and the victim would do his best to hide for a day or two, or keep within sight of the masters. But sooner or later they would be attacked by twenty or more boys of all ages, and while "fisticuffs" was strictly respected in normal circumstances, when a mobbing broke out they would kick and rip and trample, after which calm would return.

Wheatley was never mobbed. For the most part he was happy at Skelsmergh. He particularly enjoyed the monthly holiday, when the boys would go to places such as Deal, Sandwich, or Pegwell Bay. There would be "a special lunch with lemonade at an hotel", and at teatime on these expeditions there would be "all the cake we could eat" – a phrase which sets the Wheatley seal of approval on the whole business.

Skelsmergh was a good school principally because of the character of the two brothers who ran it, Sam and G.N. Hester. G.N. was the Headmaster, and Wheatley admired him. He taught geography, when he would simply tell the boys about "foreign lands" and his travels abroad. He told them about tea growing, and winter sports, and castles on the Rhine; he told them how he had sailed to Australia on a clipper ship, and what storms at sea were like; and he told them of the American on board who refused to go through the ceremony of paying homage to Neptune, barricading himself in his cabin and firing a revolver through the door. Wheatley was completely captivated.

Wheatley was still thought to be delicate, so he was taken in as a special boarder in G.N.'s own household, where there were three other boys: Oakes, Leete, and Arendt. Oakes and Leete were given to what was then known as "beastliness", which is to say they were smutty, dirty-minded characters. They gave Wheatley a demonstration of the missionary position together, on the floor. Leete also taught Wheatley how to masturbate, something he took to with enthusiasm. The adult Wheatley had a libertarian and broadly 'anti-Victorian' attitude to sex, but he did wonder if his impotence in middle age was caused by excessive masturbation when young.

Bernie Arendt and Wheatley became great friends. Arendt's father was a German waiter who became head of catering for the Great Eastern Railway: in other words Bernie was of the caste – well to do caterers and upper tradesmen – who would figure prominently and naturally in Wheatley's circle into the Twenties and Thirties. They lived at the Great Eastern Hotel, Liverpool Street, and when he was a little older it was a treat for Wheatley to go there and lunch with Bernie, the two lads being served by waiters in a private dining room. Arendt's father lost his job with the anti–German hysteria of the First War, but Wheatley met Bernie again years later as a manager at the Berkeley Hotel.

★

As the youngest boys in the household, Wheatley and Bernie had an earlier bedtime than the others. Their room was on the first floor, and one night they were going up to bed in poor light, lit only by the hallway below, when Wheatley – whose head was still at about the height of a banister rail – looked through the banister columns and saw a man's face looking back at him. The staircase turned on itself, so Wheatley was almost at the first floor landing and the man was above him, seen through two sets of banisters but not far away. The face was fat, white, and round, and the man's hand was above it, on the banister, as he crouched at Wheatley's height looking at him. Wheatley was too frightened to move.

Arendt was ahead and had seen nothing. "What a lovely moon," he said, opening the door to their room and looking out of the window. This broke the spell of Wheatley's terror enough for him to scream, as the man bounded up the stairs towards the upper storey. G.N.Hester, his wife, his wife's friend Milly Evans, and a man who had come around for the evening all came running up the stairs, and as the women looked after Wheatley and Arendt, the men went to look for the intruder on the upper floor, armed with hockey sticks.

They failed to find anyone. Telling this story in later years, Wheatley stresses that the house was a two-storey box, with no balconies, outbuildings, or fire escape. There were no nearby trees, and no sign next day of anyone having jumped to the ground. But most readers will need little persuading that there was, in fact, no one there; Wheatley had somehow spooked himself. Wheatley was comforted with cake, and Milly Evans read him to sleep. Everyone told him he must have been imagining things, and the story of the burglar was gradually forgotten.

During the First War, Wheatley met Milly Evans again. He was now a soldier, and Milly was in her thirties, and they talked about old times at Skelsmergh. Millie asked Wheatley if he remembered seeing the ghost, and the fright that he had given everybody. This threw Wheatley for a moment. "You thought it was a burglar," she said, "we let you go on thinking that because we didn't want to frighten you."

The Hesters and their circle were spiritualists, and what had happened, as Milly Evans understood it, was that holding seances must have brought some kind of entity into the house. This episode — the fear of a child — shook Milly and the Hesters badly, and they stopped dabbling with spiritualism.

Wheatley tells this story several times. By the time he wrote his autobiography, his career was so identified with the supernatural that he had a vested interest in vouching for it, but he had already recalled this episode in Thirties talks and *The Haunting of Toby Jugg* (1948). Toby remembers that as a child he saw a man on the stairs and screamed. "Almost simultaneously, like a scene in a French farce, three of the doors opened. Julia came running from her sitting room, Uncle Paul from the study with a friend of his . . . and Florrie, the little housemaid, from the dining room . . .". The men arm themselves with golf clubs and go upstairs. Years later Toby, now in World War Two uniform, meets Florrie Meddows again, and she puzzles him by asking "Did you ever see any more spooks at The Willows?"

If Wheatley fabricated this story for his occult career then his telling of it is perfect, particularly in the way that he was unaware of the significance of what he had seen until much later. The story is a gift for Wheatley's purposes, but he was probably sincere, even if its origin involved a child's imagination.

Wheatley disliked spiritualism, and in later life he followed the orthodox occult 'line' that ninety nine percent of spiritualism is fraudulent, and the other one percent exposes dabblers to the risk of contacting entities which are not, and never have been, human. Largely as a result of this experience on the stairs, he believed there really could be "disembodied intelligences" because, as he puts it, in these matters "one swallow really *does* make a summer."

It is a good story. The oddly striking detail of the man's round face being lower than his hand, and the face through the banisters being almost down at young Wheatley's level, are in their simple way more uncanny than anything Wheatley would later invent.

*

Books were already important to Wheatley, and among those from early childhood that survived into his adult collection were books on England, self-defence, and elocution. There was *Little Arthur's History of England* by Lady Callcott, originally published in 1835, in which Wheatley wrote later "I learnt my first English History from the admirable 'Little Arthur'." He also had a copy of W.H.Collingridge's *Tricks of Self Defence*. Collingridge's tricks are judo-based, and he observes "Happily, we live in a country where knife and revolver are not much in evidence." The book is illustrated with what now seem rather surreal pictures, like a woman in a crinoline throwing a man over her shoulder.

Wheatley had to equip himself with Collingridge by his own efforts – quite likely by mail order – but his mother gave him *The Practical Elocutionist*, by John Forsyth. This bore fruit, because Wheatley went on to win a copy of *Alice in Wonderland* as the Skelsmergh school prize for elocution.

The Practical Elocutionist is an anthology of pieces suitable for reading and recitation, selected for "healthiness of tone". There are pieces by Dickens, Jerome K Jerome, Mrs.Hemans (of 'The Boy Stood on the Burning Deck' fame, represented here by 'Means of Acquiring Distinction'), and many others, including a scene from Lord Lytton's play 'Richelieu.' It is thrilling stuff, and it is probably Wheatley's first encounter with the name of his greatest fictional creation, before he even read Dumas.

The emphasis of *The Practical Elocutionist* is on clear delivery: it is not about acquiring an accent. When it came to accent, Wheatley was helped by Miss Lupton, an elocution teacher who visited Skelsmergh. Wheatley's parents paid extra for him to have elocution coaching. This may have been because he had trouble with "wh" and "th" (as in the colour "ite" and the number "frwe") but there must have been a class aspect too, and this was the aspect Wheatley was most aware of. "I can never be sufficiently grateful", he writes: "elocution lessons did away with my suburban accent and gave me what might be termed an 'upper class' voice. And that is a tremendous asset to anyone."

The high point of Miss Lupton's teaching was Wheatley's role in the duel scene from Romeo and Juliet, performed at the end of term complete with swordplay in velvet and satin costumes. Ten year old Wheatley played Tybalt, fatally wounding Mercutio after exchanging some correctly enunciated banter. Romeo then steps in and draws his sword.

> Wheatley: Thou wretched boy, that didst consort him here,
>   Shalt with him hence.
> Romeo: This shall determine that.
> *They fight. Wheatley is wounded. He falls and dies.*

Being properly spoken has rarely been so exciting, but one suspects Wheatley found it quite exciting in its own right.

★

On Sunday evenings G.N.Hester would read to the whole school, giving them Wilkie Collins's *The Moonstone*, and *The Woman in White*. Wheatley was entranced, and the excitement was increased by the 'episodic' portions, with a week to wait before the next instalment.

Wheatley began inventing narratives himself, telling stories after lights out in the room he shared with Arendt, Oakes and Leete. This was "an endless serial" in nightly instalments, and it derived from books that had been read to him in the holidays, cobbled together in "a strange hotch-potch" of "lifted" episodes. Even as an adult, Wheatley's work would contain a good deal of cutting and pasting.

When Wheatley was considered robust enough to board back in the school, he continued his storytelling in the dormitory, no doubt as a way of being well-liked. On one occasion a young schoolmaster grew angry with Wheatley for talking after 'lights out' and made him stand in his pyjamas for a talking-to, in the course of which he grew even angrier and made to strike Wheatley in the face. Wheatley fell backwards, not from the blow but from trying to avoid it, and "the moment I was on the floor I realised that I had him fixed".

Like a footballer, Wheatley lay there and groaned. The master knew he could lose his job, "and with the devilishness of youth I played upon his fears". The schoolboy code forbade "snitching", but masters were not covered, and Wheatley, apparently dazed and injured, said he would tell G.N.Hester what had happened. The master and his music-mistress fiancée pleaded with Wheatley not to tell, chivvying him along with a bribe of cake, and at length he relented, "as indeed, I had always intended to do."

Wheatley's autobiography abounds in these small triumphs.

As Wheatley grew a little older he became an avid reader. He liked martial history, having had Macaulay's *Lays of Ancient Rome* read to him and being given a history of Rome by his grandfather. He liked historical novelists Harrison Ainsworth and Stanley Weyman (but not G.A.Henty or Walter Scott), and he liked Rider Haggard and Jules Verne. He liked Conan Doyle's Napoleonic books, preferring them to Sherlock Holmes. He liked E.W.Hornung's public school criminal Raffles (with his faithful sidekick, Bunny, a role Wheatley would later play himself), and he particularly liked Anthony Hope's Ruritania books, *The Prisoner of Zenda* and *Rupert of Hentzau*, and Baroness Orczy's Scarlet Pimpernel books.

As far as Wheatley was concerned, *The Prisoner of Zenda* and *The Scarlet Pimpernel* were two of the three greatest adventure stories of all time; they were almost in the same league as Alexandre Dumas's *The Three Musketeers*. This, for Wheatley, was the book of books, and when he started writing thrillers he would model his band of four friends – the Duke de Richleau [sic], Rex Van Ryn, Simon Aron, and

Richard Eaton – on the loyal musketeers, Athos, Porthos, Aramis, and their new companion D'Artagnan, who arrives as the new boy and becomes the leader. Wheatley discovered Dumas when he was about ten, and grew up to own a sixty volume set of his works. Curiously enough, all three of Wheatley's favourite books – *Musketeers*, *Prisoner of Zenda*, *Pimpernel* – involve saving endangered kings.

★

Margate lacked the social cachet of Brighton; like Southend, "Margit" was a popular destination for Cockney trippers. It had been fashionable in the late eighteenth and early nineteenth centuries, until it lost royal patronage. The town consequently failed to attract smart and wealthy Victorians, and declined.

By Wheatley's time, its main attractions for a boy were the penny arcade machines on the pier. Grandpa Wheatley's house was nearby, at Westgate – where he was in semi-retirement for his health – and during the holidays Wheatley would often be sent to stay there. Despite the fascinations of the rambling building, Wheatley found the household unhappy and gloomy. Ready Money kept his daughters, Ettie and Nell, on a tight allowance, which Wheatley felt was not ordinary meanness but revenge for the way they regarded him. They were ashamed of him because he was 'common', and they suffered for this; despite being intelligent and well-spoken, they were "the grocer's daughters." They felt they couldn't invite friends back, and although they were members of the tennis club, it rankled that "some people would never ask them to make up a set".

Aunt Ettie did her best for Wheatley. She would take him out on her bicycle, play games from Arthur Mee's *Children's Encyclopaedia*, and show him how to make sweets like coconut ice and marzipan. For all her kindness, Wheatley had reservations about Ettie, the main one being that she was somewhat do-gooding and preachy. She would also lecture Wheatley on the theme of money not bringing happiness, which was "absurd nonsense" in his book.

Wheatley grew more reconciled to Ready Money Wheatley at Westgate. He was taciturn, but at least he wasn't preachy. He would take Wheatley to the menagerie at "Lord" George Sanger's Circus, where he knew the head keeper, and to Quex Park, where he knew the head gardener. The owner of Quex Park was Major Percy Powell-Cotton, but it was so splendid that Wheatley remembered him as a Colonel. The Major had travelled in Africa and Tibet, and like old Gunn the naturalist gardener he was very keen on animals, shooting them in large quantities; his Who's Who entry records "zoology" as a hobby. The best thing about Quex Park for Wheatley was the Powell-Cotton Museum, with its collection of weapons and stuffed animals. Years later Wheatley used Quex Park in his novel *Contraband*, and the old Major showed him over the property in person.

Despite all that, Wheatley was never happy at Westgate as he was at Aspen House. The worst thing about Westgate was old Sarah Wheatley, who would creep about silently: "the grim figure of my deaf and stealthy grandmother dominated the house."

Wheatley had an unusually intense relationship to sweet things. As an old man he was puzzled by the way modern children could say no when offered sweets, and he thought this must be because "they are given as many sweet things as their young bodies crave"; an explanation with a note of something like lust. One day Grandma Wheatley caught him furtively eating sugar out of a cupboard. She regarded this as theft, and threatened him with a cane.

Cats were the love of her life, and she had a Blue Persian. Like many children, Wheatley had an invisible playmate, like a familiar spirit, called John. If adults were indulgent enough he might take an extra sweet or chocolate for John, and he would often ask John's advice, which was not always very sensible (it is tempting to think he might have got his name from irresponsible Uncle Johnny). One day they were on the upper landing, with the cat, when John suggested that Wheatley might like to push it between the banisters and watch it drop all the way into the hallway below.

Down it went, landing on its feet unharmed and running away, but the noise brought the women out. Wheatley was in serious trouble. The adults didn't want to hear any nonsense about John, and Wheatley thought that Grandmother Wheatley would have given him a severe beating if his mother hadn't been there.

According to Wheatley, old Sarah used to enjoy watching her cat jump on birds in the garden, something the other women in the family found distasteful. Years later, Aunt Nell told Wheatley that she had seen a robin come hopping into the house as old Sarah lay dying. Nell's theory was that "the birds, who had good reason to hate old Sarah, had sent the robin to fetch her soul away."

There is a country superstition that a robin in a house will take a soul, but the element of hatred is peculiar to this story. It is a strange thing for Aunt Nell to conjecture about her mother's death, if indeed she did. It is hard to know who put the twist into the final emphasis, Nell or her nephew – as if Grandma Wheatley was being dragged away to some birdland hell.

★

Wheatley and his parents were on holiday at Herne Bay when Wheatley wanted to fish from the pier, so his father bought him a simple fishing kit consisting of a hook and weights on a line, wound around a piece of wood. Wheatley went down to the pier when the tide was in, and while he was trying to fish "what we then described as "a common boy" " came up and told him he wasn't doing it right. Wheatley let his new friend show him the right way to do it, whereupon the "common boy" dropped the tackle off the pier, 'accidentally', and that was that.

Perhaps this was just class malice, or an urge to spoil things. But when Wheatley told his father, Wheatley senior made more sense of it. The lead weights would stop it from being swept away, and when the tide went out the other boy would go down and collect poor Wheatley's tackle for himself.

Wheatley particularly liked going to Brighton. He liked

the architecture and the sense of the past, with the Royal Pavilion, the Regency terraces, and the small bay-windowed shops in the old part of town. It was at Brighton, staying in a boarding house, that he first tasted French-style sauces. Wheatley's lifelong passions, food and narratives, were already in place, and around this time he started to collect cheap editions of Dumas.

A family friend named Mr. Sadler came down to the station to see the Wheatleys off. He was impressed that young Wheatley was such a keen reader, and as they left he pushed a coin into his hand, saying "Here's something to buy some more Dumas."

Wheatley thanked him and put it in his pocket, thinking it was a shilling, only to discover later that it was a whole sovereign. Unfortunately when his father found out about it he seemed to think that Sadler – "kind Mr. Sadler", as Wheatley calls him – had somehow insulted them, and he confiscated Wheatley's sovereign. He may even have sent it back to Mr. Sadler, much to Wheatley's embarrassment.

Along with petty triumphs and revenges, it is noticeable in Wheatley's memoirs how small mortifications and embarrassments stayed with him for life, sometimes quite disproportionately, as if to confirm Nietzsche's dictum that "only that which never ceases to hurt stays in the memory."

It was during another family holiday in Kent that Wheatley watched the army on manoeuvres. The two sides were on opposing hilltops, and one group made a frontal attack up a hill led by officers waving their swords. Artillery blasted away between the two groups, while the General and his senior officers picnicked on the heights. Seeing Wheatley watching, they beckoned him over, explained what was happening, and the General (Sir John French, later to be the Earl of Ypres) even offered him a sandwich; to his embarrassment he couldn't accept it, because it contained butter.

Wheatley loved playing with toy soldiers, so we can imagine how he enjoyed watching real ones. He must have particularly enjoyed it because – before camouflage, mechanisation, and modern tactics and weapons – this was an army in the last moments of its continuity with his toys, charging around in unconcealed blocks and pursuing tactics that would soon be suicidal. No attempt was made by the attackers to outflank the high ground. Nor did the defenders conceal the artillery parked on top, which was intended for old-style cannon fire on advancing troops, but was now fully exposed to other modern artillery. The General and his staff were happily perched up there as well, half officers and half umpires, eating their picnic with their gold braid and binoculars flashing in the sun. These were men for whom the nineteenth century had not yet ended. Soon it would.

★

Back at school, a craze for thieving had spread among the boys, known as "being robbers." On their way back from the playing fields they were allowed to go into the shops, and they would crowd the counter and pocket goods while other boys distracted the assistants and watched the door. Wheatley managed to steal a bar of chocolate, but the alarm was raised. A teacher searched him, and Wheatley found he had scored an own goal with his bar of chocolate. It was a plaster display dummy, and not something he could ever have bought.

It was the only time that G.N. Hester beat Wheatley. "The talking-to he gave me beforehand shook me more, because I looked up to him with respect and affection, and I felt very ashamed of myself."

Unknown to Wheatley, the Hester era was coming to an end. Joining the school train again at Herne Hill, he learned that "G.N." had retired. His replacement was a clergyman named Beaumont, and instead of Wilkie Collins, anecdotal geography, and general benevolence, the new order was Christianity, Latin, and the cane.

One day Wheatley was reading a book about a highwayman, *Tom Tufton's Toll*, by Evelyn Everett-Green. Wheatley found it so exciting he couldn't put it down, and continued reading it furtively in one of Beaumont's Latin lessons. Beaumont caught him, took his book away, and caned him. "It was a vicious beating to inflict on a boy of eleven", and more than that he resented the permanent confiscation of his book. G.N.Hester, he thought, would have been horrified at the idea of depriving a boy "from being able to learn the end of an exciting story." People were always coming between Wheatley and his reading.

Wheatley remembered Beaumont as "the very worst type of Victorian clergyman," and it was around this period that his lifelong animosity towards Christianity began to set in: "Forty minute sermons on Sundays when I was at my preparatory school made me antagonistic towards the Christian Church at an early age." The boys would be herded to Holy Trinity, Margate, where a doddering clergyman would preach away and Wheatley was bored to tears: it "was little less than torture."

Sermons would soon be the least of Wheatley's troubles. The time had come to start at another school.

CHAPTER FOUR

The Bad Man in Embryo

Wheatley's father now wanted him to go to a public school, although as Wheatley knew, "those of the first rank were both socially and financially beyond our sphere." The choice was Dulwich College, which was also conveniently close, enabling Wheatley's father to save money by sending him as a day boy. Dulwich was not in the same league as Eton or Harrow, schools where Wheatley would have been so outgunned socially that his ensuing miseries might well have dented his idealisation of the upper classes. Instead, Dulwich moulded the sons of suburban professionals and businessmen into Empire material. It should have been the making of young Dennis.

A.H.Gilkes had been headmaster since 1885, and is remembered as one of the great public school headmasters. Six foot five, with a long grey beard, he was a muscular Christian and a man of absolute moral seriousness. "Fine innings, Wodehouse", he said to P.G.Wodehouse – another pupil – after a particularly good performance on the cricket pitch, "but remember we all die in the end."

Wheatley started at Dulwich in 1909, just after his twelfth birthday, and he hated it. He hated rugby (sport was central to Dulwich, along with Christianity, Classics, and Imperial duty) and above all he seems to have hated not having real friends ("no real chums"). He was a new boy all over again; "friendless among scores of potential enemies". It was like being snatched, "by an evil twist of fate . . . from a secure and peaceful existence among a friendly community in some place that he has come to know well, and despatched to exile in a foreign land where he finds the population hostile."

He tried to bond by means of a characteristic Wheatley ploy, starting a 'Secret Society' with two friends; or at least, the friends he had to make do with. Together they swore oaths of loyalty, no doubt on the "all for one and one for all" model from Dumas, backed up with a Masonic-style threat of terrible tortures for disloyalty, and spent lunch times in a hideout in the school grounds, eating buns.

★

Instead of spending his lunch money on school dinners, Wheatley made do with buns and biscuits, and spent the rest on sweets and toys. This small embezzlement started a chain of disaster. Wheatley's father gave him money to buy a new cap in the school shop, but having kept and spent the money, Wheatley had no cap, and now he had no means of buying one.

Wheatley's father wanted to know where his cap was. Now desperate, Wheatley noticed his friend Woods had a new cap. Wheatley stole it. Woods knew what he had done, but Wheatley insisted it was his. At the same time, he knew if it came to an investigation the school shop would prove him guilty, and on top of everything else the cap was useless. It didn't fit.

Like a bad dream, the situation was closing in. Meanwhile his other friend Springfield, who was a boarder, was being bullied. Wheatley and Springfield stood next to each other at the school singing practice, talking under cover of the singing like prisoners, and Springfield said he had enough. He wanted to run away.

Wheatley took him up on this, and made a plan: they would run away and start a new life in Canada. Wheatley had a bike, and they decided Springfield should steal one. Before long they were gone, pedalling up the hill towards Crystal Palace, heading in the direction of Kent. They had a shilling between them, and the would-be epic quality of their great escape is like something out of *Chums*; 'Long Journeys Made by Boys,' for example.

Wheatley wanted to get them taken on as cabin boys on a ship going to Canada, where one of his friends at Skelsmergh had relatives. Had they been able to borrow some money at Skelsmergh, then made it to a larger port such as Southampton, they might just have been in with a chance. Looking back, the thing that appalled Wheatley about his plan was what might have happened if it had succeeded. "How my life might have developed had it done so makes me positively shudder to think."

By evening they were hungry and cold. After trying to sleep in a wood and being frightened by gunshots, they tried a haystack, but the cold defeated them and they abandoned their attempt. Cycling back without lights, they were stopped by a policeman and confessed. They were taken to Bromley police station, where Wheatley remembered the kindness of the police who gave them mugs of sweet tea and sandwiches (which, as ever, he couldn't eat because of the butter). About five in the morning, his father arrived in a hired car to collect him: "To my surprise, the little he said to me expressed sorrow rather than anger."

★

Wheatley's mother was distraught when he got home. He slept through most of the next day and was still in bed when his father returned from the office, where he had troubles of his own and was undergoing Uncle Jess-style tribulations with butlers. The firm did a large trade in Malvern water, and butlers would put refilled bottles of tap water on their employers' tables. Worse, they would tell Wheatley's father to put dozens of fictitious bottles on the bill and split the money.

Using the belt from his tennis trousers, Wheatley's father did something he had never done before, and gave him a thorough, premeditated belting. Wheatley howled, thinking his father might stop sooner, and his mother, out on the landing, started screaming in turn and hammering on the door of the room. His father had locked it.

The business of the stolen cap was still hanging over Wheatley at school, as well as running away. When he returned next day, he was told to report to Gilkes. Wheatley could never agree Gilkes was a great headmaster, and he was disgusted when a book came out in 1938 commemorating him as a splendid fellow. For all his famous high-mindedness, Wheatley felt that Gilkes didn't do anything to stop bullying. He didn't ask the boys anything about why they had run away. Instead he just caned Wheatley, then dismissed him with the further punishment of an extra Latin lesson next day, Saturday, taken by Gilkes in person.

Instead of teaching at these lessons, Gilkes would invigilate, watching the boys work in silence. Next day, continuing the logic of a bad dream, Wheatley realised he had forgotten to bring his Latin books. It was impossible to sit there under Gilke's scrutiny at an empty desk, so the best thing was not to turn up at all, in the hope of not being missed.

That evening he went straight to Aspen house, where the family still had tea on Saturdays. Returning home with his mother to Wootton Lodge, he encountered his father on the stairs, and without waiting to hear any nonsense or excuses, his father struck him in the face and knocked him down.

Gilkes had noticed Wheatley's absence and gone through his desk, where the papers of his 'Secret Society' had come to light. Deciding he was a bad influence, Gilkes had expelled him, sending the news to his father that afternoon by messenger.

*

It is not clear why Wheatley hated Dulwich so intensely ("My life was a misery and no master made the least attempt to better my lot.") It is very possible he was being bullied. He never softened, and going through his books as an adult, he came upon *The Public Schools Atlas of Modern Geography* and wrote in it "My school atlas for the year I spent at Dulwich College (1909) a bad atlas and a damn bad school."

Of the nine or ten months Wheatley spent at Dulwich, he had only one happy memory. During the summer term, when most of the boys were playing cricket, Wheatley crossed over College Road to Dulwich Park, and took a small boat out on the lake. The park was very quiet in those days, and the island in the middle of the lake was all Wheatley's, to lie in the shade of the trees and listen to the water lapping at the sides of the boat. It was an island of peace, in contrast to the "barbarous" school.

★

As for Wheatley and his terrifying father, the man whose eyes were "hard as agates" when he knocked him down, Wheatley came to realise he meant well. "It was his misfortune as well as mine that those round brown eyes of his, which lacked all expression yet seemed to hold a secret knowledge of all one's worst faults, actually masked a kind heart."

When Wheatley's father came and told him the final verdict from Gilkes – he had been down to remonstrate with him, but it was no good – he went on to say it couldn't have come at a worse time, because he was facing ruin. With his usual bad luck, he had lost money by speculating on the stock market. That was why he had lost control and hit Wheatley on the stairs, and he was sorry.

To Wheatley's embarrassment, his father then began to cry. Wheatley apologised for the trouble he had caused and, "as far as a boy of my age could, comforted him." His father confessed that the reason he was strict with Wheatley was because he feared he was going to turn out like Uncle Johnny. They parted on better terms than usual, although in due course his father's "Olympian detachment" returned, and coolness set in again.

Since Wheatley was not at school, Mrs Sharp invited him to stay over for a few days with her son Douglas, who was a great friend of Wheatley. This was a happy interlude: "To have the constant companionship of my best friend . . . and, above all, to share a room with him was a real joy." This was the kind of thing Wheatley missed after Skelsmergh, along with dormitory feasts, and now here with Douglas "we held a feast of sardines, sweet biscuits and pineapple chunks."

This was an important event to Wheatley because they had Douglas's big sister Dorothy as a guest, the girl who used to take him to kindergarten when he was five and she was nine or ten. Now, as the three of them lay on the bed after the boys' feast, with Dorothy in the middle, Wheatley

53

plucked up the nerve to kiss her. He remembered it as his first proper kiss.

While Wheatley was staying with Douglas, his future was being worked out. "The embryo bad man must be strait-jacketed," and with discipline in mind his father decided he would benefit from the hard regime aboard the naval training ship, H.M.S. Worcester.

CHAPTER FIVE

Jam Today

The Worcester was a three-masted warship from the Napoleonic era, with rows of cannon hatches still visible along each side. It was now a Nautical Training College, moored off Greenhithe on the Kent coast, and its function was to train future Merchant Navy officers, with a few boys each year receiving commissions in the Royal Navy.

A boat came out from the Worcester to bring Wheatley and his father on board, where they had their interview with Captain Wilson Barker. He was a frail-looking man with a pointed beard and "fiercely upturned" waxed moustachios, of the kind then sported by the Kaiser. Wheatley spent the next four years in terror of him.

Wheatley's father explained that Wheatley needed discipline, because he would one day inherit a quarter of a million pounds. Captain Barker was not pleased with Wheatley Senior's grasp of what the ship was about, and told him sharply that the Worcester was to be regarded as the equivalent of a good public school, not some kind of penal establishment.

This was the first Wheatley had heard about this quarter of a million (around fifteen million today). It was money which, in the event, would never materialise – he finally inherited £12,000, and not until the Fifties – but the thought of it must have shaped his attitudes and sustained him through his teens.

Wheatley went to Da Silva's tailors, near London Bridge, for a uniform. He liked his uniform, particularly his "mess kit" – a short, navy blue "bumfreezer" jacket, and a white waistcoat with gold buttons – because he thought it attracted girls at dances. Given parity of looks (and of course "address", or social class, as he characteristically notes) how could boys in school uniforms compete?

★

For all that, life on the Worcester was "not far short of Hell" for new recruits. New boys were known as "new-shits", and had to go through the ritual of "new-shits singing." Just before the first half term the boys would assemble in the gym, with the prefects sitting on stage, and the rest sitting on stepped tiers, like a theatre.

The assembled company sang "What shall we do with a drunken sailor," over and over, beating time with whatever was to hand, creating a noise Wheatley remembered as "a surge of deafening sound and excited sadism." The new shit then had to crawl on his stomach towards the stage, while a gauntlet of sixth termers hit him with knotted ropes, holding him back by the ankles if they felt like it. Having finally reached the stage and clambered up, new shits then had to sit on a stool and entertain the company with a song, until the Cadet Captain yanked the loose leg out of the stool. The first part of the ordeal was over.

The audience would then give a thumbs up or down by shouting "Walk!" or "Crawl!". If it was "crawl", the victim had to go through the gauntlet again to get back to the other new shits, but if he was thought to have shown a good spirit, it was "walk" and he could walk back. Wheatley had chosen a song calculated to please the crowd, "All the nice girls love a sailor", and he walked back.

Wheatley understood the rationale behind this perform-ance as a way of taking surly or truculent new boys down a peg, while someone who had shown willing and had "the makings of a good chap" might get off lightly. In addition to his choice of song, Wheatley knew he had made no enemies, and was glad of it. For most of his life, he writes, he "avoided trouble, like a chameleon, by assuming as quickly as possible the colour of my background."

The Worcester was like a nautical public school. There was fagging, but no matron, and boys slept in hammocks instead of beds. Like many places where people are cooped up together, Wheatley remembered it as "a pretty savage jungle".

Wheatley only had one real fight in his time there, with a Glaswegian boy named Mack, who liked to creep up behind someone who was reading a book and snatch it away from them, running round the ship with it. "I was one of the people this horrid little tough singled out to torment", says Wheatley. Mack had a tough appearance, with close cropped hair. One day Wheatley was so goaded into anger that he agreed to fight Mack, only to regret it immediately. As the boys crowded round to watch, Wheatley realised he had let himself in for something horrible.

Wheatley took up a defensive stance and waited, when for reasons best known to himself Mack suddenly lowered his head and ran at him like a cannonball. Wheatley was able to hit him repeatedly in the face, until they were separated. Wheatley had won, which increased his status, and he never had any more trouble. Throughout his life Wheatley developed a strong sense of himself as lucky, and rarely more so than here, with a public victory over a tough looking adversary who proved not to be so tough after all. He could hardly have done better if he had hired such a person to put on an act.

★

As at Dulwich, Wheatley's modus operandi of schoolboy survival included forming a secret society. With three other boys he formed a little band modelled on Dumas' three musketeers, with the motto "All for One and One for All." As ever, Wheatley identified himself with D'Artagnan. When they were allowed on shore they would hold conclaves in secluded spots and pore over Wheatley's copy of Collingridge's *Self Defence*. In the interests of greater secrecy they used invisible ink, and like miniature Masons they had their regalia (scarlet with silver braid) and "secret signs of recognition."

The boys also owned a number of weapons, including French army surplus bayonets. These sword-like items were supplied by Gamages, and had to be smuggled on board hidden down a trouser leg, which made walking difficult. Wheatley and his chums liked to pore over Gamages' catalogue, and around this time he acquired his first sword cane.

These were a lifelong enthusiasm, and the adult Wheatley knew how to use even the short variety to maximum effect: it was the swift jab, under the chin and straight up. In due course he acquired (among others) a silver mounted Malacca swordstick, which he found particularly comforting when he was abroad, venturing "into dubious night haunts."

*

Cold added to the ordeal of life on the Worcester, rowing ashore in winter and scrubbing decks with chilblains. Wheatley found the food a particular trial. Spoilt at home by his mother, he was now eating hard ship's biscuits, and "meat so bad that at times it actually stank." Wheatley's mother would send him pots of dripping to replace butter, and he was grateful for this at the time. It was only years later that he decided she could have sent him jam and cake as well.

His craving for sweet things was as bad as ever. A boy named Hobson was particularly well supplied with "tuck", and when he went down to his chest for Petit Beurre biscuits at morning break, Wheatley would loiter like a dog. Hobson knew why he was there, and with a "contemptuous smile" he would toss him a biscuit. Wheatley knew he should have had the strength to refuse this demeaning ritual, but he never could. And when he got his biscuit, he used to make it last as long as possible, nibbling the little points off first, then eating the corners, one by one, until it was all gone.

*

Back home, his father's financial bad luck forced him to sell Wootton Lodge and buy a modern semi-detached in Becmead Avenue, a suburban road near Streatham High Street. This was good luck for Wheatley, because he acquired a lifelong friend in the girl next door, Hilda Gosling, a rather fat only child. Since his little sister was much younger, Wheatley felt he was virtually an only child himself, and that he and Hilda were almost like brother and sister.

Wheatley was quite taken with Hilda's physical solidity. If it was a "matter of physical strength," he assured her, "I think

58

you could assert yourself with 9 out of 10 average girls being very well endowed in that way and I must say I can't exactly imagine you knuckling under to any body myself." Apologising for his terrible writing, he writes "Please forgive me the frightfull writing and spelling I am afraid it is shocking especially beside your own . . . but still if I can't plead that I am younger than you I can at least say you are *Bigger* than me."

Wheatley would include "spicie bits" [sic] in his letters at Hilda's request, like the seaside postcard-style story of the woman in the shoe shop who asks the assistant (struggling to get a boot on her foot without a shoe horn, and looking up her skirt) if he has the horn, to which he replies "Gaw bless yer Miss not alf I ain't." Wheatley had qualms about putting these in writing ("don't you think they are rather dangerous on paper but anyhow for God's sake don't get this caught"), and Hilda had even more. He replies to her "I quite agree with you that it is best not to put those little spicie bits in black and white, but as you asked for them I thought you would think me a fearfully unsporting bounder if I diddent send them" [sic].

Before returning to the Worcester, Wheatley wrote

> I am now employed in laying in a great stock of provisions, for going to Greenhithe at this time of the year is like accompanying Amundsen to the South Pole . . .
> I am leaving my town house at about one o'clock tomorrow and am running down to my country seat (Bow-Wow).
> H M S Worcester
>   Off Greenhithe
>   Kent
> For a rest cure having gone Rag-Time Barmy

Above all, he was anxious she should continue to write back: "Write to me again soon won't you my Mother doesn't mind at all I hope yours dosent, and when you get buried at a place like the Worcester you so much look forward to letters as the only way you know that there are other people existing as well as yourself."

★

Back on the Worcester, Wheatley was growing used to the routine. He never shone academically, and was at one stage at the bottom of his form. His spelling may have been a factor, since he seems to have been dyslexic. His reports slowly lose hope, from "Ought to work at spelling in holidays" in 1909 to "spelling still atrocious" in 1912. As an adult he owned a number of dictionaries, but had difficulty checking words because his spelling was so bad he couldn't find them.

As well as Dumas and Baroness Orczy he was now reading Stanley Weyman (he owned a twenty-five volume set as an adult), E.Phillips Oppenheim (John Buchan's favourite writer), Rider Haggard, and William Le Queux. He also read boy's papers and serial magazines such as the *Strand, Pearsons*, and less remembered papers like *The Red, The Royal, The Windsor*, and *The Story Teller.*

Wheatley's only academic distinction was the Scripture Prize, an unlikely award given his animus against Christianity. He chose Scripture as one of the safer subjects, to bolster his overall performance (unlike, say, mathematics, which he felt could go wrong on the day). He won a copy of John Masefield's *Sea Life in Nelson's Time* and later wrote in it "Used by me when writing my Roger Brook novels. One could never have expected a prize for Scripture to come in so useful."

Wheatley left some vivid pen-portraits of his peers, which not only show how he saw them, but how they saw him. Ramage, for example, was "rather a Brickey" (i.e. he was "common"). He was mean too, and "never joined in any scorfs" [sic], which was a mark against him, given that scoffing had such sacramental importance for Wheatley. When Wheatley walked past, he heard Ramage shout

> "Oh *don't you know* I'm Dennis Wheatley. I am the Gun hand *what*. I ought to be a PO only I'm not, the old man's mad or I should be." [my emphases]

(The Gun hand cleaned the brass on the 4.7 cannon, which was a privileged job, and the Old Man was the Captain). Ramage evidently found Wheatley affected, and no wonder: on being mocked like this he went back to Ramage, "bowed smiled and said I should have much pleasure in giving the Honourable gentleman a walk in the tier" (a formal fight or duel). "My conduct was, of course, straight out of Dumas", says the adult Wheatley.

Avery was another slightly "common" boy, who had never had the benefits of Miss Lupton working on his accent, and was therefore known as "Ivery from Sarthend." Avery's problem was an over-friendly manner, which could seem ingratiating. Wheatley's friend, "Squeaker" Stephens, said "he's not a bad chap Dennis old man and if he does suck up it is only in his nature you know". Consequently, writes young Wheatley, "I was never rotten to him and used to let him in his cringing way call me Old Dennis."

Jews were seen as a very distinct ethnic group in Edwardian times, and given the ambivalent depiction of Jews in Wheatley's work his picture of Robert Goldreich (a "wily Jew") is particularly interesting, and one of the liveliest in its own right. Wheatley could barely create Dickensian characters like this in his fiction.

> Robert was quite a wit and used to keep us all amused he always used to call me Mr Wheatley sir and everyone was Mr to him he was always extremely polite to anyone who was anyone always used long words and could argue a cube round, he was a great stamp collector but would do you when swapping if he possibly could, once he was swapping with Robson and he accidentally swept some stamps off the desk onto the deck then carefully put his foot on some he wanted then picked up the rest and calmly apologised as the clumsiest devil unhung – he always demeaned himself – Robson however saw the dodge and he said Oh Goldreich I think one blew under your foot and removed the object and discovered three nice stamps below it. Goldreich however was not in the

least dismayed said Oh Mr Robson sir how can I ever express how sorry I am that the clodhopping supporters of this unfortunate body should have dirtied these most beautiful and interesting specimens of yours, however I wouldn't have you lose by my clumsiness I will give you a shilling for these three although I have somewhat spoilt the faces I thank you Mr Robson sir. The latter gentleman however seeing that the specimens were not spoilt as Goldreich had taken care not to put his foot heavily upon them and the fact of the three being worth about 1/9 he declined the offer with due thanks.

Wheatley also remembered Goldreich buying some tuck for the other boys with their money, but only buying half the amount and keeping the difference; the other boys were younger, and didn't question Goldreich. Nevertheless he and Wheatley were friends, until they fell out over a younger boy whom Wheatley had a crush on; more about that later.

*

Back home, Wheatley would go on shopping trips or museum expeditions with his mother. She would take him up to the West End, the Victoria and Albert Museum, the Wallace collection, and various other sights. "I was devoted to her and she to me, so we spent many happy afternoons together either choosing her hats or sightseeing."

Wheatley also attended Miss Trail's dancing academy, where one of his fellow pupils was Ruby Miller, later to be a star. He learned the waltz and polka, as well as the newer one-step and two-step, which were gaining in popularity with the spread of American music. Wheatley would go dancing in Streatham with Hilda, to older music like The Merry Widow, or newer American numbers like The Bunny Hug, Everybody's Doing It, and Alexander's Ragtime Band. This experience came in useful when he went to Germany a couple of years later, where there was much more dancing, including the Turkey Trot and the Tango. In one his letters he asks Hilda if she can tango, hoping she can teach him.

Wheatley was indebted to Hilda for introductions to her female friends, and managed brief romances with several. He would also go out exploring South London with Douglas Sharp, partly with the object of trying to meet girls. They counted it a success if they even talked to any.

One Sunday in 1910 Wheatley and Douglas saw two girls on Streatham Common, on the edge of one of the Speakers Corner-style crowds that would listen to Socialists and religious cranks. The girls were wearing straw hats, one decorated with poppies and the other with cornflowers, and Wheatley was instantly besotted by the one in the cornflower hat, whom they named "Blue Hat."

The girls were sisters, and they walked them home and met them again on the following two Sundays. By now, "the sight of this beautiful but silly face had entirely bewitched me . . . For the first time in my life I was in love." The girls lived over a garage on a corner in Norbury, and Wheatley took to walking out there and hanging around in the hope of seeing Blue Hat.

Wheatley pined and dreamed and planned, and he continued doing this when his family went for a summer holiday to the Isle of Wight. Returning in September, he went straight down to stalk around the garage and perhaps "catch a glimpse of my divinity," only to find the family had gone. The garage was empty, the windows above it curtainless. All his life Wheatley was tenacious and now, at thirteen, he wrote to the letting agent whose board was outside, asking where the family had gone. They couldn't tell him, but they did give him the name and address of the landlord. Wheatley wrote again, but no luck.

"I had been living only for the time when I should see her again," writes Wheatley, ". . . and for many months I was inconsolable." Wheatley never knew what became of her. Fifty years later he wondered if she had become a chorus girl, fallen into the hands of "white slavers", or died in the Blitz. "More probably she married some mediocrity and is still alive . . . her breathtaking beauty now only a memory of the past."

Wheatley and Douglas also went to the newly popular movie house in Streatham, the Golden Domes, where they would watch afternoon programmes of silents with the likes of Harold Lloyd and Pearl White (now remembered for the classic 1914 serial, *The Perils of Pauline*, where she would be threatened with extraordinary perils of the 'tied-to-the-railway-line' variety, along with threats to her virtue and the fate "worse than death", like the women in Wheatley's books).

Wheatley would remember Douglas in a poem, after his early death, which recaptures one of their girl chasing adventures. In some ways Wheatley is an unashamedly unoriginal writer, a pastiche artist, and here the model is the lower-class comic monologue, and perhaps Kipling. Written on Wheatley's business notepaper – advertising Moselaris, "Sparkling Natural Table Water" – it recounts their friendship ("One for both, both for one, and together" in Three Musketeers style) and the day they spotted two girls from the top of an omnibus.

They follow them into a cinema, despite Douglas's warning ("Why, Flappers are legion in Streatham / And you've not even seen this girls face"), and when the lights come up

> . . . the girls we were sitting next to
> Were a most unpleasant sight
> Just the type of girls that you might have seen
> In Brixton on Saturday night
> Then Douglas chipped me scornfully
> In a brotherly kind of tone
> Did you think to find in the threepenny seats
> Girls you'd care to have known.

Loyalty, friendship and the Musketeers were never far from Wheatley's mind, and nor were matters of class, price and quality.

★

While Wheatley was on holiday with his parents at Lowestoft, he met a fattish man with a bald head. Over a few days this character befriended him, with his "fund of amusing stories", and they would go for walks together, when he would buy Wheatley ice creams and sweets. He then invited the fourteen year old Wheatley up to his hotel room to see his collection of tie pins, of all things, which he must have been in the habit of travelling with. Having admired them, Wheatley was bidden to look out of the window at the sea front, and as he looked, the man pressed up against him from behind and slid a hand round to his crotch.

Startled and repelled, Wheatley was swiftly out of the room. He was too frightened of his father to mention the incident, but his bald friend, no doubt fearing he would, decamped hastily from the hotel, tie pins and all.

There was no female presence on the Worcester, not even a matron, and this had its consequences. Writing to Hilda about her own single sex school, Wheatley says "of course I suppose down at Greenwood the very sight of anything in trousers is a pleasure where you have so little opportunity of seeing any boys." He continues:

> I know what it was like on the Worcester we were all like a pack of Monks in a convent and if by chance any chaps sister happened to come down for the day on a half holliday we all used to rush to ships side to see her come up the gangway and then all run down below and put on clean collers deacent coats ect and come up and parade before her like so many peacocks who havent seen the sun for ages and in consequence have not been able to air their fine feathers, and when she went away she had the whole ships company to admire her go off in the boat to the shore and then each individual person felt at least for the next two days that she simply must have fallen in love with *him*.

Inevitably there was a romantic element in the boys' lives with each other. As Wheatley explains it, older boys "took much younger boys under their special protection." These little boys who had a "special friend" among the older boys were known as "jamoirs" or "jams" (seemingly garbled French, from "amour" and "j'aime"). In his autobiography Wheatley confesses that "it was common practice to take one's jam to some dark corner of the ship in the evening to kiss and cuddle him."

Wheatley's jam was a boy named Ralph Dieseldorff, who lived with his widowed mother in Wimbledon; his father had died when he was an infant. He had blue eyes and blond curly hair, and he was German: Wheatley describes him as British-born of German parents, but in fact he was born in Guatemala, where his father had been a coffee planter, and he was still a German subject. Dieseldorff tended to wet the bed, or hammock, and the Worcester was not the place to do it. He was ribbed about his bedwetting, so Wheatley took him under his wing and protected him from jibes: "The result," he says, "was that I fell in love with him."

Goldreich made overtures towards Dieseldorff but was rebuffed, and revenged himself by writing "a lot of most insulting poetry about Dieseldorff and me" (writes the young Wheatley). Goldreich made everyone laugh with his Wheatley and Dieseldorff poems, and Wheatley challenged him to a fight. He was two years older than Wheatley, "with the strength of an ox and boxed well", so it was lucky for Wheatley that he was too civilised to take him up on it.

Wheatley's account of his relationship with Dieseldorff emphasises the idea that Dieseldorff was younger ("about thirteen"; "one of the most beautiful little boys I have ever set eyes on"; "helping him with his lessons . . . giving him the benefit of my experience"). This age difference is presented as the *raison d'etre* for the relationship, and almost the guaran-tee of Wheatley's 'normality,' so it is interesting to discover that they were, in fact, about the same age; they were both born in 1897.

Dieseldorff was the cause of Wheatley's most remarkable exploit on the Worcester, when he fell ill with appendicitis in the spring of 1913. This was extremely serious, with the prospect of death from peritonitis. Abdominal surgery had only recently become viable, with King Edward VII among the first to have his appendix successfully removed. Dieseldorff's mother wrote to Wheatley to say that she had decided he must be operated on, and that Sir Alfred Fripp, the same surgeon who operated on King Edward, was going to perform the operation at Guy's Hospital. Wheatley decided he must escape from the Worcester to visit him.

He recorded the event at the time in a letter to Hilda, explaining "as I happened to like him very much I thought I would go up and see him." Wheatley was allowed ashore for German lessons at Dartford, but it was understood at Dartford railway station that Worcester cadets were forbidden to buy tickets for London. Wheatley therefore obtained an old mackintosh and a hat and packed them in a parcel before going ashore in uniform, walking and jog trotting the three miles or so Dartford. On the way he opened his parcel to change, "going behind a hedge in respectable uniform and ralleying out the most disreputable looking rogue in a dirty mackintosh and a slouch hat my dear Hilda you would of roared if you could of only seen me there it was the devil of a joke."

Wheatley bought his ticket successfully, arrived at London Bridge Station, adjacent to Guy's, and saw his friend: "his mater was there as well and she insisted on taking me out to tea when we left him". She treated Wheatley to a "simply ripping" tea of poached eggs and cream buns and saw him off in the train at London Bridge.

Wheatley put his tramp's hat and mackintosh on again, but his troubles were not over. Getting out at the other end, who should he see but a short bearded figure in a Homburg hat coming towards him: it was Captain Wilson-Barker, the terrifying naval headmaster. "By George my heart was in my mouth how I thanked the Lord that I had on a squash hat . . . I pulled the thing right down over my eyes and held my handkerchief to my face blowing my nose violently he looked straight at me and as he passed he brushed my elbow and then he did not know me by George it was a narrow shave."

Wheatley then ducked back to the hedge, transformed

himself into the smart cadet, caught the boat back and reported to the Chief Officer as having returned from his German lesson. Affecting paganism in his old age, he comments "I have always believed that some fine old Pagan god, who does not believe in humility but does believe in audacity, gives his special protection to those who challenge Fate for not altogether selfish motives."

In Wheatley's autobiography it is Saturday not Wednesday, he cuts games instead of German, and he encounters Wilson-Barker not in Dartford High Street but Greenhithe station, travelling back to Dartford on the same train. But the core events are the same in both accounts, even if both tellings are lightly embroidered with the characteristic thrills and spills that were to become Wheatley's stock in trade. Half a century later, Dieseldorff's mother has dropped out of the story, but Wheatley still remembers the poached egg: "just time to give myself a glorious treat – a poached egg on toast at Lyons teashop –".

*

"You get such a ripping sensation when you know that if you are caught you will probably get the order of the boot", he explained to Hilda, "or else a game room licking (that's only used for the worst offences, you are strapped down to the horse in the gymnasium and they leather into you . . . there has only been one chap get it since I have been here, and I did not want to test it although that must be another ripping sensation)".

Getting caught would have been serious. The same goes for Wheatley's habit of creeping around the ship at night and stealing food. Having learned the rounds of the night watch, Wheatley had a space between midnight and two a.m., when he would sneak past the masters' quarters in his dressing gown to steal food from their galley.

The pinnacle of Wheatley's more respectable achievements came on his last Prize Day, when the ship was "dressed" with boys on the masts and rigging, for parents to admire from a nearby steamer. Dressed in full mess-kit, white waistcoat and all, Wheatley was one of two boys on the ends of the main-top-gallant yard, some hundred feet above the deck. Wheatley had learned the ropes in every sense, and by the time he was through with the Worcester he was something of an old hand, or indeed an old lag. With some cronies, he would arrive early at the beginning of term to get the comfortable new mattresses intended for issue to new boys, leaving them with the old ones.

Wheatley left the Worcester in April 1913, having done better than he expected in his final exams. His 'Scholastic' and 'Seamanship' performances were 'First Class' and his Conduct was 'Good', which in this case meant 'Undiscovered'. "I have got my certificates allright and a First Class too I am awfly bucked" [sic].

By then he was almost fond of the Worcester. When Hilda was leaving her school, he wrote

> I expect you are now rejoicing that you have only about a month more school in your existence of course one always feels like that about the last term term but I expect you will be jolly sorry to part from everybody and everything the last few days I remember I even felt a little sorry when I had my last hours Practical Nautical Astronomy drummed into me . . . The one thing I regret about school is my friends I was in such an awfly deacent set and of course I am parted absolutely now . . .

★

As for Dieseldorff, he came back from convalescence the following term, and left the Worcester in December 1913 to join the British India Steam Navigation Company.

Wheatley's father offered him three options: he could go to sea for life; he could go to sea for three years, then join the business; or he could join the business after spending three years in Europe, seeing how wine was made. He chose the third option, and in 1913 Wheatley went to Germany.

CHAPTER SIX

Good Germans

Wheatley had never been abroad before. In Belgium he saw the Pullman coaches of the Orient Express, carrying "the magic words, VIENNA, BUDAPEST, BELGRADE, SOFIA, CONSTANTINOPLE." For the young Wheatley, these words conjured up *international intrigue*. It could hardly have been more thrilling if the train was going to Ruritania.

Germany was a little different from England. Arriving at the frontier station, Wheatley and his fellow passengers were "herded" into a waiting room where their luggage was examined. Wheatley saw the most extraordinary German officer, a "resplendent and supercilious-looking being," striding about in highly polished jackboots and wearing a cloak. He had a monocle, and on his head was a helmet with a spike on the top, and a gilt heraldic eagle across the front. Wheatley's father explained that this man was, in fact, the station master.

German society was more authoritarian, and Wheatley's father warned him that ordinary policemen should be called "Sir." Even teachers tended to be "Herr Doktor". The railway stations were already under military control in readiness for *der Tag* (The Day), a prospect which seems to have worried no one. It was not thought England would be involved.

Arriving in Cologne, the Wheatleys had couple of days to kill. Going over to Bonn they went to a circus, where Wheatley saw a sword-swallower named Rogniski. Wheatley reported to Hilda that this man drank "about 20 glasses of water, then took some living goldfish, and frogs from a bowl and swallowed them . . . he then took a sword a couple of feet long and rammed it down his throat, then he brought up the fish and frogs alive and put them back into the bowl." In later years Wheatley would have trouble convincing people that he had actually witnessed this. "Listeners have expressed polite doubts about my powers of observation", rather as if he had claimed to have seen the Indian rope trick.

In the same spirit that he had been to the circus – "simply to witness an interesting spectacle" – Wheatley attended Mass in Cologne Cathedral. He was impressed by the cathedral, with its jewelled reliquaries, and the Mass, with the candles, the chanting, the vestments, "the acolytes with their swinging censers and the heady smell of the incense." Wheatley liked the aesthetic opulence of High Church ritual, and in later life he would say "If I believed in JC, I'd be an R.C."

Military uniforms were a further part of the German spectacle. In Koblenz, where the Wheatleys went after Cologne, there was a flying meeting presided over by Prince Henry of Prussia, the Kaiser's brother. Many of the officers attending were in the Wheatleys' hotel: "the Prussian Guard in their white and gold, cavalry, artillery and infantry in pale blue and pearl grey, Jager in green and, the Imperial Navy in dark blue and gold. Moving up and down the great staircase they presented a scene more colourful and impressive than the finale of any musical comedy . . ."

Wheatley had first seen an aeroplane a couple of years earlier, when his mother had taken him to see Louis Bleriot's machine being displayed in the basement of the newly built Selfridge's on Oxford Street. Bleriot had flown the English Channel in 1909, and this sensational twenty four mile flight had been front page news, with worldwide rejoicing.

Perhaps with memories of the build-up to the Second World War, when Britain was slow to arm herself with modern planes, Wheatley writes in his autobiography that "in Britain aeroplanes were still only very rarely seen and so things to goggle at. The amazement of my father and myself can therefore be imagined . . ." It sounds very reasonable, but at the time he wrote to Hilda

the flying was not good it greatley amused Father . . . [the German] people all thought it was so very fine to see a few aeroplanes go up in the air and . . . make a few circles

71

and come down again, and the joke is these Germans think that they are leading in the flying world, the French are . . . superior to them and even at our Hendon you can see for a bob any Saturday what we paid 10/- to see here.

Wheatley was more impressed by the human spectacle. It was like the Grand Enclosure at Ascot, he told Hilda, but "it was much finer because there were hundreds of magnificent uniforms." Wheatley was quite near Prince Henry ("fine looking very much like our own King") and although the flying was indifferent, "still it was worth it to see the officers there were several princes Counts etc, and one Princess flew a machine at the end of the afternoon."

Wheatley boasted to Hilda that he was in Prince Henry's enclosure, but in his autobiography he simply remembers looking into "the nearby royal enclosure." Wherever he was, it was the German officers that impressed him, with their monocles and eagle-crested helmets. They were a samurai class:

> . . . a race apart, immune from arrest by the police, they could be tried only by their own courts of honour and, if found guilty of a disgraceful act, they were simply given a pistol with which to shoot themselves. The civilian population had been conditioned to regard them with abject veneration. Ladies, as well as men, when approaching one of them in a street, stepped off the pavement into the gutter to give them ample room to pass, which they accepted as their right and did not even acknowledge by the flicker of an eyelid. Awed, and admiring, I watched them greet one another with a graceful salute, a click of the heels and a sharp bow from the waist. It was years later before I realised that very few of them had any brains at all . . .

★

Wheatley was apprenticed to Herr Julius Kayser, of the Kayser wine firm in Traben. Germany already had military conscription, and adult males like Herr Kayser were in the military reserve, with their uniforms packed ready at home. Kayser was ready to take the local railway station over within an hour or two of *der Tag* starting to roll, freeing its present commandant for the frontline. Wheatley's own status was enhanced by a photograph of himself in Worcester uniform. His new German friends thought he was a young reserve officer in the Royal Navy, and he didn't disabuse them about this.

Despite their warlike culture, the Germans were fond of the English. The British Royal family was German, and many Germans worked in England, chiefly in catering. Germans came to England on holiday to places like Eastbourne, where Wheatley's German friends had stayed. The traditional enemy of both countries was France, and while Wheatley remembers Germans were regarded in Britain as "musical, home-loving people", mildly comical in their enthusiasm for sausages and beer, the French were more suspect, "a race of dirty frog-eaters." The Germans felt England should have entered into an alliance with Germany against France, and they were shocked when Britain joined the War against them, keeping her treaty obligation to Belgium: "they felt that we had betrayed a friendship."

Wheatley was surprised by the intensity with which the Germans hated the French. This extended to French-speaking Belgians, and while he was in Germany Wheatley had a Belgian friend whom he liked because he was cheerful, well-read, and already experienced with women, but he was completely ostracised by the Germans.

The Germans could not have been kinder to "Herr Den," as he reported to Hilda: "everyone here is awfley deacent and they all like the Englander out here". Wheatley's particular friends and hosts were Herr Kayser's sons, Julius ("Juli") and Oscar. He was at first struck by the greater deference to the father in German society ("they treated their father with the deference that a subaltern would have accorded a very senior officer"), "but I soon found that they were full of fun." Again, he wrote to Hilda:

I have found some awfley nice chaps . . . awfley jolley chaps . . . there are a heap of others too I shall be very sorry to part with here, I don't think anyone could possibly have been nicer to a foreigner than these chaps were to me when I came out here altho' I could speak no German and they no English they took me everywhere and acted as if they had known me all my life, and for the first couple of months they would never think of letting me pay for a thing, they always called for me when they went out invited me all over the place and everything they are simply topping chaps . . .

★

Wheatley lodged with Julius Kayser's cousin Fritz, a hunchback who was jealous and suspicious, and accused Wheatley of having designs on his wife. This was made worse by the fact that he didn't speak English, but the wife did. She was "awfley kind", Wheatley told Hilda, "and having lived in England a long time ago she tries to think of all the English customs to make me comfortable."

The Kaysers were unhappily married, and Wheatley felt sorry for Mrs Kayser, trapped into marriage when her father's death left her family almost destitute. To Wheatley, it was "a case of beauty and the beast without any redeeming feature." It was another instance of the power of money, and the sort of arrangement that Wheatley believed was widespread in Victorian times: this was one of reasons he hated the Victorians, and what he thought of as their hypocritical religion.

Mrs Kayser may not have loved her husband, but she was devoted to her three little sons, aged three, two, and one. He had the run of the house, but he found the children so trying he stayed upstairs when he could. There was no worse bore than the doting mother, he told Hilda, and he would be reading a book when a voice would say "Oh good afternoon Den – doesn't Alfred look well. . ." A couple of lines later:

Loving Mother: Walter doesn't look well does he?

Dennis Wheatley: I think he does. [reads three more lines]

LM: But his cheeks are so pale . . .

DW: [no answer]

LM: Aren't they?

DW: [absently, thinking to end the matter] Yes.

LM: [in a surprised voice] Oh, do you really think so?

DW: Oh no, I think it was the light from the window on his face. . . [reads about twelve lines]

LM: Would you have the Doctor?

And so it would go on, with Mrs Kayser questioning him and the child regurgitating its food and spitting at him, until Wheatley finally exits upstairs, "in a most unholy state of mind, cursing the weather that is keeping you in, and all small children . . ."

★

When the weather was fine things were "awfley jolly."

Of course all those people are awfley jolly it is a great mistake to think they are stodgy and fat and stupid it is not so it is only when they are with elder people they are quiet and sedate but when you get a party of young German men and girls (of good families I am speaking) enjoying themselves in a place where they are alone or unknown there is nothing so jolly when we make up a party to go out I am always certain that I and everyone else will roar their heads off with laughter . . .

Wheatley was in his element in Germany. He liked almost everything about it, from the fairy-tale castles and toy-looking trains to the practice of eating two breakfasts an hour or two apart.

He wasn't quite a 'hearty' in the English sense of the word (he wasn't sporty enough, and too bookish) but he had become very extrovert. Not only would they dance tangos and turkey trots, he told Hilda, but one night he climbed on the table and danced a highland fling, causing great hilarity among his party. In his autobiography he tells us he climbed on the table and sang 'Alexander's Ragtime Band'.

★

It was a revelation to find that Sunday was a day of recreation in Germany, unlike England, which was "still only gradually emerging from the gloom of the Victorian Sunday." Even reading was frowned on in England, and not just among low-church sects: there was no reading on Sunday even in his second wife's family, while in his own, "to play a game of cards or tennis was unthinkable, and to have held a sing-song or dance would have been taken as a clear indication that one had sold oneself to the Devil."

Wheatley felt this was the legacy of Cromwell and the roundheads. King Charles I had refused to pass an Act prohibiting games on Sundays, saying that the common people needed their pleasure, but after "the kindly King" was beheaded "the Puritans got their way, and their spiritual descendants have ever since derived sadistic pleasure from forcing their unfortunate contemporaries to don some form of hair-shirt on the one day in the week that they don't have to work." In Germany, however, "there was no gloomy Lord's Day Observance Society fighting with myopic, tenacious bigotry to prevent people from enjoying harmless pleasures on Sundays." These sympathies and hatreds go some way to explain why he could later sympathise with the witches' sabbath.

On Sundays there would be a dance at one or other of the villages along the valley, with a piano and a fiddler, and lashings of inexpensive German wine and beer. It was in Germany that Wheatley learned to drink. He developed a lifelong taste for German wines, and remembered the much more ornate labels that they had before the First War. It was also in Germany that Wheatley discovered the drink that figures in his later parties and celebrations as "Peach Bola". This was Peach Bowle, made by pricking several peaches all over with a fork and leaving them to steep in two bottles of iced hock or Moselle, one still and one sparkling.

Wheatley enjoyed drinking binges with his German friends, who would play drinking games, challenging each other to drink toasts or linking their right arms together and drinking off their glasses in *Bruderschaft*. In order to survive these nights, and the following days, Wheatley would employ "the Roman custom, which many of them also practised," of making himself sick two or three times a night, and then continuing to drink, with "a final throw-up the very last thing before going to bed".

Wheatley loved these male drinking groups ("wonderful sense of camaraderie . . . enjoyment of wine and song") and he later regretted their passing, "doomed from the moment in the first quarter of this century when women attained a dominant voice in the ordering of our social life". Wheatley's German friends would drink until they passed out, but without becoming violent or aggressive. Instead, they would become sentimental, jolly and maudlin by turns, singing songs, laughing, and pledging friendship. Wheatley took to all this so well that he was made an honorary member of the senior students' Bund by Julli and his friends.

It was in Germany that Wheatley went to the opera for the first time, to see Wagner, but he found the plot too slow. Like poetry, pipe-smoking, and sport (the list is Wheatley's own) classical music was lost on Wheatley. Instead he was an unpretentious musical philistine who liked brass bands and sentimental or comic songs. Years later he returned from a holiday in the West Indies particularly taken by a calypso which ran

If you make an ugly woman your wife
She'll be grateful all your life
And so, from the economical point of view
Always marry a woman uglier than you!

★

There was no mixed bathing in this part of Germany, but the

girls' bathing area was opposite Herr Kayser's cellar, so Wheatley equipped himself with a telescope to watch the girls he knew from the tennis club when they came for their swim. Or so he told Hilda.

Wheatley got on well with these girls when they were face to face, and he writes to Hilda of a typical girl: "very good fun she is quite plain but brim full of fun and sport, I find all these German girls are she speaks English a little she calls me beff–stake (Beafsteak) and so I call her Wurst (sausage)."

Wheatley's girlfriend in Germany ("my jam", as he described her to Hilda) was Pia Emert, or von Emert-Kohl (the family were allowed the aristocratic 'von' but tended not to use it), a particularly attractive girl who at twenty was a few years older than him. Wheatley was impressed by her social standing as well as her looks.

As soon as he met her – in Koblenz, drinking sparkling wine while watching a firework display being launched from a castle on the river – Wheatley was smitten. His passion was cemented by the fact that he never expected, after that evening, to see her again after returning to Traben next day: she was one of those lost 'ships in the night.' A few days later someone clapped their hands over his eyes and said in English "I give you three guesses who it is" – and it was Pia, back from holiday in Coblenz to Traben, where she lived.

The jollity in Wheatley's letters from Germany is incessant, typified by a swimming episode. Wheatley was in front of the cellars one morning ("simply glorious day"), overlooking the area where the girls swam, when he saw Pia and some other girls. "So up come a chorus of shouts Hallow Beefsteak . . ." and Wheatley shouted "I do envy you lucky devils bathing how would you like me to come in too", to which they replied "Oh yes Dooo Doooo Beefsteak Do they all chorused not believing for a minute that I would."

Wheatley was not athletic but he was a very strong swimmer. A moment later Wheatley jumped in; "coat – trousers – collar – hat – boots and all amid schrieks of delight from the assembled maidens, then we shook hands all round in the water and played the fool. . ."

As he and Pia were splashing each other he saw Herr Kayser coming over in a boat, so he swam under the bathing platform and heard Herr Kayser yelling "Where have you put my little Englishman, and they replied with faces as sollem as judges I don't know where he is, working I expect, then when he had gone I said goodbye to the girls and swam ashore I did look a sight when I got out all dripping wet . . . then when I got back the Celler Master said that I had better go home and change he is an awfley deacent sort. . ."

Kayser told Wheatley he would now have to marry Pia, since this kind of public familiarity was taken to be binding in polite German society: "well Den you have done it now you have got to marry Pia Emert or pay 2000 marks for a Breach of Promise . . . of course nothing happened except we had a good laugh over it . . ."

There were nevertheless a few complaints about the badly behaved Englishman invading the women's swimming area, and Wheatley made up a comic song about it. This went down well, and even increased Wheatley's popularity. The excitable kindness of the Germans must have made Wheatley feel he could do no wrong, but it was too good to last.

★

One Saturday there was an amateur dramatic performance for charity, and Pia Emert was the female lead. Someone suggested it would be hilarious if he went up and presented her with what looked like a beautifully wrapped bouquet, but was in fact a cauliflower on a stick.

Wheatley presented it to her with his gravest bow, but at once things started to go wrong. Pia would not take the bouquet or look at Wheatley ("I felt an awful fool as absolutely everybody in Traben Trabach was there and if she did not take it and they see the joke 9/10 of them would believe that I had really presented her with a rose bouquet, which is practically an open declaration of love, and then we should both look fools").

Wheatley had to lay it at her feet and rip the covering off himself, until one of the other actors saw what it was and started laughing. In a moment the audience saw what it was and started laughing too: "they simply shrieked with laughter and I realy think they raised the roof a bit they kicked up such a row". Wheatley thought his joke was going down splendidly.

There were just a few people not laughing, notably Pia, and her father, and her mother. The crowd found it even funnier because Kohl – as in von Emert-Kohl – is German for cabbage, and a cauliflower is a kohl-flower. Wheatley didn't understand that they were envied by some of the people in the audience, for Pia's looks and their social position, and that some of the laughter had a malicious edge.

The Emerts were insulted, and Wheatley's friend Karl received a talking-to from Pia's father: "No gentelman would do such a thing and it was Karl's and Juli's and Oscar's place to stop me and tell me that people didn't do that sort of thing in Germany and I was a 'Mad Englishman' "

"Secretly I felt extremely annoyed and upset", Wheatley told Hilda, "however I diddent wish to show it so I put on the 'don't care a 2d damn' expression". He bought a bouquet and went round to make amends, but the family were not at home to him, and the door was shut in his face.

Wheatley persisted, and in the end his apologies were accepted, "but they still . . . lay all the blame on the people who were with me and had not stopped me". Soon after this it was time to return home for Christmas and he set off for England, fully expecting he would see his German friends again in the New Year.

CHAPTER SEVEN

The Curtain

Wheatley returned to a new house, 'Clinton' in Palace Road, Streatham. His father's fortunes had recovered, and this was a step up from Becmead Avenue.

Wheatley's father did not send him back to Germany after Christmas. He may have thought Wheatley was getting insufficient training – he never attended wine tastings in Mr Kayser's office – or simply that he was having too much of a good time. In a revealing expression, Wheatley writes that perhaps "the cloven hoof . . . was now coming out in me."

Instead Wheatley worked in the business in South Audley Street. Local customers included the Duke of Portland, the Duke of Westminster, Lord Howard de Walden, the Rothschilds, and the gold and diamond millionaires Jack and Solly Joel, who would buy 500 crates of Clicquot and Pommery champagne for each new vintage.

The grander wine merchants disdained to stock mineral waters and beers, so the Wheatleys did a profitable trade in them. The beer was for servants and staff, with whom the area was teeming, far outnumbering their employers. Wheatley would spend the morning working in the cellar, bottling, labelling, and bottle-washing, and then at noon – in a striking instance of his still equivocal social status – he would go upstairs to serve at the beer counter, "patronised daily by numbers of lower servants, caretakers, porters, etc."

★

Wheatley and Douglas continued trying to pick up girls at the Golden Domes cinema, and it was on a Saturday afternoon, in July 1914, that Wheatley first saw a girl named Barbara Symonds. Blue Hat was only a premonition of Barbara, who would obsess him for five unhappy years.

Wheatley and Douglas saw two girls and talked to them

leaving the cinema. As they walked along, near where one of the girls lived, they were spotted by the mother of one of the girls, who now had to invite them in. She was called Marjorie Claridge, and while they were at the Claridge house having tea Wheatley chanced to be alone with Barbara for a few moments and suddenly kissed her. Neither of them said anything, and as soon as she could Barbara ran from the room. Nevertheless, when Wheatley left the house he was in love.

They struck up a relationship, but it was lukewarm on Barbara's side and wheedlingly desperate on Wheatley's. His nervous, posturing, manipulative letters have none of the easy charm of his letters to Hilda:

> My dear Bar,
> I wonder what you are thinking now as you open this letter, perhaps you are annoyed and wish you had never seen me but perhaps you're not, anyway we will hope for the latter . . .
>
> . . . Mother either has or will send you an invitation to tennis for Saturday, and now I am going to hold you to promise that you will do your very best to come . . .
>
> So do come I'm sure you won't be so crule as to refuse, besides look at all the time I've spent on it. . . .
>
> So I am sure you'll come won't you, you can't imagine how sick I shall be if you don't all the life will of gone out of the game if you're not there I shall be thinking of the might of been all the afternoon . . .

Pleading might alternate with jokes ("you said you could not come, but I beg to differ and as you are not a suffragette you will realise that a man always knows what's best"), followed by further pleading and manipulative arguing.

They would sometimes go to picnic in Shirley Woods, with Barbara on the pillion of Wheatley's motorcycle and Marjorie in the sidecar as a chaperone. Despite Barbara's overall lack of enthusiasm, there were one or two romantic interludes, treasured by Wheatley:

> . . . I hope you don't get into trouble about being late
> I know I was a bit of a rotter to keep you so long but
> I don't think you can blame me can you Bar you were
> such a darling girl and I was so head over heels in the
> honey pot, you really were a sport to come that afternoon
> and you cant think how I appreciated it . . .

But altogether it was hopeless and Wheatley was reduced to
jealousy when he had to watch Barbara being driven off by
a friend in a car ("I did in a couple of ice creams and half a
dozen cream cakes to soothe my temper which was not of
the best . . ."). Before long he was back to arguing his case:

> . . . you say you can't get out but I have been under the
> impression for some time that where there's a will there's
> a way . . . there is no pleasure unless there is some dif-
> ficulty to overcome first . . . it is only by overcoming
> difficulty that we get pleasure, the stolen fruits are always
> sweetest . . .
>
> Do come it is so simple for you . . .

In one letter Wheatley tells Barbara of an accident he has
had on his motorcycle. Charmlessly boyish, his account is
unlikely to have cut much ice with Barbara. Colliding with a
horse-drawn van, Wheatley slammed on his brakes so hard
that his back tyre exploded "like a cannon," but he doesn't
care because he is fully insured.

Less cheerfully, after Wheatley and Douglas managed to
repair the tyre, "I saw you at the window, and you stared at
me as if you diddent know me and of course that brought me
bad luck as straight off the whole tyre collapsed again . . ."

And so it would go on, painfully, for the next five years,
with the remote possibility of marriage as "the dominant
decent thought in my existence."

★

Cousin Laurie, meanwhile, was filling in some gaps in
Wheatley's sexual education. Wheatley divided girls into two

categories, lower-class ones who were available and 'decent' middle-class girls who were not. But Laurie let him in on several great secrets, one being that women of different classes were in some ways just the same. More than that, Laurie told him that women masturbated, and thought about sex often, just as men did. Better yet, Wheatley believed that women consented to sex only with great reluctance, as a favour to men and to reward their devotion. But this was not the whole truth, explained Laurie: the fact was that some of them, sometimes, actually liked it.

This was exciting news to Wheatley, and certainly something to think about.

★

A couple of weeks before Wheatley first met Barbara there was some news from Sarajevo. On 28th June 1914 the Archduke Ferdinand of Austria, heir to the Austrian throne, had been murdered by a Serbian assassin. This kind of thing – anarchists with bombs – was well known to happen abroad, and at first nobody thought much about it.

Austria demanded reparations from Serbia, then Germany backed Austria, and Russia backed Serbia. It began to look as if there might be a war, although not involving Britain.

However, important Austrians and Germans in London were being warned by their embassies that they should return home. Among them was Baron Rothschild, a man in his seventies who lived on Piccadilly, where he had been born. Despite his Austrian baronetcy he was very English, and the War wrecked his life. One morning he was in Wheatley's wine merchants, probably settling his bill, and put a ticket on the desk almost as an afterthought. It was a ticket for his box at Covent Garden, if Wheatley wanted to go to the opera. He couldn't use it himself, because he was leaving that day.

And so the Wheatleys were present at the last night of the Covent Garden Opera that season ("in an assembly which we regarded as far above our station"), on the evening of Tuesday 28th July 1914. It was *Aida*, with Emmy Destinn in the title role, but – as at the German air show – Wheatley was more impressed by the audience.

Queen Alexandra was in the Royal Box, with her cousin the Empress Marie of Russia, the Princess Royal (Princess Louise), and Princess Maud (Queen Maud of Denmark). For Wheatley, "the spectacle on stage was far outshone each time the lights went up by that of the auditorium . . . hundreds of women were clad in every shade of silk and satin; some had velvet cloaks, others furs of ermine or Russian sable. Pearls which must have totalled thousands hung in ropes round their necks. Diamonds, rubies, sapphires and emeralds which must have been worth several million pounds glittered and scintillated from their hair, ears, necks . . ."

That night at the opera crowned an era for Wheatley. King Edward had died in 1910 but the Edwardian era really lasted until 1914. It might even be said that the nineteenth century lasted until 1914, and although Wheatley disliked a good deal about the Victorians – their religion, their hypocrisy, their unacceptable levels of poverty – the Edwardian period seemed to promise a world that would combine modernity and improved social conditions with the best of the previous century.

It was all swept away after 1914. The War killed over ten million, and more than that, this conflict between civilised countries, most of them with high literary, artistic and intellectual cultures, undermined the idea of 'progress' in a world that had, until then, seemed to have been growing steadily better since the Enlightenment.

It was an unnecessary conflict, and in the few weeks after Sarajevo it could have been avoided. There were many who thought it was virtually impossible, because of the international credit system; many of London's foremost bankers were German. Like the people in the royal box, the British and Germans were cousins, with their closely related royal families. The Kaiser was a Colonel of British Dragoons, an Admiral in the Royal Navy, and a member of several London clubs, from which he had to resign when war broke out.

Far from being "the War to end all Wars", it would lead

directly to the rise of Hitler. Democracy was battered in its aftermath, with totalitarian regimes taking hold in Russia, Italy, and Germany. To Wheatley, it was "the greatest tragedy that has befallen mankind since the Goths and Vandals brought about the Dark Ages by the destruction of the Roman Empire."

Gerald Hamilton, the original for Christopher Isherwood's Mr Norris, remembered "There was nothing about life before 1914 which I didn't like. Nothing. Then there was gracious living and happiness everywhere. Fools and their wars have spoilt it." This is only one version of the Edwardian era (in contrast, Claud Cockburn remembered it as beset by anxieties about revolution, which no doubt helped drive the booming thriller industry of the day) but it is the version that Wheatley subscribed to.

This sense of the Edwardian Eden lies behind much of Wheatley's writing, particularly in *The Second Seal* – which deals with the opening of the First War, and has the Duke de Richleau involved with the Serbian secret society of the Black Hand – and more generally in the luxury of his books. Wheatley quotes Talleyrand on the French Revolution: "He who did not live before the Revolution cannot know how delightful life can be".

The middle classes enjoyed an exceptional standard of living before the First War, and this warmed Wheatley's nostalgia for pre-War entertainments and extravaganzas like the Anglo-French Exhibition at Olympia, the London Pageants, and the Christmas Fun Fair at Olympia. At an April 1914 banquet for the Wine and Spirit Trades Benevolent Society, young Wheatley had a twelve-course dinner with Moselle and hock, Mumm's Cordon Rouge champagne, Chateau Lafite 1899, Graham's 1897 Port, and Martell's 40 year old Cognac.

That night at the opera, for Wheatley, epitomised the old world, and he was there to see the curtain come down on it.

★

As one curtain fell, another was rising. The third of August

1914 was a Bank Holiday, and Wheatley went out on his motorcycle to see Douglas Sharp and Cecil Cross, who were both troopers in the Westminster Dragoons, a relatively elite territorial regiment (socially, not martially) full of young men who had their uniforms cut by their own tailors. It was the annual camp, at Goring-on-Thames, and Wheatley went down for the regimental sports day, riding through the traffic-free open country between London and Reading.

After the sports they went to the Swan Hotel in Streatley for dinner. Eating outside, overlooking the Thames, Wheatley prepared a "peach bola" of the kind he had learned to make in Germany, and then showed them the "Rainbow" cocktail, carefully pouring red curacao, white kummel, yellow chartreuse, green creme de menthe and yellow Benedictine into a tall glass so that they stayed in coloured strata. Then they went out on a boat along the river, past the courting couples in punts, and the weeping willows. Somewhere in the distance a wind-up gramophone was playing.

Wheatley was no longer the life and soul of the party when he realised what time it was; he was in trouble with his dreaded father, who had refused him a key and instead waited up to let him in, on the understanding he would be no later than ten o'clock. Wheatley decided to stay out all night, making the excuse next day that the bike had broken down and he had slept in a barn.

His friends told their sergeant that Wheatley's bike had broken down, and got permission for him to stay in their tent. Wheatley lay awake, worrying about his father. Suddenly a head and a lantern came in through the tent flap, telling everyone to get up. It was still the middle of the night, but there was an emergency parade. Wheatley's friends thought it was probably a training stunt, like a fire drill, and he waited in the tent for them to return. They did, soon enough, only to tell him the camp was breaking up and he would have to leave. The British Army was mobilising for war.

CHAPTER EIGHT

Officers and Men

The onset of the First World War was greeted with enormous enthusiasm all over Europe, like a particularly exciting sporting fixture with religious undertones. As the midnight ultimatum rolled closer, Wheatley was in front of Buckingham Palace with Cecil Cross and Douglas Sharp. They were part of a great crowd that spread back down the Mall towards Charing Cross. Taxis were caught in the crowd, and people climbed on their roofs to wave Union Jacks. Everybody sang 'Rule Britannia!', 'Land of Hope and Glory', and 'For Auld Lang Syne'.

Drawn out by repeated renderings of 'God Save The King', the King and Queen came out on to the balcony and the crowd reached fever pitch, with frantic cheering and repeated singing of the National Anthem. The King and Queen went inside, but the undiminished noise of the crowd left them little alternative but to come out again, as if for an encore.

Wheatley, of all people, should have had misgivings about the war. Germans had been kind to him, he had loved them, and he had had close German friends even while he was in England. But he was as caught up in it as the rest. His enthusiasm was inexplicable, he wrote later; but everyone in the crowd was "completely war-mad . . . swayed by that most terrible of all evils – mob psychology."

★

The excitement died down over the next few days, to be replaced by anxiety among the middle classes. There were fears of a run on the banks, and worries about trade. Wheatley's father had built up a thriving business as the agent for a German mineral water called Moselaris (the Wheatley letterhead at this period proclaims 'Moselaris Sparkling

Natural Table Water' in a flourish of red lettering). All that was ruined.

Lord Kitchener's face was now appearing on recruiting posters, pointing a finger – aligned with his intense expressionless stare – straight at the viewer, above the words 'Your Country Needs YOU'. Wheatley took a dislike to Kitchener, based largely on his appearance ("Kitchener's face always appeared to me to be that of a narrow, harsh and bigoted man"). It may not be irrelevant that he looked rather like Wheatley's father.

Wheatley attempted to join the Westminster Dragoons so he could be with his friends, but it was necessary to ride. Wheatley lied (he had once been on a donkey at Margate, and that was the limit of his experience) but the truth became embarrassingly obvious when they put him on a horse. The Westminster Dragoons were decimated at Gallipoli in a Crimea-style tragedy of slaughter followed by disease, and he later felt he had been lucky.

Wheatley's enthusiasm for his motorcycle inspired him to reply to an advert asking for motorcycle owners to act as despatch riders in France, but he never received a reply. Once again, this came to seem lucky when he met a man who had been involved in organising the motorcyclists; most of the first batch had been killed or captured in the first few weeks.

The HQ of the 'Artist's Rifles' was near the Wheatley business, and Wheatley tried to enlist there, but he was too short, at five foot eight. It tells a grim story about the death rate that within a year or two the Army would form 'Bantam' regiments, recruiting men under five feet tall.

It transpired that Wheatley's grocer uncle, Uncle Dennis, was a former member of The Honourable Artillery Company, and he gave him a letter of introduction to the adjutant. Wheatley took it down to Artillery House on City Road, with its crenellated top edge giving it the look of a toy fort, and they put his name on the waiting list.

All this time Wheatley had been trying to enlist as an ordinary private soldier, which didn't strike him or his father as odd until a friend of his father's, a Dr Dutch who was now a major in the Royal Army Medical Corps, learned that Wheatley was trying to join the HAC as an ordinary gunner. It made him mad, he told Wheatley's father, to see middle-class officer material wasted in the ranks.

★

Like the fortunate distinction between wine merchant and grocer, this was one of the luckiest breaks in Wheatley's life – and his social ascent, the two being virtually inseparable – without which his later persona would be almost unthinkable. "There were two worlds in those days," Wheatley wrote in a filmscript, "That of officers, and that of men. I picked up a lot from brother officers who had been at Eton, Harrow, and Winchester."

Wheatley was now excited by the prospect of becoming an officer, and after seeing the officer class in Germany he had an exalted idea of what was involved. Dr Dutch gave him a note of recommendation for the colonel of the 4th Battalion, London (Territorial) Fusiliers, based in Hoxton.

Hoxton was then one of the worst districts in London, somewhere out in the mysterious East. Writing years later at his desk in Cadogan Square, Wheatley described it as "somewhere in that vast Eastern stretch of London which very few Londoners know anything about. I had never been there before, I have never been there since, and I think it highly improbable that I shall ever go there again."

The colonel that Wheatley needed to see was at a camp in Kingston. When he tracked him down the colonel interviewed him informally, asked him to sign a piece of paper, and told him he would be gazetted as an officer in due course.

★

Shortly after his Fusiliers interview, Wheatley went for two weeks in Wales with his parents. They didn't much like Wales, where the religious observances meant there were no tobacco shops open on Sunday, and no delivery of Sunday papers. They had not been back long when Wheatley's military fortunes changed once again.

Wheatley's father banked at what was then the National Provincial, on the corner of South Audley Street and Mount Street, and one day he saw his manager, a Mr Buchan, stepping out of a chauffeured Rolls-Royce in a colonel's uniform. It turned out that Buchan's father-in-law, a general, had suggested he could help out with forming a pay department.

Buchan was appalled to think Wheatley was joining the Fusiliers. "You cannot possibly go into the Fusiliers," he said, "they walk!" As a junior infantry officer Wheatley would have had to lead infantry charges from the front, walking into machine gun fire armed with a sword and revolver. This was what he was unwittingly volunteering for. It wasn't the carnage Buchan was worried about – still largely in the future – but the fatigue and indignity, and he assured Wheatley he would get him a commission in a cavalry regiment. Wheatley remembered his old problem of not being able to ride and in any case he doubted if he had enough money to be a cavalry officer.

Buchan saw Wheatley's problem with the riding, and advised him to take lessons. Perhaps the cavalry would still be too much, so he suggested the artillery. And with that he wrote Wheatley a note for an artillery colonel named Nichols. Wheatley found Colonel Nichols at the First City of London Territorial Royal Field Artillery, based in Handel Street, near Russell Square. Nichols asked Wheatley a few questions, had him fill out another form, and at last he was in; and he was an officer. He never ran across Mr Buchan again, "But I hope that the Gods have reserved a specially comfortable place in the most charming of heavens for that very charming and kindly mortal."

★

On the 23rd September 1914 Wheatley was gazetted an officer. In a telling phrase of the time – applied to officers who had received commissions only for the War, and not the old professional officers – he was now a "temporary gentleman."

Wheatley felt that his fellow Territorial officers could be divided into three categories. There were the "huntin'

91

shootin' fishin' " county types, who tended to be socially superior to their urban contemporaries. They weren't over intelligent, but they made good leaders and were popular with their men. Then there were the 'Jobsworth' officers, who predominated in the city regiments. These were people of no great social status in civilian life who enjoyed the army because it enabled them to order people about. And then, thought Wheatley, there were the men of real ability: these were rare.

Wheatley was one of half a dozen fledgling lieutenants, and began to make friends. Bertie Davis was a solicitor in civilian life (and "like myself . . . a quite undistinguished suburbanite"), while Douglas "Dolly" Gregson was a well-connected public schoolboy who had been to Winchester and lived in Kensington. Wheatley was in awe of Gregson's metropolitan life ("Mayfair . . . Claridges . . . Berkeley . . . Savoy . . .") and admired him for his charisma and unsnobbish popularity.

The early days of Wheatley's soldiering were distinctly amateur, and very different from what had been going on in Germany. The men had no uniforms, and would march in motley order wearing bowler hats, straw hats and cloth caps. As they marched up Tottenham Court Road towards Regent's Park, the public would cheer them, and run up to give them chocolate. As he led his column up the road, Wheatley noticed old ladies weeping, and old men taking off their hats and standing bareheaded to watch them go by.

Having got the men to Regent's Park, there was dismounted cavalry drill, PT, and signals practice; mainly semaphore, instructed by recruits who had been Boy Scouts. There were no guns, but an elderly carpenter made them a wooden cannon, and the men practised with that while Wheatley and his fellow officers shouted commands out of the instruction book.

Wheatley was proud of his new uniform, and before long his tendency to dandyism came into its own. His first breeches were narrowly cut, unlike his later pairs with a "beautiful full cut", giving the much prized 'elephant ear' effect on the outer thigh. Wheatley also replaced his ordinary field boots with another pair ("almost unbelievably beautiful") which had originally belonged to Baron Rothschild, the man with the opera tickets.

After the Baron had left for Germany his steward disposed of his household contents, and the boots had come to Wheatley. Let's hear Wheatley on those boots for a moment:

> Those boots must have cost a small fortune. The leather was shiny outside and velvety in: its thickness could not have been more than one-eighth of an inch, and each boot was cut in one complete piece, so that there was no break from the knee right down to the toe; and the soles were as thin as those of a pair of dancing pumps. The leather was so flexible that, apart from the sole and heel, one could have rolled up and stuffed the whole boot into one's trouser pocket.

The only problem was that they didn't fit, and if Wheatley had to keep them on for long he was in agony. "However," he writes, "I am convinced that nobody in the army had a more lovely pair of field boots, and they proved the envy of all my friends."

Wheatley was generally well-liked, but one of his fellow officers had reservations about him. Maitland was a snobbish man who had run a prep school, and he seems to have considered Wheatley to be a "bounder," a word which had connotations of ill-bred social climbing. Another item in Wheatley's bounderish kit was a monocle, still quite a common affectation at the period.

Wheatley's officer kit also included a sword, but the regulation item proved hard to obtain, and Wheatley's father found him one second-hand. Wheatley liked his sword, which made him feel like D'Artagnan. For all his enthusiasm Wheatley was not very good with it, and during mounted sword drill – an anachronistic procedure, which involved unsheathing the sword at the gallop, without injuring one's neighbour – he was distressed when he cut his horse's ear.

Wheatley was never at ease with horses; he thought they were stupid, and he was frightened of them. On one occasion he saw a young veterinary officer hit two horses with a stick to separate them when they were standing back to back and kicking at each other; a moment later he had been kicked in the face, with horrific injuries, and his war was over.

Wheatley had taken Buchan's advice about riding lessons. Having become reasonably proficient, he was on a horse one morning when it bolted down Kilburn High Road. Before Wheatley could bring it under control it mounted the pavement, upsetting fruit and veg stalls, and his misadventure was further emphasised by the practice of having a trumpeter follow mounted officers. Wheatley's trumpeter could actually ride. "He adhered strictly to his duty and made my misfortune even more ludicrous by spurring his mount then, upright and poker-faced, following me at full gallop along the pavement."

★

Several of Wheatley's fellow officers were memorable, like "Frothy" Hurst, so called because his violent temper made him froth at the mouth. One of the oddest was Wheatley's battery commander, Major William "Shitty Bill" Inglis, "a very queer individual." Wheatley believed Inglis to be "a sexual maniac", a man whose drive for women became a "pathological abnormality": "the way he used to eye any fresh young woman who was introduced to him was positively nauseating."

Inglis was unpopular, hence his nickname. He was harsh and unpredictable, forming his subalterns into a tyrant's court: "like a Roman despot he would treat one of us as a boon companion one night and, without the least scruple, have us flung to the lions the next. We soon came to the conclusion that he was slightly mental . . ."

Despite being a married man in his mid-forties and a commanding officer, Inglis would go out with second lieutenants Wheatley, still only seventeen, and Bertie Davis, eighteen, with the aim of picking up young women. This was unprofessional, to say the least, as Wheatley realised at the time. Their favourite hunting ground was the long slope up Richmond Hill, leading towards Richmond Park, with its superb view and its old pubs. In those days it was thronged by young people from all over London; "a moving crowd as thick as one would see on the Parade at any popular holiday resort."

Picking up women was easy with an officer's uniform and the excitement caused by the war, with its suspension of normal standards. Many of the crowd had come with the intention of getting off with somebody. At one point a policeman looking over the crowd said to Major Inglis – one uniform to another, as it were – "There's miles of it, sir. Miles of it, just for the asking."

One of the problems of going out for the night with Shitty Bill was that he had first pick of the women. Fortunately he seems to have been rather stupid and could be easily steered. As Wheatley remembered it, "One had only to whisper to him something such as 'Look at the width of that dark girl's nostrils. That's a sure sign she's terrifically hot stuff.' "

If the girls were agreeable then after drinks they might go to Richmond Park and disport themselves in the grass. Wheatley kept a list of women he'd had relations with between 1914 and 1921, most of them probably prostitutes. Some of the women in Wheatley's list have ticks beside them, and the end of the list he scores himself forty out of seventy, corresponding to forty ticks out of seventy women.

It seems likely these ticks mean full intercourse. "Red head Richmond" is unticked, for example, but near the Handel Street hall Wheatley seems to have had a girl in 1914 remembered as "Marchmont Street [tick]." Wheatley seems to have got down to casual fornication on a larger scale from around 1916, and ticks are rarer before that.

It is noticeable that Wheatley is likelier to reach the ticking stage with women whose names he doesn't know: Carmen, Vera, Dolly, Margery, Joan and Little Jewess Rachel are all unticked, for example, whereas things seem to have gone further with "Scotch Girl", "Florist Paddington", "Red

Petticoat", "Tavistock Square (soulful)", "Lame girl fur coat", "With Davis", "good figure", and "Whisky and soda offer", along with a few named ticks like Babs, and some fairly unambiguous prostitutes such as "Mecklenburg Square" [tick], which was then a red light district.

Wheatley kept Hilda informed of his doings throughout the war, and it is further noticeable that he associates the Devil with sex; a point which hardly needs to be laboured in its relation to his later literary output.

At one point he tells her "You may be interested to hear that if I have not been particularly good I certainly have not been particularly naughty – neither God nor the Devil seem to get much forwader." [sic] Complaining from the Western Front about a lack of women, Wheatley writes "there is not a petticoat . . . for at least twenty miles in any direction, except that of the Hun who by all accounts does himself jolly well still in the way of the way of the world, the flesh, and the devil . . ." This situation was not permanent, and later Wheatley wrote of a visit to Amiens "By Gad the Devil must have had a particularly amusing and gratifying three days at my expense still goodness knows one needs something to buck one up after the desolation of the line . . ."

Later still, having been for months "nearly always at least 10 miles from a petticoat, and even that generally a very undesirable one, I feel that I am greatly in arrears in paying Old Nick his just dues, in oats . . ."

CHAPTER NINE

The Rich Wot Gets the Pleasure

Bertie Davis suggested they should rent a cheap flat to take girls to, and he found a top floor flat on the corner of Guilford Street, overlooking Coram's Fields. Wheatley was still living with his parents, turning up for the Artillery on a daily basis, so he was only able to use the flat for evenings and Sundays except when he was "Officer of the Guard." This happened about once a fortnight, and entailed going in during the night to turn out the guard and inspect them.

Wheatley particularly remembered a relatively respectable girl he had picked up at Piccadilly Circus, after a girl he had met at Richmond had failed to arrive for the champagne supper he had laid on. She was unenthusiastic at first, and when Wheatley rushed out to inspect the guard he raced back fearing she might have gone. But having decided to stay, she was "a changed personality", and for Wheatley it was "the night of a lifetime."

It was "a jolly life on the home front" as Wheatley says, and the laziest Flashman-style cad could hardly have done better. This was not through any desire to shirk; having volunteered in 1914, he spent over three years caught up in endless courses and administration and didn't get to France until Autumn 1917. Nor was it a reflection on the Territorial RFA, which had already seen heavy action. In retrospect it looks like the luck that Wheatley always believed in.

*

Wheatley's first course was in October 1914 down at Woolwich, where he was sent to learn about field telephones. The Mess was excellent, the regular officers were friendly, and he was shown how to use a proper range finder, a splendid precision item that he never saw again. The British Army was so badly equipped that when the time came, he had to use his fingers and thumb.

Early in 1915 he was sent on another course, this time gunnery, down at Maresfield Park in Sussex. This was less pleasant, and the officers – still not regulars, but old time territorials who had been in before the war – were less enthusiastic about Wheatley and the other newcomers. The main benefit of this course for Wheatley was that he met Major Herbert Clark, an officer Wheatley greatly admired and who took something of a shine to Wheatley.

"Nobby" Clark was a kind and reasonable individual who never bullied or shouted, and took time to explain what was being done and why. After exercises he would go back over the day with the junior officers, asking each one why they had done whatever they did, and either praising them or explaining how it could have been done better. Then he would shout "Horses!" and they would race to see who could gallop back to camp first.

The next course was held at Lord's Cricket Ground, where Wheatley was sent to learn the work of an ordinary gunner. Wheatley was selected as a driver, and had to ride a pair of draught horses, sitting on one while trying to control them both. He also had to wash and comb them, no doubt while thinking of injuries he had seen, clean the harnesses with oily rags and sand, and dismantle and reassemble the gun, with its massive springs in their bath of oil.

Wheatley was getting sick of training, although he enjoyed daily outings to Hampstead Heath for drill, where the Officers Mess was a room in the pub Jack Straw's Castle. It was a three mile march there and back, and on the way back, downhill into London, the men would sing songs of the period such as Keep The Home Fires Burning, and It's A Long Way to Tipperary. There was a more modern note struck when a photographer came and photographed them dug in on a snowy day. Wheatley was surprised to see the pictures printed in a newspaper with the caption "Our Boys on the Western Front."

★

Wheatley's next course was at Ipswich, and on the 15th May 1915 he marched out of London with the regimental band playing. Being a City regiment it was their right to march through the major thoroughfares, past the Bank of England. They held the traffic up, but the public thought they were going to France and stood on the pavements cheering.

Wheatley had turned up in full marching order, which was unnecessary; no other officers had done it. None of his gear was packed and he was wearing it all: haversack, binoculars, map case, torch, water bottle, prismatic compass, pistol, and sword. He was, as he says, done up "like a Christmas tree", and probably the cause of some amusement.

Ipswich was unpleasant; the First Line Territorial officers regarded their Second Line comrades like Wheatley with contempt, and ignored them in the Mess. Wheatley was soon back, but then he was sent out there again. "It was now that my many months of purgatory with horses really began," he writes, with a hundred and forty horses being brought down in pairs to be watered at a long canvas trough:

> Often the drivers would spend ten minutes or more splashing the water gently on the muzzle of some stupid brute that refused to drink; and to send it away without it having done so was a serious offence. Many a time I have stood for over an hour watching this procedure in a mackintosh with the rain trickling down the back of my neck.

This had to be done three times a day, with a six a.m. start.

The other business on the agenda was gunnery, and Wheatley had now reached the stage, as he reported to Hilda, of firing live shells at a large square of canvas a mile or two away, representing the Hun. He had no great flair for gunnery, and wondered why he couldn't see his shells hitting the target. They were bursting in the sky because he had not adjusted the fuses properly – a moderately technical job involving a thermometer and spanner – and he remembered being gently ticked off by a General: "Look up in the air, my boy".

Wheatley was growing so bored with horses and artillery and training that in November 1915 he volunteered to join the Royal Flying Corps. "One doesn't fetch horses in the RFC," he told Hilda, having no idea that the pilots' average life expectancy would be around two weeks.

The RFC was still in its infancy, having only just got past the stage of using hand–held revolvers in aeroplanes, but it was now rapidly expanding. In May 1915 it comprised only 166 planes in total, but within eighteen months it was losing fifty planes a week. Parachutes were not issued; senior Army staff believed pilots would try harder without them. Wheatley went to Ipswich for his medical, where it transpired he was colour blind. At the time it must have been a disappointment, but it was one more lucky escape.

★

Wheatley had more good fortune a little later, "an awfley good stroke of luck . . . really a ripping stroke of luck": this was the reappearance of Nobby Clark, who had been promoted to Colonel and was now Wheatley's Commanding Officer. "He is only about 35 but very fat," Wheatley wrote to Hilda, "with a lovly round red jolly face and brown eyes that are always laughing. He is far more like a pal than a C.O."

Wheatley admired Clark's combination of dedicated soldiering and good living: "He is worth heaps of money and when he was in France he never missed having his seven course dinner . . . and yet he is a splendid soldier, knows his job from A to Z." Clark took an interest in everyone ("every day he gets letters from his men in his old Batt in France"), and he was an utterly decent person: as Wheatley put it, in a resonant phrase of the period, he was "one of God's own White Men."

Kitchener had just issued an order forbidding the smoking of cigarettes on marches, and permitting only pipes. Wheatley bought a pipe, but he hated it. He persevered for a week or two until there was a full parade, with Clark at the front as they marched down the road. After a couple of minutes Clark gave the order "March at Ease," which was associated with smoking. He then took out his cigarette case and lit up, to cheering from the troops.

Wheatley's erstwhile companion Shitty Bill Inglis was still around, and placed him under close arrest for some minor misdemeanour. This meant he had to take off his Sam Browne belt – the great emblem of being an officer – and stay confined in his room. That evening his room mate gave him a message from Colonel Clark, to say he should lower a long piece of string out of his window. Half an hour later, Wheatley found he had caught a box of chocolates on the end of it.

★

Wheatley's main recreation was reading, but more communally it was singing; the officers had an upright piano. They liked the indecent songs of the period such as "Bollocky Bill The Sailor", "Charlotte the Harlot", "Abdul El Bulbul Emir", and "Never let a sailor get his hand above your knee." Few of these have aged well, and "She Wouldn't Do Just What I Wanted Her To (So I Socked Her In The Eye)" less than most.

Wheatley's favourite was "She Was Poor But She Was Honest", with its well-known chorus:

It's the rich wot gets the pleasure
It's the poor wot gets the blame
It's the same the 'ole world over
It's a bleedin' bloody shame

This could be sung in a mock cockney accent for greater merriment. It is the story of a village girl, seduced by the local squire, who becomes a high class prostitute in the big city, mixing with "Dukes and toffs."

There are further verses, all too realistic and Victorian, about how she ends up as a poxed old crone selling matches, but Wheatley didn't like these; he preferred just to think of her as an erotic social climber. The idea of an amoral woman making her way in the world fascinated him, like Georgina

101

Thursby in his own Roger Brook books, or Amber St. Clare in Kathleen Winsor's once controversial bodice-ripper, *Forever Amber*, which he owned.

Nearly sixty years later Wheatley revisited the theme – and the song itself, quoted on the blurb – with *The Strange Story of Linda Lee*, an abysmal novel from the end of his career (sample chapter titles: 'The Transformation of Linda', 'The Price of a Lift', 'Drugged and Kidnapped,' 'Sex Rears its Ugly Head'.)

As we shall see, the degradation of women was a highly charged subject in Wheatley's imagination, whether as sadistic threats in the thriller fiction, orgiastic rituals in the black magic books, anxieties within his own family, or even national prospects in his wartime defence papers. This was so fascinatingly awful that it could never be allowed to happen, but the possibility always had to be raised as fulsomely as possible.

★

Wheatley had an erotic disappointment at Ipswich, in the shape of a girl called Sibilla. She was a nurse whom he had met back on Streatham Common, one Sunday afternoon. Wheatley and Sibilla met on several evenings and indulged in what a slightly later generation would call heavy petting. The next stage was to get her into a proper bed, so Wheatley invited her down to Ipswich, rented a room for the night at a local farm, and laid on a champagne supper.

The appointed train came in, and she wasn't on it. Thinking she might have missed the train, Wheatley waited for the later one, but still no Sibilla; it transpired that her hospital had been short-staffed and she had not been allowed her time off. Shortly afterwards, Wheatley was moved to Salisbury Plain, and that was the end of his fling with Sibilla. His list of women figures "Sibyle" [sic], but there is no tick.

Wheatley had money troubles, with a Mess bill of £29/13s/1d to be settled before they moved to Salisbury Plain, and a further £16/14s/6d outstanding from the previous month (these sums are not as quaint as they might sound, and represent about £2200 today). He had already had to sell his motorcycle, and now he went to see Colonel Clark to ask if the Mess could extend his credit. Clark was sympathetic but firm. He could lend Wheatley the money himself, or even give it to him, but this would not be good for Wheatley in the long run. He had to face up to his problems, in this case his relationship with his father: "I know that you are not on the best of terms with your father," said Clark, "but he can well afford to pay your Mess bill for you and I'm sure he will. You must write to him."

Wheatley's father paid him an allowance to supplement his army pay of £300 a year (around £14,000, and not much for the life an officer was expected to lead, but some private income was assumed) and he expected him to manage on it. Wheatley awaited his reply with anxiety. In the event he cleared Wheatley's debts, but made a point of being paid back at £5 a month (about £200). Wheatley sent off the first cheque, but was soon in money trouble again and he didn't manage to send any more.

Ten years later, Wheatley's father died, and Wheatley had the melancholy task of sorting through his effects. Among them he found his cheque, and he was moved when he realised that although his father had insisted on having it, he never banked it. Wheatley kept it for the rest of his life.

★

In August 1916 Wheatley moved to Salisbury Plain, where he was stationed at Heytesbury: he later used the area's desolate landscape for the Walpurgis Night sabbat in *The Devil Rides Out*. It was a bleaker posting than Ipswich, but he still managed to enjoy himself. He visited Bath for the first time, where he was very taken by its Georgian terraces, and he devised a gambling game for the Mess. This was a low-tech version of roulette, which could be played using a pack of cards instead of a wheel.

Wheatley found particular solace in the company of Dolly Gregson, whose social class he was pleasantly in awe of. Gregson knew the Marquess of Bath, and on one occasion he and Wheatley were entertaining Lord Bath's two daughters in the tea tent at a gymkhana when a Brigadier's wife hovered nearby, complaining to her husband that all the seats were taken by junior officers "and their shop-girl friends." Gregson was on his feet at once and told her that he only wished he could give her his own seat, but he could hardly leave his guests: "May I introduce you," he added, "to Lady Mary Thynne and Lady Emma Thynne." It must have made Wheatley's day.

It was also through Gregson that Wheatley entered his first gentleman's club, shortly after the war. He had already joined the Services Club in Stratford Place, but this was merely a sort of Mess-cum-hotel in town, compared to the Bachelors' Club on Piccadilly, to which he was taken by Gregson. This was a real club; so real, in fact, that P.G. Wodehouse's Piccadilly Jim is a member, and it features in the fiction of John Buchan.

Compared to the horror taking place in France, Wheatley was having an absurdly pleasant time. The Battle of the Somme had now started, with 57,000 British casualties on the first day, 19,000 of them dead. Wheatley was put in charge of fattening up about thirty horses, for which he had his own hut and servant, and he was free to read for most of the time. In the evenings he tried to bag pheasants from the adjoining woods with his pistol, but they were too fast for him. Ever ingenious, he decided to ply them with corn soaked in brandy, in the hope of slowing down their reflexes. He still didn't manage to bag one.

Two deaths hit Wheatley closer to home around this time: his grandfather, William Yeats Baker, died in August, and Wheatley's old best friend, Douglas Sharp, died in Egypt from blood poisoning after a camel bite. Far from glorious, Sharp's death was still sustained on active service, which seems to be the serious point in the otherwise comic poem Wheatley wrote about the two of them and the two girls glimpsed in Streatham:

> Well you wouldn't be sittin' 'ere,
> If it weren't for some like 'im, sir,

'Oo went off with a smile an' a cheer,
To gasp out 'is life in the desert,
A thousand miles from home . . .

(and Wheatley manages a rhyme with "legions of Rome").

Life on Salisbury Plain became less comfortable as winter came on, and an exercise was begun to dig trenches that would correspond to a section of the Western Front. This involved about five hundred men, with nineteen-year-old Wheatley in charge of the artillery contingent.

It rained and rained. Tents became porous, starting to let water in wherever the canvas was touched. Cooking fires were rained out, and efforts to sustain them with petrol and sugar were useless. The men were cold and miserable, in wet clothes day after day, and they began to fall sick.

Two men died in their tents, and their bodies were taken away in small wagons meant for transporting rifles. Another hundred and seventy had to be taken off the Plain and hospitalised with bronchitis and pneumonia, but still the exercise went on. Wheatley became ill, having already had three bouts of bronchitis since joining the army, most recently in April, when he had three weeks in hospital; his lungs were always his weakness.

Early one morning the head of a Captain Griffiths came through the tent flap, and asked Wheatley why he wasn't on parade. Wheatley told him that the Officer Commanding didn't take the first parade, and that he took the second parade at nine. Griffiths still said he would report him. Next day Brigadier-General Peel appeared on horseback with his entourage. It was still raining heavily, and without dismounting he had Wheatley up before him, told him he would be dealt with later, and rode away.

The exercise was finally called off and they went back to Heytesbury, where Wheatley reported sick. As was the army practice, Wheatley was shown a copy of Griffiths' report on him and given the chance to reply.

A couple of evenings later Wheatley was informally summoned by Colonel Clark. Clark gave him a drink and broke it to him that he was in trouble. He had been out riding with their new Brigadier, who told him he wasn't impressed by the Territorials and was going to find a couple of junior officers to court martial as an example. The first one he was planning to pick on was Wheatley.

Clark had a plan of defence. He thought the exercise on the Plain was a disgrace, with nearly two hundred men hospitalised and two dead, and that there would be a scandal if it became public. He told the Brigadier that Wheatley was angry about what had happened to his men, and that through his father's contacts he was thinking of having a question raised in the House of Commons. The Brigadier would therefore be well advised not to persecute him further.

Wheatley was particularly keen not to have his career fouled up at this point because he was in with a chance of being promoted to Captain and sent to France. Trench mortar batteries were being formed, and Wheatley's name had been put forward as a potential commanding officer for one of them.

Colonel Clark had made a report on Wheatley, and sent him a copy. Dated the nineteenth of September 1916, it read "I have a very good opinion of Lt. Wheatley. He has a good command of men with whom he is very popular. I consider that he has plenty of ability and he is not afraid to use his own judgement." He added a note to this report for Wheatley alone. "Please live up to it," it ran, and regarding the possible promotion:

> Please be as gay as you like, but always remember your added responsibilities, and that you will be looked up to as a leader, and as a man who can be followed: the higher authorities will rely on you as I do.
>
> If I have occasionally thought you have lacked a little 'ballast' I have always thought that the ballast was there, and I am confident that my trust in you as a good boy will not be misplaced.

Wheatley was summoned by Brigadier-General Peel, the

man who had said he would deal with him later. To his surprise, Peel made no mention of their meeting on the Plain, or Griffith's charges, or Wheatley's defence. Instead he talked of the trench mortar companies. Would Wheatley like to command them? The appointment was not for one company but three, and because it involved liasing with infantry it carried staff officer status, as a Staff Captain, which to Wheatley meant a prestigious red hat band and lapel decorations. He accepted at once.

It was a long while before he came to see this offer in a more sinister light, since few trench mortar officers survived more than a couple of months. Peel had just come back from France and he knew what conditions had become. He was sending Wheatley to the Battle of the Somme, which ground to a halt a month later with combined casualties of over a million dead for an advance of seven miles. After Clark's warning about the debacle on Salisbury Plain and questions being raised in the House, Peel may have seen Wheatley as what we would now call a 'whistle blower.' Perhaps this was why he thought France was the place for him.

Once again Wheatley's luck held, although it was another disappointment at the time. Wheatley never got his trench mortars or his red hat band, because his chest grew worse, and he was sent to hospital in London. The battalion finally went to France in January 1917, but Wheatley didn't go with them. Instead he stayed in England, where he met a strange new friend.

CHAPTER TEN

Enter a Satyr

Wheatley was sent to hospital in Marylebone at the Great
Central Hotel, before he obtained permission to be transferred home and was taken to his parents' house in an ambulance. He stayed there through January, under the care of
the family doctor, until he was ordered to report to the 6th
Reserve Brigade at Biscot Camp, near Luton.

Most of its members had been invalided out of France and
were recuperating before being sent back. There was nobody
there that Wheatley knew, but he was soon to make a new
friend. A scrap of paper survives from the Twenties in which
an unknown hand notes:

> Made friends in War with curious type of man seven or
> eight years older than himself whose views and conduct
> entirely obsessed him – His parents strongly disapproved
> of this friendship and influence and tried many times to
> break it up without success. (Eric and women!)

Wheatley's first sight of his friend was not very promising.
Reaching his two-man room, he found another officer lying
on his bed and reading; he was tall, thin, and well dressed.
He continued with his book, until the soldier carrying
Wheatley's luggage had gone, then gave Wheatley a rather
cold look, and said "My name is Gordon-Tombe. Tell me
about yourself."

Tombe perked up a little when Wheatley mentioned that
his father was a wine-merchant, and when Wheatley told
him he hated sport, Tombe laughed and quoted Kipling's
line about "muddied oafs and flanneled fools." Hating sport
was a good sign to Tombe, and he said "I think we shall get
on together."

Wheatley was never good at judging ages and just a few

years later, setting a private detective to search for Tombe, he described him as a man of about forty. This would have made the man on the bed about thirty five, but he was twenty four. Born in Nottinghamshire, then raised and educated in Ireland, Tombe had joined the Public School Corps as a private when war broke out, and later become a lieutenant in the Royal Field Artillery. He had been invalided out of France after being blown up and buried by a shell, which left him with a limp and, in the words of a journalist, "impaired in health and possibly in moral character".

Tombe had no intention of going back. People were sick of the war, especially after the Somme and the long stalemate. Voluntary recruitment had fallen — it would be interesting to know if any of the women and children who handed out white feathers ever had regrets — and at the Front the joking phrase "a separate (or "private") peace" had come into widespread use, as in "I think I'll make a separate peace." Tombe had already made his.

Wheatley remembered Tombe as Gordon Eric Gordon-Tombe, but his name was George Eric Gordon Tombe (not double-barrelled), and he was known as Eric. Tombe told Wheatley that he was estranged from his parents after running away with the family silver, and Wheatley believed it, but it was not true. Tombe was not as distant from his parents as he pretended, but he ran his life by dividing it into strict compartments, which he described as his "system of cul-de-sacs".

Witnesses would later describe him as "a very genial young man, clean-shaven . . . walked with a limp"; "a gentlemanly young fellow, well-dressed, and well spoken." Wheatley describes him as having intelligent eyes, strong eyebrows, and laughter lines making deep curves at the sides of his mouth. Above all, Tombe's charm seems to have been verbal; he spoke a language all his own, and he drew Wheatley into it.

Wheatley's father, in Tombe-speak, was "the Old Hatcher", and he lived in "The Hatching House," his office. Money was "boodle", as in P.G. Wodehouse, and women were " 'oggins" (a word better known, if at all, as naval slang for the sea). Tombe was wont to refer to himself as 'Father', as in "You can't do that on Father" and "No place for Father, me old cock sparrow."

He also seems to have made an impression on Wheatley with "Well, *of course*", and "Well, *I don't know*", and he would say that such-and-such a thing "gets me stone cold", or "stone cold I was – all of a doo da!" Another favourite expression was ". . . disappear in a cloud of blue smoke".

Wheatley's vocabulary was not very wide, but Tombe was at home with words such as *apotheosis*, which was one of his favourites. He was also something of a philosopher, and would emphasise "life is a succession of phases". "The development of one's individuality," a development with a somewhat decadent tinge to it, was of cardinal importance and much recommended to Wheatley. Tombe was also an exponent of what he called the "Masterly Policy of Inactivity" (which comes from Taoism and the *wu wei*, or principle of masterly inaction; it is quoted in the Theosophical writing of Madame Blavatsky). Wheatley later gives it to the Duc de Richleau in *The Devil Rides Out*.

Tombe's father was the Reverend George Gordon Tombe, and much of Tombe's character can be seen as a rebellion against his background. He would refer to God as "the old gentleman with a long grey beard who invariably speaks English" (another of his odd sayings was "I am so happy dear boy – that I wouldn't call God me uncle").

Looking back in old age, Wheatley felt that "In mental development I owe more to him than to any other person who has entered my life," and he dedicates his autobiography to "My father, my grandfathers and to my great friend in the First World War, Gordon Eric Gordon-Tombe, who, between them, made me what I am."

Wheatley had always been something of a bon viveur, but in a very small way. He would boast to Hilda that he had managed to sleep late, or breakfasted "sumptuously" on scrambled eggs and sausages. But when Tombe entered his life, he brought with him a more sophisticated idea of being what he called a "conscious hedonist". Tombe incarnated the late Victorian and Edwardian reaction against Christianity and morality, along with a strong current of Edwardian paganism (as in *The Wind in the Willows*, with its manifestation of the God Pan in an almost incongruous chapter, 'The Piper at the Gates of Dawn'). Tombe was interested in religion, and he persuaded Wheatley to the idea – part of the wider influence of Theosophy – that Christ, Buddha, Lao-Tzu and other sages were all equally "masters."

In short, Tombe introduced Wheatley, in a slightly belated fashion, to the whole alternative syllabus of the 1890s, the decade of aestheticism, decadence, and esoterica. Tombe was especially keen on Oscar Wilde and Walter Pater, the philosopher of nihilistic aestheticism who argued that it was not the fruits of experience, but experience itself, that was the important thing. It was a radical distinction, doing away with Victorian ideas of purpose and progress, and replacing them with a refined version of living only for the minute.

Wheatley had long been an avid reader, but mainly of historical romances and spy fiction. His spare moments in the War, of which there had been many, were not spent studying *Field Artillery Training* or *Stable Management*, but reading the likes of Baroness Orczy. It was Tombe ("the most widely read man I have ever met") who introduced him not just to to Wilde and Pater but the Russians (Dostoevsky, Chekhov, Tolstoy) and the French (Flaubert, Zola, Gautier, Maupassant, Baudelaire, Balzac, Proust).

The Tombe syllabus had a particular bias towards books that were then considered racy, such as Rabelais, Boccaccio, and Casanova, and shaded into sexology – Krafft-Ebing and Havelock Ellis, as well as Freud, shifting further into the likes of the Marquis de Sade, *The Perfumed Garden*, the Burton edition of the *Thousand and One Nights*, and the works of "Dr Jacobus X", the latter indecent by any standards but dressed up as anthropology.

Tombe also encouraged Wheatley to read about ancient civilisations and world religions. He read Plato, Ovid, Aristophanes; Lucius Apuleius's *Golden Ass*, Gibbon on ancient Rome, Wallis Budge and Flinders Petrie on ancient Egypt. He read about China, Persia, Chaldea and India. And he read the sacred books: the Koran, the Vedas, the Mayan Popol Vuh, the Zoroastrian Zend Avesta, the sayings of Buddha, and the Tao Te Ching.

Tombe's own creed was remembered by Wheatley as the "cynical but happy" *carpe diem* nihilism of the *Rubaiyat of Omar Khayyam*, which was immensely popular at the time and went through endless luxury editions; Wheatley later owned four or five.

★

One of the most damning insults in the Tombe lexicon was "imitation of gentleman." This has its ironic aspect, because it could apply to both Tombe and Wheatley. Tombe was less of a gentleman than he seemed. The hyphen was assumed (his surname was Tombe), and he was a motor mechanic. Before the war he had been living in Stoke Newington, and in 1913 he had married a local girl called Ruby Burbidge, a theatre actress. He was then calling himself George Gordon-Tombe, and he put four years on his age; at twenty, he was not old enough to marry without his parent's permission.

Some words in the Tombe lexicon are puzzling, one of them being "bimana." This seems to refer to people en masse, or ordinary people, and it seems to be derogatory. The most likely meaning is 'two-handed animals' (as in 'bi-manual'), from the eighteenth-century French naturalist Cuvier. Cuvier suggested that the human species deserved this nomenclature because it was the only manually adept animal. In Tombe-speak it seems to mean manual in a more scathing sense, almost the sense of Shakespeare's "rude mechanicals."

It is ironic that Tombe himself was a motor mechanic – or as he more genteelly put it on his marriage certificate, a *motor expert*. Being a mechanic was not only a little declassé, but it didn't pay very well, and before long Tombe found that crime was much more the ticket. Fraud and fornication were the two main activities of his short life as a gentleman criminal, in which Wheatley would find himself playing Bunny to Tombe's Raffles.

112

★

Wheatley was still trying to court Barbara Symonds, but it was hopeless. As ever, his nervous letters to Barbara have none of the charm of his letters to Hilda. Convalescing after Salisbury Plain, he tells Barbara that after her last reply he had decided never to write again, but now he has changed his mind:

> The reason is that I am so absolutely bored that I should just like to smash everything in the house, but still as one doesn't I thought I would just let off steam by writing to you instead because I simply hate doing it and I am quite certain that you will hate to read it.

He continues

> I am absolutely fed up I got a very bad attack of flu and pneumonia in November . . . and so I have been on leave ever since, and I am afraid London is getting very dull or I am probably the latter . . .

Would she meet him for lunch up West, followed by a show? "I don't suppose you will for a single minute,"

> I know you think I am just the biggest thing in outsiders that ever happened why goodness knows I don't except for the fact of the call I paid that Sunday afternoon and I only did that out of sheer devilry because you practically refused to speak to me when I saw you come out of church that morning . . .

He adds a resume of their near-affair, and the Incident:

> . . . I suppose I behaved in rather a outsiderish fashion many years ago on that Sunday when it poured in torrents and we took a cab home, do you remember my passionate avowals of love and kissing you by main force

113

much against your will, there you see out comes pre-historic man in all his glory seizing the thing he wants in spite of protests . . .

Wheatley then treats Barbara to a picture of his likely bourgeois future, balanced against the roguish possibility of Wheatley the caveman cowboy:

. . . even if I was a very terrible person then I am not so very frightful now in fact it rather terrifies me to think what a highly respectable person I am becoming twenty years hence I can see myself as a highly respectable merchant paying my weekly bills going to church on Sundays to the family pew, taking up gardening as a hobby travelling up and down in a first class smoker to Victoria inordinately fond of my roses and altogether a highly useful member of society. That is of course if the prehistoric bit in me doesn't come out in that case I shall probably turn into a cattle thief or card sharper or any of those other charming people you can see any afternoon of any day at any picture palace . . .

"I see that I have talked an awful lot of drivel," Wheatley adds, and this may have been what Barbara thought. But if she felt like taking on "the philanthropic work of cheering up a very very bored little officer," then she was invited to drop him a line mentioning a restaurant and show.

She replied as kindly as possible, saying it was really very nice of Wheatley to want take her out, and that she was sorry to have to refuse. She signed it "Yours sincerely, Barbara Symonds", an improvement on her previous "B.A.Symonds".

But Wheatley wouldn't give up, and a year or two later, with Barbara now dating a Major, he was writing

. . . my pals all wonder what has happened to the cheerful lad I used to be – if they could only know all the desperate longing that I have for you. . . the pent up maddening passion which makes me want to seize you whether you will or no – drag you even, and rush you in a car up to some tiny village in the Highlands where the peasants cannot speak English – and defy all the Majors that ever walked to take you away from me – perhaps they would understand, yet many of them are Bimina [sic], and to them understanding is not given.

That is the great mistake with me – were I only Bimina too, I would adhere to my original plan and wait confidently for the future, but I'm not, the agonies I go through are too much for me and unless I cut adrift I shall get on the rocks and do something foolish.

What Barbara thought of this business about "Bimina" is anyone's guess.

★

"Gordon Eric seemed to desire no other friends than myself," Wheatley remembered, "so apart from meals he spent very little time in the Mess." Wheatley's old hatred of Church Parade became more pointed through knowing Tombe, and Tombe gave him an erudite piece of advice. If he wanted to get out of Church Parade, Tombe suggested, he should say that instead of being C of E he was a *Neo-Nestorian* (a follower of the fourth-century heretic Nestorius, who insisted that the divine and human aspects of Christ were separate). Wheatley went along with this eagerly – probably because he wanted to *belong* as a friend of Tombe – but it may have been a joke on Tombe's part. If it was such a good idea, one wonders why he didn't do it himself.

It is just the sort of ploy that the army is good at batting back, and Wheatley found himself ordered to lead the Church Parade for the men from various dissenting and non-conformist sects. His new job was to march them to and from a distant Methodist chapel, so now instead of an hour within the Luton camp he had an eight mile march every Sunday morning.

Wheatley sometimes went up to London (although he could no longer manage it on Sundays, thanks to Tombe's clever advice) with various cronies from the Mess. If they split up in town their practice was to rendezvous at midnight in the Turkish Baths on Russell Square. This was cheaper than a hotel and a good place to sober up, so they would ask for an early call and stay until it was time to go back to camp in the dawn. Tombe would also go to London, on his own, and Wheatley noticed that Tombe never invited him along. He evidently hadn't yet found a proper place for Wheatley in his system of cul-de-sacs.

When Tombe was away, Wheatley would go to the Mess and play cards in endless games of vingt-et-un (or "pon-toon"). These would go on interminably, breaking for meals, and in one session Wheatley grew so bored with his cards that he called aloud to the Devil to give him luck, no doubt feeling this was a very rakish and Regency-Hellfire-ish thing to do.

Immediately he drew two aces and 'split,' drew again, and ended up with three 'Naturals' and a 'five-and-under'[1]. He cleaned up with sixteen times their stake from each of the other players (he wrote in the Fifties, growing to twenty-two times in his autobiography). "It scared me stiff," says Wheatley.

If, that is, it ever happened. By the time Wheatley wrote the story up he was Britain's occult uncle, and he had needed to find occult anecdotes. Nevertheless, it is possible it did happen, particularly under Tombe's influence, and it would have been subjectively very striking, like asking the Devil to make a bus come and seeing one immediately appear.

*

Wheatley was still being sent on courses: he went to courses in Buckinghamshire, Woolwich (where he noticed that the social standard of the Officer's Mess had declined badly in the course of the War) and Northampton, where he had

[1] 'Split', choosing to play them as separate hands: 'Naturals', aces and tens; 'five-and-under', five cards near 21 but not 'bust' i.e. not over 21.

to spend time in a gas-filled shed wearing a primitive gas mask. No one liked this, but they had to do it so they could assure the men it was safe.

It became increasingly clear that at last Wheatley was going to get to France, but it was an incomparably less exciting prospect than it had seemed four years earlier. Wheatley's mother bought him a bespoke armoured tunic from Wilkinson's, an early form of flak jacket, with rectangular steel plates linked together in the lining to cover most of the torso. Fearing a wound to the genitals as much as anything else, Wheatley insisted on having the lower front flaps armoured as well.

Wheatley's orders came through in July, and he took his 'embarkation leave', a period allowed before going to the front. His father made him waste a day of this going to Westgate to say goodbye to his Wheatley grandparents. He was a man of twenty going to France, perhaps to die, and Grandmother Wheatley gave him a parting gift of two shillings (about three pounds today).

Eric had meanwhile found a job with the Air Ministry in Kingsway. On Wheatley's last day in London he asked Eric to lunch at the Carlton Hotel, which stood on the corner of Pall Mall and Haymarket, and they ordered melon, Lobster Cardinal, roast duck and a rum omelette, only be told they were not allowed to have it.

A new regulation had come in forbidding uniformed officers to spend more than five shillings on a meal (about eight pounds). Wheatley sent for the head waiter, and explained it was his last day in London before going to the Front. He then sent for the manager, who was French. Still no good.

What should they do? They could have meat with baked beans, and an ice cream to follow, or one of them could go up to Piccadilly Circus and bring back a prostitute to hand over their money, if they were prepared "to suffer our Lucullan feast to be spoiled by the woman's presence." While they were deciding, the manager came rushing back after a change of heart, because Wheatley was going to fight for France: "Have what you like! Have what you like!" he said, "But remember, your mother stays in the hotel. It is she who pays the bill."

Next morning, Wheatley took the train from Victoria to Southampton. And the day after that, August 8th 1917, he finally left for France.

CHAPTER ELEVEN

The Incredible Journey

The German General Staff used to divide their officers into four categories: clever and lazy, clever and hardworking, stupid and lazy, and stupid and hardworking. The clever and lazy made good generals, the clever and hardworking made good staff officers, and the stupid and lazy were quite viable as regimental officers. The problem group was the stupid and hardworking: these were "a positive menace and had to be got rid of quickly as possible." Lieutenant Wheatley was clever and lazy, and a modest asset to his country's war effort.

Wheatley had gone over to France with a friend from Luton, Captain Colsell. They were camped just outside Le Havre, where the evening streets were full of men in khaki and French prostitutes. A large café called Tortoni's was the main venue for officers, and in Wheatley's list of sexual encounters he ticks "Havre with Colsell" and "Havre Tartoni's". Wheatley was anxious not to catch venereal disease, and Hilda Gosling remembered him as not only "always extremely interested in sex" but also "preventive methods. These ideas were almost obsessions as a young man and during the war."

VD was rife, and the situation was made worse by a decree that any soldier reporting sick with it would have his leave to England stopped. The intention was to stop the men from consorting with prostitutes, but the result was to deter men who had VD from having it treated. This was the kind of order Wheatley hated, and it added to his animus against Victorian morality and Christianity. Among the medical camps where VD was treated there was a special one for army padres and chaplains, or so Wheatley believed.

After nine nights Colsell and Wheatley received their orders to report for the front line in Flanders. They went via Rouen, where there was time for a last fling between trains.

They enquired after the town's most luxurious brothel, where Wheatley was introduced to a girl on a divan in an octagonal room covered in mirrors. Typical of a high class continental *maison* of the Belle Epoque, the mirrors were a refinement by then several centuries old. Sir Epicure Mammon, in Ben Jonson's *The Alchemist*, dreams of a room with the softest of beds, some pornographic pictures, and

> Then, my glasses,
> Cut in more subtle angles, to disperse
> And multiply the figures, as I walk,
> Naked between my succubae.

Afterwards Wheatley rushed for his midday train, which took him and Colsell on to the town of Poperinghe, behind the Ypres salient. From there, Wheatley went to the 36th Division Ammunition Column at Vlamertinghe. These were landscapes he never forgot, and years later he was drawn back to make a motoring tour, which he wrote up in a leather bound 'Motor Trips' notebook from the Times Book Club.

On the road from Ypres he remembered "up this road had to go every ounce of food and ammunition . . . an unending stream of traffic never ceasing day or night as thick as Piccadilly at midday and the Boche never ceased to shell it as he knew that it was the only road by which supplies could be got up . . . the sides were lined with a thousand and one broken motors carts lorries waggons just thrown over the side so that the stream might keep moving."

At Vlamertinghe he remembered "The Overturned Gasometer, The Lunatic Asylum (on YPRES road) the Menin Gate. This was where I was stationed when I first went out, and very badly bombed, shelled night and day, it is one of the most unpleasant places I have ever been in."

The First War is remembered as an infantry war, a war of men with bayonets running towards machine guns, but it was also an artillery war, to an unprecedented degree, with over half the British casualties on the Western Front caused by German shelling. British artillery was equally formidable, launching the Somme offensive with a bombardment of one and a half million shells, or over seventy shells for every yard of the German front.

Wheatley wrote to Hilda that on his first night "a German 8in [shell] landed quite near and the bits flew through the tent in which I was sleeping, and covered everything in mud" and then a few nights later (in his autobiography he remembers it as the first night, conflating several events) they were bombed. A bomb landed twenty yards from the Officers Mess, and on running out to see what had happened Wheatley saw his first dead man, his body twisted beneath a wagon where he had dived for shelter.

Two weeks later, Wheatley was in the Mess when the Germans bombed the lines about fifty yards away. This time there were no human casualties, but carnage among the horses. Ankle deep in blood, Wheatley had to spend the next hour putting injured horses out of their misery with pistol shots to the head.

Even here, Wheatley managed to enjoy himself. He didn't have to get up early, he had no long stable duties, and – as he told Hilda – he spent much of his time lounging in the Mess, smoking, drinking, and reading novels. This pleasant routine was broken when it was Wheatley's turn to take ammunition from the depot up to the front line artillery for the battle of Passchaendale, raging a few miles away.

There was a regulation that Field Artillery should never move faster than a trot, or, with ammunition-loaded wagons, a walk. Wheatley was at the edge of ruined Ypres with a twelve wagon convoy when howitzer shells started coming down, "with a perfectly deafening roar." They were coming one every three minutes, so Wheatley halted his convoy and waited until one had just landed. "Then did I go at a walk? – did I hell –" (an expression he had picked up from Eric). He galloped them down the main street while fragments of brick rained down from the last explosion, and he was past the danger area when the next shell came down. "So," he concluded, "artillery *does* go faster than a trot sometimes."

Self preservation was never far from Wheatley's mind. The

encampment was too wet for trenches, so they were above ground and exposed to whatever bombs and shells might burst nearby. Instead of using his camp bed, he put his sleeping bag down at ground level, then built a barricade of earth-filled ammunition boxes around it to protect him from shrapnel; an early instance of a tendency to fortification that we will see more of later.

Wheatley's first six weeks in France were his worst, although he was grateful he had escaped the fate of the infantry at Passchendaele. After a month they were pulled back from the front and a few months later he could write to Hilda that he was amused by the farcical inactivity of his service life. He then quoted the line he would often produce later in connection with his War, from an officer in Marlborough's army who described war as "long periods of intensive boredom punctuated by moments of acute fear."

★

Wheatley's division retired to a village called Waten, and they had only been there a couple of days when he was summoned to see the colonel. It was already night, and Wheatley put on his Sam Browne belt and went across a moonlit meadow to the colonel's farmhouse. Wheatley thought his lack of martial spirit must have been noticed. This was like going to the headmaster's office.

The colonel showed hardly any interest in Wheatley and referred him to an adjutant. Far from being in trouble, he was to be put in charge of something, although the adjutant was vague about what it might be. Instead he gave him instructions on getting there, by horse and rail, and a travel chit for the Railway Transport Officer (RTO). He was then to go to Headquarters IVth Corps and report to the Staff Captain for his new responsibility.

What was Wheatley to be in charge of? It might be a trench railway for ferrying ammunition, a field hospital (surely not, he thought), or some Battery positions for the divisional artillery. Whatever it was, it was essential not to be late. Honoured, frightened, and exhilarated, he was keen to take up his new responsibility. He was up at dawn, had his route planned on the map – he always liked maps – and rode off.

Wheatley reached the railway, proudly presented his voucher, and told the RTO where he was going. The RTO told him that he should report again to another RTO at Etaples, and that a train would be along at midday. Wheatley bought himself some sweets, returned to the station, and waited for three hours. Midday came and went, but not the train. Wheatley asked the RTO what had happened, and was told it had been derailed.

At about four o'clock, it arrived. Wheatley found himself a compartment with three other officers, and the train pulled out. It moved slowly, and after chugging along at about twenty miles an hour, it would stop for no obvious reason, and passengers would get out to stretch their legs. Then the whistle blew, they got back on, and it would go a little further. It was dusk before the train went through a tunnel and reached the station at Boulogne, where it stopped once again.

Wheatley was low on cigarettes and he felt like a drink. His kit – hat, overcoat, spurs, haversack, gasmask and Sam Browne belt – was all stashed in the luggage rack, so after asking his companions to keep an eye on it, he climbed from the train, nipped across the tracks, and climbed up on the station platform. There were no refreshments, so Wheatley let himself out of the station and went to a cafe across the road, where he bought cigarettes and knocked back a quick vermouth–cassis.

Back on the platform, he was about to jump down on the tracks again when an engine came out of the tunnel, pulling trucks and cutting him off from his train. As he waited for it to pass, and the first dozen or so trucks had gone by, he noticed what might for a moment have looked like an optical illusion: his own train was starting to move in the opposite direction.

Now frantic, Wheatley waited for what seemed like a hundred trucks to crawl by, until at last it was clear and he jumped down on to the track and ran after his train. It was gradually picking up speed, but Wheatley managed to catch up with it just before it completely disappeared into the other tunnel. He launched himself at the door of the guard's van, hoping to grab the handle and swing himself in, but instead he fell.

He had hurt his knee and he was winded, but as he stared after the retreating train he noticed something. It was stopping again. Wheatley now ran after it for all he was worth, eyes fixed on it, until his foot caught some kind apparatus on the track. He went down full length, cutting his hands. Picking himself up, he saw the train had started up again, and its rear lights were steadily disappearing. It was all over with him and his train.

Limping out of the tunnel, filthy from head to foot, he went back to the station and told the RTO there what had happened. The RTO told him there was no other train to Etaples that night, but there might be one at the Gare Maritime (Boulogne had two stations). It had now started to rain and there was no transport, but Wheatley limped down to the harbour.

Wheatley was by now extremely worried, and knew he was potentially in deep trouble. He had only been in France six weeks, and he might soon be in disgrace for turning his first real responsibility into a fiasco, which amounted to going absent without leave. And if he really disgraced himself, his Victorian father – already worried by his fecklessness and indiscipline – might even throw him out of the house and business without a penny. Or so he feared.

Wheatley should have been in Etaples that afternoon, and now it was already evening. Reporting to the RTO at the Gare Maritime, who seemed to regard him with amazement and distaste, Wheatley found there was a civilian train at eleven o'clock, which he would be allowed on, but this was the end of any hope of reporting that night. It would have to be next morning now, and it would look as if he had deliberately left the train at Boulogne to spend a night there.

Wanting to clean himself up and eat, Wheatley was directed to the Officers Club. He was amazed by how luxurious it was, living up to everything front-line soldiers believed about the officers at the rear. Wheatley was looking at these

124

immaculately dressed officers when one of them came up and told him that he had no right to use the club, because he was under arrest.

This was a shock, but it was a misunderstanding. The officer thought Wheatley was already under arrest, because officers under arrest were not allowed to wear their Sam Browne belt. Without much sympathy, he directed Wheatley to the wash room, where the mirror told Wheatley what an unimpressive appearance he had been cutting. He cleaned himself up and went in to dinner, where the other officers looked at him with contempt. No one asked him what had happened. Eventually it was time for his train.

It was an old-fashioned, corridorless train, and Wheatley was in a compartment filled with French civilians. There was no light, and the stations were blacked out. It stopped at every station, and sometimes it just stopped: since rural French stations sometimes had no platforms, it was hard to tell if it was at a station or not. Wheatley started to worry that he would miss his station and be carried past Etaples – one of those words not made for the English mouth, like Ypres ("Wipers") – but none of his fellow passengers could understand where he needed to get out. If he was carried past Etaples he might not even be able to report next morning to the Staff Captain, "who by then had become an ogre in my mind."

Wheatley had to lean out of the window every time the train stopped, and shout. After about a dozen stops, his shouting brought a British military policeman to the train, carrying a lantern. "If it's Atarp you want, this it, sir" he said.

It was not yet midnight, so he thought there might still be a chance of reporting to the Staff Captain's HQ, if he was still up, and Wheatley asked the RTO where he was. Unfortunately the Captain was not at Etaples at all, but at Amiens. Junior officers on journeys such as Wheatley's were never given full information as to their destination, for security reasons, but instead sent along stage-by-stage. The RTO then told Wheatley that Amiens was where the train he had just been on was going, and if only he had stayed on it would have taken him there.

The next train to Amiens was at five in the morning. Wheatley was so despondent he just sat on the platform in his wet clothes to wait, until the military policeman shepherded him down the road to a YMCA rest hut and gave him a cup of coffee. He was up again and on the train at five. Chilled to the bone without his trench coat, he arrived at Amiens, and again asked the RTO for the Staff Captain, who laughed and redirected Wheatley to the town of Albert. There was a train just leaving, and Wheatley ran and caught it. Arriving at Albert an hour later, he was redirected to Achet-le-Grand. He had five hours to wait for the train, which meant he had time to have breakfast.

Being closer to the Front, the Officer's Club was Spartan compared to Boulogne, but Wheatley got a good breakfast. He still had money, and he looked in vain for a shop where he could buy a hat and overcoat. In due course he reached Achet, where he was told to continue – he must have been getting used to this – to Bapaume.

The train was at six, and meanwhile he could spend the afternoon waiting in a Salvation Army hut. The only other occupant of the hut was a padre. Wheatley told him his story, but the man wasn't interested. Feeling cold, Wheatley would have liked a tot of rum. He had to make do with tea and biscuits, and then sat listening to the rain as he thought about the trouble he was in.

Going back to the station for the train, Wheatley fell into the company of some officers who told him this train was coming from Amiens. Had he only known, he could have spent ten hours there, checked into a hotel, had a good lunch, bought some new kit, and still been on the same train he was now joining. This was no comfort to Wheatley, who foresaw being court martialled, having the buttons ripped off his uniform, and being reduced to the ranks. He was now twenty-four hours late, after jumping off a train to buy a drink.

The train from Amiens was late. They waited, and news came that it had derailed, like the first train. It would be a couple of hours late, if it arrived at all that night. Wheatley's despair grew worse: "I visualised one thing leading to another until a whole section of the Front had been endangered owing to my criminal dereliction of duty."

One of the others suggested they should catch a lorry instead of waiting, and this they did. They climbed on the back and several hours later they reached Bapaume. This time Wheatley really had arrived, or so he thought. But on finding the RTO, there was still further to go: the IVth Corps HQ was at a village called Etricourt, some miles to the south.

The RTO ("a very decent fellow") urged Wheatley to go the Officers Club, where he could get a bath, a hot meal, and a bed, and leave Etricourt until the morning. Wheatley insisted, hoping he might still be able to report to the Staff Captain that night. Being cashiered by court martial was one thing, but if he let things get worse he might also be imprisoned. There was a train leaving for Etricourt in ten minutes, not by a fast or straight route, but it might still get there by midnight.

Unfortunately it consisted of open trucks, which had been used for transporting coal. Wheatley had no time even for a cup of tea, but the RTO gave him some empty sandbags to help him keep warm. Putting them over his damp clothes, he put two round his waist like a kilt, one on his head like a turban, and one over his shoulders like a short cape. The train was almost empty, but for a few soldiers using it to return to their units. Wheatley shared his wagon with three of these, and he was relieved to find that one of them, a Staff Sergeant, actually belonged to the IVth Corps HQ he was seeking. Now at last he was on the right track.

Or perhaps not. A couple of men didn't think this train was actually going to Etricourt. The nearest it would go was a ruined village called Ytres, which would still leave them with five miles to walk. At least there was a rest camp at Ytres, where they could spend the night, but far from being welcome news this infuriated Wheatley. By now he would like to have walked, but he was afraid to lose the Staff Sergeant.

Covered in coal dust and dressed in wet sacking, Wheatley and his companions were exposed to the wind and rain.

Within minutes, his sacks were like sodden dishcloths, and still the train crawled. The four of them huddled together in one corner of the wagon, until finally they stopped at Ytres. Wheatley was only too pleased to let the much more experienced Staff Sergeant take charge of the party. He knew the rest camp, where they were used to troops arriving at all hours and would provide tea, hot soup, and clean blankets.

Walking down the road, they came to a gate in a hedge, with some soldiers standing around. This was the place all right, said the sergeant. But where was the camp? "All the fucking tents has been blown down," said one of the soldiers. Even the fires were rained out. There was nothing to do but push on.

By now Wheatley was all in, but the Staff Sergeant knew the way. He even knew a shortcut over the moorland, which would reduce the journey to about three miles. Wheatley was immensely grateful for his presence, and more than glad to follow him.

They had been trudging along for half an hour when they found a body of water at the foot of the slope they were following. The Staff Sergeant didn't remember it. After an excursion to look at an unreadable signpost, and a new hope in the shape of a half remembered track, they realised over two hours had gone by for a journey that should have taken an hour. They were, in fact, lost.

The occasional flare had been visible over the horizon, although not with enough brilliance to light their route. But it was now that Wheatley had his inspiration. The flares were going up over the Front, and if they walked straight towards it, they would meet their own side before they met the Germans. The ground had been a battlefield the previous year, full of shellholes and barbed wire, but they trudged on, caked with mud, until finally they saw a light and made for it in a straight line. It was a radio caravan, attached to the IVth Corps HQ.

It was now five in the morning. Two clerks were up and working, while some other men were sleeping on the floor around a stove. Wheatley told one of the clerks who he was, and why he had come, and the clerk offered to wake the Staff Captain. This was not what Wheatley wanted to do at all: he didn't want to wake the sleeping ogre and drag him out of bed two hours early to listen to excuses. Instead he tried to get two hours sleep and was woken at seven to face his superior.

★

The Staff Captain looked at Wheatley, covered in mud, without his hat or coat or the all-important Sam Browne belt, and as Wheatley explained he began to smile. They had sent for an officer, he said, but they weren't expecting him for several days. Young officers generally broke their journey to have a good time on the way, and then said they couldn't get there any earlier because of trouble with the trains, so plenty of time was always allowed for them to arrive.

"You poor boy," said the Staff Captain, sending Wheatley off for a bath and lending him his own dressing gown, "You shall tell us over breakfast." And in due course Wheatley was brought to have breakfast with the Staff Captain and two other senior officers, and treated to kidneys on toast, poached eggs, real coffee, ham and fruit. Quite unlike the padre in the Salvation Army shed, they smiled and laughed as Wheatley told them the story of his journey, and urged him to make sure he had enough breakfast. Finally they kitted him out with a coat, tin hat, and gas mask, and the General sent him off for the last two miles in his own Rolls-Royce.

"Cross my heart," writes Wheatley; "every single word of the above story is true."

★

We shall never know if it is or not. Wheatley first wrote it up as a 10,000 word set piece in 1960, and he reproduces it in his autobiography. The Nightmare Journey, as Wheatley calls it, is a particularly good example of a Wheatley narrative of the kind that made his fortune, with a constant alternation of hopes and setbacks; what he later called his 'snakes and ladders' effect.

It is notable that Wheatley writes in a decisive role for his younger self when they make for the front line lights, over-riding the protests of the Staff Sergeant. This was the kind of decisiveness that, in Wheatley's judgement, "justifies a young man being given a commission and the authority to lead older men."

Above all, the happy ending shows Wheatley's ambivalent attitude towards the dog-eat-dog world of meritocracy. These men were officers of the old school, acting from a disinterested sense of duty rather than career ambition. Most officers in the post-1914 'New Army' were not like this, in Wheatley's estimation. They were Jobsworths and greasy pole climbers, "giving no thought whatever to the welfare of those under them, but driving their officers and men to often quite unnecessary exertions when they were utterly worn out, in order to curry favour with some General." The officers who treated Wheatley to breakfast, on the other hand, showed something more like *noblesse oblige*.

And now, having finally arrived at IVth Corp HQ, Wheatley found out what his new responsibility was.

CHAPTER TWELVE

Last Hope of the General Staff

Wheatley was put in charge of the 4th Corps ammunition dump at the ruined Somme village of Ytres, and looked after it through September 1917. A railway wagon would arrive each night, and Wheatley would supervise the placing and camouflaging of the unloaded ammunition.

This left him with time on his hands, and he began his first novel. Inspired by a local chateau, it was called 'Julie's Lovers' and featured an English and German officer staying at the chateau just before the war, both falling in love with the daughter of the house.

After his stint with the ammunition dump, Wheatley went to nearby Equancourt, where the Division was sent to rest after Ypres. This suited Wheatley, since Amiens was nearby. Wheatley remembered the best of the brothels as Madame Prudhomme's, run by a dignified old lady with white hair. Clients were presented to the girls in the drawing room, so that a girl could veto a customer if she wished. Wheatley had five or six girls in Amiens, including Colette, "Big Fair", and Marie, all of whom are neatly ticked in his list. Later in life he collected books.

"Amiens with Colsell" is another ticked entry. One night he and Captain Colsell picked up two girls in a café and the girls took them for a long taxi ride to a house where a dentist practised in the daytime, but where it turned out there was only one bedroom free. They tossed a coin, and Wheatley and his girl had to make do with the dentist's chair, before joining the others upstairs and swapping partners.

Wheatley's parents wrote regularly, and his father sent him a generous cigarette allowance of five thousand a month, straight from Cairo, so he could offer them to the men. From his father's letters, Wheatley learned that London was being bombed by Zeppelins. Eclipsed by memories of the Blitz, the bombing in the first war was traumatic enough, particularly since nothing like it had occurred before. Several hundred people were killed, and the famous department store of Swan and Edgar's on Piccadilly Circus was hit.

The manager of the Wheatley shop had left London to escape the bombing, and the window had been smashed by a bomb in South Audley Street, after which there had been looting. Drink was running short: bottles of Kummel had increased in price from five shillings to three pounds (at modern prices, from about eight pounds to about a hundred) and even gin was becoming expensive. Food was also short, and Wheatley's father had started keeping pigs and rabbits.

Wheatley's mother wrote more frequently, although he found her letters trivial. She was frightened by the bombing and spent time at Brighton, from where she complained to Wheatley about the number of Jews who were there, having fled the bombs. General Allenby was having a storming success in Palestine, where he took Jerusalem, and Mrs Wheatley sent Dennis the quip of the day: Allenby had taken Palestine to relieve Brighton from the Jews.

Close to Equancourt was Etricourt, where Wheatley was quartered in the garden of an old chateau, destroyed by the occupying Germans when they were forced to withdraw. Not wanting to spend winter under canvas, the Major decided that two men who had been bricklayers could make an Officer's Mess from the bricks in the rubble. It was built as a lean-to in a corner, and inspired Wheatley to try his hand at what would later become his hobby. He built a two room 'house' for himself and the officer he was sharing with. He drew a map of it in his 'Motor Trips' notebook, labelled 'My House.'

Wheatley knocked up a very creditable building, with a fireplace and a hot water tank to heat above it. His friends named his house "Crooked Villa", and he went to look for it when he eventually returned to France, but never found it.

While he was bricklaying he had a strange experience. He

left the Mess after dinner one night and started work; if the moon was good, he would lay bricks until one or two in the morning. While he was working he had an unpleasant sensation of being watched from the ruins of the chateau: "I saw nothing, but felt myself to be threatened by a spiritual force of overwhelming evil . . . I felt . . . some incredibly evil thing had its gaze riveted on the back of my neck . . . Suddenly my nerve broke." Wheatley ran to his tent, lit his light, and sat on his camp bed shivering.

There was no one there, but Wheatley had felt as if a tiger was about to spring on his back. His only explanation was that the chateau had been a German field hospital (on taking over the site, the men had found bloodstained uniforms and some pickelhaube helmets, much prized as souvenirs). Germans had probably spent their final hours there in agony, and he believed this was related to the hate-filled presence he had felt watching him.

Wheatley makes no mention of this in his letters to Hilda, his 'Motor Trip' journal, or his First War reminiscences in *Saturdays with Bricks*. It is only in his late autobiography (and *The Devil and All His Works* of 1971, where he suggests he was menaced by an "elemental" spirit) that he produces this story. It belongs with another experience from the same period – whether the period is 1917 or the 1970s is hard to say – when the officer he shared Crooked Villa with (Picquet in his autobiography, Pickett in his letters) came back from leave in England.

Picquet had been home to be with his sister, who was mortally ill. She died while he was beside her deathbed, and as she was dying (their father having died some years earlier) she had said "Hello, Daddy." Her brother-in-law Jacques was a captain in the French army, and the stranger thing was that she had then looked surprised, and said "What, you here too, Jacques?" As far as anyone knew he was alive, but next day a telegram arrived to say that he had been killed the day before Picquet's sister died. This story, says Wheatley, "fully convinced me of the survival of personality after death", a subject that was very close to his heart in the

Seventies. Again, he makes no mention of it in his letters to Hilda[1].

Picquet or Pickett, however, certainly existed. Wheatley wrote to Hilda that he was much consoled to have with him

> one Pickett a subaltern of the old school to wit a most amusing card quite one of the best people, and when we get away in the evening to our house which I hear the Mater told you about we wile away the time by a little "game of chance" or reading to each other books (Some books I can tell you I got them in Harve [sic] and will show you some at Christmas) or telling each other little tales of adventures with the fair but frail . . .

Wheatley seems to have granted Hilda honorary exemption from the 'fair but frail' category. The dated usage '*Some books, I can tell you*' means they were *hot stuff*, or at least very warm.

*

Having been sent on another course and returned to find the camp moved, Wheatley was at Bertincourt on the morning of November 20th, 1917, when the Battle of Cambrai began. This was an Allied offensive using the new secret weapon, the tank.

Attacks had previously been preceded by a massive artillery barrage, often lasting a week, during which the Germans were effectively warned and took cover in deep shelters. This time the barrage was simultaneous with the tank attack, followed by infantry, taking the Germans by surprise in what at first seemed like an extraordinary victory. Wheatley later noted "from the ridge you get one of the finest views in France, you can see CAMBRAI plainly and from here I watched the main phases of the seven days battle that followed the push."

Before long the advantage was lost, and after several days

---

[1] Nor have I found a likely girl among British death certificates during the period that Wheatley was in France.

Barbara Symonds.

Hilda Gosling.

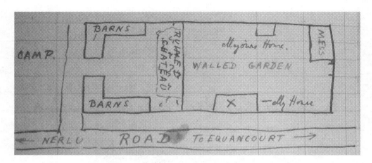

"My House": the little brick house Wheatley built on the Western Front during the First War.

Wheatley as a lieutenant in the Royal Field Artillery.

the result was an inconclusive reshaping of the front line, but for a while it was a moment of glory. Bells were rung across England for the victory. "Let me hasten to add," says Wheatley, "I played no part in the actual fighting. I performed only my allotted and inglorious task of keeping some of our guns well supplied with ammunition. But I was there, and privileged to witness the glorious triumph of British arms".

After Cambrai, he was sent on yet another course. He spent a lot of time on these, and in November he had been on a PT course, where he joked with the instructors that he had trouble raising his hand higher than his mouth. "Still, there it is," he wrote to Hilda about the course, adding the very First War sentiment "I certainly did not ask to come but some madman sent me."

The new course was a month's artillery course, but Wheatley spent three weeks of it in bed with bronchitis. His bronchitis had been playing him up almost from the start, and he was hoping it would get him home. He wrote to Hilda, "the Gods have been kind to me so far so I hope I shall not be in the last boat [back to Britain], anyway I think it's very unlikely as my bronchitis has started off again . . ."

He wasn't back for Christmas as he hoped, but he was recovered enough to celebrate in France, writing to Hilda "I went on a gunnery course over Christmas and on the way back I managed to get three or four days in Amiens which is quite a first class town Restaurants, Hotels, Shops Girls ect . . . the Devil must have had a particularly amusing and gratifying three days at my expense".

It was a hard winter. Wheatley's division were sent to back up the French at St.Quentin, where they suffered severe casualties. The trek there was a horrible experience of nineteenth-century style soldiering, with Wheatley on horseback through snow and ice, concentrating hour after hour to prevent his horse from slipping and breaking a leg. The cold was bitter, and one of the men died while billeted in a barn. Wheatley dressed as heavily as he could and kept rum and brandy in his pistol holsters, together with cigarettes, biscuits and bars of chocolate.

Their destination was the village of St.Simon, which they reached via the small town of Ham. It was at Ham that Napoleon III had been imprisoned, but made his escape disguised as a workman; escaping monarchs always caught Wheatley's imagination. At St.Simon he was entrusted with the construction of horse-lines, and standing there frozen (whereas he thought the men at least kept warm with digging) he told the sergeant in charge, a Sergeant Watkins, to hurry up: "Waiting for you to get this job done is like waiting for the second coming of Christ!". Next morning he was summoned before the Colonel and severely reprimanded. Watkins was a member of some zealous Christian sect, and he had complained about Wheatley's blaspheming.

Wheatley and Colsell shared a billet at St.Simon in the local chateau. This had been blown up by the retreating Germans, but Wheatley found a single room with a turret roof. It was hexagonal, with one of its sides attached to the remains of the chateau, while the other five had tall windows with metal shutters. Wheatley described it as his "Pergoda" [sic].

Wheatley's love of creature comforts extended to furnishings, and now he rode to the nearest town and bought wall paper and even some chintz, as he told Hilda: it had been a "a frightful hole" but "for the last few days we have had a "hen father papered the parlour' sort of stunt"; a reference to the music-hall song[2].

"We have made it really tophole now, quite luxurious in fact," reported Wheatley: there were "little tables (with table cloths) . . . rugs on the floor, and a glorious marble fire place (quite ancestral)" – this last 'baronial' detail oddly looking forward to the decor of Hammer horror films – and in short, "we've really put up a jolly good show."

This wasn't Wheatley's first attempt at interior decoration. While he was stationed at Ipswich he had picked enough

[2] "When Father papered the parlour / You couldn't see him for paste / Dabbing it here! dabbing it there! / Paste and paper everywhere / Mother was stuck to the ceiling / The children stuck to the floor / I never knew a blooming family / So stuck up before."

wild flowers to make himself a bowl of pot pourri. Sated with novels and cards, he also had enough free time to take up the study of palmistry. Like ancestral fireplaces, this may have felt like a return to a reassuringly nineteenth-century world. Wheatley's disrespect for Christianity had increased with the War. He was well aware that both sides attended Church Parade (the Germans even had their famous slogan, 'Gott mitt Uns', God With Us), and for many people the War involved a wider loss of faith in civilisation, rationality and progress.

It is against this loss of faith in the ideals of the Enlightenment that Wheatley's absorption in palmistry on the Somme seems particularly appropriate. He started off with Cheiro's *Guide to the Hand* and *Palmistry for All* (the latter under Cheiro's other pseudonym of Louis Hamon), reinforced by Edward Heron-Allen's *A Manual of Cheirosophy* (1885) and Katharine St.Hill's *The Grammar of Palmistry* (1889). From palmistry Wheatley went on to numerology (he owned Cheiro's *Book of Numbers*) and astrology.

Life was quiet, and as Mess Secretary Wheatley arranged to have tinned cream and similar luxuries sent out from the Army and Navy Stores in Victoria. He also rode to Ham once a week, to the French grocer. The only thing that spoiled this otherwise pleasant trip was that Wheatley had to ride past a Chinese labour camp. They had been hired from China (Wheatley thought they might have been convicts, which was not true) and they had little interest in the war. They would line the road as Wheatley and his orderly rode by, hissing and gesturing and trying to frighten the horses.

The quiet life was soon to end, and the war in Wheatley's region began to intensify, partly caused by British efforts (initially regarded as foolhardy and unsporting) to stir up what had been a relatively amiable stalemate between the French and Germans. The man who commanded Wheatley's division, General Sir Oliver Nugent, had boasted that a double decker London omnibus would hold all the men he intended to bring home alive.

Russia's new Bolshevik government had made peace with

the Germans, which freed their army on the Eastern front for France, and an onslaught was expected. German prisoners were questioned as to when this was due, but they had all been instructed to say it was tomorrow, keeping the British front line in a state of perpetual false alarm, manning the trenches at four o'clock every morning against an attack that never came.

One night Wheatley was having dinner with some other officers when they heard German bombers going over towards Paris, a sound they had become used to. A moment later there was a horrifying series of explosions; the target in this instance was not Paris but St.Simon. One of the officers Wheatley was with, "a splendid chap" who had come up from the ranks and won the Military Cross, suddenly dived under the table sobbing. He had cracked from the cumulative trauma of being at the Front. Wheatley and the others brought his case to the attention of the Medical Officer, and managed to get him sent home with shell-shock.

Colsell was home on leave, and Wheatley was alone in his chintz and wallpaper decorated pagoda when the last great German offensive started on the 21st March at 4.40 in the morning, launching seventy-six German divisions at twenty-eight British divisions. It began with a five hour artillery bombardment that included poison gas, followed by immense numbers of infantry.

Wheatley timed the onslaught to 4.43, when shells began bursting in such numbers that the sound merged into a continual roar. He was terrified, thinking his room would be hit at any moment. Eric had encouraged him to hold the Christian God in something like contempt, but Wheatley now lay on the floor and begged God to get him out alive, promising to pray every night for the rest of his life.

He bent the rules here, and from the safety and comfort of fifty or sixty years later, he wrote "He, or – shall we say – they, got me out. And I've kept my promise, although I don't kneel down and it is to the Lords of Light that I pray."

Wheatley pulled himself together enough to get dressed and see what was happening. Shells had made craters and overturned several limbers, but it was clear the real target was further on, at the village of Ham. The density of the barrage lessened, and individual heavy shells could now be heard going overhead with what Wheatley remembered as a noise like a train.

The men waited anxiously, and the order came through to pack up. While they were doing so they saw the occasional man rushing past from the Front, as if on some urgent errand towards the back of the lines; nobody realised at the time that they were deserting.

Wheatley's column retreated in good order to Olezy and made a camp there, when the Major in command sent for him: they were now to move to Aubigny, and because Wheatley's section was nearest to the exit of the field, he was to lead. Aubigny was closer to the front line, which seemed to Wheatley to be the wrong direction to be going in, but there was nothing he could do.

After a good few miles and several villages, an English officer on foot asked him where he was going. He then told him the Germans were already in Aubigny, and – when Wheatley asked where the front line was – told him he had already come through it. The officer himself was on a reconnaissance in what was now No Man's Land, and after telling Wheatley to turn his men around or have them massacred, he slipped away.

Wheatley slowly turned the ammunition wagons around as quietly as possible, knowing that if the Germans heard them they would open fire. Years later he found out what had gone wrong: there were two Aubignys, one of them further back from the front, not closer to it. This was where he was meant to go, but the Major had pointed him towards the wrong one on the map. This was why he had retreated closer to the enemy, which struck him as odd at the time, but "Theirs not to reason why."

The start of the last great German offensive was the nearest thing to a rout the British had experienced since the War began, although at terrible cost to the Germans. Wheatley couldn't lose his way to Ham, because the sky above it was

141

glowing. Burning buildings lit the night, and he saw the main street choked with retreating British troops.

The men were exhausted and Wheatley called a halt. They had only had the camp set up for a few hours when a man galloped past shouting "Get out! The Germans are coming!". Later Wheatley was told that the Germans had sent English speakers ahead in captured English uniforms to spread panic. Drake's famous words about finishing his game of bowls before defeating the Spaniards were then more widely known, and when there was a sudden move to get up from the table, Wheatley said "Gentlemen. Let us finish our coffee first and run from the Germans afterwards."

This ("one of the few wisecracks that my slow mind has ever been inspired to make") caused considerable amusement. They then moved off, in good order, and for the next few days took part in what became known as the March Races, racing to see who could retreat fastest towards Paris.

Wheatley had minor discipline problems, but he was backed up by a solidly professional Sergeant-Major, a Boer War veteran, and over the next ten days, having lost touch with his Major, he was effectively in charge of around a thousand men, including stragglers and even deserters. He kept them together until he met a larger British force, and Wheatley's men were inspected by Brigadier-General Henry Brock. Brock was a professional soldier of the old school, who had recently won the DSO, and he kept a cow on hand at all times so that he could have fresh milk in his tea; whenever his HQ moved, an orderly was to be seen among the baggage carts, leading the cow.

Wheatley was proud of his efforts, particularly in rounding up stragglers from the Front and forming them into platoons, which were now marching in columns of four abreast behind the main section. Wheatley and Brock sat side by side on their horses as they watched the men go by. Brock said nothing: he asked no questions about the rout and retreat, and had no curiosity about who the men marching at the back might be. When the men had gone by, he turned to Wheatley and said "I see a number of your men have lost their steel helmets.

Take their names, have them up tomorrow morning, and see that they are crimed for it."

This was the less attractive side of the old style officering that Wheatley had been so enamoured of after his nightmare train journey. Recalling General Brock years later, Wheatley wrote "it seems to me a terrible thing that anyone so insensitive and mean in spirit should be given authority over other human beings." In the event he didn't have anyone crimed for losing their helmet. Instead he told the men that the Brigadier was pleased with them for having got back in such good order, particularly after what they had been through.

★

Wheatley and his section were now sent to Hornoy, near Amiens, which Wheatley lost no time in revisiting. The great German push had been largely halted, but Amiens was now within reach of German shelling, and the civilian population had been forced to abandon it. The streets were empty and the windows shuttered, with military policemen to discourage looters.

Wheatley hoped the Salon Godbert restaurant might still be open, but he had to ring the bell. A one-legged old man came to the door, and invited him to look around. It was like the Marie Celeste; the comparison that struck Wheatley was the Castle of Sleeping Beauty. Every place had a half-eaten plate of mouldering food, with glasses of wine beside it. Ice buckets full of water held magnums half full of flat champagne.

The place had been full of British officers when the order came to leave, and the exodus had been so final that the staff had left too. Wheatley went out and found a café still open, and as he walked around the town afterwards he met an English-speaking girl who told him all the other girls had left for the country. This was stupid of them, she said, looking straight at Wheatley, because in the villages there were no British soldiers to pay for "jigijig."

This was a clear invitation, and in a few minutes they were

in the girl's apartment, in one of the tall old-fashioned houses that formed a valley-like corridor for the entrance of the railway into the town station. Wheatley noticed several of these houses were in a state of ruin. While they were in bed there was a tremendous explosion, and the sound of bricks falling nearby. As Wheatley writes it up in his autobiography, "I went rigid, but the girl did not stop her movement for a second and was impaled upon me so I was a prisoner beneath her. She simply smiled down at me and said 'Eet is le bombardement. The Boche, 'e is a creature of 'abit. 'E always starts at four o'clock.'"

Having seen the newly shelled ruin a couple of doors away, Wheatley hoped she lived to enjoy the money she was making. He may have fine-tuned this story, but there was a real basis for it: "Amiens under bombardment" gets a tick in his fornicator's Game Book.

*

All this time, Wheatley had a picture of Barbara Symonds around his neck in a locket. At Christmas 1917 he had sent her a box of French chocolates – now almost impossible to obtain in England – and to his delight she wrote to thank him, so he felt he could resume courting. She added that she was bored to death by the War because there were so few young men at dances, so she hoped it would be over by her 21st birthday, on the 27th November.

Wheatley also hoped it would soon be over. In January he wrote to Hilda that his friends thought "providing the Hun doesn't send them a special packet, the war might end in time for them to be present at the christening of their great grandchildren, but who knows, the Boche is fed up and we are fed up, both fighting more or less for something that will not benefit either of us individually one iota".

This was the period of General Haig's famous "backs to the wall" order. Like many men who served in the War, Wheatley was extremely critical of Haig. Wheatley's judgement was that you have to break eggs to make an omelette, but you don't have to break them on the floor.

The second stage of the German offensive was launched on April 9th, and just before it began Wheatley's Division was sent north, apparently to recuperate. This was a blunder, because the second attack came in the north. On the 14th April Wheatley had what he remembered as his worst day of the War, when the division entrained at St Roche, in the suburbs of Amiens. They had to get several hundred horses into vans, eight to a van, while the station was being shelled and the horses reared and kicked in panic. Several horses were killed, and more had to be put down. A number of men were also killed, and at one moment a shell hit an engine, blasting hot coal and boiling steam.

Wheatley had a more prosaic aggravation to deal with in the wake of his earlier retreat from the Front, since it was discovered that the Section's cash box had gone missing during the journey. Along with the tin hats, this was the only thing lost, but Wheatley was held responsible and made to pay up.

Wheatley's travails were coming to an end, although he didn't yet know it: "praise be to the dear Gods, my days in France were nearly numbered." It was bronchitis that brought him home in the end, as he had been hoping it would almost from the day he arrived. His cough had been getting worse, and in May he reported sick. The MO sent him to a British Red Cross Hospital in Boulogne and on May 14th he wrote Hilda a cheerful letter: "I hear you murmur, 'the poor fellow, struck down in defence of King Country & Co, brave lad', but no – it is nothing so tragic – merely my dear old friend the enemy Bronchitis."

Wheatley's bronchitis may have been aggravated by the presence of gas, since the Germans were using gas shells, but it doesn't seem to have occurred to him at the time. His comment in *Saturdays with Bricks*, "There could be no doubt about it; I had been badly gassed" is distinctly retrospective. Compared to many gas victims (". . . floundering like a man in fire or lime . . . As under a green sea, I saw him drowning . . . He plunges at me, guttering, choking, drowning") Wheatley had got off lightly, as usual.

Wheatley's army career had not been glorious, but he had done his duty; no less, if no more. He was well-liked by the men, seemingly because he was cheerful and humane. In later years he became President of the Old Comrades Association, where he was able to meet the men socially and get a better sense of what they thought of him. Far from seeing him as a monocled *ubermensch*, it seemed they regarded young Lieutenant Wheatley as a kind of mascot.

But for now he was coughing and writing to Hilda. "Oh to be in England now that Spring is here, how I should love it but I am afraid it is not to be, the Army cannot spare me".

Let me tell you a secret Hilda, – I am the last hope of the General Staff, for nearly four years they have played the fool . . . but they know that without me they are lost . . .

Glorious news

Sister has just come in to say that I am to go off to England after all, have decided to leave the General Staff in the lurch, see you soon . . .

CHAPTER THIRTEEN

The Only Girl

Wheatley arrived back in England on the 15th May 1918. He was put on a hospital train for Charing Cross, then carried on a stretcher to a waiting ambulance. Each ambulance carried two "stretcher cases", and the other man was badly wounded; he was all but inanimate, and Wheatley never saw his face, which may have been a mercy.

The journey in the ambulance turned into one of the high points of Wheatley's life. Leaving the station, the ambulances went left down the Strand and into Trafalgar Square, then up the Haymarket to Piccadilly. Visible as he sat up at the window, Wheatley found that people in the crowd were cheering.

There is a morbid side to the cultification of military ambulances – on a slippery slope towards the wheelchair rallies for Hitler, which were to be a feature of German life within a few years, with hundreds of prosthetic arms punching the air – but that day it seemed entirely innocent. Women blew kisses, and the traffic in Piccadilly was so slow that they bought flowers from the flower sellers who were then clustered under the statue of Eros, throwing them in bunches at the ambulances. Wheatley waved back, looking out of the window like a hero or a monarch, and found he was laughing and crying at the same time.

★

He had truly arrived back in England; "dear old England." He was taken to a charitable hospital for officers in Regent's Park run by a wealthy woman named Mrs Hall Walker. Sussex Lodge was her own house, and she appointed herself matron, employing doctors and nurses from Guy's Hospital and a French chef.

Hilda Gosling was now at Girton, and Wheatley wrote to

her explaining that he wasn't yet allowed to get up properly but spent every day in pyjamas and dressing gown, sitting in the garden, "which is perfectly gorgeous, it is about twice the size of Chatham House garden or more, with the most beautiful green lawn surrounded by great chestnut trees."

Hilda had met a man and, continuing his association of sex and sin, Wheatley writes "I hear your news in re the Devil with much surprise." As for himself, he told her he was "greatly in arrears in paying Old Nick his just dues, in oats". He was able to pay these a month or so later, when he was allowed out for the afternoon. He made for the Regent Palace Hotel off Piccadilly Circus, where the lounge was known as the best place in London to pick up women. He caught the eye of an attractive brunette and managed to get into conversation. She was called Marie, and before long Wheatley put his cards on the table: "I told Marie that it was a year since I kissed an English girl and I wanted to kiss her, but I could not do it there and had no idea when I would be let out of hospital again. It was a good plea from an invalided officer." (It was not unlike a plea for what is sometimes known as a 'sympathy leg-over'; a direct approach not unknown in Wheatley's fiction).

Wheatley took Marie to Kettners in Soho, in those days a great restaurant. It had been founded fifty years earlier by a former chef to Napoleon III, but aside from the food Kettners was in business as a *maison de rendezvous* with short-stay bedrooms and "private dining rooms" or *cabinets particuliers*.

What were *cabinets particuliers* like? Ann Veronica, eponymous heroine of H.G. Wells's 1909 novel, is taken by a man called Ramage to a private dining room where she dimly apprehends an "obtrusive sofa". They are welcomed by a waiter with "discretion beyond all limits in his manner", who later closes the door "with an almost ostentatious discretion", after which Ramage locks it before pouncing. Again, in Jean Rhys's *Voyage in the Dark*, the heroine is taken to a private dining room with red furniture and red lampshades, with a bedroom discreetly en suite behind a curtain, where the waiter closes the door "as if not coming back".

Private dining rooms must have been prime locations for what is now known as 'date rape', although most girls probably understood what they were about. At the same time they were a genuine amenity, like the 'love hotels' of Japan, and they were popular with officers on leave.

Wheatley installed them in a private room and ordered a bottle of champagne. Marie, he says in his autobiography, "proved incredibly passionate and while gasping with pleasure kept on sighing: 'Oh, Dennis darling, do be different!' " It is not clear what she meant by this; perhaps she wanted him to him to be "different" from all the other men who had used her. She may have been more of a veteran of the private dining room than Wheatley suspected.

When it was time to say goodbye, Marie asked Wheatley for her "present." This was a shock to Wheatley's self esteem ("it had never occurred to me that she might be a tart"), and an embarrassment, because after the room and the champagne Wheatley had no money left. Wheatley took her address and sent her some silk stockings, for which she wrote him a "glowing" letter of thanks and continued to write "very sweetly" now and then; "So I was able to flatter myself that it had not been altogether a commercial transaction."

They never saw each other again, but of his two hours in bed with Marie, Wheatley was to write fifty years later "I can recall the two hours . . . more clearly than I can a casual *affaire* with any other girl." This is a mystery, because in his almost contemporary sexual list there is no mention of Marie and no one who corresponds to her, and yet the circumstantial details – the "do be different", the disappointment at finding she wanted a present, even the silk stockings ("two pairs . . . one pink and one pale blue. That seems a strange choice now . . .") – have a distinct ring of truth.

After eight prostitutes in France, Wheatley had returned to London to have "Baker St. little fair girl", "Tavistock Sq. (soulful)", "Gt.Portland St. (ring)", "Dolly W. Fair" and "Oxford Terrace" [now Sussex Gardens], along with "Brixton. On bus", and "Victoria (middle age)". They are all ticked, so Marie is probably a composite figure, a fictional amalgam of other women he had at this time; or, just possibly, perhaps their transaction affected him emotionally and he didn't list her in his usual way.

★

Around the end of June, Wheatley left the hospital to go to a convalescent home, the Prince of Wales Hospital for Officers at Staines. Wheatley made a new friend at the Prince of Wales Hospital, a cheerful and chubby tank lieutenant known as 'Tanks' or 'Tanko' Moate. His time there was also enlivened by a rich and charitable woman named Mrs Mosscockle, who would entertain officers to lunch on Sundays at her Windsor country house, Clewer Park.

Mrs Mosscockle had literary aspirations, and had published several volumes of verse. The matron would select which officers should go, seemingly less by whether they deserved a treat and more by whether they would do the hospital credit. The social class of officers had declined considerably as the war had gone on, and although he had been a bounderish "temporary gentleman" at the start, Wheatley's social polish was now higher than average and he was often chosen.

Mrs Mosscockle's other hobby was motoring, and she owned a Rolls-Royce with a gas balloon on top. The purpose of this Heath Robinson device was to save petrol by reducing the weight of the car, although if it had any effect at all, apart from increasing air resistance, it must have been to slightly weaken the traction of the tyres against the ground.

On certain Sundays Wheatley and two other officers would take the train to Windsor, where the Rolls-Royce would meet them at the station. After lunch Mrs Mosscockle would walk them to the river, where she had a full-sized steamer, suitable for a couple of hundred passengers. The steamer would then take them down to Maidenhead and back, while they ate strawberries and cream on deck.

Wheatley and Tanko were also keen on messing about on the river in a punt. They met a cheerful girl called Peggy, and went punting with her most days. On another occasion, recalling his extrovert exploits in Germany, Wheatley spotted a "luscious blonde" and deliberately fell in the water to attract her attention, but she was married, and the results went no further than "a jolly tea and drinks afterwards".

★

Unfortunately the love of Wheatley's life was still Barbara Symonds, to whom he had posted a bottle of scent while he was at Sussex Lodge. He continued to suffer, and when things reached a particularly low ebb the following year, he wrote that "ever since I was seventeen it [i.e. the hope of one day marrying Barbara] has been the dominant decent thought of my existence, however remote the possibilities of gaining her affection."

Barbara had started to thaw towards him, or so it seemed, and even to encourage him a little. And then Wheatley had his memories:

Lady Dear
Thanks very much for your little letter, it came I think from the Barbara with a very large heart – the girl who drove with me one night a very long time ago, from Kettners to Victoria and kissed me of her own accord, – and who once wrote me a letter forgiving and forgetting after I had behaved like a brute and a beast, – who once, when I was very hard up went one evening to the pictures with me and when on the way home we paused beneath a tree and I asked her if she did not care just a little, replied. "Yes, I think I do – a tiny bit."

While Wheatley was at Staines, Barbara wrote to say that if he "really" wanted to take her out, she wouldn't mind dinner at the Waldorf, followed by a play at the Gaiety Theatre. But she added "Perhaps the river scenery will cure you of your (imaginary) wound without much effort on my part. It's really quite time you recovered, don't you think?" This imaginary wound was the one Wheatley felt Barbara had inflicted on his heart.

Things went so well that Barbara even came to visit

Wheatley at Staines, bringing her friend Dot with her to make a foursome with Tanko; the four of them had lunch and then went out on the river. Things were going beautifully, but the following month disaster struck. Wheatley and Tanko had taken the two girls out for the night, and the four of them were in the back of a car, being driven to drop the girls back in Streatham. Wheatley kissed Barbara, and then discreetly put his hand inside her dress. She seemed not to object until Tanko and Dot were out of the car, when she suddenly turned on him and accused him of treating her like a Piccadilly tart. "How dare you?" she said, "How *dare* you?"

Wheatley's world must have fallen in. He got down on his knees and actually grovelled for her to forgive him, but it was no good. A few moments later she had let herself out of the car, slamming the door, and she was running up her garden path into her house.

Wheatley sent letter after letter, drafting and redrafting them before they were posted. After a few days a letter arrived back from Barbara, now on her summer holidays: "I would prefer to say no more about Thursday night," she wrote, "if you are sorry it is no use crying over spilt milk and it cannot happen again. I regret the incident more than I can say and shall do my best to forget it entirely." In the end Wheatley was forgiven, for better or worse, and his passion crawled on.

*

Shortly after the death of Ready Money Wheatley, from cirrhosis of the liver in July 1918, Wheatley was sent for another Medical Board examination and they found him fit enough to go to a 'Light Duty' camp at Catterick. Duties were very light indeed, and included dancing classes. On Saturday evenings Wheatley could practise new dances such as the Boston and the Bunny Hug, but sadly there were not enough women to go round, and the men usually had to dance with each other. Wheatley drew the line at this.

Wheatley's duties also allowed him to finish *Julie's Lovers*, the novel he had begun on the Western Front, and his father paid to have it typed up. It was sent to the publisher Cassells, but they rejected it.

It was at Catterick that Wheatley saw the end of the War. He was a keen armchair strategist, following the progress of the War on maps, and when the news came in early November that Austria had fallen, he judged that things were nearly over, winning a bet on it when the Armistice was announced. Celebratory drinking was the order of the day, and Wheatley charged about the camp hiccuping and shouting "Victory urges me to shout, HOORAY! Victory urges me to shout, HOORAY!"

Wheatley had taken a gamble to get him to London for the victory celebrations, applying for service again as a fit man, simply to get the two week's leave that automatically preceded such service: the only danger being that he might then be required to do the service itself. His leave got him into London four days after the Armistice, with the "mafficking"-type celebrations still going strong. People roamed the streets waving Union Jacks and singing, and great bonfires were lit in Trafalgar Square, damaging the lions at the foot of Nelson's Column. These bonfires were still alight when Wheatley arrived on the scene.

His gamble paid off, and he was never ordered to report for duty (or notified that he was discharged). In later life he liked to joke that his file might still be gathering dust somewhere in the Army bureaucracy, marked "on leave." After Christmas at the Grand Hotel in Brighton with his parents and sister, he rejoined the family wine business in January 1919.

*

Barbara still continued to be his "dominant decent thought." Wheatley had been sending her presents, despite her kindly objections. He sent her scented cigarettes tipped with rose leaves from the Bichera de Paris, a scent shop opposite Aspreys, and chocolates: Barbara told him she was using the chocolate box ribbon for her camisoles ("I was thrilled," wrote Wheatley, as no doubt he was meant to be).

From Catterick he sent her some sheet music, chosen with the help of Tanko. Never very musical, Wheatley asked Tanko to choose a couple of songs, but the third was his own: "it is neither classical or good style . . . but when it is played softly and slowly in the evening when things are quiet and I've got a cigarette on, I am afraid I'm idiot enough to think the chap who wrote the words meant it for something better than for the King of Comedies to make a farce of."

One of Wheatley's all time favourite songs was "If You Were The Only Girl in the World (and I were the only boy") from *The Bing Boys are Here*, a 1916 musical show at the Alhambra. It was particularly popular with young officers on leave, and would always remain associated with London in the First War. It starred George Robey ("Crown Prince of Mirth") as Lucifer Bing, and his masterstroke, although the show was a comedy, was to sing the show's great song, with its very distinctive tune, sentimentally 'straight' ("I would say such wonderful things to you / There would be such wonderful things to do . . ."). The song that Wheatley sent to Barbara was probably something in the same line, and quite possibly this very song.

After the Armistice celebrations Wheatley and Tanko took Barbara and Dot out on Friday and Saturday night, but on the Monday a letter arrived from Barbara reminding him that she was still serious about not letting him maul her in the taxi home, and if that was what he wanted then he should go out with someone else.

Later in November Wheatley and Tanko took the girls to a Thanksgiving Ball at the Cannon Street Hotel, and he saw quite a lot of Barbara around this period. Despite his quiet exit from the army, Wheatley revelled in the beautiful uniform of Blues he'd had made that October, a few weeks before the War's end, with its high collar and its red stripe down the outside of each leg. He felt this really "cut a dash."

*

Wheatley was effectively 'dating' Barbara now. Ever the strategist, he composed a long memorandum for himself, 'Rules of Procedure in re B', i.e. regarding Barbara. This peculiar work of planning and would-be control has around fifty points inscrutably numbered from 1–8, 1–4, 1–12 all the way down to 19–11, 19–14, 19–21. Some of them have a weirdly homiletic, 'fortune cookie' quality that suggests they may be gathered from somewhere else.

"Make a secret with her," Wheatley advises himself. If need be, "If she wants a secret, invent one rather than have nothing between you". When things are not going so smoothly, "Don't make her go into long explanations rather let a misunderstood remark pass, and look wise." And of course, "Do not discuss deep subjects that she is unlikely to understand."

When it comes to flattery, "Don't flatter too thickly"; "avoid generalities and go into details"; "Mention any new clothes but don't forget her old ones." Better yet, "Praise her for what she hath *not*." Failing all that, "If flattery is useless, make a quarrel, but see that you are in the wrong."

Along with a few elaborate dicta, such as item 8.5 ("A poem to the foolish, a conundrum to the wise, a kiss to the chaste, and a handclasp to the unchaste") much of Wheatley's list is entirely reasonable ("Do not talk too much of yourself"; "Avoid underhand methods"; "Never make either her or yourself look ridiculous"). At the same time, there is a calculating or even would-be predatory streak in it, such as "Don't propose when she has on a new frock or when she is happy" (15.9), followed by "But when she is ill or weary and needs someone to comfort her."(15.10).

It was nothing short of a campaign, as 19.10 suggests: "If she give the many reasons she can be persuaded, if but one the case is hopeless." "Persevere and be patient," Wheatley advises himself. "Don't be deceived by the undemonstrative", but at the same time, "Don't hurry, she goes into love as water little by little". Later, "Do not go timidly to work, when you have worked her up, go in and win"; "By her eyes only can you tell if she means her commandments to be broken or not. Never take no for an answer."

And where did all this planning get Wheatley? It got him nowhere.

As we have seen, Wheatley's nervous calculations with beautiful Barbara never had the charm of his spontaneous fun with plain Hilda, and he strikes one bad note after another. On one occasion, he wrote and told her that his love for her – because it stopped him chasing loose women and prostitutes – was actually saving him money:

> if it had not been for your kindness since my return from France, I should not be as I am, floating along pretty well, but instead heavily in debt . . . and the prospect of the devil of a row with the Pater . . . after our little lunch together at the Piccadilly it was quite obvious that if we were going to be friends it was not fair to you for me to have anything to do with any of the ladies of Vanity Fair . . . anyhow it's an expensive pastime, and through you dear little girl although I hate to consider you in the tawdry light of a financial speculation . . . I'm a jolly sight better off . . .

Wheatley knew he lacked the light touch, and he knew why:

> A man can only be cheery and amusing, really sympathetic and helpful, if he has nothing on his mind, but when he is worrying and worrying until he is almost ill, he becomes hopelessly dull and uninteresting because being depressed to the very depths he cannot possibly be gay and light hearted – at least, I can't, perhaps super-men could, and I am very ordinary.

Things had taken a serious turn for the worse at the beginning of January. When Wheatley had returned from Brighton after Christmas he met Barbara, and she told him of the new man in her life, Cyril, whom she hoped to marry. Barbara now sought to convert Wheatley into a confidant, complaining to him about Cyril's "lack of ardour".

Despite item 7.5 of his Rules – "If she talks much of another you have no rival & Vice Versa" – Wheatley was in misery. He drafted a long letter, with a last desperate offer of marriage or parting ("unless I cut adrift I shall get on the rocks and do something foolish. My love for you is so great that I must have all – or nothing.")

> Without you I know that I shall never reach real happiness, the want of you started when I looked into those wonderful eyes of yours across the Claridges tea table when we were young and ever since I have known that you were the only girl in the world.

> This waiting – thinking – waiting is killing me by inches, you are literally never absent from my thoughts – and my thoughts since Jan 1st 1919 have been Hell! – the people cannot understand why I have become so dull and apathetic, why I never go out and enjoy myself, and when I do go out, why I return home more depressed than ever, my pals all wonder what has happened to the cheerful lad I used to be – if they could only know all the desperate longing that I have for you . . .

Wheatley now worried that she might not have been serious, because she thought he wasn't serious, and he put his cards on the table:

> . . . to prevent the least possibility of a mistake I tell you now that I love you, adore you, and that if you would become engaged to me, now, I mean properly engaged, with rings blessings etc., and at once, I would give you a life times love and devotion. I swear to you that you should never regret, entrusting yourself to me, and that my every thought should be for your happiness.

This did little good, and the worst was yet to come.

★

Wheatley's lungs were still bad, and his father sent him on a cruise to Madeira. They had a rough time crossing the Bay of

Biscay, where conditions were so bad that the captain changed course to lessen the risk of capsizing, so the ship would cut the waves front on, instead of being hit from the side. Three days later, Wheatley felt privileged to see the literal source of a metaphor, pouring oil on troubled waters: "the Captain had a large barrel of oil poured overboard. The effect was astonishing. Within a few minutes the rough seas for a mile around the ship subsided."

There was unrest in Portugal, with prisons thrown open and a general strike, so Wheatley was pleased to see a British destroyer conspicuously present and flying the White Ensign in Lisbon harbour: "woe betide anyone who dared to lay a hand on a British subject or his property," he writes in his autobiography. "Those were the days."

Madeira impressed Wheatley chiefly by its corruption, with the Governor giving his blessing to the illegal gambling scene and taking a rake-off. The real power seemed to be Mr Blandy, of the drink shipping dynasty, who gave Wheatley a tour of his estates. It was also in Madeira that Wheatley got into serious difficulties while swimming, close to a harbour wall he was unable to get a grip on, and nearly drowned.

The relief he felt at finally hauling himself out alive must have been tempered by a letter that he received in Madeira from his friend Cecil Cross. He had introduced Barbara to the good looking Cecil in those happy months before Christmas, and now Cecil was writing to say that he felt a terrible cad but he was obsessed with Barbara, and the two of them were engaged.

This destroyed Wheatley's friendship with Cecil, but on his return he continued to see and write to Barbara. In one of his letters he wrote

If ever you chance to be in any difficulty or trouble which your father and brother or husband cannot sweep away for you I shall be very happy to help you in any way that I possibly can, because whatever may happen to me whether I marry or not no man can love one girl, and want her, and think of her, for five long years as I have of you and afterwards completely forget and be unresponsive to her in whom his whole soul had been centred during the first years of his manhood, so of you ever need a friend, remember,

　Your Unchanging,
　　Dennis

Fast-forwarding a moment, we find Wheatley in June 1922 re-reading his draft of this letter and putting heavy brackets around "(because whatever may happen to me whether I marry or not no man can love one girl, and want her, and think of her, for five long years as I have of you and afterwards completely forget and be unresponsive to her in whom his whole soul had been centred during the first years of his manhood)".

He then scrawls heavily and almost vengefully:

the years have gone
all wrong all wrong
I have forgotten
June 1st 1922 / Dennis

★

But for now, there was little comfort. What cheer there was, perhaps, was centred on the fact that Eric Tombe made a grand re-entrance into Wheatley's life.

CHAPTER FOURTEEN

Eric's Crimson Nights

In July 1919 a massive victory parade marched through London. It was led by the commanders of the thirteen Allied countries, followed by their troops and bands. Behind them came the British and Empire Troops, with their heavy artillery, bands, and hundreds of regimental standards borne aloft. Wheatley and his parents watched it from the office of a friend in Pont Street, probably the narrowest street it passed through, and they saw the spectacle at close quarters. Wheatley thought it was like something from the days of Rome.

But on the morning of his hung-over victory breakfast, on the 12th November 1918, he had shared a table with an elderly officer who had no cause for celebration. With a sad smile this man explained that now his life was going to change: after drawing full pay for a desk job, with social status and a servant and even a horse, he was going back to lodgings in Cheltenham, scraping along on his pension. "So there were two sides to that wonderful event," writes Wheatley: "I felt truly sorry for that nice old man."

The *Times* Personal Column is dotted with ex-officers down on their luck and seeking work ("motor driver, speaks French, excellent character"). Many would end up in depressing jobs such as prep school teacher or travelling salesman, and the situation must have been doubly difficult for "temporary gentlemen" like Wheatley and Tombe, for whom being an officer had, in terms of social class, been their taste of honey.

Wheatley was far from well off, but at least he was working in his father's wine business. He was now a Liveryman of the Vintners Company and he attended his first Vintners' dinner, with mock turtle soup opening a multi-course feast of the sort he always approved of. His day-to-day duties were less grand, selling wines and beer at the cash counter, and helping

160

in the cellar, and doing the books. In the mornings he was expected to go around the great houses in the area calling on the head servants, a two-faced caste who operated, as we have seen, on a system of bribes and backhanders.

Wheatley found a few of these men likeable, and enjoyed having a glass of their master's wine with them by their fire-sides below stairs, but most of them were "far from pleasant . . . they secretly hated their employers and their only interest was racing. To me, some of them were unpleasantly servile and others openly rude." Consequently Wheatley stopped calling on the majority, and had to spend his mornings slop-ing off to a Lyons Tea House until it was time to reappear in the office.

*

Eric Tombe had meanwhile been employed by the Air Ministry on Kingsway, where his engineering background had set him up for a job administrating aircraft production and visiting factories. At the Air Ministry he had fallen in with a new crony named Ernest Dyer. Son of a brewer's drayman, Dyer had been a gas fitter before going to Australia, where he tried his hand at engineering, pearl fishing, fruit farming, and horse breeding.

He enlisted in the Australian Engineers as a sapper and was invalided out after being blown up by a mine at Gallipoli. He subsequently re-enlisted in the Royal West Surrey Regiment as an officer and transferred to the Royal Engineers, becoming a captain before being wounded again.

War suited Dyer. In later life he always carried a revolver – people remembered it as a mysterious object under his coat that his hand frequently went towards – and he once said "Yes, I was in the Army. I was a soldier, and I'm a soldier of fortune now: I'll tackle any proposition."

Dyer was always interested in horse racing, and in 1920 he allegedly put the whole of his War gratuity on the horse Furious, which was running in the Lincoln Handicap at odds of 33 to 1. It won, and netted Dyer a payout of £15,000 (well over £350,000 today). This may well be true – the recklessness sounds in character – although large on-course wins were also used as an alibi for laundering money.

Tombe left the Ministry when the war ended, but Dyer stayed on through 1919. His job was to oversee compensation claims from factories, for work begun but no longer needed, and Tombe conceived the plan of sending in invoices from non-existent companies, to be approved for payment by Dyer. Tombe printed bogus company letterheads, opened bank accounts, and even had telephone lines answered by one of his mistresses. Tombe and Dyer did well out of this, and Eric set himself up in an expensive serviced flat in Yeoman House on the Haymarket, where he could entertain women.

★

Tombe and Wheatley had been in touch since Wheatley's return to England, when Tombe had visited him at Staines, and now they went for nights out on the town with girls; Wheatley was womanising to dull the pain of Barbara, and he had a number of minor romances going around this time.

Tombe's private life was complicated. He had several casual girlfriends and a mistress called Dolly Stern, a secretary who lived in Nevern Place in Earls Court. Always keen on lists, Wheatley catalogued them as "Nellie . . . Kittie, Peggy, Beatrice, Desiree, la Belle Americaine, Mrs Hall, and of course Dolly"; but the real love of Eric's life was Beatrice, a dignified and intelligent older woman who was married to a wealthy Northern manufacturer in Huddersfield: Tombe seems to have met her on one of his factory viewing trips for the Air Ministry. Wheatley and Tombe referred to her husband as " 'Undreds and 'Undreds" (probably something Tombe had heard him say), and Tombe had every expectation that Beatrice would one day inherit Undreds's money.

Beatrice had three children, and from time to time they lived almost as a family with Eric in London. He had meanwhile managed to convince Dolly that he was a British agent who had to go abroad on anti-Bolshevik missions. When Wheatley enquired after Dolly and "the menage" – Tombe, Dolly, and another girl – in the Haymarket, the answer was quintessentially Eric. "She grows more splendid every day," he said:

> — last night we had a long discourse on Masochism and Sadism — she wanted me to buy a dog whip and experiment — I tell you Dennis it warms my old heart — the way she laps up our delightful doctrine, of the maximum of Sensation, and of the Value of Experience. I've enjoyed our fortnight tremendously, never once have we committed the sin of being bored, but on Tuesday next *I go on a short mission to Poland*, poor Dolly resumes the humdrum of her clerical life and thinks of me wrapped in a great fur *shutka* making my way across eternal snows, and tracked by bearded Bolshies who bristle with automatics, thirsting for my innocent blood — While actually I meet Beatrice and the kiddies — with whom I resume our peaceful existence at the Hyde Park Gate Hotel.

*

Tombe and Wheatley collaborated together in an organisation called the Anti-Prohibition League, which Tombe seems to have been involved in setting up. In January 1919 America had embarked on a disastrous attempt to ban alcoholic drinks, so that a man in Michigan was sentenced to life imprisonment for possession of half a bottle of gin.

Wheatley had a newspaper clipping which put the case in stark terms. Headed ' "Wets" Final Drink', it said

> January 16th in the United States will go down to history as "Fanatic Friday" . . . "Such a centralisation of power over the lives and habits of the individual", says the New York World today, "has never before been realised outside the boundaries of Russia."

One of the most prominent Prohibitionists in America was William "Pussyfoot" Johnson, so named for the stealth with which he and his men crept up on illicit alcohol. Feelings ran high, and when Pussyfoot came to England in 1919 he was attacked by pro-drink medical students in a prank which went wrong, resulting in the loss of one of his eyes.

Pussyfoot was a heroic man in his way, and he capitalised on this experience with a song, 'What I See With My Blind Eye.' He saw a drink-free Britain in five years, and a subsequent rally at Central Hall, Westminster, was held under a banner proclaiming "Pussyfoot's eye will make England dry. / 1920 – England to be dry – 1925"

In opposition to all this, the *Times* of July 16th 1919 carried a small announcement in its personal columns, then on the front page. Along with the usual mysteries ("Jack – absolutely nothing doing, old bean – Ivy") we find

> Publicists, Literary Men, Scientists, Statisticians, Doctors and Clergymen who are OPPOSED to the INTEM-PERATE and EXAGGERATED CLAIMS of the PRO-HIBITIONISTS and are willing to assist in propaganda work are invited to COMMUNICATE with the Anti-Prohibition League, 33-34 Chancery Lane WC.

There was a small item inside the paper, recording that 'The Anti-Prohibition League, "in an announcement in our advertisement columns," was asking for help in its propaganda work.

Letters were being sent out from 33–34 Chancery Lane, under the auspices of Sir Augustus Fitzgeorge KCVO, outlining the situation: the Prohibitionists were more powerful and serious than was generally realised; Prohibition itself could lead to Bolshevism (presumably by encouraging sober discontent among the working classes); and it would also lead to a considerable tax increase to make up the shortfall in revenue. More than that, it would be an encroachment on personal liberty.

With all that in mind, "We believe that you may be sufficiently interested to know how you can help us, and for this purpose Mr Gordon-Tombe will shortly be calling upon you."

This had taken months to set up, and Tombe had sought

Wheatley's advice back in January. Wheatley had given him an account of the London drinks trade and some of its key players, with a brief breakdown of how each firm operated, and its specialisation: one was concerned with "treating sick wines, turning sour wines sweet etc. Old established and wealthy," while another specialised in Australian wines: "We do practically no trade in Australian Wines," added Wheatley, "but in the suburbs there is a great deal consumed."

The Anti-Prohibition League was an early instance of Wheatley thinking about publicity and propaganda; these were always key ideas in his mind. The word propaganda was widely used between the wars, to such an extent (for example) that a 1928 booklet offering "Tasty Fish Recipes" is blazoned with the words "Fish Trade National Propaganda Association."

Wheatley stressed the importance of reaching "the man in the street", and drafted an advert for "BRITISH LIBER-TY'S DEFENCE FUND", formed to resist the Prohibition Movement

And to fight by Press, Platform and Parliament all bodies who shall endeavour *to undermine or restrict the individual liberties* and freedom that is the splendid inheritance *of every British citizen.*

In due course Wheatley became an agent for the cause, with a discreet, private detective-style card:

Telephone:- Holborn 2790
D.Y.WHEATLEY
Special Representative
THE ANTI-PROHIBITION LEAGUE
33–34 Chancery Lane
London, W.C.

★

Wheatley's chest was again bad in the winter of 1919, and that spring his father sent him on a cruise to Jamaica. He sailed on the SS Canuto, a Fyffes banana boat carrying sixty passengers, bearing with him a letter from the League: "We wish to make known to you Mr D.Y.Wheatley our special representative."

Wheatley noticed that although Jamaica was a British possession, it was dominated by America. With Prohibition now in force, the US Fleet and Cuba ("virtually a US colony") were dry, so American sailors would use Jamaica for binge drinking, making the streets dangerous and finally being thrown into patrolling lorries when they were too drunk to walk.

Wheatley's most memorable experience of his trip was a shipboard affair with a girl named Jean, travelling with her parents. Jean was above Wheatley in terms of class, and he felt it, which must have been part of her appeal. Her family had probably never met a tradesman socially and were surprised to learn how Wheatley made his living, but "after the initial shock" they quite liked him.

After their shipboard romance was over, Wheatley and Jean saw each other only twice; she had him to tea in St.John's Wood, and years later she came to hear him speak at a Foyle's Literary Luncheon. In fact they had almost nothing in common: she was of a good county family, with a life of point-to-points and hunt balls, and Wheatley was suburban and he knew it; "Yet for a brief spell the Gods had blessed us with perfect companionship."

*

Returning to Britain, Wheatley resumed a fast life with Eric. Wheatley had a beautiful sheath-like overcoat made, modelled on Eric's overcoat, which had no pockets so as not to disturb its tight drape. Together with their girls they would consume bottles of "the Boy" (a deliberately outdated nineteenth-century slang for champagne), and go to restaurants and clubs such as Oddenino's ("Oddie's") on Piccadilly Circus; Ciro's on Orange Street, famous for Ciro's Club Coon Orchestra; and Rector's on Tottenham Court Road: this was a particular favourite of Eric's, and its basement dance hall featured a big block of ice in the middle to cool the room.

On a not untypical evening Eric took a girl to the Savoy for dinner and dancing, and on leaving the Savoy he said "Look here, what about calling at the flat, I've got a bottle of the Boy there and a nice fire, we can have the bottle and then go on to Rectors." They never got to Rector's, as he told Wheatley by the same-day post of the time: everything went "according to plan – of course she bought it and everything very splendid – but – we fell asleep – and here we are – all in our top hats – tail coats and evening cloaks – add to which we have run out of money and cannot sally forth to Bond Street to get more in this get up – so will you please beg borrow or steal a fiver and a Bottle and come along here as soon as you can."

Wheatley needed no prompting, and before long he was at Yeoman House with an overnight suit case and seven bottles of champagne. Wheatley liked Tombe's friend ("very clever and amusing") and the three of them had a "a very merry lunch." Afterwards Wheatley collected a girl of his own; the porter at Yeoman House, "the excellent Sims", was a confrere of Tombe's, and he let them have a flat (letting flats for the night and pocketing the money was a profitable sideline). They rejoined the Tombe party for dinner, after which, reported Wheatley at the time, "we drank 6 remaining bottles between the four of us – and – there I draw the curtain—"

★

Sometimes Wheatley would see Eric with two girls he knew, usually Dolly and a friend, and at other times he would simply be with Beatrice, who knew nothing of his other lives. "Dear old Beatrice," he once said to Wheatley (and then "for a moment his face grew quite tender"); ". . . you know Dennis this orgy business is all very well – in fact it's necessary to me, if I didn't have a week of it now and then I should scream – it is the only thing that enables Beatrice and I to live together so happily – I've never lived with any other woman for half the time, it's three years now, and . . . we're as happy as a couple of kiddies together. I'm awfully fond of her."

"My dear old chap," said Wheatley, "I do wish you'd give up the other business, you know how often I've spoken to you about it." No, said Tombe, "it is necessary to me. If I were faithful to her I should hate the very sight of her within six months – as it is we may go on for years and years together."

Wheatley liked Beatrice, and the three of them would often dine together and go to the theatre, particularly to short *grand guignol* programmes. On another occasion it was Eric's birthday, and Eric, Beatrice and Wheatley had a champagne dinner at the Savoy before going on to Oscar Asche's orientalist extravaganza Cairo at His Majesty's Theatre, which featured a real camel.

They had already seen his more famous Chu Chin Chow at the same theatre, a lavish tale based on Ali Baba and the Forty Thieves. Cairo was criticised in its day for its orgy scene, which led an organisation called The London Council for Public Morality to pass a resolution against it. As for Tombe, Wheatley and Beatrice, they felt it was not as good as Chu Chin Chow; "nevertheless", said Wheatley, "some of the colours are gorgeous, a perfect feast for the senses, and the orgy was very fine from a spectacular point of view" to which Eric said "my dear old boy, we can do that sort of thing so very much better at home."

*

Wheatley had been on stage earlier in the year. He had spent Christmas at the Grand Hotel Brighton with his parents and some family friends, including Sir Louis Newton, who had recently been Lord Mayor of London, and a Mr. and Mrs. Hilton, whose son persuaded Wheatley to join a South London amateur dramatic group, The Nondescript Players, chiefly for reasons of alcoholic conviviality.

After a rehearsal Wheatley grew more than usually drunk, and discovered it was immense fun – and very amusing for his friends as well – if he smashed every street lamp they passed. He was happily doing this when a policeman took hold of him.

Wheatley stupidly attempted to bribe the policeman – a far more serious offence than smashing street lamps, had the policeman chosen to make something of it – but was taken to the police station. The police were quite well disposed to a middle-class young man like Wheatley, and they let him sit in the office instead of being taken to a cell. It was here that he had another idea, to make a sudden run for it down the corridor. Moments later he was lying on the floor with a policeman on top of him, "But they were awfully pleasant about it."

On the following Monday morning he had to report to Bromley Magistrate's Court, where his friend Bertie Davis pulled out all the stops to defend him, stressing his war service and general good character. As usual, Wheatley got off lightly.

There was a sequel to this incident, when Wheatley and his father were over at the Newton's' for Sunday lunch. While having a pre-dinner drink, Wheatley noticed that Sir Louis had left the local paper casually open at the report of Wheatley's arrest and appearance in court for drunkenness, which gave Wheatley a tense few minutes. "Ever-smiling but secretly malicious", Sir Louis evidently hoped that Wheatley's father would see it. Little wonder Wheatley disliked and distrusted him, but unfortunately, within a few years, he is going to marry Wheatley's mother.

★

Later that year Wheatley went on holiday with his favourite uncle, Dennis. They went to Corsica via Marseilles, where they saw the famous red light district, later demolished by the Germans. While they were there they went to a brothel, and Wheatley saw his first and only blue movie. Being the keen Dumas reader that he was, he also made a visit to the Chateau d'If, as in *The Count of Monte Cristo*.

Reaching Corsica, in those days "unspoilt" and with only one hotel, made of wood, Wheatley saw the house in which Napoleon was born, and the steep precipices around Corte, in the mountainous centre of the island, later gave him the idea for his short story 'Vendetta'. On their return journey they went to Monte Carlo and motored along the coast, which was the beginning of Wheatley's lifelong love of the South of France. "Those were the days," he wrote later, "when something of the glamour which attached to it before the First World War still lingered."

*

Back in England, Wheatley's rackety life with Tombe continued, with what he calls "romps" and "hectic nights" with women at Yeoman House. For Christmas 1920 Tombe gave him Havelock Ellis's *Studies in the Psychology of Sex* in the complete six volume edition, inscribing it "To my very dear friend wishing him a happy Xmas, and all the happiness he has always given me."

Wheatley read these books closely, and wrote in them "Eric called these six volumes 'The Family Bible' and he was right. For an intellectual sensualist like himself they are truly 'the book of books.' " "Every page is full of interest," wrote Wheatley, and "much information is given on the customs of the ancients, and Savages." He decided Volume IV was particularly interesting, "as it discusses the effect of scents, music, wine, colours, etc etc on the human passion. In the hands of an unscrupulous man it is a dangerous book, but extremely interesting to the psychologist." Altogether the six volumes were "a monument of patience and learning *to which too high a tribute cannot be paid*. His postscript is *beautiful*."

*

Tombe was still heavily involved in fraud, although Wheatley claims in his autobiography that he was unaware of it at the time. This was far from being the case. Among Wheatley's papers is a draft of a mining offer by Tombe, selling some land with mineral rights: we can be fairly sure the land had no minerals, or that it wasn't Tombe's to sell, or both. This was just the tip of the iceberg.

Tombe and Dyer had both left the Air Ministry and had a new venture in a racing stables and stud farm at Kenley. Dyer had bought a large house there called The Welcomes with a stable block attached, where he employed a trainer, stable man, and a number of stable lads. He had bought it for £5,000 and insured it for £12,000.

On the night of April 12th 1921, Tombe went out to Kenley dressed in his finest evening clothes: white tie, tails, and top hat. It was important to look his best, because if the police should stop him, he could say he was going to a big dance that was being held in the area. But in fact he wasn't going to a dance at all: he was going to burn down The Welcomes for the insurance money.

Dyer had packed the place with combustibles and gone to Brighton for the evening. When he got back, he stood in the still smoking ruins with the tears pouring down his cheeks, looking for all the world like a man who had lost everything, instead of a man laughing all the way to the bank. Psychopaths often have a talent for acting. Apropos of this very perform-ance, "after he had plotted the burning of the Welcomes", Tombe told Wheatley that Dyer was "the most wonderful actor he had ever seen."

Wheatley's role in all this was to provide Tombe with an alibi. Wheatley, Dolly and another girl dined that evening in Tombe's flat, and Tombe joined them around midnight; the idea being, of course, that if need be they would say he had been with them all the time. The girls didn't know what Tombe was doing, apart from a "night job", but Wheatley did. Tombe was suitably grateful, writing to Wheatley later "It will always cause me a thrill of happiness to remember how wonderful you were on the evening of my famous stunt that night – I do not forget things like that, my friend."

The strain was beginning to take its toll on Tombe, who had started to suffer from fainting spells; he wrote to Wheatley "I think it was time I pulled up a wee bit, when that fainting business began." He started to spend more and more time away with Beatrice – on the Isle of Wight, in America, in Austria and Italy – leaving Wheatley to mind his criminal and romantic affairs in his absence.

CHAPTER FIFTEEN

Scheherezade in Streatham

In his autobiography Wheatley recalls what a splendid era the Twenties were; at the time he had mixed feelings. In autumn 1921 he complained to Hilda that he was broke, Christmas was coming, and he had to spend it at Bexhill with the Newtons. "This will mean spending more money," he wrote, and standing around in a crowded bar. Instead,

> If I am going to drink – I like it to be with my own friends, – I like it to be in a quiet and secluded spot – *not a bar* – I like it to be a good wine over which I can linger, with joy, – not continual rounds of gin and vermouth – and if I dance, I like it to be with one girl all the evening – and one who enjoys it in the way *I enjoy it* – revelling in the sensuous movements of the music, the light, the colour . . . *from the aesthetic point of view.*

"Of course," he added, in their way

> I suppose these people are very nice – their parents I believe term them "jolly young people", and they term each other "cheery souls" a terrible expression! – but it annoys me so to think that they go home and tell all their friends that they have had "the time of their lives" and moreover believe it – poor people, – well one day perhaps they will know what it is to Live with a Capital L – but I doubt it.

Wheatley had acquired these "aesthetic" and condescending values largely from Eric.

★

Despite their own forays into living with a capital L, Wheatley had been lonely through 1921, without a girl. Then one morning in Bond Street he saw the Chinese goddess Kwan-Yin, Queen of Heaven, in the window of Asprey's. Wheatley prayed to her to send him a mistress.

As if in answer, he saw an attractive girl's reflection in the window as she walked past, walked after her and managed to strike up a conversation. They had lunch, and she agreed to see him again the following Saturday, when he took her down to Yeoman House, slipped Sims some money, and spent the night with her. She was eighteen and an artist's model from a poor background ("but her accent was not common"). They continued to see each other for a few weeks.

Wheatley's loneliness was made worse when Hilda Gosling married John Gardner, a dealer in old prints. He was not long out of uniform, but in due course he became a respected dealer with a shop on Buckingham Gate. Wheatley was best man at their wedding, and made a characteristic list of expenses ("Tea 1lb Souchong 5/6"; "Special mouthwash 4/-" and so on) coming to £16/9/6 against the £12/10 he was given for the occasion, with an invoiced shortfall of £3/19/6.

Wheatley wrote an Orientalist paean to their happiness immediately after their honeymoon: "My dear, dear People," he wrote

> . . . The joy which I derived from seeing you both so happy – was greater than the joy contained in many bottles – many dinners – and any that a Maiden has to offer, in Allah's Garden – beneath which rivers flow.
>
> You see – the choicest bottles – leave a bitter taste, the morning after – the most Lucullan feast – a heaviness and tension, undesirable – and even the most seductive Houri – one sometimes grows – a little weary.
>
> But in the spectacle of your happiness together – I find a wine, of which I can drink long and deep – but yet it leaves no bitterness because – I love you both. – In your companionship – I have a dish – in which there is no

legacy of heaviness – instead – it lightens wonderfully my burdens – how much so you can never know – and in your friendship, I can thank the Gods – there is no chance of waking up one morning – satiated and disillusioned.

. . .

One thing only – do I say – never rob me of my wine – let me drink of it for many moons, even unto the time when we shall pass into the land which no man knoweth.

Wheatley was looking forward to seeing them again, because time was going slowly on his own: "Sunday is a miserable day I find now – particularly the mornings – therefore forget not that you are wealthy – let a few crumbs I beg fall from your table."

A couple of weeks later he wrote again: "Will you please forgive an ordinary mortal – if for a few moments he breaks in upon the peace and happiness of the Elysian Fields in which you dwell . . .". Continuing the Oriental theme, he thought John had shut himself up in his Palace,

eschewing all the works of man, – happy, in hunting the game within his pastures and revelling in the joys of Allah's Paradise that lie within his gates . . .

They had all but disappeared into their happiness, Wheatley wrote a couple of weeks later, "like divers into so deep a sea that we do not even see the bubbles . . . rising from your helmets."

*

With the time on his hands, Wheatley tried to write a play. He envisaged the life of a writer, complete with Oriental rugs and Eastern decor:

if I could get a novel published or a play accepted – it would mean so much to me – I should not be such a fool as to give up business, but it would mean independence

174

and the things I love – a little flat somewhere, with eastern rugs – hanging lantern and the room of a thousand cushions . . .

This would be a place "to entertain my few very dear friends" (Wheatley was still living with his parents), and "it would be another lease of life for me, and before I am too old to appreciate the joys that a bachelor can have."

As for the alleged joys of being a bachelor, Wheatley wrote hopefully to Hilda and John about a girl at the wedding: "also when you write – tell me of the girl in grey who was at the wedding and the Station afterwards – who is she – I thought her very charming –"

★

A few weeks later, Wheatley's parents held a dinner party and invited a friend of theirs from Harrogate, a Mrs Robinson. Mrs Robinson's daughter Nancy, a blue-eyed blonde, sat next to Wheatley, and they were very taken by one another. Wheatley escorted her home, bowed and kissed her hand. Next day he telephoned her and they had lunch. He wrote again comparing her to Scheherezade, and she wrote back to her "Prince of a Thousand Charms." Within a week they were engaged.

Wheatley had once written over ninety stanzas of lugubrious doggerel for Barbara Symonds, but Nancy inspired better efforts. Wheatley was still in Oriental mode, and his verses came straight from the mystic East of J.E.Flecker, Omar Khayyam, and Oscar Asche:

> If I were King of Babylon and Tetrarch of Judaea,
> The Lord of all Assyria and Mighty in Chaldea,
> I'd overthrow the Idols and slay the Sacred Bull
> That men might worship thee instead – my own most beautiful.

And so it went on, splendidly: divans and caravans, a marble temple "with Crystal Lamps set in a Mystic Sign", oriental carpets, silks from far Cathay, secret gardens, fountains flow-ing wine, a Marble Lotus Pool, and Nancy's myrrh-perfumed breasts. Nancy wrote back a sixteen page story called 'The Legend of the Lovers Nancia and Denesco'.

Wheatley's parents were not displeased by the fact that Nancy was not only beautiful but an heiress, with the Nugget Boot Polish fortune behind her.

★

Wheatley wrote and told Tombe about "Scheherezade", and Tombe wrote back from Austria, where he and Beatrice were staying: "how wonderful it is, and I am so glad, dear boy, if, and I am sure she is, the little lady is all you say, it is truly wonderful, and you have achieved the miraculous. She sounds so curious in the strange Eastern setting you give her – and your progress is that of Adonis himself. Well, one cannot wonder that she is attracted . . . I am deeply inter-ested, and so glad for you." And here Tombe modestly took a little credit for himself:

How often I have told you of this strange Elixir of Life, now you experience it, and all is well. It is very good of you to say all you do about my teaching, such as it is and has been – I have done very little – you over appreci-ate me dear boy. I but long for your happiness, and the ability to taste of the fruit of *all* [underlined twice] the trees in the Garden, using each one to the more perfect development of your individuality, and appreciation of the beautiful in all things. "To cure the senses by the soul, and to indulge the soul by means of the senses", that is our gospel.

"The fruit of all the trees" is from Oscar Wilde's *De Profundis*, while "our gospel" is (mis)quoted from his *Picture of Dorian Gray*, where Lord Henry Wotton explains to young Dorian "that is one of the great secrets of life – to cure the soul by means of the senses, and the senses by means of the soul."

All this time Tombe had been continuing with Wheatley's education. "Do not, amid all you have to do, neglect your reading", Tombe urged him: particularly since it would be "one's chief pleasure in one's later years." Tombe was a conscious disciple of Wilde, and from Wilde he discovered Walter Pater. Pater's famous 'Conclusion' to *The Renaissance* would become Tombe's bible for the rest of his short life: "it is true that I find many of my own ideas crystallised, but he goes further than I had ever dreamed of. My whole philosophy you will find epitomised in his 'Conclusion' – to which I most earnestly draw your attention."

Along with Wilde, Pater, Flaubert, and Lao Tzu, Tombe was particularly fond of cultured erotica, a taste later reflected in Wheatley's own library. When Wheatley went to Marseilles, Tombe asked him to look out for a copy of *The Perfumed Garden*, and Tombe's own preferred book shop was The London Foreign Book Company at 2 Langham Place, which was run by a Russian named Ohzol. He recommended this to Wheatley, adding "mention that you were recommended to call by Major Macsweeney and Major Coode" (a Major Gilbert Macswiney was secretary of the Anti-Prohibition League, so Coode seems to be a Tombe alias).

"I visited our Russian bookselling friend the other day", Tombe reported, "and bought *The Principles of Lao Tze* and also a most amusing little book in three volumes, which you must read – its astonishing crudity smacks of Swift at his zenith – but it is most amusing." Before long Mr Ohzol was writing to Wheatley: "With reference to your enquiry I beg to say that I have now an opportunity of purchasing the following, viz. Krafft-Ebing, *Psychopathia Sexualis* at 31/6 and Bloch's Book at 32/6." This was Regina Bloch's *The Book of Strange Loves*, which Wheatley annotated as "delightful."

Tombe kept Wheatley under his spell with his unceasing solicitude and flattery, granting Wheatley membership of a highly superior club of two. When Wheatley sent Tombe a copy of a speech by Tanko, Tombe said "I should imagine it will exactly suit the hoi polloi [sic] it is intended for –"

Has it ever struck you that the ideals and life of the latter, while excellent for them per illos, constitute for us the very dread inspired by the head of Medusa, without, of course, its grandeur!

However, ordinary people had their compensations: "Perhaps the abysmally uncultured have more chance of domestic happiness than we intellectuals."

It was important for superior beings to stick together and remember their duties to each other, which in Wheatley's case included making the effort to write regularly, and Tombe had to admonish him: "Now, part of the vital creed is that we never do anything which we are disinclined to do – but frankly I miss your letters as the public do not matter to me!!!"

Tombe was not quite the intellectual he imagined. As the error of "the hoi polloi" – i.e. "the 'the people' " – suggests, he was operating at the limits of a self-educated vocabulary. "Thank you over and over again for your so charming gifts," he wrote to Wheatley: "you forget nothing, not even such lacunae [sic] as my penchant for crystallised fruit."

At one point Tombe congratulates Wheatley on his style: "your style is excellent, and graceful – while your soupcon of 17th century maniere titillates my artistic palate. The pupil is far outstripping the master!" For all that, pupil and master were beginning to diverge in their tastes: Tombe was leaning decadently towards pure style while Wheatley – anticipating the research-packed world of his fiction – was finding that what he really liked from books was information. "Our ways of ascending the mount of Olympus may be slightly different," Tombe conceded,

But the same translucent beacon beckons us both – and the combination is wonderful. To me literature is beauty – beauty of language – and poetry of rhythm – information, qua information, takes a secondary place; it has taken me all my life to reach this – and I have only fully realized it during the last 3 or 4 weeks – so you must forgive my somewhat boyish enthusiasm!!

Tombe recommends Walter Pater to Wheatley, while Wheatley recommends Lord Chesterfield's *Letters to His Son* to Tombe. Described by Doctor Johnson as teaching "the morals of a whore and the manners of a dancing master", Chesterfield's *Letters* are essentially a handbook of social climbing[1].

The pair of them, Tombe felt, still had a great deal to learn, including the Greeks ("the Pagan coupled with the worship of beauty in its all and every form") and "the Eastern point of view" ("I think that you are very right when you say that we shall find our philosophy . . . there"). "How short one's life is," Tombe wrote, "for all one must do and experience!"

★

Tombe had made a new base with Beatrice in Totland Bay, on the Isle of Wight, and he was also abroad for much of the time. His letters come back to Wheatley as if from a world tour. From America he sent postcards from New York and the Grand Canyon, and reported from California that not only was the bathing wonderful ("One can actually see the bottom of the sea at a depth of 90ft") but "This is the paradise of 'oggins! Imagine *all* the women do it . . ."

Writing from the Hotel Continental in the rue Castiglione, Tombe reports "Paris is wonderful, what a change from London and the stolid ones who live there!! Save your wonderful self, who indeed possess the Gallic soul and art."

Vienna was even better ("the air like champagne, and the people are charming") particularly because things were so cheap. Tombe writes excitedly about the price of silk socks, champagne, night clubs, and pearls. "The excellent kroner is now 29,500 to the pound and we grow fat thereon." As for the charming Austrians, Tombe reported innocently – one of several ominous notes in his correspondence – that they couldn't afford anything: "whole town is packed with foreigners, a good many of them Jews."

---

[1] They were also a favourite of the popular novelist Catherine Cookson, whose own edition of Chesterfield was subtitled A Strategy for Rising in the World.

Italy was just as good: "dear boy, a heaven on earth." In Taormina (in those days "a synonym for Sodom", associated with the photography of Baron von Gloeden and others), Tombe treated himself to some pictures: "quite perfect studies (photographic), and in the nude, of the purely Greek-type of boy one sees here so much – they are rather wonderful." Palermo was "Paradise (complete with houris)", even lovelier than California. The women were marvellous, and "here one dreams one's life away – lotus eating . . . It is really considered bad form to do any work here – and I never felt so much at home anywhere in my life."

In Rome they went to see the dead Pope, Benedict XV, in all his robes:

> It was a most impressive spectacle, yet curiously pathetic – to see how utterly helpless is even the head of the greatest church in Christendom before the Reaper.

"I wonder if he was sufficiently Pagan to have no regrets?" Tombe wondered, adding – straight from Pater's 'Conclusion' to *The Renaissance* – "For I do not suppose that my gospel – experience for the sake of experience, and not for its fruits – would have appealed to him."

★

Tombe's grand touring alternated with spells of domestic bliss on the Isle of Wight, where he and Beatrice rented a house. Wheatley went to stay, going via Lymington; this was probably his first experience of Lymington, where he would later live.

Beatrice's letters to Wheatley reveal a more fragile side to Tombe: his arthritis is less severe than it used to be, she says, he manages to play a little tennis, and "really gets about quite a lot". All in all, "we are as happy as the day is long." Sometimes Tombe had to absent himself on missions of one sort or another, but "when Boy" – as she called him – "is here it is Heaven itself . . . hoping before long he will be back again, so we can be ideally happy once again."

Tombe was getting about quite a lot more than Beatrice rea-lised, and Wheatley was helping him. Wheatley was instructed to send them a wire that read "Important business, come to town as early as possible tomorrow. Bill." ("Just that, no more. I have my reasons"). When Wheatley went to Marseilles, Tombe sent him a letter to re-post from there, "on June 21ˢᵗ, *without fail* . . . PS will you stamp enclosed letter old man." As for Dolly, "I am in the East, and you have not heard from me." All this was typical Tombe: even in Paradise, Tombe's movements were clandestine, and he wrote from Palermo "I want you, dear boy, to regard all information re our movements as absolutely confidential, as a curious contre-temps has taken place in England – which I will relate when I see you."

★

Wheatley entered into the spirit of all this and suggested writing to Tombe in code, which Tombe greatly approved of ("The word for the key word of the code you suggest is admirable, and I commend the whole idea.") Tombe added that if he was writing a coded or otherwise confidential letter, Wheatley should write a harmless letter to go into the same envelope, which he could show to Beatrice, "and all will be very well!".

Tombe conducted his criminal as well as romantic deceits from a letter drop at 131 Jermyn Street; this was only a min-ute or two from his flat in Yeoman House, but it formed one of his "cul de sacs". The mining fraud, for example, was conducted from 131 Jermyn Street. When Tombe was out of London, it was Wheatley's job to attend to business at 131. There was a code for this, when Tombe would simply put an 'X' at the top of letters. This meant "will you go to 131 Jermyn St and fix up", and occasionally it had to be emphasised: "Will you attend to 'X' at once?"

And so it went on. "I was so glad you fixed things up all right at 131 . . . be very careful to destroy (burn) both letters and envelopes . . . Acknowledge receipt of this letter by a cross at the top of your letter, but do not allude to it in any other way. Will you like a good chap post enclosed letter to D anywhere in the West End." On another occasion Wheatley had to make a telephone call:

As soon as you get this ring up Mrs BELL, Hammersmith 1447, do not ask to speak to her specially, unless a man should answer, and do not give your name. Simply say "Please give Mrs Bell this message," "that Mr Gordon-Tombe will arrive in town on Friday next, and will ring up at about 5 o'c pm."

That's all. Quite simple. The comic idea being, as your astute brain will guess, that I wish her to think I have been abroad in foreign lands! *Quelle vie*!! All the very best dear old boy, and burn this.

★

Among the Tombe materials in Wheatley's personal archive are some odds and ends which resemble nothing so much as the material 'clues' in Wheatley's celebrated 'Crime Dossiers' of the Thirties. There are some theatre tickets; and a key label, marked "D. Key", which on closer examination evidently comes from Harrods; and there is a scrap of paper with some authors jotted down (Rabindranath Tagore, and Henri Murger with his *La Vie Bohème*) along with the words "David Watson 131 Jermyn St."

It is possible that the D Key is Dennis's duplicate key, perhaps to a Harrod's safe-deposit box owned by Tombe. And – given that people choosing pseudonyms often keep the same initials – it is also possible that "David Watson" is a Wheatley alias for use at no.131. It is difficult to know where these clues really lead, if anywhere, but *quelle vie*.

★

Mrs Bell, a.k.a. "Desirée", was a new passion in Tombe's life, the only one who really competed with Beatrice. She was a minor actress, married to a doctor, and what made her particularly exciting was that she was relatively intellectual, with a strong if somewhat neurotic character.

Tombe had spent a week at Yeoman House with Desirée before going to America with Beatrice, and there was now a possibility that he would leave Beatrice on his return, while Desirée would leave not only her husband but her children. Wheatley was deputed as go-between in Tombe's absence, and his account reads like a literary work in its own right.

★

Desirée is a semi-invalid, almost unable to eat. She has been in bed since Eric left for America, getting up only for a single taxi journey around midnight, when she went to look at Yeoman House.

Now she has recovered enough to ring Wheatley and invite him over to 25 Shepherd's Bush Green, where she lives with Dr. Hugh Bell. Wheatley was not impressed by Shepherd's Bush, with its cheap coffee stalls and a Bolshevik disturbance in progress at the tube station. The pavements were thronged with "bimina", and what with "the haggard looking women, the ornamented, ready-tongued girls in their cheap finery, the round shouldered, dirty-looking youths, it's hardly a place that even the most elastic-minded estate agent could term 'a high-class residential district'."

This led Wheatley to think on urban decline, something he had seen in South London. Like "Brixton, Camberwell, Catford, Lewisham etc" the area had seen better days, and Desirée's house was of the type once lived in by a prosperous city merchant, when it had fields nearby. Wheatley paints a fanciful picture of the upstairs room, with bygone Richard and Arabella, but now, "Gone is Arabella with her blushes and her bun, gone is Richard with his magnificent waistcoats . . . Gone are the horse hair chairs and waxed fruits that under glass cases adorned the mantle." Instead we have "Desirée in her own setting. An eastern room."

> The walls patterned with a striped pattern paper of a dark reddish colour, giving warmth and comfort . . . dark hangings of an oriental stuff . . . in Chinese design, Eastern rugs upon the floor, a long low divan before the fire,

183

which burnt brightly despite the warmth of the evening, flanked by two armchairs, all having coverings of material embellished with oriental patterns, over the low back of the divan a large square of Chinese silk bright crimson, flowered with gold, making a brilliant patch in the rather sombre apartment, a few small tables, otherwise little furniture except a large stand upon which incense was burning in Chinese holders, the whole lit up by the soft light of a hanging lamp covered with red silk.

How far it seemed from the trams and tubes that run within fifty yards, and the jostling puppets of fate who throng the pavements outside.

The eastern room has all the cheap exoticism of Desirée's neurasthenic desire for a better life.

Wheatley talked for a while with Dr. Bell, a progressive Socialist, "rather a dreamer and a missionary" and in Wheatley's estimation a good, unselfish man who would not object if Desirée left him, if he thought it would make her happier. Dr. Bell left after twenty minutes, and Wheatley and Desiree spent the next three hours talking about Eric, until it was time to make a dash for the last tube train.

Wheatley found all this a delicate responsibility, since he was mindful of both Beatrice and Desirée's children, and he urged Tombe not to string Desirée along. This bore directly on whether Wheatley should, as he put it, be helping her to build the house of her dreams, "her house of love and sacrifice," or whether he should be watering the cement.

Wheatley proceeded to weigh up the pros and cons. There was Desirée's mind: "She undoubtedly possesses a mind far above the average woman and you have already tasted to a certain extent the pleasures of each others conversations. She is a woman in a million and one who might even when she had lost her beauty retain your affection by her intellect alone . . . She firmly believes that by these powers she could overcome for once and all the loneliness that comes upon you at times so much so, that even when she is not with you she swears that if she once possessed you, you would never be lonely again."

184

Then there was the intensity of her passion for Eric: "she is just like the convent school girl, she has a few scraps of your writing which she treasures, your favourite handkerchief, and greatest treasure of all the famous piece of artichoke."

Wheatley proceeds to dream on the perfect, self-contained relationship, very similar to the sort that he envisaged Hilda and John enjoying, and which he longed for himself.

> In her love there are boundless possibilities; if you had as much for her, you might rank with Abelard and Heloise or Helen of Troy and Paris. If you went away together you might almost defy the Gods and find on earth the peace that passeth all understanding.
>
> If you took your courage in both hands you might really take a little island, with palm trees and a lagoon, there are many such scattered down the coasts of Africa and America and there you might sample the joys that come only to one in a million, the perfect peace of mutual dependence . . .

And yet even then, says Wheatley, the exile in sunny lands hankers for Piccadilly Circus at night, the call of the news boys in Trafalgar Square, even "the sight of the multitude that we despise."

Comparing Desirée to Beatrice, Wheatley conceded that Eric would never have such "thrilling discussions" with Beatrice, "because all she knows you have taught her yourself." On the other hand, "remember that there are great possibilities here for she is the child of your brain, to a great extent, and to watch her open and develop as a flower the seed of which you have sown would be wonderful."

And in any case, Wheatley thought, the whole intellectual business is overvalued and grows less interesting as one gets older. "These glorious talks are a great joy but all the same it does seem to me that we wander in a circle, older people seem to realise this more particularly; they shrug their shoulders and pass on where they see the younger generation expounding new theories, and wandering knee deep in the

185

philosophies of bygone times. I sometimes think that Old Omar was right when he said

> Myself when young didst eagerly frequent
> Doctor and saint, and heard great Argument
> About it and about: but evermore
> Came out by the same door as in I went."

Tombe too, when older, might be less interested in "abstruse questions."

Tombe had suggested to Wheatley that Desirée could join in his life of fraud, but "Last night she told me that her dearest ambition was that you should give it up, far from aiding you she will seek to deter you . . . Her idea is that you will never learn what real peace is until you do give it up. In this I must say I think there is a great deal . . ."

Wheatley never had any illusions about the importance of money, and he points out that Desirée might be a financial liability. And yet even without much money, Eric and Desirée could still afford to live on a little island. Wheatley mentions that one in the Channel was recently let for 99 years at £100 pounds (still only about £2500 today): "and there is much to be said for it during the Revolution that is coming here."

*

Beatrice, on the other hand, offered security, and if he stayed with Beatrice he could give up crime. Eric and Beatrice should have "great expectations . . . they may take a few years to mature but they should come to fruition someday", on the death of old 'Undreds.

Beatrice also offered emotional stability, and on this point the twenty-three year old Wheatley writes a treatise on the great difference between women: "All women from the age of Puberty onwards are one of two things – either A Mother or a Prostitute."

A woman who has no children may be a Mother.

A woman who has never committed the sexual act may be a Prostitute.

This is a close relative of the Madonna / Whore polarity, and Wheatley argues that while some women offer calm, family-type stability (Beatrice as Mother) others offer precarious and demanding romantic excitement (Desirée as Prostitute). "To marry a Prostitute is to court Divorce" says Wheatley, whereas

A Mothers love is more lasting than a Prostitutes
Love is the greater part of her being
Mother love is not so intense so it is not so exacting
To love a Mother is to have always a refuge . . .
. . .
To marry a mother is to marry a life long friend
The love of the Mother is hard to kindle . . . but gradually brightens to a steady light . . . the brighter as the years roll on.

Underlining his definitions of Beatrice and Desirée as "Mother" and "Prostitute" respectively, Wheatley foresees a tranquil and happy future for Eric with Beatrice, becoming increasingly necessary to each other as time goes by.

Taking up the attack from another angle, Wheatley compares the two women to wines:

God who is the Maitre de Hotel of Fate bows before you in the Restaurant of Life which is the World. On one hand he holds a bottle of the Widow Clicquot '06, in the other a bottle of Chateau D'Issan.

He holds them carefully because they are both his children and he loves them well.

He murmurs softly:

"What will monsieur take to drink?"

It is the difference between a champagne and a good Burgundy.

You hesitate, knowing that the Widow as she is will warm you through and through, that if you drink her your eyes will shine, your red blood will rush in your veins for very joy of life, your tongue will loosen and wit will flow from your lips, your brain will unfold as the moon flowers in the moon light, your being will be filled with exaltation and her sparkle will turn you from a man into a demi-god.

And yet the effect will not remain, finally the reaction will set in; you will need more and you will find the bottle empty. It is the wine of youth.

But with reliable old Burgundy Beatrice,

You turn to the Chateau D'Issan . . . you know it will not make you gay and sparkling, it will not cause your brains to reel with the joy of great sensation, and yet it will give you warmth and comfort over you will steal the gentle feeling of well being and of contentment out of its mellow depths will come the sense of quiet happiness and of companionship it is the wine of age.

When you have finished the bottle, you will not require another; the sense of contentment and that all's well with the world goes with you as you leave the restaurant and make your way to bed. Your mouth is not parched or dry, and its beautiful bouquet lingers in your nostrils long after the bottle is empty.

So that was the choice.

God who is the Maitre D'Hotel bows before you in the Restaurant of Fate which is the World.
He murmurs softly.
"What will Monsieur like to drink?"

CHAPTER SIXTEEN

Dangerous Liaisons

Wheatley was having trouble with his teeth, which were now so bad they were beginning to spoil the pleasure of constant sweet eating. In his early twenties he had them all pulled and replaced by dentures. This was a common practice, and Wheatley said he never regretted it. Eric was predictably solicitous and concerned: "I am so very distressed . . . poor old man, how terrible for you, I truly sympathise, but as you say, it may be for the best – I only hope so."

Wheatley was increasingly uncomfortable about Desirée, and in the absence of clear instructions from Eric he took the decision to gently disillusion her before she decided to leave her husband. He went once more to 25 Shepherd's Bush Green, as he told Eric, "firmly determined to shatter some of her illusions regarding your charming self."

Dr Bell was there, but left to see the first night of a play Desirée should have been in, had she not been ill. In the event, however, there was to be more acting going on at number 25.

Desirée told Wheatley she had been through hell, and talked about sacrifice. She showed him photos of her children. They talked for a couple of hours, with Wheatley still very conscious that he hadn't managed to do the deed, when she suddenly said, "I wonder what Rosa [the Maitre d'Hotel] thinks of Eric and all his women that he takes to Oddies."

Of course [reports Wheatley] I saw the trap at once, as I have gathered from one remark and another that Oddies is considered sacred to you two: – so I promptly fell in without moving a muscle, just a little laugh and my reply.

"Oh I don't know, he must be rather amused, I should think."

I was lying back upon the divan gazing into the fire as

I spoke, and I could not see her face or the effect of my words upon her, but she wished to make quite certain and went on again casually.

"I suppose you have been there with him and a good many of them too."

With all the guile of the Serpent in the Garden I continued to smoke and gaze into the fire, as I answered lightly and with the air of pleasant memories.

"Why no, I wouldn't say that, but I've been there with one or two you know . . ."

There was a little silence and then she said with great intensity.

"So he did lie to me after all then."

Wheatley shifted about uncomfortably, trying to give the impression that he had accidentally let the truth slip out. Desirée then began to rail against Eric

"Oh why did I trust him? Oh why need he have told me again and again that I was the only woman he had ever taken to Oddies, and I thought of him as my affinity, a God, and he's only a man, just like the rest, what a fool I've been and now I have to begin the long search all over again – . . . I merely despise him now, that is all, poor fool, he doesn't know what he has lost."

"I really felt quite sorry for you old bean," writes Wheatley: "I knew that you didn't deserve a word of it and it was I who'd told a whacking great lie, having never been into Oddies with you and a woman other than Desirée in my life."

★

Wheatley had to make a rush for the 12.07 tube, but before he left Desirée reminded him that they had agreed to go out for dinner and a show, asking him to get tickets for *The Blue Lagoon* and take her anywhere but Oddie's.

Next morning, when he rang her to say he had the tickets, she had changed her mind about the restaurant; she now thought it would be "rather pleasant" to go to Oddie's after all. She turned up looking pale and ill, having had a relapse and gone back on to a milk diet. Desirée could not be persuaded to take anything but a plain omelette and some milk, while Wheatley addressed himself to an Homard Victoria — lobster with truffles — followed by a partridge and a Praline Ice. He helped all this down with a Martini, a comforting bottle of Chateau D'Issan — the wine he had compared to Beatrice —, a coffee, and a glass of Green Chartreuse. They talked quite cheerfully about Eric, until Desirée suddenly looked Wheatley in the eye and said "Why would you be glad if I gave him up?"

Wheatley was taken aback ("She's quite uncanny"). Rather than try to convince her she was wrong, Wheatley pretended to put his cards on the table; "principally some of the material ones . . . the sort that she would expect from the pudding head devoted to your interests that she believes me to be."

Wheatley told Desirée he had great ambitions for Tombe's future, and "that we all sooner or later had to return to respectability (at least outwardly)". He thought a liaison with Desirée might delay this, which she disputed: "Did I not think that she was capable of rising herself to that future, and moreover by her love assisting you to climb?". Nor would she cost Eric money, she said, because she could support herself by acting. This brought out the puritan in Wheatley:

> Personally I could not bear to have the woman that I cared about working in any form, and it would be particularly repugnant to me to have her mauled about upon the stage by all sorts of actor people, I am perfectly aware that there is nothing in it and all that, still I am sufficiently narrow minded to resent the mauling . . .

Wheatley assumed Eric would feel the same way, so "She utterly astonished me by saying that you had already discussed it, and not only were you perfectly willing for it but liked the idea."

It was then that they got on to more serious matters.

Knowing Eric's "constant striving for companionship," said Wheatley, what would be Desirée's attitude if he consorted with other women: " 'Need you ask!' " said Desirée, "with a look which made me positively shiver for you . . ."

"My dear old boy," Wheatley counselled Tombe, "it's either to be or not to be like dear old Hamlet, there is no middle course"; "you can't monkey with this . . . don't try any funny business or you will get it in the neck good and hard some fine morning."

*

After dinner they went to the theatre, and then to another restaurant, where Wheatley persuaded her to tackle another omelette and some more milk.

Shivering in the street, Desirée was clearly unwell, but for all her frailty Wheatley seems to have been terrified of her. She told him that if Eric let her down she would devote the rest of her life to wrecking his, and that killing him would be a kindness besides the things she would do. "Of course with the ordinary woman one could afford to laugh at this," said Wheatley,

> Yet I dread for you should such a contest come about, with all your wit, and your brain, big as you are, because this is no ordinary woman, but one who is diabolically clever, who understands the world, who understands the underworld, hers would be no ordinary vengeance.

Wheatley remembered a story he had read of a woman seduced by a pimp, promised marriage, and instead sold into a brothel in New York. Having at last escaped, "always planning planning planning to have her revenge," she finally found the man again, struck up a further liaison, "then she deliberately went with another man in the last stages of syphilis and then passed it to the man who had seduced her."

Yet since syphilis was no longer incurable, Desirée wouldn't do that. She would do worse. Aside from wrecking Eric's illegal ventures ("remember her connection with the C.I.D.")

192

she would have access to her husband's laboratory, and its bacteria samples. Arming herself with "a tube of Cancer baccili, knowing that to be your pet aversion," she would run Eric to ground and inject him: "The prick of a needle and Hey Presto, you might perhaps kill her but the damage would be done."

> I only wish to show you the sort of thing that I consider it is really very possible might be your fate if you took this woman (with her terrific knowledge of the underworld and her diabolical cleverness and her practically unlimited capacity for love and hate) for a few months or a couple of years even – and then sent her the way that all the rest have gone.

Wheatley was hamming it up for Eric's benefit, but Desirée does seem to have made an impression.

He met her again, a few days later, after work at Barbellion's Tea Room, 79 New Bond Street. No doubt adding to Wheatley's sense that she might be slightly deranged, Desirée opened up a new line of argument: it was her duty to lead Eric back to "My Friend" (seemingly Jesus). "This is the only thing that I care about at all, I must save him, it is a crusade that has been given to me, and somehow I feel that you are standing between us . . ."

Wheatley walked her to Bond Street tube. She was leaving in a few days to convalesce in France. Much as Wheatley admired her intelligence, he was relieved to see the back of her.

★

Desirée wrote to Wheatley around this time, explaining her state of mind. "You came and shattered my trust. Quite unwittingly, bless you" – or not, as we have seen – "and immediately put me on the defensive." But now she was unrepentant:

> In reality I only live for the moment when he shall

return, and I don't care if you, he, and all the world know it, for if it be all a dream, I shall be past caring. As for the unmaidenly behaviour it was, as I said, pure fetish worship.

"Au revoir my friend," she closed. "Once again I find myself wishing that I were a man entirely. We could all be such wonderful friends, unhampered by the constant sex antagonism."

★

Wheatley's letter about Desirée ran to forty pages, and it was his greatest literary effort to date: it is hard to believe that 'Julie's Lovers' or his play were a patch on it. Tombe was suitably impressed, thanking Wheatley "ever and ever so much" for his "wonderful letter and extensive report"; "it is a masterly letter, the apotheosis of Dennis".

Tombe, in America with Beatrice, was still thinking seriously of Desirée. "She has the extraordinary capacity for thrilling me 6,100 miles away."

I find that I continually think of her – and am convinced that she and I could climb the heights together. With her, I feel I can and would do great things, and, most important of all, she understands. I shall, of course have to talk over the whole position financial etc very very frankly with her – and we shall have to see what can be done, and how far she is willing to face comparative poverty with me.

Tombe greatly appreciated Wheatley's efforts on his behalf, and had come to think of the pair of them as David and Jonathan, the Biblical friends who had a love for each other "surpassing the love of woman" (see 2 Sam.1:26). He would sign off "Much love. Your affectionate pal, David", and observed "You know, Dennis, I think that this David and Jonathan business, is just about all that makes life worth living."

★

Chums: Eric Tombe with his arm around Wheatley.

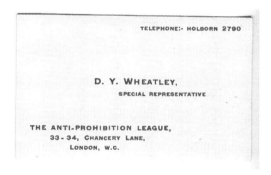

Agent Wheatley: Wheatley's calling card from The Anti-Prohibition League.

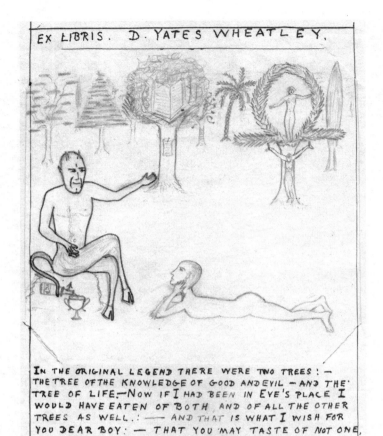

EX LIBRIS. D. YATES WHEATLEY.

IN THE ORIGINAL LEGEND THERE WERE TWO TREES : —
THE TREE OF THE KNOWLEDGE OF GOOD AND EVIL — AND THE
TREE OF LIFE.—NOW IF I HAD BEEN IN EVE'S PLACE I
WOULD HAVE EATEN OF BOTH, AND OF ALL THE OTHER
TREES AS WELL.: —— AND THAT IS WHAT I WISH FOR
YOU DEAR BOY: — THAT YOU MAY TASTE OF NOT ONE,
BUT OF ALL; THE TREES IN THE GARDEN.

Wheatley's own design for his bookplate: Eric as devil, pouring champagne with his tail.

David had his Bathsheba, Tombe had Beatrice, Desirée and the rest, and now Wheatley had Nancy, his Scheherezade. Tombe's congratulations were characteristic: "To have found Scheherezade in Streatham, & in Clinton, & among your mother's friends; my dear boy, the feeding of the multitude in the wilderness was nothing to this!"

After Eric and Beatrice met Dennis and Nancy, Tombe wrote "the more one sees of Nancy, the more charming and delightful does she become . . . *We* both send *you* both our love." Nancy, however, had reservations about Tombe, principally because of his influence on Wheatley. "She had always regarded Eric with suspicion and distrust," Wheatley recalled later, in an unpublished memoir of their friendship, "– not on his own account she thought him quite charming tho' a terrific poseur, but as a disturbing element as far as I and she was concerned."

> . . . she knew of course that he had been to me, guide philosopher and friend, as far as nearly all my exploits of the last few years were concerned and intuitively she understood that tho' he might show every satisfaction at my happy engagement and approaching marriage instinctively he could not help but feel antagonism to her, since she was separating from him the boon companion, of his purple nights.

More than that,

> . . . nothing would please him better than that after the glamour of my marriage had worn off I should play to Nancy the role he played to Beatrice, and continue to participate secretly in those Haymarket seances, of wine and women – although he had never even hinted at such a thing, respecting me too much to endeavour to tempt me – I recognised infallibly that he would welcome and encourage any deviation from path of virtue on my part – it would have been contrary to his every principle to do otherwise.

"Nancy instinctively recognised this too," says Wheatley.

Wheatley always liked to put his case in writing, and the day after an argument, he wrote to Nancy about "the matter of our talk last night, 'Eric and my relations with him.' " Nancy was worried that Eric would get Wheatley involved with other women. Wheatley said this was exactly the fear he had when Nancy flirted socially with other men, and yet he overcame it. As for himself and women, he said, he derived "no kick" from casual flirtatious attractions:

> The kick in life which I get comes quite another way – it is concentrated, into the few moments when one has the unusual, such as my expeditions with Eric. At such times, I am generally in situations such as the ordinary man . . . very rarely finds himself, sometimes, truly, these evenings end in immorality of one kind or another, but usually something unusual, and therefore from which I derive immense kick, often however I am merely a spectator . . .

Wheatley compared this to Nancy's flirtations, where she unconsciously attracted men without caring for them, "yet always wishing the *possibility* that you might be attracted in turn."

So in Wheatley's case, like Nancy's, "I get a kick from these expeditions, the bizarre and the unusual, as a looker on – yet by going along each wishes the possibility of being drawn into active participation."

★

Preparations for marriage were well advanced, and Wheatley and Nancy looked for a flat. They settled on one at 20a Trebovir Road, Earls Court, and on Wednesday 19th April 1922 Wheatley viewed it again with Eric. The two of them walked from his office to Down Street tube (now one of London's 'ghost' tube stations, between Green Park and Hyde Park corner). "Both of us thoroughly enjoyed the little time we had together," Wheatley remembered: "As always we talked of books, and art, women and money."

At the flat, Tombe examined it and questioned the land-lord, a Mr Winning, as though he were going to take it himself. "Marching from room to room with his long rapid strides, he measured and gauged – vetted the floors and walls, took the direction of the sunlight, and at last having satisfied himself on my behalf, admired the height and spaciousness of the rooms, the general convenience of their arrangement and agreed that it was both reasonable in price and capable of being, when neatly decorated, not only comfortable but handsome."

For all Eric's questions, neither Wheatley nor Tombe were as clever as they thought. In due course "a nasty little man" turned up claiming to be the landlord, which in fact he was, and Winning disappeared with Wheatley's money.

For the time being, however, after Winning left them alone, they strolled about the empty rooms smoking and talking of Eric's criminal affairs. First there was a fraud on a man named Stephens:

"Dear Boy", said Eric, "that little piece of business that I spoke to you about is shaping splendidly"

"Good!" said Wheatley.

"Old Bill [Dyer's nickname] has got that fellow going splendidly. Next week we shall have our little meeting, and he will be poorer to the tune of several thousand pounds."

"Do you appear in it?"

"Nup! – I'm the feller that stands outside – a prospective investor – you know the idea my interests are his, etc – the only thing I have to do is to bolster up Bill's banking account. You see this time next week he'll have to show this fellow a balance of £2,000 under his own name at the Purley branch as a guarantee of good faith, – of course poor Old Bill's about on his uppers – so I've to transfer the boodle from my own account. I'm going down to Purley to fix it up tomorrow night."

With hindsight, this may have been a fraud by Dyer on Tombe; two thousand pounds is about £75,000 at today's values. Then there was the insurance fraud; how was that going?

> "That's shaping well, dear boy, the sous should come on in a fortnight's time."
> "You're sure they don't know anything," said Wheatley "– there's no hitch? I'm frightened of that since they've delayed so long."
> "They haven't got an earthly, my dear fellow I've had the three biggest insurance experts in London on the case – it's as sound as a bell."
> "But you never know, at the last moment they may bring some fresh evidence."

Tombe smiled disdainfully. "You can't do that on Father," he said – i.e. on Tombe himself – "We've made them show their documents they're only holding out to the last minute to get the best terms. If we'd take £7,000 they'd close tomorrow – but we don't mean to settle for a penny under eight."

Then there was the racing. It is sometimes said that the way to make a small fortune by gambling is to start with a large one, but Tombe had a scheme. Wheatley implored him to get out of racing ("I've always hated it, and it's never done you any good") but Tombe said that for the moment he had to stay in, out of loyalty to Dyer. Then after the insurance was settled, he would quit, after one last "grand slam".

In those days betting debts were not enforceable by law: this gave the gambler on credit or cheques a final loophole, but added to the undercurrent of threat and violence that surrounded turf betting.

> "I just hate the thought of all those bookies spending my good money," said Tombe.
> "Evade the Betting Act, you mean?" asked Wheatley.
> "That's the spirit, our credit's excellent, Old Bill's got a

splendid name on the Turf. Between us we can easily lay on £10,000 among the twenty Bookies that we deal with. You see we've always spread our dealings so as to keep open the maximum number of accounts – you know how I always work these things – We put the money on a good horse that we think has a chance to win at fairly decent odds say five to one – if it comes in, alright! we get our boodle – if not we refuse to pay . . . All they can do is to bar us from the Turf, but who cares . . ."

"What about the Bookies' gangs?" said Wheatley: "You'll have to be careful or they'll beat you up."

For a moment Tombe became thoughtful, then he smiled. "It's not an easy matter to beat me up, dear boy. When I run to earth I'm hard to find. You know the old game of *cul de sacs*."

"I can look after myself as well as most people and as for Bill, well somehow I'd just hate to beat up Bill – he's a terrible fellow when roused – a great big burly devil – do you remember what he did to the feller trod on his foot in the tram, eh, and the taxi who wouldn't take him further than Croydon? . . ."

Oh yes, Tombe continued,

"Bill's a murderous devil . . . and anyhow Dennis if they did catch us napping £10,000's worth a beating. They dare not go too far, they know too much to do you in – Think of all the bottles of the Boy [champagne] and little dinners at Oddies there are in ten thousand pounds."

This brought Wheatley to his last question: the prospect of Beatrice and Tombe inheriting "Old 'Undreds's" money, which he hoped wasn't far away. "I hope so too," said Tombe.

"The Star of the Bluestones is in the ascendant, dear boy. What with Stephens, the Insurance, the Bookies, and the prospect of 'Undreds breaking up, our prospects have never been better."

They shook hands at Earl's Court station. "Well, dear boy," said Tombe, "I've enjoyed *so much* having one of our *little chats* together . . ."

Wheatley never saw him again.

CHAPTER SEVENTEEN

. . . In a Cloud of Blue Smoke

Next day, Thursday, Tombe telephoned. As usual, he said a first gruff "Hello" until he was sure who he was talking to, then reverted to his normal voice. He was going down to Purley that night to see Dyer and would be staying over, so he wondered if Wheatley would like to go to Haymarket and have dinner with Dolly and a friend (a similar set up to the alibi dinner of almost exactly a year before). Wheatley knew Nancy would be angry if she found out, and this time he declined.

Nancy was down at Margate, and this worried Wheatley. "I knew full well," he wrote, "that these few days out of my influence might easily destroy the patient work of months." He knew Nancy loved him, but he knew it was "purely for my personality – that was all – " and this made him insecure. Her love was safe, "providing only I could be present with her to make my influence felt."

Characteristically, Wheatley felt his engagement to Nancy had been not only a delight but a "a battle – an up hill game":

> She had had so many love affairs, known so many men, had so many romances . . . I had to be ever watchful, ever alert, to catch the faintest signs, to soothe with my voice and encourage with a smile from my eyes – these were my only assets – one must remember that I had little or no money compared with that which her previous suitors had had, I was not tall or well dressed, as she liked men to be – I could not even dance well and that was her favourite pastime, almost her life before she met me – the life she had with me was alien [to her] . . . and she was only getting used to it gradually – with my insistence, because I knew it was the only possible life in which one could settle down to real peace and happiness. –

And now

> . . . she was suddenly cast back into the old environment and at Margate where of all places except perhaps Monte Carlo she had had more affairs, more dancing, more everything that was opposite to all that I desired – and I was forced to remain 75 miles away for a number of days – and my personality, all that I possessed, ceased entirely to have any influence with her.

Wheatley was as calculating and embattled as ever, even in love, and he wouldn't have been Wheatley had he not also been aware that he was bagging an heiress.

He discussed this with Tombe, who assured him Nancy's wealth actually made their relationship possible: the "boodle-fiend" was not going to make things difficult in this instance, "as having means herself, she can afford to ignore the lack of it in others."

Wheatley was overjoyed to have Nancy back from Margate that Friday, not only for the pleasure of her presence but because "I felt that the only dangerous patch of our engagement had been safely tided over by her return to me in the same mental state as she had left."

*

On Monday morning Ernest Dyer rang Wheatley at the office, sounding worried. Did Wheatley know where Eric was? No, said Wheatley; they hadn't spoken since he said he was going to stay with Dyer. He had been down, said Dyer, "but we parted early so he didn't stay the night . . . it's an awful nuisance his dashing off like this without leaving any address, I want to see him about some business."

Eric was always coming and going mysteriously, and Wheatley thought no more about it. Next day, however, Dyer rang again. Any news of Eric yet? "No," said Wheatley, "hasn't he turned up?" Dyer reminded him that Beatrice was due to arrive at Paddington with the children, and Eric always made preparations for their arrival. For the first time, this now struck Wheatley as odd, but he put a brave face on it: "There's no need to worry," he told Dyer, "you can bet he'll be on the station to meet her with the usual flowers."

"No," said Dyer: "I don't think he will."

★

Dyer now revealed that he had received a telegram from Eric, the morning after seeing him down to Purley station, which read: "Going overseas back in Seven Days, look after things while I'm away. Eric." Dyer was annoyed, because Tombe had sloped off just when he was needed for some important business, but Wheatley was reassured: "I was so used to his goings and comings, his wires, and the complicated arrangements of this quadruple life."

That afternoon, Beatrice rang in a very agitated state. Where was Eric? Wheatley said he hadn't seen him Wednesday. "Oh Dennis," she said,

> I'm dreadfully worried, dreadfully worried, I can't imagine what happened to him. – you know he always writes to me every day when I am away, – well I had Thursday's letter, on Friday and not a word more, – not a single word and I don't know what to do – he hasn't been to the Hotel for a week, then only his heavy luggage here – do you think anything's gone wrong?

Wheatley did his best to reassure her, particularly since he didn't want her to involve the police in Tombe's affairs. "Dennis," she said, "you're not concealing anything from me are you?"

Wheatley was still not as worried as Dyer and Beatrice: "I knew far more of his complicated existence than either of the others, and therefore his sudden disappearance did not appear as strange to me as to them." Wheatley assured himself Tombe would soon turn up, "with a plausible explanation for everybody and some remarkable tale (possibly the truth) for my private ear."

Next day, Wheatley met Dyer and Beatrice at the Hyde

Park Gate Hotel. Dyer was quiet, and Beatrice's eyes were "violet lined" with unhappiness. She made Wheatley swear and swear again that he didn't know where Eric was, and that he wasn't concealing anything, and then she broke down:

Oh there must be another woman. – but why why? Why? Couldn't he tell me – oh I don't know what to do – Dennis, do you swear he has not gone off with another woman?

Wheatley swore that Eric was absolutely faithful to her, and that his last words at the tube station had been about how he missed her and was looking forward to her return.

As they went down to lunch it began to hit Wheatley that Eric might really not reappear. It was so unlike him not to meet Beatrice at the train, which he always did with presents for the children, having arranged for flowers at the hotel. And Eric wrote daily, and telephoned whenever possible: Wheatley remembered times when the two of them had been dining with other women, and Eric had slipped away from the table to make his daily call to Beatrice.

Dyer was morose and preoccupied, but he began to complain about Eric leaving him in the lurch. Since Wheatley knew their criminal dealings, he took this to be about the £2000 needed for the fraud on Stephens.

And then, as he looked at Dyer, something else occurred to him. Suppose he had lured Eric down to Purley on Thursday night, imprisoned him in a cellar and made him write a large cheque? Then, after the Stephens deal and the insurance had paid off, he could skip the country, "leaving Eric to find his way home as well as he could, confident that he could not give him away to the police since he was too deeply implicated himself."

It was all horribly like a penny novelette, Wheatley thought – but there was no limit to what a desperate man like Dyer might do. He remembered Eric talking about him:

"There's only one man who could really make me feel afraid, and that's Bill – he's such a bluff good hearted fellow that everybody likes him, but you watch his eyes, those deep black cruel eyes of his make me shudder sometimes, he'd be a murderous devil to be up against."

Wheatley asked Dyer about the telegram. Dyer didn't have it with him, but he said it was sent from a small office in a baker's shop near Purley at 11 o'clock on the Friday morning, the day after he had last seen Eric.

This was odd in itself. Why was Eric still in Purley next day, if he had gone down to the station the night before? If he was going abroad, why hadn't he sent it from Charing Cross or Victoria? Perhaps Dyer had drugged or chloroformed him, Wheatley thought, "and carried him down sleeping to the cellar of my imagination."

Wheatley felt Eric would otherwise be capable of defending himself, and remembered his theories about how to use a stick or umbrella to deadliest effect by jabbing at the eyes, and how to use bottles in a fight (his notional favourite, due to its weight and thickness, was the broken champagne bottle).

Beatrice suggested that Eric's bank account might hold clues, since he couldn't survive long without money. Had he withdrawn a large sum before disappearing?

Beatrice could hardly go to the police without revealing that she was Eric's mistress, and Wheatley was similarly tied, as Dyer would know, by the fact that "I . . . knew something of Eric's questionable dealings and therefore for Eric's sake should be extremely loath to go to the police."

Unknown to Dyer, however, Wheatley had an unexpected card up his sleeve. About a year earlier, Tombe had given Wheatley power of attorney over his bank account, so Wheatley decided to see the manager.

Dyer walked back to wine merchant's with Wheatley, and they talked about things they couldn't mention in front of Beatrice. Thinking that "look after things for me while I am away" referred to Dolly and her friend at Haymarket, Dyer said he had sent them home and settled the bill. Dolly was used to Eric's "anti-Bolshevik, Secret Service, Diplomat coming and going from the ends of the earth" and took it in her stride; she had already been expecting him to leave for Poland on the following Tuesday.

Wheatley asked Dyer what he really thought had happened to Eric, and, "in the Voice of a Master," he assured Wheatley it must be a woman ("you can take it from me"). He had gone off with a woman and left Dyer in the lurch. Worse still, it made him sick to see what Tombe had done to Beatrice by disappearing:

> he's cleared out with some woman and let me down properly – this will break me, absolutely break me, – still I'm fond of Eric and there may be something in it that we don't know about – still the way he's treated Beatrice makes me sick, I tell you she was in the hell of a state last night, it absolutely broke my heart and that's not easy.

If he was lying, thought Wheatley, "he was a consummate actor, and never have I seen a finer display of the histrionic art – even I was moved by it to feel tremendously sorry for him, despite the fact that I had it in the back of my head that he was the villain of the piece all the time, and had been told by Eric that he was the most wonderful actor that he had ever seen."

Beatrice had said Dyer was "an angel," and she didn't know how she would have managed so far without him.

*

After parting from Dyer, Wheatley went round to Eric's bank to see the manager, Mr Sampson, who remembered him from his visit with Eric about the power of attorney. Wheatley told him of Eric's disappearance, and how very distressed his "sister" Beatrice was, and asked if his Power of Attorney was still valid. This was a difficult matter, said Mr Sampson: "You see, the power of attorney granted to you has been superseded by one granted elsewhere. And curiously enough only a few days ago."

This was a surprise, and the conversation turned cagily to Dyer. What did Wheatley think of him? Cautiously,

Wheatley said he didn't altogether like or trust him, which didn't surprise Sampson; "To be equally frank, Mr Wheatley," he said, "I don't think I'd care to trust Mr Dyer very far either – mind you I know nothing against him but we get a lot of funny characters here and he doesn't strike me very favourably."

Wheatley told him some of his suspicions, trying not to damage Eric's reputation or Beatrice's good name. In return, Sampson said he felt justified in telling Wheatley to whom the new power of attorney had been granted: it was Dyer.

It has been issued on Monday the 24th, four whole days after Eric's disappearance. "Then perhaps there is something in my wild theory of the cellar and coercion," said Wheatley, but things were more complicated. Tombe had asked Sampson in person, when he had called in on the preceding Wednesday or Thursday, to transfer a large sum to his bank in Paris.

Stranger still, they had spoken on the telephone on the Saturday; he had said he was sending the form, and it had arrived on Monday. "He spoke to you on Saturday," said Wheatley – "That was two days after he disappeared – are you quite sure it was him?"

"Oh quite, you couldn't mistake it over the telephone, could you, you know his voice is quite out of the ordinary. I always recognise it in a moment."

"Well this is most extraordinary, you've no idea where he spoke from I suppose?"

"No, none, but I should think that it was in London, his voice was quite clear."

Then they examined the Power of Attorney itself. It was typed from Yeoman House, but the interesting part was the signature: "it was his usual signature, but so jerky and irregular that it looked as if he had an attack of ague when he wrote it." Wheatley thought it was either forged, or written under coercion, "when he had been starved or doped into an exceedingly weak condition".

Even the unexcitable Mr Sampson had to agree there was something in this: "It is this signature which lends a certain amount of probability to your idea . . . of course since Mr Gordon Tombe spoke to me about it before hand I naturally concluded that it was alright – but I admit the signature is very shaky."

Given their suspicions, Sampson declared that Wheatley's Power of Attorney could still be considered valid since it had never been formally concluded. They then drafted a letter together, as from Wheatley to Sampson, requesting him to stop all cheques and cancel Dyer's Power of Attorney until such time as Tombe might reinstate it in person.

*

Sampson had been helpful: he took a personal interest because, as he told Wheatley, he had a very strong liking for Tombe. Almost everyone liked Tombe, the two notable exceptions – who would have a decisive effect on Wheatley's conduct in the case – being Wheatley's father and Nancy.

Wheatley tried to discuss the disappearance with Nancy, but she wasn't very interested. Wheatley felt she might even have been pleased. She had always suspected and distrusted Eric, and felt he must resent her taking away "the boon companion of his purple nights." It was Eric's nature to "encourage any deviation from path of virtue on my part" and Nancy instinctively recognised this; "therefore I could not wonder that she was not anxious for his reappearance . . ."

Nancy disapproved of Wheatley being involved in the case, and he began to feel a paralysing conflict of loyalties. As he puts it, "I adopted Eric's "Masterly Policy of Inactivity" and shelved the affair."

*

Wheatley was shaving next morning when his father called him to the phone. It was Beatrice, who had been awake all night. Wheatley arranged to see her at the Hyde Park Gate Hotel and slipped away from the office, supposedly to see customers.

Dyer had now borrowed money from Beatrice, suggesting that she virtually owed it to him, since Eric had defaulted on their deal. Her attitude to him had changed, and she was now sure he was holding Eric prisoner. Dyer was a desperate man, almost bankrupt, and he knew Eric had money. He also knew Eric had no relatives to miss him – or so he thought, along with Beatrice and Wheatley – and that he was too deeply involved in their criminal schemes to go to the police.

Beatrice had hardly slept, "but falling into a doze in the early hours she had seen Eric in a sort of vision – he was very pale and weak lying head up in a cellar at the bottom of a flight of stone stairs and he was calling to her to help him. She declared that she could see the whole thing as clear as daylight."

Wheatley didn't put too much faith in this dream. "Nevertheless – there was still a possibility that there might be something in it. I am by no means a disbeliever in thought transference particularly when it is between two people who have been very closely associated as had Eric and Beatrice."

It still remained to account for Eric's phone call to the bank manager. Could it have been done by Dyer himself? "He was an excellent mimic and had heard Eric speak so many hundred times upon the phone that he could probably do it very efficiently, I felt myself that I could have quite well reproduced it, especially considering that he had so many curious characteristics in his way of speaking . . . "

Wheatley and Beatrice were in a bind. They were reluctant to involve the police, for her sake and Eric's. And as Wheatley added, there was still "the possibility that he had gone off of his own free will and might deeply resent the measures we were taking." Finally they reached a compromise: they would put a private detective on the case.

CHAPTER EIGHTEEN

Mr Meyer Investigates

Wheatley engaged a Mr Hugo Meyer in Queen Street, Westminster. Meyer was short and squarely built, with a "bulldog face, iron grey hair . . . and an old briar pipe which he continually puffed as he meditated."

Wheatley was in a difficult position. Even the fact that Meyer struck him as "extremely intelligent" was a mixed blessing; "I made up my mind to go very carefully in what I told him." He had to conceal Eric's criminal dealings, and he had to be careful what he said about Dyer, since he and Eric were associates. He had to keep Beatrice out of the picture as much as possible, as well as Dolly: "she might learn of Beatrice's existence or worse Beatrice of hers, a thing that Eric would not take pleasantly, secondly for my own sake" (with Nancy).

If Eric had been murdered, and it came out, then there would be "a very nasty case". This wouldn't bring Eric back, but it would cause "needless suffering" elsewhere. So, Wheatley reasoned, it was actually his *duty* to keep quiet about Dolly, "not only for her own sake but also because she was the only person who knew of the Orgies in which Eric and I had participated, and if she were dragged in she might disclose much that while serving no useful purpose would damage me considerably."

Wheatley was worried about his forthcoming marriage, and he was in a difficult position. "If any one who reads this" – Wheatley's private account of the disappearance – "will glance back and endeavour to tell the story of Eric's disappearance, excluding the four vital facts" (i.e. Eric's criminality, Dyer's criminality, Eric's relationship with Beatrice, and Eric's relationship with Dolly and Wheatley), "they will realise that it is hard, but I can assure them that it is very much harder indeed when you are sitting opposite an

212

intelligent man . . . with sharp eyes which probe you all the while".

It was a tough half hour. Meyer knew Wheatley was lying, Wheatley knew he knew, and Meyer knew that too.

What was Mr Gordon Tombe's business? asked Meyer.
He has no business.
Has he private means?
Yes, to a certain extent.
And he supplements this by occasional deals as you call it, associated with Mr Dyer.
Yes.
Do you consider any of these to be transactions of a questionable nature?
No.
But you believe Mr Dyer to be of doubtful honesty?
Yes – but I believe Gordon Tombe is perfectly straight.
Has he never told you anything of the nature of these transactions?
No.
Don't you consider that strange, since you have known him for a long time intimately?
Not necessarily – he knows that I am a wine merchant, but I never discuss my business with him.
Where does he live?
Hotels, principally.
No fixed abode?
No.
What hotel was he living in before he disappeared?
The Hyde Park Gate.
Was he living alone?
("dangerous ground" thought Wheatley) – No, with his married Sister, it is on her behalf as well as my own . . .
What about *Women*, Mr Wheatley, do you know anybody in whom he was particularly interested? I understand he is a single man.
No, I don't know of anybody particular.
But you know someone?

I know nobody who could have had the slightest connection with his disappearance.

Wheatley felt Meyer was extremely capable, and if he could only tell him the truth he might solve the case, but there was so much he had to suppress, "on my own behalf and on others". What would happen if he revealed Eric's dealings and Eric turned up again?

Wheatley went to 131 Jermyn Street on the chance that there might be a letter for him. Then he visited Yeoman House, where Sims told him a woman had been in and collected some letters that had arrived since Thursday: Wheatley recognised this as Beatrice, collecting her own letters to Eric: "I thanked God that Eric was so particular to keep his affairs in separate watertight compartments, otherwise she might come across some compromising epistles."

Wheatley slunk back in to the wine merchants by the side door. Shortly afterwards a Doctor Atkinson called to see him, "a tall slim boyish man of thirty . . . beautifully dressed and in morning coat and topper, a very typical handsome Englishman of the upper classes." This was Eric's doctor, who had become a friend. It was typical, Wheatley thought: "Atkinson the doctor, Simpson the bank manager, the people at the hotel, even Walter, his tailor, and Sims of Yeoman House, had all fallen under the spell of his charm and declared themselves his friends . . . tho actually not one of them except perhaps the discreet Sims knew anything about him at all."

Dr Atkinson was now attending Beatrice. She had told him the story and he had offered his help, which Wheatley was glad of: "I felt that he was an eminently honest straightforward Englishman," yet still Wheatley tried to conceal from him things he didn't want Beatrice to know.

Atkinson wasn't having it. "Now look here, Wheatley," he said, "what about the other woman?" Atkinson knew more about Tombe than Wheatley realised, because while he was treating him they had had "some rather interesting conversations on morality and sexual relations."

Atkinson's theory was that Tombe had gone off with another woman. Wheatley was sure this was not the case, but once again he couldn't explain why: to acknowledge Beatrice as Eric's financial mainstay "would have been to acknowledge that Eric was a financial adventurer."

They agreed Dyer knew more than he was telling, but Atkinson couldn't believe Wheatley's "penny novelette theory" could take place in reality. He was so sure Eric had gone off with another woman, and that Dyer knew about it, that even Wheatley began to wonder.

The only other woman Wheatley could think of was Dolly, "since he had recently given me such glowing accounts of her . . . it was barely possible that he might have decided to take her on the south sea tour of happiness which he had once planned with Desirée"; the woman Wheatley had feared might take a murderous revenge on Eric.

Wheatley left the office and went to a call box. He wanted to check whether Dolly was still in her flat. She was, and she confirmed that Eric had left her to go to Purley on Thursday. Then on the following Saturday Dyer had arrived bearing the telegram, packed Eric's clothes and paid the bill. Wheatley reassured Dolly nothing was wrong, but he noticed that Dyer's story of going over to Haymarket on Friday didn't match hers.

Atkinson, Dyer, Beatrice and Wheatley met at the Hyde Park Gate Hotel that evening. Dyer had brought the telegram as promised. It looked in order to Wheatley, but unknown to him, or at least unmentioned in his memoir, Beatrice had become convinced the telegram was a fake: she was sure Tombe would never have used the word "overseas."

★

Wheatley's account of Tombe's disappearance is as vivid – perhaps more so – than his fiction, and the next chunk deserves to be preserved whole.

> We were in the single room that Eric had engaged for himself – Beatrice came in with the keys of his trunks – a

large travelling Innovation and a leather hat box – she handed them to me.

"Dennis I thought we might find a clue in them," she said pointing to them, "but I waited until you were here to open them, I thought it best."

I took the keys and unlocked the hat box – two grey Homburgs were all that it contained – the Innovation did not contain much, a mackintosh, some dirty dress shirts and socks, a number of books among which were two or three of mine, and a newspaper cutting.

The latter was an account of the burning of the Welcomes, it was curious that he should leave such a thing to show his interest in the affair if he had gone off on his own. I handed it to Bill – [or rather] I secreted it at once not wanting Atkinson to see its contents and later handed it to Bill – suggesting that it was best to destroy it. He agreed and I burnt it.

Only one item of interest did we find among the luggage, that was a very ordinary shilling cloth edition of Oscar Wilde's *Selected Prose* – actually its value a few pence only, since it had been much used – but psychologically to me it was of great interest.

Ever since I had renewed my acquaintance with Eric after the war he had had that little book – it accompanied him everywhere – it had been with him in America, in Austria, Paris, Italy, Sicily, the Scilly Isles and Totland Bay – always it was in his bedroom upon the chest of drawers or dressing table, and in odd moments he would pick it up and delight in the music of the words – he considered Wilde 'The Great Master' – if it could speak that little book could tell of passionate nights indeed, – it knew all his mistresses and his friends – the occupant of his bed might change often but his little friend the shilling book never – that was typical of Eric's mentality.

That he should have gone leaving it behind seemed almost incredible – Beatrice noticed it at once and mentioned its significance, even Bill who took no interest in books admitted that he recognised it.

Yet I had to admit, that had Eric really gone off of his own free will it was just what he would have done to have left it. In my mind I could see his close lipped smile as he had placed it in the trunk with the others, – reckoning upon us finding it and delighting in our saying to each other "Certainly, he is dead, – he's met with some accident and we shall never see him again, he would never have left behind this little book." It was just such strokes of genius which gave him greatest pleasure.

★

At the same time, most of Eric's "splendid wardrobe" seemed to be missing. Wheatley remembered the dinner jacket, the evening overcoat, the black pearl dress studs, the silk underwear, the white trousers, the silk shirts, the Chinese dressing gown . . . where had it all gone? Its disappearance seemed another point in favour of the theory that Eric had gone somewhere of his own free will.

Nancy arrived to have dinner with Wheatley and Beatrice, but the evening was far from happy. Beatrice tried to show an interest in the wedding preparations, but she also poured out her troubles, to which Nancy was not particularly sympathetic. She was quiet, "because she did not like to disclose her true feelings, yet she evidently did not care to go so far as to act a sympathy and interest she did not feel."

On the way home, Nancy urged Wheatley to leave the affair alone. Wheatley was always tied up with business when she wanted him to see furniture, but here he was "flying all over the place" to help Beatrice. And then there was his father: Wheatley was always saying it was necessary to keep him happy, and yet here he was getting involved with something particularly prone to annoy him, given his intense dislike of "Gordon Tombe and all his works."

Nancy was implacable. Wheatley should forget about Tombe, and consider all previous ties cancelled by their engagement. Her wishes should come first; had she not given up all her friends for Wheatley? This wasn't quite a fair argument, Wheatley thought, since all her previous friends seemed to be men, but he said nothing.

*

Returning to Streatham, Wheatley was alone with his thoughts. If Eric was really in trouble he had to help him. At the same time, he could see Nancy's point of view. And yet he owed Eric almost everything: "an enormous debt of gratitude."

> Had not my whole nature expanded under his careful tuition? Did not I owe to him everything, which went to make me no longer a suburban youth? – even indirectly Nancy herself, since she would never have taken any interest in me, had I not had the culture that was the gift of Gordon Tombe? – It was not too much in my mind to say that to him I owed a second and a greater life, for under his tuition I had indeed been born again, certainly in the Biblical sense of "in the spirit".

Up in his bedroom, Wheatley continued to think over the facts of the case, "twisting and turning them in my brain, ever evolving new combinations, new speculations, suspecting everyone in turn, piecing out theories endlessly, until the grate was scattered everywhere with cigarette ends." If Eric had really left, how could he have abandoned Beatrice, and why had he not told Wheatley, "his friend, whom he knew would think no worse of him whatever he did."

*

Next morning the seven days mentioned in the telegram were up, and Wheatley hoped Eric might have reappeared. He rang Beatrice, who had been hoping the same thing, but no; "every time the lift had come up she had thrilled with hope," until she watched the dawn coming up over the trees of Hyde Park.

Wheatley had another appointment with Hugo Meyer, "if possible a more unpleasant half hour than before, under his

218

penetrating gaze". Meyer stressed that their conversations were strictly confidential ("Oh of course, quite," said Wheatley; "quite so.") Meyer didn't think Wheatley had been entirely *frank* with him on certain points, and this was impeding the very investigation Wheatley wanted done. "Nobody knew that better than I," writes Wheatley.

Wheatley had told Meyer that Tombe was living at the Hyde Park Gate Hotel, had he not? Yes, agreed Wheatley. But in fact, continued Meyer, Tombe hadn't been there for over a month. "Oh!" said Wheatley, as if surprised.

And so it went on. "Bitterly I resented having come to see Mr Meyer," writes Wheatley, since Meyer was only being paid to discover things Wheatley knew already, and which he didn't want aired. Wheatley was no longer 'on side' with his own inquiry: "As far as the Haymarket went, I felt pretty safe Mr Meyer had absolutely no clue pointing in that direction . . ."

As for Dyer, Meyer had found he was a gambler, short of money, and regarded by the police as suspicious. He had also been in prison, which Wheatley hadn't known. Wheatley was relieved that Meyer hadn't found anything suspicious about Tombe, but Meyer pressed on: did Wheatley know that the Welcomes had been burnt to the ground under mysterious circumstances? Wheatley knew of a fire, he said, "but I didn't know there was anything mysterious about it."

The interview ended inconclusively. Meyer thought that Tombe, who was after all a man of forty (or so Wheatley had told him) had gone away for reasons of his own. He was "a mysterious individual. He has no business or profession, no permanent place of residence, it is quite on the cards that he has affairs of which you know nothing."

Wheatley left the office, "very glad once again to be out of the sight of this intelligent gentleman."

★

Beatrice was now convinced Eric was dead: she had accused Dyer of murder, and talked of putting the affair in the hands of Scotland Yard. Dyer didn't want this to happen, as he explained to Wheatley: "Once Scotland Yard get put on to a thing, they sift it and sift, and Lord knows what won't come out and where it will end."

Wheatley agreed Scotland Yard should be kept out. Dyer then opened up a second line of argument: expressing his deepest sorrow and sympathy for Beatrice, he said they shouldn't allow her to "sacrifice herself" for Eric. If she went to Scotland Yard, it would come out that she was not Eric's sister, and her husband would divorce her. They shouldn't allow her to ruin her life, and her children's – and she probably wouldn't if she knew about Dolly and the others.

"This was nasty," thought Wheatley, who felt it was his duty to Eric to shield Beatrice from this knowledge. If Dyer thought he was Eric's friend, said Wheatley, "there was no better way that he could prove it than to never give Beatrice the slightest hint that Eric had ever been unfaithful to her".

But it was a hundred to one against Eric reappearing, said Dyer, and they could save a good deal of needless suffering to a woman who had been a friend to both of them. Wheatley took the opposite line: "to tell her would be extremely cruel, it would deprive her for ever of the belief that whatever had happened to him, while he was with her he had loved her truly and faithfully. – to snatch away that consoling belief was to my mind the unkindest thing we could finally do."

It was being cruel to be kind, said Dyer, and later she would be thankful that she had not wrecked her life for a man who was unworthy of her.

Wheatley felt his first duty was to Eric, and for this reason he was against telling Beatrice, just as he was against going to Scotland Yard. If he changed his mind about the latter, however, he realised Dyer had him in a "polite blackmail"; in effect, "You go to Scotland Yard and I will tell her everything that you do not want her to know about Eric."

★

Wheatley lunched with Beatrice and Dr Atkinson at the hotel, where Beatrice was in a worse state than ever: "He's dead Dennis, he's dead," she said, "I know it, I know it as surely as if I could see him, – he was alive yesterday but now he's dead, that murderer has killed him!"

Atkinson then took Wheatley aside. "I think we ought to tell her about the other woman, she says that she's going to Scotland Yard this afternoon, and it's not fair to let her run the risk of spoiling her whole life unless she knows the truth about the sort of man she is exposing herself for." Dyer had won him over with his argument.

This was difficult, but Wheatley persuaded him not to tell her anything for the time being. He then had to persuade Beatrice not to go to Scotland Yard. Beatrice was not easily put off. Eric was dead, and nothing could hurt him now; "she was the only one who would suffer by an enquiry therefore she had the right to say, and she would cheerfully suffer anything for the sake of seeing justice done on behalf of the man who had been everything for her."

"It was pitiful," thought Wheatley, "to witness the desolation of her grief, and I admired tremendously her unhesitating courage in being so ready to ruin everything."

Wheatley had one last card to play. He was going down to see the original telegram message that afternoon, and they would then know if it was sent by Eric or by Dyer. If it was Eric, then they had no right to interfere. But if the telegram did turn out to have been written by Dyer, then and only then it would be time to involve the police. "I made her promise that she would do absolutely nothing until my return."

★

Wheatley was going to see the original telegram with one of Mr. Meyer's subordinates, and at 2.30 he was in Meyer's office. The subordinate was not there, allowing Meyer to give Wheatley "a further twenty minutes inquisition".

At the Post Office he was presented with various forms to fill in, but no one cared about his power of attorney. It seemed only the sender or recipient could exhume a lettergram, so he had to forge either Dyer's name or Eric's. He decided on Eric's, knowing he was getting himself in deeper. "Unless I was frightfully careful I might be involved in a very nasty mess, – first there was Eric and his crimson nights, in which I had participated,"

next I might be accused of being an accessory after the fact to the affair of the burning of the Welcomes, and further, and by no means the least disagreeable, be called as the principle witness in Hundreds divorce petition against Beatrice, or worse, if he got really nasty, be cited as co-respondent, since I had virtually taken over her protection since Eric's disappearance and been seen with her as such, – added to all these delightful possibilities, I did not want a little private affair on my own of false representation and forgery with the Post Office authorities.

They then asked him which office he had sent the telegram from, and to his embarrassment he didn't know. Was Wheatley sure he had handed his telegram over a counter? Was he sure he hadn't just phoned it into the main office? He said he was, now hating the whole business. Guessing what had probably happened, he took his chance to leave and "withdrew cursing."

It seemed likely that telegram had been phoned, and there was no hand draft. "I felt sure that was what had happened – if either Bill or Eric had wanted to mislead us they would have been sure to have done it that way."

Meyer's subordinate was indignant at Wheatley's impersonation ("it was a most serious matter to falsely represent oneself at the GPO"), and Wheatley gave him money to keep quiet.

★

Wheatley rushed back to the wine merchants: he had been watching the clock with horror ("how the devil was I to explain this lengthy absence to my father?") and expected to find his father raging. Instead he found Beatrice, Atkinson and Dyer in his private office, and a row in progress. Beatrice turned to him:

222

"Dennis! Oh thank God you're here at last! Now tell me it's not true about the other woman, it's not true is it?".

The balloon had gone up.

"What other woman?" said Wheatley.

"Oh it's no use lying," said Beatrice, "– I know every-thing, everything, all about Yeoman House, how I've been lied to and tricked . . ."

Atkinson, Dyer's unwitting collaborator, explained what had happened. Beatrice was going to Scotland Yard, he said, so "we thought it our duty to tell her the truth about Gordon Tombe."

"I considered the possibility of sticking to my guns and lying black was white," says Wheatley, but it was useless. Then came what Wheatley remembered as a terrible scene:

> She accused me of the basest ingratitude – had I not so often said I was her friend? had I been fair with her? I had accepted her hospitality while I aided Eric in his treach-ery – I had come like a thief in the night – lied to her while I smiled in friendship – hadn't I sworn time and again during the last few days that there was no other woman? hadn't I played the hypocrite even to manu-facturing a speech of Eric's when I last saw him about how glad he would be when she returned? how he looked forward to her return? while all the while he was living with another woman . . .

Silently, Wheatley "faced the storm, letting her wear her-self out – I thought she would never have done". It wasn't the abuse that troubled him, in fact "I felt that I was paying a little of the debt I owed to Eric, by bearing the brunt of her wrath on his part". It was only when she began to cry and asked him what she had ever done to him, to treat her like this, and reminded him how happy she had always been to have him around with her and Eric; that was when it began to hurt.

And it was true. Wheatley hadn't behaved well. For two and a half years Beatrice had been in his daily life, "always with pleasant thoughts and a thousand little kindnesses . . . always so thoughtful for my comfort." In fact, in his early life, "no other woman ever held the place in my affections which Beatrice did." She was, in a Platonic way, Wheatley's type: "The element of sex did not enter into our relations, she was to me as an older sister."

But as Beatrice exhausted her misery, so Wheatley was gathering his powers. When Beatrice had quietened down, Wheatley asked for silence, and spoke in Eric's defence. He could, he began, honestly say he knew Eric better than anyone else, and he could understand Eric's actions towards Beatrice. "His," said Wheatley, "was a peculiar nature",

> one full of affection and a love of placid comfort surrounded by the people of whom he was fond. None knew that better than she and her children. That he loved both her, and them, very deeply I was perfectly certain in my own mind – in fact, it was the one really good and deep affection of his life: time and again he had spoken to me with joy of the prospects in the future, and how when she was free he had hoped to settle down. But at the same time, now and again there came over him an immense craving for excitement – he could not help it, he did not love them less – but this enormous craving took possession of him completely and upon her periodic visits to the north, he gave vent to this feeling with other women. There was *no* woman, I insisted upon that, it was different women at different times, as soon as the craving for excitement was appeased he was utterly indifferent to them and hating his unfaithfulness he came back upon her return rejoicing. – it was a case of Dr Jekyll and Mr Hyde, a thing entirely mental – an aberration perhaps, for Eric was not entirely normal – yet much as he regretted his inconstancy to her, and though I had pleaded with him again and again, pointing out that sooner or later she were bound to come to know, he said that he could not give it up, it was totally necessary to his existence – when one of these fits was upon him, and if you were not going

north for another month or six weeks, he said he used to become depressed and irritable, a burden to himself and a distress to you – he had tried many times to suppress his cravings but it was hopeless, he knew that if he did not give his brain the relief it needed at least twice a year by one of these wild fortnights – he and you would quarrel miserably, and separate for good before the year were out. So – he regarded these deceptions as absolutely necessary to your happiness as to his own. That is the whole truth. – you must not think he loved you less because of it – he did not – often he has told me that after each bout of his excitement, he returns loving you more.

Wheatley was wasted in the wine trade; he should have been a barrister.

Wheatley then called Dr Atkinson for the defence, and asked him to recall his conversations about morality with Eric. It was true, Atkinson admitted, Tombe had told him "he considered that it was not wrong to deceive a woman if it were for her happiness, and strange as such a doctrine may seem, in Eric's case it was the truth." Furthermore, he admitted that when Tombe told him this, he was suffering from arthritis, and had appealed to him "for some speedy remedy since "his sister" was going away and he was about to enter upon one of his periods of wild excitement."

Beatrice was now more collected. She said she understood – "*in a way* she understood" – and she forgave Eric. "Of course, should he now return things could never be as they had been, but she would always love him, and nothing could induce her to give up the search for him."

*

The room was calm. Wheatley had succeeded. He hadn't removed Beatrice's love for Eric, and yet he had restored the situation.

I had shifted the blame of Eric's infidelities from his own shoulders, onto some mysterious exterior power which seized upon him stronger than himself, – I had made of him a kind of martyr – and created a subtle difference in the view which Beatrice took of the facts which we could not deny.

Wheatley's writing and spelling make it look as if the word is "monster", although "martyr" makes more sense. In any case, this picture of Tombe is martyr and monster both: not a reasonable and integrated being, but a man possessed by almost demonic forces.

★

And at this point, a little demon seems to start smiling and cackling inside Wheatley himself.

It was all very well for her to say that things could never be as they had been before but let Eric return and we should see. I had made the bridge over which he could walk, and I had terrific confidence in his power to walk over it if he liked – he would return like the prodigal son, nobody could plead so eloquently as he, I could see him at it in my own mind – there would be tears, protest-ations, – he would tell her all about his horrible bouts of neurasthenia – depict the sufferings he had undergone to allay his cravings and finally she would forgive him, he would undergo a special course of psychoanalytical treat-ment with some big specialist to exorcise the devil – then come to me and laugh like Hell about it – wire to Dolly the first time Beatrice went away, and the domain of Eric would be "in status quo".

★

Now, with one battle half won, Wheatley conceded another. He finally agreed to go to Scotland Yard.

226

CHAPTER NINETEEN

Marriage – and a Horror

Dennis and Nancy continued to prepare for their wedding. Wheatley's grandfather had never knowingly allowed a Jew or a Catholic into his house, but Nancy was a Catholic, and she refused to give up her religion. Religiously mixed marriages were still difficult, so it was Wheatley who had to pretend he might be interested in converting.

They went to see a priest at Margate, and Wheatley took to him at once. For one thing he liked his library, full of crumbling leather-bound books. The priest said it was quite clear nothing he said would make Wheatley take up the faith, and they proceeded to talk about Eastern religion. Wheatley then signed a document to say that any children would be baptised as Catholics, and the priest gave him his dispensation.

There was just one thing the priest wanted. "I would like you to promise to read Mallock on *Doctrine and Doctrinal Disruption*," he said, and added "But you must not read the last chapter." Wheatley acquired a copy of the book (subtitled *Being an Examination of the Intellectual Position of the Church of England*) and admired Mallock's thorough demolition of the Protestant case. Naturally, having been told not to, he then had to read the last chapter. In it, Mallock conceded that although Catholicism was the only form of Christianity sanctioned by God, there was no proof God existed: so while Catholicism was the only way to be a Christian, it was quite possible not to be a Christian at all. This amused Wheatley.

*

Wheatley's father and Nancy were both adamant that he must cease to meddle in Tombe's disappearance. This meant Wheatley had to pull the drawbridge up on Beatrice. He let her pay Meyer's bill and settle his own expenses, for which he

227

had made characteristically detailed accounts. He had been to Scotland Yard, he told Beatrice, but they were not very interested and felt Eric might have his own reasons for disappearing. Now Wheatley had to draft quite firm letters to both Beatrice and Doctor Atkinson telling them that he could do no more:

> I am strongly advised both by my father and his legal adviser that I must not take any further active part in prosecuting further enquires. As you know, I am more than busy getting my flat ready for my forthcoming early marriage, and having done all that I could to assist you in this very unfortunate affair, any further action I must not take, for my own safeguard [crossed out and replaced with 'reputation'] and that of my future wife I cannot, of course, allow any scandal to attach to her name or my own.

Beatrice – the only person who comes out of this whole business with much credit – was now ill. Wheatley still had various of Eric's possessions – Cartier watch, gold cigarette case, tie pin – but Beatrice had no interest in them, "only to know the Boy who was dearer to me than life itself is safe and alive."

The thing she did want back was a photograph of Tombe in a suede case, which Wheatley had given to Meyer for identification purposes. Beatrice had broken down under the strain, and she wrote to Wheatley from Rochdale, apologising for her handwriting as she was sick in bed, pleading with him to tell her the truth. The uncertainty was killing her, she said. She promised not to divulge anything Wheatley might tell her. She wanted the truth, however cruel, and even if Eric had committed the most terrible crime she would rather know. "I only pray and long for death, but if you have it in your powers to give me any help, then I ask you as a last request to do so."

Wheatley really didn't know what had happened.

And then, a few months later, he happened to meet

Desirée again. More than slightly flaky, as we have seen, this was the woman who alternated between dreams of introducing Tombe to her friend Jesus on the one hand, and murderous revenge on the other. She was back from the continent, and she had some startling news for Wheatley. She told him that she had caught sight of Eric, alive and well and in Madrid.

*

Wheatley's wedding came around on the 17th June, 1922. His father wanted him to come to the office for drinks on the morning, but he wanted to be alone and spent the morning walking around a park. He would only have been human if he had at least some thoughts of Beatrice and Eric. He then had a glass of champagne at the Savoy with Bertie Davis, his best man, and Tanko Moate, and they went with him to St. James's, Spanish Place, the Catholic Church in Marylebone. Owing to the mixed nature of the marriage, the priests decreed that lavish display was not appropriate, and they were allowed just two vases of flowers on the altar before a brief ceremony.

A reception followed at the Grand Central Hotel. Nancy's mother had asked them if they would prefer a quiet wedding and £500 towards furnishing their flat (around £15,000 at today's values), or a grand reception. They plumped for the latter, and "wisely" notes Wheatley: "Between them some 500 guests sent us over 300 presents which, when I later had them assessed for insurance, were valued at more than £800."

Nancy gave him *The Masterpiece Library of Short Stories*, a twenty-volume red leather set subtitled 'The Thousand Best Tales of All Times and All Countries', inscribing it "To my darling One with all my love, in memory of June 17th 1922."

Wheatley wasn't himself that day. Having wanted to spend the morning alone, now – after the enormous cake had been cut, and the health of the bride and bridegroom drunk – he refused to reply to the toast. This wasn't the Wheatley who sang songs, climbed on tables, and took public speaking in his stride. "Some contrary devil had got into me."

Wheatley and Nancy left for the Savoy, where they were spending the first two nights of their honeymoon. Two mornings later they took the train for Dover, and for once Wheatley's obsession with money had temporarily abated: "the expenses had led to my being £114 overdrawn," he writes. "But I could not have cared less."

*

They went to Belgium for their honeymoon, where Wheatley visited Waterloo. Back in London, Wheatley totted up his outgoings and income, Mr Micawber style, and found things were quite tight, but with the addition of Nancy's money they managed. It was a fairly comfortable life at 20a Trebovir Road, where they had a maid. Having just the one was something of a privation, but it was becoming a feature of modern life: *The One Maid Book of Cookery* had been hailed by the Pall Mall Gazette as a good idea, "Now that so many people live in flats, and have only accommodation for one maid."

There was another marriage in the summer of 1922, shortly after Wheatley's own, when Barbara Symonds married Cecil Cross at St.Leonard's Church, Streatham, with a reception at the Parish Hall. Wheatley's years of suffering were over, and he now felt a sense of one-upmanship: "I had passed out of the suburban society of Streatham into wealthier bourgeois circles."

Wheatley wore a grey morning suit complete with waist-coat, grey top hat, and spats on his patent leather boots. Better yet, beside him stood Nancy, "a blue-eyed blonde, every bit as lovely as Barbara – and an heiress to boot – wearing a huge befeathered hat and clothes that came from Paris."

Wheatley's satisfaction must have increased when Cecil came to see him a month or so later. Barbara had left him, the day after their marriage. "I could only condole with Cecil," writes Wheatley in his autobiography, "but it did now seem that the Gods who protected me had saved me from what might have proved a most unhappy marriage." Wheatley seems to be putting in his own parting shot by hinting that Barbara was frigid, as if to explain their own unhappy relationship.

★

Nancy brought Wheatley a new life and new friends. One of these was Cyril Eastaugh, known as Bobby, who had earlier courted Nancy. Bobby was a tall, distinguished man who eventually became a notably conservative Lord Bishop, but like Wheatley he wasn't quite out of the top drawer. Born in South London, he was the youngest of thirteen children. Having been a scholarship boy, he became an officer in the war and won the Military Cross.

At the time Wheatley met him, Eastaugh was secretary to Maundy Gregory, a flamboyant but sinister character. The monocle-wearing Gregory collected first editions and manuscripts, and became a stalwart of the Wine and Food Society. He was an honours broker under the Lloyd George government, illegally fixing peerages for cash, and one of his associates, Gerald Hamilton, remembers he rigged up his office to impress guests and pretended to have a private phone line communicating directly with the Prime Minister. More discreetly, the drawer of his desk was solidly stuffed with fifty pound notes.

Hamilton saw him as a "kind, jovial" man, with "a great hatred of any form of Socialism". Gregory had worked for MI5 since 1909, and was later involved in propagating the Zinoviev Letter, which helped to defeat Labour at the 1924 election.

Gregory was the particular *bête noire* of an independent socialist MP named Victor Grayson. Gregory had been spying on Grayson for the Special Branch since 1918, and Grayson's counter-investigation discovered that Gregory was selling honours. After threatening to expose him, Grayson was attacked on the Strand early in September 1920, probably on Gregory's orders.

On the 28th of September 1920 Grayson was drinking with friends when he received a telephone message. He left, telling them he was going to a hotel in Leicester Square, and

231

he was never seen again. A witness recognised him entering a house beside the Thames, and the mystery of his disappearance only became clearer in the 1960s, when a new investigation revealed that the Thames-side house belonged to Maundy Gregory.

Gregory also seems to have murdered his own wife for her money. Wheatley's autobiography vaguely suggests Gregory's murky career might have come later (he "later became notorious") but it was in full shady bloom while Eastaugh was his secretary. No doubt Eastaugh knew little of the full picture, but working for Gregory must have been an interesting apprenticeship on the way to being the very worldly cleric that Eastaugh became.

Since Bobby had religious leanings, a rich elderly lady paid for him to go to Oxford to study theology, and in due course he became the Bishop of Kensington, and then the Lord Bishop of Peterborough with a seat in the House of Lords. "During over half a century," says Wheatley, "we have spent many a happy evening enjoying good conversation and the finest wines."

★

It was also at Margate that Wheatley met Joseph Gluckstein Links, another lifelong friend. Links's father was a furrier at the bottom end of the market, who specialised in skunk. His mother died when he was twelve, and when he was fourteen his father became terminally ill. Knowing he was soon to die, he took Joe out of school to learn the fur trade. Joe's mother's relatives, the wealthy Glucksteins – who owned the Lyons teashop chain – urged Joe to come into business with them, but Joe stayed with fur. In due course he became a leading furrier with the firm of Calman Links, and eventually gained the post of Furrier to the Queen.

Joe Links was probably the most cultivated of Wheatley's friends. *Venice for Pleasure*, by J.G.Links, has been described as the best guidebook to any city ever written, and he later became a world authority on Canaletto. He shared Wheatley's taste for German white wines, and looking back in old age,

Wheatley wrote "I am very proud to have had such a man as an intimate friend for over fifty years."

Wheatley also made a lasting friendship with Frank van Zwanenberg, who had made his fortune as a bacon importer, and more particularly with Mervyn Baron, whose family business was lead smelting, and who became the model for Simon Aron in Wheatley's fiction.

Along the lines of the old anti-Semitic cliché, "Some of my best friends are Jewish . . ." it is interesting, given what look like flashes of anti-Semitism in his work, that not just some but most of Wheatley's best friends at this period really were Jewish. For now, we can see that Wheatley positively liked Jews. It may be that to Wheatley, who was highly class-conscious and snobbish, but painfully aware that he was merely middle class, Jewish company could offer a little holiday from the English class system. Better yet, he could have had the benefits of what one might hope upper-class people are like – charming, highly civilised, and so on – without the drawbacks of what they really are like, much of the time.

Wheatley was impressed by Nancy's step-brother-in-law, one Clement Spindler. Born on the Continent, Clem Spindler had lived in Margate and, by the time Wheatley knew him, "lived in a fine Regency house in Hove . . . He had a fine library of beautifully bound books, loved fine wine and was so selective that he would eat only the undercut of a sirloin of beef."

*

Wheatley's own book collection was getting under way. He had a definite taste for multi-volume sets, of the sort he would be photographed against in later years, and he already had Nancy's twenty volumes of short stories, and Tombe's six volume Havelock Ellis. In 1920 he bought the *Secret Court Memoirs* in twenty volumes, and not long after he bought the works of Le Sage in six volumes, including *Gil Blas* and *Asmodeus or The Devil Upon Two Sticks*.

He was also starting to build up a collection of modern first editions, and in July 1923 he bought James Joyce's

Ulysses, a recent and still controversial book, from the London Foreign Book Company. He judged it to be "The ravings of a lunatic possessed of extraordinary erudition."

> I had heard this book spoken of as "a man's thoughts during a day set down without reserve," if it were this alone it might be readable, as it is it is several people's thoughts – and unfortunately one often does not know who is thinking or speaking. It is both sacrilegious and vicious – but this is nothing against it *if* it is supposed to be a study of the psychology of human brains. If so it is a work of Genius, considering that the author has taken types lower than the average.

In Spring 1923 Nancy had become pregnant, and things were well advanced by the autumn, when the expectant father received a nasty shock. A major news story broke on September 14th, giving rise to headlines such as Surrey Farm Murder, Body in Cesspool, The Kenley Horror, Farm Sensation, and Garden's Grim Secret. The previous morning, police had recovered a hideously decomposed body from a cesspit at The Welcomes. It was Tombe.

*

Wheatley subscribed at once to a press-cuttings agency, Romeike and Curtis on Ludgate Circus, in order to miss nothing about the case. Cuttings arrived thick and fast, filling several scrapbooks. A Mr Tombe, Tombes, Toomb or Toomber – or in one case Tom Tombs – had been shot in the back of the head with a pistol, a revolver, a rifle, a sporting gun or shotgun. His skull was partly blown off and his body had been dumped down a well. Foul play was suspected.

It transpired that he had been shot, by Ernest Dyer, at close range behind the right ear with a shotgun. The body was fully dressed, and from the clothes it was wearing he was probably shot outdoors. He may have been shot by surprise, and must have been killed instantly. Without removing Tombe's engraved gold watch, Dyer put the body down one of several well-like cesspits in the area, covering it with an overcoat and a quantity of bricks, rocks, lumps of cement and debris from the burned stables. By the time the body was found, under about ten feet of water, the filled-in pit was grown over with grass. After the murder Dyer had proceeded to impersonate Tombe and tried to empty his bank account.

The Tombe murder was a newspaper sensation of 1923, sharing the headlines with the Madame Fahmy case. Wheatley's intense study of the murder must have been tempered with anxiety about exactly what would be revealed about Tombe's criminal past. Were the police, for example, seeking to trace a David Watson who frequented a letter drop at 131 Jermyn Street? They were not. Were they looking into Tombe's movements on the night the Welcomes burned down? They were not. Were there any revelations about Tombe's orgiastic private life? There were none ("Tombe was a sober, hard-headed business man," reported one paper, "careful of his expenditure and never given to excesses.") As usual, Wheatley's luck was holding.

Wheatley found the murder very distressing, and for the rest of his life it was a subject he refused to talk about. Anyone who cared about Tombe and followed the case could hardly fail to wonder if he really was killed by surprise on the night he went down to the Welcomes, or whether – as Wheatley had originally suspected – he had been held captive there before being killed. The remains, so decomposed that they had to be taken to the mortuary in a sack, were beyond revealing any signs of violence. With the body was a long length of leather strap, which might have been used to lower the body down into the cess pit, but could have been used to tie Tombe up before he was shot. None of the headlines read "Ordeal of Kenley Farm Victim", but there may have been one, and it must have occurred to Wheatley that if he had acted at once he might even have saved Tombe's life.

There was a further twist to the Tombe case which kept it in the headlines. It was widely reported at the time, and in several books since, that Tombe was only found after his clergyman father – or in some accounts his mother – dreamed that the body was down a well, and insisted the police re-open the case of his disappearance. This is the account Wheatley gives in his autobiography, but fifty years earlier he had followed the real story.

'Dream Drama', ran the headlines: 'The Dream Vision', 'Gruesome Discovery Through A Dream', 'Terrible Drama Revealed by Mother's Dream'. His father was reported to have had an extraordinary dream; then his mother ("It was she, and not her husband, as had been reported, who dreamed that her son was buried in the garden. 'In my dream,' she said, 'I heard him say, "Oh, let me out." I felt that he was shut up somewhere and could not get free.' "). Then they both denied having a dream, and finally "The Rev.Gordon Tombe ridiculed the report that that his conduct had been influenced by a dream."

The real story was hardly less extraordinary, giving rise to headlines such as 'Relentless Trail of a Parson-Detective.' Tombe was not as distant from his parents as he pretended. He was now their only child, following the death of his brother in a fire in America, and he wrote to them regularly. They had last seen him for dinner at the Strand Palace Hotel, when he was arranging to help them move into a new house. No sooner had Tombe gone missing than his father was on the case, placing adverts in The Times, and exploring his haunts in the West End.

Visiting a hairdresser that Tombe used, John Richards at 59 Haymarket, he asked if there was anybody who might know anything. Looking into his customers' book, Richards found an entry reading "Ernest Dyer introduced by Mr Eric Gordon Tombe." He went on to disclose Dyer's bad reputation, and the fact that the insurance company had refused to pay up for the fire at the racing stables. Immediately the Reverend Tombe felt that Dyer and the stables had something to do with his son's disappearance.

At Tombe's tailor, Walkers in Albemarle Street, the Reverend Tombe discovered several uncollected suits which Eric

who called Tokay the *vinum regnum, rex vinorum*: "Wine of kings, king of wines."

Wheatley sold the contents of the Royal Saxon cellars, and this time he hadn't filled them himself. They contained about twenty dozen bottles of Imperial Tokay, from 1649 to the turn of the twentieth century. Alec Waugh remembers drinking some:

> Tokay exists no more. It was, I suppose, scarcely a wine at all; it was really a liqueur . . . Each bottle was numbered and distributed by the Austrian Emperor. It never reached the market. The bottle that I drank had come from the Imperial cellars . . .
>
> An Hungarian once said . . . "think of the most beautiful picture you have ever seen, the most wonderful symphony you have ever heard, the most beautiful sunset on earth, the fragrance of the most exquisite perfume, in the company of the person you love most in the world. Add a touch of original sin – and there you have Tokay!"

Wheatley found the best year was the 1806. He always liked time-travelling through wine, and when he drank a bottle of the 1649 – "no longer a great wine and had gone almost as pale as water; but when opened it still had a delicious perfume and was quite drinkable" – he was very aware this was the year in which King Charles I had been beheaded.

Along with Imperial Tokay, readers of Wheatley's fiction will remember Hoyo de Monterrey cigars, the Duke de Richleau's favourite brand. They are the Duke's "especial pride," and in the opening pages of *The Devil Rides Out*, as he ponders the mystery of Simon Aron's absence, "the Duke inhaled the first cloud of fragrant smoke from another of those long Hoyos which were his especial pride".

Hoyo de Monterreys were considered the best cigars in the world, and it was Wheatley's friend Mervyn Baron, the model for Simon Aron, who suggested they should go into business selling them. Baron was a great cigar aficionado and a friend of Cecil Hart, whose firm – Melbourne Hart – was the sole importer. Baron put up half the capital for the firm of Baron Wheatley Ltd, and Wheatley installed a cedar-panelled cigar room in South Audley Street.

Baron produced a cigar expert, Monty Sternberg, to run this part of the business. Around this time Wheatley had written to an Orientalist writer and translator named Norman Penzer, remembered for *The Harem*, and asked him to sign a book, his edition of *The Ocean of Story*, a ten volume Indian precursor of *The Arabian Nights*. They became friends, and Wheatley took him on, at Mervyn Baron's suggestion, to help Monty Sternberg.

Liqueurs were an obvious line for the newly luxurious business, largely ignored in Wheatley Senior's day. People often asked for obscure liqueurs they had discovered on the Continent, and Wheatley and Son usually advised them to try Fortnums. Now Wheatley made an effort to obtain every available liqueur in London, which came to well over two hundred, and in another marketing inspiration he printed his list as a scroll, several feet long, which he sent out wrapped round a tube. When the average price of a liqueur was 17/6, Wheatley's list included eighteenth-century Chartreuse at £25 a bottle (about a thousand pounds today).

It must not be assumed, Wheatley wrote, that these lesser known liqueurs were all sickly sweet. "Many are famous in the countries from which they come, as tonics and restoratives, producing that appetite and vigour which is the true joy of mankind", and he added "Messrs Wheatley and Son cordially invite inspection of this unique collection by all who are interested in the curious and the rare."

★

Wheatley was continuing to collect Oscar Wilde, and in 1928 the rare booksellers Dulau, on Bond Street, brought out a catalogue of Original Manuscripts, Letters and Books of Oscar Wilde. The first copy of a limited edition of 105 was given to Wheatley, inscribed "To D.Yates Wheatley with the publisher's thanks for his having suggested this large-paper issue, November 1928."

In 1928 Wheatley decided to have a new bookplate, the one that he would keep for life and put inside the majority of his four thousand books. It features himself and Tombe, with Tombe as a Pan-like satyr sitting on a stump discoursing to Wheatley, who sits in a flowery forest glade before him, looking up and drinking in his words. "One admires EVE for having tasted the FORBIDDEN TREE OF KNOW-LEDGE," Tombe is saying, quoted from one of his letters "– But what a WONDERFUL EXPERIENCE she missed when she overlooked the TREE OF LIFE. I should have eaten of not ONE, but ALL the trees in the garden – and THAT; dear boy – is what I hope for YOU."

The scene is the Garden of Eden, and while we are usually told the tree in the Garden was the tree of Knowledge (the tree of the knowledge of good and evil) Wheatley and Tombe mention a second one, "the tree of life". The tree of Knowledge is from Genesis ii.16–17, but there is also a reference to the tree of Life in Genesis iii.22–4, and this was the further tree that Adam and Eve were expelled before they had a chance to eat; indeed, stopping them before they managed to eat that one seems to have been one of God's motives in expelling them, before they become "like Us".

Wheatley's chosen artist was Frank C. Pape, who had illustrated James Branch Cabell's *Jurgen*, which Wheatley owned. Wheatley gave Pape thorough instructions: the most important part of the picture was Tombe's face, and the cigarette he was smoking had to be held not between the finger tips – which Wheatley would have thought looked 'common' – but in Eric's more suave manner lower down the fingers, like a cigar. Behind them is the barren tree of Knowledge, with a book in its branches, and further back the tree of life, with a naked woman within a flowery Egyptian-style ankh or *crux ansata*, above a crucified figure. Beside Eric are the tokens of a fast 1920s life; a bottle of champagne in an ice bucket, a saxophone, and even an opium pipe. The saxophone was a late and lucky inspiration, and it has worn better than the ukelele – crossed out in his instructions – that Wheatley originally wanted.

Wheatley provided photographs and a couple of his own sketches for the design. In the first of these, Tombe is not merely a satyr but the Devil himself, with a pointed tail as well as hooves and horns. The tail is prehensile, and he is using it to pour a bottle of champagne. Looking forward to the brand-naming within Wheatley's fiction, this isn't just any champagne but VCP, Veuve Clicquot Ponsardin; 'the Widow.'

Wheatley was pleased with his bookplate. There was a distinctly obsessional and perfectionistic strand in his character, with a great capacity for planning and taking trouble (he always enjoyed cataloguing and making lists, which he remembered his father enjoyed before him, and in later life he kept scraps of string and paper). Now he carefully steamed his old bookplates from inside the front covers of his six volume Havelock Ellis from Tombe, re-stuck them into the back covers, and replaced them at the front with his new bookplates.

★

Wheatley's marriage was as good as over. Nancy had her own circle of friends, who enjoyed tennis and dancing, and in this set her particular friend was a man named William 'Doc' Kelleher, an Irish doctor. Good looking and a good dancer, he also became a distinguished physician, developing the Kelleher Breathing Machine for polio patients.

The relationship between Nancy and Doc was less furtive and more innocent than that between Wheatley and Gwen. It was the latter's practice to have sex in Wheatley's office a couple of evenings a week, just after the shop closed at six o'clock. One day in November 1927, Nancy and Doc were in the area, in Doc's car, and they thought they would drop round to South Audley Street and give Wheatley a lift home after work.

Wheatley was expecting Gwen, and this put him in a dilemma. With only moments to spare he got into the car with Nancy and Doc, leaving Gwen, on her way to the now locked shop, to catch a glimpse of them in the car and recognise Nancy from a photo in Wheatley's office.

Wheatley knew he would be in terrible trouble with Gwen next time he saw her, but if he thought he had averted more serious trouble, he was wrong. It was only just beginning, because Gwen had his home telephone number. The phone rang, and it was Gwen, "almost delirious with rage . . . she positively screamed at me . . . In vain I pressed the receiver hard against my ear. Nancy was sitting within a few feet of me. She would have been stone deaf if she had failed to hear a woman's voice hurling abuse at me . . ."

Wheatley now had to admit that Gwen had been his mistress for the past couple of years. It was a relationship that was making no one happy. Wheatley couldn't possibly marry Gwen because she was common, which made Gwen unhappy. Wheatley, meanwhile, was in agonies of jealousy because he knew Gwen was seeing other men. And now Nancy was miserable as well.

Dudley was still on the scene. One evening Wheatley was round at Gwen's flat in St George's Square when the bell rang. "It's my boyfriend", said Gwen, warning Wheatley that Dudley was much bigger than him and an Oxford boxing blue. Dudley knew about Wheatley, she said, he was very jealous, and he had come round to beat Wheatley up. "Please don't go down," she said – she would go down instead, and send Dudley away herself. "As I have a horror of being hurt," Wheatley remembered, "I then did what I always think of as being the bravest thing I've ever done in my life."

Wheatley confronted Dudley, who proved to be a pleasant man of about Wheatley's size or smaller. Telling him to stop bothering Gwen, Wheatley closed the door in his face.

Wheatley now set Gwen up in a flat at 183 Westbourne Terrace, but she still continued to see Dudley without his knowledge. When he found out they had another row, and he slapped her face ("the only time I have ever hit a woman"). This was out of character, and he wrote a poem around this time:

The woman, the dog, and the walnut tree
The more you beat 'em, the better they be

That's a saying that's true, as true can be
But oh my dear, What a hope for me
Whose every thought is a tender plea
That life may be kind to my loved one

(the ugly little proverb is not, of course, Wheatley's invention).

Gwen had led Wheatley to think that Dudley was 'bothering' her, and in due course Dudley received a solicitor's letter telling him to stop molesting her. Wheatley tried to bolster what he hoped was Gwen's resolve to break with Dudley and gave her a bunch of flowers to wear when she was with him, so that when they were together she would think of Wheatley: "Don't let him get you alone anywhere to create a scene, be firm, smell my little bunch of flowers and refuse when he pleads with you to go to the flat or for a run in his car 'just for the last time', because that's what he will do."

But still Gwen – having been caught out once again, with another terrible row – found justifications for continuing to see Dudley. She had to see him because he was threatening her. She had to see him because she felt sorry for him. She had to see him because she wanted to make him fall in love with her in order to revenge herself upon him. She had to see him because he was a potential blackmailer, and so she had to protect not just herself but Wheatley. She had to see him because she couldn't help bumping into him in the street.

The pivotal issue was marriage: Dudley said he wanted to marry her (" 'Oh but Dudley wants to marry me' I think I must have heard you say that dozens of times"), and she wanted to have children. Wheatley could hardly believe Dudley really wanted to marry her, and in any case it would be bigamous, as Wheatley reminded her, with the prospect of prison. In addition to love letters, Wheatley wrote her long letters about the situation, one of them a three page typed letter outlining her position as he saw it, complete with red type for emphasis and two lists – very Wheatley – outlining the lengths that Gwen would have to go to keep the marriage secret (five items) and ways that Dudley's mother might find out (eight items). If she was going to marry him, Wheatley advised her to do it at once: "he'll be a very different man on the marriage question if he's got rid of me and been living with you for a month."

Eventually Wheatley and Dudley had a meeting, and they got along quite pleasantly. Dudley had met her in a hotel at Oxford, and after a couple of drinks she had invited him straight up to "see her room." Despite the fact that he thought she was a prostitute, he was in love with her and really did want to marry her. Wheatley bowed out gracefully, on the condition that Dudley took over the rent for Gwen's flat.

Late in their relationship, Gwen had given Wheatley a remarkably prescient present. It was a copy of the *Malleus Malleficarum*, the notorious fifteenth-century witch hunting manual, in the 1928 edition by the Reverend Montague Summers. Why she gave it to Wheatley we shall never know, but he later used it in writing his books, wrote his own introduction to an edition in 1971, and for a while he even became a friend of Summers.

★

Gwen and the 'Kwan Yin' girl were both "artist's models," but in 1929 Wheatley was briefly involved with a woman from a very different sphere. For several years he had been aware of a girl he thought of as "The Lovely Lady of Berkeley Square," whom he would see walking along Hill Street or Charles Street to the Square. She was "a goddess," says Wheatley: "tall, stately, with a firm step and the most beautiful woman I have ever seen in my life."

One day a local nobleman came into the shop and complained that some mineral water had been added to his bill. It had been ordered by his daughter, and he resented paying her debts. This man was the goddess's father, and the upshot of his complaint was that Wheatley learned who she was; she was called Gladys (or, as I believe, Gwladys).

New Year's Eve 1929 found Wheatley in the Hungaria restaurant, in a less than riotous foursome comprising his mother and his sister Muriel, with Norman Penzer pulled in to make a fourth. Across the restaurant, however, he spotted

Gladys. Wheatley's mother and Muriel left shortly after midnight, and Wheatley and Penzer continued to observe the goddess from a distance. Wheatley asked Vecchi what he knew about her, and learned that her friend was Italian, and that she was fluent in the language. When she and her escort finally got up to leave, Wheatley was after them. Her friend had a car, so Wheatley quickly commandeered a taxi from another couple: if they would "follow that car", he said, he'd treat them to a magnum of champagne.

Gladys was dropped off not far from Wheatley's office, where Penzer and their new friends cracked open a magnum. Having already seen her friend drive off, Wheatley doubled back to Gladys's and rang the bell. As he hoped, there were no servants up at two in the morning, and she opened the door herself. Wheatley declared his love, told her that he had seen her for years, and invited her back to his office for champagne. Gladys took all this calmly and pleasantly, but said no.

Next day Wheatley bought a beautifully bound volume of Italian love poetry, and sent it to Gladys asking her to have pity on him and let him take her out to dinner. A couple of days later she called at the shop to thank him for the book, and agreed to have dinner. Two nights later he took her to the Savoy: "I have never felt prouder than when I accompanied this superbly beautiful woman in full evening dress down the steps to the restaurant."

A couple of nights later they dined again, and went back to Wheatley's office for a final drink. By now they were getting to know each other. Gladys was a great Italophile, and would rather have been Italian than English. She had refused many offers of marriage. And since her allowance didn't match her lifestyle she was also quite heavily in debt, to the tune of about £400 (around £15,000 today). Wheatley could do something about this, and he had £400 delivered to her in cash.

A few nights later they dined again, and again they went back to Wheatley's office for a final drink, before Gladys very kindly offered to make love with Wheatley. Wheatley's autobiography, while not altogether reliable, is at the same time candid, and he is keen to spare himself nothing:

Nancy, Wheatley's first wife.

"The Lovely Lady of Berkeley Square."

Wheatley with Joan, his second wife, in 1933.

The Forbidden Territory (1933), with Joan's cover design.

"Laughing happily," he writes, "we set about it, then to my utter horror I suddenly found that I had become impotent . . . I was terribly ashamed of myself and for one of the few times in my life burst into tears."

Gladys, however, was "very sweet about it."

Wheatley's sexological books reassured him that this was not unusual, and indeed he remembered it happening to him on another occasion, "when a woman that I had long desired offered to let me enjoy her". Gladys and Wheatley had supper again, this time in Yeoman House, which Wheatley thought would be a better erotic setting than his office, but the moment had passed: Gladys liked Wheatley well enough, but she had her own life, her own friends, and her own sphere.

★

Wheatley does an admirably un-caddish job of not spelling out the identity of Gladys, who was still alive when he wrote his autobiography, and the story of her letting him pay her debts and agreeing to have sex with him might cause offence even now. I believe Gwladys was three years younger than Wheatley and the daughter of an earl, with one of his family houses on Berkeley Square, and she spent much of the year in Italy. She was married to an Italian count, and had been since 1924, although she may not have shared this information with Wheatley. Perhaps as a result of some dalliance during this stay in London, she had her only child nine months later in November.

Gwladys had a regal manner. Rebuked by a teacher when she was a schoolgirl, she lowered arrogant eyelids and said "Insolent creature!" Wheatley's estimation of her looks may show his changing taste in women, as he climbed the social ladder. While Nancy was definitely 'pretty', in a way that Wheatley would later come to think of as suburban, Gwladys was a different type: she had a large, handsome, patrician face of the sort he would find again in his second wife.

★

Around this time Wheatley consulted a 'psychic' or 'clairvoyant' named Henry Dewhirst, "the only true seer that I have ever known." Dewhirst lived with his wife at 14 Chepstow Mansions, not far from Wheatley, and it was in this flat that he gave consultations. Wheatley remembered him as a Swede or a Dane, and he was a frail man who was already in bad health. His death certificate describes him as a "psychologist".

Dewhirst and his clients found each other by a network of recommendations, and Wheatley was recommended to see him by a friend. Dewhirst insisted that clients tell him nothing about themselves when making the appointment, not even their names, so that he could start with an impressively blank slate. "Your initials are D.I.W." he said, when Wheatley arrived, after a searching look from his pale blue eyes. It seems likely that he actually knew who Wheatley was, and was careful to make the middle initial a near-miss so as not to give the game away.

They sat in armchairs on either side of the fireplace, and Wheatley was treated to a variety of what is known in the trade as 'cold reading', in which the psychic or other manipulator will feel their way in from vague assertions to a reasonable knowledge, particularly by studying the client for non-verbal cues and small signs of blankness or recognition.

"I see a lake . . ." the cold reader might say, "a body of water . . . perhaps the sea . . . yes, the sea . . . with an older person . . . I see an older person . . . perhaps the older person is you . . . with a younger person . . . a child, perhaps a son . . . a daughter . . . I see you at the seaside with your daughter . . ." It was extraordinary, the happy client will be able to say later: he'd never met me before, and yet he knew we'd just come back from taking Ethel to the seaside.

This can be combined with widely applicable horoscope-style insights of the "you have an artistic side" variety, or "you have some weaknesses, but you are generally able to compensate for them." Addressing Wheatley as "my child," Dewhirst told him to sit silently and not answer any questions while Dewhirst thought out loud, embarking on a tentative monologue ("Obviously," says Wheatley, "for the purpose

264

of tuning his mind in to my circumstances and personality"). This enabled him to get in touch with Wheatley's psyche, saying such things as "You have recently crossed the water – no I am wrong, but you have been at the seaside." Wheatley made a longer stab at reconstituting his spiel in *The Devil And All His Works*:

Have you been abroad lately? Yes, but not far. Perhaps only to the seaside. But you have crossed water, haven't you? What do you do for a living? I think you are in some profession connected with art. But perhaps it is only a flair for using your imagination.

And so on. Dewhirst's stock in trade seems to have been a mixture of psychic flummery with sound counselling, and he proceeded to talk with Wheatley about his marriage and mistresses.

Wheatley was still intending to stay with Nancy, and use their marriage as a stable base for his affairs. Dewhirst thought they should part, since their marriage had fulfilled its purpose (it had been "ordained" as a "path" to bring Anthony into the world). As for Gwen, he said "My child, I am so glad you had the strength to break with that woman." She too had been sent for a purpose, the purpose of giving Wheatley the sexual satisfaction he had needed at the time, but Wheatley had moved on: "You don't really need her any more because your sex life is over."

This was worrying news, but Dewhirst explained. He simply meant that sex would not dominate Wheatley's mind as it had, and that it would be a more manageable impulse. He was predicting the relief from intense sexual drive that would come as Wheatley moved into middle life, the shift that Sophocles once said was "like being unchained from a lunatic."

Wheatley would not have to rely on casual affairs in future, Dewhirst told him. He would find a new partner, perhaps the sister of a close friend, and perhaps Wheatley would meet her through his work. She would have been married before. It would be a mature and stable love. This was all sound advice for a single thirty-something and Dewhirst added a final gracious flourish: "She is a wonderful child, and you do not know how fortunate you are to be."

And a new woman did indeed come into Wheatley's life, in the shape of Bino Johnstone's sister.

CHAPTER TWENTY-TWO

Falling in Love Again

Wheatley prided himself that his customers included "three Kings, twenty-one Imperial, Royal and Serene Highnesses, twelve British Ducal Houses, the Archbishop of Canterbury and a score of millionaires." It was a subject he loved to expand on: "Kings of Italy, Rumania and Egypt; a score of Princes (including his present Majesty King George VI); another score of Ambassadors and Dukes. Rajahs and millionaires, cabinet ministers and film stars all came to buy those lovely things in which I specialised."

Wheatley's wares were expensive, but they were costing him a great deal of money to stock: for an exceptional port he was paying £350 per pipe (cask); "a price which far exceeds anything ever paid by any other merchant."

★

On May 3rd 1929 a woman named Joan Pelham Burn had come into his office to order champagne for a ball, and Wheatley had got to know her socially because she was Bino Johnstone's sister. Joan's appearance was entirely in tune with Dewhirst's prediction, which always impressed Wheatley. He had even seen Wheatley meeting her in a wood-panelled room – his wood-panelled office, in some retellings – although this was not unlikely, since Wheatley was leading a rather wood-panelled life.

Joan had been married twice, and had four children, Bill, Jack, Diana, and Colin. She was divorced from her first husband, Scottish Baronet William Younger, and had lost her second, Captain Hubert Pelham Burn, in a car crash. Joan and Wheatley became friends, went out regularly to venues such as the Savoy, and the old Quaglino's, and went into business together with a firm called The Burn Trading Company. This supplied restaurants with equipment, from carpeting to china and cutlery, and could take advantage of Wheatley's restaurant contacts such as Vecchi.

He had been planning to do this for some time, and his strategic plan was to attain a drinks monopoly, supplying so many key restaurants that he could dictate terms to his own suppliers, rather in the way that the big commercial lending libraries had been able to make or break publishers.

Gradually Wheatley and Joan fell in love. The Noel Coward song 'I'll See You Again' from *Bitter Sweet* became the theme song of their relationship, and it was a great thrill for Wheatley when they met Coward while selling drinks and cigarettes at the 1929 Schneider Trophy seaplane race. They had Coward to lunch, and he later signed Wheatley's books.

As their relationship deepened, Wheatley's demands on Joan increased. With his lifelong tendency to 'state his case' in writing – as he wrote to her, "I am able to put my ideas (not more grammatically – dear me no but perhaps more clearly) on paper" – he explained his feelings and worries:

> Am I unreasonable? Of course I am, because I have no earthly right to expect anything except that which you choose to give me – but it does raise my horrid complex – not jealousy . . . but the feeling of which I spoke to you . . . that the more one gives the less one gets, one becomes accepted.

"I am capable of such unutterable devotion to you," he wrote. He was putting his cards on the table, but was he doing the right thing?

> Does it pay? Such experience as I have had goes very definitely to show that it does not – the reaction of the women is "Oh why can't he be sensible, the man is becoming just a bore." – Are you different from the rest – Oh how I pray to God you are.

They were now a couple, although this didn't stop Wheatley from taking advantage of the prostitutes available when he visited Madrid with Bino that November, where he found himself in the most luxurious *maison de rendezvous* he had ever seen, with a sunken marble bath *en suite* to his bedroom. He also noticed the hatred that many Spaniards had developed for the monarchy. When Bino's Spanish friends showed them the Royal Vault under the Escorial Palace, filled with dead kings, they pointed to the last vacant space and said emphatically "Alfonso Thirteenth; then *finish*."

Wheatley had been consulting another soothsayer, a blind woman, and she told him that he should make his position clear to Joan in every respect, which he did. He was leading "this farce of married life," but he had been slow to end it because he was depressed, "and again because it is repugnant to me to cause anybody of whom I have been fond, and who is a good friend, pain." Altogether

> I am tied up . . . I have been unhappy for a long time now about this hopelessly unsatisfactory home life of mine but if I thought about it at all, it was to feel with a certain amount of cynicism that most people's home lives were not particularly jolly anyhow, that mine was no exception, and that in the future, one had at least, a wife who was certainly fond of one in a friendly kind of way – a child who would be no worse for having a father present as he grew up – and for the rest, – one took an interest in developing one's business – in art and literature, and knew that women more or less desirable would surely come along and from time to time provide interludes from which one would derive a certain pleasure – it never occurred to me that I might fall in love.
>
> . . . for a long time now I have regarded myself as almost an old man – my youth was so full and so hectic, and it has long since gone. It did not surprise me yesterday when Miss Craven looked at me with her poor blind eyes and said, – You are a man of about 45, I should suppose – How terribly near to 50!

He was 33.

> . . . the war put ten years on my generation – and now
> when I thought I was past love – I'm just down on my
> knees – full of shame that I should have monkeyed with
> life as I have, yet filled with the understanding which
> monkeying with life over a long period gives, – that now
> I have met someone superbly different, and I am filled
> with undying gratitude that you should feel I am suf-
> ficiently unsullied to give me your hands and your lips.

He also explained to Joan that on the business side he was
seriously undercapitalised: "actually the whole thing is based
on borrowed money . . . given a few years, I may be secure
and reasonably well off . . . on the other hand – a few really
big bad debts – a sudden calling in of loans by the bank – and
then! Where should I be?"

Wall Street had crashed in October, an event which took a
while to catch up with Wheatley, but already he returned
from Spain to face business problems. He had over expanded,
taking on too many staff and venturing into schemes which
looked good on paper.

Wheatley's last push for the luxury market was his catalogue *At The Sign of the Flagon of Gold*, a beautiful gold–on–
black covered production from the spring of 1930. This was
themed around 'Old Masters, Old Brandies and a few Great
Wines'; the Old Masters being reproduced engravings of
Van Eyck, Holbein, and Durer, among others. The original
engravings, "for many years in the possession of His Imperial
Majesty The Tsar," could be viewed at Wheatley's offices.
Wheatley captioned each picture with a smattering of art
history (". . . may be said to have been the founder of the
Flemish school . . . One of the greatest of the early masters,
he lacked somewhat in composition, but his heads, which
were copied from nature, are charming . . ."[1]).

Drinks on offer included a Chateau d'Yquem from 1870,
and a brandy which had been repeatedly ordered by no less
than two English dukes. Wheatley therefore called it Ducal

[1] On Jan Van Eyck.

Brandy and, while allowing the dukes to remain unnamed, appended a note from his accountants, Messrs Carter, Clay and Lintott, to confirm that they had examined the books and that dukes were indeed buying.

Most impressive of all was the 1789 Champagne Brandy and the 1830 Cognac, the latter having been Tsar Alexander's, and now being sold by Wheatley at twelve guineas a bottle (about five hundred pounds today). Both of these had been served at the Inaugural Luncheon of the Gourmets' and Connoisseurs' Circle. This was organised by none other than Mr Stambois the rare brandy importer, whose letter of gratitude to Wheatley was reproduced in the catalogue. Writing from Marlow Lodge, Buckinghamshire, for all the world like a disinterested country gentleman, Stambois wished to place on record the fact that all the brandies served were from Mr. Wheatley's "remarkable stocks," omitting to mention that he was supplying them to Wheatley in the first place.

The Gourmets' and Connoisseurs' Circle held its first Luncheon on November 13th 1929; if the name is anything to judge by, it might be seen as a slightly more vulgar and ostentatious forerunner of Andre Simon's Wine and Food Society, founded in 1933. "How this fat, rather tattily dressed, little Polish Jew succeeded in getting to know the people he did I have no idea", Wheatley wrote of Stambois. This first lunch was presided over by Lord Decies, who had had a distinguished military career and won the DSO with the Somaliland Tribal Horse. Diners enjoyed pheasant, remarkable brandies, and Imperial Tokays from 1763 and 1837.

Before long Stambois persuaded Wheatley to host a dinner for the Circle at his shop. Thirty guests, dressed in white tie and tails, sat down to plover's eggs followed by roast sucking pig, and the evening was a great success. Guests included painter Sir John Lavery; Harry Preston, hotelier and boxing promoter; and Wing Commander Sir Louis Greig, who was to play an important role in Wheatley's life.

Preston was an exceptionally tough cockney who made his fortune from the only recently respectable sport of boxing – legalised in 1925 – and had since become well known for his charity work. He seemed to know everyone, from Arnold Bennett and Arthur Machen to Sir Louis Greig and the Prince of Wales, and his passport had been "good fellowship", an idea which became important to Wheatley. Being a "good fellow" could transcend class and forgive politics.

Sir Louis Greig was Gentleman Usher in Ordinary to the King, and Equerry to the Duke of York, later to be King George VI. He was a man of great charm from a relatively ordinary background. Although he was far from being a committed fascist, he was to be a regular attender at Sir Oswald Mosley's January Club. Whereas the British Union of Fascists had a largely working class membership, the January Club – sometimes seen as a 'front' group brokering fascism to the more influential classes – was a more Establishment group for the broadly sympathetic discussion of the various varieties of fascism, bringing together people who were "interested in modern forms of government"; with hindsight a rather chilling phrase.

★

Joan was keen that Wheatley should leave Nancy, and in the Spring of 1930 he moved out. Joan found him a flat at 11 Manson Mews, just round the back of her own flat at 48 Queen's Gate. Meanwhile the slump was beginning to bite, and Wheatley's over-expanded and under-capitalised business was starting to feel more and more precarious. When a friend suggested he should try upmarket bootlegging to 'dry' America, Wheatley was excited by the idea and gave it a go. ("Oh yes," he wrote of his rum-running in a Thirties newspaper column, "I've seen life.")

In fact Wheatley's career as a bootlegger amounted to very little. He took Joan – still in separate cabins – and samples of his wares. Having travelled from New York to Miami by train, and been shocked by the state of America's black population in the shanty towns they passed through, Wheatley established a base at Nassau, in the Bahamas, where he was advised to store his wares in a shed. The shed was duly broken into, and everything stolen. Wheatley returned home with nothing but a bad case of sunburn.

As the slump bit harder, Wheatley had to start sacking his staff. Norman Penzer's job had for some time amounted to smoking Wheatley's cigars, and making coffee laced with brandy. Monty Sternberg and others also had to be laid off (and it was now Wheatley tried to sack the tenaciously parasitical Bino, who laughed and refused to go) but this was not enough to save the business.

Gordons Gin would now only deal with Wheatley on a cash basis, and his tailors and hatters were asking for their money. Most embarrassingly of all, Dulau's, the rare book firm with whom Wheatley had enjoyed such a good relationship, were threatening legal action.

Wheatley's mother was wealthy, but she was little help. That summer she had married Sir Louis Newton, whom Wheatley felt had always been against him; now Sir Louis showed Wheatley a "Cheshire cat" smile and made smooth noises about throwing good money after bad. Sir Louis's son Sidney was Wheatley's lawyer, and he advised Wheatley to declare himself bankrupt.

It was now that the people Wheatley remembered as his "Jewish friends" – Mervyn Baron, Frank van Zwanenberg, and J.G.Links – rallied round him. They urged him not to go bankrupt, and lent him a thousand pounds – about £40,000 today – to stave off his creditors. Wheatley's book collection was now stored in his office, so Joe Links took it away to the furrier's to prevent it from being seized.

Mervyn Baron had a contact with the firm of Block, Grey and Block, who were looking to expand, and the upshot was that their parent company, Fearon, Block and Co, bought Wheatley out. They swallowed Dennis Wheatley Ltd, Baron Wheatley cigars, and the Burn Trading Company restaurant suppliers, along with the premises, stock, and goodwill of 26 Audley Street, and in return they made Wheatley a director.

Bankruptcy had been averted, but Wheatley was not happy with the new firm. Having been his own boss, he was now the junior of eight directors. Nor was he even particularly solvent under the new arrangement, which paid him about a quarter of his former salary.

He was still saddled with personal debts, but Joan had an unearned income of about £40,000 at today's values, and she was subsidising him. Nancy and Anthony were very unhappy that Wheatley had left them, and Wheatley can't have been unmoved when Anthony wrote to say "please come back home Daddy, Mummy and I are crying." Nevertheless he steeled himself to go through with the divorce.

On or about the seventeenth, eighteenth, and nineteenth of August, 1929, Wheatley was with a woman whom Nancy thought was called Sylvia (she was actually called Sybil Shore) at the Red Lion Hotel in Henley. On or about the nights of the 15th and 16th of February, 1930, he was in the Hotel Russell, Russell Square, with a woman unknown. Nancy filed for divorce on the grounds of adultery, but it seems to have been insufficient, and on or about the 22nd to 25th August 1930 Wheatley was at it again in Brown's Hotel, Dover Street.

Finally the divorce came through, costing Wheatley £88/ 2/4 in legal fees. He then had to pay Nancy alimony, and later find the money for Anthony's school fees, with which the Vintners Company gave him charitable help. It was a man facing a straitened financial future who finally married Mrs Hubert Pelham Burn at Buckingham Place Registry Office on the 8th August 1931, with a church blessing the next day at St. Ethelburga-the-Virgin in the City.

Wheatley was proud of Joan's aristocratic lineage, which went back to the Norman Conquest and the de Talbots, and she was dimly related to most of the European monarchies. Joan herself seems not to have been free from a certain snobbery; "*Come along Dennis*, we'll be *late for the Duchess*" was a not untypical exit line, which caused some amusement after the door had closed.

Old Nick Block, the only member of the firm that Wheatley liked, urged him to take six weeks off for his honeymoon, because of the strain he had been under. To raise the money, Wheatley hit on the idea of selling some of his erotica to a friend, Leah Barnato, who was married to former silent movie actor Carlyle Blackwell. Knowing her tastes, he went round to see her with an illustrated edition of Aretino and a valuable eighteenth-century set of the Marquis de Sade. She gave him a large cheque, and Wheatley's honeymoon was on the road.

Going to Paris, they stayed at the Hotel St Regis on the rue Jean Goujon, which Wheatley remembered as the most delightful hotel he ever stayed in. From there they went to the coast, and in due course they went to see some of the claret families in Bordeaux, where they were lunched handsomely. One in particular, Ronald Barton of Barton and Guetier, invited them to stay.

Barton turned out to have been at Eton with the ubiquitous Bino, and Wheatley was impressed by the history of the firm. When the French Revolution had entered the Terror phase, the Barton of the day had to abandon his estate and flee back to Ireland to save himself from the guillotine. After the Napoleonic Wars intervened, it was a quarter of a century before he went back to see his former property, which he assumed had long been confiscated by the State. Instead he was welcomed by his faithful clerk, Guetier, who had kept the business going and carefully banked Barton's money for him. Barton was so pleased he made Guetier a partner in the firm, which still exists today.

It was a lotus eating existence for the Wheatleys at Chateau Barton, with Krug before meals and Chateau d'Yquem afterwards. Unfortunately, however, they were marooned there by what seemed like revolution in Britain, because while they were in Paris the British Navy had mutinied at Invergordon. It was this which had caused them to accept Barton's hospitality in the first place, because they found their money was almost worthless. Trotsky had already pronounced Britain to be ripe for revolution and, thinking it was now imminent, the French were reluctant to change British money.

Indirectly caught in the same slump that had done for Wheatley, the sailors had refused to obey orders after pay cuts. In retrospect the Invergordon Mutiny was a very reasonable affair, hardly worthy of the term mutiny at all, but at the time it caused a great shock and contributed to Britain being taken off the Gold Standard.

The Wheatleys returned home, where another crisis blew up. Accountants and lawyers were looking into the books, and Wheatley was accused of fraud.

CHAPTER TWENTY-THREE
First Blood

Wheatley had included his own overdraft in the firm's liabilities, causing Fearon and Block to settle it for him when they took over. When this was brought to their attention by accountants they denied having agreed to it. There was about £4000 at stake – around £150,000 today – and Wheatley was afraid that he was facing prison.

Wheatley probably did think of his overdraft as part of the firm's business; spelling out his position to Joan in November 1929, he had described himself as "virtual owner," with "a personal credit for any reasonable amount which goes with such a position." But now he was suspended as a director pending investigations.

It had been Wheatley's practice to drop in on the office in the evenings to see if any cheques had arrived. Now, fearing that the locks might be changed, he made one last raid-like visit. Joan drove them over, and Wheatley rescued his love letters and personal papers.

Wheatley was still heavily in debt to tradesmen. He owed rent on Manson Mews, he had burdened himself with expensive extra cellarage, which he was finding hard to get rid of, and he had to find Nancy's alimony. The take-over problems deepened when debts owed to Wheatley and counted as assets had subsequently failed to materialise, turning into bad debts ("the Slump had played the very Devil with everybody's finances"). The sum in dispute was now over £6,500.

The story of how Wheatley started writing was part of his personal myth, and it became pebble smooth with telling. The idea was all Joan's ("wonderful Joan"). "Why don't you write a book?" she said. Wheatley didn't think he could, but in the hope of making perhaps fifty pounds he turned his hand to a thriller.

In fact, as we have seen, he had long wanted to be a writer.

He had written a novel, tried to write plays, and completed several short stories when he lived with Nancy. The new factor was that now he had time on his hands; as a still captive director of Fearon and Block, he was effectively barred from working for another firm. There was really nothing to do but write.

★

Wheatley always seems to have inspired loyalty, and before long a letter arrived from his old cellarman, Lewis. Writing from Willesden, he told Wheatley he heard he was writing a book and hoped it would be a success, adding that there were still Wheatley ghosts in the cellar; "I don't like the outsiders coming and upsetting them."

Within a few years Lewis will figure in Wheatley's fiction. For now, however, he sat down to write 'Who Killed Her Ladyship?' The title is an uninspired juxtaposition of pure genre with snobbery, but the answer is interesting. Wheatley had come to resent and even hate his mother and Sir Louis Newton for not helping him, and Her Ladyship, Lady Elinor, is based on Wheatley's mother. She has remarried to Sir Gideon Shoesmith, a man not unlike Sir Louis. Her son from her first marriage, Richard Eaton, is a bibliophile facing bankruptcy, who runs a small press like the Golden Cockerel (Wheatley collected Golden Cockerel books). He has doubled his business but is undercapitalised and gets caught up in the Slump. He receives no help from his mother, who is under the malevolent influence of Sir Gideon.

After repeated blows to the base of the skull with a blunt instrument, the unconscious Lady Elinor is drowned in the bath. Sir Gideon hangs for her murder, and in due course Eaton inherits a fortune. In a striking instance of the pleasures of authorship, it is clearly the wishful writer who "dunnit."

The book is largely of interest as the first meeting of the four friends who figure in Wheatley's fiction: along with Richard Eaton, who faces prison and even spends time on remand, we meet his loyal friend Simon Aron, who has a

278

"pronounced Semitic nose, a pendulous lower lip and very quick, black eyes." Meeting for the first time on the night of the murder, and initially regarding Simon Aron as a suspect, are the Duke de Richleau and Rex Van Ryn.

Richard and Simon are based on Wheatley and Meryvn Baron, but the Duke and Rex are ideal creatures of his imagination, representing all that Wheatley thought was best about the Old and New Worlds. Rex Van Ryn is a hulking American aviator – combining very Thirties preoccupations with flying and physical stature – and entirely modern; he even *surfs*. On the evening of the murder he is missing the new Noel Coward revue because his father has urged him to have dinner with the old Duke: "We people spend a lot of time seeing the Pyramids, and Notre Dame, and Stratford, and places – well, the Duke, to my mind, is all these in one, he'll give you the idea what Europe really stands for."

The Duke de Richleau is a distinguished, delicate-looking man with "devil's eyebrows." He is living in exile from his beloved France, after his role in a plot to restore the French monarchy, but fortunately he is a keen Anglophile. He has great respect for the British sense of individual liberty and "sporting fairmindedness" along with their breakfasts; he doesn't want kidneys and kedgeree himself, but he is glad to know they are there.

The Duke has a flat full of old treasures in the same building as the sterile, *nouveau riche* flat of Eaton's mother, but he first entertains Rex at his club, the Mausoleum Club, "behind closed doors through which the word socialism has never penetrated." The Duke is, as he explains, somewhat "out of tune" with modern democracy.

Almost from the start of his career Wheatley was labelled as a distinctly reactionary writer, but it is worth noticing that his first novel refuses the anti-Semitism of the period. In lower genres such as the thriller, particularly in the hands of once popular writers such as Sidney Horler, remarks about oily Jews and "Levantines" are routine. The work of Graham Greene had to be tactfully edited after the Second World War to remove anti-Semitic passages, and there are flashes of

279

anti-Semitism in writers as respectable as Isherwood and even the early Orwell ("it would have been a pleasure to flatten the Jew's nose," he writes of a genuinely loathsome individual in *Down and Out in Paris and London*).

Anti-Semitism was sweeping the planet: a Japanese acquaintance explained to Harold Acton that the Chinese were vile because they thought of nothing but money; "they are the Jews of Asia". In London the celebrated black American musicians Layton and Johnstone, who played at society parties, also performed at the Café de Paris. On a quiet night around 1930 Johnston looked at the sparse audience and went back to his dressing room shouting "They're Jews! I'm not going to sing to such a small crowd of terrible people."

London hostess Emerald Cunard was giving a party for the Prince of Wales, and when it was going sluggishly she exclaimed that she hated all Jews. Immediately the party seemed to spring to life. "Not that I really hate them," she explained next day, "but I wanted my party to be a success."

We might have to look more closely at Wheatley's peculiar consciousness of Jews later, but for now we can give him a clean bill of health. In fact, by the grotesque standards of the day, Wheatley's creation of a steadfast band of loyal chums, one of whom is thoroughly Jewish and plays an admirable central role, is almost heroically not anti-Semitic. ("I tell you, Van Ryn," says the Duke about Aron; "I like this young man")

The larger model for the chums is the Three Musketeers: De Richleau is Athos, Rex is the good natured giant Porthos, Simon is the clever and subtle Aramis, and Richard Eaton is the character Wheatley had always identified with: "a more restrained, English version of the inimitable D'Artagnan." It was to be several years before Wheatley's novel was published, and then under the title of *Three Inquisitive People*, but there was no stopping Wheatley now that he had taken up writing. Before finding a publisher, he was already sending the friends off on a new adventure, this time deep into Bolshevik Russia.

Spending his days at home, Wheatley was seeing more of Joan's children and taking an interest in their education. History was always his subject, and to bring home the reality of time he made a "history kite" with string. This showed that if six thousand years was ten feet, then the French Revolution was only three inches behind 1932.

Wheatley was still working hard on short stories but he had little luck with them, and eventually gave up on short fiction altogether. Whatever makes Wheatley's novels viable is largely absent from his short stories. Several read like the work of an early twentieth-century English school-boy: Wheatley prints his first story, written at the age of fourteen, in *Meditteranean Nights*, and it is no worse than some of the others.

Wheatley was dining one night with Alan Sainsbury – later Lord Sainsbury – and his wife Doreen at their house in Chelsea when Doreen drawled, "I thought of the *most* lovely title for a story the other day. I am sure it has *enormous* possibilities, though I can't think *what* they are. Dennis, do write a story called '*Orchids on Monday*'."

Always keen to fit in and be fun, Wheatley promptly rushed off and did just that ("That's them – *orkidds* they is. I never did 'old wiv 'is way of doin' things.") There are more ghastly working class types in 'The Deserving Poor', from the same period. This is a tale about the dangers encountered when giving money to down and outs ("Gawd bless yer, Lidy"). Aside from the usual obsession with money and a keen mistrust of the lower classes, it is notable for two things: firstly, the observation that a heightened emotional state – in this case being in love – can prevent one from becoming drunk, an observation that recurs several times in Wheatley and wouldn't be out of place in a better writer. Secondly, the mention of a master villain called The Limper ("strewth! You won't 'arf cop it when the Limper 'ears.") He is an ex-officer wounded in the First War – hence the limp – who has turned to crime. We have met him before, or someone very like him.

Wheatley leaves no cliché unturned when it comes to foreigners. Chinese villainy was such a stereotype that Ronald Knox's Ten Commandments for Crime Fiction[1] decreed "No Chinamen must figure in the story." No surprise that Wheatley's story 'In the Underground' reminds us "the Chinese are queer people," and hinges on "subtle oriental poison" in a curio box; "one of those Chinese puzzle boxes."

Worst of all, however, was Wheatley's attempt to write in what he hoped was the manner of P.G. Wodehouse, about which no more needs to be said.

★

Among the many friends of Bino was Gerald Fairlie, the man who continued the Bulldog Drummond stories after the original 'Sapper' left him the character in his will. Joan had Bino round to lunch with Fairlie and Fairlie's literary agent – Bill Watt, of A.P. Watt – and the upshot was that Watt took 'Who Killed Her Ladyship?' away with him.

Wheatley went to see Dewhirst the seer shortly after this, and Dewhirst at once said "You've written a book!" (it is likely Wheatley had confided on a previous visit that he hoped to write). Again and again, Wheatley would tell the story of how Dewhirst predicted good news on the 22nd of the month – in some versions with a publisher beginning with H – and how it all came true: Watt sold his book to the firm of Hutchinson.

Wheatley wrote a number of short stories featuring Neils Orsen, a supernatural investigator inspired partly by Dewhirst and partly by William Hope Hodgson's character Carnacki the Ghost Finder. Like the Carnacki stories, their central idea is that the anomalous events are sometimes truly supernatural and sometimes the work of earthly trickery.

Wheatley hoped Dewhirst would advise him about his business troubles, but around this time he seems to have had a stroke of luck. Among his papers he was able to produce a

[1] In his introduction to his *Best Detective Stories of the Year 1928* (Faber and Gwyer, 1929).

carbon copy, albeit typed by himself, of the list of liabilities he had given to Fearon and Block for the take-over. It included his personal overdraft. At the same time Sir Louis Newton – perhaps not as malevolent as Sir Gideon Shoesmith after all – persuaded Wheatley's mother to pay Fearon and Block the disputed sum on Wheatley's behalf in a £5000 settlement.

It may be that Wheatley was less vindicated than he would like readers of his autobiography to believe. His account is not entirely consistent: he claims his innocence was proved, and yet the £5000 was still paid back, and his mother long resented it.

Whatever the finer legal points, Wheatley was now free to reclaim his valuable furniture from the office, resign, and offer his services elsewhere. He went to Justerini and Brooks, and kept up a lifelong friendly relationship with the new firm.

Wheatley had now finished *The Forbidden Territory*, which Hutchinson felt was a better book than 'Who Killed Her Ladyship?'; the latter was held over indefinitely, and *The Forbidden Territory* scheduled for January 1933. Meanwhile Wheatley had his first short story accepted for publication.

Inspired by a walking stick owned by a friend, Colonel Roland Lawrence, 'The Snake' features an African witch-doctor whose cane turns into a black mamba. Left on someone else's premises, it can kill in the night and be innocently collected next morning. A similar item had already figured in Sax Rohmer's *The Devil Doctor*, with a more this-worldly Holmesian emphasis, but Wheatley's story concerns "Black Magic" and "the Black Art." Like the shape-shifting Malagasy in *The Devil Rides Out*, who turns into the Goat of Mendes, the witch doctor himself somehow becomes the snake.

'The Snake' displays a brisk knowledge of dodgy foreign types ("he looked a good half-dago himself, for all his English name, and dagoes always believe in that sort of thing") and, like many of Wheatley's short stories, it suffers from a gimmicky twist-in-the-tail ending of the sort then admired.

Wheatley was as pleased as Punch with 'The Snake' and its

acceptance. It was simultaneously published in the January 1933 issue of *Nash's* magazine and *Cosmopolitan* in the States, and Wheatley sent copies out in December as Christmas greetings, writing "First blood!" on them.

★

The Forbidden Territory was published on the 3rd January 1933. This time Rex is in trouble, jailed in Russia, and the other three rescue him: "Together they had learned the dangerous secret of 'The Forbidden Territory' and travelled many thousand verts pursued by the merciless agents of the OGPU."

Just ahead of publication, Wheatley wrote letters to almost everyone he knew: "Dear Colonel"; "Dear Maundy Gregory"; "Dear Scholte" (his tailor). He sent them to ambassadors, lords, opticians, owners of West Country cider firms and debt collectors. He even managed to send one to Buckingham Palace, thinly disguised as an apology for the non-appearance of that year's Wheatley and Son diary.

Recipients were urged to ask for the book at their library, and recommend it to their friends. Some of them were quite distant acquaintances ("I fear you will hardly remember my name . . .") but people Wheatley knew better were asked to "scatter" the leaflets enclosed, and doctors were requested to put them into the magazines in their waiting rooms. "It does not pretend to be a great literary achievement," Wheatley wrote, but "with such thousands of books coming out every year, it is exceedingly difficult for a new author to get his work before the public"; "I should be most awfully grateful . . ."

Wheatley paid for 2,000 promotional postcards, featuring the map from the book's pictorial endpapers. Again, these bore a request that people should ask for it at their library, and friends were often sent a dozen more to pass onto their friends in turn. This seemed to pay dividends, so Hutchinson printed a further 15,000.

The book was launched with a party in Justerini's cellars, underneath the arches at Charing Cross. There were plenty of journalists and a few celebrities including Harry Preston, who made a speech and proposed a toast – these old Edwardians loved their puns – to "the two best *sellers*". A couple of days later Dennis and Joan threw a smaller party at No.8. Guests played a quiz game about Russia and the book (' "Crossing the Forbidden Territory", with Mr and Mrs Dennis Wheatley') and copies of the book were given as prizes.

It took off almost at once. The first printing was 1500 copies, but orders came in so fast that there was only time to put the pictorial endpapers into the first batch; the rest had to go out plain. Wheatley told Hutchinson's to plough his royalties back into further advertising, and the book reprinted seven times in seven weeks.

Wheatley's self-promotion was unrelenting; he went round the bookshops and bookstalls asking if they stocked his book, and took the manager of the W.H.Smith's at King's Cross station for a drink, after which King's Cross sold seven hundred copies. Wheatley was not only good at writing books, after a fashion, but he was extremely good at selling them.

Westerners were interested in Russia. Not only was the *New Statesman* predictably full of adverts for trips to the Soviet Union, books from the Russia Today Book Club, and Soviet periodicals in English, but Herge's first published book – like Wheatley's – was set there, with Bolshevik agents pursuing its hero in *Tintin in the Land of the Soviets*. *The Forbidden Territory* became even more topical shortly after publication, when six British engineers were arrested by the OGPU and subjected to a show-trial that Ian Fleming covered for Reuters.

Hutchinson's described *The Forbidden Territory* as "a novel of Russia as she is today", but a sharp reviewer in the *Times Literary Supplement* suggested Wheatley might have done better to set it in Ruritania, for it was "essentially Ruritanian and good of its kind."

Many books are "good of their kind," but Wheatley's career never looked back. Before long he was 'Public Thriller Writer No.1' and 'Prince of Thriller Writers', and as late as 1966 one of his books would shift 100,000 copies in ten days.

Within a few years *The Forbidden Territory* had been translated into fourteen languages, and a mid–Thirties jingle ran:

Patagonia to Alaska, Iceland, East to Mandalay
Wheatley thrills his thousands *every* hour of *every* day

What was the secret of Wheatley's success? He was a notoriously bad prose stylist, but this is not to say he was a bad popular *writer*. His writing is clichéd but rhetorically fluent, and it has a powerful sense of narrative: moments of crisis, relief, and further crisis are alternated relentlessly (in what Wheatley came to think of as "snakes and ladders"). Scenes of crisis and action are extended in prolonged accounts, never thrown away in brief summary, and the narrative is broken at critical moments – often chapter breaks – like the old "cliff-hanging" breaks of *Chums*-style adventure serials.

Wheatley's fictions also have a strong romantic interest. They are love stories: in *Three Inquisitive People*, Rex has a tragically sentimental love affair, and in *The Forbidden Territory* Richard Eaton meets the woman he is to marry, Princess Marie-Lou, and brings her back from Russia. This enlarged Wheatley's appeal and market, and his books were read by women as well as men. He was even commissioned to write a straight love story for *Woman's Own*.

Wheatley would further explain that he always wrote two books for one and laboriously dovetailed them together: firstly there was the story, "boy jumps into bed with girl" as he summarised it, and secondly there was the research. Wheatley's books were nothing if not educational, whether it was geography, history, or occultism. And when there were foreign locations, Wheatley's books were a holiday abroad in the days when ordinary readers didn't travel.

"People who live in miserable rows of grim little houses," Wheatley said, "don't want to read about other people who live in miserable rows of houses." Wheatley's books were the absolute incarnation of what a reviewer nicely called "the luxury traditions of the cheap novel." Wheatley's own persona became inseparable from this, as he settled into the role of the smoking jacketed gentleman with a splendid library and a fine cellar.

The Duke de Richleau's Curzon Street flat is furnished with his treasures:

> A Tibetan Buddha seated upon the Lotus; bronze figurines from Ancient Greece. Beautifully chased rapiers of Toledo steel and Moorish pistols inlaid with turquoise and gold, Ikons from Holy Russia set with semi-precious stones and curiously carved ivories from the East. The walls were lined shoulder high with books, but above them hung lovely old colour prints, and a number of priceless historical documents and maps.

From Ouida to Thomas Harris, an air of kitschily exaggerated and sometimes woefully inaccurate[2] connoisseurship has often been part of popular fiction. But in Wheatley, particularly where food and drink are concerned, it is well informed. Before Ian Fleming, Wheatley was probably the first writer to use real brand names, along with real shops, restaurants and hotels, sometimes with an element of what would now be called 'product placement.' The Duke and his friends not only enjoy Hoyo de Monterreys and Imperial Tokay, but also go to the Hungaria, buy drink from Justerini's, and smoke Rashid cigarettes : "I think they're the best in London," says Simon Aron.

With their attention to drink and food ("the *bécasse* is a bird for which I have a quite exceptional partiality"), their old English values, and the manifest decency of their leading characters, the luxury of the Duke de Richleau books has an almost Christmassy warmth about it, but it is not Dickensian; it is an *aristocratic* warmth, or an idealised suburban fantasy of it.

---

[2] "Entering her palatial music-room filled with all kinds of instruments, Eloise sat down at a spinet incrusted with lapis lazuli and silver, and flooded the room with the rich, voluptuous strains of Wagner's Tristan and Isolde." (Ouida)

As Wheatley explained to an interviewer, the people in those grim little rows of houses wanted to read about "dream lives." Looking back on his life, he put his success down to hard work, telling a good story, "and never mentioning the kitchen sink."

★

Wheatley had heard that Edgar Wallace could write a book in a week, and he wanted to try, so he borrowed a cottage from Joe Links and scribbled out *Such Power is Dangerous*. It took seventeen days.

The power in question is media power, and the book features an attempt to form a world monopoly of film companies ("Combination and Amalgamation are the business watchwords of this era") masterminded by Lord Gavin Fortescue, a criminal dwarf. Along with the usual love story and plenty of ethnic stereotyping, it shows an acutely Thirties awareness of what literary critic I.A.Richards called "the more sinister potentialities of the cinema and the loudspeaker." In the opening chapter, 'A Plot to Dominate the World', Lord Gavin explains that through a film monopoly they could not only achieve limitless wealth but

> ... our sphere of influence would be unbounded. By the type of film which we chose to produce we could influence the mass psychology of nations. Fashions, morals, customs, could be propagated by our will – we should even be able if it suited us to fill a whole people with a mad desire to make war on their neighbour... We should have power to do endless good or boundless evil. No king or emperor would ever have had such power in the world before!

"You're right," says his colleague, an American gangster, "– the President of the United States himself would be small fry compared to us – I guess it's dangerous to think how precisely powerful we'd be." Wheatley was intensely aware of the power of the mass media, in a period obsessed by the notion of 'propaganda': press baron Lord Beaverbrook even described Christ as a "great propagandist".

Wheatley had meanwhile written *Old Rowley*, a biography of Charles II. He had hoped this might go into a series of royal biographies published by the firm of Peter Davies, but they turned it down because Wheatley was insufficiently well known. In the event this was for the best: Wheatley sold it to Hutchinson, pitching it to editor Joe Gaute as a good advertisement and promotional vehicle for his other books. They made a good job of it, with illustrations by Frank C Pape, and as an in-joke Pape depicted Joan as the young Countess of Shrewsbury, to whom she was related.

Old Rowley shows Wheatley's affection for Merrie England and dislike of the Puritans. He sounds a number of contemporary notes, relating the 1660s to the pyjama parties and "bright young people" of the 1920s, and the religious bigotry of the seventeenth century to the "loathing which was engendered in our own population by an exceedingly able Ministry of Propaganda in the late war." Just as the English believed the Germans crucified prisoners and gouged out the eyes of the wounded, so the Anabaptists believed Catholics ate Protestant children.

Britain was deeply troubled in the early Thirties, with unemployment seemingly beyond the power of parliamentary government: Churchill said that democracy itself was "on trial", and popular columnist J.B.Morton ('Beachcomber') wrote "The machinery of parliamentary government, which works clumsily and laboriously, is incapable of dealing with the kind of crisis we are facing today. You might as well expect a Mother's Meeting to conduct a military campaign."

That was Morton not in the *Express*, where he is remembered, but in the Mosleyite paper *Everyman*. It is with this national crisis, and the age of dictators, that *Old Rowley* had its most contemporary resonance, since Charles II dissolved his quarrelling Parliament and ruled as a benevolent autocrat. Timely Thirties lines include "general unrest had reached such a height that revolution was feared by many"; the Whigs, pledged to overthrow the Tories, included "the fanatics and madmen who pester every Government, the human dock rats from Wapping, the hooligans, the jail-birds, and the very scum of the London gutters"; and in due course Charles dismissed Parliament and its "would-be Kommisars".

In Wheatley's celebratory summary, Charles dismissed Parliament as "A House of Talkers", and through his so-called "despotism" he brought about a "happy, prosperous England"; so "Charles, reigning without a Parliament – stands justified."

In one of the book's most striking lines, Wheatley recalls the King finding his way "through the stormy night to the shelter and safety of Mosley." It could be entirely fortuitous, but some readers might consider the careless grandeur of this statement to be an unnecessarily resonant way of telling readers that the King went to the Lancashire town of Mosley.

★

Wheatley hoped to turn *Old Rowley* into a film, and drafted a script. Imperilled kings were central to his imagination – as in his three favourite books, *Zenda*, *Pimpernel*, and *Musketeers* – so the story of Charles excited him: "chased through the length and breadth of England . . . for six whole weeks he was hunted like a hare . . . this 'Flight of the King' is the greatest epic of escape in history . . ."

Nothing came of his film script, and for years he was unlucky with films. Wheatley and his wife were friendly with the Hitchcocks, and Hitchcock admired *The Forbidden Territory*. There was a plan for Hitchcock to film it, with Gerald du Maurier – already acclaimed as Raffles and Bulldog Drummond – playing the Duke. Wheatley inserted a bold piece of publicity into *Such Power is Dangerous*: "I figure to make this picture The Forbidden Territory," says a character:

> . . . It's a great story – sledge scenes in the snow – aero-planes – a gun-fight with the Reds in a ruined chateau, and a dash to the frontier in a high-powered car – marvel-lous material to work on. It's by a feller named Wheatley – who he is, God knows, but that don't matter. There's

290

plenty of love interest too . . . It's got the makings of
a master film – great spectacle, human interest – and
educative value as well.

In another writer this overlap between art and life might be
almost avant-garde, despite the asterisk announcing it was
available from Hutchinson at 7/6d. In Wheatley's case, however, a reviewer complained "I do not approve of an author's
boosting a previous book of his own in the text of his
new book, and I am astonished that his publishers did not
discourage such a breach of literary manners."

Gerald du Maurier died and was replaced by Ronald
Squire, better known in light comedy roles, and instead of
Hitchcock it was directed by a B-movie director. Wheatley
was disappointed. In the event his mass medium was not
to be cinema but print, publishing books that contained
deliberate messages, polemic, 'editorialising,' and 'spin' of a
kind more usually associated with newspapers.

★

Wheatley was now settling into the identity of a writer.
He joined the Society of Authors and, thinking it was something writers did, he also joined the PEN Club. Then as now,
PEN ("Poets Essayists Novelists") was a worthy organisation,
a kind of literary Amnesty International, much concerned
with the civil rights of overseas writers.

Wheatley went to a PEN dinner, with H.G.Wells as
Chairman, but he was disappointed when he looked around
the room. Where were the famous authors? There seemed
not to be any there. He persevered with a second dinner,
but at this one a member of the Christian revivalist 'Oxford
Group', associated with Frank Buchman's American 'Moral
Re-Armament Movement' – felt the need to stand up at the
table and make a public confession of her sins. That was the
end for Wheatley, who was further appalled by the fact that
PEN organised tours for members to visit other countries
and meet foreign authors: "It seemed sad that Britain should
be represented by such people." He resigned.

Far more useful was the Paternoster Club, "the only important literary club in Britain, which is quite unknown to the general public." This was founded in October 1933 by Bruce Graeme, author of the 'Blackshirt' thrillers (*Alias Blackshirt*, *Blackshirt Takes a Hand*, *Blackshirt Inteferes*, *Blackshirt Again*, and so on). He had been to the Dutch Treat Club in New York, where authors, journalists, and publishers met, and it gave him the idea of starting something similar in Britain.

The Paternoster Club met once a month at the Cheshire Cheese in Fleet Street. Wheatley became Chairman in the second year, and he introduced more journalists including Tom Driberg, who wrote the William Hickey gossip column in the *Daily Express*, and Bunny Tattersall and Lord Donegall, who held similar posts on the *Daily Mail* and *Sunday Dispatch*. The Paternoster Club also included booksellers, from the Librarian at Harrods to the managers of W.H.Smiths railway station branches, and the buyers for the great libraries such as Boots. "Our Hon Sec buys 8,000,000 new books every year, and it can safely be said that 85% of all the books bought in the British Empire pass through the hands of certain of its members . . ."

Wheatley derived special benefits from being a member of the club's inner circle, the committee, along with Bruce Graeme, Joe Gaute of Hutchinson, Freddy Richardson of Boots and Cecil Hunt, literary editor of the *Mail*. As Chairman, Wheatley kept an efficient card index on its one hundred and fifty members, including their CVs, special subjects, recreations and other clubs. Members had a considerable influence over what the reading public were fed with, although they were strictly forbidden to mention the Club itself, leading Wheatley to dub it "The Nameless Club". It was a superb machine for mutual back scratching,

Through another friend on the committee, Victor McClure, Wheatley became a member of the Savage Club, a club associated with writers. In Wheatley's day it occupied premises on Carlton House Terrace, but Wheatley was not very excited by it, perhaps because it was not socially exclusive enough. Before long he had set his sights on being a member of Boodle's.

★

Wheatley was unhappy with the quality of *Such Power*, but he was told that it was a writer's third book that really counted, and he put the best part of a year into writing *Black August*, a novel of Bolshevik revolution in Britain. It is set in about 1960, and yet it often seems more like 1926 or earlier, with communist cavalry clattering down the streets.

Poland and Germany are at war, there is a Fascist puppet king on the throne on France, and Britain is in chaos, with Jewish pawnbrokers kicked to death in the East End, troops firing on crowds, and a "mob" burning the "lovely furniture" of Queen Elizabeth II. Minor characters include Choo-Se-Foo, a wily Chinaman and fraudulent practitioner of Modern Art, but the book is more significant for the appearance of the "cad" who is to be its hero: "The scar which lifted the outer corner of his left eyebrow gave his long, rather sallow face a queerly Satanic look."

It is Gregory Sallust, the resurrection of Eric, who is to figure in Wheatley's fiction for another thirty-five years. He lives on Gloucester Road as the lodger of his old army manservant, Rudd, who is based on Wheatley's old cellarman, Lewis. The orders for *Black August* were so strong that it reprinted half a dozen times before publication. "Terrific!" said the Press: "It would be a dull dog who could lay it down for longer than it takes to wolf a quick Martini," said A.G.Macdonnell (a friend of Wheatley). "Mr Wheatley . . . never lets you down," said Howard Spring in the *Evening Standard* (a Paternoster); "I do not remember a more vividly or more cunningly told story" said Ralph Straus in the *Sunday Times* (another Paternoster). Wheatley's third book was home and dry.

★

Wheatley had published four books in a year and it was time for a holiday, so he and Joan went to South Africa. Bino was

293

now living there in Gandhi's old house, having married a well-off South African woman, and the Wheatleys stayed with them. Bino showed Wheatley the Johannesburg slums and told him about the violent communist uprising there in 1922, which Wheatley used for a short story, 'When the Reds Seized the City of Gold'.

Apartheid had not yet been introduced but there were already serious ethnic problems and it was not safe for whites to be outdoors after dark. Despite that – since real life is never quite as black and white as Wheatley's fiction – when Wheatley lost his wallet, with his money, passport and tickets, he was pleasantly surprised to find one of the local blacks handed it in.

The Wheatleys returned home via Gibraltar, where Wheatley was "strangely delighted" to see the Gibraltar police wearing English uniforms. Back in London, the Younger boys Bill and Jack were now in their teens and were spending more time with their mother and Wheatley. Wheatley took to the two boys, and Bill in particular – an intelligent boy who had been stricken with polio, which left him small in stature and with a partly withered right arm – became the apple of his eye, somewhat overshadowing his real offspring.

Despite his age, Wheatley said the Younger boys were like "younger brothers" to him (not sons). It is a revealing description, because – perhaps because he had disliked his own father and paternal grandfather – he was not very good at paternal relationships. As for the boys, Wheatley thought they liked him because he had a "happy disposition" and a "jolly time" was guaranteed, while their father was gloomy and bad tempered.

Wheatley put his South African holiday to work with *The Fabulous Valley*, featuring a lost valley strewn with diamonds, but his research was showing. "This is the place, I've not a doubt," cries a character. "Look! It is exactly as described in Hedley Chilver's book *The Seven Lost Trails of Africa*."

Howard Spring, Ralph Straus, James Hilton (another

friend) and several other reviewers praised the book, but a less friendly reviewer said "Mr. Wheatley should make up his mind whether he is going to write a thriller or a travel book."

Now Wheatley had a new inspiration. He would write a book where his research really would show, and to spellbinding effect. He was going to write a book about black magic.

Luncheon with the Beast

About a head taller than Wheatley and far better spoken, Tom Driberg was securely upper-middle class and quite left wing; he went into politics and ended up as Chairman of the Labour Party. At first sight his politics make his friend-ship with Wheatley unlikely, but only at first sight. He was also a member of Andre Simon's Wine and Food Society, eating turtle fins with the likes of David Tennant and Sacheverell Sitwell, and at his birthday party, as an old man, he crowed "One duke, two dukes' daughters, sundry lords, a bishop, a poet laureate — not bad for an old left-wing MP, eh?"

Along with High Church ritual — he could have made a memorable bishop — Driberg adored the aristocracy and working-class men, but he hated the middle classes and women. In his posthumous autobiography he flaunted the amount of time he spent haunting public lavatories, and he became a friend of the Kray twins, who supplied him with East End youths. When he wasn't chasing the lower orders he could be foul to them — his rudeness to waiters reduced them to tears, and his friends were embarrassed to go into restaurants with him — and yet he genuinely seems to have wanted to bring a more Christian ethic into public life. Psychiatrist Anthony Storr described him as the only person he ever met who could truly be called "evil".

In later life Driberg developed a face and manner that would do credit to a Wheatley villain, but at this time he was a personable and charming young man. He lived at 5 Queen's Gate Place Mews, in Bino Johnstone's old house, with a former lavatory attendant as his manservant. This was just around the corner from Wheatley and Joan, and one night — Driberg having made an enemy of some kind — Wheatley was pressed into service to escort him home.

The two of them walked into the dark mews with some trepidation, Wheatley armed with his swordstick, but fortunately there was no one there.

★

When young, Driberg had been an associate of Aleister Crowley, the self-styled Beast 666. He considerably misrepresents their relationship in his autobiography. According to Driberg, he was an undergraduate at Oxford when Crowley read something in a newspaper about Driberg's avant-garde poetry performance, 'Homage to Beethoven,' and invited him to lunch. He thought Crowley was eccentric, but they continued to see each other occasionally.

What really happened was that Driberg read Crowley's novel, *Diary of a Drug Fiend*, and sent him a fan letter. This was the beginning of their association, which for a time amounted to discipleship on Driberg's part (thanking Crowley for a photograph, he writes it "will be an inspiration . . . it does convey, if I may say so, a distinct impression of power and wisdom, and of the presence of a Master").

This discipleship could be quite grovelling: at one point Crowley delegated Driberg to buy some aloes, needed for the preparation of a magical incense, and Driberg bought the wrong sort:

Dear Sir Aleister,
    Thank you so much for your letter: it really is good of you to bother about anyone as ignorant and disappointing as myself – and I am sorry about the aloes: they gave me "black" aloes, and said it was exactly the same as lignum aloes!

On surer ground within his own field of interest, politics, Driberg assured Crowley that democracy was over – it was a "a sham" – and firm leadership was the order of the day: the strength of the Communist Party (of which Driberg was a member) was that "the majority could always be led and controlled by an intelligent and clear-sighted minority."

This would have struck a chord with Crowley: from his own far-Right 'Thelemic' position, he desired that the "few and secret . . . shall rule the many and the known."

Crowley had some 'Forms of Acceptance' of the Law of Thelema (in effect Crowley's own religion) but filling them in seemed so much like the traditional signing away of one's soul that Crowley had difficulty getting people to put their names on them. Driberg signed, and was entrusted with recruiting others: "I enclose a copy, filled in, of the 'Form of Acceptance': I am taking great care of the copies, and will only show them to really promising people."

★

As Driberg grew older, the balance of power shifted. Increasingly washed up and short of money, Crowley would tap Driberg for cash and meals, but Driberg didn't always respond and Crowley complained in his diary "Tom Driberg's unforthcomingnesses are really unschooltiesome."

By the time Driberg put Wheatley in touch with Crowley, the latter's fortunes were ebbing: he was sliding from being The Great Beast to the great joke and finally the great bore, and his reputation wouldn't revive until the Sixties, when occultism became part of the counter-culture and he appeared on the cover of the Beatles' Sergeant Pepper.

Crowley was always on the look out for promising young men to spread the word and if possible subsidise it. He was an indefatigable self-publicist, and his magnum opus, *Magick in Theory and Practice*, has a distinctively modern and almost transatlantic air of hucksterism when it announces Magick is for all, including "the Poet", "the Golfer" and "the Stenographer".

Wheatley would certainly have known Crowley's reputation for depravity and wickedness, fostered by the yellow press of the Twenties. It was bold of Wheatley to meet this potentially distasteful character, even though he had become a somewhat pathetic figure by 1934. People meeting him for the first time often feared that he would make indecent advances, but in practice he was more likely to borrow a fiver.

Wheatley invited him to lunch in May 1934 at the Hungaria restaurant on Regent Street.

Wheatley and Crowley both liked good food and drink, they were both rather Edwardian, both high Tories, and in later life they were both proud of their resemblance to Churchill. They should have got on. So it is remarkable that Wheatley never says anything whatsoever about this lunch; it provided him with not a single anecdote, and he never even describes Crowley's appearance, although he sometimes exaggerates their acquaintance to the extent of claiming he and Joan had Crowley round to dinner several times.

At the time of their lunch Crowley was preoccupied with a court case. Hoping for damages, he had launched a libel action, in the course of which he was the last man in Britain to wear a top hat in the witness box. He lost. Anthony Powell lunched with him within a week or two of Wheatley, finding him absurd and yet "intensely sinister, both in exterior and manner." He reminded Powell of an old time music hall comedian, with a "steady flow of ponderous gags." Powell was struck by his great bald head, "so shaped as to give the impression that he was wearing a false top to his head like a clown's." Beneath it his features were "strangely caught together within the midst of a large elliptical area, like those of a horrible baby."

Powell would occasionally see him in the street afterwards, often wearing green plus fours. He was wearing these, set off with an enormous tartan bow-tie, when he lunched with Maurice Richardson. As was his wont, Crowley began with his own grace, "Do What Thou Wilt Shall be the Whole of the Law", and they ate and drank prodigiously while Crowley indulged his ponderous humour: indicating a piece of lobster in the bisque, he said "Looks like a devil roasting in hell, does it not, Mr Richardson?".

Meeting Crowley again in a public house, Richardson noticed a smell of old operating theatres: this was because Crowley had started the day with half a pint of ether. Asked what he wanted to drink, he plumped for a triple absinthe, not in honour of the 1890s – although in many ways this would have been appropriate – but because by this time he was more or less an alcoholic: he had two more triple absinthes before a gourmand lunch washed down with a bottle of burgundy and several further brandies.

As well as the bald head and the grandly dated clothes (this time a tail coat and sponge-bag trousers, "like a Duke in a musical comedy") Richardson couldn't help noticing Crowley's famously hypnotic eyes: "it was difficult not to keep staring at them . . ."

Like Richardson, Arthur Calder-Marshall was struck by those notorious eyes. Calder-Marshall found Crowley sordid and disenchanting, from his having checked Calder-Marshall's family in *Who's Who* ("you have great possibilities . . . Have you any money of your own?") to his attempt to get him to stay the night. In the end it came down to "this shagged and sorry old gentleman trying to outstare me across a table."

It was a great anti-climax for Calder-Marshall, who had wanted to meet Crowley for reasons not irrelevant to Wheatley's fiction: "In a world where blacks and whites were breaking up so fast into various shades of grey, The Beast was the last of the graven images, an obsidian monolith of evil, a simple and reassuring devil." In the event, he was forced to conclude that "Evil was never Pure."

★

Overshadowed by the court case, lunch with Wheatley doesn't rank a mention in Crowley's diary, although he does mention meetings around the same time with Driberg and fellow occultist Rollo Ahmed. Soon afterwards however, he did give Wheatley a specially customised copy of *Magick in Theory and Practice*. Where the title page read "Published for Subscribers Only 1929", Crowley altered it to "This unique copy . . . Published for Dennis Wheatley only 1934 e.v." [era vulgaris], added a photograph of himself captioned "The Beast 666" and inscribed the book to Wheatley "in memory of that sublime Hungarian banquet."

He drew a diagram of the Qabalah at the back of the book,

with a squiggle representing the Babe of the Abyss, and wrote in the inside cover "Recommendations to the Intelligent Reader humbly proffered," which included "Study Liber XV pp.345 etc" – his 'Gnostic Catholic Mass' – "with a view to putting on this ritual in London as it is done in Hollywood. Amen" and "Read 'Hymn to Pan' aloud at midnight when alone with INTENTION to get HIM." Wheatley was not tempted to try this.

★

Wheatley wrote a polite thank you letter (it was a "magnificent gift", a "delightful addition" to his collection, especially due to the "kindly" inscription; he was looking forward to reading it "with the greatest interest") and he sent a couple of his own books: "I fear that in interest and value they can in no way be a fair exchange but if you like a thriller, The Forbidden Territory may serve to while away an evening and as we agreed on Charles II being the most intelligent of English Kings, I hope Old Rowley may find favour with you."

This agreement on Charles II is one of only two things we know about their conversation. The other is that Crowley wanted to sell some manuscripts – he may have tried to sell them to Wheatley – and Wheatley recommended he should try the bookdealer Percy Muir, from whom Wheatley often bought first editions.

A letter from Crowley hopes that Wheatley's work is "swift and successful" and leaves him "some leisure soon," which suggests he had been using work as an excuse not to see Crowley.

In lieu of any experiences of his own, Wheatley had two stories about Crowley that he never tired of telling. When Crowley was an undergraduate at Cambridge he wanted to put on a production of Aristophanes, but the Master of his college forbade it. Crowley and his "coven" met in a moonlit field, and Crowley went to stick a pin in a wax image of the Master, but one of his comrades scrupled to jog his arm and he only pierced the figure's foot. Next day, the Master slipped and broke his ankle.

There seems to be no truth whatever in this, even as an exaggeration or a coincidence. It is very vulgar, magically speaking: pin in doll, moonlight, coven; this is witchcraft, or its popular image. Crowley's principal undergraduate interests were chess, mountaineering, and writing poetry. Magic came slightly later, from the end of his time at Cambridge, and it was magic of a relatively exalted sort, writing a letter to A.E.Waite for advice and joining the Order of the Golden Dawn. Not pins in dolls.

This story seems to come from Driberg, as did Wheatley's second story. Wheatley told Driberg he thought Crowley was intellectually wonderful, but harmless; he didn't believe he could harm a rabbit. Perhaps not now, Driberg said, but he used to have real power, before *that terrible affair in Paris*.

Crowley and the other twelve members of his coven – an obviously bogus detail – were in a hotel in Paris when Crowley and a disciple attempted to raise Pan in an upstairs room. The others were ordered to wait downstairs and not intervene whatever they heard, while applying themselves joylessly to a "cold collation" and getting "stale tight". Shouting and banging was heard and the temperature dropped, but it was not until morning that they went up and broke down the locked door: the disciple was dead, and Crowley was reduced to lunacy, after which he had to spend six months (or sometimes four months, as if for a greater ring of circumstantial truth) in an asylum.

Driberg himself – named only as Member of Parliament "Z", in one of Wheatley's accounts – was supposed to have been one of the party downstairs, and "an eye witness". In Wheatley's introduction to Crowley's novel *Moonchild* this "friend of mine who later became an MP" is quoted at length in his own voice, telling Wheatley how he went up, broke the door in, and found Crowley "a naked, gibbering idiot in one corner."

The most likely apportioning of blame for this extraordinary farrago of nonsense is that Driberg's presence in the story is a Wheatley invention – the temperature dropping in the presence of evil, getting "stale-tight", and Satanic cold collations are all suspiciously like Wheatley's fiction – but that Driberg did tell Wheatley a fantastically garbled account of 'The Paris Working.' This was a series of sexual invocations performed in Paris in 1913–14 by Crowley and his then magickal partner Victor Neuburg, primarily concerned with invoking Jupiter and Mercury.

Nobody died and it all took place without the attendance of eleven people downstairs, but Neuburg did have a nervous breakdown of sorts afterwards: he went into psychotherapy with Dr E.T.Jensen, an early Freudian with magickal leanings, after which he got married and took good care to avoid further dealings with Crowley.

One of the main objectives of the 'The Paris Working' was money, Jupiter being associated with its arrival, and Crowley noted in his magickal diary that since they had begun operations a letter had arrived "which should bring in £500 within the next two months", and moreover the bank rate had fallen to three percent and Consols had gone up, bringing him a profit of over £1,400. So the Working was good news not just for the magickal duo, as Crowley's biographer John Symonds notes drily, but for the public at large; or at least, for those members of it with overdrafts, mortgages or Consols.

Crowley and Neuburg had earlier invoked Bartzabel, the spirit of Mars – oddly germane, as we shall see, to *The Devil Rides Out*, where Crowley is a model for Mocatta – and here the news was not so good. Speaking through Neuburg in 1910, Bartzabel had prophesied war involving Germany. In fact, looking back over his magickal record for 'The Paris Working', Crowley felt the two of them had perhaps been responsible for the outbreak of the First World War.

★

Leafing through the French Fascist paper, *Gringoire*, George Orwell noticed no less than thirty eight advertisements for clairvoyants. He remembered this when he was trying to fathom the relationship between occultism and right wing politics. For one thing, occultism replaces the idea of progress and the untidy reality of change with a timeless and reassuring vision of eternal myth, instead of real history, as if nothing essential had changed since the days of ancient Egypt. Secondly, occultism and fascism share a sense of spurious elitism, esoteric knowledge being the dominion of a special few and the guarantee of their superiority. More than that, it offers a transcendence of ordinary life, and an idealist fantasy of pure mental power without normal economic or social restraints. In a larger sense, it is no coincidence that Crowley's magickal philosophy was centred on the notion of the Will, and that Leni Riefenstahl's immortalisation of the Nuremberg rallies was entitled *The Triumph of the Will*.

Crowley's diary entries from the Thirties show he had hopes of Hitler's Germany as a possible vehicle for his own philosophy, and he had dreams about Hitler: in one of them the Fuhrer, who was very tall, had all Crowley's books translated and made official reading in Germany. In another one, more elaborate, Hitler figured along with cigars and the idea of Magick, and in this dream Crowley was actually running Germany on Hitler's behalf.

In 1904 Crowley had received a communication from his Guardian Angel, a being called Aiwass. Aiwass and Crowley proclaimed the coming of a new Aeon, the Aeon of Horus; the era of war. Crowley was not a vulgar Satanist – in any case virtually non-existent until the 1960s – but he did identify Aiwass with the Egyptian god Set, a forerunner of Satan notorious as the first of the dualistic "bad" gods, and pivotal in *The Devil Rides Out*.

"Deem not of change", Aiwass said in *The Book of the Law*; "The kings of the earth shall be Kings forever: the slaves shall serve." Aiwass believed in strength and joy: "We have nothing with the outcast and the unfit: let them die in their misery. For they feel not. Compassion is the vice of kings: stamp down the wretched and the weak: this is the law of the strong: this is our law and the joy of the world. [. . .] on the low men trample in the fierce lust of your pride, in the day of your wrath. [. . .] Pity not the fallen! I never knew them. I am not for them. I console not. I hate the consoled and the consoler."

War for its own sake was a central theme: "I will give you a war-engine. With it ye shall smite the peoples; and none shall stand before you. [. . .] I forbid argument. Conquer! That is enough . . . worship me with fire and blood; worship me with swords and with spears. [. . .] Mercy let be off: damn them who pity! Kill and torture; spare not; be upon them!"

And so on. Crowley's friend Gerald Yorke annotated a copy of *Mein Kampf*, noting its similarities with *The Book of the Law*. It has to be said, Crowley's book is the kind of thing that gives Fascism a bad name. It is a Nietzschean rant, and inasmuch as it lacks the socialistic elements of actual fascism it is, in a real sense, well to the right of Hitler.

The next of the people Wheatley met through his researches, however, and the man who probably had more influence on him than anyone else, was the Reverend Montague Summers. He hated Satanists and witches with a vengeance, and on unexpected grounds. He thought they were engaged in a Bolshevik conspiracy.

CHAPTER TWENTY-FIVE

Top Chaps in the Field

Of all the "top boys" that Wheatley befriended through his research, none was more important than Montague Summers, who has been described as "a mysterious figure, with his large moon-like face, wearing a black shovel hat and flowing cape, flitting bat-like across the literary scene of the twenties and early thirties . . .".

With his silvery locks and his outdated clerical garb, Wheatley thought he looked like a Restoration bishop. Summers's extravagantly ecclesiastical outfits were notorious, and one witness remembers him in a purple stock, black cassock, wide black silk cincture with a foot-deep purple fringe, and large silver buckles on his patent-leather shoes.

And this was despite the fact that there were doubts about whether he was really ordained as a priest: he was frowned on by the ecclesiastical authorities. When he lived in Hove he acted as private chaplain to the Hon. Mrs. Ermyntrude Greville-Nugent, who had a private oratory in her house where Summers would officiate, until the Bishop of Southwark put a firm stop to it.

Wheatley used Summers as the model for Canon Copely-Syle in *To The Devil – A Daughter*, but it could further be argued that it was Summers who stood behind Wheatley's entire occult output, with his view of Satanism as a criminal conspiracy posing an enduring menace to society. For Summers, witchcraft and Satanism were real; they were "still" practised (something of a paradox, because they are largely modern inventions) and they were all around us. More than that, they had a political aspect.

Summers's 1926 *History of Witchcraft and Demonology* set the subject back four hundred years. It was an ultra-orthodox fire-and-brimstone compendium of witch hunting lore, and its credulous details of Sabbaths, Black Masses, and infant sacrifices would provide the raw material for numerous other books on the subject.

Wheatley prided himself on his research. This plays a special role in his occult books, where the accumulation of quasi-factual information suspends disbelief and enfolds the reader in the books' distinctive atmosphere. This effect is already a feature of Summers work, where mountainous quantities of scholarship tend to overwhelm scepticism and draw the reader in.

Summers recounts a story from 1895, when the agents of Prince Borghese regained possession of a flat in the Palazzo Borghese from an uncooperative tenant. Having gained entry, they discovered why he wanted to be left undisturbed.

> The walls were hung all round from ceiling to floor with heavy curtains of silk damask, scarlet and black, excluding the light; at the further end there stretched a large tapestry upon which was woven in more than life-size a figure of Lucifer, colossal, triumphant, dominating the whole. Exactly beneath an altar had been built, amply furnished for the liturgy of hell: candles, vessels, rituals, missals, nothing was lacking. Cushioned prie-dieus and luxurious chairs, crimson and gold, were set in order for the assistants; the chamber being lit by electricity, fantastically arrayed so as to glare from an enormous human eye.

Compare the passage in *The Devil Rides Out* where the Duc de Richleau is explaining the reality of modern Satanism to Rex Van Ryn:

> '. . . Borghese's agents forced an entry. What do you think they found?' 'Lord knows.' Rex shook his head.

The principal salon had been redecorated ("at enormous cost", a very Wheatley touch) and converted into a Satanic Temple:

'The walls were hung from ceiling to floor with heavy curtains of silk damask, scarlet and black to exclude the light; at the farther end there stretched a large tapestry upon which was woven a colossal figure of Lucifer dominating the whole. Beneath, an altar had been built and amply furnished with the whole liturgy of Hell; black candles, vessels, rituals, nothing was lacking. Cushioned prie-dieus and luxurious chairs, crimson and gold, were set in order for the assistants, and the chamber lit with electricity fantastically arranged so that it should glare through an enormous human eye.'

De Richleau hammered the desk with his clenched fist. 'These are facts I'm giving you Rex — facts, d'you hear, things I can prove by eye-witnesses still living.'

Summers's story is not factual. It was concocted by the nineteenth-century hoaxer Leo Taxil in order to smear the tenant of the flat, an Italian politician named Adriano Lemmi.

Recent examples were another Summers speciality. The Duke de Richleau asks Rex when he thinks the last trial for witchcraft took place. "I'll say it was all of a hundred and fifty years ago", replies Rex, to which the Duke pulls out his trump card: "No, it was in January, 1926, at Melun near Paris." It was the Madame Mesmin case, a bizarre story from Chapter V of Summers's 1927 book *The Geography of Witchcraft*.

The sheer matter-of-factness of Summers's belief is coercive, along with an intellectual snobbery that is completely in conflict with modern thinking, but so confident that it seems to have not only the moral but even the intellectual high ground. Summers regarded his opponents as "vulgarians," and he liked to quote the reply of a priest (or in his phrase a "Prince of the Church") to the woman who told him she was a freethinker: "Free, Madam, I doubt not, but a thinker, no."

★

"The cult of the Devil", says Summers, "is the most terrible power at work in the world today." As in Wheatley, his belief in the absolute conflict between good and evil is allied to cultural pessimism, with "monstrous things below the surface of our cracking civilisation". Witches are the continuation of heretics, who were in the business of "revolution and red anarchy"; they were "red hot anarchists" who fully deserved to be burnt at the stake, while "The Black International" of Satanism has always been in the business of fomenting revolutions, including the French and Russian.

More significant than the alleged politics of a largely fictional group, however, is the fact that Summers found occultism such a satisfyingly arcane field for his obsessional and reactionary scholarship. Like his dress, it was part of the anomie he felt in the modern world:

> Above all, I hate the sceptic and modernist in religion, the Atheist, the Agnostic, the Communist, and all Socialism in whatever guise or masquerade.

Summers explained the issues when he talked about witchcraft with Lord Balfour, a former Conservative Prime Minister. Balfour was an intellectual who had published several books on philosophy and theology, and he questioned Summers on the "ultimate aim and object" of witches. As Summers tells it, Balfour "found it hard to believe from a metaphysical point of view that there could be people who craved evil for evil's sake. His intellect was, I think, too noble and too lofty to conceive of such degradations and culpability, unless we had explained the problem by sheer lunacy." But lunacy was not a sufficient explanation of the problem as Summers conceived it, so he "ventured to stray into the political arena":

> "Well, Lord Balfour," I answered, "you have only to think of the political views of some of your opponents." And I cited certain persons whose ideas appeared to be

fundamentally anarchical and to end logically in absolute nihilism. "That is the witch philosophy," I said.

H.G.Wells made a perceptive point about Summers's world view in his 1927 article, 'Communism and Witchcraft'. After reading Summers's *History of Witchcraft and Demonology* alongside various utterances about Russian Bolshevism, "I find a curious confusion in my mind between the two." Wells quotes Summers's condemnation of the witch as "an evil liver; a social pest and parasite; the devotee of a loathly and obscene creed; an adept at poisoning, blackmail, and all creeping crimes . . ." (and so on) and then observes that any reader of the British newspapers of the time might be unsure whether this passage is describing Gilles De Rais, Lunacharsky, Old Mother Shipton, or Lenin.

Wells's tolerant view of Bolshevism has dated, but his wider argument is still of interest. He cites the "interesting views" of "that great historical writer, Mrs.Nesta Webster" – he is being ironic, since she is better remembered as a con-spiracy theorist and anti-Semite – on the fact that "modern Communism is the lineal descendant of the black traditions of mediaeval sorcery, Manichaean heresies, Free Masonry, and the Witch of Endor."

This is exactly what Wheatley claims in *The Haunting of Toby Jugg* and elsewhere. Perhaps, says Wells, "mankind has a standing need for somebody to tar, feather and burn. Perhaps if there was no devil, men would have to invent one."

*

Things were not so black and white in Summers's own life. He has been described as "one of the most enigmatical fig-ures of the century," and most people found him to be a delightful old gentleman. His *Who's Who* entry, which lists among his recreations "talking to intelligent dogs, that is, all dogs," makes him seem rather engaging. He was also a devotee of that great Victorian pastime, the toy theatre (or as he preferred to call it, "the miniature stage") and he liked nothing better than to read a good book, cosily "chair-croodled" – his English was highly idiosyncratic – beside a blazing fire.

At the same time, some people found him indefinably repellent and sinister, like a "split personality" or "a man wearing a mask", and perhaps they were right. It turns out that Summers was a Satanist himself.

The person who has gone most convincingly into the mystery of Montague Summers is Timothy d'Arch Smith, who first presented his findings in a talk given to The Society ("The Society is a society in London", he explains in a footnote; "In accordance with occult precepts it requires no further advertisement.")

As a young man Summers had been steeped in the atmosphere of the 1890s and the work of Oscar Wilde, and he was in the habit of saying "Tell me *strange things*", a request with a very Nineties feel to it. His first published work had been a 1907 volume of poems entitled *Antinous*, condemned by one reviewer as "the nadir of corruption" and containing poems such as 'To A Dead Acolyte,' in which some sort of ceremony seems to be in progress – Summers was always of a ritualistic bent – watched over by an ancient figure:

. . .
Across the crowded palace
His bright eyes gleam with malice,
When we uplift the chalice,
   Brimful of sanguine wine.
No mass more sweet than this is,
A liturgy of kisses,
What time the metheglin hisses
   Plashed o'er the fumid shrine.

He dreams of bygone pleasures,
Whose passion kenned no measures,
Of all his secret treasures,
   The lust of long dead men.
And thro' dishevelled tresses,
He smiles at our caresses,

        To know that he possesses
        As great power now as then.

Metheglin, evil as it might sound, is just a type of mead,
but the "He" in question is the Old One himself. "This
is Satanism", says d'Arch Smith, "Satanism celebrated by
Montague Summers in 1907 with as much fervour as in
1926 he would denounce it in his *History of Witchcraft and
Demonology*."

A man calling himself Anatole James had met Summers in
1918, and they found they had things in common. In consequence, on Boxing Day, 1918, Summers had asked James to
his house in Eton Road, Hampstead, to take part in a Black
Mass. Satanism being a recent invention, a recent academic
book accords this Boxing Day performance the unexpected
status of "the earliest Black Mass for which there is reliable
evidence". Unaware that he was at a historic event, and
not being sufficiently religious to find it either shocking or
exciting, James was merely bored, but he understood well
enough that what was going on was a perversion of the
Catholic rite.

James was not invited to the Black Mass again, but he
continued to see Summers socially: heavily made up and
perfumed, drunk on liqueurs, Summers would cruise the
London streets in search of young men. One day Summers
confided his particular taste: "He was aroused only by devout
young Catholics, their subsequent corruption giving him
inexhaustible pleasure."

And so Summers might have continued, but something
seems to have happened. Around 1923 he cut James dead in
the street and embarked on his fevered and credulous series
of inquisitorial, rack and hellfire invectives against witchcraft,
Satanism, demonolatry, diabolism, and black magic. Was there
an element of hypocrisy in this later career, as has been suggested, or even showmanship? D'Arch Smith thinks not,
intuiting instead that Summers received a violent spiritual
shock, and learned a lesson which he phrases in terms more
Manichaean than anything in Christian theology:

he had discovered (and not a moment too soon) that the god he worshipped and the god who warred against that god were professionals.

★

Wheatley was aware that there were sinister rumours about Summers, and that his ordination as a priest had been questioned, but they should still have got on well. Wheatley was charming, respectful, and eager to learn, and both men were keen bibliophiles, reactionary in their politics, and fond of liqueurs.

Wheatley was a receptive ear for Summers's stories, like his experience of carrying out an exorcism in Ireland. A peasant woman was possessed by a demon, and when Summers arrived at the cottage she was foaming at the mouth and had to be physically restrained. Summers performed the ceremony of exorcism, with 'bell, book and candle', and then – so he apparently told Wheatley – a small black cloud came out of the woman's mouth. She became quiet, and the black cloud disappeared into a leg of cold mutton that was sitting on the table for supper. A few moments later, it was swarming with maggots.

In fact this anecdote – which Wheatley re-tells several times – appears to be taken from a short tale by R.H.Benson, 'Father Meuron's Tale', in a book of Benson's stories entitled *A Mirror of Shalott*. Benson's short fictions had also appeared in *The Ecclesiastical Review* and *The Catholic Fireside*, both of which one can imagine Summers curling up with.

After dining with Dennis and Joan, Summers invited them to stay for the weekend. He was living at Wykeham House at Alresford in Hampshire where, as at his other residences, he set up his own private oratory. It is likely that Summers's interiors were something of a moveable feast, so a visitor's description of the decor in another Summers house – this one at Richmond, where he also had a statue of Pan as the "garden god" – may approximate to the ambience Wheatley would have encountered. The house was rather gloomy, and this gloom was heightened by old-fashioned furnishings and

This unique copy of

MAGICK

IN THEORY AND PRACTICE

BY

THE MASTER THERION

(ALEISTER CROWLEY)

The Beast

6   6

6

Dennis Wheatley

PUBLISHED FOR ~~SUBSCRIBERS~~ ONLY

1929 34 EV.

Wheatley's customised copy of Magick, from Aleister Crowley.

314

The Reverend: former Satanist and dubious clergyman Montague Summers.

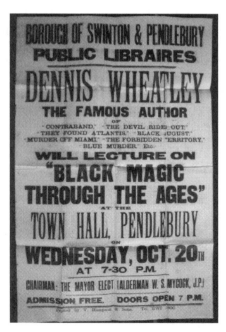

On the road: one of Wheatley's Thirties lectures on Black Magic.

a large number of Italianate and 'Gothick' oil paintings. The oratory was in an upper room, and at one end was a large altar, with gilt candlesticks and damask hangings, surmounted by a heavily framed oil painting of a saint. "It has been said", continues the visitor, "that the house was sinister. It never struck me as such, but exactly the kind one would expect as the home of a man possessing the tastes of Summers." He was received in the library by Summers, with his soutane and "twinkling eyes". Twinkling eyes were not to be the aspect of Summers that he revealed to Wheatley.

Wheatley and Joan "motored down" to Alresford on the Friday afternoon, and while they were being shown around the garden, Joan saw an enormous toad. "He is the reincarnation of a dear friend," explained Summers benignly; "I'm just looking after him."

The room that Summers had given the Wheatleys to sleep in seemed to be full of large spiders. Feeling Summers must have known this, and that it was at the very least inhospitable – almost a malevolent practical joke – Wheatley had no hesitation in whacking them with a shoe. When Wheatley complained, Summers simply said "I like spiders".

After dinner (or possibly the following morning: Wheatley's accounts vary) Summers showed Wheatley into a small room with a large pile of books lying on the floor. Picking up a leather bound book, Summers assured Wheatley it was very rare (he could have described it as being "of the last rarity", a phrase of which he was fond) and that it was just the thing Wheatley needed. Not only that, but – although it was worth far more – he could let Wheatley have it for a mere fifty pounds.

Wheatley didn't recognise the title, didn't feel he could afford it, and didn't want it. As politely as possible, he said he no longer collected that type of book. A moment later, he had never seen such an expression come over a human face. Summers' mask slipped, and from benevolent calm he suddenly became "positively demoniac" with fury, throwing the book at the floor.

Goodwill had broken down, and the Wheatleys were

anxious to escape. There was a well-known wheeze of the time for escaping from dull country house parties, and this is what they used. (A 1933 manual of etiquette gives the drill: "You must be careful not to telephone or telegraph from the house and, in every other way, to cover up your tracks . . . evolve some telegraph code for your family. You wire "How is Fido?" and promptly receive a message: "Grandma dying come home immediately.")

Wheatley left Summers's house on Sunday morning for the Post Office, where he sent a telegram to the nanny, asking her to send a wire saying young Colin was ill. It arrived at Alresford shortly after lunch, allowing them to pack hastily and leave. They motored home, and Wheatley never saw Summers ("the perhaps not so Reverend gentleman") again.

★

At any rate, that is the account that Wheatley gives in his autobiography and elsewhere, but Summers's surviving letters to him tell a different story. Although Wheatley had drawn heavily on Summers's work for *The Devil Rides Out* he didn't make contact with him until after it was published, when they struck up a warm correspondence.

Summers enjoyed *The Devil Rides Out* immensely: he found it so unputdownable he had to delay work on correcting the proofs of his own book *The Playhouse of Pepys* until he had finished it. He was particularly impressed by Wheatley's power of narrative and by the way he blended fact and fiction ("one stops now and again to ask oneself where the first ends and the latter begins, which is a very subtle achievement").

Some of this so-called fact was from Summers himself, of course; he commended Wheatley on the accuracy of his description of Prince Borghese's Satanic temple, although he had to tell him it was in Rome and not Venice. "I actually saw the *Templum Palladium*," he added, "and naturally at the time the thing caused a resounding scandal."

Summers visited the Wheatleys in London in July 1935,

317

when he talked and talked and talked; Joan may have found it a strain. They nevertheless went down to stay with Summers and his partner, Hector Stuart-Forbes, at Wykeham House, Alresford, for the weekend bridging August–September, and they seem not to have fallen out too badly because correspondence continues cordially (although Wheatley told him how busy he was, as he had with Crowley) into the Autumn, by which time Summers had moved to Brighton. They met again in London, and at Christmas 1935 Summers seems to have given him an inscribed copy of his book *The Werewolf*.

Wheatley's story about the rare book may be inspired by Summers trying to borrow five pounds – more than it sounds, in 1935[1] – in October, and offering him the Gothic novel *Varney the Vampire* ("a rarity of the first order") as security on the loan, telling him it was worth a hundred pounds. Wheatley evidently checked and found it was worth no such sum, leading to Summers's wonderfully diplomatic but unmistakably 'caught out' reply "It is very good of you to have made enquiries about Varney the Vampire. . . . How prices have dropped !"

★

Wheatley's relationship with Summers cooled, and he may not have liked Crowley very much in the first place, but he always remembered Rollo Ahmed with affection. Ahmed was a magical acquaintance of Crowley, whose diary records a demonstration announced by Ahmed in which he was to drink a bottle of whisky and remain completely sober, due to his mastery of the mystic arts. The appointed time came and there was "one absentee: Rollo."

Ahmed was to all intents and purposes West Indian, but he claimed to be from Egypt, which increased Wheatley's respect for him. He had apparently travelled extensively in the jungles of South America and in Asia, and it was in

---

[1] At today's values about £250 by purchasing power or £1000 by earnings, which were relatively lower then.

Burma that he had taken up yoga, at which he was now an expert.

After the great success of *The Devil Rides Out* a publisher asked Wheatley to write a non-fiction book on magic, which he felt unqualified to do. Instead he recommended Ahmed, who wrote *The Black Art*. Originally to have been entitled *The Left Hand path: A Study of Black Magic*, this was a global condemnation in the Summers tradition but with more attention to anthropology and the horrible doings of "primitive peoples." He dedicated it to Wheatley, who wrote a warm introduction, and he followed it with a novel, *I Rise: The Life Story of a Negro*.

Wheatley had three stories about Ahmed. On one occasion he had Ahmed round with a man from the Society for Psychic Research, and the man asked Wheatley if he had seen the little black imp hopping about behind Ahmed. Wheatley hadn't, and it did cross his mind that the man might be pulling his leg. Later he heard that Ahmed had bungled a ritual and failed to master a demon, who made all his teeth fall out. On a happier note, Wheatley was very impressed that when they had Ahmed round to Queen's Gate one cold evening, Ahmed had come all the way from Clapham without an overcoat and yet his hands were "warm as toast".

This was apparently due to his mastery of yoga, and he drew up a course in it for Dennis and Joan to follow. Most of it was about health and correct breathing, and Wheatley was keen to get on to more advanced areas, notably awakening the Kundalini power, but Ahmed replied "I think that the Kundalini or spinal concentration is just a bit dangerous for you at the present, as you have not yet established the Breathing. I am anxious to give you the best, but feel that we must make haste slowly."

Instead, Ahmed substituted "Transmutation of the Reproductive Energy for Brain Stimulation"; "The energy thus transmuted may be turned into new channels and used to great advantage."

Wheatley failed to stick at his yoga. Ahmed was meanwhile

having trouble with what he called "the demon finance" – already known to Tombe and Wheatley as "the Boodle Fiend" – and making a precarious living by giving public lectures on the South Coast, such as 'The Magic of the Mind' by The International Lecturer and Psychologist Rollo Ahmed: "Extraordinary demonstrations, and a brilliant demonstration by the only coloured author in Europe". There would be a silver collection afterwards (a half crown, two and sixpence, was about five pounds today) and the further offer of instruction in Yoga, "adapted for Western vibrations".

Ahmed lived in a fourth floor flat at 23 Old Stein, Brighton, but with Wheatley's help as a referee he was trying to rent a house or bungalow in the Worthing or Hove area, particularly for the benefit of his sick wife, and he eventually found one in Shoreham. Unknown to Wheatley, Ahmed had already served two prison sentences for fraud, and was to go down for a longer one in 1946. Wheatley found him some work with MI5 at the beginning of the war, but afterwards they lost touch.

There may have been an element of showmanship in Ahmed, but Wheatley liked him. He remembered him not only as the most interesting of the occultists he met, but as "a jolly fellow", and that always mattered to Wheatley.

*

Another top chap in the field who had an element of showmanship was Harry Price, psychical researcher and "ghost hunter"; this would have reminded Wheatley of Carnacki the Ghost-Finder. Price was a skilled amateur conjuror who pioneered the scientific investigation of psychic phenomena and exposed a number of fraudulent mediums, although suspicions of fraud subsequently arose around Price himself. He seems to have ruthlessly exposed nine-tenths of supposedly supernatural events but then become excessively enthusiastic about the remainder, with an element of gullibility or worse. "They don't want the debunk," he once said of the public, "they want the bunk, and that is what we'll give them."

Price had recently been involved in what can only be

described as a publicity stunt, when with the collaboration of the once famous Professor Joad, later to come unstuck through travelling without a railway ticket, he staged the performance of a mediaeval ritual in Germany. This involved a virgin girl and a goat, which was supposed to metamorphose into a handsome young man. The goat remained unchanged, surprising nobody, and Price claimed that this exposed the fatuity of Black Magic in the modern world.

A year earlier he had told a journalist that there were many Satanists in England.

> The devotees are a degraded type, and they find secrecy one of the allurements of the cult . . . I am of the opinion, however, that the headquarters are not here. I know there is one in Lyons, and also there are many followers in Paris . . . I have attended a Black Mass in Paris. It was both spectacular and startling, but most of the performances are reserved for the initiates. They are to be guessed at rather than described.

Price had a private income, accumulated a library of around 20,000 books, and was a member of the Reform Club. Wheatley and Joan could have him to dinner at Queen's Gate without fearing he would behave badly, unlike Crowley. He was very English in manner (like Wheatley himself, "Price was as totally English as a man can be," remembered a friend, "a person impossible to think of as other than English") and he radiated boyish enthusiasm, which would no doubt have rubbed off on Wheatley.

Price's finest hour came in the investigation of Borley Rectory, supposedly "the world's best authenticated haunted house". Price went there with a suitcase full of recording gadgets and a hamper from Fortnum and Mason, although Fortnums were not to blame when a bottle of Gevry Chambertin turned into black ink. Price wrote no less than three books about the complicated web of events at Borley, which included a possible murder, a coach, a nun, and some poltergeist scribblings.

Witnesses included a servant girl, a clergyman and his family, and a second clergyman and his wife: the Reverend and Mrs Foyster. It now seems Marianne Foyster played the lead role in faking phenomena, but Borley was the site of multiple frauds and collusions. Colluding parties may have included Price himself, who had stumbled into a network of what one commentator calls "cruel tricks played upon one another by the members of a household which lived in an atmosphere of obsessive love, sexual jealousy and suspicion."

When it comes to fraud, however, a desperate former army officer, one Captain Gregson, trumped the lot of them in 1939. He torched the place and burnt it to the ground for the insurance money, in a Welcomes-style fire.

★

Wheatley had mixed feelings about occultists, and in some ways he found them rather wretched. For one thing, they never seemed to have any money: they were always trying to cadge or sell him something. "No saying is less true than that 'the Devil looks after his own' " he wrote; "I have never yet met anyone who practised Black, or even Grey, Magic who was not hard up."

Now he was ready to write his masterpiece, the book that would virtually invent hardcore occultism – or its popular image – for the twentieth century. It was "a new adventure featuring the four friends from The Forbidden Territory," originally entitled *Black Magic* and *Talisman of Evil*; but it is better known to us under its published title, *The Devil Rides Out*.

CHAPTER TWENTY-SIX

The Devil in his Decade

Things were looking ominous in the Thirties. Unemployment reached two and a half million in 1931, and abroad, in addition to the spectre of Bolshevism, there were rising dictators and the possibility of war. To Auden it was a "low dishonest decade," while for *Sunday Dispatch* editor Collin Brooks – an associate of both Crowley and the press baron Lord Rothermere – it was nothing less than "the devil's decade".

Hitler had come to power in 1933, and paganism had become official in Germany. Third Reich historian Michael Burleigh has argued that Nazism itself is best understood as a political religion. The economist John Maynard Keynes made a similar point about Russia: "If Communism achieves a certain success, it will achieve it not as an improved economic technique but as a religion." Irrational forces were now abroad. Wittgenstein caught this atavistic return to a pre-Enlightenment world when he said of the Nazis: "Just think what it must mean, when the government of a country is taken over by a set of gangsters. The dark ages are coming again. I wouldn't be surprised . . . to see such horrors as people being burnt alive as witches."

People expected a new war to be like the last, but worse. There would be Somme-like attrition, but there would also be new weapons such as "death rays", and the poison-gas bombing of cities. The technology of aerial war and bombing was known to have improved, and it was widely believed London would be completely destroyed in the opening hours of a new conflict. "We thought that the war would be as depicted in H.G.Wells's film, *Things to Come*," remembered writer Robert Aickman, "involving almost universal and nearly instantaneous obliteration."

When Alfred Hitchcock contacted Wheatley and asked

him to write a screenplay about the bombing of London, Wheatley remembered "the terror depicted on his normally cherubic countenance" and the vividness of the scenario: "as he talked to me about it I could almost hear the bombs bursting."

★

Conservative and Establishment opinion saw Hitler as the lesser of two evils, and even as a useful bulwark against Bolshevism. Respectable figures like Lloyd George could admire what Hitler was doing for Germany – he wrote an enthusiastic piece about it in the *Daily Express* in 1936 – and as late as 1937 Lord Halifax, the Deputy Prime Minister, could say to Hitler "on behalf of the British Government I congratulate you on crushing communism in Germany and standing as a bulwark against Russia." Wheatley was very much of this persuasion.

The anti-war faction covered a whole spectrum from pacifists to fascists. Prominent advocates of peace included the novelist Sir Philip Gibbs; press barons Lord Rothermere, Lord Northcliffe and Lord Beaverbrook; the Aga Khan; conservative politician R.A. 'Rab' Butler; Lord Londonderry; the Duke of Westminster; Montagu Norman, the governor of the Bank of England; and many others. The *Times* newspaper was also notably in favour of Appeasement.

Wheatley particularly admired Sir Philip Gibbs, whose loathing of war came from being a war correspondent in the First, and in the Thirties he wrote several anti-war novels. Another honourable example was Lord Beaverbrook, for whom Appeasement was a less craven policy than the word suggests. Beaverbrook's emphasis was on Isolation: he believed Britain should keep out of Europe and stay close to her Empire, while re-arming. He had helped prevent Britain going to war with Turkey in 1922, and liked to quote Bonar Law: "We cannot act alone as the policemen of the world."

Historian A.J.P.Taylor commented in his biography of Beaverbrook that if the British people had been told "the price of overthrowing Hitler would be twenty-five million dead, they might have hesitated . . . they might even have hesitated . . . if they had been told that that the price of destroying Germany would be Soviet domination of Eastern Europe."

"Do not be led into a warlike course by our hatred of dictators," Beaverbrook wrote in the *Express*, "Let the people who are misgoverned free themselves of their autocrats." In 1934, a few months before *The Devil Rides Out*, the *Express* produced a book of war photographs with a skull on the cover entitled *Covenants with Death*: "The purpose of this book is to reveal the horror, suffering and essential bestiality of modern war."

One consequence of the *Express*'s anti-war line was that Tom Driberg, in his Hickey column, regularly assured the public there would be no war (as late as 1939 "Hickey" was writing "My tip: no war this crisis."). When he collected his Hickey columns for book publication he quietly suppressed his anti-war statements and said he always knew that war was inevitable.

Driberg and Wheatley both exaggerate how early they were prepared for war in their later recollections, along the lines observed by Rupert Croft-Cooke in his comments on Munich. When Chamberlain proclaimed "Peace in our time", "The rapturous crowds at the airport who cheered him hysterically as he waved that ridiculous piece of paper were not exceptional people – they cheered for all but a tiny minority of not necessarily wiser Britons." To which he adds the very apposite footnote, "Though in that tiny minority, I have since been interested to note, were almost all the autobiographers of the future . . ."

★

Beaverbrook, meanwhile, was producing rhetoric that wouldn't be out of place in *The Devil Rides Out*: "The powers of darkness are gathering," he wrote in July 1934, reminding readers that interference in Europe would mean war. Later the same month, he added "The British Empire

325

meddling in the concerns of the Balkans and Central Europe is sure to be embroiled in war, pestilence and famine"; invoking the Four Horsemen of the Apocalypse: War, Pestilence, Famine, and Death.

Beaverbrook played an exceptional role in both wars. He was Minister for Information in the First (a war he bitterly regretted, believing no British interests were threatened and that it was caused by secret promises made to France) and in the Second he became Minister for Aircraft Production: in this role he helped win the Battle of Britain, true to his vision of a fortress island. Rothermere's pro-Appeasement stance, on the other hand, was more tainted by his political sympathies.

Rothermere believed "The sturdy young Nazis are Europe's guardians against the Communist danger," and he was a supporter of Mosley: he gave Mosley a weekly page for Blackshirt material in the *Sunday Dispatch*. Mosley found the paper's coverage a mixed blessing, and in May 1934 he wrote to the editor:

> All this human interest business – "Blackshirt patting head of mastiff"; "Come to the cook house door"; "Girl fencers" etc – cuts no ice for the purposes of our organisation, and I imagine are liable to bore your public. It may have been a good thing to do it for the first week or two in order to show that Blackshirts have no horns or tails, but beyond that it serves no good purpose and may even do harm.

Rothermere's flagship paper, *The Daily Mail*, was also strongly pro-Mosley; so much so, that in January 1934 it carried an illustrated piece by Rothermere himself, with the headline "Hurrah for the Blackshirts."

And so it was that on Halloween 1934 the *Mail* began a thrilling new serial novel ("Startling! Provocative! Romantic!"), about a struggle to avoid a new war with Germany. It was *The Devil Rides Out*, by "master of sensation" Dennis Wheatley.

★

"The Duke de Richleau and Rex Van Ryn had gone into dinner at eight o'clock," it begins, "but coffee was not served until after ten." Continuing the formula established in the first two Richleau books, one of the chums is in trouble and misses their reunion dinner. This time it is Simon Aron, "a young man brought to the verge of madness by his greed for gold": he has fallen in with Satanists in the hope of obtaining clairvoyant powers to play the stockmarket.

After dinner, Rex and the Duke are driven to St.John's Wood in the Duke's Hispano, where Simon has leased a house. Anthony Powell writes of the area's "Victorian dis-repute as a bower of love nests and houses of assignation," and its "tradition of louche goings-on". William Sansom expands: it is "bizarre and dramatic . . . hushed . . . [with] conservatories, thick bushes, covered drives and reticent windows . . . The Wood . . . among the decorative lilacs and laburnums, was discreetly orgiastic. Relics of this time are still to be seen – a number of high front garden doors, stoutly placed between pillars surmounted by eagle or pineapple, still have peepholes."

This is just the place for Wheatley-style luxury Satanism, and for Wheatley's readers the very words "St.John's Wood" have acquired an aura. Like the words "Hoyo de Monterrey" and "Imperial Tokay", the magic of Wheatley is upon them.

Simon's house is at the end of a cul-de-sac, in reality Melina Place. The doors set in the street wall, some of them leading straight into entrance halls, add to the ambience of leafy seclusion and slightly sinister privacy. The upper storeys are visible above whispering trees, and it is in one of these upper storeys that Simon has built an astronomical observa-tory with a pentagram on the floor.

Politely gatecrashing Simon's party, Rex and the Duke meet the Satanists. One of these is the lovely Tanith, with whom Rex falls in love, but the others are an extraordinary bunch: like the Napoleonic marshals that Wheatley collected in later life, they would make a fine set of porcelain figures.

There is a "Chinaman" in Mandarin costume; an albino; an Irish bard with a kilt and a pot belly; a "Eurasian" with only one arm, the left; a red-faced "Teuton" with a hare lip; a "Babu" Indian; a scraggy American woman with beetling eyebrows that meet in the middle; an elderly French woman with a beaky parrot nose who smokes cigars; and a man with a mutilated ear, Castelnau, a French banker who introduced Simon to Satanism.

Their grotesque qualities show a simplistic characterisation of evil by physical disability, and it is also noticeable that most of them have the misfortune not to be English. The fuller significance of their physical idiosyncrasies is probably the popular Adlerian psychology of the inter-war years. Alfred Adler believed that inferiority complexes were a driving force in human nature, an idea which spread into the saloon bar wisdom that Napoleon and Hitler caused trouble because they were short. Similarly, Wheatley's friend Anthony Powell wrote in his notebook "No doubt it was Tamerlaine's bad leg that made him such a nuisance to the world."

The leader of the Satanists is Damien Mocata, a defrocked priest whose physical features – bald head and hypnotic eyes – were based on Crowley, while his refined fruitiness and preciousness probably owe something to Summers. "He does the most lovely needlework," Simon explains:

> . . . petit point and that sort of thing you know, and he's terribly fastidious about keeping his plump little hands scrupulously clean. As a companion he is delightful to be with except that he will smother himself in expensive perfumes and is as greedy as a schoolboy about sweets. He had huge boxes of fondants, crystallized fruits, and marzipan sent over from Paris twice a week when he was at St.John's Wood.

Now and then he has strange fits that send him out on missions unknown, returning unshaven and stinking of drink in torn clothes, as if he "had been wallowing in every sort of debauchery down in the slums of the East End."

328

Mocata's background – half-Irish, half-French – is in keeping with Catholic diabolism, since France was thought to be the place where Satanism flourished. However, his name, which now seems so perfectly part of his character, is about something else again: it is a distinguished Portuguese Jewish name, predominant in the London gold market since the seventeenth century, and evidently part of Wheatley's heightened consciousness of Jews. A Thirties piece in the National Socialist League Monthly – unsigned but seemingly by William Joyce, better known as Lord Haw-Haw, whom we shall meet soon at one of Wheatley's parties – complains about the financial power of the "Rothschilds, Sassoons, Mocattas, and Goldsmids".

Rex and the Duke rescue Simon with a sock on the jaw. Getting him into the Duke's treasure-packed Curzon Street flat, with its ikons and Buddha and ivories, the Duke first hypnotises him and then places a supernatural charm around his neck to keep him safe. In one of the stranger moments in Thirties fiction, it is "a small golden swastika set with precious stones". "He'll be pretty livid," says Rex: "Fancy hanging a Nazi swastika round the neck of a professing Jew."

The Duke explains that the swastika is "the oldest symbol of wisdom and right thinking in the world . . . used by every race and in every country at some time or another." The swastika was still not as associated with Nazism as it has been since the War. As an Eastern charm, the swastika appeared on the books of Kipling (and, perhaps less innocently, it was given away as a lucky watch fob by Coca-Cola, who later sponsored the Berlin Olympics).

The Duke's comments are not pro-Nazi: he says that although "the Nazis bring discredit on the Swastika, as the Spanish inquisition did upon the cross, that could have no effect upon its true meaning" (and Wheatley later propagates the idea that Nazi swastikas go "the wrong way", like the Christian cross inverted; this is not very convincing, because ancient swastikas go both ways, but it is an attempt to reinforce the idea of Nazism as evil).

Germany is, however, specifically exonerated from having

caused the First War. "I thought the Germans got a bit above themselves," says Rex mildly, to which the Duke says "You fool! Germany did not make the War. It came out of Russia." It was caused by Rasputin, in his role as Black Magician. This exemption from blame is part of the book's central message: to borrow a phrase from Noel Coward, "Let's not be beastly to the Hun."

Now Mocata and the Satanists are trying to cause another war. "The Four Horsemen of the Apocalypse," says the Duke: "War, Plague, Famine and Death. We all know what happened the last time those four terrible entities were unleashed to cloud the brains of statesmen and rulers"; ". . . if they are loosed again, it will be final Armaggedon"; "to prevent suffering and death coming to countless millions we are justified in anything."

Wheatley's earlier title for the book was *Talisman of Evil*, and the Satanists plan to start the War by finding the Talisman of Set, a mummified Egyptian phallus belonging to the god Set: "a forerunner of the Christian Devil, Osiris's younger brother." If they can get their hands on this cigar-like object then (as Wheatley was able to inform newspaper readers) "those dread four horsemen would come riding, invisible but all powerful, to poison the thoughts of peace-loving people and manipulate unscrupulous statesmen, influencing them to plunge Europe into fresh calamity."

★

As we have seen, Crowley felt his 'Guardian Angel' Aiwass was a version of Set, and he thought his "Aeon of Horus" would be the era of glorious war. Crowley liked to believe the publication of his books had caused wars: successive editions of *The Book of the Law* had caused the Balkan War, the Great War ("the might of this Magick burst out and caused a catastrophe to civilisation"), and later the Sino-Japanese War and the Munich crisis.

Wheatley's novel was in tune with more than he fully understood, and he was getting extraordinary mileage from a smattering of occult knowledge. The Duke's great spiel about magic[1], repeated almost verbatim in later books, begins with the reality of hypnosis. It moves down a slippery slope to telepathy, then the powers of the human will, and before long the reader is plunged into the conflict between the forces of Eternal Light and Eternal Darkness.

Many occultists began with Wheatley's books, although they may not always admit it. From *The Devil Rides Out* alone, the main planks of an occult worldview are clear: mind rules matter; spirit is transcendent; the human soul is eternal; we move through successive incarnations, "towards the light"; and there are "Hidden Masters" and "Lords of Light," who tend to be Tibetan. The theosophical and Gnostic elements in all this come largely from Maurice Magré's 1931 *The Return of the Magi*, which Wheatley read, with more archaic and picturesque details picked up from Grillot de Givry's 1931 *Witchcraft, Magic and Alchemy*.

Wheatley's writing tends to be research-heavy, and this research plays a special role in the occult books. *The Devil Rides Out*'s encyclopaedic packing with occult lore is so insistent that not only do readers learn about the astral plane, elemental spirits, the inner meaning of alchemy, familiars, grimoires, scrying, and the rest, but it tends to cause a suspension of disbelief. It is also richly atmospheric, with the Golden Dawn grades – Ipsissimus, Magister Templi, Neophyte, Zelator and so on, – and "passing the Abyss", the "dispersion of Choronzon", "St.Walburga's Eve", the "Clavicule of Solomon", "Our Lady of Babalon", and what-have-you.

Within the book's occult framework, Wheatley had now found his central idea: that of Manichaeanism, the conflict between the forces of light and dark, or absolute good and absolute evil. Umberto Eco describes the James Bond books as Manichaean, but the universe of Wheatley is *literally* Manichaean in the theological sense. The Duke de Richleau explains it, and Richard and Simon complete his explanation: "Surely you are proclaiming the Manichaean heresy? . . ."

[1] In Chapter Three, 'The Esoteric Doctrine.'

"Even today many thinking people . . . believe that it holds the core of the only true religion."

Back in the fourth century, Saint Augustine had rejected Manichaeanism as psychologically inauthentic, in the sense that everyone can do some bad and some good. In the words of T.S.Eliot: "pure villainy is one kind of purity in which it is difficult to believe. Even the devil is a fallen angel." But this all-out conflict between good and evil is useful for pulp fiction and propaganda. It corresponded to something intrinsic to Wheatley's psyche, a tendency to 'split' the world into good and bad, and a lifelong ability to see things in reassuringly simple, black-and-white terms; or perhaps an inability to see them otherwise.

★

Occult fiction had tended to be a relatively subtle affair, like the quality ghost story, but Wheatley dragged it firmly into the thriller genre, combining black magic with hand grenades and car chases. So generously thrilling is *The Devil Rides Out*, in fact, that it ends on a plateau of rolling climaxes, any one of which would be good value in a lesser book.

First comes the siege in the pentagram, borrowed from the occult fiction of William Hope Hodgson. The friends are holed up in a pentagram on the floor of a country house library, and their ordeal ends with an attack by the Angel of Death, who rides a black horse and can never return empty handed (borrowed from an anecdote of a similar siege in Alexander Cannon's 1933 *The Invisible Influence*, a book the Duke recommends to Rex). It is only defeated by the Duke's pronunciation of two lines from "the dread Sussamma ritual" (again borrowed straight from Hodgson, along with "ab-humans" and "saiitii").

As if that wasn't enough, the Eatons' little daughter Fleur is then snatched by the Satanists, who intend to sacrifice her. The friends track Mocata and his associates to an empty Satanic temple in Paris, only to be mistakenly arrested as Satanists in a French police raid. Escaping after a fight, they follow Mocata in an aeroplane chase to a Greek monastery

The Black Art (1936) by Rollo Ahmed.

Rollo Ahmed performing a ritual.

The Devil Rides Out (1934).

"The lovely Tanith."

where the Talisman is hidden. Here, "the perverted maniac playing the part of the devil's priest would rip the child open from throat to groin while offering her soul to Hell".

Mocata is just raising the knife when Marie-Lou remembers *The Red Book of Appin* (taken from Montague Summers). She has seen it in a dream, and she utters a sentence she saw written in strange characters: "They only who Love without Desire shall have power granted to them in the Darkest Hour". All Hell breaks loose: the ground is rocked as if by an earthquake, the crypt spins, the Talisman of Set falls uselessly to the floor. The phallic power of the Satanists has been defeated by the power of love.

"Time ceased, and it seemed that for a thousand thousand years they floated." The friends find themselves back at Cardinal's Folly, as if it had all been a shared dream. Only the fact that the Duke still has the phallus of Set, which he throws in a furnace, suggests it has been something more. With the world moving steadily towards war, escaping the process of time was a popular motif in Thirties fiction – most famously in *Lost Horizon* (1933), written by Wheatley's friend James Hilton, with its fabulously timeless Tibetan-style kingdom of Shangri-La – and the Duke explains in the book's closing line: "it is my belief that during the period of our dream journey we have been living in what the moderns call the fourth dimension – divorced from time."

★

It has been widely observed that the crisis of the Thirties led many writers "to Moscow or Rome", to Communism or the Church, and Wheatley's turn to supernaturalism is a variant of the latter. Given the link between occultism and right-wing thinking, it is oddly appropriate that the greatest occult novel of the twentieth century should have a subtext of peace with Nazi Germany, and have first appeared in the pro-Blackshirt *Daily Mail*. In all his interviews about his career and the genesis of *The Devil Rides Out*, Wheatley never once mentions the salient fact that it is an Appeasement novel.

Wheatley's masterstroke was to put a disclaimer at the front, insisting that he had never been to an occult ceremony and warning readers not to dabble. Framing the alleged reality of Black Magic ("still practised in London, and other cities, at the present day") so negatively was more powerful and convincing than any other stance on it could have been.

Wheatley's life would never be quite the same again. He had hit the occult vein that would immortalise him in popular culture, like Agatha Christie's demon brother. Wheatley was far from confident about what he had done: he worried that there was too much research showing in *The Devil Rides Out* and that "the data was overwhelming the plot", not realising that the "data" was so atmospheric in itself that for many readers it made the book. He originally put a questionnaire at the back of the first edition (page 329, excised from most copies), asking readers if they thought there was too much complicated background in the way of the plot. "Or do they find subjects such as the occult lend additional interest to thrilling action?"

Reviews were largely favourable. Compton Mackenzie quibbled Wheatley's Latin and his haziness about theology but admired the "cracking pace." The reviewer in the *Times Literary Supplement* conceded it was "a good story" but complained that the powers of evil were not evil enough. "There is no torture," he wrote, and as for the "boiled baby", it "appears to have died naturally." TLS reviews were anonymous in those days, but this man must have been the paper's Resident Fiend.

*

Wheatley soon discovered that his occult books drew a different postbag from the rest. A man in Edinburgh signing himself "The Christ" wrote a series of letters about the Book of Revelations. Another wrote from Broadmoor to say that since the worship of Christ had failed to stop wars or improve anything over the previous 2000 years, it was time we gave the Devil a chance.

Wheatley seems to have had little sense of whether writers

were pulling his leg. One man wrote to quibble the location of the Satanic temple in St.John's Wood, and said it was on the other side of the Finchley Road ("I went there to a meeting some little time ago, but I suppose you thought it policy not to give away its actual situation in your book"). Wheatley could now cite this letter as further evidence for the reality of Satanism.

One of his most involved correspondences came from a woman in Essex who claimed to have been sold to the Devil by her father (or mother: Wheatley isn't quite consistent in his telling of this story, but there does seem to be a real woman behind it). Wheatley met her, and she told him she was unable to go into a church without feeling sick, and that she had to be careful not to be angry, because bad things would happen to people if she wished them ill.

Wheatley thought she was like someone resigned to having a rare and incurable disease. She made no effort to borrow money or seek Wheatley's help in having anything published. "I am convinced that there was nothing whatever evil about her," Wheatley remembered, "but it certainly seemed that she was *a focus for evil* and she spoke of her sad fate with such simple candour that I found it extraordinarily difficult to believe that she was romancing deliberately." Her story later became Wheatley's inspiration for *To The Devil − A Daughter*.

★

Crowley had written to Wheatley since their lunch at the Hungaria. "I would love another chat, esp. about *Magick*, as you're on a book; I'd like to hear what you think of mine." Wheatley was not keen to continue his acquaintance with Crowley, and made the excuse of being too busy with work.

Having failed to make a useful disciple of Wheatley, Crowley's correspondence took on a more jibing quality. "Most ingenious," he wrote at one point, "but really a little Ely Culbertson, to advertise your love of rare editions in a thriller blurb!" (Ely Culbertson was an American bridge player, whom Crowley evidently found vulgar).

Now, the day after the first *Mail* instalment appeared, Crowley wrote him a brief note on the letterhead of the Hotel Washington, Curzon Street, Mayfair. "Dear Dennis Wheatley," it said, "Did you elope with the adorable Tanith? Or did the witches get you Hallowe'en?"

The Right Kind of Dope

Along with *The Devil Rides Out*, Wheatley wrote a short anti-war polemic entitled 'Pills of Honour'. King Alexander of Yugoslavia had been assassinated at Marseilles in October, reminding Wheatley of Sarajevo, and a plebiscite for the Saar – part of Germany given to France after the First War – was coming in January.

> Hitler will be a ruined man if he fails to secure the return of the Saar as an integral portion of the Reich. France, armed to the teeth, is determined to act if he tries to force the issue. A few shots fired by either side and *we are liable* under the pact which our government has made to enter into a war . . .

Wheatley recommended the novels of Sir Philip Gibbs; "should be compulsory reading in every school". Together with a "truly patriotic" section of the press, such books fostered "the growing opinion that Great Britain should stand out in splendid isolation, refusing absolutely to be involved in any further continental squabbles"; "no matter how many bullies may wave their swords on the continent, nothing but the defence of our Empire and our homes can possibly justify our taking up arms again."

The alternative, if Britain felt obliged to honour "criminal pacts" made by old gentlemen in pleasant spots such as Locarno, would be apocalyptic. At least in the First War the nation had time to adjust to war conditions "before the bulk of us went down into the maelstrom that cost the nation a million lives and the accumulated treasure of three generations", but next time would be different, due to bombing. "If war were declared tonight, large areas of London and many of our other provincial cities would be laid waste before the dawn."

Wheatley's evocation of the bombing and the horrors of war – dwelt on at some length – is very much of its time, but his emphasis on curtailed freedom and the onset of wartime bureaucracy is more distinctively his own: "those of us who survive the first aerial attack will collect our ration cards from the local authorities in the morning."

Every soul in the country will find himself in the grip of those relentless ordinances which did not quite smother personal liberty in the last war until 1917. The steel shutters of the war machine will have closed down upon every form of protest and argument.

As for the war itself, and the enormous sacrifice of youth ordered by a few old men, Wheatley had a suggestion. To show they were really sincere, the Cabinet should make an honourable example and commit suicide en masse: "If Mr Macdonald is so anxious that Britain should lead the world to a permanent peace, let him cease reducing our armaments to below safety level and instead give *this example*."

"The frontier of Britain lies upon the Rhine," declared Mr Baldwin loudly.

"Quite," murmured the chief official of the government laboratories. "And tomorrow, all of us who still remain alive will know you have died with that conviction. Would you now kindly take a pill please."

"By honouring our obligations we set an example to the wo-r-r-ld," announced Mr Ramsay MacDonald dreamily.

"Exactly, Sir, and the remnants of the British nation will honour the memory of your cabinet which so unhesitatingly sacrificed itself to the spirit of true leadership."

The chief official of the government laboratory again held out his box. "Would you also kindly take a pill. Their action is rapid and quite painless, Sir."

★

The Devil Rides Out was launched with a party at the Prince of Wales Hotel in De Vere Gardens, Kensington, where Harry Preston laid on a three-round boxing match as part of the night's entertainment. The party doubled as the launch for the first of Joan's six novels, *No Ordinary Virgin*, written under the pseudonym of Eve Chaucer (others included *Better to Marry*, *It is Easier for a Camel*, and *Silk Sheets and Bread-crumbs*). These were quite racy, perhaps not unlike the novel that bookshop assistant Gordon Comstock urges on a cus-tomer in Orwell's *Keep the Aspidistra Flying*: "Something modern? Something by Barbara Bedworthy for instance? Have you read *Almost A Virgin*?"

The Paternoster machinery rolled into action behind *The Devil Rides Out* and The Crime Book Society (publishers of The Crime Book Magazine, from Paternoster House) made it their January Choice. Reviews were good: Wheatley's friend James Hilton, writing in the *Telegraph*, described it as "the best thing of its kind since *Dracula*."

There was a dissenting voice in *Time and Tide*, where "Roderick Random" attacked Wheatley as a symptom of declining standards. "There is at present, particularly in England and America, a very widespread movement to degrade contemporary standards and values," he said, and Wheatley ("merely a dummy figure, a target selected by chance for the arrow of attack") was a case in point, although unaware of what he was doing and "unimportant except as one example of a vicious tendency."

Also in the dock was reviewer Mr Ralph Straus, guilty of claiming he could not remember "a more vivid or more cunningly told story". There were only three possible explanations for this: either Straus's memory was bad, his reading was very limited, or he really did take Wheatley's work seriously, in which case "he is to be pitied". (Random overlooked a fourth explanation, that he was a friend, which was in fact the case).

Singing from the same sheet as the Leavises, with their

attack on "cheap and easy" reading pleasure in *Fiction and the Reading Public*, Random dissected Wheatley's "insidious and dangerous" work, which amounted to "the crudest forms of sensationalism plus a style that makes one wince." Wheatley's reader survey at the back of the book was further evidence against him: it was just a way of saying "Am I supplying you with the right kind of dope? Let me know if I'm not and I'll do better next time."

Wheatley wrote back. He could appreciate Mr.Random's point of view, he said, because he read serious modern fiction such as Huxley, Waugh, Norman Douglas, Radclyffe Hall, James Hilton, and Baron Corvo. Unfortunately appreciating literature and being able to write it were two different things, and Wheatley stressed that thriller writers like himself had "no pretensions to literary merit"; in fact, he was "perhaps better aware than most of my short-comings where fine English is concerned."

Wheatley's defence was that in "these days of uncertainty and general trouble" people needed exciting books to distract them from their worries, and they were too tired after work to read "the finest type of English novel". If it wasn't for work like Wheatley's, "the great bulk of the present reading public would give up reading books altogether and turn for their relaxation to the cinema instead" – a prospect to fill a Thirties Leavisite with dread.

★

That Spring the Wheatleys went to Rome; it was Wheatley's first visit. Wheatley greatly admired the ancient Romans and the civilising effects of their empire: "The benefits they conferred upon the people they ruled were inestimable . . . With the fall of Rome in AD 410 the light of Western civilisation went out . . ."

Wheatley was fascinated to walk in the old Forum, which had been a slum until Mussolini cleared and restored it, and to see the floor of the Senate House where Caesar died, which had just been cleared of 1500 years worth of accumulated rubbish. Wheatley was a great admirer of Mussolini.

"Mussolini made Italy a far more law–abiding and less smelly place than he found it, and performed that miracle without, apparently, interfering very much with the happiness of the average Italian."

Wheatley's enthusiasm for Mussolini may seem naive now, or worse, but it was widespread. Back in the Twenties, Lord Rothermere had written an article in his *Sunday Pictorial* entitled 'Mussolini: What Europe owes to him.' Readers were told "He did much more than save Italy, for he really saved the whole Western world." Macdonald, Chamberlain and Churchill[1] all saw him in positive terms, and J.C.Squire saw him as "a nice Napoleon, with less education, an equally strong historical sense, and more compassion." In February 1934 the *Saturday Review* ran a full page picture captioned "Mussolini: the World's Most Benevolent Ruler": "He has dragged Italy out of the mire of Socialism and in a few years has made it the most successful and prosperous country in Europe." Better yet, "he sets an example of kindness to animals and birds."

Despite all that, there were fears that Britain would go to war with Italy over the invasion of Abyssinia, and Wheatley had a contingency plan to escape to France if this happened while he and Joan were in Rome, so they could avoid being interned as enemy aliens.

Wheatley and Joan had dinner with the British Counsellor in Rome, Sir Noel Charles, and Sir Noel produced some Hoyo de Monterrey cigars: he had got them especially, because the Duke de Richleau smokes them. Like Wheatley, Sir Noel had been through the First War – he had won the MC – and he didn't want to see another. As they went to get their coats before going to a night club, Sir Noel assured Wheatley there would be no war, and they did a little dance together in the hall.

*

[1] Churchill told Mussolini "If I had been an Italian, I am sure I would have been wholeheartedly with you from start to finish in your triumph-ant struggle against the bestial appetites and passions of Leninism."

Back home, the Wheatleys were doing a lot of entertaining at their newly rented house in St.John's Wood, and when Wheatley published a book they would give a champagne supper party for about a hundred people. Along with old friends like Links, Eastaugh and Baron, Wheatley's newer and more writerly friends at this period included Gilbert Frankau, James Hilton, Howard Spring, Pamela Frankau, and Michael Arlen, and he also knew a motley bunch of right-wing extremists, anti-Semites, and cranks.

Wheatley had become very chummy with Peter Cheyney, "Prince of Hokum". Cheyney wrote endless crime fictions in the American 'hard-boiled' style – *Dames Don't Care*, *Can Ladies Kill?*, *Dangerous Curves*, *Don't Get Me Wrong*, *I'll Say She Does* (as in "Does she go?") – and he was the creator of "Lemmy Caution", "Alonzo MacTavish", "Abie Hymie Finkelstein", English private detective "Slim Callaghan" and many others. Cheyney ran his own private investigation agency, and the boundaries between fact and fiction in his own life were distinctly blurred.

Originally known as Reg, Cheyney had been born in the East End, where his cockney father worked at Billingsgate fish market. Cheyney tried out various names including Evelyn and Everard, and was at one stage Peter du Sautoy Cheyney, before settling on the story that he was descended from the ancient Irish family of du Cheyney. Wheatley believed his real name was Leper, and that he had at one stage been a barrow boy.

Like Wheatley, Cheyney's big break came when he became an officer in the First War. His *Who's Who* entry mentions being "seriously wounded" and for a while he managed to claim a pension, which was stopped when his wound turned out to be a nick to one ear. Cheyney took an active role against the 1926 General Strike, where he made important contacts in the intelligence and police communities, and in 1931 he joined Oswald Mosley's New Party – a forerunner of the British Union of Fascists, funded by the car manufacturer Lord Nuffield – where he was head of the thug section, Mosley's so-called "Biff Boys."

Cheyney was a big man who boxed and fenced, and he affected a cloak and a gold monocle. When Wheatley first knew him he was still working as a writer-cum-private-detective-cum-journalist (he was news editor of the *Sunday Graphic*), but he concentrated on fiction after his 1936 best-seller *This Man is Dangerous*, and in 1937 Wheatley wrote a warm introduction to *You Can't Hit A Woman and Other Stories*, detailing the heroic and extraordinary life of 'The Remarkable Peter ("Ten Thousand Smackers") Cheyney.' Entering into the Americanised spirit of Cheyney's work, Wheatley told readers he was confident that "I am putting them on to a real good thing."

Wheatley remembered Cheyney as a tremendous liar but "great fun." When he stayed with the Wheatleys during the War, he arrived bearing a case of Kummel and a case of whisky: "It was enormous fun to watch this great, big, bald tough, whisky glass in hand, striding up and down our drawing-room telling the most extraordinary tales about his exploits" ("desperate encounters from which he always emerged with flying colours"). Evidently Cheyney was another "good fellow," and that excused any faults he might have had.

★

Although he had been in the New Party, Cheyney didn't follow Mosley into the BUF. Another of Wheatley's friends, William Tayleur – soon to be prominent in the new trade of "publicity" and PR – was more in touch with the evolving progress of British Fascism. "I knew Tayleur to be in sympathy with the Fascists" writes Wheatley in his autobiography, "but I thought no worse of him for that as I also inclined towards them".

Tayleur corrected Wheatley's proofs, a demanding job made worse by what Tayleur believed was Hutchinson's use of cheap unskilled labour. The texts of Wheatley's books are abysmal (*The Devil Rides Out* includes "aesthetic" for "ascetic" and "Stravinsky" for "Stavisky") and Tayleur now battled with "the worst galleys I have ever seen" thanks to Hutchinson's "inserted errors" and "blithering ineptitude."

It was through Tayleur that William Joyce came to one of Wheatley's parties. Joyce – later to achieve notoriety as "Lord Haw-Haw" for his propaganda broadcasts from Nazi Germany – was a hardened Fascist whose face had been razor-slashed from mouth to ear when fighting broke out on stage at a 1924 meeting against the Communist MP Saklatvala (and not, as he liked to claim, when he was attacked by a gang of Jews in the street)[2]. Ironically Joyce was intensely patriotic, in his fashion, but early exposure to the violence of Southern Ireland – where his family were 'ethnically cleansed' by the Catholic majority and forced to flee – made him extreme and unstable. Distantly related to James Joyce, he had a first-class degree in English and earned his living as a private tutor while working as a Director of Propaganda for the BUF.

By the time he met Wheatley, Joyce had split with Mosley and founded his own party, the more extreme and anti-Semitic National Socialist League. He outlined his ideas in *National Socialism Now*, a book Wheatley owned, with a preface by his sidekick John Beckett.

Joyce knew Wheatley's Duke de Richleau books, and probably enjoyed *The Devil Rides Out*. Along with an early interest in hypnotism, one of Joyce's personal quirks was the constant doodling of a Devil's head with a crown on it, to such an extent that MI5 noted in his file: "one curious point that might interest a psychologist . . . he could never come within reach of a pencil and paper without drawing a coronated Devil's head." Perhaps these doodlings could have been used to trace him across the wastepaper baskets of the

---

[2] There is no mystery or ambiguity about this, although Joyce's untrue story has been repeated in print. In a vivid eyewitness report, an MI5 observer saw him slashed after the meeting at Battersea turned into a general melee, with attempts to storm the stage and seize the Union Jack. Bleeding massively, his life was probably saved by a policeman who half carried him to medical help, while an associate named Webb marked his assailant and brought him down with a blow to the head from a heavy spanner. Public Records Office, file KV2 / 245.

Reich; at any rate, it is a neat instance of the links between Satanic imagery, violent disaffection and unmerited elitism. Joyce was also devoted to Marlowe's *Doctor Faustus* (he had it with him when he was captured) to such an extent that when his Nazi boss and mentor, Dietz, gave him a *Punch* cartoon of himself he signed it "from Mephistopheles to Faust."

Joyce told Wheatley it was a great pity that the Duke de Richleau books could not be published in Germany, because Simon Aron was Jewish. Nevertheless, he said Goering read all Wheatley's books and was a great fan, and he urged Wheatley to come over to Germany with him and meet the Nazi leaders.

Given Joyce's personal intensity – which grew worse with drink – his remarkable razor-slashed face, and the even more remarkable news that Goering was a Wheatley fan, you might think that having met him wouldn't easily slip Wheatley's mind. This is just what it seemed to do, however, as we shall see.

*

It is unlikely Joyce would have found much to talk about with Louis Golding, another of Wheatley's friends. Golding was a gay Jewish novelist who enjoyed the company of children (he put "cherub collecting" as a hobby in *Who's Who*) and did a great deal of work for charities and Boys' Clubs. Legendarily tight-fisted (he once gave a two-and-sixpenny edition of one of his own books as a wedding present) Golding was also vain and insecure, and worried that his books were not taken seriously by other writers, laughing at him behind his back. In this respect he was safe with Wheatley, who was no enemy of the second-rater. Golding used to give Wheatley lifts in his car, and Wheatley described him as "the wittiest man I know." Judging by the ponderous and fussily well-turned inscriptions in the books he gave Wheatley, this was generous.

It is even harder to believe Golding would have got along with Graham Seton-Hutchison, another cordial acquaintance of Wheatley. Lieutenant-Colonel Seton-Hutchison had won the DSO and MC in the First War, been wounded three times, and developed a sentimental fondness for ordinary working-class soldiers. This was expressed in his *Biography of a Batman* (an officer's soldier-servant) the story of an orphan, Piper Peter McClintock, "who now sleeps, forever young" in a military cemetery in France.

Seton-Hutchison wrote popular thrillers – *The Viper of Luxor*, *Eye for an Eye*, *Scar 77*, *The K Code Plan* and others – under the name of Graham Hutchison, combining these with non-fiction under his full name such as *Footslogger* and *Arya: The Call of the Future* (1934), which Wheatley owned. In 1933 he founded the tiny fringe Fascist party the National Workers Movement, which in 1936 became the no larger National Workers Party. Seton-Hutchison seems to have been the only member.

Seton-Hutchison was also a member of the Nordic League, along with Captain Archibald Ramsay (who led the Right Club, a coalition of extremists), William Joyce, and Crowley's old disciple Major-General J.F.C.Fuller. Originally called "The Hooded Men" or "The White Knights of Britain" the Nordic League was set up by Germans and was effectively the Nazi Party in Britain, actively dedicated to the German cause: for this reason MI5 considered Joyce, Fuller and Seton-Hutchison to be German agents.

Seton-Hutchison believed the Franco-Soviet Pact was "an armed alliance, not between nations, but between the criminals, all of whom are Grand Orient Freemasons or Jews." Interestingly enough Wheatley blamed Grand Orient Masonry for the decline of France in his Fifties newspaper articles, and he even attacks it in *The Devil and All His Works*, in the Seventies.

Seton-Hutchison was a decent man and he even had a sense of humour, drawing a caricature of himself in one of the inscribed books he gave to Wheatley. At the same time he was insanely anti-Semitic. He not only authored the pamphlet *Don't Send Your Son to the Shambles of a Jew-Made War* but he was far more extreme than Mosley, and it is clear in his case that anti-Semitism at this level is not some kind of moral failing but a mental illness: Seton-Hutchison distrusted Mosley because he thought he was controlled by Jews.

A good deal of more mundane Thirties anti-Semitism had a left-wing, anti-capitalist quality (an old French description calls anti-Semitism "socialism for fools") but it is the paranoid and irrationally totalising quality of this really full-blown anti-Semitism that led Orwell to isolate it as something distinct from xenophobia, amounting to "an essentially magical doctrine."

Crankier still, but harmless, were the British Israelites. A well known piece of doggerel from the period ran "How odd / Of God / To choose / The Jews", and it might seem eccentric of Him until one realises that references to Jews in the Bible should actually be read to mean "the British", specifically those of Anglo-Saxon descent, who are therefore "God's Chosen People." This radically changes our understanding of the Bible, particularly the Old Testament.

The word "Saxon" itself is derived from "Isaac's Sons", and "British" from the Hebrew "Berith" (covenant) and "Ish" (man) so the British are strictly The Men of the Covenant. The Oxford English Dictionary seems completely unaware of this and is little help to the British Israelite cause, which also argues that the prophet Jeremiah was born on an island off the coast of Scotland and that Jerusalem was actually Edinburgh.

Regarding the Anglo-Saxons as a Lost Tribe of Israel did not entail anti-Semitism, and most British Israelites regarded 'real' Jews as kindred rather than impostors, although later American developments of British Israelitism have been more morbid, and at least one believer has been shot dead by the FBI.

The British Israelites were very interested in Pyramidology, which may be how Wheatley encountered them: he owned a number of books on this, but he also owned books about British Israelitism itself, and books by prominent British Israelites on other subjects, suggesting he may have known them socially. It seems unlikely that Wheatley believed in British Israelitism, although he may have found it intellectually entertaining. The belief that the Anglo–Saxons were God's Chosen People was not taken lightly, however. It was less about superiority than duty, and a special responsibility to guide and even save the world: this would certainly have struck a chord with Wheatley, and with many others of his generation.

★

One night the Wheatleys went to a party at a flat in Hallam Street, given by the socialite and horror writer Sir Charles Birkin. The young crowd were mainly debutantes and Dennis and Joan felt like "fish out of water" until they met a more serious guest, a tall man in his mid–thirties with immense charm and a striking Wellingtonian nose. This was Maxwell Knight, a very queer fish indeed, who was a key player in MI5 and became an inspiration for Ian Fleming's spymaster 'M'.

Like Wheatley, Knight had been on the Worcester, he was a great fan of John Buchan, and he was interested in the occult. The Wheatleys invited him over for drinks at St.John's Wood and gradually got to know this strange man, whose great passions were jazz – he played the clarinet and drums – and animals. He generally had something living in his pockets, and visitors to his flat might encounter grass snakes, a parrot, a couple of ferrets, some salamanders, a giant toad, or a bush baby. It was this side of his life that later made him a popular children's naturalist and broadcaster, 'Uncle Max', author of books such as *How To Keep an Elephant*, *Be A Nature Detective*, and *Reptiles in Britain*.

Knight dabbled in crime fiction and was a member of the Paternoster Club: the Paternoster file simply lists his profession as "Author". He had published a thriller, *Crime Cargo*, and as their friendship grew, he dedicated his second book, *Gunman's Holiday* (1935) to the Wheatleys. Like Wheatley, he had combated the General Strike and had been involved in the murky overlap between the State and private intelligence, where merging and interdependent far-Right organisations such as the "Industrial Intelligence Bureau" and

Admiral Sir Reginald "Blinker" Hall's "National Propaganda" and "The Economic League" all flourished.

Knight had worked for the Industrial Intelligence Bureau and been a member of the early British Fascists (or Fascisti, in the Italian style, led by a remarkable woman named Rotha Linton-Orman, not to be confused with the later British Union of Fascists). He was their Director of Intelligence from 1924–27. On leaving, he published a letter in their paper, *The British Lion*, assuring his comrades that he had not been dismissed for stealing the office dog's milk and he had not joined the Communist Party, but "I *am* going where I can still keep an eye (or even two) on any undesirables, inside or outside the movement, who may seek to make trouble for us."

Knight's fiction shows the casual prejudices of its period, and in person he loathed not only foreigners and Communists but Jews and homosexuals. Knight had three unconsummated marriages, and is now generally believed to have been homosexual himself. The period he met the Wheatleys was an unhappy one because his first wife had committed suicide: at the time this was rumoured to be due to Crowley's influence, but it was due to marital difficulties. In retrospect, a former MI5 colleague thought "his flair for espionage was all of a piece with his feeling for the occult and his clandestine sexual leanings."

Although his own feelings were for the Right, Knight was in charge of MI5's department B5(b), which scrupulously monitored and infiltrated both left and right-wing extremists. Despite personal tragedy, professionally he was coming into his prime: over the next few years, the period of his closest friendship with Dennis and Joan, he broke the Woolwich Arsenal spy ring (pro-Russian), wound up Captain Ramsay's Right Club (pro-German), had Mosley interned, and thwarted a plot which came frighteningly close to keeping America out of the war. It was only when he hounded a harmless pacifist named Ben Greene on suspicion of being a Nazi agent, forging a letter to frame him, that he was felt to have overstepped the mark and his star began to wane.

★

The Wheatleys came to call Knight "Uncle", and he became a pivotal figure in Wheatley's life. He was a ruthless and manipulative man, making use of associates as varied as Tom Driberg and William Joyce, and Wheatley himself seems to have been a victim of his deviousness.

For now, Knight wanted to know what was going on at Oxford University. In February 1933 the Oxford Union had passed a motion, proposed by Professor Joad, "That this house will in no circumstances fight for its King and country." This was widely reported and Hitler took it as an encouraging sign, easing the world further down the path to war. Many undergraduates and *bien pensant* young people, like the Auden gang, were also attracted to Communism; one of them later remembered singing songs "of unbelievable absurdity," like the one about the Soviet Air Force with the chorus "And every propeller is whirring "Red Front" / Defending the USSR!"

Bill Younger was now an undergraduate at Christ Church, and Knight asked Wheatley if he could have a word with him; he wanted Bill to keep an eye on the student body. This was the beginning of Bill's career in MI5, and he soon learnt that his history tutor, J.C.Masterman, was also an MI5 man.

★

Along with extremists of the Left and Right, Knight seems to have thought occultists needed watching, perhaps because of their potential for Masonic-style networking. One of his early employers, Sir George Makgill of the British Empire Union and the Industrial Intelligence Bureau, was concerned to monitor "all forms of subversion including Communism . . . the international traffic in drugs and the traffic in women and children . . . [and] unmasking the cult of evil of which Aleister Crowley, alias the Beast, was the centre."

Aside from his professional interest, Knight was fascinated by Crowley. If Knight felt himself deviant in any way, then Crowley's outré reputation would probably have appealed to him, and he was also philosophically interested in the occult for its own sake ("always searching for other meanings to life, other reasons for being, and he used to discuss them . . . avidly").

Wheatley is sometimes said to have introduced Crowley to Knight. Knight told his young nephew Harry that he and Wheatley both went along to Crowley's "occult ceremonies" (and that "They jointly applied to Crowley as novices and he accepted them as pupils") but this seems like one of Knight's lies. Crowley wasn't conducting ceremonies at this period; he wasn't likely to initiate anyone into much more than the mysteries of a good lunch, and then only if they were paying; and as we have seen, Wheatley was hardly in a pupil or novice relationship with him. But it was a good story for a nephew, especially given Wheatley's public image as the author of *The Devil Rides Out*. As Knight used to tell his agents, "If you are going to tell a lie, tell a good one and stick to it."

★

The Devil Rides Out was still Wheatley's only occult book, and the Orientalist streak in his psyche was just as strong. During the filming of *The Forbidden Territory* Wheatley had met George Hill, a flamboyant, swordstick-touting former British agent in Bolshevik Russia. Among his many stories, he had apparently brought the Tsarist crown jewels out of Russia. Hill also had experience in Turkey, and now Wheatley drew on this to write his seventh novel, *The Eunuch of Stamboul*.

Set in a Turkey which, "despite its surface modernity, still held all the beauty, cruelty, romance and intrigue of the time-less East," *Eunuch* features a conspiracy to overthrow Kemal Ataturk's recent modernisation and start an Islamic Jihad, which could spread from Turkey to the Balkans and beyond. The action begins in London, where Captain Swithin Destime saves Diana, an English woman, from being sexually assaulted by an arrogant foreigner, Prince Ali, socking him on the jaw. Before long Destime finds himself in "that cruel city of the Sultans" face to face with the grotesquely obese

353

eunuch, Kazdim; police chief, monster of elaborate cruelty, and "completely Oriental – subtle, shrewd, sadistic." The British Embassy represents a haven of decency.

The Eunuch of Stamboul gives the reader a Turkish travelogue (including the mysteries of the kebab, a delicacy then unknown in Britain) and an insiderishly informed insight into current affairs and recent history. All this is interwoven with Wheatley's characteristic snakes and ladders – "Mr Dennis Wheatley is a past-master," said the *Morning Post* "at getting his heroes out of one danger that looks inevitable and deadly and putting them at once into another, still more inevitable, still more deadly, and getting them out of that" – and his equally characteristic trademark love story. It climaxes with the spectre of dreadful female degradation just narrowly avoided, as Diana is told she will have to "kiss the feet of the Descendant of the Prophet" – none other than Prince Ali – "and, receiving, permission to advance, [press] her lips to each of his legs in turn, inch by inch as she crawls forward on her belly . . ."

The Eunuch of Stamboul sold well, and it was filmed in 1936 as *The Secret of Stamboul*, with James Mason. Wheatley wasted no time before embarking on his next book, the first of his 'lost civilisation' novels, *They Found Atlantis*, in Wheatley's account a sunken land that once stood in the Atlantic, "the original Garden of Eden as far as the White Races go." William Beebe had recently set a new record for diving in his "bathysphere" and published an account of it in his 1934 book *Half Mile Down*. He found more life down there than anyone expected, including unknown species at depths previously thought to be almost lifeless, and observed the phenomenon of "submarine blue":

> We were the first living men to look out at the strange illumination: and it was stranger than any imagination could have conceived. It was of an indefinable translucent blue quite unlike anything I have ever seen in the upper world, and it excited our optic nerves in a most confusing manner . . . the blueness of the blue, both outside and

inside our sphere, seemed to pass materially through the eye into our very beings . . . It actually seemed to me to have a brilliance and intensity which the sunshine lacked . . .

Wheatley was inspired by *Half Mile Down*, and as they submerge his argonauts find "the light had darkened to a deep violet blue and still had that eerie unearthly quality about it". They include deep-sea explorer Herman Tisch, a young duchess named Camilla, a Russian count, and a "dago"film star, who all find themselves hijacked at sea by super-crook "Oxford Kate."

The effetely sophisticated Kate, a man, is one of Wheatley's oddest creations. He embodies exaggerated "Varsity" sophistication of the Brian Howard variety, but with criminal cronies whose talk recalls The Limper's henchmen: "Oxford's no skirt an' he'll make it hot fer you plenty if you don't make it snappy".

There is plenty of action and romance in the submarine paradise they discover, until things are ruined by the dago, who is a cad. It is one of Wheatley's best non-supernatural thrillers and Wheatley dedicated it to Beebe, who wrote him a two page letter praising it.

It is a precarious Eden. As "small warm pagan goddess" Lulluma explains to the count as they lie down together, their cardinal rule is never even to mention Evil. In a decade that was ticking away towards war, Wheatley's Atlantis has effectively survived outside of time and passed into "that happy state where it no longer has any history to record" (a "Happy state indeed," says Doktor Herman Tisch, "for history is only a record of man's brutality and folly caused by fear.")

Along with *Half Mile Down* and Conan Doyle's lost world stories, notably *The Maracot Deep*, there is more than a touch of Shangri-La about this beautiful Atlantean civilisation, which also happens to revere the ancient sign of the swastika:

Then she proceeded to give them both the benefit of the cumulative experience of the women of her race . . .

355

When she had done she kissed them both, [and] made the sign of the Swastika on their foreheads, breasts and thighs with a curiously scented oil from a little bottle.

Despite their narrative power and their oblique engagement with current affairs, *They Found Atlantis* and *The Eunuch* are a generically backward-looking and dated style of thriller. Soon, however, Wheatley would surprise himself, and put together a book so radical it would even be mentioned in a *Times* editorial.

CHAPTER TWENTY-EIGHT

Like Spitting on an Altar

A craze for crime fiction gripped the Thirties. Auden and Eliot suggested the detective story was ultimately religious, like a quest for the Grail, while Wyndham Lewis compared it to the situation in Europe. What with Italy and Germany, he said, and terror in Russia, and the Stavisky scandal in France, Europe had "gone Crime Club": "how like a shilling shocker continental politics have become."

One night over dinner, Joe Links suggested to Wheatley that he should write an illustrated murder story with real evidence. Crime fiction had too much narrative: "Why can't we just have the facts and the clues?" At first Wheatley didn't see what Links was getting at, but then he became excited by the idea and the two of them produced their first 'Crime Dossier', *Murder off Miami*, in which British financier Bolitho Blane is found dead on board his yacht. The cast includes the Bishop of Bude, Miss Ferri Rocksavage, Count Posodini and others, but they are upstaged by some hair in a cellophane envelope, a photo of some cigarette stubs, and a spent match from a hotel.

There was little enthusiasm in the trade. WH Smith's railway station managers gave it a unanimous thumbs down ("Words fail me," said a Mr Iron at Liverpool Street). Hutchinson pointed out that it would have no library sales, being fragile and only usable once, so he could only charge 3/6d, of which Wheatley and Links could only have a royalty of one penny (£8 and 20p). Wheatley and Links persisted.

Gordon Selfridge was one of the few to see the book had potential, taking a thousand copies and throwing a launch party at the store. Hatchards only took six copies, but Queen Mary came in on the day of publication and bought them all. Suddenly the book took off: its gimmickry made it a journalistic novelty, and it was the subject of a *Times* editorial.

"The contents of the book include human hair, blood-stained chintz, a letter in Japanese, blueprints of a yacht, match-ends, and finger prints," reported the *Times*. Where would it end? A small phial of perfume "will convey the devastating qualities of the heroine's perfume far more vividly than her creator ever could." Once books contained real substances, critics would be reduced to saying "the hay in Mr Blank's pastoral scenes is definitely the best he has given us yet" or "Miss Dash's picture of nursery life is marred by an unimaginative use of tapioca." On the facing page from all this cosy footling, meanwhile, was news from Spain: churches were being burned, and some priests and army officers who had tried to defend one were shot after they came out under a white flag.

Before long Wheatley was caught up in the Thirties crime craze like everyone else, and he even took young Anthony to see what he hoped was TS Eliot's new murder mystery on stage, *Murder in the Cathedral*. They left at the interval.

*

Murder off Miami was a sensation at the 68th Foyle's Literary Luncheon, July 1936, upstaging the book for which the Luncheon was given, *Six Against The Yard*. Very much of its time, this featured Dorothy Sayers, Ronald Knox, Margery Allingham, Freeman Wills Crofts and others pitting their wits against a real policeman, Ex-Superintendent Cornish of the CID. No less of its time was the party given by Wheatley's friend Lord Donegall, where he invited a number of writers and challenged them to find the safe: Peter Cheyney was the winner.

In a similar spirit, the writer Rupert Croft-Cooke thought he had discovered something unknown about a murder case, and he felt it would make a viable book if some detective writers could be persuaded to solve the crime. After *Murder off Miami*, he felt Wheatley was the man to advise him, and one evening he went round to see him. Wheatley was interested but unsure, and wanted the advice of a third party, whom he telephoned.

Unfortunately the man he called wasn't nice Mr Links but nasty Mr Cheyney. He arrived, immediately striking Croft-Cooke as "a cad and a potential con man," and began to give him the third degree. What was the clue? How did Croft-Cooke expect him to judge the book without knowing the clue? Didn't he know how serious this was? If he really knew something unreported and withheld it, he could go to prison. How could he drag other people into this situation? So what *was* the clue? Did he really have one – or was he just bluffing? He was just trying to get publicity out of Wheatley, wasn't he?

Croft-Cooke felt all this must have made Wheatley ("a man of breeding and principle") very uncomfortable, and that it was only Wheatley's presence that stopped Cheyney from using violent methods of interrogation. He vowed never to speak to this "overbearing cheapjack" again.

★

There was no stopping the Dossiers now. *Murder off Miami* had shifted around 200,000 copies[1], and Wheatley and Links started on a second one, *Who Killed Robert Prentice?* This was another cache of facsimiles including a torn up blackmail photograph featuring a naked woman, a Belgian stamp, a railway ticket and a letter in an envelope: at one stage Hutchinson's had forty girls in Watford putting stamps in cellophane packets and tearing up photographs.

Wheatley had spotted a further potential of the genre, and the fictitious newspaper enclosed, the *South Sussex Chronicle*, contained extensive publicity for the Sir Harry Preston Memorial Fund and Wheatley's other books, along with some real advertising which netted Wheatley £300. Again, almost everyone was thrilled, although the *Times Literary Supplement* complained (as they had with *Murder off Miami*) that it was too bulky to read comfortably in bed.

There was a stronger complaint from Germany, where the book was unexpectedly banned due to the loose life of the

[1] According to the jacket. Reg Gadney says 80,000 copies in 18 months.

dead man's secretary, Miss Suzanne L'Estrange, and particularly the torn-up nude photograph. "Its moral character must be designated more than inferior," said the censor, "created for English conditions, not German ones."

★

Meanwhile Wheatley published another conventional thriller, *Contraband*. This featured our old friend Gregory Sallust, "a cynical but brainy devil" with a "Mephisophelean appearance", while the villain was the twisted, malcontented, power-mad Adlerian dwarf Lord Gavin Fortescue, from *Such Power is Dangerous*. This time Fortescue is smuggling foreign agitators into Britain. They are going to spread discontent, followed by "illicit arms . . . bombs, and poison gas and every sort of foulness to desecrate England's green and pleasant land". As Gregory explains, "These birds are out to wreck the old firm of J.Bull, Home, Dominions and Colonial."

1936 was a bad year for the old firm of J.Bull, with worrying international news, a royal death, and an abdication. Dying of cancer, George V had whispered "Is all well with the Empire?" – although his last words were more popularly 'known' to have been "Bugger Bognor", as he dismissed any hope of convalescing there – and been killed with a lethal injection, so that his death would catch the next morning's *Times* instead of dragging on to break in "less appropriate" evening papers.

He was succeeded by Prince Edward, a democratic and popular figure with a slight Cockney accent (picked up from his nurse) and a real concern for issues such as unemployment: his accompanying Nazi sympathies were not widely known at the time. He had hardly become Edward VIII when he was forced to abdicate over his love for an American divorcee, Wallis Simpson, despite the fact that the majority of his people supported him. Wheatley was among them, and he felt so strongly that he sent the King a telegram. Beseeching Edward not to give up the crown, he wrote "If only you would rely on the love, sympathy and understanding of the masses, your will would be done."

It was not to be: despite overwhelming popular sympathy, the King was forced out by a *petit bourgeois* moral elite led by Stanley Baldwin, the *Times*, and the Church. He was succeeded by King George VI, and when *Cavalcade* magazine wrote to Wheatley the following year, asking his opinion on "The Man of The Year", he chose the new King, "who probably worked longer hours than any of his subjects during the terrific strain of the Coronation Season and sustained the ordeal with a dignity and affability which must be the admiration of us all; thus success in his particular task of stabilising the Throne after the unparalleled crisis which shook it to its foundations last year." The old firm was still in business.

The new King was present at the 1937 Coronation Derby, during a day of perfect summer weather. Wheatley was there too, and he put an each-way bet on Le Grand Duc, thinking of the Duke de Richleau. It was an exceptionally exciting race, with Le Grand Duc in the lead at one stage, and Wheatley was still pleased when he came in third at 100–9.

★

Abroad, meanwhile, the Spanish Civil War had broken out in July 1936, the month that Mussolini's invasion of Ethiopia – effectively the end of the League of Nations as a force with any power for peace – reached Addis Ababa, and Germany breached the Locarno Pact by remilitarizing in the Rhineland. Germany was now ready to press territorial claims against France, a country Britain was pledged to defend.

This particularly worried Wheatley, as we have seen in 'Pills of Honour', and the Wheatleys stayed in the British isles for their summer 1936 holiday. Wheatley took them to the Isle of Mull. Ever careful, no doubt remembering what had happened to him in France after the Navy mutinied, he took £50 worth of silver coin – in those days made of precious metal – in case there was trouble and a paper money crisis.

The situation blew over, and that autumn Dennis and Joan let Diana stay with a family in Munich to learn German. Like Angus Wilson's character Elspeth Bungle, Diana loved Germany and came back full of enthusiasm for its new way of life ("Elspeth Bungle used to attend ALL the Nuremberg rallies in the 1930s, but that was when we only knew the GOOD side of Hitler!").

Even after the War broke out, Wheatley had trouble getting her to take an interest in the Allied cause.

*

Wheatley was now working on *The Secret War*, a bit of peace-mongering that tried to put Mussolini's invasion of Ethiopia in an understandable and sympathetic light: the TLS noted the book's impartiality. The Secret War is being waged between international financiers who want to turn the Abyssinian conflict into a profitable world war, while another secret organisation trying to stop them. Wheatley even manages to write his unpublished 'Pills of Honour' into the book, attributing it to the hero.

Wheatley had never been to Ethiopia but he had an impression of it as hopelessly backward after reading Evelyn Waugh's *Black Mischief* (1932) and *Waugh In Abyssinia* (1936; published in the *Daily Mail* as despatches in 1935). "In common humanity it was high time that white men took over the administration", wrote Wheatley, and the Italians would "make life safe, human and decent for the people of the country." There had been outrage in the civilised world over the news that Mussolini was using poison gas against primitive tribesmen, the Danakil, who were themselves notorious for their atrocities against anyone they captured. Wheatley felt they were savages and that their atrocities merited gas as the safest way to deal with them – this was also Churchill's opinion – and at the end of the book his protagonists are rescued from the Danakil by Italian airmen. After the War Jack Younger married an Italian princess, Marcella Granito, the Princess Pignatelli Di Belmonte, and Wheatley inscribed a copy of *The Secret War* for her: "We weren't all pro-Abyssinian."

Wheatley was sincere about the benefits of Empire. Visiting pre-war Eastern Europe, Wheatley and Joan found Vienna delightful, Prague dull, and Budapest especially enchanting, particularly for its food and cafés: "Budapest had lain within

The blackmail photograph, before being torn to pieces in Who Killed Robert Prentice? (1937).

A new sport: "balloon hopping."

Strange Conflict (1941), with a jacket by Frank C. Pape.

Total War (1941).

the Roman Empire so for many centuries its people had inherited a civilised mentality." Wheatley returned from Budapest laden with foie gras, and in December 1937 he wrote a piece for the *Mail* entitled 'We Don't Eat Enough at Christmas.'

Writing as "thriller novelist and student of gastronomy" Wheatley extolled the virtues of English gluttony, beginning sentimentally with Bob Cratchit's goose and moving greedily on to old royal feasts of sturgeon, swans, peacocks, and wild boar. Then he found space for oysters, turkey, and Joan's Christmas pudding recipe, all washed down with a variety of drink including mediaeval garhioflac (white wine with cloves); Burgundy with the bird ("say Chambertin or Richebourg 1923"); and Bismarck's favourite "black velvet" of champagne and stout. This is a favourite drink in Wheatley's novels, and he recommended it for the "morning-after": "there is no finer pick-me-up".

★

Who Killed Robert Prentice? came out that summer, but Wheatley's next major book was *Red Eagle*, showing broader political sympathies than one might expect. Marshal Tukachevsky and other high ranking officers had been shot in the Russian purges, and Wheatley had started to wonder about the man who came out on top, Marshal Voroshilov, as a subject for a biography. As usual it was researched with the help of "top boys", notably Sir Vernon Kell, who had founded MI5.

Red Eagle became the story of the Russian revolution, with Voroshilov in the central role. As Wheatley told the British Russia Club, when he lectured to them, "Conditions for Russian working men were very bad; there were no unions to protect them . . . They were absolutely in the clutches of the capitalist." He made the ruthless Voroshilov a sympathetic figure, and having been an army officer himself, he admired not only Voroshilov's tactical flair but his devotion to his troops, teaching them to read. More than that, Wheatley's Voroshilov is a "good fellow", fond of wine, women and song, and his origins – born to a peasant and a servant girl, begging in the street as a child – have elements of the Victorian-style 'poor boy made good' narrative; that always appealed to Wheatley.

Wheatley had picked a winner with Voroshilov, whom Queen Elizabeth later had to address as "my good friend", despite his having slaughtered eleven thousand White Russian officers who should have been treated as prisoners of war.

★

Wheatley's next book, *Uncharted Seas*, was one of his more bizarre offerings. Ethnic conflict is a central theme, after the Swedish ship Gafelborg runs into serious trouble at sea. Along with the admirable Swedes ("first-class sailors. The Viking blood you know; we've got a dash of it ourselves") the passengers include Unity, a sturdy flower of English womanhood, a lecherous Venezuelan, and a sympathetic Frenchman with a "D'Artagnan moustache" who admires the English and is given to musing on national characteristics.

The danger comes from sixteen-stone black stoker Harlem Joe, a convicted murderer who sees his chances when civilisation breaks down in the shipwreck: "Harlem Joe said nothing, but the half sly, half arrogant, smile which he gave his coloured companions as they moved forward held a world of meaning."

As if that wasn't enough, the party also face Sargasso weed, a monster octopus and some giant crabs straight out of Rider Haggard. Coming close to land, they are surprised to see strange spider-like creatures with round bodies above four stilt like legs; one of these creatures is being chased by a pack of others. As they watch, they realise these creatures are people with balloons on their backs, propelling themselves across the surface of the weed with leg stilts and hand sticks, like ski-sticks, which all have smaller feet-like balloons at their ends.

It is characteristic of Wheatley that these balloons were based on a real inter-wars sport, "balloon jumping", and no less characteristic that the balloonist in front is a white woman being chased by a group of black men. Rescuing her, the Gafelborg party find that she belongs to a lost island society still living in the seventeenth century, ruled by descendants of Sir Deveril Barthorne who was marooned there in 1680. The constant danger in their lives is the nearby savage island, Satan's Island, inhabited by marauding blacks.

The structure of *Uncharted Seas* splits and re-formulates with the logic of a dream, as ethnic conflict on board the ship is followed by the discovery of a black island and a white island. As we have seen, Wheatley tended to split the world into an absolutely black and white, Manichaean system of good and evil, and he was not the sort of man often likely to say there was a little bit of good and bad in everybody. So it is interesting that it should be in *Uncharted Seas*, of all Wheatley's books, where Unity says to Basil Sutherland "Still, there's some good in the worst of us and a streak of bad in the best of us, I suppose, as the old cliché has it." It is as if the polarised structure of the novel is so overt and solid that it allows space for this repressed idea to surface, like an over-secure political party falling prey to internal dissent.

William Joyce's friend and tutoring partner Angus Macnab spotted it was a re-hash of *They Found Atlantis*, as Tayleur reported in a letter. Wheatley knew this, and he felt it was not as good as the previous book. As before, Diana did the drawings for the endpapers; they are exceptionally kitsch.

★

Diana had caused the Wheatleys a lot of worry over the past year. In February 1937, returning from a ski-ing holiday with some friends of the family, she had been in a car crash near Dieppe. Another girl in the party was killed, and Diana's head injuries left her vague and flakier than ever; the Wheatleys took to calling her "Little Woolly Head."

It was Diana's debutante season – she was presented that summer at Balmoral – and she recovered sufficiently for Mrs Wheatley to throw a party for her at No.8 that March: the girls wore masks, with the name badges of film stars.

Morecambe Bay shrimps, truffled game pie, nectarines and Black Velvet were provided. During the same season, there was a ball at the Brazilian Embassy, and Wheatley – always alert to possible danger – became worried by the number of people standing on the staircase: fearing it might collapse at any moment, he took Diana and their party off to the Berkeley instead.

This was nothing compared to the worries they had had when Diana went out to Africa, staying with Bino and his wife Louise while the Wheatleys were in Budapest. Reports reached them that she had been playing strip poker, and getting drunk on cocktails and whisky until she couldn't stand and had to be put to bed. The drinking seemed to start at eleven in the morning, day after day, and in one of her infrequent letters Diana had said "Bino and Lou say I am the grandest drunk they have ever met because I am so amusing when I'm tight," adding "I'll write again when I feel better."

The Wheatleys were worried sick, as Dennis telegrammed a friend: "Joan so worried about Diana doctors fear complete breakdown Stop." They got her back intact, after which Wheatley composed a double-edged thank you letter for her to copy: "I can never thank you enough for the marvellous time," it began, continuing "It is tragic that I should have left under a cloud . . . It hurts me a lot to think the parties we had are not well looked on . . . Please believe that I enjoyed every moment of it – except the hangovers . . . Anyhow, in spite of these rotten stories that are going around, I do thank you . . ."

Wheatley's own thoughts were not so nicely couched: "Lou ought to be in an asylum," and Bino was a liar, thief, fraud, and "a queer bird and not quite normal," so no wonder he could "sink to such depravity." When Diana returned, Wheatley wrote her a long letter in the form of a present-tense diary from December 2nd to February 21st entitled "All That I Knew Of What Was Going On," so she would know how he had felt.

The crux of the matter was the fear of female degradation,

on which Wheatley's books often pivot. "Stripped naked and put to bed", Wheatley thought. And Lou and Bino thought it was amusing to see her "wild eyed and excited; just as we used to think it funny to get the Regimental Goat drunk."

"The thought of her as she may be tonight (New Year's Eve) dishevelled, blear-eyed, sodden with drink, makes me almost physically sick. It is like spitting on an altar for these people to spoil her loveliness . . ."

CHAPTER TWENTY-NINE

The Mystery of the Black Box

That winter Wheatley and Joan went to Egypt, travelling in the quintessentially Thirties luxury of a flying boat. It had twenty or so seats arranged in pairs, padded and adjustable with footrests like dentists' chairs. Passengers could get up and walk around – there was plenty of space – and the view from the slow, low-flying plane was superb. Wheatley thought it was like looking down on a map.

Wheatley saw the Pyramids and they were shown into a tomb by a French archaeologist they met, where Wheatley saw a mummy, and representations of the soul double or ka, as in his novel *The Ka of Gifford Hillary*. In the temple at Karnac he saw a figure of the god Set, and claimed to feel "a definite sense of evil, although I sensed nothing of that kind in any of the Tombs of the Kings." The only problem Wheatley had in those was in the tomb of Thotmes III, where he was three hundred feet under ground when his "filthy Arab guide" threatened to make off with the only light unless Wheatley gave him some baksheesh.

Given the routine xenophobia of Wheatley's work, he had an interesting experience when he went to Greece on this same holiday. He had already written a filthy Greek into his short story 'Athenian Gold' ("I say nozings – you maka me present, eh?"), where the narrator thinks "I should just love to have hit him in the middle of his oily face." Wheatley had never met any Greeks, and he had a surprise when he discovered what decent, dignified, intelligent people they actually were, "proud of their lovely country and its magnificent contribution to civilisation" and wanting their guests to understand and enjoy it too. What is more, they had a lot of respect and liking for Johnny Englishman. Wheatley regretted 'Athenian Gold,' and later dismissed it as "more than usually unlikely".

In Egypt, meanwhile, the Wheatleys had an introduction to "Russell Pasha", Sir Thomas Russell, head of the Egyptian police and founder of the Camel Corps. Through him, Wheatley met Count Laszlo Almasy, the original for Michael Ondaatje's English Patient (although quite unlike the Ondaatje character, he was a gay Nazi). Solo desert travel was so dangerous that it was usually regarded as foolhardy and bad form, but Almasy was engaged in a series of lone explorations. Wheatley believed he was looking for treasure, but this seems to have been a bluff; in fact, unknown to Wheatley, Almasy was probably exploring for small oases, laying the basis for a desert expertise that led Rommel to give him the Iron Cross.

Nevertheless Almasy's cover story, filled in by Russell Pasha, provided Wheatley with the germ of a future book, *The Quest of Julian Day*. After the Persian king Cambyses conquered Egypt, the Persian army marched across the desert with a fabulous loot in gold. Unfortunately they were dependent on Egyptian guides who misled them, and after a week's march into the wastes they were lost. The entire expedition perished, and the treasure is somewhere out there to this day.

★

The Spanish Civil War had been under way since July 1936, with the left-wing Republican side (the former coalition government, fallen into chaos) having widespread support in Britain against the right-wing Nationalist side (rebellious and eventually victorious) led by General Franco. Nancy Cunard's questionnaire, published as *Authors Take Sides on the Spanish War*, found about 125 authors for the Republicans, sixteen neutral, including H.G.Wells and T.S.Eliot, and only five for Franco, notably Evelyn Waugh and Arthur Machen.

There would have been six if Cunard had asked Wheatley ("he had my vote every time . . . To me it was inconceivable that any sane person should wish to see Spain in the hands of the Communists.") Wheatley's position was rare among writers but not as isolated as that might suggest. Conservatives generally agreed with him, and Churchill, who later described himself as neutral, had written in his *Evening Standard* column that Franco's forces were "marching to re-establish order" in opposition to a weak Leftist government that "was falling into the grip of dark, violent forces coming ever more plainly into the open, and operating by murder, pillage and industrial disturbance."

Wheatley was particularly proud of his Spanish Civil War novel, *The Golden Spaniard*, based on Dumas's *Twenty Years After*, when the four musketeering friends were divided by civil war in seventeenth-century France. In Spain, "Quite naturally the Duke would be in sympathy with the Spanish Monarchists, and Richard, as a staunch supporter of the best Conservative tradition, would be with him; whereas Simon, the Liberal Jew, and Rex, the Democratic American, would equally naturally espouse the cause of the Spanish Socialists."

The *Morning Post* saw Communistic tendencies in Wheatley, while the *Daily Worker* accused him of being a Fascist. The *New Statesman* slipped in a further allegation, noting that although Wheatley "judiciously divides his sympathies . . . The sadistic touch, the *specialité de la maison*, is provided in a rape – perpetrated by the Reds."

The Thirties were highly aware of sadism. It was also in the *New Statesman*, just a little later, that John Betjeman wrote 'Cookery for Sadists' ("Slash some turnips with a sharp knife, rub salt, curry powder and cayenne into the cuts and truss them tightly"). There was a new attention to psychopathology and its jargon, an awareness of brutality on the Continent, and a sadistic new sensationalism in American-style hard-boiled writing: Julian Symons credits Peter Cheyney with pushing the boundaries and "exploiting the public taste for cruelty . . . Lemmy Caution is the first 'good' man in crime fiction to torture for pleasure." *No Orchids for Miss Blandish* (1939), a book Wheatley owned, was another landmark in the tendency, featuring the abuse of a female captive by a criminal gang.

Wheatley's work does have a sadistic streak and he was predictably interested in spanking ("lots of girls enjoy a playful hiding sometimes") or *technique Anglaise* as it is known in France. Roger Brook flagellates a Russian woman with an umbrella, of all things, but Wheatley knew from his reading of Tombe's Havelock Ellis that Russian women enjoy being beaten. The dash of sadism in Wheatley – the prospect of a girl being Satanically deflowered on a bed of nettles, for example – is usually buffoonish stuff compared to the more sophisticated and unpleasant sadism in Ian Fleming, but it is sufficiently there to qualify Wheatley for the "three S's" that Cyril Connolly saw as the winning formula of the James Bond books: Sex, Snobbery and Sadism.

★

Wheatley felt it was time to create a new character. Julian Day – the name, as in the Julian Calendar, makes him a counterpart of Gregory and the Gregorian Day – is a young man caught in a scandal which ends his career in the Diplomatic Service and his timely dreams of "one day averting another world war as Britain's youngest yet most brilliant Ambassador." Perhaps through Bill, Wheatley was now taken with the glamour of the "Varsity." In addition to a baronetcy, Julian has a Double-First, and he was "the best man with an epee in my year at Oxford." Along with the treasure Wheatley had learned about in Egypt, *The Quest of Julian Day* (1939) has a Monte-Cristo style revenge theme, but perhaps Julian was too embittered, or just too smug: the public didn't take to him.

Characters like Julian Day and Swithin Destime, out of the Buchan and Sapper stable, were now dated ("that's – devilish sporting of you" says Swithin to Tyndall-Williams, one of our men in the Istanbul embassy). A new style of thriller came in with Eric Ambler's 1939 *The Mask of Dimitrios*, which was realistic and no longer relied on the clean-cut gentleman hero grappling with proletarians and foreigners.

If Wheatley was dated he hardly noticed: his career was going great guns, and while working on Julian Day he had got into *Who's Who*. Largely on the strength of the Crime Dossiers, he was described as a "novelist and inventor . . ."

The Dossiers were continuing, and when Wheatley went to Egypt he had left J.G.Links to finish *The Malinsay Massacre*, about the murder of a Scottish baronial family. It was weaker than the previous two, and Wheatley was particularly annoyed by the photographs, which he felt were taken in insufficiently baronial locations.

A fourth dossier in the summer of 1939, *Herewith the Clues!*, about the murder of a London night club owner by an IRA gang, descended into self parody. Boasting on the cover that it had "*Five times* as many clues as in any of the previous dossiers," it also emphasised the (frankly minor) celebrity of the people who posed for the photographs as if this was another technical innovation. It flopped.

There was a postscript to the Dossiers early in the War when William Butlin, later to be Sir Billy, offered Wheatley a generous fee to write a Dossier mystery featuring a Butlin's holiday camp. These were still new, the first one having opened at Skegness in 1936, and provided economical holidays for the masses. Given the luxury appeal and *snobisme* of Wheatley's work, and his later attribution of his success to "never mentioning the kitchen sink", Wheatley's reply was almost inevitable. Butlin's was too much like taking the kitchen sink on holiday, and he declined.

*

In October 1937 Wheatley had met the last of the figures who would shape his occult world view, Joan Grant. She became famous after her 1937 novel *Winged Pharaoh*, supposedly based on her memories of a previous incarnation in ancient Egypt. Other books dealt with her past lives not just in Egypt but the Holy Land and pre-Columbian America. Wheatley had always had a leaning towards belief in reincarnation, but his friendship with Grant intensified it.

Reviewing *Winged Pharaoh* in the book trade paper *Current Literature*, Wheatley recommended it to "those who are interested in things of the spirit but not necessarily members of any church" because it had "an inner message which makes it one of the most important books for our time."

Three decades later he still felt it had "as much wisdom and light in it as in any sacred book of East or West." The Grant worldview became almost a religion for Wheatley. At the end of his tether with Diana, he warned her:

> Then there is the greater future. You believe in *Winged Pharaoh*. This time you have been given many blessings and, whatever you may think, a very easy path . . . If you continue Selfish, Lazy, Loose in your mind and entirely self-contained you will be throwing it all away.
>
> You won't get such a good deal next time . . .

Wheatley could be ingenious in his arguments for reincarnation, which he believed had been central to every great religion until Jewish monotheism suppressed it. Christ's words that "the sins of the fathers shall be visited upon the children, even unto the third and fourth generation," must refer to His own belief in reincarnation:

> Is it conceivable that so gentle and sweet-natured a man could possibly have meant that an unborn child should suffer because his grandfather had been a brutal rogue? His meaning was that everyone is the father of his next incarnation. . . .

Wheatley first met Grant at a cocktail party, shortly before the publication of *Winged Pharaoh*. He got to know her better in the following year, and she would probably have told him her Aleister Crowley story. When she was seven, a visitor came to see her mother; "a kind of human toad," as she remembered him. He poured fulsome compliments over Joan's older step-sister Margery, who was around twenty, and outstayed his welcome after tea.

Finally "the Toad took his black pearl tie-pin from his purple satin cravat and stuck it into Margery's arm. He pretended it was an accident and blotted the bead of blood with his handkerchief . . . Margery was too terrified to shriek, but when he tweaked out a strand of her hair she squeaked "Mother!" She was so frightened she sounded like a mouse."

"Now," said the toad, "you are in my power, for I have your blood and your hair," at which point Grant's mother, who had re-entered the room without him noticing, broke the spell and threw him out. "What a very disagreeable man," she said.

Joan left her husband, Leslie Grant, for Charles Beatty, and he too became a friend of the Wheatleys. Dennis and Joan often went to stay with Charles and Joan at his old mansion, Trelydan Hall, and despite Wheatley's life-long insistence that he had never been present at a magical ritual, it was here that he witnessed something very like one, 'The Ceremony of the Roses.' Charles sprinkled Joan's naked body with rose petals and made a series of passes over her, invoking the 'Powers of Light'. Joan then went into a trance and began talking from one of her Egyptian incarnations.

These trances were a standard practice of hers when she composed her books, and the Wheatleys saw them many times. Romantic novelist Barbara Cartland was wont to do something similar: "Lying on her sofa in a darkened room, which she used to call 'the Factory', she tapped into her romantic dreamworld and dictated a fresh chapter every afternoon to her faithful secretary Mrs Eliot."

Wheatley had mixed feelings about Charles: he admired Charles's devotion to helping those in distress, through which he eventually lost Trelydan Hall, and came to feel "I have met only one living saint – Charles Beatty." On the other hand, he also felt that Charles's devotion to rituals and symbols actually had a damping or wearing effect on Joan Grant's imagination, and perhaps even "ruined the natural psychic link that she undoubtedly had with Powers of Good."

Beatty was an interesting man in his own right, and one of his formative experiences caught Wheatley's imagination. He was the nephew of Admiral Beatty, the hero of Jutland – later Viscount Borodale – and when the Irish Troubles began, Admiral Beatty sent Charles to defend the ancestral home at Borodale, County Wexford. The big houses in the area were being burned down, and Charles lived at Borodale alone for months, living in one room with a supply of tinned food: a scenario like the paranoid sieges Wheatley enjoyed so much in Charles Hope Hodgson books such as *The House on the Borderland*.

Beatty spent much of his time at Borodale meditating in the lotus position, and put the months to use in a study of Buddhism and mythology. Writing as Longfield Beatty, he published a book, *The Garden of the Golden Flower*, a study of myths, and in later life inclined towards Jungianism.

★

Always sensitive to decor, Wheatley compiled a folder of eight 'Ideal Home Mystery Rooms' for the 1938 Ideal Home Exhibition, in which readers were invited to guess which famous person each room belonged to, with a £200 first prize (about £10,000 today). In the course of it he met Baroness Orczy, whose Scarlet Pimpernel stories had meant so much to him as a boy.

Wheatley had given a number of talks on Black Magic in the late Thirties and in 1939 he gave one to the Eton Literary Society. His stories were smoothly in place by now; the man who went mad raising Pan; the woman given to the Devil in a pact when she was a child; the exorcism that drove a heap of maggots into a joint of meat; and his own experience with the man on the stairs as a child. "Mr Wheatley," reported the Eton Chronicle, "ended with an earnest appeal not to dabble in black magic."

Wheatley enjoyed being invited to Eton, and he particularly admired the way the boys were given a degree of freedom to run it themselves. The most important thing was to be popular, which didn't strike Wheatley as pernicious; to him it was another instance of the importance of being a "good fellow."

In the same week Wheatley appeared on an 'Authors versus Publishers' wireless quiz, where the authors' team included Pamela Frankau, Louis Golding and Peter Cheyney, and on a very early television broadcast with Tom Driberg,

Lord Donegall, and Lady Eleanor Smith. The producer offered a copy of *Who's Who* as a prize for the best performance, won by Lady Eleanor, only to take it back as soon as the programme finished, saying it was just a gambit for the viewers.

Lady Eleanor wasn't having that; she seized the book saying it was now rightly hers and she was going to sell it, at which point Wheatley gave her a pound. Wheatley's pleasure at this bargain was barely dented when Tom Driberg trumped the pair of them, in his supercilious public-school drawl. "Silly of you, Dennis," he said; "Waste of a pound. You should have made the office buy you one; they always do for me."

★

The office Driberg had in mind was probably the *Sunday Graphic*, where Wheatley ("Noted Author and Man About Town") wrote the 'Personalities Page.' This was only part of his journalistic output: he also wrote 'Men, Women and Books' in *Current Literature*, and pieces for various other papers including the *Mail* and the *Evening Dispatch*, on subjects such as the Bacon Shakespeare controversy and 'Crime as a Science'. In the latter, which bears a similarity to his conspiracy-oriented views on occultism, Wheatley revealed that there were "schools on the Continent" where "forgery, safe-blowing, confidence tricks, white slave traffic, and black mail, are learnt under the tutorship of experts."

Wheatley used his columns to promote friends such as Joan Grant, and he also let his house be used as a venue for talks on reincarnation by two associates of hers, a Mr Wyeth and Mr Neal. In this same period he was also promoting Jacques Penry on physiognomy, the old-style reading of character from the face in a manner akin to palmistry. In a sense physiognomy – something also associated with old-style bad novelists, where a strong chin might denote bravery, a retroussé nose innocence, and so on – completed Wheatley's pre-Enlightenment beliefs, along with numerology and the rest. With the world drifting onwards to war, Wheatley seemed to be drifting backwards to the Middle Ages.

Along with friends and even family – Wheatley got plenty of mileage out of Diana – Wheatley's columns included trivia of a distinctly Thirties kind. After an anti-Nazi joke about the difficulties of dentistry in a country where no one is allowed to open their mouth, Wheatley reported "Anglo-Saxon stock is going up in Germany": Hitler had announced that English girl Marian Daniels was the best dancer he had ever seen. "Here are the measurements of Hitler's ideal girl," Wheatley told his readers:

Height 5'4"
Bust 32 ½"
Hips 37"
Waist 25"
and she wears size 5 shoes with 2½" heels

★

War was now clearly on the cards: after the Munich Agreement and "peace in our time" in September 1938, Hitler seized the rest of Czechoslovakia in March 1939.

Reviewing an anti-war book, *Danger Spots of Europe* by Bernard Newman, Wheatley agreed with Newman that "the greatest force for good or ill in the world today is Propaganda." He managed to incorporate it into his topical board game, *Invasion*, which had the dual message of re-arming while staying out of war if possible. It was played as a game of strategy across a Europe featuring place names such as Kitsch, Cliché, and Ersatz, along with Wurstanworse, Wuntzbit and Twyceshi, while the character of Angleland was suggested in places such as Dolittle, Flanelhurst, Fogey-on-Booze, and Blimps Bluff. A betting system was suggested in the rules, with the pool to be divided between the winners, but "To be logical, **as no country ever makes anything out of a war**, the contents of the pool should go into a charity box."

Wheatley bent his newspaper columns to the task. Supporting an Appeasement-oriented politician named Sir John

Simon, Wheatley told readers "How amazingly young Sir John Simon looks! That doubled my interest in a prediction recently made by my favourite astrologer. He tells me that Sir John's stars mark him out as more likely to succeed to the premiership than any other leading statesman."

Never one for the visual arts, Wheatley singled out "a fine dynamic painting of the famous 3.7 anti-aircraft gun in action" for praise at the Royal Academy, and he used his column to run a food hoarding competition: "Don't wait for emergency and start hoarding. Do it now. I laid in my iron rations at the time of the Abyssinian crisis, and I have been urging all my friends to do the same since." The housewife who sent in the best list of "iron rations for the home" won £3 worth of her chosen items. "Few mentioned chocolate," said Wheatley, "but I recommend it."

Wheatley had an amusing confirmation of media power through his column, when he and some other journalists, reporting a dance, agreed to invent a beauty named Ermintrude Wraxwell. Offers immediately starting coming in from agents and film companies: "had we named a real girl, we could have made a fortune for her."

★

Home Secretary Sir John Anderson, remembered for Anderson bomb shelters, formed a panel of celebrity speakers to tour the country raising volunteers for the Territorial forces, Air Raid Wardens and nursing. The panel included various sportsmen, actor Charles Laughton, writer Ralph Straus, and Wheatley. Characteristically – like the questionnaires he sometimes put in his novels – Wheatley asked readers for help with these speeches in his newspaper column: "I am anxious to have unofficial tips on best lines that will appeal to audiences – three guineas for best suggestion." In the event Wheatley's speeches went down well, and he closed them by leading the audience in what must have been an emotional rendition of 'Land of Hope and Glory.' Two million volunteers were raised by Anderson's panels in three months.

Wheatley focused on the dangers of political extremism, Fascist and Communist ("I do not suggest for one moment that these extremist parties should be suppressed. To attempt to do so would be the negation of the freedom that we stand for. But I do suggest that it is in our vital interests to see to it that their numbers grow as little as possible.") The important thing, said Wheatley, was for his listeners to remain free to vote for whichever party they thought would serve the interests of the country, "and so ensure yourselves of a continuation in your freedom of choice of government and the certainty of a healthy opposition which will preserve our liberties."

In private, as we shall see, Wheatley had more mixed feelings about democracy than this might suggest. Historically, the promotion of democracy by people without left leanings had arisen largely in opposition to Bolshevism and later Fascism. Before that it was a less universally positive word, and an observer at a socialist meeting in the nineteenth century described a meeting of "characteristically democratic men with dirty hands and small heads, some of them obviously with very limited wits."

Wheatley managed to knock off one more thriller before war broke out, *Sixty Days to Live*. The sixty days are those remaining before a comet hits the earth and a tidal wave finishes off the entire human race; entire, that is, but for a Surrey squire and three young couples who happen to include a film star and a millionaire.

Absurd as it is, it includes some compelling descriptions of a frozen England, anticipating Anna Kavan's *Ice*, and the *TLS* judged it to be "an excellent book for war time." Not everyone was so generous. Responding in the early science fiction fanzine *Sardonyx* to an American fan deprived of his regular fix of Wheatley, English writer Christopher Youd wrote:

Witness the anguish of Fred W. Fischer, who apparently dwells in the picturesque li'l burg of Knoxville, at being unable to obtain the works of Dennis Wheatley, a defect which makes me think more highly of the American publishing trade. The especial mention — "Sixty Days to Live" — is, my dear Fred, one of the latest and worst specimens of undiluted tosh to radiate from the well-known Wheatley pen. If, in America, you cannot reach Wheatley, thank once again the deity who created your native land. For we, in England, cannot get away from him . . . Wheatley, by the way, is another of our pseudo-Fascists, who, on Italian intervention, suffered a pseudo-change into patriots.

★

Diana was still a source of worry. Now eighteen, she had fallen in love with Brinsley Le Poer Trench, a charming man some ten years her senior who was the son of an Irish peer. His family were ancient and distinguished: one of his fore-bears had married the fourteenth-century witch Dame Alice Kyteler, who was accused of murdering three husbands and having relations with a demonic incubus named Robert Artisson — as in the Yeats poem 'Nineteen Hundred and Nineteen'[1] — while the fictional protagonist of H.P.Lovecraft's story 'The Rats in the Walls' is a de la Poer descendant.

Brinsley had, at one time, had a large fortune, but his affairs were now in the hands of trustees. He was tall and handsome, and all accounts agree how personable he was: he was a dis-tinguished but amiable individual, with a rather haunted, faraway expression and a taste for elegant braces.

In due course Brinsley and Diana wished to marry, which on the face of it might have pleased Wheatley. Wheatley was nothing if not class-conscious, and in that respect Brinsley — the son of the Earl of Clancarty, albeit only the fifth son — was certainly the real thing. Wheatley was impressed by the fact that Joan could trace her ancestry back to the time of the Norman Conquest, but Brinsley could do even better.

---

[1] "There lurches past, his great eyes without thought /. . ./ That insolent fiend Robert Artisson / To whom the love-lorn Lady Kyteler brought / Bronzed peacock feathers, red combs of her cocks."

He could trace it from 63,000 BC, when beings from other planets first landed on the earth in spaceships. Most humans, Brinsley was to explain in later years, were descended from these aliens, who came from more than one planet: "This accounts for all the different skin colours we've got down here." The majority of extra-terrestrials still out there were friendly, but Brinsley gathered that at least one group were hostile, and needed to be watched. Brinsley was eventually to reveal the existence of aliens living inside the earth, communicating with our surface world by secret tunnels erupting in places such as Tibet, and infiltrating agents among us in preparation for an eventual take-over. Many UFOs had in fact come not from outer space at all, but from this alien civilisation inside the earth, emerging from holes at the North and South Poles.

"I haven't been down there myself", Brinsley admitted, "but from what I gather they are very advanced." When the time came, Brinsley was to be a gift for his *Telegraph* obituarist. Brinsley had once produced a photograph showing "a large circular blob" amid the ice of the North Pole, which he said was the entrance to an alien tunnel: "He remained adamant even when it was pointed out to him that he was looking at part of the camera."

Brinsley's eminence as a UFOlogist was still in the future, but somehow Wheatley felt he was not the man for Diana. Apart from anything else, he had no money, forcing Wheatley into the role of Victorian-style father. Brinsley's intentions might be honourable, but how could he keep Diana in the style to which she was accustomed? All he had was a lowly clerking job at the Bank of South Africa.

Wheatley became angry when Brinsley announced that he wished to marry Diana. Diana arrived shortly after his outburst, insisting that she loved Brinsley and she wanted to marry him. Wheatley and Joan put forward their most sensible arguments, but finally they gave in, with the proviso that it should at least be a long engagement.

Brinsley took up lodgings in the house next door but one, and his charming presence was much in evidence at No.8

itself until at last, after almost a year, his status as one of the family became official. Brinsley and Diana, now twenty, were married by Wheatley's friend Cyril 'Bobby' Eastaugh. As Wheatley gave the bride away he was filled with misgivings, even as he hosted the champagne reception at his house. Penniless, the couple went down to 'Pen's Porch' – a cottage on Lady Carnarvon's Highclere Castle estate in Hampshire which the Wheatleys had leased – for their honeymoon, before Brinsley was conscripted into the Artillery at Amesbury, and Diana took a small flat in the town to be near him.

Wheatley's misgivings about the marriage proved to be well-founded, and it collapsed during the War. Through Wheatley's own war work, Diana met and fell in love with an American academic working in intelligence, Professor Wentworth 'Went' Eldredge of Dartmouth College, New Hampshire, and she obtained a divorce from Brinsley.

Wheatley liked Went, who later worked for the CIA, and he was relieved to see the back of Brinsley, who went on to unforeseen heights. Wheatley's former son-in-law found work selling advertising space for a gardening magazine opposite Waterloo Station, while editing the *Flying Saucer Review* and founding the International Unidentified Object Observer Corps. It was said that Brinsley spent his working time selling space, and his spare time gazing into it. Brinsley Le Poer Trench became well known to UFOlogists, with a string of books. His work anticipated the 'God was an astronaut' thesis of Erich von Daniken, and he also became big in Japan. Mr Honda, the motor manufacturer, came to London to question him about UFO energy and its potential uses in the automobile industry.

Wheatley did not live to see Brinsley's finest hour. After years of modest living in *Kind Hearts and Coronets*-style straitened circumstances, at last Brinsley's ship came in. Some unexpected deaths in the family propelled him into the House of Lords, when he became the eighth Earl of Clancarty, Viscount Dunlo, Baron Trench, Viscount Clancarty, and Marquess of Heusden. Brinsley's greatest triumph came when he instigated the House of Lords UFO debate in 1979, two years after Wheatley's death ("Is it not time that Her Majesty's Government informed our people of what they know about UFOs? I think it is time our people were told the truth.") He was also instrumental in introducing the *Flying Saucer Review* into the House of Lords Library.

Before we take our leave of Brinsley Le Poer Trench, eighth Earl and sometime Wheatley in-law, with his elegant braces and his haunted look, the last word should go to John Michell, who wrote a gentle and respectful obituary of him in the *Fortean Times*: "Friends from all periods tell of his great kindness, and those who laughed at his beliefs were often disarmed by the simple courtesy with which he defended them."

★

With war impending, Wheatley wanted the family to holiday in Ireland, but Joan insisted on the South of France. While they were there, Max Knight sent them a coded telegram: "Uncle has taken a turn for the worse and, if you wish to see him before the end, you should return home at once." In the event it missed them: they were already on their way back, just in time.

Back at No.8, Wheatley began preparing as if for a siege. He had already deposited a "large black box, roped and sealed" with his bank for safekeeping. It contents are unknown. Perhaps every book should have an unsolved mystery within it, like a vault, and this is ours. Quite likely it was Wheatley's personal archive and papers, containing things like his account of Tombe, in which case it held much of the present book.

He now asked Justerini and Brooks for empty champagne cases and built a half-submerged air raid shelter with them, packing them with rubble and making a protected space big enough for himself, Joan, the cook and two maids. Wheatley split his wine cellar into four, keeping a quarter, sending a quarter to Justerini's for storage, and dividing the rest between Joe Links and Charles Beatty, who had places in the country. Wheatley had stocked up on food, and his greatest fear was food riots and public disorder in the aftermath of bombing. Characteristically, he was as fearful of mob rule as he was of the Germans: "I had planned to make my household, of myself, and five women, self-supporting until the Government had got things under control."

Like families all over Britain, the Wheatleys – that day including Bill, Diana, and Colin – were gathered to listen to the wireless on the Sunday morning of the third of September 1939. Britain had given Germany an ultimatum to leave Poland, expiring at eleven, but there had been no response.

Consequently, said Chamberlain in his broadcast, "this nation is now at war with Germany."

CHAPTER THIRTY

Death of a Fifth Columnist

When Joe Links dropped round to No.8 on that first Sunday afternoon of the war, wearing the uniform of a Flying Officer in the RAF Volunteer Reserve, Wheatley felt a vicarious pride in his old friend's appearance; officer's uniform was "the proper dress for any gentleman when Britain is at war". This is probably not the first thought that would have occurred to TS Eliot on seeing a Jewish furrier swanning around dressed as an officer, and it shows a more inclusive vision of Englishness, despite the oddly schizoid attitude to Jews in some of Wheatley's writing.

Links invited Wheatley up to Hampstead for lunch at the Officers' Mess, which he had generously set up in his own house on Pond Street. After lunch he gave Wheatley a chance to throw a Molotov cocktail – a home-made petrol bomb – at a dummy tank. Never very athletic, Wheatley botched his throw, and it went up in a ball of flame just a few feet away from them.

Wheatley felt he might have a role with propaganda and he tried to get into the newly formed Ministry of Information, but as he recalled in an after-dinner speech years later, "They wouldn't have me as a gift". He applied again when he discovered the names of the two senior civil servants appointed to do the recruiting, but once again he didn't even receive the courtesy of a reply.

The ever capable Joan, meanwhile, who was a keen motorist, had found work with M15 as their "Petrol Queen," using her knowledge of different cars to dole out tailored fuel rations. Bill Younger, who had already been unofficially employed at Oxford by Max Knight, was now taken on to work in Knight's office, beginning what was to become a full time career in MI5.

The Wheatleys found work for Diana as a filing clerk for

MI5, but she was sacked after five weeks, and Wheatley wrote her another of his long letters. She'd shown a bad attitude, he said; clattering about in high heels, wearing a beauty spot, making her face up in work time, going around the corner for furtive cigarettes, and exercising her wit on the women she didn't like, just "for the sake of raising a laugh among a few other stupid girls."

She was rude, vain, snobbish, bad-mannered, and obsessed with young men, which led her to dress and behave in a "flashy" "shop girl" manner, going around the West End with tarty furs, heels and "incredible nails," and "the way you let your breasts hang half out of your dress at Quaglino's the other night . . . honestly made me writhe."

And so it went on, for four thousand sensible words. Wheatley complained that Diana had no real female friends: "A girl can have any number of lovers yet still cultivate other women. Yet you haven't got a single real intimate girl friend . . . there are times when women can do for a woman things no man can and you'll regret it later." He appealed to reincarnation: if she continued to live so selfishly "you won't get such a good deal next time."

She seemed to take no interest in the War ("It's no good blaming us for it") and then there was Brinsley, who also took no interest and seemed to Wheatley to be a no-hoper. If everyone behaved like Diana, said Wheatley, we would lose, with Communist revolution and German invasion: "You wouldn't find it much fun being conscripted for forced labour or having to become the mistress of somebody you hated for the sake of enough food to eat and their protection. But that's what is happening to Czech and Polish girls . . ."

Wheatley's autobiography veers to the other extreme when he tells his readers that Diana was parachuted into France on secret missions with the Special Operations Executive. There seems to be no evidence for this[1].

[1] Neither I nor Diana's brother Major General Sir Jack Younger could find any trace; and if it is true, it is suprising that Wheatley doesn't say more about it.

Through Wheatley, the shadowy occultist Rollo Ahmed also seems to have found work with MI5. Wheatley sent notes on him to Knight, and Knight wrote back to say he would be grateful if Wheatley would "sound him out very gently particularly with a view to finding out if he would be willing to do this sort of work abroad." Discreet as ever, he doesn't say what sort of work it is.

The one person Wheatley couldn't place with MI5 was himself. He asked Knight for work, emboldened by the fact that he also knew MI5's founder Sir Vernon Kell, but Knight didn't seem to want him, and told him the best war work he could do would be to keep the public entertained with his thrillers. Knight had other plans for Wheatley.

★

The day before war was declared, the police had raided William Joyce's basement flat, only to find he had just fled to Germany: someone had tipped him off. It was almost certainly Knight, despite the fact that he disliked Joyce (a "pompous, conceited little creature" with "that romantic streak common to all Celts which makes them double effective and doubly dangerous.") In the long run it was Knight's helpful tip that led to Joyce being hanged. Without it, he would have spent a relatively safe war interned under Regulation 18B with the likes of Sir Oswald Mosley, Admiral Barry Domville, and Archibald Ramsay. In the short run it ensured that the police found absolutely nothing in his flat "except old National Socialist League propaganda and evidence testifying to the couple's abject poverty."

Knight rang Wheatley to ask him about Joyce, and Wheatley – despite the fact that Joyce was razored from mouth to ear, and had told him how much Goering liked his books – said he couldn't remember him. "Oh yes you do," said Knight, "He was at one of your parties." And then he had some surprising and perhaps uncomfortable news for Wheatley: when MI5 had raided the flat, they had captured his papers, which included a file on Wheatley. Joyce had apparently reported to his German superiors that Wheatley could be an excellent collaborator after the invasion of Britain, and would even make a good Nazi Gauleiter for North West London. This is one of the best known stories about Wheatley, and it has gone from Wheatley's auto-biography to books on Knight and even Joyce, but there is no evidence for it.

Knight had plenty of good stories: he told Wheatley that a soldier had been found with a slip of paper bearing suspicious names such as Carlotta Casado, Heinrich Hauser, Pauline Vidor, and Serge Orloff. The list was sent to MI5, where Knight spotted that the man had simply been playing Wheatley's *Herewith The Clues*. Very droll. It could be true, of course (like Knight's stories of sitting next to a Marx brother in the cinema and taking jazz lessons from Sidney Bechet, although they start to seem cumulatively unlikely) but his story that he and Wheatley had attended Crowley "ceremonies" and been "initiated" by him was definitely untrue, as we have seen. Knight had also fabricated a letter to help his case when he framed the innocent pacifist Ben Greene as a Nazi.

This compromising piece of information about Wheatley the potential Gauleiter – people had been interned for far less – could have been very damaging, but as Wheatley says, "fortunately Max knew all about me; so we had a good laugh over it." It is possible that Knight was having a better laugh than Wheatley.

*

Hardly had they finished laughing when Knight asked Wheatley for a favour. Wheatley would have done all he could to help anyway, but Knight probably felt the Joyce story increased his hold over him. As Joan Miller remembered, "he liked to control people".

Knight had a newly arrived Austrian girl named Friedl Gartner or "Fritzi" working as a double agent, and he wanted a respectable member of the public – safely outside MI5, in case the connection should be discovered – to provide her with employment and vouch that they had known her for several years. Wheatley was more than happy to do this, and employed her as a research assistant for his wartime novels, paying her by cheque while Max forwarded him untraceable cash.

Wheatley and Joan met another agent, this time a genuine Nazi, at a cocktail party of Charles Birkin's. Wheatley describes her as a Hungarian named Vicki, married to a peer. Max Knight ("having learned by his own mysterious means that we had met her") then filled Wheatley in on her background. He wanted the Wheatleys to entertain her at No.8 and generally cultivate her, which they did, and they also made the acquaintance of her friend, a dark-haired baroness whom they nicknamed The Black Baroness.

Knight had Vicki so well under surveillance that when she threw a party for thirty-odd people, her guests included Wheatley, Joan and Diana; Bill Younger with Fritzi; Charles Birkin, Bunny Tattersall, and a colleague of Bill named Grierson Dickson; and Max Knight himself, who tapped his nose and told Wheatley the room was full of his operatives. Vicki was, Wheatley realised, "more or less throwing her party for MI5".

★

Wheatley was meanwhile working hard on the wartime adventures of Gregory Sallust. Pitting Gregory against the Germans gave him a chance to shake off the slur of fascist sympathies that some reviewers had felt in the first two Sallust books. Writing sixteen hours a day, from ten in the morning until two the following morning, Wheatley managed to produce his 172,000 word novel *The Scarlet Impostor* in seven weeks.

It was a phenomenal success on its publication in January 1940. Its bestseller status caught Wheatley in a trade battle between his publisher and the big libraries – Boots, Smiths, Harrods, and The Times – who in those days could make or break a book. Hutchinson used Wheatley's name to force a two shilling price rise from 8/6 to 10/6 (£16 to £20 today; in the days before television, novels were relatively expensive). The reviews were excellent and the book was

391

selling well, but the libraries refused to buy it. Wheatley argued with them, saying they would be damaged if they refused to stock the books their customers wanted, and he even wrote to Freddy Richardson at Boots with a version of an old music hall favourite:

> We don't want to fight, but by Jingo if we do,
> We've got the book, we've got the quotes,
> We've got the money too.

Finally the advertising campaign, in addition to word of mouth, created such a clamour for the book among library subscribers that the libraries were forced to give in and stock it.

Along with whatever charm they found in Gregory – whose amorality and worldly savoir-faire make him the major precursor of James Bond, as distinct from the cleaner and tweedier heroes of John Buchan – the public devoured the Sallust books for their extraordinarily well-informed narratives and news-like coverage of the war.

Allowing that Wheatley's place "may not be the loftiest niche in the mighty edifice of the world's fiction," one reviewer nevertheless praised him as "as a dealer in magical spells of sensationalism" and noted "the book is so up-to-date that you can even read that the Royal Oak was torpedoed at Scapa 'on the 14th' Phew!"

This newsiness continued through the next two Sallust books, *Faked Passports*, and *The Black Baroness*, published in October 1940. "I have been reading Dennis Wheatley's thriller called *The Black Baroness*," a journalist wrote, "in which he refers by name to the capture by the Germans of Major-General Victor Fortune, who commanded the 51st Division . . . and yet it was only on October 3 that Major-General Fortune's name appeared in the list of prisoners of war."

The public were only given *The Black Baroness* because they voted for it. Wheatley put a questionnaire in the back of *Faked Passports*: "Shall I send Gregory to Norway and perhaps to other fronts as the war develops, or have you had enough of him for the time being? The alternatives are a story of strange happenings in the West Indies . . . or a new departure for me into Historical Romance. Any postcards stating a preference will be gratefully acknowledged and, as a servant to the public whose business it is to entertain, I will write the book that gets the largest vote." The largest vote was "more Gregory". Wheatley had put a questionnaire into a book before, but given his cinema speeches it is not too far fetched to think this one emphasised the importance of voting and democracy.

Sallust also led to Wheatley's attendance at a Foyle's Literary Lunch with the theme of "Spies". Wheatley had become a founding patron of Christina Foyle's 'Right Book Club', which Frederic Raphael remembers his parents subscribing to, receiving "a succession of furiously fascistic books (in nice tweedy covers)". Wheatley hoped it would counter "the spate of subversive stuff . . . pouring from the Left Book Club under the aegis of Victor Gollancz."

Wheatley met Sir Paul Dukes at the Foyles lunch. Dukes had been a British secret agent in Tsarist and Bolshevik Russia, and he was a former associate of the man known as Sidney Reilly, "Prince of Spies". He was also adept at Yoga, a subject on which he eventually wrote books, and interested in reincarnation. Wheatley told an acquaintance that Dukes was the sort of man he would like to have been.

★

When the Spanish Fascists had attacked Madrid, they claimed they not only had four columns of troops marching on the city but a "fifth column" of secret supporters already inside. It became a famous phrase of the time (Hemingway wrote a play called *The Fifth Column*) and the idea of infiltrators caught Wheatley's imagination. He drafted a script for a BBC broadcast "with a view to putting the fear of God into Fifth Columnists and as a warning to misguided people to disassociate themselves from bodies such as The British Union, the Peace Pledge Union, etc." Many of these people were guilty of holding the same sort of views that Wheatley himself had held a few years earlier.

Describing the Fifth Column as a "sinister force" which had been active with devastating effects in Norway, Holland and Belgium, Wheatley considered it in England. There was Mosley ("this ranting schemer") and his followers:

> His lieutenants and helpers believe that they would be the Himmlers and Gauleiters of this country. They are mostly small-time people who have become embittered through lack of success in honest occupations and having been tempted by the Devil, have bartered their soul with him for a chance of power.

"I can tell you that we have lists of several hundred British-born traitors," said Wheatley, and "and every single day some of these people are leading us to others who do not belong to any particular organisation and who normally we would never have suspected."

The likes of Mosley and Captain Ramsay had got off lightly. "As this is not Germany, they will not be beaten with steel rods until the flesh hangs down in gory strips from their backs." Instead they would be interned. But for smaller fry, caught aiding the King's enemies, there would be no such good fortune.

> I do not suppose that many of you have ever seen a firing squad execute a spy. It is a grim business. Such executions are usually carried out in the early morning. The scene is generally the cold grey yard of a military barracks. Perhaps there is a little pale sunlight giving promise of a lovely day which the spy knows that he will never live to see as he is led out of his cell.
>
> He is escorted to a large post driven into the ground and tied to it, because sometimes traitors lose their nerve at the last moment and show a desperate desire to run away. The victim's hands are tied behind his back and a canvas mask is drawn over his face. But he has already

seen the little group of soldiers loading their rifles and a cold sweat breaks out upon his forehead. Those soldiers are uneasy because they hate the job they have to do. When the traitor has been blindfolded, he can still *hear* what is going on. The officer's orders, the clicking home of the bolts of the rifles. He tenses himself for the last ordeal and perhaps begins to pray.

'Fire!' cries the officer. The rifles crack. The awful split second has come and the victim tenses himself to receive the bullets that will end his life. Another split second; another second. Dully, he realises that he is still standing there unharmed. For an instant, he may believe that he is already dead, but a moment later he hears the officer giving fresh orders and realises the horrid truth. The soldiers, each not wishing to be responsible for his death, have all fired high. They can be punished for that, but they do it all the same. In consequence, the sweating victim stands there in an agony of apprehension while the whole appalling ordeal has to be gone through all over again.

But at the second attempt, the victim is rarely killed. Nine times out of ten, the troops, hating their work, do not aim at the heart or head, and after the second volley, the wretched traitor hangs groaning from the post — five or six bullets having smashed into his body — but still conscious. He hears footfalls as the Provost Marshal, whose duty it is to finish him off, crosses the yard. After what seems to him an interminable time, the cold barrel of a revolver is placed against his temple and his brains are blown out. The still quivering body is cut down and dragged away to be cast into the lime-pit of the prison yard. That is the end reserved for traitors. It is also the fate of misguided idealists who are led into aiding the enemy by placing their personal theories before their country's safety in time of war.

Wheatley's fear of Fifth Columnists was the mainspring for a series of stories he wrote in 1940 for the *Daily Sketch*, featuring a new hero, "The Man With The Girlish Face." This was

Vivien Pawlett-Browne, whose "lazy smile and brown eyes with their ridiculous curling lashes might have caused him to be thought effeminate, had it not been for his good jaw and strong, well-shaped hands." Wheatley had already experimented with the effete sophistication of the super-criminal Oxford Kate, and Diana also had some input into the new character.

Pawlett-Browne specialises in rooting out treacherous Jews and suspicious foreigners in general. When bubonic plague breaks out in "cosmopolitan" Hampstead, he traces it to a refugee librarian ("definitely non-Aryan and spoke with a heavy accent") who is handing out free Union Jack bookmarks impregnated with plague bacilli. And so it goes on: German Jew Jacob Bauer is a radio engineer with access to top secret transmitter plans, fortunately cut short by Pawlett-Browne: "It's curious that your name rhymes with Tower, isn't it, dear Herr Bauer, since it's at the Tower of London that we shoot people like you." And a Miss Marlowe turns out to be of German descent, despite her father changing his name by deed poll back in 1928: "how right you were, *my sweet*, about our cherishing snakes in our bosoms."

Stories one might wish Wheatley hadn't written, but entirely of their time. 'INTERN THE LOT' ran the Beaverbrook headline, and Sir Neville Bland's pamphlet *The Fifth Column Menace* told readers that "The paltriest kitchen maid, with German connections, not only can be, but generally is, a menace to the safety of the country." It was one of those moments when the outer world and the inner world are in tune, because it chimed with a lifelong fear of contamination in Wheatley's mind. One of the things people often remember about his occult books is the importance of keeping dust and dirt out of pentagrams and magic circles, in case evil spirits should use it gain a foothold in the purified "astral fortress".

The struggle with the Fifth Column came close to home. When MI5 raided the flat of a pro-Nazi American cipher clerk, Tyler Kent, they captured Captain Ramsay's notorious "Red Book": a leather ledger with a heavy lock, containing the Right Club's membership list. Along with the likes of William Joyce it contained the name of Brinsley, "Le P Trench, B."

Wheatley was still writing hard – he published nine books during the war, six of them new novels – but other war work continued to elude him, until one day Joan was chauffeuring an MI5 officer named Captain Hubert Stringer. It seemed clear Hitler would soon invade Britain and it was part of Stringer's job to think of counter-measures, but he wasn't finding it easy to come up with ideas. "Why don't you ask my husband?" said Mrs Wheatley, "That's rather his cup of tea."

CHAPTER THIRTY-ONE

Strange Conflict

With Poland already occupied, the spring and early summer of 1940 saw Blitzkrieg victories over Norway, Denmark, the Netherlands, Belgium and France. It became increasingly obvious that the British Expeditionary Force was in trouble until it had to be rescued from the beach at Dunkirk, isolated and facing total defeat. As Wheatley later summarised it in a document for limited circulation, the fact was that "an army of 350,000 well-trained and well-equipped men were converted in the course of a few days into a rabble, which had to be taken off in its shirts." But the flotilla of ships that brought them back included civilian volunteers in all manner of small boats, and this moving detail caught the public imagination, transmuting "a highly successful fuck-up" (as one of the rescued put it) into a spiritual victory for British amateurism. Like Scott's last expedition and the Charge of the Light Brigade, "the Dunkirk Spirit" entered the national mythology.

Just as the Dunkirk rescue was beginning, in the days following the 27th May 1940, Wheatley was working through the night of the 27th–28th to write his first paper for Captain Stringer, 'Resistance to Invasion'. Believing there might only be a fortnight or less to prepare, and that the bulk of an invasion would hit the South East coast in the area between Beachy Head and Cromer, Wheatley envisaged desperate low-tech counter-measures. Since searchlights would soon be shot out, beaches should be covered by burning beacons every few hundred yards, built by civilians. Fishing nets should be placed offshore to foul propellers, and barbed wire should be requisitioned from farmers and placed in the shallow water. Rowing boats filled with explosive should be anchored off the beach and detonated as the Germans came amongst them. Nails and broken glass should be used, set in planks and concrete.

As the enemy came ashore and inevitably gained ground, trees should be brought down on tanks, petrol stations mined to explode, and petrol supplies mixed with water ("if the enemy use the captured petrol it would then have the effect of choking their carburettors"). Shallow trenches should be dug, filled with oil and smoke bombs, "which can be ignited on the approach of a superior enemy . . . making a serious barrier . . . and enabling our own units to retreat to a new position, unmolested, under cover of the flames and smoke . . ."

Most famously, Wheatley suggested that road signs should be taken down, along with railway station names and even pub signs; this measure was adopted, and – as it turned out – "put a lot of people to a lot of inconvenience and all for no purpose." In a final Wheatley flourish, he envisaged a pamphlet to be dropped over the continent: "Come to England this summer and sample the fun we have prepared for you. Try bathing in our barbed-wire enclosures . . . Try jumping in our ditches and get burnt alive. Come by air and meet our new death ray . . . England or Hell – it's going to be just the same for you in either."

★

Captain Stringer ("delicate, charming man and a real patriot") came round for drinks a couple of nights later. He liked Wheatley's paper and had passed it on, but he warned Wheatley that the machinery was very bureaucratic, and the Germans might already be here before anyone could use his ideas.

Wheatley asked if he might send the paper to contacts of his own, including Admiral Sir Edward Evans, Colonel Charles Balfour-Davey, and Sir Louis Greig, who was now a Wing Commander and Personal Assistant to the Secretary of State for Air. Around three weeks later Greig telephoned and asked Wheatley to lunch at the Dorchester. Also at the table were a Czech armaments manufacturer and Wing-Commander Lawrence Darvall, later to become Air Marshal Sir Lawrence Darvall. The war had moved on: France had surrendered, Italy had come in on the German side, and the Dunkirk evacuation had been a success, although the British Army had abandoned its tanks, artillery and even rifles on the other side of the Channel.

Greig and Darvall also liked Wheatley's paper, particularly its guerrilla-style aspects. Unlike many amateur dreams of the time, involving grandiose, science-fiction style plans for putting immense electric fences across the country, or encasing London in a giant concrete fort, Wheatley's approach was influenced by his study of the Russian and Spanish civil wars. At the end of the lunch Darvall suggested another project for Wheatley: this time he was to consider himself a member of the German High Command, and produce a plan for the invasion of England.

On his way home Wheatley went to Geographia in Fleet Street and bought two maps of Britain, one physical and the other showing density of population. Over the next forty eight hours, with the help of three magnums of champagne and two hundred cigarettes, Wheatley wrote a 15,000 word paper entitled 'The Invasion and Conquest of Britain'.

"There must be no humanitarian considerations," said Obergruppenfuhrer Wheatley. Advocating the use of poison gas and bacteriological warfare, Wheatley imagined the German occupation as the payback for a long-held German grudge. In a characteristic detail, he observed that "Not until British women lick the boots of German soldiers while British men look on can we be certain that we have achieved our final objective and that Britain will never menace us again."

The British middle class were to be destroyed, with the bombing of public schools and universities, "because these contain Britain's officer class of tomorrow." All Service officers over the rank of army Captain, naval Lieutenant or Flight-Lieutenant were to be shot, along with members of the House of Lords, MPs, and prominent journalists, writers and sportsmen: excluding, of course, those "on our special list."

Fifth columnists and collaborators would come into their own during the invasion, spreading chaos by every possible means. Wheatley had always feared that the refugee influx would contain a number of German 'plants', and he envisaged that even real refugees with families still on the Continent could be forced to co-operate. Poisoned cigarettes and chocolate would be distributed. Reservoirs would be poisoned with bacteria, or dynamited to cause water shortages. Gas mains would be broken by false roadworkers. Prisons, lunatic asylums and zoos would all be thrown open. False BBC-style broadcasts would be made. Cabinet Ministers would be assassinated. Letter and parcel bombs would be sent to thousands of homes, and men with key posts would be told their wives and children had been killed, to spread "mental distress and to hamper coherent thought."

Ireland would be occupied prior to the full invasion (where "resistance would be almost negligible," particularly with "the very strong Fifth Column elements there") as a base to strengthen the Atlantic blockade, preventing supplies reaching Britain from America. On the straightforwardly military side, Wheatley made detailed plans to get 600,000 men across in the first five days, followed by a further million once the lines of supply and communication had been set up.

He expected heavy casualties, but it would be worth it: "the conquest of Britain means the conquest of the world."

★

It was a great satisfaction to Wheatley when it was revealed a few years later that Operation Sea-Lion, the German plan of invasion, was to be a massive assault on the South East Coast, just as he had predicted. Britain's official strategy was prepared to resist an attack further north, on the East coast. Meanwhile he delivered his paper as instructed to "Mr Rance's Room, at the Office of Works": a cover name for the the Cabinet War Rooms, the Whitehall bunker complex where the Joint Planning Staff had their HQ.

Wheatley's prediction of how the Germans might behave as an occupying force was based on their treatment of the

Polish, and on the research he had been doing for his Gregory Sallust books. As he later told a journalist, "Gregory and I had been looking pretty closely at the Nazis for quite a while."

Darvall and his colleagues were shaken by Wheatley's paper, particularly by its sheer swinishness. "We've been playing this war like cricket," they said, "but Wheatley thinks like a Nazi."

*

Among the smaller trials the people of Britain endured were propaganda radio broadcasts from an unknown Briton with a hectoring and supercilious manner, soon nicknamed "Lord Haw-Haw". Lord Donegall was instrumental in discovering that this man was, in fact, none other than William Joyce. His talks were initially appreciated for their comic value, but they slowly began to wear their listeners down. Among his more picturesque suggestions was the idea – since prayer and church services were clearly failing to help the British cause – that Aleister Crowley should be invited to celebrate a Black Mass in Westminster Cathedral.

On the material plane, meanwhile, Stalin said "It was not Germany who attacked France and Britain but France and Britain who attacked Germany, thus assuming responsibility for the present war. The ruling circles of Britain and France rudely declined both Germany's peace proposals and the attempts of the Soviet Union to achieve the earliest termination of the war."

Stalin and Hitler were now comrades, after the Russo-German Pact, and British Communists (previously in favour of war, on anti-Fascist grounds) now attacked the British government as Imperialist war mongers. They staged an industrial go-slow campaign to sabotage the war effort, and in February 1940 they fought a by-election in East London on the slogan "Stop This War".

Wheatley now wrote another paper, 'Further Measures for Resistance to Invasion'. Reiterating his fears about Fifth Columnists, he suggested that just as Fascists had been interned, so similar measures should be taken against Communists, who could do great damage in areas such as Clydeside. Above all, Wheatley urged diehard civilian resistance to invasion. If the Germans put in a million troops, as seemed likely, they would still be outnumbered forty to one: "If one in forty of us can kill a German, we'll win. After the first phase, it won't be a matter of guns and tanks; we've got to prepare the people to fight with knives."

After another lunch with Darvall, Wheatley produced his most desperate paper yet, 'Village Defence,' written in the form of instructions for the public. Each village, acting as an isolated unit ("don't rely on support from neighbouring villages or attempt to give it to them") would be prepared to dig in and die in an attempt to slow down the German advance: "No one expects you to hurl back the advance of a German armoured division, but you can delay it"; "Delay — delay — delay. That is your function."

Everyone over the age of ten was to play a part. Children were to hand in their lead soldiers to be melted down for ammunition. Old tyres and hot water bottles were to be collected together to make noxious fires for smoke screens. Paving stones were to be pulled up and used for makeshift fortifications, along with headstones from the village graveyard ("these are just the right shape"). This wasn't disrespectful to the dead, said Wheatley: "If they could rise again they would carry their headstones for you."

Some of Wheatley's planning shows clear tactical thinking; defenders were not to mass together in a central redoubt, for example, but deployed around it at lesser strong points, "so that enemy tanks, smashing through it, should not annihilate the defenders concentrated in one building. After the tanks had passed, the majority of its defenders would still be at their posts and capable later of delaying the advance of enemy infantry." This was combined with attention to morale, so preliminary meetings were to be preceded by a short church service "for those who wish to attend". After singing 'All Things Bright and Beautiful', the sermon would stress the militantly atheistic aspects of Nazism, and that this was a war "in very fact against the forces of Evil." The service would then end, like Wheatley's cinema talks, with 'Land of Hope and Glory'.

★

Wheatley modestly acknowledged that there was a certain 'comic opera' element to some of his defence plans, but he could hardly have been more in earnest about their over-all picture. Years later, interviewed by a smirking journalist who raised his eyebrows at the idea of singing 'All Things Bright and Beautiful' as a preparation for last ditch defence, Wheatley said ("wearily"): "It is impossible to explain now that it was that sort of emotional touch which meant so much then, how eagerly people responded to a community gesture, how spirits could be livened . . ."

Rounding off 'Village Defence', Wheatley produced a line that could have come from one of his occult novels: "Remember that we are the champions of Light facing the creeping tide of Darkness which threatens to engulf the world."

★

The real German invasion was scheduled for mid–August 1940, preceded by the Luftwaffe's attempt to destroy the RAF. They were narrowly beaten back in the Battle of Britain, and from the seventh of September a new strategy appeared with the Blitz. This was bombing on a scale the world had never seen before, almost of the kind feared and predicted in the Thirties: two million homes were destroyed, and 60,000 civilians killed. Wheatley was dining with Joe Links one night at Hatchett's, a newly popular basement res-taurant in Piccadilly where Django Reinhardt and Stephane Grappelli played, and they came up to see Burton's the tailors completely ablaze, lighting Piccadilly up like daylight.

They were lucky not to be in the Café de Paris, another popular basement venue a hundred yards further east. Thought to be bomb proof, the deep and heavily mirrored ballroom received a direct hit through a ventilation shaft in the same raid, and the ensuing scene was made even more nightmarish by looters scrabbling around among the dead and dying for valuables and jewellery, cutting off fingers if need be.

In September 1940 Wheatley wrote a paper on 'Aerial Defence', much of it taken up with fulminations against incompetent official policies. The rest combines practical suggestions with close attention to issues of morale, and some wilder, lateral-thinking inspirations of the kind Wheatley specialised in: he suggested, for example, that devices giving off a bomber's drone should be drifted at altitude over Germany, wrecking the population's peace of mind and making it harder to tell where real raids began and ended.

It was against the background of the Blitz that Wheatley wrote his next occult novel – still only his second – entitled *Strange Conflict*; a title that would serve for almost any of Wheatley's occult books. Not only was the Blitz approaching its height in September, but Britain was suffering from a U-boat blockade, with 160,000 tons of shipping sunk in that single month. Sir Pellinore Gwaine-Cust, an old friend of Gregory Sallust, needs urgent advice on the shipping losses, so naturally he invites the Duke de Richleau to dinner. De Richleau plays a role not unlike Wheatley's own, with "no official position at all" but the "fresh mind" of the non-specialist, with "imagination and a great reservoir of general knowledge."

The Duke discovers that German Intelligence are working with a practitioner of voodoo in Haiti, one Doctor Saturday, who uses uses occult means to spy on shipping convoys. The main supernatural plank of *Strange Conflict* is "astral projection", one of the most appealing ideas in popular occultism, in which the "astral body" of a dreamer or a waking adept can leave the physical body and fly.

Wheatley had been discussing this with Maxwell Knight, who was very interested in the subject and probably gave Wheatley information. Knight even seems to have fancied himself as a practitioner. His MI5 assistant Joan Miller felt she "had to contend with M's extra-sensory perception," and one night she saw him "standing by a chest of drawers in the moonlight when he was, in fact, in bed asleep; I have since learnt that this phenomenon is known, in theosophical circles, as 'projecting one's astral body'. At the time I was simply overwhelmed by the spookiness of the occurrence." She seems to have been in awe of him.

Astral projection for purposes of espionage might sound just the sort of nonsense that belongs only in the world of Wheatley, but the American government later poured an estimated 20 million dollars into military clairvoyance experiments, under the concept of "remote viewing," notably in the CIA's notorious Stargate Programme.

As was usually the case with Wheatley's occult fiction, there was a careful propaganda cargo being smuggled across with the supernaturalism: Wheatley was writing like a one-man Ministry of Information. In particular, the seductive idea of flying around on the astral plane was calculated to remove the fear of death – the Duke discusses exactly this aspect, as he encounters the spirits of the departed rising from blitzed buildings – and to prepare a wartime readership to endure widespread bereavement (without sending them anywhere near spiritualism, as had happened after the First War). Wheatley had already decided there was a morale benefit in the reincarnation beliefs put across in Joan Grant's novel *Life as Carola*:

> At this present time it is of immense importance because it carries the message that Death is not to be feared . . . The comfort, reassurance and shining hope to be found in these pages are an armour which would turn even a craven into a paladin . . . and the light shines again in this darkest hour when the dread shadows of War are all about us. That is why every family, even if they have to save their pennies, should give with their love copies of LIFE AS CAROLA and its glorious predecessor, WINGED PHARAOH, to their fighting men.

There was a further message in *Strange Conflict*, concerning the Blitz. Not only had the Blitz fallen heaviest on industrial areas, inhabited by the working class, but many middle–class people were able to leave London for the country, a freedom resented by those trapped in London "for the duration." For the most part the Blitz stiffened resolve by increasing public hatred for the Germans, but it was also proving socially divisive, as the Germans knew it would.

In the previous war, a relatively few bombs falling on East London had caused some East Enders to stage a "Call The War Off" demonstration, and now the bombing was incomparably worse. Harold Nicolson's diary reports a hear-say account that the King and Queen were booed, and that "everybody is worried about the feeling in the East End, where there is much bitterness." When Buckingham Palace was bombed, Queen Elizabeth famously said "I'm glad we've been bombed. It makes me feel I can look the East End in the face."

It is against this background that the Duke and Sir Pellinore make a positive point of staying in London. "I wonder you don't clear out to the country," says Sir Pellinore, but they agree they are not going: "I loathe discomfort and boredom," says the Duke, "but no amount of either would induce me to leave London when there are such thousands of poor people who cannot afford to do so."

And with that agreed, the Duke embarks on one of Wheatley's most richly characteristic books, chalking up a pentagram (complete with the words INRI ADAM TE DAGERAM AMRTET ALGAR ALGASTNA, taken from *Rembrandt's Faustus* in Wheatley's copy of Grillot de Givry) on the floor to serve him and his chums as an "astral fortress".

Strange Conflict is a product of the most Churchillian, "fight them on the beaches" stage of the war. America, destined to grow rich through the war, was still not in (that took Pearl Harbor, and Hitler's subsequent declaration of war on America) and Russia was still on the other side, supplying the German planes in the Battle of Britain with Russian fuel. Britain was alone, leading to the Duke's final oration on the last page:

407

"As long as Britain stands the Powers of Darkness cannot prevail. On Earth the Anglo–Saxon race is the last Guardian of the Light, and I have an unshakable conviction that, come what may, our island will prove the Bulwark of the World."

★

Joan stayed in London throughout the War but Wheatley left for a couple of months at Pen's Porch. He went there with his secretary in October 1940, not to escape the bombs but to protect Pen's Porch from being requisitioned by Newbury Council for the use of refugees; the Wheatleys had sent all their best furniture and possessions down there for safety.

Wheatley continued to come up to London a couple of days a week, sometimes spending the night at No.8, but in December 1940 No.8 was bombed. Joan moved to Oakwood Court in Kensington, and Wheatley joined her there in a separate flat in January, relinquishing Pen's Porch to the refugees. Wheatley became an ARP warden at Oakwood Court and was elected as head of fire-fighting by the other tenants, but in February the Wheatleys found a flat together at 10 Chatsworth Court. Wheatley kept his Oakwood Court flat as an office, since it was only ten minutes away from Chatsworth Court, where the Blitz had resulted in around three quarters of the 200 flats being unoccupied.

★

Wheatley was now writing for fourteen or fifteen hours a day. *The Black Baroness* – the book he had interrupted to write the first 'Resistance to Invasion' paper – was published in October 1940, and *Strange Conflict* in April 1941, after which he gave Julian Day a second outing in *The Sword of Fate*, published in September 1941.

Meanwhile he continued to write papers for Darvall and the Joint Planning Staff. He wrote on keeping Turkey neutral, keeping morale up at home, and getting supplies across the Atlantic by using convoys of crude wooden rafts drifting on the Gulf Stream (an idea he re-used in his postwar novel,

The Man Who Missed The War). He suggested a deal with General Franco, swapping Gibraltar in return for Tangier. And he developed an obsession with his plan for invading Sardinia and making it a "new Gibraltar", pushing for it in paper after paper.

Wheatley's plan nearly came off: eventually, in 1943, it was in the balance whether the Allies invaded Sardinia or Sicily. The Joint Planning Staff were persuaded to Sardinia (the target also favoured by Eisenhower) and it was only with difficulty that Sir Alan Brooke, Chief of the Imperial General Staff and later Viscount Alanbrooke, managed to swing the decision in favour of Sicily. Wheatley never forgave him.

"I still maintain we would have won the war a year earlier if we had gone into Sardinia," Wheatley said, "And we would have been in Vienna, Berlin and Budapest long before the Russians. Think what a difference that would have made to the world situation to-day!" Lawrence Darvall, Commandant of the NATO Defence College in Paris, looked back in 1959 and wrote "the long slog up the leg of Italy need never have taken place. From Sardinia a relatively quick entry into Austria, South Germany, and Hungary might have been possible."

Wheatley also believed that the world's religious faiths were being insufficiently mobilised against the atheistic menace of Nazism: prefiguring a secret assignment he was later given in the Cold War, he pointed out that the Muslim world had not understood the nature of Nazism, which had made successful overtures to Islam: "150,000,000 Mohammedans are waiting for 'the word', and who gives it to them? Only Dr Goebbels . . ."

International Jewry, too, was insufficiently organised against Nazism, or so it seemed to Wheatley. Through a Jewish refugee at Oakwood Court, one of his team of fire watchers, Wheatley knew that the New Zionist Organisation had offered to raise an army of at least 100,000 men to fight the Germans, under the Allied High Command, but that the British Government had considered the proposal and turned it down.

Wheatley advocated a similar scheme, believing that the free world's Jewish population could raise and fund an army of 250,000 men. Ewen Montagu, one of Wheatley's wartime colleagues – the two men didn't like each other – later poured scorn on this idea in the *Jewish Chronicle*, and particularly scoffed at Wheatley's eccentric idea for a Jewish homeland. Believing the Jews would have to be promised a homeland after the war, Wheatley suggested giving them Madagascar.

The argument behind this was that the Jews were originally from the Yemen and arrived in Palestine, which had an indigenous Arab population, around 1500 BC: by this logic it was no more their birthright than it was of later occupiers such as the Romans or Ottoman Turks. As for Madagascar, this might seem one of Wheatley's typically lateral thinking suggestions, but in fact it is an idea with a more sinister history.

Writing in the Nazi paper *Der Sturmer* in 1938, Julius Streicher noted "When Der Sturmer suggested some years ago that a way to solve the Jewish Question would be to transport the Jews to the French colony of Madagascar, Jews and their lackeys mocked the idea and declared it inhumane. But today our proposal is being discused by foreign statesmen." Its origins seem to lie with a French writer, Paul de Lagarde, back in 1885. Both Japan and Poland considered settling their surplus populations on Madagascar and Poland even sent a commission to look into it and held discussions with the French, while the native Malagasys held demonstrations against immigration.

This last detail would hardly have bothered Wheatley. In *The Devil Rides Out*, Mocata's black manservant – an "ab-human" whose eyes glow red, and who assumes the form of the Goat of Mendes – is specified as being a Malagasy, from "the home of voodoo", and the island and its people are vilified in some detail.

*

Wheatley also had some idiosyncratic suggestions about how

to prevent another war: after the experiences of 1870, 1914 and 1939, he believed the Germans should ideally be sterilised. Failing that, continental Europe's twenty-two countries were to be rearranged into eight new states, including the Balkan Union, the Central States, and – between France and a much smaller Germany – a United Provinces.

His masterpiece of the period, however, was *Total War*. Brigadier Sir Dallas Brooks felt that Britain was not yet fighting a "Total War", and he asked Wheatley to think about how this would be done. Wheatley produced a 9,000 word paper almost at once, but then worked on it over the following year until it ran to over 100,000 words. Wheatley argued that while the First War had been a tribal war, the Second was better understood as a civil war (an idea which must have made particular sense to Wheatley after being a fellow traveller of the other side only a few years earlier). This had serious consequences, since while tribal wars could end in compromise, and the concession of territory, civil wars continued without compromise until the total annihilation of one cause or the other. "The nature of total war is, therefore, that of civil war deliberately fomented and organised down to the last detail."

Further, "Total War" was idea war: "the decisive sphere of Total War is the Mental Sphere," and "The primary Power Instrument of Total War is not Armed Force, but propaganda." Armed force came third in Wheatley's estimation, below propaganda and military intelligence; in fact, "Armed force must be considered as the backing for propaganda power." As for propaganda itself, "the science of influencing ideas," it "loses its value if it is recognised as propaganda."

Wheatley also suggested that the Germans benefited from the strong brand identity of the Swastika, and that Britain should adopt a similarly recognisable symbol, such as a stylised shield with St George and the dragon. A 30,000 word adaptation of *Total War* was published by Hutchinson, but the *Times Literary Supplement* had misgivings about it. Considering the St George logo, as well as Wheatley's suggestions of executing Rudolf Hess and sending undercover "tourists" into neutral countries, the reviewer noted "If Mr Wheatley had his way, there would be much less difference than now between our methods and the enemy's."

The reviewer's misgivings would have been startlingly confirmed if he could have seen the unpublished version, with its italicised passages for strictly restricted circulation. Believing "Expediency, not morality, is the sole criterion of human conduct in total war", and against the implicit background of America's slowness to come into the war, Wheatley argued for the hypothetical torpedoing of a ship:

> *For example: if it were calculated that the sinking of a neutral ship would bring that neutral into the war, thus shortening the war and bringing victory nearer, statesmen of a nation at war would be perfectly justified in ordering one of their submarines to sink it. The loss of a few hundred lives must be placed in perspective against the loss of a few hundred thousand.*

In one of the more bizarre diplomatic episodes of the Second World War, Eamon de Valera, the head of the Irish government, presented the German ambassador with the Irish people's condolences after Hitler died in the Bunker. If Wheatley had had his way, this would never have happened: de Valera would have been assassinated.

Wheatley found de Valera's neutrality offensive, and believed that his refusal to lease Irish bases to the British Navy and Air Force further stacked the odds against Britain's Atlantic supply line. *"Logically therefore, since thousands of British lives are being lost in the Atlantic, and southern Ireland may become a base for German operations against this country while we allow him to continue as President of the Eireann Republic, steps should be taken for his elimination."* Perhaps Wheatley was still thinking like a Nazi.

*

Wheatley's papers run to over half a million words. It is not easy to say what effect they had, other than causing inconvenience with road signs, but Wheatley looked back on them as "perhaps my most satisfying work", with their "rather small, select readership of four – King George VI and the Chiefs of Staff."

In fact they had a larger readership than this, because Wheatley would post them to any contacts and acquaintances who might prove influential, but the King did take a keen interest. Louis Greig, who had been Equerry to the King when he was Duke of York and remained a friend, knew the King liked Wheatley's fiction – Wheatley was sometimes said to be the King's favourite author – and showed him 'Resistance to Invasion'.

The King was so impressed that he asked to be given copies of subsequent papers, and when the JPS and the Directors of Plans were discussing Wheatley's scheme for Sardinia, and found they only had one copy between them, Louis Greig telephoned Buckingham Palace, a few hundred yards away, to borrow the King's copy. The King addressed the envelope himself, adding "Personal and Urgent," and Greig was thoughtful enough to save the envelope for Wheatley, who in due course had it framed as "my most precious souvenir of the war."[1]

Wheatley's paper on 'The Invasion and Conquest of Britain' was studied by a committee on invasion set up by Churchill and headed by General Denning and Air Marshal John Slessor (later to be a friend of Wheatley, and written into his novel *They Used Dark Forces*). Dallas Brooks later told Wheatley that parts of *Total War* had been filtered up to Churchill, and, according to Wheatley, Admiral Sir Brear Robertson told him years later that Churchill had been given an outline of Wheatley's Sardinia plan and found it "magnificent".

For the most part, Wheatley's papers remained in the realm of the fantastically hypothetical; this may have been

---

[1] Not to be confused with the envelope on the cover of *The Deception Planners*, another wartime souvenir. The King's envelope was photographed in 1959 for the serialisation of *Stranger Than Fiction*.

what Wheatley meant when he gave them, in their published form as *Stranger Than Fiction*, to Bobby Eastaugh with the inscription "these strange adventures in wonderland." At the very least, their "boyish, Biggles-like optimism" may have helped to keep morale up at the most senior level, which is no mean achievement.

★

The effect the papers had on Wheatley's own life was far more tangible, giving him an entry to the highest circles in the nation's military establishment, and providing a springboard towards the next stage of his career. Darvall was promoted abroad, and his successor was Wing Commander Roland "Roly" Vintras. Vintras asked Wheatley to bring a paper direct to the JPS in "Mr Rance's Room," and while he was there Vintras introduced him to his chief, Group Captain Sir William "Dickie" Dickson, later a Marshal of the Royal Air Force. Wheatley became friendly with Dickson, and Dickson's successor as Air Planner, Wing Commander "Tubby" Dawson (later Air Chief Marshal Sir Walter Dawson) even invited Wheatley to have a drink in the JPS. In due course Wheatley became a fairly frequent visitor to Mr Rance's Room and befriended the JPS staff, getting on lunching and dining terms with them and becoming an accepted feature of their world.

Darvall, Vintras and Dickson had all mentioned informally that they would like to get Wheatley a proper role with the JPS and Wheatley, never shy of promoting his own cause, dropped a reminder at the end of his 1941 paper 'Atlantic Life-Line.' Perhaps his idea about drifting raft convoys on the Gulf Stream was nonsense, he said, "but if it is not, I really think that I shall deserve either a KG[2] or a very small hard bench in the draughtiest room of the Joint Planning Staff."

One day in November Dickie Dickson asked Wheatley to lunch. There was another man there, Oliver Stanley, whom

[2] i.e. being made a Knight of the Order of the Garter.

Churchill had put in charge of a newly reorganised version of the JPS; the FOPS or Future Operations Planning Section. There might be a place in it for Wheatley, Stanley said, and if so would he like to come in as an officer or a civil servant?

CHAPTER THIRTY-TWO

In the Stratosphere

Given the choice of having a civil servant post or an officer's commission, Wheatley wanted to be an officer, although it meant he had to start as a Pilot Officer, a junior RAF rank. Having been a naval cadet and an army lieutenant, it was his third uniform. After his frankly undistinguished service in the First War as a gunner subaltern, he now found himself in the "strategic stratosphere", part of a small team that formed the guiding vision over almost ten million men and women in uniform.

Wheatley had a strong sense of his own good fortune, like a 'boy makes good' story from *Chums*. "Success stories of the poor boy who becomes a millionaire are innumerable," he wrote later, pitching his wartime memoirs, "but for a civilian to be specially commissioned in order that he should become a member of the Joint Planning Staff in the midst of a war is a different kind of success story, and one that is unique."

★

Wheatley's new career began with a two week intake course at RAF Uxbridge, "to learn not to slap Air Marshals on the back." There was a good deal of square-bashing, but among the other six hundred recruits was His Grace Freddy the Duke of Richmond. He was a charming man – and it would, in any case, have been unlike Wheatley to leave a duke unbefriended – and they became great comrades. There was no alcohol in the camp, but Wheatley had the foresight to bring a flask of old brandy, and after parades Wheatley and His Grace "could be seen sneaking off like two schoolboys to smoke cigarettes behind a haystack," as Wheatley remembered it in after-dinner speech years later: "By these means we kept body and soul together and from the illicit drinking a delightful friendship sprung."

416

Wheatley also had his greatcoat lined with red satin, and (against regulations, since RAF officers were not supposed to carry sticks or canes) had Wilkinson's make him a couple of short swagger sticks, like those often carried by army officers, but covered in blue leather and hiding fifteen inch blades in case of trouble during the blackout. Years later he left one to Freddy in his will.

Deception is almost as old as war, but its founding genius in the Second World War was Lieutenant Colonel Dudley Clarke. He was a small man with quick, bright eyes, fascinated by conjuring tricks, and Wheatley noted his "uncanny habit of suddenly appearing in a room without anyone having noticed him enter it." He was also the first British officer to set foot on the Continent again, after Dunkirk, leading a small reconaissance unit, "so he was, in a sense, the Father of Commando Raids as well as the Father of Deception" and he seems to have introduced the terms commando and "Special Air Service" to the British army. Clarke became a legendary figure to his colleagues, although his sanity was questioned after he caused a diplomatic incident in Spain, fraternising with German agents while dressed as a woman.

Clarke had masterminded a number of brilliant deceptions for General Wavell in the Middle East and was chiefly responsible for misleading the Germans about where Montgomery's main attack would come at Alamein. In due course he built up his own deception network, known as 'A' Force, and in October 1941 he gave an account of his work to the Chiefs of Staff in London. They were sufficiently impressed to create a small unit at home which would liaise with 'A' Force, and explore the possibility of deception in Europe.

A three-man team was proposed, comprising officers from all three services. The Army nominated Lieutenant-Colonel Lumby, then teaching military intelligence at the Army Staff College, the Navy promised a man who never appeared, and the RAF declined to spare anyone for this nebulous task, so Wheatley was recruited for it instead.

Wheatley's career in deception began gently: Colonel "Fritz" Lumby OBE turned out to be a kindly and agreeable one-legged Indian Army man who spent an hour every morning doing the *Times* crossword in their shared office. On Wheatley's first day, a trews-wearing Royal Scots officer named Eddie Combe invited him to lunch at Rules in Maiden Lane, where he kept a regular table for six or eight, and these lunches were to be a major feature of Wheatley's war. Contacts were made there between people working in "cloak-and-dagger" roles, and "sooner or later one met . . . everyone involved in any secret activity in the war".

"Lunch at Rules with Eddie Combe was a good invitation," Wheatley remembered. It would start with two or three Pimms before moving on to harder stuff; Combe liked a dash of absinthe, or "Chanel No.5" as he called it. Lunch would consist of smoked salmon or potted shrimps, then Dover sole, salmon, jugged hare, or game, with Welsh rarebit as a savoury to finish. After their wine with lunch, they would end with port or kummel.

Combe, who had won a double MC in the First War, was a fat man of about fifty, but on returning to the War Office he would make a point of running up three flights of stairs. Wheatley, in contrast, had to lie on a bed for an hour, having arranged with a friend to wake him if he was needed.

★

Wheatley and Lumby were marginal figures, isolated in their office up on the third floor without a clear role. Wheatley's most idiosyncratic plan during the time he worked with Lumby was a paper called 'Deception on the Highest Plane' in which he proposed to spread rumours of a new Christ-like figure emerging in Germany as an alternative to Hitler; its Messianic aspects may have owed something to John Buchan's *Greenmantle*. Nothing came of it.

Lumby disliked deception work, and he was pleased to get a transfer to a senior staff post in Africa. There was a change of gear when his successor Lieutenant Colonel Johnny Bevan arrived, becoming head of the reorganised "London Controlling Section", as the team was now called. A modest, unassuming man with a Military Cross, Bevan was good at rescuing situations. A contemporary at Eton recalled "when things were looking pretty bad for his side at cricket, he would shuffle in, about sixth wicket down, knock up a hundred and shuffle out again looking rather ashamed of himself."

Bevan lobbied the Chiefs of Staff to give deception a more definite role, and he moved himself and Wheatley – still a two-man team – down to the basement of the war rooms, where they would be better integrated with the JPS machinery and be taken more seriously. Deception was a difficult field to work in, and many senior figures were initially unconvinced of its worth, particularly since it required not just rumours and false messages but thousands of real troops moved around the globe and massed in places that would – unknown to almost everyone involved – never lead to action.

The first major job for Bevan and Wheatley was to provide deception for Operation Torch, the Allied invasion of North Africa in November 1942. Bevan masterminded a complex series of feints to tie up as many German troops as possible in Western Europe, including Solo I (a notional invasion of Norway) and Overthrow (a fictitious plan to establish a foothold in the Pas de Calais).

Torch was a great success. After the telegrams came in, the team treated themselves to a lunch at the Berkeley, and Wheatley bought himself a couple of top hats. Returning to the basement, Wheatley found a duplicated memo in his in-tray, from Churchill to the Chiefs of Staff: "The news of our early successes in North Africa is most gratifying. But it is over a week since I have heard anything of our plans for going into Norway. Pray let me hear most of these as a matter of urgency."

It was a joke, at least of sorts, to discourage complacency. Wheatley didn't have personal contact with Churchill, although Bevan did, but he was a great admirer. One morning he "souvenired" (his word) an ashtray that Churchill had used at a midnight meeting of the War Cabinet.

As time went by the LCS took on more members, several of them to become enduring friends of Wheatley. Along with

Johnny Bevan, these included Major Neil Gordon Clark, Colonel Sir Ronald Wingate, Commander James Arbuthnott, and in particular Major Derrick Morley, who smoothed Wheatley's entry into clubland after the war.

Other friends included General "Pug" Ismay, Churchill's Chief of Staff; Air Chief Marshal Sir William Elliott; Major Eric Goudie, ("gayest of all my friends") and the legendary Dudley Clarke himself, who became another enduring friend: almost any post-war career would be an anti-climax, and in later years he worked quietly at Conservative Central Office. Wheatley left him a pair of Chinese Immortals in his will. "We formed a happy band of brothers," Wheatley said later, and these were among the best years of his life, with full outlets for his own gaiety and bonhomie.

At Christmas 1942, for example, he gave William Elliott some Chateau Petrus Pomerol 1921, and Elliott gave him some Floris scent in return. "Spirits are a very poor return for wine," he wrote, "but I am hoping that you may like them in this rather sybaritic form. If not I can only pray that your wife does. Secretly however I would like to feel that you share the shocking weakness which I have for scent. But for Rosemary you would find me redolent of Caron and Chanel." As a postscript, he added about the wine "I wish Goering and Laval knew that I had these bottles of the famous year."

As for the Floris, "Joan will, I know, love it," wrote Wheatley; "that is if I can bring myself to spare her a single drop. But that is doubtful as I too am a devotee of joyous smells. Alas! This decadent age and my wife forbid me to move abroad with scent upon my person; but I make up for that as well as I can in the seclusion of the bathroom . . ."

Following Coombe's example, Wheatley began hosting his own lunches, and his behaviour with his seniors (or "bigger boys", as he thought of them, as if fixated on his schooldays) was an unusual mixture of formal and informal. To begin with, Wheatley stuck to the behaviour expected from junior officers during the First War, and on being shown into the room of a General or Admiral he would stand rigidly at attention until he was addressed. They might smile and invite him to sit down, or offer him a cigarette. When business was concluded, Wheatley might then say "I wonder, Sir, if you happen to have a day free to lunch with me?"

This was slightly unusual but they generally accepted; many of them in any case knew of Wheatley as a writer. Wheatley would lunch them at the Hungaria and he was a good host, with exceptional wine from his own cellars. As well as colleagues and the occasional writer he lunched a host of others including J.C. Masterman (Bill Younger's old tutor, the MI5 man who later wrote *The Double Cross System*), Peter Fleming, Brigadier Colin Gubbins, who scotched Germany's atomic bomb plans with a raid on its deuterium or 'heavy water' plant, Ian Fleming, John Slessor, Max Knight and a legion of others, often in groups of four or six; over a hundred and sixty guest lists survive in his papers.

Wheatley's lunches were a great success; "I spent my war Eating for Victory," he said later. He would move from lunch invitations to dinner, and by this means he built up a good network of contacts. The work of the LCS involved endless liaising with other officers, and Wheatley's capable networking undoubtedly smoothed Bevan's way with senior colleagues and generally oiled the wheels.

All Wheatley's life he was noted for his jolly demeanour, and he was never happier than during the War. Not only was he happy with his friends, but he was happy with his enemies. Conflict with the unambiguous evils of Nazi Germany fitted perfectly with his tendency to see things in invigoratingly black and white terms, instead of letting any depressing grey areas creep in. As Bertrand Russell once put it, "Few people can be happy unless they hate some other person, nation or creed."

In Spring 1943 the JPS moved to larger room in the fortress-basement. Feeling the new room was bleak, Wheatley took the opportunity to decorate it with his some of his best furniture, which also protected the furniture itself – then costing money to store – from bombing. He brought in a dining table, a set of Chippendale chairs, a bronze figure of a dancing faun for the table, and some oriental rugs. Seeing all this for the first time, General Ismay looked at Wheatley and said, "Dennis, where are the girls?"

It was a move that almost never happened. Allocating rooms was the responsibility of a pompous Lieutenant-Colonel named Denis Capel-Dunn, "the Papal Bun", and he denied the JPS request for more space. When Wheatley complained, he told Wheatley that his decision was final, and that for a junior officer to argue with him was "an impertinence". Wheatley outwitted him by appealing to a more senior figure that he was on lunching terms with, and the JPS gots its extra space. Wheatley then magnanimously invited Capel-Dunn to lunch, becoming friends with the man later immortalised as the model for the odious Widmerpool, in Anthony Powell's *Dance to the Music of Time*.

★

By summer 1943 the Allies were ready to invade Sicily, beginning the Italian Campaign, so it was Bevan's job to convince the Axis that an invasion of France was imminent instead. To this end he had banknotes printed with the inscription 'British Army of Occupation in Northern France.' Wheatley and other colleagues would carry these, and when they paid the bill in a restaurant or bought something in a shop they would accidentally hand one over, snatching it back when the recipent had seen it.

Wheatley had less to do with Operation Mincemeat ('The Man Who Never Was') than he let people believe in the Fifties – it was largely engineered by Ewen Montagu – but he was involved in 'Monty's Double' (Operation Copperhead), in which a peacetime actor and lieutenant in the Pay Corps named M.E.Clifton James, who bore a remarkable resemblance to Montgomery, visited the Mediterranean days before the invasion of Normandy; if Monty was in the Mediterranean, then it seemed obvious no cross-Channel invasion was imminent. At the last moment someone realised "Monty" might be airsick, ruining the illusion, and Wheatley took him up in a plane to check he could fly.

The most important deception of the war was the

protection of Neptune (the D–Day Normandy landings) by Operation Bodyguard. Bevan and the LCS created false operations including Fortitude North, leading the Germans to expect an invasion of Norway, and Fortitude South, for which an entire fictitious army of invasion was built up in Kent. This was so successful that even as the Normandy landings were happening, the Germans believed they were only a feint and continued to keep the bulk of their armoured divisions uselessly in the Pas de Calais, where they expected the real attack. This ensured the success of D–Day.

Allied deception was one of the great triumphs of the War: by the strategic legerdemain of arriving in large numbers where they were not expected, the Allies saved thousands of lives on both sides, avoiding the attritional horror of a grinding, head–on struggle with a fully prepared enemy. Even Churchill, for the most part excessively sanguine, suffered from nightmares about the possible loss of life in invading Europe. Worse still, there was the almost unthinkable possibility that the landing might have failed altogether and been pushed back into the sea. This would have been the ruin of three years planning, the exposure of technological 'secret weapons' like the Mulberry harbours and DD amphibious tanks, which could never again have the same surprise value, and the loss of an army.

Instead the Chiefs of Staff came to record that Bevan and the LCS had an unbroken record of success that was "unique," and in particular that it had made a "decisive" difference to the retaking of Europe. Johnny Bevan was made a Companion of the Bath, as was Dudley Clarke. Wheatley didn't feel this was enough: he thought Bevan should have had a Grand Cross of the Bath and the rest of the team, including himself, "CBs or, at least, CBEs." In the event he had to be content with an American Bronze Star, a medal one grade above a Purple Heart[1].

---

[1] The citation was simply for "meritorious service to the US army while serving as London Controlling Section representative on the Inter-Service Security Board from August 1943 to August 1944."

Bevan modestly dissuaded Wheatley from writing about the team ("No one will want to read all this nonsense about the sort of people we are") but he wrote and told him that without Wheatley's "enthusiasm" he would have been tempted to pack the job in. They remained friends, and after the war Bevan looked after Wheatley's investments as his stockbroker. When he came to make his will, Wheatley wanted Bevan to have the bronze faun that had been on their table in the War Rooms basement.

★

Wheatley's last real assignment came in June 1944, with the D-Day Landings. Air Chief Marshal Sir Richard Peck thought the Americans would soon believe they had won the War single-handed, and he wanted war correspondents and known writers with 'names' to cover the British assault and write pieces pitched at the American press.

General Ismay declined to let Wheatley go, not because he was too useful – his work had effectively come to an end – but because he knew too much to be captured if his plane was brought down over Europe. Peck then said that even if he had flown over the beaches he wouldn't have seen much more than clouds of smoke, and instead sent him to down to Harwell to cover the launch of the British 6th Airborne Division under Major-General Gale, whose parachute and glider troops spearheaded the assault by capturing bridges. Wheatley turned in a suitably upbeat piece about "the great crusade which was to bring light back to Europe", befriending Gale in the process.

The piece, entitled 'The Opening of the Battle of the Century' seems never to have been used; perhaps Wheatley's account of taking down a "a very special bottle of wine" (a Rupertsberg Hoheburg Gewurztraminer Feinste Edelbeer-Auslese 1920, "the greatest Hock I have ever drunk") was not what the American public needed.

Wheatley had ascended in rank as his war went on, from the keenly saluting middle-aged Pilot Officer (a rank more suited to someone in their twenties) through Flying Officer,

Flight Lieutenant, Squadron Leader and finally, in July 1944, acting Wing Commander. But by now there was nothing for him to do, and he spent his time collecting together thematic groups of stamps – Queen Victoria heads from around the Empire, Rajahs, gods and goddesses and so on – some of which he later put under glass on tabletops.

Wheatley's fiction career had come to a halt in March 1942, with the publication of the Gregory Sallust book *V For Vengeance*, and he wanted to get back to it. Britain, in a famous formulation, would proceed to win the war and lose the peace, and there was going to be more for Wheatley to worry about in the coming years. But for now, it was time to get out of uniform.

CHAPTER THIRTY-THREE

Grove Place

Wheatley's war ended at Christmas 1944: like a schoolboy breaking up for the last time, he was free to go on the 22nd of December.

Having been released, he began a new novel, *The Man Who Missed The War*. This was another of Wheatley's 'lost civilisation' tales, and the public rationale for its "far from here" setting was that he was now so steeped in inside knowledge that he dared not write another contemporary spy or war story, for fear of breaking the Official Secrets Act. There may have been some truth in this, but it was also a canny way of promoting a certain image.

Based on his wartime 'Raft Convoy' idea, *The Man Who Missed the War* is the story of a man who leaves America on a raft hoping to drift into European waters. Instead he is carried to the Antarctic, where he discovers a previously unknown area with a warm climate, inhabited by a lost race who practise human sacrifice. Meanwhile he discovers that he has a stowaway on his raft, in the shape of a beautiful redhead. Together they not only survive their encounter with devil worshipping Atlanteans in cahoots with the Third Reich, but they also meet the narrator's ghostly guardian, some pirates, some giant man-eating crabs which seem to have migrated from *Uncharted Seas*, and a bloodthirsty Russian aristocrat, hell-bent on becoming the ruler of a lost race of pygmies.

It was, according to Hutchinson, in "the true Wheatley tradition of adventure, rising to a terrific and truly satisfying climax". Wheatley was Hutchinson's prize author, and he had a good working relationship with Walter Hutchinson, so Hutchinson's advanced him a sizeable loan[1] for his new

---

[1] £5,000, or about £150,000 by today's standards: property was relatively cheaper then.

house. Grove Place was at Lymington, a notably "unspoilt" small town on the coast near Southampton. In mediaeval times it had been a major port, and its prosperity lasted until the mid-nineteenth century. Lymington had been entitled to two Members of Parliament (among them Edward Gibbon, whose *Decline and Fall of the Roman Empire* Wheatley owned in eight leather-bound volumes) but by Wheatley's time it had become little more than a long, sloping High Street, the Northern side of which had once belonged to Nell Gwynne, given to her by "Old Rowley." In a word, Wheatley found Lymington "picturesque."

Grove Place was a Georgian house built around 1770. It had ten principal rooms, with high ceilings, tall windows and a curving main staircase. There were four acres of land and it particularly benefited from the view beyond them, sweeping over four miles of fields and woods down to the River Solent, followed by the sea and the distantly visible Isle of Wight. This vista owed a great deal to the fact that a previous owner and three other landowners had covenanted together that none of them would have any building on their land without the consent of the other three, so the view remained unbroken by suburban sprawl.

The previous owner had been an old widow, Mrs. Hall, the sister-in-law of Sir Reginald "Blinker" Hall (founder of The Economic League). Mrs. Hall had been unable to keep the place up, and the lawn and terrace were overgrown. Wheatley's account of it in a 1946 letter shows a characteristically die-hard approach to gardening: "We moved to the country last summer and have since been fighting a furious war against dirt, decay and weeds to get the lovely old Georgian house really habitable again. It has been a great fight but we are now well on the way to victory."

Wheatley kept a twelve bore shotgun in his bedroom, and would shoot out of the window at rooks. His daughter-in-law remembers walking towards the house when he shouted out "Stay where you are!": a moment later Wheatley had blasted another rook, with a cry of "Death to the invaders!"

Wheatley had to do further battle with ants ('Nippon' ant

killer, with its mushroom cloud logo, was a familiar item in the post-war British garden shed) and rabbits, for which a landed friend advised ferrets. "Leave it with me," he wrote, "and I will do my best before you are invaded".

A far nastier pest appeared at Grove in the form of a potential blackmailer. Wheatley spent more money on renovating and decorating than wartime economy regulations allowed, and they remained in force in this state-centred era just after the war (Earl Peel was caught spending his own money on the upkeep of his stately home and fined £25,000: about half a million pounds today). A local man discovered what Wheatley was doing and came round to see him with a proposition. He knew that Wheatley had overspent, and he offered not to inform the police if Wheatley would like to make it worth his while.

Wheatley asked for time to think, and the man agreed to come back the following morning. When the would-be extortionist returned, Wheatley's builder (a Mr Bower) was hiding within earshot. Having invited his tormentor to put his cards on the table, Wheatley then produced Mr Bower. "You are attempting to blackmail me, and I can call Mr Bower as a witness", he said: "One word about the decorating, and I'll have you in the jug." And that was the end of that.

★

Wheatley's war had hardly been austere, but now he was keen to throw off what few privations there were. In 1946 he wrote to the firm of Maurice Meyer, drink shippers, to re-establish his supplies of Aurum and Kummel. The Aurum factory was still out of action, having been looted by the Germans for steel and copper, and ordinary pre-war Kummel was now fetching £8 to £15 a bottle (£200 to £400). Meyer's were gratified by his request: "It is pleasing to receive your refreshing letter", they wrote: "Asking for Hunting Kummel and Aurum seems like a breath from the past." Meyers promised to advise him when they were again in possession of Aurum and Kummel, and meanwhile invited him to drop in for a cup of tea if nearby.

It is a pre-war Kummel – pre-First War, in this case – that Gregory Sallust and Sir Pellinore Gwaine-Cust split a bottle of in *The Black Baroness*. "Hurrah! The fatted calf!" says Gregory, seeing the cobwebby bottle as he enters – where else in a Wheatley book? – *the library*. "What's that?" says Sir Pellinore; "Oh, you mean the pre-1914 Mentzendorff's Kummel . . . They don't make stuff like this in Russia these days; but there it is – the whole darned world's gone to pot in this last half-century."

Wheatley's luxurious tastes were quite widely known. A letter arrived at Grove Place in 1946 to introduce a budding actor, formerly in the RAF, by the name of Christopher Lee. Lee is a great friend of the letter writer, and the two of them have just been drinking port and talking about Wheatley, of whom Lee is an "enormous admirer": "Although he has never met you he knows your life history and your love of the good things of life."

Wheatley was now "established" at Grove Place in a more gentlemanly style than he had ever really enjoyed before: these were to be some of the best years of his life, if relatively uneventful. The thrills and spills were largely over. Wheatley's main activity in the post-war years was writing.

Wheatley was not a believer in waiting for inspiration, and found it would come to order if he first forced himself to write. He tried various methods of getting his narrative down, including dictation, but he never mastered the writerly trance in the manner of Joan Grant or Barbara Cartland, and found dictation went too fast to develop situations. Instead he found the best method for him to think and write was to use a soft pencil, with an eraser handy, giving an ease of composition that he didn't get with a pen. He averaged about four sheets of foolscap a day and at that speed he could finish a book in seven months, since – being anxious to give his reader-customers good value – his books were around twice the length of the normal thriller, averaging 160,000 words.

Wheatley worked with self-discipline and absolute ser-iousness ("You couldn't go and stay while he was working"), beginning at about nine in the morning. He would spend an hour or two with his secretary, dealing with the post from his public, then at around ten thirty or eleven he would press on with the current book. At one he would have a simple lunch, followed by another hour or so of work until around half two, and then he would go to sleep to pre-empt the afternoon slump (like Churchill, he believed "work in the afternoon has almost invariably to be done again"). He would sleep on his sofa until four, when a cup of tea was brought to him, and he roused himself to write until dinner. After dinner he would go back to work until midnight or, if it was going well, until two o'clock in the morning.

Wheatley worked solidly like this for seven or eight months of the year, including Saturdays, during which time he was effectively "in purdah", as a friend put it. He also travelled abroad with Joan for two or three months, which doubled as research for settings and local colour.

One of the great pleasures of Grove Place for the Wheatleys turned out to be the proximity of Constance, Duchess of Westminster ("Sheila" to friends), who became a great friend to both of them. She was a strong woman of the sort Wheatley admired, and he was particularly impressed by an adventure she had in Istanbul before the First War. She heard that a great ceremony was to be held at Ramadan inside the Hagia Sophia mosque – then far from being the tourist destination it has since become – but she was warned that it was impossible for her to see it, since women were forbidden. Ordering one of her sailors to hand over his clothes, she infiltrated her way into the ceremony, alone and disguised as a man, despite the fact that (as Wheatley understood it) "if discovered she would be torn to pieces".

The less attractive side of this forceful character was that she could be arrogant, and would often speak to her second husband "Fitz" – Wing Commander James Fitzpatrick Lewis – as if he was a servant. But Wheatley was spellbound by her stories of life in the great Edwardian houses, and he must have found pleasure in the fact that she was the former wife of Hugh Grosvenor, Second Duke of Westminster, who had made such an impression on Wheatley when Wheatley

Wheatley at Grove Place, painted by Cynthia Montefiore.

Wheatley the amateur bricklayer, with some of his handiwork.

DENNIS WHEATLEY
GROVE PLACE
LYMINGTON
HANTS

TEL: LYMINGTON 315

FRUIT, FLOWERS, VEGETABLES & HERBS

Grove Place.

OF VICE AND VIRTUE.

An Eastern Romance

by

Dennis Wheatley

———————

Privately commissioned by

For
translation into
Arabic, Persian, and other Eastern Languages

1950

Commissioned by? Wheatley's own copy of his Islamic propaganda novel
Vice and Virtue.

was his wine merchant: he figured as "His Grace the Duke of Blank" in *At The Sign of the Flagon of Gold*, and he was the owner of Eaton Hall. Wheatley would not have been Wheatley if he hadn't been at least a little gratified by the fact that he was now a good friend of His Grace's former wife.

★

Largely as a result of contacts made during the War, Wheatley's post-war circle was now more aristocratic and military than it had been. It is probably fair to say that Wheatley took a certain pride in knowing members of the aristocracy, and that he was never quite unconscious of their rank.

When Wheatley wasn't working he was often entertaining. "I thought I ought to let you know that by approx 11 o'clock this morning we had both nearly recovered from your most wonderful luncheon of yesterday. It truly was the most enjoyable time we have spent for ages and Helen and I thank you both a thousand times . . . Paradise we are told exists in another world, but I am beginning to suspect that such a story is but a cover plan put about by the nonconformists and their like and by the Cripps[2] and other killjoys that inhabit this island of ours." The same man, an impecunious earl, writes on another occasion, "Thank you a thousand times for your hospitality and may God bless you for the hock – that delectable hock."

Another friend, a colonel, writes "What with you, Moet and Chandon and that hat – not to mention the bricks – what more could one want??". The hat might well be the extraordinary straw number that Wheatley is wearing in the photograph on the back of *The White Witch of the South Seas*[3].

---

[2] I.e. the Rt.Hon Sir Stafford Cripps, (1889–1952), Labour politician.

[3] The bookseller's note in my copy says "one of the most extraordinary author portraits I've ever seen", while the photo caption reads "Here we see the author about to go for a swim from a palm-fringed island in one of the lovely blue lagoons of the South Seas." With its brickwork and yew it looks more like the garden at Grove.

More about bricks later, although another friend writes "I would like to thank you for a most enjoyable weekend, even though I think I laid some of my bricks slightly, only slightly, out of the perpendicular." The wife of the Hereditary Falconer of England (the 13th Duke of St Albans, formerly in Military Intelligence and Psychological Warfare) writes to thank Joan for a delightful evening with the Richmonds (i.e. Freddy, Duke of Richmond, and his wife Betty) and says how much she enjoyed seeing Joan's needlework.

And so the thank-you letters go on: "just a line to thank you . . ."; "A really lovely evening . . ."; "Thank you both ever so much for a most delightful visit which we enjoyed greatly – I much enjoyed meeting "the 18B man" [i.e. a man interned as a Fascist during the war under Regulation 18B] who I thought was very amusing and entertaining but probably one doesn't want to see him too often . . ." Even allowing for the high level of politeness among Wheatley's friends ("How kind of you to invite me and how base you must think me not to have replied before") it is clear that a good time was had by all – "P.S. the lunch was terrific!"

★

Wheatley's next book, *Codeword: Golden Fleece*, published in May 1946, is another instance of his responsive relationship to his readers. It arose from a throwaway line in the first chapter of *Strange Conflict*, when the Duke de Richleau mentions to Sir Pellinore Gwaine-Cust that the four of them were in Poland at the start of the War. Readers wrote to Wheatley, asking what had happened and what they had missed, and so *Codeword: Golden Fleece* was written to fill in the story. As Francois Truchaud has written, "It is a beautiful example of the autonomous life of novelistic characters obliging their Creator to tell their adventures".

Whatever misgivings Wheatley might have had about the Official Secrets Act, *Codeword: Golden Fleece* was a World War Two story involving economic sabotage of Germany's oil supplies. The 1963 Arrow blurb added "It can now be revealed" that the plot was based on facts given to Wheatley, as a member of the JPS, by a Foreign Office colleague: a French nobleman had succeed in acquiring a controlling interest in the Danube oil barges, and getting them into Turkish waters, depriving the German air force of fuel. Six months later Wheatley followed this with another Gregory Sallust, *Come Into My Parlour*, then shelved Sallust's wartime adventures for another twelve years. A new hero was about to be born.

CHAPTER THIRTY-FOUR

Rogering Roger

Wheatley's overdue departure from improbable 'lost race' tales and stories of wartime intrigue arrived with a new hero in the person of Roger Brook, a British agent during the Napoleonic era. If Sallust was Tombe, Roger Brook was an ideal version of Wheatley, and the Georgian ambience of Grove Place reinforced his identification.

Decor had always been important to Wheatley (he was, after all, the man who not only put a rug in his World War One billet but managed to wallpaper it) and the uxorious dedication in the first Roger Brook novel involves a very English blurring of the distinction between cottage and stately home: "For my darling wife JOAN:"

> This, my first historical novel – inspired by "Cosey Cott", which she has done so much to make the smallest stately home – with all my love.

Along with Grove Place, Wheatley bought in to the mid-twentieth-century ideal of Regency, as in the historical fiction of Georgette Heyer, the paintings of Anna and Doris Zinkeisen (all crinolines, uniforms, carriage rides and bow windows), and what was for many years the packaging of 'Quality Street' confectionery. Like the slightly earlier passion for bygone coaching inns, a related look could be seen on Christmas and other greeting cards well into the Sixties and Seventies, with a richness of decanters, model cannons, leather-bound books and the rest.

The first Brook novel, *The Launching of Roger Brook*, opens in 1783 with the bookish Roger still at school, confronting a bully named Gunston who is insulting Brook's mother and her Jacobite sympathies. Contrary to the received wisdom of schoolboy fiction, Gunston is not a coward, or the sort of bully who caves in when stood up to. He is genuinely tough, and he is just about to give Roger a thorough pasting when another boy, "Droopy Ned", steps in to save him. Droopy, more properly Lord Edward Fitz-Deverel, son of the Marquess of Amesbury, is a strange boy, possessing natural authority and a wisdom beyond his years:

> In an age when blood sports occupied nine-tenths of the thoughts and leisure of every English gentleman, Droopy Ned made no secret of the fact that he abhorred bull-baiting, fox-hunting and cock-fighting; he also displayed an aloof disregard for all schoolboy crazes, ball games and field sports. Instead he concerned himself with strange expensive hobbies, such as the collecting of antique jewellery, the study of ancient religions and experimenting on himself with eastern drugs . . .

Clearly admired by his author, Droopy Ned is an archetypal Wheatley character with similarities to the Duke de Richleau, showing Wheatley's lifelong faith in connoisseurship and aristocracy. This love of all things upper-class is itself vulgar, as any really competent snob could point out, and it is likely that had Wheatley had a less suburban background he might never have developed it.

Young Brook lives at Lymington, in a Georgian house with high ceilings and tall, white-painted windows, giving a fine view of the Isle of Wight across the sea. Attached to the house is the remnant of an older dwelling ("a low-roofed building faced with old red tiles which was now used as the kitchen quarters") which in the twentieth century was to be occupied by the Wheatleys' live-in couple, Captain Georges Pigache and his wife Betty.

Late in life, Wheatley was the subject of a film, and at one point he pulls down an indistinct character figure from his collection of Napoleonic figurines and holds it, saying "And this is Roger Brook; *he was born here at Lymington*." Wheatley's fond, indulgent little joke is like a jump of seventy-odd years back to Charlie, the doll who nearly suffocated.

Period detail is applied with a trowel, and Roger finds his father having a jovial drink with none other than Lymington MP Edward Gibbon ("I've read all three volumes that Mr Gibbon has so far published and am athirst for more", says another member of the party). We have already been invited to notice the kitchen beams "festooned with hams, tongues and flitches of bacon, while the table could hardly be seen for joints, game, pudding-basins and vegetables" – rationing was still in force when Wheatley wrote that – and now in the dining room we see the main table ("a good modern one made only a dozen years before in Mr.Chippendale's London workshop"), with its highly-polished surface reflecting a somewhat Christmas-cardy spread: "a brave array of china, glass, gleaming silver, white napery, crystal bowls of fruit and filigree baskets holding bonbons, comfits and candied peel . . ."

Young Brook has a pleasant face, and in due course he will "play the very devil with the women". It is not too far-fetched to think that one of Wheatley's main associations for the name Roger was "rogering". Towards the end of his life, he bemoaned the amount of sex in modern fiction: "some of these modern novels are too explicit. They have chaps doing absurd feats, *rogering* everyone. It's impractical. You can't *roger* that many women, even in your youth."

Despite Roger's endless liaisons the love of his life is an independent and amoral older girl named Georgina, another name with clear associations. The adventures of rogering Roger and Georgian Georgina eventually ran to twelve volumes over twenty-seven years of Wheatley's life, covering the period 1785–1815, with the court of Marie-Antoinette, the French Revolution, the rise and fall of Napoleon, Napoleon's campaigns in Egypt, and Roger's missions to Turkey, Persia, India, Brazil, the Caribbean, America, St.Petersburg and almost everywhere else that Wheatley went on his travels. Wheatley put his heart into the Roger Brook series.

George Macdonald Fraser, author of *Flashman*, was generous enough to say that the Roger Brook series "makes James Bond seem like an infant gurgling in his play pen". But the

Brook books are flawed by their unconvincing direct speech, and they have an uncertain 'feel' for the period, although they have a staggering amount of facts about it. As Anthony Lejeune has noted, Brook is prone to say "Talleyrand, tell me what's been happening", after which several pages of straight history will follow.

Wheatley prided himself on the fact that his books were educational, and within a certain idea of history they unquestionably were. Wheatley's taste in history is not unlike that of the old-school English critic John Bayley, as expressed in Bayley's novel *George's Lair*, where George finds he "only really cared for dates, personalities and battles, or details about armour and archery. That was not the way it was taught now, and he was expected to interest himself in social and economic trends . . ."

Wheatley's research for the Brook series was extremely thorough, from Edward King's *Old Times Re-visited on the Borough and Parish of Lymington, Hants* to Burgo Partridge's *History of Orgies*. As well as standard works of reference such as the *Dictionary of National Biography* ("invaluable") it included twenty-four books on Napoleon alone, six on Pitt, three on Talleyrand, and many others.

Wheatley was enjoying himself with Brook, and his next novel, published in 1948, was another Brook story, *The Shadow of Tyburn Tree*, in which Brook goes on a mission to Russia after the mysterious death of Georgina's husband makes it imperative for him to leave England. While in Russia he becomes the lover of Catherine the Great, and finally returns to England and Georgina just in time to save her from being hanged.

Meanwhile, Wheatley had written one of his strangest works, in durable ballpoint on the back of a pencilled Roger Brook manuscript. It was his message to posterity, buried in a bottle.

CHAPTER THIRTY-FIVE

The Message in a Bottle

Diana had been staying at Grove Place for the first nine months of 1946. She was waiting for her divorce from Brinsley to come through, so that she could marry Wentworth Eldredge, and in September she took a plane for America.

Wheatley was meanwhile building and gardening assiduously; he made a maze, planted a glade of young forest trees, and opposite the front door he planted lilacs, laburnums, peaches, cherries and magnolias. The colours made him think of Renaissance painting, so he called it his "Botticelli garden"; something the Eatons already have in *The Devil Rides Out.*

Around the house Wheatley put a stone balustrade and some Georgian urns. Believing Grove Place would last for centuries, it was here that he secreted his message to the future.

Wheatley invited Diana to post a message to the future from America, to be buried in the bottle with his. He seems to have thought it up half in a spirit of fun, but his message is more remarkable for its anxieties, and for the way it deepens rapidly from the thoughts of a loyal subject to calls for revolt and assassination.

The idea was already several months old (Diana had posted her message in July) when Wheatley got down to write on Thursday the 20th of November, 1947. His immediate inspiration was the marriage of Princess Elizabeth to Prince Philip, and his fears for the future of the monarchy.

Wheatley begins with a precis of his life, and makes no big deal out of being a famous writer in the twentieth century. He has simply been a Naval Cadet, Artillery Lieutenant, Wine Merchant, "Author from 1932", Wing Commander, and latterly "the owner of this property (on which I have planted over 1200 trees and bushes)."

Wheatley reflects on the immense changes he has seen in his lifetime. He was born in the reign of Victoria, and "At that time even the thought that one day the British Monarchy might be abolished was inconceivable. But in the 50 years of my life greater changes have been wrought in the habits and mentality of the world's population than in any 500 years of previously recorded history." London had no telephone system, there was no wireless, and there were no motorcars on the streets. Vehicles were horse-drawn, and "the idea of travelling by air was as remote and unreal with us as it was with the Romans".

But now "the electric age, having its infancy while I was a schoolboy . . . has revolutionised thought." In particular, people are now at the mercy of the mass-media and the messages of "professional politicians", in a process that Wheatley briefly traces; "the cinematograph", for example, "soon became one of the most insidious weapons for political propaganda."

In consequence, people took on "ready-made" thoughts, and an immense change took place in their mental life. Now they thought about political ideologies, and abstract theories of government:

> Worst of all, the masses came under the immediate influence of the political demagogues who labelled themselves as the 'representatives of the people', who held that 'all men being equal' all power should be vested in the majority rather than in the intelligent minority . . .

Wheatley's preference is for the old system of "Priest-Kings", subject to the safeguards of oligarchy ("It was generally recognised that a throne could be permanently maintained only if it were the apex of a solidly supporting pyramid of aristocracy . . . as a general rule the Priests/Nobles/Senators exercised a power at least equal to that of the Priest-King"). Wheatley cites the Magna Carta here, and adds that the priestly and noble classes were "constantly being added to by the rise of men of exceptional ability and talent among the masses, as witness King Henry VIII's great minister Cardinal Wolsey, who began life as a butcher's boy."

In opposition to this system came the idea that all men are equal, which threatens the idea "that the direction of human destinies should remain vested in a limited number of individuals who are, on average, better educated and more intelligent than the masses."

Wheatley traces the spread of equality, from the aristocracies of Egypt, Greece and Rome, all the way to post–1945 Britain, and the propagandist nature of modern life.

> The coming of the machine age enabled the politicians of the 'all men are equal' school to get into ever-closer touch with the masses. Under the banners of liberation they preached against every form of privilege, thus making the masses discontented with their lot; and later, as socialists, they openly advocated equality in all things with supreme power vested in the House of Commons . . . It was not, however, until the elections of 1945, that the 'all men are equal' propaganda resulted in the return of a Socialist majority to Westminster . . .
>
> Up to the end of the last century the difference in condition between the very rich and the very poor was obviously too great to justify on any count, but much had been done to bridge the gulf long before the Socialists came to power . . . No one would seek to deny that the worker's own representatives and the trade union movement played a great part in bringing about these reforms; yet the fact remains that the laws concerning them were mainly introduced and passed by just-minded and humane legislators drawn from the old ruling classes.

But now, where would it end?

> . . . while workers are being protected and provided for, whether employed or not, from the cradle to the grave, they are no longer putting in a sufficient number of

working hours to pay for the benefits they receive. To continue on these lines can only end in national bankruptcy, or a reversal of policy by which, as in Soviet Russia, the vast majority of the theoretically classless society are compelled to work appallingly long hours to maintain the state bosses and a huge non-productive bureaucracy. . . . And this is the slippery slope to which the new socialist government 'of the people, by the people, for the people' has now brought a once rich and prosperous Britain.

If this went on, said Wheatley, you wouldn't be allowed to put up so much as a shelf in your own house without a special permit. No doubt he remembered the decorating blackmail.

Worse, "this Dictatorship of the Proletariat, instead of gradually improving the conditions in which the lower classes live . . . must result in reducing everyone outside the party machine to the level of the lowest, idlest and most incompetent worker."

Man began as a member of a herd. He became different from the animals only when the urge to become a real person – an individual – gave him the courage to back away from the herd. . . . The triumph of communism means the reconverting of civilised men back to the herd . . . There is not a shadow of liberty left. Everyone is compelled to labour to the limit of their endurance in return for their bare subsistence. They can be arrested and imprisoned or shot without trial. There is no justice and no freedom of either thought or action. Few have any conception of the joys that go to make life worth living. The Russian people now know no other form of life than that of state slaves. Day after day they labour on like harnessed animals. From their dreary lot there is nothing to look forward to, no future and no escape.

And *this* is the *ultimate* outcome of the false, pernicious doctrine that 'all men are equal'. Socialism is but a halfway house.

"All men are *not* equal", continues Wheatley: "Some have imagination and abilities far above others. It is their province and their right to take upon themselves the responsibility of leading and protecting the less gifted."

By now Wheatley was fully into his stride, imagining a grey future without freedom or monarchy, whipping himself up until his message to the future becomes a manifesto of leaderless resistance, and he begins to hit Churchillian notes of the 'fight them on the beaches' variety:

Therefore, if when this document is discovered, the people of Britain are bound to a state machine, *my message to posterity is REBEL.*

We are sent into this world to develop our own personality – to use such gifts as we have been given and to set an example to others by our courage, fortitude, sympathy, generosity and *self-reliance.* Any state which controls the lives of the people and dictates where they shall live, what work they shall do, what they shall see, say, hear, read and think, thwarts the free development of personality, and is therefore EVIL.

It will be immensely difficult to break the stranglehold of the machine, but it can be done, little by little; the first step being the formation of secret groups of friends for *free* discussion. Then numbers of people can begin systematically to break small regulations, and so to larger ones with *passive* resistance by groups of people pledged to stand together – and eventually the boycotting, or ambushing and killing of unjust tyrannous officials.

Your life does not matter, but your freedom does. The age–old wisdom tells us that death is not to be feared, for it is but a release from life, leading to rebirth, and if one has lived and died courageously, as a finer, stronger personality. Therefore, if need be, fight for your *RIGHT to live, work and love, how and where you will.* If need be die for it. Your death will be an example to others that it is better to die fighting for your freedom and happiness than to live on as a slave.

This is splendid Wheatley stuff, its defiance oddly complimented by the historical potboiling on the other side of the page (' "Nay", gasped Roger . . .'). Finally, like a lone man sending a message out into space, Wheatley signs off, and he does so on an equally characteristic note:

May the courage and wisdom of the Timeless Ones, who order all things, be your support and guide. They will never fail you if you have faith in yourself.

Blessings be upon you; freedom and love be with you.
   Dennis Wheatley

★

It is hard to say what Wheatley's intended audience in the distant future would have made of these "Timeless Ones." Perhaps he hoped to start something like a new religion, spread by whispers and rumours, with the message that the Timeless Ones would help.

The idea of the Timeless Ones is perfectly in accord with the reactionary quality of Wheatley's fiction, since the Timeless Ones are not only a benevolent oligarchy, of the kind very familiar in occultism – like the Lords of Light, Secret Chiefs, Ascended Ones, Great White Brotherhood, Hidden Masters, and the rest of them – but by definition they are safely outside of historical change.

In due course time and change caught up with Wheatley's message itself, and far sooner than he expected.

★

Diana's buried message is hardly more than a postcard to posterity, although she does seem to have inherited something

445

of her mother's grand manner. Telling us about her new life, she adds that she has come to love America for its little simple people.

Wheatley's extraordinary message is absolutely pitted against the era he lived in. His whole career was spent in conflict with the two main tendencies of 'progress' in the post-nineteenth century world: science and democracy, or materialism and the masses. Instead he placed his faith in elitism and the supernatural, their common denominator being the primacy of mind or 'spirit'.

At the same time, it is absolutely of its era as a response to post-war Socialism. Churchill had been voted out in 1945, and the country had its first post-war Labour government. Churchill himself wrote a quasi-supernatural short story in the late Forties called 'The Dream', in which he dreamed that his father came back from the dead to ask him questions about the 20th century; Churchill senior was particularly concerned that the country might have turned to Bolshevik republicanism under a Labour government.

Meanwhile the West End theatres were full of comedies about the perceived plight of the middle classes. Writers such as L.P.Hartley, Angela Thirkell, Somerset Maugham, and Evelyn Waugh all wrote about their anxieties in the post-war world, and Waugh told Harold Acton "We'll all end in a concentration camp". As for Acton, an English Communist friend visiting him in Italy said "How lovely it will be when your villa and garden are handed over to the proletariat!" Acton immediately saw them stoning the statues, wrecking the flower beds, and killing the goldfish. "But you would be employed as caretaker" his friend said soothingly, "if you behaved yourself."

Above all, Wheatley's message in a bottle and its concerns about the tyranny of "the State machine" are exactly con-temporary with the writing of George Orwell's *1984*, the title famously intended as an anagram of "1948".

★

Along with extensive planting, Wheatley had also taken up

446

amateur bricklaying again, building on his experience with "Crooked Villa" in the First War. The methodical streak in Wheatley's character came out in his bricklaying as much as his writing; he applied himself seriously, and laid over sixty thousand bricks. Unusually for him, he drank beer during his exertions. His sweet tooth generally put him off beer (if he wanted a long drink he preferred cider), but he found it was the most thirst-quenching drink for bricklaying. He started off by walling up the entrance to the stable yard, then embarked on his major achievement, a 200 foot long serpentine wall.

Wavy serpentine walls are believed to have originated in Brittany, and there are a number of them around South Hampshire, dating from the Napoleonic wars. They are mostly the work of French prisoners-of-war, who had the misfortune to be captured during a conflict that lasted twenty-one years. They were treated as humanely as possible and let out to work as gardeners, when they built the walls. Wheatley knew all this – it is his account that I have borrowed here – and his serpentine wall accompanies the Roger Brook books as a similar conjunction of place and period.

Being wavy, the wall has the extra strength of corrugation; a wall one brick deep risks being blown down, unless it is buttressed with pillars, whereas a one-brick wavy wall will stand without extra buttressing, and it will also conduct warmth and ripen fruit. Over the next few years, Wheatley followed up his serpentine wall with a sunken rose garden and a 250 foot terrace, and by 1958 he was confident enough to build an arch.

Amateur bricklaying was also a hobby of Sir Winston Churchill, along with painting, and this must have confirmed it in Wheatley's mind as a good hobby for the right sort of chap to have. Wheatley would wear a boiler suit for his bricklaying. This was largely on practical grounds ("its long sleeves protect one's arms in summer and early autumn from the attention of mosquitoes") although it is hard not to over-look the fact that it is also an item of clothing associated with Churchill.

Wheatley liked to imitate Churchill's voice as a party

piece, and he was very gratified during a Christmas game that required players to guess the identity of a famous personality. In this case it was a man who wrote, had travelled widely, had false teeth, disliked exercise, read a great deal of history, served in the First War, went to bed in the afternoon, had a fanatical belief in the virtues of the Empire, liked champagne and old brandy, and whose hobby was bricklaying. It must be Churchill, said Wheatley. "No," said the family, "it's you!"

In due course Wheatley wrote a book about his bricklaying, his 1961 *Saturdays with Bricks*, and he dedicated it to Churchill, "Our most illustrious amateur builder and architect of victory".

The concept of DIY had taken off in the Fifties, and Wheatley was well aware that he couldn't write an authoritative book of "the 'How to do it yourself' type that is now frequently produced by experts", so his publisher suggested interspersing *Saturdays with Bricks* with anecdotes. Wheatley interspersed it with anecdotes about the First War. It is a modest and engaging book, and above all a document of amateurism, which was for a long time something of a cult and a valued space with the English, notably in their detective fiction[1].

Not only were Wheatley and Churchill both bricklayers, they were both writer–amateurs who wrote books about their hobbies; Wheatley's *Saturdays with Bricks* followed Churchill's *Painting as Pastime*, and they were both preceded by Biggles author Captain W.E.Johns's *The Passing Show: A Garden Diary by an Amateur Gardener*.

Saturdays with Bricks is a better title, but Wheatley did much of his bricklaying on Sundays; he was still working six days a week, and on Saturdays he was hard at it with pencil

---

[1] Holmes is the great amateur. English writer Dorothy Sayers has her amateur detective, Lord Peter Wimsey, whereas Continental writer Georges Simenon has his professional detective, Maigret. Showing the same division in the work of a single writer, Agatha Christie has her English amateur, Miss Marple, and her Continental professional, Hercule Poirot.

and eraser. He felt his next book, *The Haunting of Toby Jugg*, was one his best, particularly as an exercise in suspense. It also has some very peculiar messages lurking under the surface, not buried in a bottle this time but broadcast in a million-seller.

CHAPTER THIRTY-SIX

An International Spider

Shortly before the Second World War, MI5 investigated the progressive co-educational school at Dartington Hall, in Devon. Famous for its music and its liberal discipline, Dartington Hall had begun as an experimental arts community, on the lines of the Bauhaus, founded by Leonard Elmhirst and Dorothy Whitney. By the late Thirties M15 had become worried that it might be a place of Communist indoctrination, and also that its emigré staff might unwittingly harbour Nazis in reach of the South West Coast. It gave refuge to the dance innovator Laban, for example, who had mounted Nazi dance shows (before falling foul of the regime, supposedly because he was a Mason). The idea of MI5 investigating Dartington now seems ridiculous, although in fact Dorothy Whitney's son Michael Straight did spy for Russia after being recruited by Anthony Blunt.

In 1938 Maxwell Knight had written to Wheatley, in order to put Bill Younger on the Dartington case. (MI5's findings are preserved at the Public Records Office as HO144/21511, 'Allegations of teachings of communist doctrines at Dartington Hall Co-Ed School 1932–41': they remain closed until 2042).

"I had heard about a school in Devonshire," says Wheatley, where "pupils were allowed complete licence to attend classes or not as they liked, lie in bed all day if they wished and even abuse teachers that they disliked." Wheatley claims there were rumours of pupils being encouraged to attend Satanic gatherings in a nearby ruined church, which is surely a little flourish of Wheatley's own, unless Uncle Max was pulling his leg again.

This inspired Wheatley to put Gregory Sallust on the case in 1939, but it was shelved with the war. Picking the idea up again afterwards, Wheatley left Sallust out and built it around a new hero with new, topical concerns.

Bedridden and partially paralysed from a wartime spinal injury, ex-RAF pilot Albert "Toby" Jugg slowly realises he is being held captive in his family castle by his apparently benign but increasingly sinister guardian Helmuth, who was a teacher at the school Toby attended. Toby is unable to tell anyone about the enormous, half-spectral spider which fingers the window of his room every night with its legs, casting a horrible shadow in the moonlight as it tries to get in. Ordinary spiders from all over the building also converge on Toby's room, somehow directed by Helmuth, and Toby's letters are intercepted before they can reach the outside world. It transpires that Helmuth wants Toby's inheritance, as heir to the Juggernaut engineering fortune, and if Toby refuses to sign it over, Helmuth will have him certified as insane and gain control by default.

One of the strangest aspects of *Jugg* is the nature of the ideas that run through Toby's mind as he lies bedridden. You might think that the state of British democracy, and the fact that it is too easy for extremist foreigners to be elected to Parliament, would be the last things a man being menaced by a giant spider would worry about. But that would be to overlook the book's allegorical dimension and political message, in which the spider and the foreign Communist menace are bound up together.

After all, thinks Toby, it is not that we want to prevent all foreigners from settling in Britain; and "neither, shades of Disraeli, do we want to discriminate against our own Jews." But then Disraeli was all right; "his family had been resident in London for nearly a hundred years before he first sat at Westminster". The book plays out a drama of Englishness versus foreignness, the latter exemplified by the evil Dr Helmuth Lisicky.

All the indications are that Helmuth is a thoroughly bad egg, right from the fact that he despises stamp collecting (Wheatley, of course, was a keen collector). "Wasting your time with those silly little bits of coloured paper?", he asks

451

Toby. But Toby is not wasting his time; he is using his stamp albums to hide the diary of his ordeal, which becomes the novel itself.

Helmuth is a very bad egg indeed: he is a Communist-Satanist. Unfortunately, it is sinister on a less amusing level when, on top of everything else, Toby suspects him of being Jewish: "the fact that his ears are set low on his skull suggests that he may have a dash of Jewish blood."

Toby, in contrast, is a distinctly Aryan type, blond and formerly nicknamed "The Viking", but the real issue is less Jewishness than xenophobia. The problem is not that foreign Jews are Jewish but that they're foreign, and therefore prone to political extremism, which in Britain was associated with Continental emigrés.

Throughout Wheatley's lifetime, extremist politics of a kind supposedly 'alien' to the British way of life tended to come from abroad, with East End Russian anarchists before the First War, Italian Fascism and German National Social-ism, and – the Continental far-Right having been defeated – the foreign Left making post-war emigré inroads into higher education, the media and the Labour Party. This was a con-cern of Orwell's at the end of his life, and his controversial denunciation of a number of individuals to MI5 was handled by Wheatley's friend Colonel "Sherry" Sheridan. More about Sheridan later.

This foreign-English theme in *Jugg* is further played out in the contrast between Jugg's two nurses. Jewish Deborah is a thin-lipped intellectual, and although she is perfectly decent in a humourless way (and not party to Helmuth's plan for Toby) Toby is shocked to find that she is a Communist and wants to stand for Parliament. Toby's other nurse is a strap-ping English girl named Sally Cardew, and she is much more Wheatley's cup of tea: she is well bred ("much better born than I am," and in that respect like Wheatley's own Joan) and not too brainy ("a nice healthy English hoyden, not over-burdened with brains, of the sort who has been brought up to believe in God and the King"). She is just the sort of girl John Betjeman might have liked, right down to the fact that she is "a hefty wench"; as Betjeman was wont to say, "I wouldn't mind being pushed round the park in a perambulator by her".

★

Jugg's main supernatural plank is a sensationalistic treatment of hypnosis, which Toby teaches himself from a book he finds among the books-by-the-yard furnishing the castle library and uses in his attempts to escape (it is J.Milne Bramwell's *Hypnotism*, a book which Wheatley owned). Like the two earlier occult books, *Jugg* also features plenty of argument to suspend disbelief in the supernatural, and Wheatley puts his childhood experience of 'the Thing on the stairs' into Toby's schooldays, brought about by the school staff dabbling with the occult.

"Weyland School" was a Satanic recruiting ground, with Crowley's old Rabelaisian motto of 'Do What Thou Wilt Shall Be The Whole of the Law', but Satanism has considerably expanded in *Jugg*. The Satanists in *The Devil Rides Out* were an international gang, but they have now become a global conspiracy, The Brotherhood, with a new totalitarian programme in the guise of Communism.

This identification of Satanism and Communism was a major innovation in Wheatley's propaganda career, and one that would continue in his subsequent occult books. Leaving aside, just for a moment, the fact that it is ludicrous, there is nevertheless an esoteric justification for this equation, pivoting on the idea of materialism versus idealism.

Wheatley believed in idealist 'light' and 'spirit', whereas Satanism is a materialism, exalting the things of this world. The upright or 'good' five-pointed occult pentacle (bearing some resemblance to the human form with outstretched arms) represents among other things mind over matter, in the unity of spirit – the one point – above the division of matter: the two points. The inverted or 'bad' Satanic pentacle (bearing some resemblance to a goat's head, with horns, ears and chin) represents divided matter exalted over spirit, comparable to the way in which Marxism or 'dialectical materialism' exalts the economic base over the cultural superstructure.

453

On a simpler level, if Satanists aim to sow dissent, discord, stupidity, conflict, darkness and ruin, then Wheatley believed that the Left was the modern vehicle for this. Further, Left atheism is anti-Christian and therefore a potentially useful stalking-horse for Satanism; an opinion not unknown among Christians in America. But whatever its niceties or obtusities, Wheatley went to town with the idea in *Jugg* and never looked back.

As Helmuth explains,

> Communism is the perfect vehicle for the introduction of the return of Mankind to its original allegiance [i.e. to the Old One, Satan]. It already denies Christianity and all the other heresies. It denies the right of free-will and the expression of their individuality to all those who live under it. Communism bows down only to material things; and my real master is not Stalin but the Lord of Material Things; Satan the Great, the Deathless, the Indestructible . . . He has taken the very word Communism as his new name, and he even mocks those who no longer believe in his existence by having them demonstrate in favour of rule by the Proletariat on the first of May. Have you never realised that it is his anniversary, and that it is born of May-day Eve – Walpurgis Nacht – on which we celebrate his festival?

Walpurgis Night, or St. Walburga's Eve, should be familiar to Wheatley readers from *The Devil Rides Out*, and May Day, the old pagan festival and more recently workers' day, was the occasion of a massive military parade of troops, tanks and missile launchers through Moscow, once a familiar annual sight on British television.

Just as the Satanists in *The Devil Rides Out* were defeated by a woman and the power of love, so the Satanists in *Jugg* meet their end within a familiar Wheatley scenario: Sally Cardew has been taken prisoner and is going to be ritually ravished by the Satanists at the climax of their Black Mass, before the general orgy begins, and there is nothing that Toby can do about it except pray.

Toby's old, mad Great-Aunt Sarah, who lives elsewhere in the castle, has been at work for many years on a secret tunnel, leading her – so she believes – towards rescuing the man she once loved. The idea of tunnelling was in the air in 1947, with British prisoners having tunnelled out of German POW camps, and so was the bursting of dams, after the Dam Buster air raids. In a *deus ex machina* ending that is extraordinary even by Wheatley standards, these ideas are brought together when, just in the nick of time ("Night after night for over forty years she had laboured for love's sake") Great Aunt Sarah's tunnel strikes a lake, and her dead body comes flying out of the tunnel entrance towards the Satanists in the sunken chapel, borne by thousands of gallons of water that pour in and drown them all.

Only Toby and Sally survive, and in due course they pray together, "for the happiness of that spirit which for a little time lived in the body of Sarah Jugg – who yesterday was old and mad, but today is young and sane again."

To be fair to Wheatley, he doesn't try to suggest this is simply an extraordinary coincidence. Instead it is the working of "an inscrutable Providence" to save two lovers, perhaps even an answer to prayer. And in any case, literary quibbling is beside the point. Highly improbable, full of unintentional humour for the modern reader, *Jugg* is nevertheless one of Wheatley's best books, full of plot twists, hopes raised and dashed, near escapes failing at the last moment, Toby's Hitchcockian frustrations at not being believed, and his love for Sally.

It is as plausible in small details as such an allegorical story could be, combining – for example – the entirely naturalistic nickname of "Toby" for a man in the Forces surnamed Jugg, together with its more symbolic invocation of Olde England under threat, via the familiar character jug modelled as an 18th century drinker in his three-cornered hat; a figure almost as archetypal as John Bull. Wheatley had one of these Toby jugs on his desk.

The Haunting of Toby Jugg was published just in time for Christmas 1948 and it was a great success, clearing the one million mark. "It propounds a theory that under a new disguise the Devil is still intensely active", said the blurb, no more than hinting at the Cold War theme. It may have been helped by another extraordinary Frank Pape cover illustration, which — like most of Pape's Wheatley jackets — has to be seen to be believed.

A lone man, on crutches, confronts a gigantic and amorphous spider-creature which towers over him: it is greenish, and looks to have soft, pale, toad-belly flesh. The creature wraps right around the book and behind it, on the back jacket, there is a suggestion of smoke or incense rising above a naked blonde who is about to be sacrificed on an altar by figures in black cowls. The title of the book is carried on the beast's face and legs, with the T of Toby in red looking something like a hammer while the tails of the 'g' letters drop into red, hooked curves. Taken together, they form a suggestion of the red hammer and sickle.

★

The spider-creature in *Jugg* also resembles the Jewish spider or octopus, often seen getting its tentacles around the planet in anti-Semitic propaganda. Inasmuch as some Jews might be specifically seen as a menace, Wheatley was following a line also to be found in Churchill. In his 1920 essay, 'Zionism versus Bolshevism,' Churchill's argument was that Jews were everywhere behind revolutions (his point being, since he was a Zionist, was that they would cause less trouble if they had a homeland):

> This movement among the Jews is not new. From the days of Spartacus-Weishaupt to those of Karl Marx, and down to Trotsky, Bela Kun, Rosa Luxemburg, and Emma Goldman . . . this worldwide conspiracy for the overthrow of civilisation and for the reconstitution of society

456

on the basis of arrested development, of envious malevo-
lence, and impossible equality, has been steadily growing.

★

There is another flash of ambivalence to Jews in Wheatley's
immediately postwar novel, *Codeword: Golden Fleece*, set in the
early days of the war in Eastern Europe:

> Rex had often discussed the Jewish problem, thinking in
> terms of the flashy Americanized Jews who throng the
> second-class cinemas and restaurants of the great cities of
> the Western world, and by their overbearing brazenness
> give a false impression of their numbers. He knew, too, that
> there existed a small sprinkling of really cultured Jews –
> men of quiet demeanour and unshakeable integrity, such
> as his own friend Simon Aron – and he had often argued
> that, in spite of their reputation for sharp practice, the
> average Jew was honest and industrious and made a useful
> contribution to any country in which he settled. Here, for
> the first time in his life, Rex was brought face to face
> with the real Jewish problem, and he wondered unhap-
> pily how any country could make useful citizens out of
> these dirty, stupid-looking off-scourings of humanity.

Wheatley probably attempted this as a serious historical
point, trying to give a picture of the perceptions that contributed to Continental anti-Semitism in the Thirties. It is
also possible that his friend Michael Balcon, the film director, introduced him to the idea that Sephardic Jews – like
Balcon himself[1], and Simon Aron – were aristocratic, while
Ashkenazi Jews were a teeming problem.

As ever, it shows Wheatley's tendency to 'split' the world.
We might refine the old cliché to say it wasn't just that some
of his best friends were Jews; rather, some of his best friends
were *nice Jews*.

---

[1] Balcon and the Sephardic-Ashkenazi distinction: see Peter Parker,
Isherwood Picador 2004 p.280.

The Jewish theme in *Jugg* doesn't seen to have bothered anyone at the time. Satanism, however, was a much more alarming prospect, and before long an unwelcome letter arrived through Wheatley's door.

Into the Cave of Bats

Wheatley's postbag always swelled after his occult books. Shortly after *Jugg* was published he received a letter from a woman who claimed she had been present, in 1934, at a Black Mass held in Brighton with the specific intention of bringing about the death of King Albert of Belgium. The following day, in a climbing accident, he had indeed died.

Another unwanted letter arrived in January 1949, in a House of Commons envelope. It was a brief handwritten note from Sir Waldron Smithers, Conservative MP for Orpington, and it simply told Wheatley he wanted to see him in London, suggesting the Central Hall of the House as a place to meet.

Wheatley's curiosity was evidently not piqued by this somewhat peremptory letter (he may well have guessed what it was going to be about), and it seems to have put his back up. He waited a couple of weeks before replying, and wrote

> I have your letter, opening "I want to see you." Your brevity suggests that you are a very busy man. I most certainly am, and in these days I rarely come to London.
>
> Unless urgent business requires my presence there, I shall not go up again till I have finished the book on which I am now engaged – which should be some time in March.

Wheatley also asked for some indication of what Smithers wanted to see him about. Smithers wrote back more formally, this time typed and on House of Commons notepaper. What Smithers really wanted, he said, was to find out if Wheatley had any concrete evidence of Black Magical practices, with facts, places, and names. If he did, then Smithers was going to pass it on to the police so that firm action could be taken.

Wheatley was not particularly keen to be questioned about this, and in fact he must have known that however useful it might be for potboiling and propaganda, there was an embarrassing shortage of Satanic practice in Forties Britain.

The occult revival of the Sixties was still in the future. Kim Philby's 1940s reports to his Russian masters had been padded with unreliable material, including the assertion that RAF officers in London were being induced to part with information by German spies who had them "under the influence of drugs, alcohol, sexual orgies or Black Mass", but this was just Wheatley-style invention.

Wheatley had not kept in touch with Aleister Crowley, who had recently died, in 1947, a heroin addict in a Hastings boarding house. Louis Wilkinson had declaimed Crowley's 'Hymn to Pan' at the funeral, and this had scandalised the local council, who promised to take "all necessary steps" to prevent anything of the kind from happening again.

Gerald Gardner's witchcraft "revival" was yet to make itself felt. There were a few respectable esoteric groups such as The Society of the Inner Light, and some provincial offshoots of the Golden Dawn were still soldiering on, but all this was a long way from Black Magic.

Far from being a rampant menace to everything we hold dear, Black Magic was largely confined where it belonged, safely between the covers of Wheatley's own books. He let the correspondence with Smithers lapse.

★

Justerini and Brooks had commissioned Wheatley to write a company history for their 1949 bi-centenary. They had been at the same address – No.2 Pall Mall – since they began, and Wheatley celebrates the firm as an enduring British institution, "like a little rock of Gibraltar".

In the course of the book it survives fire and bombs, as well as the "black year of 1780", when the wine merchants had to put up their shutters and reach for their flintlocks during the Gordon Riots: "Had it not been for the King's firmness this week of anarchy might well have developed into a revolution."

The riots left over eight hundred dead, and – like Dickens in *Barnaby Rudge* – Wheatley's account shows his fear of the "rabble" and the "lawless mob". He sees the Riots as preventing later revolution in Britain: "the middle-classes of London profited by the lesson. They had seen for themselves the bestial excesses of which a drunken mob was capable, and realised the danger of supporting the wave of anti-monarchical feeling which was already sweeping Europe". The ideas of Rousseau were all very well, but "the King stood for law and order."

After the French Revolution and the Napoleonic Wars, trouble again broke out on the continent when Karl Marx – probably not a figure Justerini's expected to find in their company history – issued the *Communist Manifesto* in 1848, the year of revolution across Europe. In April 1848 Justerini's shutters went up again, as Chartists paraded across London armed with iron pikes fashioned from spear-topped railings, but Britain (already constitutional, and far ahead of the Continent in social legislation) escaped lightly. Her people were not in sympathy with the rioters, "and serious trouble was avoided".

Amid all this upheaval and reaction, Wheatley gives a detailed account of changing tastes in middle-class British drinking, including the discovery of whisky (formerly despised), the arrival of cocktail and sherry parties, and the practice of having a drink before dinner. "In Victorian times people never drank anything before eating, for fear of impairing their palate for the wines that would accompany the meal", but the early twentieth century saw the rise of the aperitif: "Perhaps it was the nerve-strain of the war which led to a great increase in the consumption of spirits and the general desire to put away not one but several drinks before dinner".

The book is completed by numerous recipes, including cherry brandy, which Wheatley used to make at Grove Place (pricking each cherry twenty times), "peach bola," and the eighteenth-century drinks ratafia and negus: it also included two new cocktail recipes from Wheatley and Alfred Hitchcock.

Wheatley made a solid job of *The Seven Ages of Justerini's*, while perhaps casting the scope of the book wider than Justerini's expected, with everything from the Black Hole of Calcutta to Darwinism. It shows an impressive knowledge of British history, and at heart it is a celebration of quality and continuity.

★

Anthony Wheatley – no longer in the Army, having contracted tuberculosis in Germany and been invalided out – had meanwhile met and fallen in love with Annette Webb, a vivacious and attractive woman who was the daughter of a military scientist, and in 1949 they were married. Confectionery and chocolates were always bound up with affection for Wheatley, and before they drove off on honeymoon, Wheatley told Anthony that when they reached the hotel in Dover, en route to the continent, they should enquire about a package. It proved to contain a big box of chocolates from Charbonnel et Walker, a magnum of vintage Veuve Clicquot and a copy of Wheatley's latest book, *The Rising Storm*.

The Rising Storm is the third of the Roger Brook series, bringing Roger into the French Revolution. The Brook series were becoming popular, and Wheatley resolved to include all major events of the period, carefully digested into what he called "history without tears".

Wheatley proceeded to write one of his major achievements in this genre, and his own favourite among his books, *The Second Seal*, published in 1950. Set in 1914, it fills in the earlier life of the Duke de Richleau and deals with the events leading to the First War. De Richleau becomes involved with the Serbian "Black Hand" secret society, mixes with the Imperial Family in Vienna, goes to the Kaiser's HQ at Aix, and is finally involved in the Battle of the Marne.

The Second Seal shows Wheatley's nostalgia for the world before the First War and, as usual, there is a stronger romantic interest than in most male popular writers, as the Duke becomes a colonel in the Archduchess Ilona Theresa's Hussars, falls in love with her, and marries her.

The Second Seal is a careful novelisation of its period, populated by real characters such as Generals Ludendorff, von Moltke, and Joffre. Wheatley used books by Arthur Schnitzler and Stefan Zweig for Viennese background, and for his history he used Churchill's *The Great War*, Ludendorff's *War Memories*, and many others, including the anonymous *My Secret Service*, written under the memorable pseudonym of "The Man Who Dined With The Kaiser".

Wheatley later visited Bavaria, where he stayed for a few days with Dr Kurt Hahn. Wheatley admired Hahn, a German Jew who had founded Gordonstoun School, the Outward Bound courses, and the Duke of Edinburgh's Award scheme, among other things. Hahn is sometimes regarded as the greatest educator of the twentieth century, with his dictum "there is more in you than you think."

Wheatley, of course, was particularly aware of Hahn's royal connection, since Prince Charles and several other members of the royal family attended Hahn's school. Wheatley was extremely gratified when he gave Hahn a copy of *The Second Seal*: Hahn apparently admired its historical accuracy, its fairness to Germany and Austria, and its readability, saying he would get two hundred copies for his students.

Wheatley was still writing two new books a year, but he was about to slow down a little; he still published two books a year through the Fifties, but the new formula was usually one new book and one omnibus edition of previous books.

Wheatley and Joan went to the South of France in 1950, staying in Nice, where Wheatley took an apartment for two months on the Boulevard des Anglais. As a guidebook, Wheatley brought *The Coast of Pleasure: Chapters Practical, Geographical and Anecdotal on the Social, Open Air and Restaurant Life of the French Riviera* by the publisher Grant Richards, who had died in 1948. Wheatley had known him slightly, remembering him as a charming man but not a very successful publisher (in fact he had published James Joyce, although he may not have been financially successful by Hutchinson standards; it was said of Walter Hutchinson that he had never read a book in his life but he knew how to sell them). Wheatley found Richard's book useful, although it must have been dated by 1950. It was published back in 1928, but no doubt part of Nice's appeal was that it didn't change too much.

The Wheatleys had friends in Nice, Diane and Pierre Hammerel, and the Hammerels took them to see "The Cave of Bats", which Wheatley was to use in *To The Devil – A Daughter*. Its unusual feature was that it was partly man-made, and possibly used by the Phoenicians when they dominated the Mediterranean, bringing with them what Wheatley thought of as their horrible Gods and Goddesses, such as Astarte (prototype of Astaroth, who figured in *Jugg*) and Baal, the latter also known as Moloch and associated with human sacrifices. As Wheatley later put it:

> Wherever the Phoenicians went, they took their terrible gods with them, and the priests performed their magic by the spilling of blood and semen. Some years ago, when I was in Nice, a friend took me to see a Phoenician temple.
> It was deep underground, its only entrance being a well-like cavity on a hill-top some miles outside the city. One shudders to think of the revolting rites that had taken place in those subterranean chambers.

Wheatley was always alert to the possibility of *Evil*, and he had another hair raising experience in Nice while he was in a night club. One of the cabaret turns featured an emaciated old man who recited a few indecent poems and then, as a finale, recited the Lord's Prayer backwards. Some of the audience may just have thought this was a feat of memory, perhaps in bad taste, but its blasphemous aspect was probably intended to be part of its effect. Reciting the Lord's Prayer backwards is often held to conjure up the Devil, and any frisson of wickedness in the night club was probably not accidental, particularly in France, with its strong anti-clerical tradition running right through the literature of Satanism and Surrealism.

Wheatley, however, saw even more in this performance, and he put the man into *To The Devil – A Daughter* as a Satanist:

> There is an old priest at Cagnes who has a pretty grue-some reputation, and a fortune-teller in Monte Carlo who does not stick to telling the cards. There is one man in Nice, too, who might know something – if only we can persuade him to talk. He is an elderly cabaret singer with a husky bass voice, and he does his act in a dirty little dive off the Place Massena. One of his stunts is to intone the Paternoster backwards.

In real life Wheatley believed the act contained a hint, to any interested parties in the audience, that they could contact him after the show:

> Most of the audience took it, no doubt, as a feat of mem-ory; but I felt certain that it was a covert invitation. Had I put it to him afterwards that I could pay handsomely for a wax image to be made, and that to be done which had to be done so that I could inherit from a rich uncle, I do not doubt he would have obliged me.

*

What has been described as the main period of Wheatley's success – the "second quarter of the twentieth century", according to American academic J.Randolph Cox – was coming to an end. But far from his time being up, he was going to become even more of a household name in the third quarter of the century.

And before that he was going to write a book that nobody was to know about: a book he remained unwilling to discuss for the rest of his life.

CHAPTER THIRTY-EIGHT

Eastern Assignment

During the war Wheatley had met Colonel Leslie "Sherry" Sheridan, "a cloak-and-dagger chap with whom I had numerous friendly dealings". Sheridan had been a Fleet Street journalist and then a barrister, but the war transformed his life and brought him a senior role in the Special Operations Executive (SOE), the controversial organisation responsible for "ungentlemanly warfare"[1], or propaganda, subversion and sabotage.

Such things were traditionally despised by the military establishment, but in 1940, with Europe under German occupation, the time had come to consider them. The SOE's brief, in Churchill's phrase, was "to set Europe ablaze", and its methods necessarily involved "varying degrees of illegal or unethical methods, which would violate normal peacetime morality and would not only be improper but often criminal; untruths, deceptions, bribery, forgeries of passports, permits or currencies, acts of violence, mayhem and murder."

The SOE was formed from the remains of two earlier clandestine organisations; the black propaganda unit known as 'Electra House', and the sabotage branch, section "D", for Destruction, of the Secret Intelligence Service, SIS or MI6. Before long, it had a global network of agents under Sheridan's direction: "Starting in the Balkans and using his widespread contacts with Fleet Street journalists and foreign correspondents, Sheridan built up a network of agents

---

[1] It was originally founded under the auspices of the 'Ministry of Economic Warfare', widely known as the "Ministry of Ungentlemanly Warfare", a description of Churchill's. It remains controversial because despite the bravery of its operatives, and the deaths that many of them met after being captured, civilians were caught up in its activities (in the derailing of trains, for example).

that, by 1941, covered the principal neutral capitals of the world."

Agents were often placed under the 'cover' of being Fleet Street foreign correspondents, while others worked for Sheridan's own brainchild, a supposedly commercial "news agency" set up in 1940 called Britanova Ltd, with offices just off the Strand in Norfolk Street.

When the war ended there was no going back to Fleet Street or the Bar for Sheridan, although his new career would still be concerned with mass communications and winning arguments. In 1946, in partnership with another ex-SOE man, Sheridan set himself up with an office at 47 Essex Street, again just off the Strand, as a practitioner of public relations.

Meanwhile the Cold War was getting under way. In 1946 Churchill spoke of an 'Iron Curtain' coming down across Europe (a phrase echoed in Wheatley's Cold War thriller title *Curtain of Fear*). The following year British Foreign Secretary Ernest Bevin found himself swamped by a wave of Soviet propaganda at the United Nations, and this was also the era of Soviet front organisations such as the 'World Federation of Trades Unions' and the 'World Peace Council'.

The Foreign Office needed to respond, so a new unit called the Information and Research Department was founded to organise anti-Communist publicity. The name was deliberately bureaucratic and bland: "It should be noted that the name of this department is intended as a disguise for the true nature of its work, which must remain strictly confidential"[2]

There has been a certain amount of paranoia on the Left about the operations of the IRD, but its aims were entirely reasonable. "I think the work we were doing was a good thing", IRD officer Celia Kirwan has said, "because people were misinformed about Communism in those days in a big

[2] FO 1110 / 383. In the event this draft explanation was not used, and a more anodyne definition was substituted.

way. And it was about time they got the record right." The IRD sought to alert people to the reality of the Gulag and the Soviet forced labour camps, and to show that life in Stalin's Russia was not all it was cracked up to be. In that respect the IRD hardly deserved to be controversial (as a well informed individual of Establishment sympathies said to the present writer, "Oh, they just told people socks were badly made in Bulgaria, that sort of thing".) The IRD was, nevertheless, instrumental in bringing down the Sukarno regime in Indonesia, and by the end of its existence there were concerns that its operations had exceeded its remit, both abroad and on the domestic front.

★

The Islamic religion was looking like a spent force in an increasingly modern world; nobody in 1948 would have predicted the revival of Islam by the end of the twentieth century. The IRD, however, decided to sponsor its resurgence as a Cold War strategy, bolstering it up to act as a Middle Eastern bulwark against the influence of the atheistic Soviet Union.

To this end the IRD planted articles in the Arab press such as 'The Life Giving Principles of Islam are a Sound Basis for a New Pattern of Life' by Zahid Hussein, planted in the Egyptian press by IRD Cairo. However, the problem with British-originated propaganda was that it tended to be pitched at too high a level for the local readership. In December 1949 the IRD had planted 'Moscow Attacks the Koran' and other articles in the Persian press, but the British Embassy complained that the material was too intellectual for the "earthy press of Persia". Or in the words of IRD Baghdad, in the Minutes of a Meeting of Information Officers in March 1948, ' "Propaganda must always address itself to the broad masses, and must fix its intellectual level so as not to be above the heads of the least intellectual of those to whom it is directed."(*Mein Kampf*)'

The breakthrough came with the idea of publishing pulp fiction, as minuted by IRD Cairo in February 1950:

19. Among the pamphlets and books, the following categories might be used for carrying propaganda . . .

b. The paper-backed novelette, dealing normally with sex or crime themes. This is apparently the staple diet of the half-educated *effendi*.

It was with this half-educated *effendi* in mind that IRD Cairo wrote, in a March 1950 memo marked 'Secret', that "IRD would arrange the production of drafts in English of short love or detective novels, or thrillers, embodying anti-Communist propaganda but following their local counter-parts as closely as possible . . . the IRD, Cairo, would arrange for the drafts to be re-written in Arabic by local hacks . . .". In June, however, in a document marked 'Top Secret', a more senior figure replied

The task suggested . . . is not, I think, a very feasible one. Mr.Sheridan has already seen an example of the sort of short story commissioned by the more lurid press, and I am sure the IRD could not begin to compete at that level of pornography.

Sherry Sheridan had meanwhile become an early and key member of the IRD in London (and had supervised the production of Orwell's *Animal Farm* as an anti-Communist comic strip for the Islamic world; it was particularly viable in this respect because the evil animals were pigs).

Using his PR office as a front, Sheridan rushed about in a succession of meetings and lunches with journalists and other opinion shapers at various restaurants and clubs, and he would lunch with Wheatley at the Hungaria Restaurant and the Savile Club.

Sheridan asked Wheatley to write a propaganda romance for the Middle Eastern world. Sheridan was luckier than he knew with Wheatley, given the Orientalist strain in Wheatley's psyche from his earlier years. Wheatley owned a number of books that he thought of as being about Islam (he catalogued them under this heading) including James Elroy

Flecker's *Hassan*, Norman Penzer's *The Harem*, four or five illustrated editions of *The Rubaiyat of Omar Khayyam*, E.Powys Mather's *Red Wise*, and a copy of *The Qur'an*.

Wheatley – and probably the Foreign Office men themselves – would have been familiar with the idea of Islam holding the balance of power in the Middle East from John Buchan's 1916 thriller *Greenmantle*; it was one of Wheatley's favourite books, and his copy was inscribed to him by Buchan. In it – and this much was historically true, oddly enough – Kaiser William has proclaimed a Holy War, calling himself Hadji Mohammed Guilliamo and claiming that the Hohenzollerns are descended from the Prophet Mohammed[3].

The British are forced to take counter-measures. Buchan's Sir Walter Bullivant – the man who sends Richard Hannay on his missions, and seems to be the model for Sir Pellinore Gwaine-Cust in the Gregory Sallust books – muses:

> The ordinary man again will answer that Islam in Turkey is becoming a back number, and that Krupp guns are the new gods. Yet – I don't know. I do not quite believe in Islam becoming a back number.

Wheatley's instructions, probably from Sheridan himself, were imaginative and detailed. In two typed sheets headed NOVEL FOR THE MIDDLE EAST, the Foreign Office specified the setting and four chief characters: the Heroine ("a beautiful Islamic girl"), the Hero, and the Villain, a Russian Embassy official who runs a spy ring ("Inter alia he has on his staff a number of loose, flaunting women imported from Russia, who treat the local inhabitants with arrogance"). There was a particular cultural sensitivity in the fourth character, the Sage:

> – venerable old gentleman, possibly father of hero, who gives good advice, and maintains (but not at too great

---

[3] As Queen Elizabeth II is said to be, via the Moorish Kings of Spain.

length) the importance of the good life, the necessity of following the customs and practices of Islam, and their complete incompatibility with Communism. The old gentleman should, it is thought, have a hard life, being continually robbed, beaten up and so on, at the instigation of the Russian official; but right, of course, will triumph in the end.

Overall, there should be "a fairly continuous suggestion of sex, but nothing actually pornographic, i.e. the reader should see people going into the bedrooms, but should not follow them in."

Wheatley rose to the task magnificently. Ayesha, sales-girl in Souliman's scent shop, is eighteen "and in the full flower of her beauty", whether sitting in a simple cotton frock under the date palm behind her mother's house, or wearing "traditional costume" at work with "filmy Turkish trousers caught tight with bangles at the ankles" (Wheatley doesn't actually say where this costume is traditional; perhaps Seragliostan) and of course a yashmak, revealing just her beautiful eyes. It was the proviso she could work veiled that secured her now-dead father's consent to her taking a job, because he was a "strict Mohammedan and old-fashioned in his views."

Ayesha has been noticed by Sergius Razoff, a high ranking official in the Soviet secret police. He wants her to be his mistress, and warns her that when the Communists come to power in the near future, in a planned coup, she will be his for the taking. This sounds strange and alien to Ayesha:

In Islamic countries, through centuries of convention, women have always enjoyed a special protection, and to Ayesha it seemed almost impossible to visualise a state of things in which an official, however powerful, could take a woman against her will . . .

It is all the more alien because she finds Razoff repulsive, with his "flat Mongol face and small dark eyes that peered avidly at her, seeking, she felt with repulsion, to strip her of

471

her garments. The thought of being embraced by him made her shudder."

Ayesha loves Selim, handsome and clever son of the scent shop owner. He is university educated and runs the laboratory where the perfumes are made. Ayesha wants to get an education so she can work in the scent lab with Selim: "Prostrating herself, she begged Allah, the Merciful, the Compassionate, would hearken to a maiden's prayer." – and in due course she does get to work there. Ayesha's devout Mohammedan father, meanwhile, has been "a strong supporter of the movement to found an Arab league as the best means of maintaining the independence of the Islamic countries from encroachment by Jews, the Western Powers, and Soviet Russia alike . . ."

An Armenian named Melkon gives Ayesha a lift in his newly acquired car, but he tells her "my new master is both rich and generous" and drives her to the Russian compound against her will, where his new master Razoff is waiting: "At the thought of brutal hands upon her shrinking flesh, and his flat Mongol face, hot and leering, within a few inches of her own, a shudder ran through her." Ayesha struggles to escape. Melkon says "You spawn of Iblis!" – the Devil in Islam – and produces a knife: "Were it not that I mean to produce you to my master in good shape, I would slit you across the face with this in payment for that bite you gave me."

> She was a highly imaginative girl, and had been brought up on the immemorial romances that for a thousand generations have been the literary treasure of the Arabian lands. Ever since she had been old enough to understand anything of life, she had dreamed girlish dreams of a happy marriage. Even if there were no longer Caliphs in Baghdad, and princes no longer sought adventure disguised as poor princes to the Holy Cities, there were still their modern equivalent in the handsome, cultured sons of rich merchants – young men like Selim. It had been her highest ambition to unveil ceremoniously and give herself joyfully, as a bride, to such a one. But beyond that small stout door in the wall lay the very antithesis of all

472

such dreams, and an hour of horror that would render them for ever unrealisable.

Just as Melkon is dragging her through the door Wheatley suspends the action, cliff-hanger style, and treats readers to a chapter on Selim and his progressive beliefs. He debates the pros and cons of Marxism, revolution and reform with his friends, one of whom, Hassan, says "To play with Moscow is to play with fire . . . if we had a Communist Government here, what is to prevent it inviting Soviet troops to march in on the excuse of maintaining order. No thank you!"

Ayesha has meanwhile stabbed Melkon with his own knife. Terrified, she feels doubly culpable because she accepted the lift, but she still hopes to get away with the murder. Somehow she finds enough calm to discuss politics with Selim, and asks him if he has ever met anyone who has lived under Soviet rule and escaped. This is the cue to introduce the Sage, her Uncle Ishak: "Old Ishak was completely bald; his face was covered with a thousand wrinkles . . ."

"Young sir," Ishak says to Selim,

your generation makes a mock of Holy Things and its ears are deaf to the voice of truth and wisdom. It would be profitless for me to weary you with the tale of my sufferings, for Iblis, the accursed, has befogged the understanding of all such young men as yourself. You would go from here only with cynical laughter in your heart, judging me a dotard who seeks refuge in lies to excuse the failure he has made of his life. It is far better that you should employ yourself in converse with my niece, while admiring her physical perfections, for that is surely the true purpose which has led you to honour us with your presence.

"Oh uncle!" protests Ayesha, turning crimson. Ishak's eyes lose their dullness and glint with a sudden light as he continues:

Then be warned by me. Repent in time and return to

Islam. Above all, have no truck with Communists, for it is such as they who are referred to in the Koran where it says "For these are the fellows of the fire, and they shall burn therein for aye."

"But what it would really interest me to know [says Selim] is why you consider that Communism is necessarily evil."

"Because it destroys the soul. It teaches men to deny their God and robs them of their individuality." [. . .] "Red is the symbol of the fire, and these are the fellows of the fire. For Allah sees all, and even as it is written in the Holy Book, they shall burn therein for aye."

While a discussion of 'equality', educational brainwashing, and the realities of Russian life is going on – and Ishak describes what happened to the family carpet business under Bolshevism – Razoff suddenly arrives. He threatens to send Ishak back to Dagestan, draws a gun on Selim, and announces Ayesha is "as succulent a morsel as I've seen in all the years I've been stationed here . . . you will kindly regard her as my property."

"You must be crazy to think that you are on such an easy wicket," says Selim, "Praise be to Allah the Communists haven't a hope of getting a clear majority." But Razoff has the upper hand because he knows Ayesha murdered Melkon, and she sees her future all too clearly:

He might not even stop at blackmailing her into becoming his concubine. Even if she let him have his way with her, rather than face exposure, her degradation might not end at that. When he had tired of her, he would be able to renew his threats and force her to prostitute herself in order to get him information, as she had heard it said he did with the Russian secretaries on his staff.

The thought of such a prospect made her flesh creep.

Razoff announces he is taking her straight back to his villa in his car, where

I shall first strip you naked, so that not only I, but all my people, can have a good look at you. I shall then proceed to the full enjoyment of your charms at my leisure. When I have done with you I shall give you over to my men to do as they like with you. Finally, I shall hand you over to a Chinese eunuch who is an expert in devising measures to make pig-headed people talk. After half an hour with him you will be screaming yourself hoarse to be allowed to tell me what you have done with that letter. How do you like the idea of being the central figure in such a programme?

"You beast! You inhuman brute!" sobs Ayesha, "May Allah be the witness to your persecution of me! May he repay you for it by casting your soul to Iblis, so that it will forever burn among the damned." "I don't give a fig for Allah," says Razoff, "and I've no time to waste in talking mythology."

Things look bad, but Wheatley has more snakes and ladders in store. Selim has managed to escape and summon the police. Safe from Razoff, Ayesha is now rejected by Selim because he thinks she was Melkon's mistress. She still has Razoff's letter, letting slip the plan for the Communist coup d'etat, but she will implicate herself in the murder if she reveals how she came by it.

For a quarter of an hour she wrestled in torment with her soul. She was convinced that to produce the letter would bring about her own death; but if she did not, her country would be given over to the Godless inhuman Molochs of Moscow. The people would be enslaved: in the months to come countless women would suffer the degrading fate with which Razoff had threatened her; Selim, and every man likely to give trouble to the new Soviet masters, would be shot. Yes – Selim would be shot.

So she tells Selim everything, and the planned coup and Razoff's plans for women are made public (he had told her "under Soviet rule every woman had to submit to any official who took a fancy to her"). "Allah, what a scoop!" exclaims a journalist. Ayesha has saved her country.

Now there is only the murder to worry about, and at this point Wheatley searched his Koran to find a passage he remembered dimly from years earlier, and the white-haired magistrate declares

> Is it not written in Chapter 24 of the Koran, that even a slave girl shall not be compelled to prostitute herself. We have before us an honest woman who, under extreme provocation, did what she has done in defence of her chastity. I find no case to send to a higher court.

Sobbing with joy, Ayesha walks into the street with Selim and their friends and families. It is election day, but now the Communists have no chance, thanks to Ayesha's revelation. Quoting Razoff's letter, a newspaper headline reads "COMMUNIST PLOT TO SEIZE GOVERNMENT" and another "PROMINENT SOVIET CITIZEN STATES ALL WOMEN PROPERTY OF OFFICIALS UNDER COMMUNISM."

Communism is defeated, and boy and girl live happily ever after.

Sheridan was well pleased with Wheatley's effort, particularly his adroit use of the Koran. In his typically all-out, Manichaean, black-or-white fashion, Wheatley entitled the book *Of Vice and Virtue*. It was published in Beirut in 1953, with the Arabic title changed to *Ayesha*.

★

Wheatley was always keen to evade the tax man. Indeed, his pre-war Fascist friend W.H.Tayleur – now another public relations consultant – wrote in a mid-Fifties letter that Wheatley's request to be paid (for a proposed advertising campaign selling razor blades) with a greenhouse was just not practicable. His clients might be able to put something portable through their books as an expense, from a TV set to a motor car, but the greenhouse was taking creative accountancy too far.

For *Vice and Virtue*, the agreement was that Wheatley should be paid in cash. "It was . . . suggested that for such an operation the use of Secret Funds was fully justified, and these would be tax free". Wheatley went to 47 Essex Street for his money, but he had been seized with anxiety about carrying a large sum in notes, in case something should happen on the street. Like the old SOE man that he was, Sheridan took Wheatley's security arrangements in his stride (what they really needed was item ns.306 in the SOE quartermaster's catalogue of Special Devices, the Calico Money Belt). After putting several hundreds of pounds worth of notes into Wheatley's trouser pockets – several thousand by today's values – he pinned them shut with safety pins, and Wheatley walked away down Essex Street with the money safely trousered.

Wheatley professed himself unable to discuss *Vice and Virtue* in his lifetime; perhaps partly to foster a certain image of himself, but also from a real sense that he had entered into something clandestine with the IRD. He wrote to a bibliographer in 1972

> . . . in fact I [would not have] allowed it to be mentioned at all in the Hutchinson's pamphlet, but for the fact that it is now a long time since I wrote it. I am, however, still uncertain that I may not get into trouble from the Foreign Office by having done so, as the whole thing was a highly confidential business and I certainly cannot allow any particulars about it to be printed.

In due course he had his typescript bound by Sangorski and Sutcliffe in blue morocco leather, with *Pro Rege et Patria*, For King and Country, stamped on the cover.

★

Under the umbrella of the nuclear stand-off, Wheatley was very conscious that Cold War was an ideas war. As Gifford

477

Hillary argues in *The Ka of Gifford Hillary*, "as for destroyers, cruisers, and other conventional craft I'll admit that they have a certain use in a cold war, for showing the flag in foreign ports; but if we spent the cost of their upkeep in radio programmes for the Arab and Asiatic nations, aimed at countering Soviet propaganda, we would get infinitely better value for our money."

Working with the given premise that "communism is only a cloak for the most sinister imperialism the world has ever seen", the IRD had a complex task in the Middle East. They had to be careful not to push Western-style 'democracy', which might be unsuitable for the Arab world and prove destabilising; they had to be careful not to mention Communism too much, which might have the effect of publicising it; and yet they had to emphasise the threat of Russia, and its Godlessness. And at the same time, to their credit, they resolved to avoid Islamic fundamentalism, reminding themselves in a memo "Don't back reaction". Wheatley's book was as good a contribution to the struggle as could be expected and, like a number of his books, it is notable for a strong female character in the decisive role.

Wheatley and Sheridan remained friends until Sheridan's death in 1964. Sheridan spent the latter half of his life as a professional Cold Warrior of great flair and integrity, and he was the case officer for George Orwell's 1949 denunciation of a list of people whom he considered to be "crypto-Communists and fellow travellers."

As for the IRD, it was finally closed down in 1978. Its hawkish hard line and apparent autonomy had become a cause for concern; "a frequent complaint from the more detente-minded in Whitehall was 'We have one foreign policy, IRD has another.' " There were also concerns that despite being a part of the Foreign Office, the IRD had taken an over-keen interest in domestic affairs, particularly the Trades Union movement, and was producing propaganda material with unacknowledged 'spin' for the home market.

This was what Wheatley did for four decades: *Vice and Virtue* is only part of his propaganda career, and the anti-Communism of his post-war books follows the IRD agenda. The IRD had stressed that Nazism and Communism should be closely equated (and even tried to gain credibility for the term "Communazis") which is part of the message in *Jugg*, and again in *The Satanist*, where a character named Lothar is an old Nazi, Communist and Satanist all in one. Wheatley no doubt held these opinions independently, although they may have been reinforced and sharpened over lunches – and by the IRD journal of comment, *The Interpreter*, which Sheridan was regularly sending to him.

Of Wheatley's eight occult novels, seven have a distinct propaganda function. As we have seen, *The Devil Rides Out* was an early Appeasement novel, written to prevent war with Nazi Germany, and *Strange Conflict* was written for the war effort. An anti-Communist line then goes through *Jugg, To The Devil – A Daughter, The Ka of Gifford Hillary* and *The Satanist*, with increasing attention being paid to the menace of Trade Unionism, and in *Gateway to Hell* Wheatley turns his attention to the Black Power movement.

It is fitting that Wheatley's occult novels should be propaganda vehicles, since propaganda and magic both involve the manipulation of reality by means of words and images. The propagandist and the magician are both interested in changing consciousness, within an idea-led, thought-driven view of the world.

Wheatley had spent formative years in the propaganda-conscious period between the wars. It was in the Thirties that Captain J.F.C. Fuller – tank expert, occultist, and a friend of both Crowley and Hitler – told readers of the *Occult Review* that magic remained a "formidable weapon under the name of 'propaganda' ", and added "Is not Dr.Goebbels a magician?"

*

By now, Wheatley was in many respects a member of the Establishment. He had certainly had "a good war", and he was close to senior officers in the Army and Air Force, as well as several members of the peerage. He had worked near

Churchill, and he had close links with MI5 and other intelligence organisations.

There was, however, another establishment that would never really accept him, and that was the literary establishment. This was a club he could not join so easily, and it has to be said his name might sit oddly with the likes of C.P.Snow or Ivy Compton-Burnett.

Wheatley had had his disappointing experience with the PEN Club, some years earlier, but now the time seemed ripe for him to try to enter the Royal Society of Literature.

Clubland Heroes

Founded in 1820, and bearing a reassuringly regal title, the Royal Society of Literature had included Yeats, Conrad, Beerbohm, Buchan, Maugham, Kipling, Eliot, and Wodehouse among its many Fellows. Churchill had recently become one, in 1947, and Montague Summers had been elected back in 1916: "a distinction," he wrote bitchily, circa 1948, "in those days not so generally awarded as it is to-day."

Wheatley's friend Gilbert Frankau, author of the once celebrated novel *Peter Jackson, Cigar Merchant*, was also a Fellow, and in March 1950 Frankau wrote to the RSL Secretary, Miss Rudston Brown, nominating Wheatley for a Fellowship: "As a writer", he added, "Mr Wheatley needs no recommendation. It is not so widely known that he served as a volunteer in both wars." He chased this request up a few months later, and Rudston Brown mentioned that since Wheatley didn't know he was being considered for membership, his feelings couldn't be hurt whatever happened. Frankau's further reply introduces an unfortunate and delicate note: "I quite understand the position. *Privately*, Dennis and I are such very good friends that I told him I'd put his name forward."

Neither Frankau nor Wheatley could have foreseen the difficulties ahead, which might have been more likely from a gentleman's club. Gaining membership of a gentleman's club could be a hazardous procedure. Candidates had to be proposed by one member, seconded by another, and – crucially – not objected to by any others, hence the custom of the anonymous "black ball". Members of the club would place white or black balls into a bag when a candidate was up for membership, and if even a single black ball was found, he was rejected; a custom which could lead to long-pursued feuds and vendettas. Unsuitable, oiky, nouveau riche candidates could even give rise to a bag that looked, as one writer puts it, "like a helping of giant caviar." Worse still, the member who proposed them would then feel honour bound to resign.

★

Wheatley had already had problems trying to get into a club. He had joined the Savage in the mid-Thirties, but found it socially undistinguished (many of its members were writers, a number of them also in the Paternoster). The club he pined to join by the end of the Thirties was Boodles, and he made typically strenuous efforts to get in, canvassing the support of members he knew. These efforts culminated in an alarmingly forward letter to the Chairman, Mr Bagge.

"You may, perhaps, recall giving me lunch at Boodle's about a year ago," writes Wheatley. He then recalls a conversation with a friend about clubs: "I remarked that mine, the Savage, interested me so little that I never went into it from one year's end to another; but that there was one club to which I would really like to belong – Boodle's – on account its lovley [sic] house, charming atmosphere and excellent food." He concludes "there should be no difficulty about the letters necessary to support my candidature. But it occurred to me that since you are the Chairman of the Club, if you cared to write a line saying that I am personally known to you, that would be of the very greatest assistance."

What Sir Picton Bagge thought of this we don't know, but we hear no more about Wheatley and Boodles.

★

Wheatley's "Qualification" on the RSL application form was filled in as being the author of *The Forbidden Territory*, *Mediterranean Nights* "and numerous thrillers", but this was not good enough. The application was turned down by the RSL Council. "As his name was only a suggestion", the Secretary wrote to Frankau – evidently having forgotten Frankau's earlier letter – "and Council was to consider the suggestion before Fellows approached their nominees, there will be no unpleasant duty before you, nor will anyone's feelings be hurt." But there was an unpleasant duty before Frankau, and Wheatley's feelings were hurt. Frankau now felt he had no alternative but to resign.

The Secretary urged him not to, and to nominate Wheatley again, since the earlier rejection was not a judgement on Wheatley but merely meant that they were unfamiliar with his work. If Frankau would re-nominate him – slightly more formally, with two other Fellows seconding the proposal – then he would be reconsidered. Frankau agreed to withdraw his resignation temporarily, but added that unless Wheatley was made a Fellow by the end of the year, he would have no alternative.

Different clubs suit different people, and in January 1951, while Wheatley was having his troubles with the RSL, Labour minister Aneurin Bevan dined at White's club one evening as the guest of Wheatley's friend Sir John Slessor (Chief of Air Staff and Marshal of the RAF; Wheatley had worked with him during the War and wrote him in to *They Used Dark Forces*). White's is often thought to be the most prestigious of the gentleman's clubs, and Wheatley would eventually become a member.

On this particular evening White's air of respectable calm was ruffled when the Honourable Denzil Fox-Strangways, who was drinking in the bar, was alerted to the fact that there was a Socialist on the premises. Fox-Strangways had been prone to erratic behaviour since the War, and although lamed from wounds he left the bar at once and caught up with Bevan on the club steps, which he attempted to kick Bevan down. He was forced to resign, but fortunately he was also a member of Brooks's, handily placed just across the road.

*

Frankau filled out another nomination form for Wheatley on Boxing Day 1950, this time proposing his 'Qualification' as "Probably the most widely read adventure-story writer of his generation". Once again, Wheatley was not elected. This time the Secretary added what was clearly intended to be the conciliatory suggestion that the Council would welcome Wheatley as an ordinary member. Frankau resigned.

The members of the Council who rejected Wheatley, deciding that his work did not qualify as "published work of value to the literature of the country," included Charles Morgan and, curiously enough, Louis Wilkinson, the man who had read 'Hymn to Pan' and passages from *The Book of the Law* at Crowley's funeral. Of all the committee members, Wilkinson is the most likely to have had an attitude of informed derision towards the author of *The Devil Rides Out*, with its Crowley-inspired villain. Wilkinson's presence on the Council raises the picturesque possibly of what Wheatley would no doubt have interpreted as a fellow traveller of Satanism operating behind the scenes.

★

George VI was very ill, and knowing how much the King liked his books, Wheatley had sent him an advance copy of his latest novel in the autumn of 1951, to read during what was to be his final illness; he received a letter of thanks from Sir Michael Adeane, the King's Equerry, which he framed. Perhaps unfortunately, the book was entitled *The Man Who Killed The King*.

On the sixth of February 1952, the King died. A friend of Wheatley's wrote from London: "Everyone is most depressed, all theatres closed, even the BBC, and the general feeling seems to be sadness at losing an elder brother who really worked himself to death."

In due course Dennis and Joan were very pleased to attend a ball at Hampton Court, given by Officers of the Household Brigade, at which Queen Elizabeth was present, just a couple of days before her official coronation. This was the coronation which Wheatley had feared in 1947 he might never see. A few years later, at a Coldstream Guards cocktail party organised by Jack Younger on the polo ground at Windsor,

Wheatley was even more gratified to be presented to the Queen in person.

⋅★

In 1954 – Gilbert Frankau meanwhile having died in 1952 – Wheatley tried once more for Fellowship of the RSL. This time he had the support of Lord Birkenhead (Chairman of the Council, no less) and his 'Qualification' was more carefully honed. Now there was no mention of "numerous thrillers", and instead the emphasis was on History, the most gentlemanly of subjects and the grandest genre in classical painting. Wheatley was the author of "Charles II, a Biography, *Red Eagle*, a biography of Marshal Voroshilov, *The Man Who Killed The King*, and other historical adventure novels". And now, at last, Wheatley was elected. "Would you be kind enough", he wrote to the Secretary, Mrs Patterson, "to express on my behalf to the Council at its next meeting how sensible I feel of the great honour they have done me."

Having been elected, Wheatley was required to turn up in person to sign the Roll. Unfortunately, however, he had to postpone this, because he was going for a brief holiday in Germany, so he would present himself after Easter. The Society assured him that this was not a problem, and that there were suitable meetings after Easter on April the twenty-second and May the thirteenth.

Wheatley's friend Eric Gillet was giving a talk at the Society on May the thirteenth, so this would clearly be a good time to attend. However, it then transpired that Diana was to return from America on that day with her two boys. The Society then suggested a subsequent meeting on June the tenth, which included a poetry reading. William Younger was a poet, so Wheatley decided to come that evening with Bill as his guest. May the thirteenth came and went, however, and still No. 1 Hyde Park Gardens had seen nothing of Wheatley. His assurance to the Secretary on the twenty-fifth of June now has an almost plaintive note: "short of some entirely unforeseen circumstance, *I really will* present myself at Hyde Park Gardens at 4 o'clock on Thursday next, the 1st of July."

And this time he did. After all the trouble involved in gaining entry, Wheatley's membership of the RSL was uneventful to say the least, although he did donate copies of his books to the library. Perhaps its most poignant feature is the fact that Gilbert Frankau never lived to see it. Years later, after Wheatley's own death, the Secretary asked Mary Lutyens, the wife of Joe Links, if she would write a short obituary of Wheatley for the Society's report. Lutyens was glad to do so, and she asked for more details of Wheatley's membership. The reply was brief and a little barren: "I have very little to tell you about his Fellowship as he never lectured to us and he did not often come to meetings."

CHAPTER FORTY

To the Devil – A Daughter

Wheatley remained on warm terms with his RAF friend Freddy, the Duke of Richmond, and around 1951 it was Freddy who introduced him to the subject of flying saucers. This led to one of Wheatley's worst books, *Star of Ill Omen*.

Published in 1952, *Star of Ill Omen* is an early manifestation of the flying saucer craze, which became part of the Fifties zeitgeist. Despite RAF sightings going back to 1943, it really took off in post-war America and came to Britain in 1950 with newspaper serialisations of American books. The *Sunday Dispatch* ran a splurge in October 1950 headed "The Story That May Be Bigger Even Than The Atom Bomb Wars." Mountbatten took an interest and Lord Dowding, head of Fighter Command during the Battle of Britain, went on record as a strong believer.

It is against this background that British agent Kem Lincoln finds himself thinking about flying saucers. He is on a mission to investigate Argentina's nuclear capabilities, because this might affect Britain's ability to fight for the Falklands.

In a counterpart to the 'suspension of disbelief' spiel in Wheatley's occult novels, Wheatley runs through several UFO cases and reviews the data, including the appearance of what Aldous Huxley's friend Gerald Heard termed "Thinking Lights", in his 1950 book *The Riddle of the Flying Saucers*, which Wheatley used for research.

After this careful beginning, Kem is rolling around on a bed with the lovely Carmen when her husband Colonel Escobar bursts in. Kem finally subdues Escobar in the fight that follows, but he has barely regained his breath when a gigantic hand reaches in through the window and picks Carmen up.

The great hand belongs to an alien, and Kem, Carmen and Escobar soon find themselves abducted on a spaceship heading for Mars. The aliens seem to be lumbering brutes (shaped like "homo sapiens, only of the most primitive type") so Wheatley's assumption is that there must be a more intelligent race controlling them. This proves to be a breed of hyper-intelligent insects who buzz around like bees and give telepathic orders.

Time goes slowly on their journey, living on water and nutritious beans, although Escobar provides some swathes of popular science about space. The three of them manage to get along surprisingly well in the circumstances, although "Kem would have given a great deal to be able to bestow Anglo-Saxon mentalities on his two companions." In particular, he wishes the Catholic and guilty Carmen could develop a more pragmatic attitude to having sex with him, especially since her husband gives them his blessing to get on with it (' "Thanks," said Kem, a little awkwardly. "That's damn' decent of you." ')

There are three other humans already on Mars, who turn out to be Russians. There is political fanatic Zadovitch; Anna, whose no-nonsense Slavic brutishness grants Kem the sex that he is unable to have with Carmen; and Harsbach, a former Nazi who is now a Communist, and who harbours a fanatical hatred of the British that goes back to the Boer War.

The humans cause mutiny on Mars among the "loutish lower-race people" and succeed in flying a spaceship all the way back to earth. By now they are split into two polarised camps of good and bad, living on opposite sides of the ship.

Harsbach has the upper hand, and he plans to drop an atomic bomb into the Thames, causing a vast cloud of radioactive steam, before flying on to Russia. Escobar having been murdered by the Russians, Kem and Carmen manage to swap themselves for the explosive in the bomb, and are dropped to land in the river near Tower Bridge, no more than bruised and shaken. Harsbach is then blown up by the real bomb.

Star of Ill Omen is an extraordinary performance, with its characteristically fraught and tender Wheatley love story (quite unlike James Bond and his girls) embedded in a mind-bogglingly improbable Cold War potboiler. Realistic details are combined with a larger naivety about space that wouldn't be out of place in Dan Dare, and there are moments whose sheer weirdness compares with the work of proto-surrealist Raymond Roussel; when, for example, the insects show them black and white films of great moments in human history, and

> the bee-beetles who controlled the machine again pressed the lever; again the machine whirred and the words came, "Music while you work," followed by the rumba.

Wheatley never attempted science fiction again.

★

In contrast to his tribulations with the RSL, Wheatley had a smoother time with the Royal Society of Arts (more fully the Royal Society for the encouragement of Arts, Manufactures and Commerce; a title appropriate to Wheatley's industrial output). They made him a Fellow in January 1948.

Wheatley was invited by the RSA to deliver the first of three Cantor Lectures, on the subject of 'The Novel', followed by lectures from a publisher and bookseller. Wheatley was regarded in many quarters as a successful hack (a superior Fifties newspaper interviewer referred snidely to his difficulties in getting into the RSL, "whose acid test is whether a writer has produced literature of value") but the RSA were treating him with respect, and he responded with a carefully prepared April 1953 lecture 'The Novelist's Task', which gives a number of insights into his own work.

First of all, the writer must choose their public ("He, or she, can aim to wring the factory girl's heart"). Wheatley attributed what he liked to think was his crossover public, from thriller readers to serious readers, to his thorough research. Some people might say his books were only thrillers, "But I like to flatter myself they are not altogether a valueless contribution to our literature, if only from their educative aspect."

Serious psychological novelists, says Wheatley, build up their characters from birth to the moment where the story starts: "by visualizing the childhood, school–days and early adult life of his characters the author comes to know them as real people", even though "the greater part of this material never appears in the book." For the action novelist, in contrast, the priority is strong plotting, and the middle of the book consists of a series of episodes. Here – like Toby's hopes in *Jugg* – "the more it resembles a game of snakes and ladders the more likely it is to hold the reader's interest."

Determined to give his lecture audience good value, Wheatley tells them of a poll he once conducted among booksellers to find the outstanding books of the century. The results now give a strong sense of the ephemerality of literary success. Arnold Bennett, Norman Douglas and Samuel Butler occupy the first three positions, and then (along with Lawrence, Joyce and Woolf) come works by C.E. Montague, William McFee, George Douglas, and Gilbert Frankau, with his famous novel *Peter Jackson, Cigar Merchant*.

With hindsight, one of the most salient points in Wheatley's lecture comes early, when he considers the purpose of the novel. The novel entertains; it can also be written to edify; and then, "the novel is often used as a vehicle for propaganda."

Star of Ill-Omen was no qualification to pontificate about the writing of novels, but Wheatley followed it, three months before his lecture, with an incomparably stronger performance. It might almost be the work of a different man, right from its elegant title, like a parody of a birth announcement in the *Times*: *To The Devil – A Daughter*.

★

To The Devil – A Daughter is the story of Christine, who becomes possessed by Satanic forces every night after darkness falls. It had its distant inspiration in the Essex woman who had written to Wheatley after *The Devil Rides Out*, and who had told him that her father had sold her to the Devil as a child, but it has even closer affinities with the literature of multiple personality disorder, a subject which was rising in the Fifties.

Christina is no doubt named after Christ, but she has an ancestor in Christine Beauchamp, the girl in Morton Prince's 1906 case history, *The Dissociation of a Personality*. Prince's Christine had a "bad" self and told him she was sometimes possessed by a devil. As a critic has written of her case, "what is now called dissociated personality would not long ago have been described as demonic possession."

The subject reached best-seller status in the Fifties with the *Three Faces of Eve* in 1957 (a book Wheatley later refers to in *The Satanist*), in which a woman has her good self, "Eve White", and her bad self, "Eve Black". It is strange to think this ever passed for the cutting edge of psychiatry, when it now looks more like a moment in popular culture.

Christina's dual personality gave this book an extra frisson, especially to female readers; the message was, as it were, that you could be a good girl but sometimes you could be a bad girl too. I remember talking to a woman at a party who told me how exciting she and her adolescent girl friends found this particular book in the early Seventies, and the critic Lorna Sage has written

> I'd read and reread Dennis Wheatley's *To The Devil A Daughter* (a 1950s best-seller and another of Uncle Bill's anthropology books), all about how the baser forms of eroticism threaten the very fabric of Western civilisation. The heroine is nice in the daytime, but when dusk falls she dresses up, drinks, gambles, kisses men with her mouth open and shows signs of being able to look after herself. . . .

*

Middle-aged female thriller-writer Molly Fountain is writing at her modest villa in the South of France when she becomes fascinated by her new neighbour, a girl. Molly is a widow who worked for British intelligence during the war, and she is a friend of Colonel Verney, or "Conky Bill" ("C.B."), who has a nose like Maxwell Knight. Together with Molly's son John, who falls in love with Christine, these three form

491

Wheatley's familiar small band of friends who combat the powers of evil.

Christine has been pledged to the Devil by her father, a businessman who turned to Satanism for material success. Worse than that, she is now going to be sacrificed by the Satanic priest Canon Copely-Syle, who is going to sacrifice her so her virgin blood can give life to the homunculus he is creating. Copely-Syle is based very recognisably – with his silvery locks, antiquated ecclesiastical garb, silver-buckled shoes and general appearance of a "Georgian parson" – on Montague Summers, safely dead for the past four years. Wheatley was not a literary writer but the name "Copely" is inspired, and conjures up something grotesquely ecclesiastical with the word "cope", a High Church vestment, as in Andrew Marvell: "Under this antic cope I move / Like some great prelate of the grove."

To The Devil – A Daughter includes some memorable set pieces, including another pentagram fortress. Beddowes has become terrified of Satanic forces, and he is living on biscuits and bottled water up in an attic, inside a pentangle made of neon tubes.

> . . . the thing that first sprang to the eye was a great five-pointed star. It was formed of long glass tubes, all connected together in the same manner as strip-lighting designed to show the name over a shop; and through their whole length glowed electric wires that gave off the cold blue light. Five tall white candles were placed in the points of the star; but these were unlit, so evidently there only against an emergency failure of the electric current . . . More faintly seen were two thick circles that had been drawn in chalk on the floor . . . Between the two were chalked a number of cabalistic formulae . . .

Like the pentangle in *The Devil Rides Out*, this has its prototype in William Hope Hodgson, with Carnacki's "Electric Pentacle" in *Carnacki The Ghost Finder*.

Posing as a Magister Templi, a magical grade borrowed

from the Golden Dawn system, C.B. talks to Copely-Syle, who is himself an Ipsissimus. The two of them go over the hoary old Crowley story from Driberg, and the circumstances of *The Devil Rides Out*, with Mocata and the house in "Medina Place".

Copely-Syle then shows C.B. over his chapel in the crypt, which doubles as alchemist's laboratory and satanic temple, where he is producing homunculi in large glass jars. There is a horrible moment when C.B. finds that Copely-Syle's work is underpinned by vivisection; there are animals in the laboratory, "crouching or lying in unnatural positions with their limbs pinioned . . . Many had had their genitals removed, some had had legs amputated, others lacked eyes or had had their claws cut out. From the bandages of several of them small bottles and test tubes protruded, into which was draining the fluid from their wounds." With these "small martyrs to Evil" Wheatley has been unusually successful in finding an image of Satanic horror which is free from being kitsch, camp or salacious.

The homunculi theme is lifted from Somerset Maugham's novel *The Magician*, in which the protagonist is based on Crowley. Cutting-and-pasting at speed, Wheatley makes little effort to cover his sources: Maugham's Oliver Haddo talks of a book which

> . . . contained the most extraordinary account . . . of certain spirits generated by Johann-Ferdinand, Count von Kuffstein, in the Tyrol, in 1775. . . . There were ten homunculi . . . kept in strong bottles . . . and these were filled with water. They were made . . . by the Count von Kuffstein and an Italian. . . . the Abbe Geloni . . .
>
> [. . .] Once a week the bottles were emptied and filled again with pure rain-water . . . at certain intervals blood was poured into the water . . .

Compare *To The Devil – A Daughter*:

Among those who had trafficked in these forbidden

mysteries was a Count von Kuffstein, and C.B. remembered reading in an old book of the experiments he had carried out in the year 1775 at his castle in the Tyrol. With the aid of an Italian Abbé called Geloni, the Count had succeeded in producing ten living creatures, who resembled small men and women . . . and had to be kept in large strong glass jars that were filled with liquid. Once a week the jars were emptied and refilled with pure rain water . . . and human blood on which the homunculi fed.

Along with toads, bats, voodoo drums, two love stories, the Soviet menace and an evil French count, *To The Devil – A Daughter* has plenty of "snakes and ladders"-style thrills. "You're mad!" says C.B., "You can't do this!" "Oh, but I can . . ." says Copely-Syle. "It is only a little after half past ten, so there is plenty of time to put you on the line before the train passes"

It all builds to a climax in the Cave of Bats at Nice, just as Christina is about to be sacrificed. As before, the denouement invokes the power of love, and features a decisive female role; this time, following Fleur's mother and mad Aunt Sarah, it is Molly Fountain who finishes the Satanists off with an old wartime Mills bomb, justifying the slaughter with a definitive Wheatley line: "They were all horrors and menaces to everything decent in life."

★

The appeal of "black magic" in popular culture was ultimately erotic, and this is especially true of Wheatley. David Langford has noted that the charm of his Black Magic books was "a spice of wickedness that particularly appealed to adolescents." Professor John Sutherland, when he was asked to name the most erotic book he had ever read, confessed "I don't find them erotic anymore. When I was an adolescent, however, Dennis Wheatley could always make me lively around the groin." The writer Matthew Parris, when asked the same question, said "I used to find Dennis Wheatley's satanic stuff very exciting."

Wheatley-style Satanism tends to involve an atmosphere of impending group sex, and the perverse nature of the weird crew attracted is often mentioned: "They get hold of pederasts, lesbians and over-sexed people of all ages", C.B. explains in *To The Devil – A Daughter*, "and provide them with the chance to indulge their secret vices."

Thanks to Wheatley's unfailingly useful idea of what a Black Mass might involve, the promised orgy has for its central focus the impending violation and degradation of a woman, often on an altar. In *They Used Dark Forces*, Malacou has his own daughter on an altar after they have stripped off their zodiac robes; in *Toby Jugg*, Sally is to be spreadeagled on a bed of nettles before the Devil's altar and violated by Helmuth; in *Gateway to Hell*, Miranda is to be gang raped in a "Satanic marriage", and something similar awaits Mary Morden in *The Satanist*, where the head Satanist slowly licks his lips as he explains

> Later I intend to perform a ceremony of initiation. The neophyte Circe [Mary] is to be received among us as a Sister. She is of unusual beauty; so no doubt most of you will wish to perform with her the Sacred Rite of Creation when she offers herself for Temple Service.

And in *To The Devil – A Daughter*:

> . . . instead of removing her clothes garment by garment they tore them from her body shred by shred, till she stood swaying among them stark naked except for her shoes and stockings . . . Christina, still struggling was forced back upon the altar and stretched out on it. John could see her long, silk-stockinged legs dangling over the right-hand end of the altar . . .

In this instance the sacrifice is not directly sexual – it is her blood that Copely-Syle is after, not her body – but the ambience is almost indistinguishable: "Really!", says the cynical Frenchman Jules, when the nature of the impending crisis is

495

explained to him, "That sounds very intriguing. Ellen, or Christina, or whatever you like to call her, would look pretty good stretched out naked on an altar."

The climactic double-bind of Wheatley's plots is that the dreadful ravishment and fate-worse-than-death can never be allowed to happen: like Pearl White tied to the railway line, the girl must be saved, and she is. The result is almost family reading, even if it does appeal to adolescents. One of my paperback copies of this book is inscribed in a young, girlish hand "To Gill, Happy Birthday Love Beth xxxxx PS Lynne said it was good so don't blame me if it's not!"

The last word on Wheatley, sex and magic should go to Timothy d'Arch Smith.

> Wheatley actually did the occult a great disservice in that he reduced hermetic science to the rogering of virgins on altar-tops, but goodness what fun the books were.

★

Molly Fountain's bedtime reading in *To The Devil – A Daughter* is a "a new William Mole thriller". Mole was the pseudonym of William Younger, now a career MI5 officer, who had published his first thriller, *Trample an Empire*, in 1952.

"Mole" followed *Trample an Empire* with *The Lobster Guerrillas* and *Goodbye Is Not Worthwhile*, before writing his masterpiece, *The Hammersmith Maggot*, which features an amateur detective (he is really a wine merchant) named Casson Duker, who is at home in clubland: he is a member of "Canes", and has friends in White's. The maggot of the title is a blackmailer, John Perry, a cold little man who has acquired a connoisseurial taste for classical antiquities and antique furniture, although he remains "common".

The book is interesting as a study of class; Duker despises Perry for his naive snobbery, yet at the same time he looks down on him for being common. Perry dreams of being upper-middle class, and before he is hanged he says "Cane's, St.James Street. I should like to have gone into a club before I died."

There is little sympathy for the maggot, although his passion for collecting is beautifully described, with his George II candlesticks and Bristol blue glass goblets. In a museum he sees a case of exquisite old watches, all stopped: "He had felt that both he and the watches had escaped the dull, daily round into a timeless universe of jewellery and enamel and figured silver."

Mole is a considerably better writer than Wheatley, who writes of Molly Fountain, "As a writer she could not help being envious of the way in which Mr.Mole used his fine command of English to create striking imagery . . . ."

Bill had married Nancy Leslie, a young war widow, and they lived in Knightsbridge. Nancy was always known as Poo, and Wheatley dedicated *The Shadow of Tyburn Tree* to her: "For the Life and Soul of the Party: The Incomparable Poo." Bill was similarly celebrated as a 'life and soul' type, whether he was at a carnival in the West Indies or doing his impression of a chorus girl.

Wheatley's industrial output continued, and in 1953 he managed two books, the second of them the Cold War story *Curtain of Fear*. He also devised a new game, *Alibi*, a Cluedo-style whodunnit in which players travel around the towns and cities of the British Isles (learning some geography in the process) trying to deduce the killer. The victim is himself a high-class criminal, and the murder is discovered by his butler-valet, "Beals": a name we shall encounter again.

★

Wheatley's relationship with his mother had not been close for many years. He blamed Sir Louis Newton for turning her against him, and he had, of course, killed off the pair of them in *Three Inquisitive People*, which may not have helped if they read it.

Since Sir Louis had died, Wheatley's mother had lived with Wheatley's unmarried sister, Muriel. Muriel felt trapped, but she worried that if she moved out, their mother might leave her money to Dennis. Dennis, on the other hand, feared she might leave it to Muriel. With this in mind, when Muriel came to stay at Grove they made a pact that however their mother left her money they would split it equally.

In 1949 Wheatley had at last dedicated a book to his mother: "with love and in grateful memory of my first visits with her to Paris, Versailles and Fontainebleu." It is a charming dedication, although it was his thirty-ninth book. Previous dedicatees had included his Aunt Nell, his secretary, his cousin Laurie, his publisher, his agent, and Bino Johnstone.

In 1954 she died. It turned out that she had left two thirds of her money to Muriel and one third to Dennis, but since he was now a comparatively rich man he didn't hold Muriel to their bargain. Money-minded as ever, he was struck that he only received about £12,000 (two hundred thousand today), out of the quarter of a million that his grandfather had left (ten million today).

*

In the autumn Wheatley published his new book, *The Island Where Time Stands Still*. It begins with a letter from Gregory Sallust to his author, like Tombe back from the grave:

> I am all the more touched to hear that still, after all this time, a week seldom passes without some of your readers writing to ask what has happened to me . . .
>
> P.S. I still have a little of the Pol Roger '28 you sent me in return for my last batch of notes, and it is now so good I'm keeping it for very special occasions . . .
>
> P.P.S. I am hoping to be back in England shortly, and that will definitely be an occasion for us to knock off a bottle or two of the '28.

The book opens with a shipwreck in which Gregory is washed up on a Chinese island, appearing on nautical charts only as "Leper Settlement Number Six". Here a group of enlightened Chinese are keeping the old Imperial civilisation alive, and Gregory goes with them to San Francisco's Chinatown to find their new monarch, a missing princess.

There is good local colour throughout and it is a rattling yarn in the usual Wheatley fashion.

The theme of saving a threatened monarch was close to Wheatley's heart, and the time theme remained central to the conservative aesthetic of his fiction. Wheatley described the book as involving "the old China of dignity and beauty" as opposed to "the new Communist China of today". A very few things have changed (Wheatley has improved the condition of women), but otherwise, with their wisdom, the high-caste Chinese have achieved "the carefully planned salvaging of their ancient civilisation".

They have no ambitions, as a Mandarin explains:

> Only to live graciously, and to perpetuate a way of life that long experience has shown leads to the well-being of the spirit. In that we are successful, while the outer world is disrupted by irresponsible men seeking power through innovations. Here we live like a placid stream – ever unruffled yet ever renewed. We have learned the wisdom of making Time stand still.

"Please allow me to offer my congratulations, Excellency", says Gregory:

> In this age of instability and disillusion it is a remarkable achievement to have created a Utopian state. I could almost believe that I have arrived in Shangri-La.

At first the Mandarin doesn't understand Gregory's reference to the Thirties classic, *Lost Horizon*, "Mr James Hilton's beautiful book."

Time was not standing still in the larger world. In 1949 China had become the Communist Republic under Mao-Tse Tung, and there had been a Communist purge in Hungary with the use of torture and show-trials, while in 1950 the Korean War began, there were riots in South Africa, and Wheatley's old hero Voroshilov announced that Russia now had the Bomb.

At home the iron and steel industries had been nationalised, and taxation was reaching undreamed of heights. Wheatley might not have gone as far as Evelyn Waugh's complaint that "The trouble with the Conservative Party is that it has not turned the clock back a single second", but he would have found some common ground with the man who complained "Reform, reform – aren't things bad enough already?"

Time was also spreading its depredations with suburban sprawl, the ruin of the countryside, population growth, and tourism: all those phenomena which have made "unspoilt" a key word for understanding the twentieth century. A few years later, a friend wrote to Wheatley about the Algarve in the spring. "Beautifully green, lots of mimosa and quite good wild flowers of which the best were narcissi and little dwarf iris. What was even more interesting was to see the way in which the English proletariat has taken over there. The whole coast was crammed with them . . ."

Bill and Poo had left Knightsbridge and bought a house called Pelling, near Windsor (Wheatley was amused when Poo told him about the woman she bought fish from in Windsor town, who had said "It's only you, mu'm, and them up at the castle what really appreciates a bit of good fish"). But the charm of Pelling was blighted when the adjacent fields were turned into a housing estate, and the Youngers moved back to London.

Wheatley would take this theme up in his next novel, where Gifford Hillary comes back from the dead to see his house under threat ("The idea of its being turned over to demolition squads in order that rows of jerry built bungalows might be built on the site made me see red"). This was going to strike a lot closer to home than he could have foreseen: time still had some unpleasant tricks up its sleeve for Wheatley.

Sir Gifford Comes Back From the Dead

Wheatley's next book, *The Ka of Gifford Hillary*, was about a man who comes back from the grave with a freshly acquired social conscience. This was something of a new departure.

Its main supernatural plank was the Egyptian idea of the "Ka", a kind of astral body. Wheatley had long been interested in Egypt – when his secretary Audrey went to Paris in the mid Thirties, the two places he particularly advised her to visit were Prunier's for its lobster and the Louvre for its Egyptian galleries – and he owned a bronze figure of the Ka, along with another of the resurrected god Osiris.

Gifford is a military shipbuilder, and he has employed a Professor Owen Evans to develop a "death ray". Short and bearded, Evans is a parody of a redbrick professor, and in this instance not merely provincial but a stage Welshman ("Land of my fathers!").

Gifford goes trustingly with Evans to a demonstration of the death ray, only to feel a pain in his chest. Looking downwards, he is astonished to see his body lying there in its burgundy velvet smoking jacket. Evans has murdered him, but his consciousness survives.

Evans has been having an affair with Gifford's promiscuous wife, Lady Ankaret, carried away by her beauty and social class, but she is not serious about him, and she is appalled by what he has done. Wheatley goes to town on Evans's Welshness as the pair fall out ("Is it mad you are, woman?"). Ankaret helps him dispose of the body, then kills him. Gifford forgives her for leading Evans on: she was "a born pagan but in no way evil. I longed to comfort her."

The Ka Of Gifford Hillary was one of Wheatley's top five best-sellers. Much of its appeal comes from the depiction of Gifford's existence after death: as *The Times* once wrote of

Wheatley, "He makes the unbelievable seem absolutely real". Gifford finds he can now fly, although it is not quite as he expects:

> Naturally, I supposed that, as a disembodied spirit, I should be able to flit from place to place without effort and, having no weight, I – or rather the mind of which I now solely consisted – could remain poised high up in the air or sink to any more convenient level as I desired. But it did not prove quite like that.
> [. . .] . . . I rose slightly and drifted in the direction I wished to go, but only for a few yards, after which I became static again till I once more made a conscious effort to advance. The movement can best be likened to that of a toy balloon which having been thrown with some force bounces in slow graceful arcs across the floor. It was a most pleasant sensation and I recalled having on rare occasions experienced it in dreams.

It has the appeal of books on 'astral projection' and the fraudulent best-sellers of Carlos Castaneda, which also featured out–of–body–experiences.

Gifford realises he must rejoin his body and try to re-animate it (the concession to plausibility is that the death ray has somehow not fully killed him), but having rejoined his body he is trapped in it, and comes close to dying permanently. Wheatley gives the reader a vivid treatment of being buried half alive, dehydrated, almost too weak to move, and trying to attract attention. *Ka* has a generous quota of desperate setbacks and a superbly orchestrated plot, which involves Gifford clawing his way back from near-death only to be found guilty of murdering Evans and sentenced to hang.

When Gifford's Ka glides about London he sees the evil that goes on behind walls and doors, brightened only by a couple of voyeuristic moments, and in particular he sees how the poor live in areas such as Notting Hill and Walham Green, Fulham (slummy in the Fifties). "That must not be taken to imply that I became a sudden convert to Socialism", he adds.

Gifford's position is closer to so-called "One-Nation Toryism". The character of his suburban and selfish first wife, Edith, is made to stand for the modern rich and their middle-class lack of duty and *noblesse oblige*:

> Helping to run the Women's Institute, visiting sick cottagers, reading to the elderly bedridden poor, and other such good works to which most women of any position in the country consider it incumbent on them to devote a certain amount of time, were entirely foreign to Edith . . . the fact of the matter was that not having been brought up to talk to labouring people as fellow human beings it embarrassed her horribly, apart from giving them orders, to have anything to do with them at all.

Just as Jugg found time to ruminate on the nation's ills while being menaced by a giant spider, so Sir Gifford, despite his desperate situation, decides that neither Socialism nor higher taxation are the best answers in the long run, and pins his faith on duty and charity.

Wheatley originally wrote another ending to the book, not used in the published version. After his last minute escape from the hangman's rope, Sir Gifford gives away the bulk of his fortune and resolves to become an itinerant knife grinder, pushing his knife grinder's barrow and working with ordinary people.

> Believing me to be poor they will tell me their troubles freely and without ulterior motive. Wherever I find genuine hardship or distress, particularly in old people struggling along on very meagre incomes, I shall be able to relieve it a little. I can hardly wait for the thrill I shall get the first time that, having sharpened the knives of some poor housewife who is going through a bad time, I can push a few pound notes under a plate on her kitchen dresser without her finding out what I have done until after I have left.

He seems to have become half George Orwell and half the reborn Scrooge, as at the very close

> after all my tribulations, I shall find contentment and a real freedom, sharing the joys and sorrows of my fellow men, as through sunshine and rain I tramp the roads of England.

This was all removed from the published version.

The Ka of Gifford Hillary is a big-hearted book: Wheatley's work is generally humane, but this is positively sentimental. Its benevolence extends to Sir Gifford's first family, his ex-wife Edith, son Harold, and daughter Christobel, with whom he makes amends after realising that he has neglected them.

There are several points of similarity between Sir Gifford and his author. Sir Gifford has "a comfortable late Georgian house" with "really beautiful views across the Solent to the Isle of Wight". Lady Ankaret is Gifford's second wife, and better bred than he is, but he has already been married to Edith. He remembers the attraction was mostly physical, and looks back on her as a suburban woman with bad taste, but at the same time he worries "had I been justified in leaving her?" This question is all the more heart-tugging when he remembers Harold, his son, asking "Why don't you come home and live with Mummy?"

Sir Gifford seems to express something of Wheatley's pain and guilt in the aftermath of his first marriage. Thinking of the way Harold and Christobel have turned out, he asks "Would they have been two quite different people had I carried out my full responsibilities as a parent?"

*

In November 1955 Wheatley was invited to take part in a debate at the Oxford Union, to argue the proposal 'That Equality is in Theory a Pestilential Heresy and in Practice a Pitiful Illusion'. His star opponent was the publisher Victor Gollancz, the man behind the Left Book Club.

The evening began badly with a power failure, leading to candlelight and delays. At last, just before nine o'clock, the motion was presented to the House. Various undergraduates spoke, with the star speakers being kept until the end.

Unfortunately Wheatley had no experience of this kind of debate. He opened with a dictionary definition of debating, and told long and unfunny stories. The nearest he came to rigour was his early observation, "that all men are born equal is not self-evident". He then presented a historical analysis which led to his main theme: the advantage of Plural Voting – i.e. weighted voting power, and not universal suffrage on the 'one man one vote' basis – for which he said the criterion should be "superior mentality".

This went down badly. Wheatley said that he was going to stick his neck out, and the student paper Cherwell reported "Mr Victor Gollancz, who spoke sixth and last, seized the metaphorical chopper and hacked off same at its thick-set base." Gollancz airily dismissed Wheatley's point that egalitarian revolutions have always led to massacres, and said the idea that some people have superior mentality was "damn impudence." He argued that all men have a right to develop their potentialities as far as possible, and made the fine-sounding but rather nebulous claim that until we respect everyone simply because they are human beings, the threat of war will always be present. Finally he appealed to Christianity, to which he had converted after a nervous breakdown.

The proposal was "defeated by acclamation". Wheatley had been trounced, and by the man who had refused to publish Orwell's *Animal Farm* because it was "unfair to Stalin". Cherwell wrote the debate up under the headline 'These Men Were Not Equal'.

*

Plural voting was something of an *idée fixe* with Wheatley, and he had deep misgivings about the workings of universal suffrage. Ancient Greece is generally credited with inventing democracy, but Greek voting was limited to a relatively small section of the population: only those who were property owners and bore the burden of taxation were eligible to steer the community in its democratic decisions, and not *hoi polloi*.

This system, "the soundest possible form of government", according to Wheatley, is not to be confused with the present arrangement; "this very sensible form of government has now degenerated into something very different from the original".

Wheatley liked Disraeli's idea of 'Fancy Franchises' where the number of votes a voter had would depend on the extent of his education and the amount of tax he paid. He also liked the similar idea put forward by the novelist Nevil Shute, who suggested everyone should have one basic vote, but then to weight the system towards more intelligent decisions, certain qualifications should entitle people to extra votes, so people might have up to six votes. Higher tax was one qualification, and the others now have a period flavour: having had a commission in one of the Services, having a university degree, and having lived abroad.

Wheatley could get quite excited about these issues: reading the letters of John Cam Hobhouse, a friend of Lord Byron, he noted Hobhouse's hatred of Viscount Castlereagh (also hated by Byron and other romantics, who saw him as an oppressor, responsible for the Peterloo Massacre). Wheatley annotated as he read:

> Castlereagh was like a red rag to a bull to the author Mr Cam Hobhouse who was a most poisonous lot. More or less of a Bolshevik – a believer in popular assemblies – parliaments & all inventions of Satan

Some form of weighted voting – like a literacy test for juries – has a perennial appeal to a certain temperament. Wheatley was later appalled by the abolition of the property qualification for juries in 1973, whereby instead of householders over 21, jury service could now be done by anyone over eighteen, including "young fellows who tear up the seats of railway carriages."

*

The Ka of Gifford Hillary also contained a new propaganda message about nuclear armaments. This was very topical: the

CND was founded in 1957, the year after the book was published (Wheatley was not in favour of the CND, and probably regarded it as Russian-funded). He wanted to see Great Britain armed to the teeth, because without nuclear status, "Britain will be as much a thing of the past within ten years as Greece or Rome."

The crux is that Britain must reduce her conventional weapons, the 'Old Look' and in particular her expensive conventional navy, in order to afford the 'New Look' of nuclear weapons, and the public – despite their sentimental attachment to the Navy, and resistance to cuts – must be brought on side. A well-placed friend tells Sir Gifford that the heaviest burden in a democracy is "that of persuading the mainly ignorant masses to accept a programme that sound evidence has shown to be best for them."

It is sometimes said that anyone seeking real power would do better to own newspapers than seek elected office, and Gifford and his friend discuss the role of the Press Barons in influencing public opinion, with Lord Northcliffe's role in the First War as an example. The friend asks Sir Gifford if he will raise public awareness of the issues by rejecting a Ministry of Defence order for conventional warships, despite the impact on his firm's profits, and writing a letter to the *Times* to explain exactly why he has done so.

The Ka of Gifford Hillary was a remarkably topical and informed book, slightly ahead of the 1957 White Paper on Defence. In publishing a million-seller with these pro-nuclear discussions, Wheatley achieves the same publicity mission that Sir Gifford is asked to undertake within the narrative.

★

Wheatley had always said he would be dead at sixty, with an air that he was fully resigned to it, or would even welcome it. On Wheatley's sixtieth birthday a card arrived at Grove Place from Annette Wheatley, Anthony's wife. "Hypodermic follows", it said. Wheatley understood the joke, but he was not amused.

Wheatley was fond of Anthony and Annette, in his fashion, and he would sometimes bring them spectacular confectionery as a token of his affection: a big garden trug full of crystallised fruit, for example, or an enormous chocolate egg from Gloriette, the Knightsbridge patisserie. Joan was less fond of them; understandably, to a degree, since they weren't her family, and she may have resented Wheatley having other ties. They sensed a certain coolness from her, and felt that she tried to keep Wheatley away from them.

Annette had converted to Catholicism and they began to raise a family, having six children. Wheatley was pleased to be a grandfather, and in his notes for a speech a few years later he wrote of Anthony:

> We share a love of good wine and any other things; and he's a better man than I am, Gunga Din! I only produced one child – that is as far as I know – but he has given me six fine grandchildren – so that the name of Wheatley should not perish from the earth.

Wheatley liked to have Annette over to stay at Grove Place when she was expecting a new baby, for fresh air and feeding up. On one of those visits Joan told her that she was doing some charity work for Ceylon, adding "Of course, they breed like rabbits."

It may have been a perfectly innocent remark, but as the children grew older, Joan managed to produce further statements that may have been put-downs: "I don't know *why* you teach them to ride, when you *don't live in the country*", for example.

On one occasion the family were down at Grove Place when their youngest daughter climbed up to an open bookcase with a display of Venetian glass on the top shelf, and accidentally proceeded to smash it. Annette was talking to Joan but she ran into the room as soon as they heard the glass starting to go and managed to save the rest. In this instance, Joan had the grace and presence of mind to say "You know, I never liked that Venetian glass anyway."

★

508

Wheatley's new book for 1957 was *The Prisoner In The Mask*, which covers the Dreyfus case. It is the earliest Duke De Richleau novel (he was born in 1872) and fills in his background, mentioned in *The Devil Rides Out* and elsewhere, of being involved in an unsuccessful plot to restore the French monarchy. It is clearly inspired by Alexandre Dumas' novel *The Man In the Iron Mask*.

It was in this year that Wheatley wrote the introduction for another Dumas novel, *The Queen's Necklace*, concerning a scandal which enmeshed Marie-Antoinette, and his introduction is chiefly interesting for the way it shows his identification with Dumas; so much so, that he seems to be writing about himself. Dumas was a hack who wrote for money, sometimes at great speed. And yet no one can read him without being gripped by the plot (or so Wheatley believes, perhaps optimistically). More than that, his books have two wonderful features. Whatever is happening, "there runs like a golden thread the doctrine of *Noblesse Oblige*", and young people are influenced by his books into developing "loyalty, courage, and fortitude". This is what Wheatley said about his own books.

Secondly, his books are highly educational. They are a form of "history without tears", and just as Kurt Hahn complimented Wheatley, so the French historian Michelet had already complimented Dumas: "You have done more to teach the people history than all the historians put together."

It is for these reasons, says Wheatley, that although the work of many finer writers has passed into oblivion, the work of Dumas has achieved immortality, despite the carping and quibbling of "small-minded literary purists".

★

Wheatley's literary stock had not risen very much since the days when *Time and Tide* complained about him, although he had picked up some spectacular accolades from the popular press. The *Times Literary Supplement* had virtually ceased to review his fiction since the War, compared to seventeen books before and nine during (the latter perhaps covered partly on patriotic grounds). Compared to its more gentlemanly and amateur pre-war range, the paper's post-war face was a little more austere and professional. It was less likely to recommend undemanding thrillers, or to complain that books were too big to read comfortably in bed.

Much of the problem even with Wheatley's better books was his prose style, not helped by Hutchinson's editing. This allowed him to place the capital of Sweden in Denmark, use "infer" when he meant "imply", and similar errors.

Literary critic James Agate was at a party in the Reform Club one evening, talking with Humbert Wolfe and Pamela Frankau, when the conversation turned to the extraordinary literary phenomenon of Dennis Wheatley. Wolfe said Wheatley had told him that his novels had been translated into every European language except one, adding "I can't think which."

"English," said Frankau.

CHAPTER FORTY-TWO

The Best Revenge

Wheatley was now very well established indeed, as he would stress to interviewers who came to visit him at Grove Place: "My books have earned me half a million pounds", he told one, "I think you can call me a success." By this time in his life Wheatley had something more than a little Toad of Toad Hall about him.

He was always conscious of money, but this stress on earning it was probably made more emphatic by the knowledge that he wasn't taken quite seriously as a writer. "I write to make it plain to the reader what's going on . . . If the highbrow critics don't like the way it's put, well, they can go and write better books, make more money."

"This is the way to live" he said, gesturing around him, "If I save money, the taxman gets it." Wheatley liked the phrase – which had been a Peter Cheyney title – "no pockets in a shroud". He was as fond as ever of his foie gras and lobster and partridges, his hock and vintage champagne and Imperial Tokay. The times might change, but Wheatley still had his smoking jacket and his well-stocked cellar and his library.

It is the smoking-jacketed Duke de Richleau, in *The Devil Rides Out* back in the Thirties, who considers private ownership will last out his time, although " 'After him', of course, 'the Deluge', as he very properly realised." This was the Deluge Wheatley thought was coming in 1947, when he put his message to posterity in a bottle. Taken together with his cultural pessimism, Wheatley's lifestyle adds up unmistakably to the notion that "Living well is the best revenge"[1].

★

---

[1] A saying which originally meant something very different; in the work of George Herbert and elsewhere, it means the Christian life.

Wheatley had assembled some very gratifying personal effects – some "good kit", as auctioneers used to say – and this was a crucial part of being Wheatley. He wrote his books at a mahogany table desk which had belonged to Joan's father, sitting in an Empire armchair. Elsewhere there was plenty of Chippendale, including a bookcase and a gilt mirror; a Louis XV bookcase; a few bits of good Georgian silver; some old Rockingham and Dresden china, including Dresden candlesticks; and a plate from Marie-Antoinette's dinner service.

Wheatley liked porcelain and figurines. There were china figures of Napoleon's marshals on top of his bookcases, and he also owned china figures of the Dumas musketeers. He had a bronze of Napoleon on horseback, ivory figures of Louis XIV, Louis XVI, Marie Antoinette and Madame de Pompadour, a bust of Marie Antoinette and a bronze figure of Charles I, another royal martyr.

He owned a bronze bust of Homer, and an ivory and ebony figure of Zeus (chief of the Gods and the "Jove" of the bygone exclamation, still used by Wheatley). Striking a similarly pagan note, in his bedroom he had a bronze satyr and nymph, each forming a two branch candelabra; a bronze dancing faun (the one he had taken down to the War Cabinet); and a bronze group of three cherubs and a ram.

Wheatley had a fondness for things Chinese. He admired Taoism and Confucianism, the latter for its combination of meritocracy and social order, and among his Chinese odds and ends were a Ming bowl, a pair of T'ang horsemen, a blue dragon on his bedroom mantelpiece, a wooden figure of an Immortal on a twisted root base, and two white vases with dragons, used in the hall as umbrella stands. These might be found in any country house, but items with more personal meaning included an ivory carving of Kwan Yin, Queen of Heaven, the goddess he had prayed to in a shop window, and two figures of Ho Toi, the Chinese God of Happiness[2]: by

---

[2] The Kwan Yin and the better Ho Toi can be seen in *The Devil and All His Works*, facing pages 111 and 132.

Wheatley's ivory figure of Kwan-Yin, Chinese Queen of Heaven.

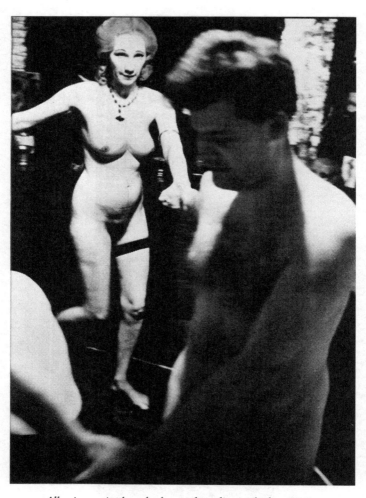

All going on in the suburbs: occult nudity in the late Sixties.

this time Wheatley would describe himself to interviewers as "a consciously happy man."

Wheatley also owned a rosewood treasure chest, originally from Arundel castle, and five rapiers wall-mounted on a bracket, the effect being somewhat suburban-baronial. He had a few pictures too – some of Birket Foster's very English scenes, inherited from his grandfather, prints of Waterloo and Curacao, a collection of miniatures, and an alleged Brueghel, optimistically attributed – but he was more interested in rugs.

Wheatley thought of himself as a collector of Oriental rugs (he lists it in *Who's Who* as a hobby, along with Georgian furniture and stamps). There was a Bokhara rug in the hall, and he had a couple of Caucasian rugs, but his particular taste was for Persian rugs in silk. These are technically very fine, and prized by Middle Easterners, although they have a bourgeois or even nouveau riche look (compared to the more Bohemian or scholarly look of tribal rugs, as on Freud's couch). Wheatley's bourgeois taste in rugs may have been influenced by having the shop window of "C.John", carpet merchants to the King, just across the road from him back in his South Audley Street days.

Wheatley loved his possessions, and he took an almost naive delight in them. "His books urge facts with a collector's absorption", noted one of his most astute profilers; "He *is* a collector, obsessive, comprehensive, boyish."

Along with his library, Wheatley had his stamps. In addition to his main collection, kept in safes, he liked to display stamps under glass on table tops. British Empire stamps were a particular favourite, showing Victoria's head on all the territories to which the Empire had brought the benefits of British civilisation. Visitors sometimes thought Wheatley had trimmed the perforations off his stamps, but their trimmed appearance was because they preceded the introduction of the perforation. It would have been quite in character for him to make them neat, but very much out of character for him to damage his investments.

"That's full of first editions", Wheatley said as he showed a journalist a book cabinet, "Wells, Kipling, Huxley, Dreiser.

Those must be worth a lot of money." Another journalist, less sympathetic to Wheatley's success, noted that "Mr Wheatley stroked the top of a small table inlaid with foreign stamps – catalogue value £715."

This £715 (about £11,000 today) is a rather snide detail, as if Wheatley bumptiously volunteered their value himself. Perhaps he did, but I like to think things might have gone something like this:

> CRAFTY JOURNALIST (*sensing an opportunity to get a rise out of Wheatley*): What nice stamps. They must be . . . ah . . . worth a few bob, eh?
> FAMOUS AUTHOR (*innocently taking the bait*): £715 actually!

As well as putting his stamps under glass, Wheatley also cut out pictures of fish and applied them to his bathroom walls, swimming about here and there and congregating in corners with a naturalistic, aquarium-like effect.

His masterpiece in this line was his bedroom ceiling, blue and slightly domed, which he carefully covered in paper stars. They represented the Milky Way and the major constellations, like a planetarium, and they were laid out as they would have been at the moment of his birth, while around the walls were large signs of the Zodiac.

More portable items of Wheatley's kit included his malacca swordstick (and he still had his blue morocco covered swaggerstick from World War Two), some gold Persian coins made into cuff links, a crocodile leather note case, and a "rolled gold fountain pen that lights up".

While he wrote, Wheatley was surrounded by the homelier items on his desk.

He had two teddy bears, a Chinese soapstone pencil holder, an old cash box, a Wedgwood biscuit barrel, a wooden cigarette box, a large onyx ashtray (an object that appears in his Duke de Richleau books), a glass vessel filled with Alum Bay sand, a pen stand (holding four pens, like something from a bank manager's desk), and an octagonal crystal-sided and ormolu-mounted box with a miniature painting in the lid. This thoroughly bourgeois little item, a token of Frenchified late nineteenth-century taste, had belonged to his mother, and he used it for paper clips.

He owned more than this, of course, but these items give a sense of his possessions, and they will have to serve here as a *musée imaginaire*; The Wheatley Museum.

Wheatley also liked joss sticks and big cushions, and in addition to his plum-coloured smoking jacket he had an Arab robe and a Chinese dressing gown with a dragon on the sleeve. This was the exotic Wheatley. People often remarked on the colourfulness of his clothing. "Bright as a rainbow trout", Kenneth Allsopp reported when he went to interview him, and found him in an azure blue shirt and a yellow paisley smoking jacket. To write he would generally wear a coloured shirt, untucked and often short sleeved, over a pair of equally bright trousers ("tangerine, all sorts of colours"). This was the casual Wheatley.

Around 1960 Wheatley had a large painting of himself done by Cynthia Montefiore – reproduced on the back of *Vendetta in Spain* – with Grove Place in the background and Wheatley in the foreground, looking like the monarch of all he surveys. It is in a neatly double perspective, with Wheatley sitting beside an urn on the balustrade of the simultaneously distant house. Fictitiously, on some brickwork, as if on a coloured plaque, is a coat of arms consisting of Wheatley's assumed crest above Joan's shield.

Wheatley is wearing a plum smoking jacket with a dress shirt and a black bow tie. In his hand is a glass of hock, and the glass has a gold dolphin for a stem (he had six of these glasses from Venice, and one of them is visible beside him, on his desk, on the back of his 1970s Arrow black magic paperbacks). Montefiore's portrait is distinctly flattering, with Wheatley's visage austere and commanding. He looks less like the portly middle-aged author with a drinker's red nose, and more like an older James Bond. In fact he seems to have borrowed not only the Duke de Richleau's jacket, but Gregory Sallust's face.

CHAPTER FORTY-THREE

Nice Work

1959 was a milestone for Wheatley. He had been an author for twenty-five years, and now he modified his image by publishing some of his wartime papers as *Stranger Than Fiction*. This launched Wheatley the war planner, maverick thinker, and senior backroom boy.

The party for *Stranger Than Fiction* doubled as a celebration of Wheatley's quarter century of authorship, and it was held at the wine merchants Justerini and Brooks. Justerini's had moved from Pall Mall to 153 New Bond Street, with new decor themed around the Regency.

Thursday 29th January was an exceptionally bad night of old-style "pea-souper" fog in London, with low visibility, traffic halted, breathing trouble, and red-rimmed eyes. Guests had to battle their way to New Bond Street. Along with the Press, there were around sixty friends and comrades, mostly with their wives, including, Dudley Clark, Peter Fleming, General Sir Colin Gubbins, Colonel Sir Ronald Wingate, Maxwell Knight, Sherry Sheridan, the Marquis of Donegal, the Duchess of Westminster, several lords, a Russian prince or two, J.G. Links, Bino Johnstone, and several Air Marshals and Air Chief Marshals. Lord Mountbatten telephoned his apologies at the last moment, while Air Marshal Sir Laurence Darvall flew back from Washington. Bobby Eastaugh turned up in full ecclesiastical purple ("stranger than fiction just about suits it", he said to Wheatley) because as Bishop of Kensington he had to go on to the St.Paul's Cathedral Dinner.

Inside the party – in "the mahogany twilight of one of those green-glass and deep-carpet wine merchants in Bond St" – the air smelled of Patou's *Moment Supreme*. Wheatley, just turned 62, tubby and red-faced, was wearing an unflattering double-breasted suit of somewhat gangsterish effect and handing round treble whiskies. He was in his element presiding over the raffle, at which the Duchess of Westminster drew the lucky numbers and presented the prizes, chiefly drink and books.

Wheatley was having fun, after a fashion, but it was hard work. His conversation with journalists generally consisted of a bonhomous gallop through his *curriculum vitae*. He circulated the room, spending "ten seconds or so having a lightning conversation with each of the small groups of friends." It was then time for him to be whisked off for a television appearance. Wheatley mislaid his glasses and insisted that he had left them in Television House, which was searched thoroughly before they turned up in his bedroom. "I felt a bit foolish", he said. But it had been a good party, and he had done well. "Thank *you* for the party," wrote Eddie Tatham in reply to Wheatley's prompt letter of thanks.

Wheatley had meanwhile finished another book, *The Rape of Venice*, and with that and the party out of the way, he and Joan flew out for four weeks on the Italian Riviera.

★

Wheatley had to give a number of interviews about *Stranger Than Fiction*, which generally took his success and comfortable lifestyle as their starting point. Wheatley was the "£10,000 a year thriller writer", the man with 37 books translated into 23 languages, and total sales of around 14 million. They were still selling at the rate of half a million books a year, and all thirty seven were still in print.

Wheatley was genial and hospitable ("first let me fill up your glass, and I'll tell you about it") but he was also somewhat self-regarding and self-mythologising: war planning, he said, was "an ideal job for a man *steeped in espionage*" [my emphasis]. More than that, "I was gassed in the first world war. As a result, I couldn't play games. I had time to study international politics instead. Rather funny, that. The Germans gassed me – and gave me time to learn how to beat them in war."

As far as gassing went, Wheatley had got off very lightly compared to many, if he was gassed at all. He didn't play games anyway. He had always been a voracious reader. And his immersion in Alexander Dumas and Baroness Orczy perhaps played a less decisive role in bringing the Reich to its knees than he manages to imply.

Pre-war journalism had a jauntier style and it was heavily oriented towards twists and novelties in its headlines; by modern tastes, it tries too hard. Even the *Stranger Than Fiction* coverage produced lines such as "The arch-intriguer of the lending libraries was put to plotting actual dare-devilry," and "In the midst of war, PEACE was his aim." It was probably his experience of pre-war papers that led Wheatley to feed journalists neat lines and little twists ("rather funny that") suited to old-style journalism of the 'No Games for Wheatley Meant No Fun For Hitler!' variety.

The reviews of *Stranger Than Fiction* were exceptionally mixed. Depending which paper you picked up, it was either an absolutely fascinating book about a valuable contribution to the War, or it was a pointless waste of time and an embarrassment to all concerned.

Wheatley's Sardinia plan provoked discussion, for and against. Wheatley did what he could to air it in interviews, and tried to gain publicity for it with potential reviewers ("Thank you for the autographed copy . . ." wrote one of them, "I certainly hope that I will be able to write about the question of the Sardinian landing"). A number of commentators were convinced by Wheatley's plan and thought the Allies could have avoided the slog up the coast of Italy, arriving in Germany far ahead of the Russians and changing the course of history.

Wheatley kept all his reviews together – good, bad, and indifferent – and put them carefully in an album, together with letters about the party.

One review riled him, and this was a piece by Ewen Montagu in the *Jewish Chronicle*. Montagu, who had been awarded an OBE and a CBE, had already annoyed Wheatley with his 1953 book about deception planning, *The Man Who*

Never Was. Noting in passing that Wheatley's papers were of inordinate length and detail, he then turned to Sardinia.

> The wildness of Mr Wheatley's ideas can be indicated by mentioning that his pet strategic plan, to which he returns again and again, was that we should invade and occupy Sardinia *in 1940*! The reader who remembers what it cost us to supply and maintain Malta can gain an idea of Mr Wheatley's strategic thinking even without knowledge of our lack of suitable material at the time.

Montagu also raised an eyebrow at Wheatley's idea of Jewish regiments, funded by "World Jewry", with a homeland promised in some unspecified place other than Palestine. He then ridiculed several other ideas (fortunately not adopted, or "those of us who survived would now be speaking German") before concluding "Mr Wheatley's many fans will indeed be sorry that he has seen fit to publish these papers."

Wheatley made a typewritten note and put it in his album with Montagu's review:

> Montagu was only a Lt.Cdr.RNVR (Intelligence). He could not conceal his bitter jealousy of us in the War Cabinet. We laughed and nicknamed him "Highland Laddie". In his eagerness to take a crack at me he has even ignored convention by reviewing "S than F" 10 days before the date of publication; yet I would have thought him more intelligent than to compare Sardinia with Malta – poor Ewan!

★

Wheatley's new reputation as a lateral thinker and talented non-specialist inspired a friend to write to him about the subject of noise. Inventor Peter Kooch de Gooreynd wrote to say that he had been talking to a mutual friend about his latest idea which concerned the elimination of noise. Leslie Hollis remembered Wheatley's plan for droning bomber noises to spoil the German night. Kooch de Gooreynd's

521

object was the reverse, but he nevertheless hoped Wheatley might have some ideas.

Another unexpected commission came from the managing director of Nu-Swift, the fire extinguisher manufacturers. Mr Graucob had read Wheatley's book and been so impressed that he wrote to Wheatley in March 1959 with a business proposition. He wanted Wheatley to look over his factory and his sales organisation in the hope that he could suggest improvements.

Wheatley's first concern was tax. Graucob offered Wheatley a generous four hundred guinea fee (about six thousand pounds) and Wheatley was immediately alert to the possibility of being paid in cruise tickets or similar.

In due course Wheatley produced a careful document, divided into numbered and lettered subsections. From "2. The Object of the Operation" ("To increase the sales of Nu-Swift Fire Extinguishers") Wheatley proceeded to consider "3. Factors in favour of the achievement of the Object" (a–d) and "4. Factors against the achievement of the Object" (a–c). And so it went on, for fifteen detailed pages.

Unfortunately, once in receipt of the Report, Graucob had to break it gently to Wheatley that it wasn't altogether useful. Part of the problem was the two men's different outlook. Graucob knew he had an excellent product, but he also knew that the majority of fires occur in the homes of the elderly and the poor, and that these are precisely the groups who tend not to have fire extinguishers. This was the kind of problem he wanted to address.

Wheatley's approach was instead based on prestige, and targeting the fears of special interest groups. He advised Graucob to get his extinguishers fitted in Rolls-Royce cars, then use the fact in his advertising, and he further suggested targeting yachtsmen, private schools, and stamp collectors, the latter fearful of their precious collections going up in smoke. In fact Wheatley's dual approach was a mixture of prestige and anxiety (or in simpler terms, snobbery and fear) not unlike his thrillers.

Graucob was still keen to give Wheatley his fee, which

Wheatley now felt was too generous. He insisted on half the sum, and said that if Graucob would care to treat him and Joan to air tickets to Rhodes, "we should regard that as a very friendly gesture."

★

Wheatley's guerrilla war with the tax authorities became a strategic conflict in 1960 with the formation of Dennis Wheatley Ltd., a company which would employ Wheatley to write books.

Wheatley had dreamed this up in 1959, and originally wanted to call the firm 'Bestsellers Ltd.'. The essence of his idea was that he should cease to be a freelance author, writing on his own account, and should instead be employed by a company formed for the purpose of marketing his books.

Wheatley was to be paid a modest £1000 a year, with expenses, but all his financial needs were to be met by the company. They would pay for his secretary, his "accommodation in which to work", which he already had, his entertaining, his travel between Lymington and London, and his months abroad "for local colour". In return he would provide one novel a year.

More ambitious possibilities included letting his house to the company, employing Joan as his assistant, and perhaps even receiving no salary but very generous expenses. Wheatley was helped in all this by his accountant, Neville Hayman. Having thought of almost everything, he drafted a letter for Hutchinson's to send back to him, beginning "Dear Mr Wheatley, In reply to your letter of [blank], I do fully understand that the present tax laws bear harshly on authors such as yourself, and it certainly seems most unfair . . ."

The upshot was that in February 1960 Dennis Wheatley Ltd was launched, an event that Wheatley would refer back to happily in a speech.

> In 1960 I handed myself over bound hand and foot to the Company . . . Time was when I could work or not as I liked. Things are very different now . . . For example I

might have spent next January February March quietly in my own home. But not a bit of it. I have my orders now and must obey.

His orders were to go to Mexico and climb an Aztec pyramid, go to India, and spend some time in the South Seas. "And all this in the depths of winter," he added, as if it was further hardship.

The Company continued to send its author off to various locations, no doubt after a little input from Wheatley himself. In May 1962, for example, a letter arrived at Grove Place from Dennis Wheatley Ltd ("Registered Office: Grove Place"). "Dear Mr Wheatley", it said,

> It has occurred to the Directors that no book by you has as its background the Adriatic Coast of Italy and the Dalmatian Coast.
>
> As there is much fascinating history in connection with this part of Europe, the Directors would like you to consider making use of it and, with this intention, they suggest that you should spend a few weeks in the Adriatic.

As Wheatley's generation used to say, nice work if you can get it.

CHAPTER FORTY-FOUR

The Satanist

If Sir Waldron Smithers had written to ask Wheatley about "Black Magic" just a few years later, Wheatley might have had more news for him. Occultism had started to bubble up again in the Fifties, and there was a witchcraft revival under way, spearheaded by the publication of Gerald Gardner's *Witchcraft Today* in 1954. Gardner's synthetic brand of witch-craft owed a lot to his own peccadilloes, notably flagellation, and the climax of his ceremonies was the 'Great Rite' of intercourse between priest and priestess.

There was also a swell of tabloid interest, much of it influ-enced by a small cast of key players, principally Wheatley and his old associate Rollo Ahmed (whose own book, *The Black Art*, had been published on the back of *The Devil Rides Out*) with the work of Montague Summers standing behind both of them. At times there is an elegant circularity, when allegations that seem to have come from reading Wheatley then lead to commentary from Wheatley himself, citing them as further evidence for contemporary Satanism.

The *Sunday Pictorial* was on the case as early as 1951, with the help of a mysterious "Mr.A"; in fact Ahmed, out of prison again after a third sentence for fraud. "It is the cult of many organized groups," readers were told: "they include people who are nationally and internationally famous." Mr.A was back again in 1954, by which time things were really warming up. He told *Pictorial* reporters "I want to prove that people in Britain are interested in magic", and to show that strange rites went on, he was photographed performing one himself.

In the same year Fabian of the Yard – a retired policeman with a distinguished record – published *London After Dark*, in which he told readers of a temple of Satanism in Lancaster Gate, W2, an area of West London then associated with immigration. In a house of bedsitters, we go down to the cellar, through a small doorway, and into another house, the front of which faces a different street. Then we go up a spiral staircase to a door padded with black felt. "Beyond this door is a private Temple of Satanism!"

> . . . a large room, sickly with odours from two tall brass braziers. The room is dimly lit by wick lamps that burn a dark green fat which smells abominable, and seems to have some stupefying power. I think the acrid smell conceals the fact that the temple is probably densely sprayed with ether or chloroform.
>
> At one end of the long room is an altar, exactly as in a small church – except that the altar candles are black wax, and the crucifix is head downwards.

We know it well. But in a newer twist:

> Pentagrams and sigils . . . are on the low ceiling. On the left of this altar, is a black African idol – the ju-ju, obviously, of some heathen fertility rite. It is nearly five feet high, squat, repulsive, and obscenely constructed. It is rubbed to a greasy polish by the ecstatic bare flesh of the worshippers.

The Police knew where the Temple was, but they were powerless to act. It was too dangerous:

> Not even the London policeman or policewoman can guarantee to be immune, in an atmosphere thick with perfumed ether, throbbing with jungle drums and chants.

The *Sunday Pictorial* upped the ante in May 1955. This time they had a real witness – not just Rollo Ahmed in a mask – in the form of a Mrs Jackson of Birmingham. Mrs Jackson had seen it all: "How at ceremonies lasting into early dawn orgies were practised while everything decent in life was mocked." (She seems to have been reading *To The Devil – A Daughter*, with its Satanic menaces to "everything decent in life"[1]). There was an inverted cross and a cockerel sacrifice, along with an altar and a virgin girl to be initiated. The whole business was a "passport to debauchery".

Mrs Jackson continued her revelations throughout the Fifties, changing her story as she went and making progressively less impact. Then in June 1956, as the climax of a story the paper had been building since March, *Reynolds News* acquired a dossier on black magic. In true Wheatley style, *top people were at it*. Under the headline 'Peers on Yard Black Magic List', the newspaper revealed

> The list reads like pages taken from Debrett! It includes two or three of the most famous names in the peerage and that of a former ambassador at the Court of St.James. It also names a number of wealthy people, including one with two country mansions and a luxurious West End flat.

This story duly fizzled out, but now it was time to bring out the big guns. The *Sunday Graphic* launched a short series of non-fiction pieces on Black Magic by "the man who knows more than anyone else about this strange, evil cult." It was, of course, Dennis Wheatley.

In *Gunmen, Gallants and Ghosts* Wheatley confesses that this commission came about due to the interest raised by the woman in Birmingham, Mrs Jackson. The series offers a good resumé of Wheatley's occult spiel almost midway through his career. Whereas the wish of God – in whom Wheatley didn't actually believe – is that we should all lead "*peaceful, orderly lives*" Satan wishes to cause disorder and misrule by every possible means, such as "trade disputes".

Wheatley then encapsulates the central, Manichaean conflict:

---

[1] "They were all horrors and menaces to everything decent in life." TDAD (Hutchinson, 1953) p.383.

The dual principle of Good and Evil, which is the basis of every religion, must continue in perpetual conflict until the end of time. On the Right hand we have light, warmth, growth and order; on the Left hand, darkness, cold, decay and chaos.

Like its simple 'Black/White' polarity, this 'Left/Right' language of magic might well have a larger resonance.

As for Black Magic, "Such Magic is of the Devil and can be obtained" – i.e. supernatural power can be obtained – "only by such sexual depravity and bestial rites as are described in the official reports of the initiation ceremonies of the Mau–Mau."

Yet it is not only in Africa that such abominations are practised. A few years ago women were giving themselves up to hideous eroticism with a great carved ebony figure, during Satanic orgies held in a secret temple in Bayswater, London W2.

Wheatley produces some old stories about Summers and Crowley and adds a few contemporary touches, such as the widely reported "ritual killing" of a farm worker in 1945 (the murder of Charles Walton in Warwickshire; in fact almost certainly not magical).

Wheatley also points the finger at Grand Orient Freemasonry (a Continental Masonry, distinct from Grand Lodge Masonry). The inner circle of Continental Masonry are descendants of the German Illuminati and Rosicrucians, says Wheatley, and in the past two hundred and fifty years they have been responsible for causing "many revolutions." In particular, "it is the Grand Orient, more than all other factors together, which has reduced France, once the most powerful nation in Europe, to her present pitiful condition."

But now the Grand Orient is being surpassed by the Communists. Marxism advocates "the destruction of the middle classes by every means *including violence*." Wheatley then repeats, verbatim, the paragraph already cited: "Good

528

and Evil . . . every religion . . . perpetual conflict . . . Right . . . warmth, light, growth and order . . . Left . . . darkness, cold, decay, and chaos."

The idea of a great occult conspiracy – as in *Jugg* and *The Satanist* – is given a flourish towards the end, when Wheatley recounts something an M15 man said to him in 1938:

> Believe me, Dennis, I would rather be up against a combination of the most dangerous German and Russian agents I have ever known, than up against "The Brothers of the Shadow".

Wheatley knew two MI5 men very well – Maxwell Knight and Bill Younger – and this man ("one of my oldest friends") sounds like Knight. Knight seems to have enjoyed telling Wheatley tall tales, perhaps finding him to be excitable and gullible, but in fact he was doing him a great favour. He was providing him with what writers used to call "good copy".

★

Wheatley had already revealed in *Jugg* that Communism was the new vehicle for Satanism. Now, in *The Satanist*, he would turn his attention from Communism in general to the British Trades Union movement in particular, surely one of the most unlikely guises ever suggested for the Prince of Darkness.

It makes the book very much a document of its time. It was published in 1960, just a year after the Boulting Brothers comedy *I'm All Right, Jack*, with Peter Sellers as the Stalinist shop steward. In 1958, the London docks had lost some 340,00 working days through industrial action. Demarcation disputes, wildcat strikes, and the cry of "All out!" were becoming a routine part of post-war life, the subject of numerous jokes and cartoons.

John Calder remembers that in 1959 the unions seemed to have the country "by the throat". Where the dockers' militancy was politically motivated, elsewhere the problem was apolitical greed. The printers of the time were well paid, but they had a powerful union and it was, as Calder puts it, the period of "I'm alright, Jack!" attitudes: it pushed "the middle classes, together with those who did not have the power of the biggest and most powerful unions behind them, into a state of boiling resentment . . ."

Communist influence was widespread and systematic, and ballot-rigging in the Electrical Trades Union led to a court case in which the Communists were found guilty. The Judge, Mr Justice Winn, found that Communists in the ETU had "conspired together to prevent by fraudulent and unlawful devices the election of the plaintiff Byrne in place of the defendant Haxell as general secretary", and that the Union was in fact "managed and controlled by Communists."

Inevitably the Information and Research Department (IRD) were taking a very keen interest in this state of affairs. Wheatley's friend Colonel Sherry Sheridan had met with Vic Feather, the TUC Deputy General Secretary, as early as 1950 to discuss the placing of anti-Communist articles. The IRD publishing firm 'Background Books' later published Feather's *Trade Unions: True or False*, and another IRD company, Ampersand, published *Use and Abuse of Trade Unions* in 1963.

Wheatley, meanwhile, was doing his bit for the struggle with *The Satanist*. Chapter One is largely given over to an emotive and almost suspiciously well-informed discussion of Trade Unionism and its problems. It is a strange beginning for an occult thriller.

★

The Satanist opens in the office of Colonel "Conky Bill" Verney, Wheatley's Max Knight character. He has a photograph on his desk showing the dead body of one of his agents. Teddy Morden has been found in an alley near Bermondsey Dock, with his throat cut from ear to ear and the marks of binding on his wrist and ankles. He has, it will transpire, been crucified upside down in a ritual murder.

C.B. is showing the photo to another of his agents, Barney Sullivan, who is also the Earl of Larne, although he tends not to use the title (and is in that respect like Bill Younger, the baronet). "Now; how about it?" asks C.B., inviting Sullivan to pick up the case where Morden stopped.

> "I'll play, Sir." Barney's reply came after only a second's hesitation. "I hardly knew Morden, except to pass the time of day with; but he was one of us and I'm game to have a cut at the swine who did that to him."

"Good show, Sullivan", says C.B., "I had a hunch that in you I'd picked the right man . . ."

This dialogue is really sterling, pukka stuff, and it must have been at least forty or fifty years out of date even when it was written. Tom Driberg once said he thought Wheatley's famously bad style was for the benefit of translators, but much of it almost defies the translation of its full resonances, with a richly dated idiom that conveys a whole way of life. How many other writers could talk of a "Satanic beanfeast"?

Sullivan doesn't immediately get C.B.'s point about the Devil being involved: "Morden was after these Communist saboteurs, they rumbled him and knocked him off," he says; "I can't see how the Devil comes into that." C.B. lets the point pass for a moment, and then Wheatley deftly introduces the subject of the Trades Unions. C.B. has been at a meeting with some Cabinet Ministers and "some of the big shots of the TUC", in order to discuss "a matter which for a long time past has been giving a lot of responsible people headaches; namely, the hold that Communism still has on Labour."

Suddenly we're deep into the subject:

> "Did you happen to see a booklet published last year that was called *The British Road To Stalinism*?"
> "Yes. It was a warning to trade-unionists put out by the Industrial Research and Information Service about the danger of Communist infiltration."
> "That's right. And the I.R.I.S. is no Tory-backed set-up. Its chief is Jack Tanner, a former chairman of the T.U.C. and president of the Amalgamated Engineering Union . . ."

This is all real life material – sitting oddly in a book which is shortly going to produce all the excesses of Wheatley-style *diablerie* – and highly topical. *The British Road To Stalinism: The Communist Menace to Britain Exposed* had been published by Industrial Research and Information Ltd in 1958. As for the IRIS not being a "Tory backed set-up", this is a moot point: IRIS meetings of the period seem to have manifested an unlikely alliance between moderate trade unionists and retired senior officers from the Army and Navy. Harold Macmillan had started funding the IRIS directly by 1963, and it was also funded by an anti-Communist body called Common Cause.

Well-informed as ever, Wheatley points out through Conky Bill that although there are eight million trade unionists and only twenty-five thousand Communists, the Communists hold posts out of all proportion to their number. General apathy, to an almost irresponsible degree, allows extremists and special interest groups to dominate the unions, while ordinary employees work in their gardens or go to the pub. Wheatley is at some pains to stress that ordinary decent workers are not the problem ("The average British working man is as sound as a bell"), just as in *The Ka of Gifford Hillary* Sir Gifford had praised "a Trade Union Leader, who is a patriot through and through and has more good, sound, common sense than any man I know."

And so Wheatley's public address goes on, dramatised into dialogue that stops just short of creaking.

> Barney nodded. "Yes, apathy's the root of the problem; but from what one hears, it's not only that. A lot of the elections are rigged."
> "Ah! Now you're talking, young feller."

*

The Satanists wield their influence over union affairs by ruses such as employing a fortune-teller to frighten a moderate candidate, while the larger story concerns an American air force officer, Colonel Henrik G Washington, the Satanist of the title, and two telepathic brothers, Otto and Lothar Khune. Lothar is an old Nazi turned Communist, showing the continuity between the two totalitarian movements; he is a "Communazi", to use the word that the IRD tried to put into the language.

Among its other characteristic features – including its pornographic salaciousness (considerably toned down for the published version) and a decisively heroic female role in the character of Mary Morden – the book includes a black imp (something that a psychic once told Wheatley they could see hopping about behind Rollo Ahmed) and a Satanist's Georgian house, in the run-down Cremorne area of Chelsea, at the river end of Lots Road, with an Adam fanlight and an interior described by a character as being "like that of a nobleman's mansion, as seen on the films". It is a description that now seems to conjure up a definitively Wheatley ambience, and looks forward to Wheatley's cinematic association with the House of Hammer.

The Satanist also features a memorably xenophobic picture of the wicked Indian devil-worshipper, Mr Ratnadatta, a rotund man with protruding teeth whose breath has "a curiously sweet yet unpleasant odour like that of bad lobster." Among his many wickednesses is a desire to break Mary in to cacophonous modern music and ugly modern art which, Mary privately knows, "could bring pleasure to few people other than those with twisted minds."

> "I don't think much of it", she tells Ratnadatta.
> "You are wrong," he told her severely. "And you must learn to like it. In recent times the arts haf made great strides. Musicians, painters, sculptors, haf broken away from tradition. That ees good; very good. They no longer follow slavishly tastes set by bourgeois society. This shows that they are persons fitting themselves for advancement and acceptance off the hidden truths."

★

Bill Younger ("William Mole") had continued to write, and

533

had grown so serious about it that he had recently left MI5. He continued to be the apple of Wheatley's eye. Not only had Molly Fountain been reading a Mole book in *To The Devil – A Daughter* (his "new book"; it would have to be *The Lobster Guerrillas*) but in *The Ka of Gifford Hillary*, Lady Ankaret is reading a travel book about Portugal entitled *Blue Moon in Portugal*; another real book, written by Bill and his wife Poo.

Now, early in 1961, Bill and Poo went on holiday to Sicily, where Bill caught Asian flu. He had been in bed for a few days, and seemed to be recovering. He got up and went out for a walk, but that night he had a relapse. The doctor was called again, but before he arrived Bill was dead.

This was one of the most grievous events in Wheatley's life, and when he received the news he broke down and cried. Bill didn't live to see it published, but he had just completed a monumental history of wine, entitled *Gods, Men, and Wine*. Even in his fiction he had written memorably of wine as a living creature, "an animal that one drinks", and his book was highly regarded when it appeared. Wheatley was moved by the now posthumous dedication, "For Dennis, who taught me to love fine wine."

★

Since 1950 Wheatley had been a member of the now vanished United Hunts Club, in Upper Grosvenor Street. By the time Wheatley joined it was less horsey than it might sound, and it was owned by Captain John Sleigh, who had had a "system" at Monte Carlo and consequently lost a fortune. He was reduced at one point to running a cupboard of a club in Soho, the Abyssinian in Archer Street, which had only one table and one chair. But he had bounced back to own the United Hunts, with its Italianate staircase and its heavily panelled and chandeliered dining room.

Wheatley must have enjoyed the Club's particularly fine stock of wines, and the fact that the club offered exceptional value would certainly not have escaped him (in 1963 a 'country member' like Wheatley paid five guineas a year, still less than £70 at today's values). For some years he used it like a hotel whenever he and Joan came up from Lymington.

As time went by, they took to staying instead at Brown's hotel, in Dover Street, Mayfair, and he let his membership of the United Hunts go. Founded in 1837 by James Brown, a former manservant, Brown's was one of the oldest and most traditional hotels in London. Literary patrons had included Kipling, but Wheatley was probably more impressed by the fact that King George II of Greece spent several years of exile there in the Twenties and Thirties, and that the Dutch Government had declared war on Japan from Room 36.

In 1961, however, Dennis and Joan decided to go for a flat of their own in London, to use as a *pied à terre*. Wheatley was still friendly with "Don", the Marquess of Donegall, whom he had known since Don's days as a Thirties gossip columnist. The Marquess was having trouble getting a divorce and wished to marry another woman, Maureen, and had been advised that if he and Maureen lived together for a while in Switzerland, this would strengthen his case. Maureen had a flat in Cadogan Square which she wanted to sell because of the Swiss move, and Don told Wheatley about it over dinner.

Wheatley rang him the next day to say that he and Joan would like to buy the flat. This was very convenient, and the Marquess generously threw in the fittings, curtains, and carpets for nothing. This arrangement saved Wheatley "several hundred pounds", a fact which pleased him so much he mentions it in his autobiography.

The Wheatleys now had a foothold in Cadogan Square, in the ground floor flat at No.60. Wheatley would end his days in this pleasant backwater of Knightsbridge, with its trees and its tall, red brick, Queen Anne style buildings. Congenial neighbours must have given the pavements a village feeling: both his stepson Jack Younger and the actor Christopher Lee, soon to become a friend, lived nearby on the Square.

★

Wheatley's mail bag was as full as ever, and he did what he could to answer it, although he found it a trial. Characteristic of Wheatley's polite and unpatronising replies is a letter he wrote to a teenage girl living at the top of a high rise on a Kentish Town council estate. "Dear Miss Walker," he begins,

> Many thanks for your letter . . . It is always a pleasure to hear from readers who have enjoyed my books and I note your particular interest in those with occult backgrounds.

Wheatley then notes the immensity of the literature on the occult and recommends consulting a "really good librarian" for advice on the field, and the particular areas Miss Walker might be interested in, before disclosing a few books he has found "particularly informative" himself.

These are *Witchcraft, Magic and Alchemy* by Grillot de Givry, *Death and its Mystery* by Camille Flammarion, in three volumes, and the works of Montague Summers. The Flammarion is a daunting book to recommend, but Wheatley was entirely sincere. He had annotated his own copy "so many really well attested occurrences of the supernatural – after reading these pages, the most rational could no longer doubt."

Wheatley had now published around forty novels, and he was pleased when Robert Lusty at Hutchinson decided that they merited a uniform edition. Just in time for Christmas 1961, Hutchinson published the first six titles in the Lymington Edition, with another four coming out in time for Christmas 1962 (although most of them were swallowed by what in those days was the public libraries' insatiable demand for Wheatley). They are attractively produced, with black cloth, gold lettering, and a wheatsheaf crest, and Wheatley signed the first thousand copies of the first book in the edition, *The Forbidden Territory*. Like the Wessex Edition of Thomas Hardy, the world now had the Lymington Edition of Dennis Wheatley.

CHAPTER FORTY-FIVE

The Reich Revisited, and the Death of the Duke

Writing in an early Sixties number of the glossy magazine *Queen*, Quentin Crewe mounted a pseudo-anthropological study of the British upper classes. When it came to friendship, "Membership of the group entitles the member to about five thousand friends."

> By this arrangement it is possible for the group to meet anyone of importance and to save hotel bills abroad. In far countries the group will ask anyone to stay who is a bona fide member. The term friend is more loosely, but more usefully used than in other classes. There is no need to like a friend, but the duties owed to him are clear.

Despite its satirical exaggeration this bears a distinct resemblance to the way Wheatley travelled. He sometimes stayed in hotels, but he was more often entertained by a large network of old Service friends and friends-of-friends, particularly British diplomats (and in later life he felt he would like to have been a diplomat). He once complained that it was "hard work being entertained straight off the plane by ambassadors and tycoons."

In 1963 Wheatley and Joan embarked on a round the world trip, flying out to Ceylon, followed by Singapore, Hong Kong, Japan, Manila, Honolulu, and America. Hong Kong also furnished Wheatley with the background for a subsequent book, *Bill For The Use of a Body*.

*

Writing a perceptive profile of Wheatley in the *Times*, a columnist noted that although Wheatley travelled, his books didn't, and added "He is British. His hazel eyes moisten at the compliment."

Even more specifically, Wheatley was English, and his whole character embodies the archetypal traits of the twentieth-century middle-class Englishman. He believed in an orderly, cohesive and benevolently hierarchical society (notably in the mixed blessing of the class system); he had a grain of eccentricity, or at least individuality; a code of good form, allied to a sense of fairness; a sense of voluntary service; a respect for amateurism; and a lasting boyishness, with his stamps, his paper stars, and his cut-out fish[1].

Wheatley always liked joining things, and in 1963 he became a member of the Royal Society of St.George. Patriotism has become rather compromised, but the Society of St.George is an entirely respectable organisation with the Queen as its Patron, and it exists to celebrate Englishness and English values ("freedom, gentility and human decency").

Wheatley was introduced into the Society by a friend named Hugh Smyth, who also knew Odette Hallowes, the French-born British agent who had been tortured by the Gestapo and sent to a concentration camp. She still walked with a slight limp after having her toenails pulled, and – within the large 'small world' that Wheatley moved in – she was married to a director of Justerini and Brooks. She was another member of the Society of St George. Wheatley's membership conferred on him a lapel decoration and a tie, which he evidently liked; he can be seen wearing it in several photographs.

[1] Wheatley also scores highly on the schema of The British Character given by the cartoonist Pont in his 1938 book of the same name, including Importance of Breeding; Enjoyment of Club Life; Proneness to Superstition; Tendency To Think Things Not So Good As They Used To Be; Failure to Appreciate Good Music; Love of Detective Fiction; Refusal to Admit Defeat; Importance of Not Being an Alien; Love of Writing Letters to The Times; Love of Never Throwing Anything Away; Tendency to Put Things Away Safely; Tendency Not To Join The Ladies; Importance of Not Being Intellectual; Enthusiasm for Gardening, and Passion for the Antique.

For much of 1963 Wheatley was working on a new Sallust thriller, provisionally entitled *The Devil's Disciple* and later published as *They Used Dark Forces*. It is set in the final days of the Third Reich, where Gregory is now in league with a Jewish Satanist and astrologer named Malacou. Gregory finally insinuates himself into the bunker with Hitler, where he advises the Fuhrer on astrology and reincarnation, and possibly hastens his suicide by assuring him he will be reincarnated as a warlord on Mars.

It is an impressive performance, particularly in the way that Wheatley inserts Gregory – like Woody Allen's Zelig – into historical situations, carefully keeping him within an accurate chronology. The book reads like an insiderish, Procopius-style 'secret history' of Hitler's court, as he records the very different characters involved, with their dissents and rivalries.

As if to underline a virtuoso performance, Wheatley gives himself a cameo role. Various friends and associates are written in, including Jack Slessor, Colin Gubbins, Richard Gale and Sir Richard Peck, and Gregory lunches with an unnamed friend who "had been a Cadet with him in H.M.S. Worcester and, since 1941, had worked in the Deception Section of the Joint Planning Staff."

Within Wheatley's story, the "They" who use dark forces refers to Gregory and Malacou, but even on the cover and blurb, the emphasis has slipped to the Nazis and their involvement with the occult. There was considerable interest among senior Nazis in paganism and occultism, and they also claimed to believe in cosmological theories such as the 'frozen world' and 'hollow earth'. Hess, Himmler and certain factions in the SS had occult interests, and during his rise to power Hitler seems to have been influenced by a Jewish astrologer named Erik Jan Hanussen, and later by another astrologer, Karl Ernest Krafft.

British Intelligence went as far as to keep an astrologer on the payroll – a man called Louis de Wohl, whom Wheatley knew, and who gave Wheatley a copy of his novel, *Introducing Doctor Zodiac* – not because they believed in astrology themselves but because they wanted to work out what the Nazis might be thinking. De Wohl was employed by the SOE, who later found a more active role for him in developing astrological propaganda.

Nazi occultism has become part of twentieth-century mythology and spawned a heap of trashy – almost *definitively* trashy – books, symptoms of a public appetite for morbid kitsch and Nazi trivia, as well as the overlap between the esoteric and ultra-right sensibilities. Wheatley's 1964 novel was one of the first books to broach the subject, and helped launch it into the popular consciousness. Air Marshal Dowding is on record as saying that Hitler was a black magician, in terms which echo Wheatley. There's no doubt about it, he said (circa 1970): "he used dark forces."

*

Wheatley was invited to give a talk in the book department at Harrods, his subject being 'Magic and the Supernatural'. It was very well attended, and among the people in the audience was Christopher Lee. Lee went up to Wheatley afterwards, and introduced himself as a fan. They talked for a while, and Lee remembers Wheatley's friendly manner as "graciousness itself."

Wheatley was still assiduously collecting books. Before the War he had bought many of them from Percy Muir, a major figure in the London book trade (it was Muir that Wheatley had recommended to the hard-up Crowley, when he wanted to sell some manuscripts) but now he was buying them mostly from Sam Joseph on the Charing Cross Road, and Harold Mortlake, who had a small dark emporium nearby on Cecil Court.

Mortlake specialised in nineteenth-century books, with a sprinkling of the sensational and esoteric. Montague Summers had been a customer, and Mortlake had the uncanny experience of receiving a cheque from him seemingly written and dated a week after his death. "It could have been postdated, of course," concedes one of Summers' chroniclers, "but one wonders."

Mortlake kept a stock of Wheatley first editions, and Wheatley knew him well enough to haggle, and even to try for a reduction on books already ordered; not a practice to be recommended. Wheatley was in cahoots with Mortlake when it came to providing signed copies of his books, which he may have done for credit or discount. It was Wheatley's usual practice to inscribe his books to people rather than simply sign them (which most collectors would prefer, but almost all 'signed' Wheatleys are 'inscribed') so when he signed books for Mortlake, he put fake inscriptions in them. He writes to Mortlake:

> I sent off the 60 copies of my own books to you this morning in four parcels by rail. It took me quite a time to autograph them as I tried to make the inscriptions as varied as possible.

This might explain why – along with all the Wheatley books signed to people with quite ordinary names, often bookshop managers or bona fide fans – many of them are signed to slightly peculiar names such Mr Jaz, Harry Hardon, Constance Tofts and Lily Palmay.

The lovely Constance Tofts was surely an actress – you can almost see the cigarette card – while Lily Palmay sounds like a music hall star. Of course, all these names could be absolutely genuine, but one wonders, especially knowing that 'Palmay London' was the cable address of Mortlake's shop.

*

In May 1964 Wheatley catalogued his library, a task he probably enjoyed. He had around 4,000 books, including a signed first edition of *Ulysses*, and books by Evelyn Waugh, Sax Rohmer, and Zola. The purpose was to sell the library to Dennis Wheatley Ltd.

Wheatley's cataloguing offers a revealing breakdown of

his interests. Categories include "Baconia" (i.e "Bacon was Shakespeare"), "Books" (i.e. publishing and book collecting), "Character" (how to read character, including faces, phrenology, and handwriting), "Egypt", "Erotica", "Greece", "History" (the largest category, with seven subsections), "Islam", "Memoirs", "Mysticism", "Napoleon", "Occultism", "Psychology", "Palmistry", "Religions", "Rome", "Sexual psychology", "Space", "World War 1", "World War II", "Wine and Food", and "Wheatley, Dennis"

The Wheatley section includes a full set of his own books, bound in blue morocco by Sangorski and Sutcliffe; the Arabic edition of *Vice and Virtue*; his 'Mystery Rooms' pamphlet from the Ideal Homes exhibition; an inventory of the contents of his childhood house, Clinton; and a number of manuscripts including 'Julie's Lovers', 'The Trees in the Garden', notes on the *Perfumed Garden of Sheik Nefzoui*; 'Scenes and Portraits', comprising over a hundred pages of historical notes on his stamps; and two handwritten exercise books devoted to 'Books I have Read, and Opinions Thereon.'

Wheatley's distinction between 'Occultism' and 'Mysticism' is not based on the usual definition of mysticism as the direct apprehension of God. Instead he tends to file his more serious occult books under 'occultism', while 'mysticism' tends towards mumbo-jumbo and crankery. 'British-Israel' theories are prominent, along with pyramidology, dubious Biblical exegesis, and even a book combining Horbiger (the Nazi 'frozen world' man, with his doctrine of eternal ice) and Madame Blavatsky. Entitled *Blavatsky and Horbiger: Reconciliation*, it is surely a reconciliation the world could live without.

Wheatley's library also included a number of books by Thirties far-Rightists. His idea of political wrongdoing included both the far-Left and far-Right, and he had a number of extremist tracts catalogued together as "Pamphlets, A Collection of several subversive, some under the guise of patriotism and others on wild-cat economic policies."

Wheatley had a good number of books in his 'Erotica'

collection, with more in 'Psychology', such as *Phallism: A Description of the Worship of Lingam-Yoni in Various Parts of the World, and In Different Ages, With an Account of Ancient and Modern Crosses, Particularly of the Crux Ansata and Other Symbols Connected With the Mysteries of Sex Worship* (n.d., circa1890). Wheatley's bookplate figures the *crux ansata* in the shape of a tree.

Wheatley's erotica collection also included Aubrey Beardsley prints, erotic Japanese paintings on silk, nearly a hundred etchings illustrating the adventures of Casanova, and even twelve ivory carvings of "*La Vie Privée du Chine*", all duly catalogued. The man who catalogues not just his dirty pictures but his filthy carvings as part of his library is a true bookman, at least of a sort.

★

They Used Dark Forces was Wheatley's fiftieth book, so it was an occasion for more celebrations. There was a drinks party, complete with raffle, at Justerini's, but the great event was a more select dinner at the Garrick Club on the night of November 20th 1964. On the menu were Crab Eggs Gregory Sallust, Homard Princess Marie-Lou, Stuffed Chicken Roger Brook, Canard Duc de Richleau, Frucht Salat Erika Von Epp, and English Christmas Cake Georgina.

Thirty-odd male guests (no women were allowed in the Garrick) included chief deception planner Johnny Bevan, Eric Goudie, Eddie Combe, Hugh Astor, Joe Links, Anthony Wheatley, Derrick Morley, Bill Elliott, and the Duke of Richmond. Wheatley made a well prepared and entertaining speech, recounting the story of his life so as to focus on the guests around the table. Between them they included a duke, a marquess, a bishop, two lords, a director of Hambro's Bank and the Chairman of the Stock Exchange.

"This is certainly one of the happiest moments of my life," said Wheatley, and went on to say how proud he was to be the centre of such a distinguished gathering. Just before finishing his speech, he praised his publishers: "I have always met with kindness and consideration from every member of the firm", he said: "Hutchinson's have done a wonderful job for me over thirty years and no author could have had a better publisher." This was a generous assessment, but Wheatley knew what the moment demanded.

★

Around this time Wheatley was grossing over half a million pounds a year for Hutchinson, about a seventh of their entire turnover. He had fifty-five books in print, with a print-run of 30,000 copies for a new hardback, while Arrow, Hutchinson's paperback subsidiary, was shifting 1,150,000 Wheatleys a year, or around a quarter of its total sales. When *The Wanton Princess* came out in 1966, Wheatley could dedicate it – with characteristically self-regarding gratitude – to "the Sales Representatives of the Hutchinson Group in appreciation of their having sold 20,000,000 copies of my books."

Wheatley was flying high. In July 1965 *Queen* published an 'In' and 'Out' list reflecting "new social attitudes." Along with "Art Galleries to be seen in" (Robert Fraser) and "Comic Strips" (Modesty Blaise and Flook, yes; Rip Kirby and The Gambols, no) we find "Authors to read." It's thumbs down for Kingsley Amis, John Wain, and John Braine, and thumbs up for Iris Murdoch, Malcolm Lowry and Dennis Wheatley.

★

Not everyone liked Wheatley, however, nor would he always meet with kindness and consideration from every member of the firm of Hutchinson. A bright young man named Giles Gordon had just moved from Secker and Warburg to "the middle-brow mediocrity of Hutchinson", famously bankrolled not just by Wheatley but by the hardly less profitable Barbara Cartland.

Like the trouper that he was, Wheatley turned up in person to deliver his latest manuscript. Wheatley tended to see a different editor each time he went in, which can't have impressed him. The reason for this, unknown to Wheatley, was that the most junior editor was always given the job of processing his books, and as soon they were promoted, they could pass Wheatley on to their successor.

There seems to have been nothing about Wheatley that Gordon liked. He didn't like his centre-parting, which he thought was a sign of right-wing leanings ("always a give away as to lack of liberal stance and even, in my experience, latent fascism in the wearer"); he didn't like his raincoat ("of the kind labelled 'dirty' "); and he certainly didn't like his books, not least because he never deigned to read them.

Wheatley didn't attempt any small talk with Gordon, nor did he smile. He may have sensed that Gordon didn't like him; or, in a changing world, he may have sensed that Gordon was the *type* who didn't like him. Gordon went back to his office carrying a great slab of typescript. He didn't remember the title ("if indeed I ever noticed it"), but it was probably *Dangerous Inheritance*, the book in which Wheatley sends the Duke de Richleau on his last mission.

Wheatley liked to say that his books were written to teach young people the virtues of courage and absolute fidelity to one's friends, and *Dangerous Inheritance* is no exception. The now elderly Duke de Richleau blames himself for getting his friends incarcerated in a foreign prison, and he feels it his responsibility to get them out again, which he does by threatening to set off some plastic explosive taped to a wooden handle. After his friends are released, the explosive is revealed to have been no more than a bar of soap, with a battery and some wires. But the strain has been too much for the old Duke, and as he is flying back towards England together with his friends, he suffers a heart attack and dies.

Poor old Wheatley's musketeering nonsense was no match for the serious literary fiction that Gordon preferred. Gordon had, in fact, recently made the great discovery of Barry Unsworth's first book, *The Partnership*, a "novel . . . about two homosexuals making plaster gnomes in a cottage in Cornwall."

Gordon had a wicked idea for Wheatley's manuscript. He sent it to one of Hutchinson's 'readers' for a report, deliberately selecting "the most acerbic and intolerant", and concealing Wheatley's identity by losing the title page. In due course the report came back.

> This author can tell a decent, if irretrievably old-fashioned story, and his (it must be a he) plotting is sound. The book is terribly hackneyed, and it is hard to imagine that it would appeal to readers today. Above all, he cannot write. Regretfully decline.

Gordon was "more pleased with myself than I can say" about this, because "I resented having to soil my brain cells with the likes of Wheatley."

Gordon requested a meeting with Bob Lusty to tell him the good news about his best-selling author. As a Scot, Gordon was lucky enough to be outside the English class system, whereas Wheatley and Lusty had had to negotiate it as best they could, and Gordon sneeringly describes Lusty as "the one-time Kent Messenger-boy trying to rise to the ranks of the country's rulers." He blames this for his "curiously strangulated voice . . . which made it difficult for him to speak loudly, let alone shout." Nevertheless, when Lusty learned what Gordon had done he shrieked at the top of his voice: "Mr Wheatley's books are not to be read; they're sent straight to the printer!"

Somehow, says Gordon, "in spite of my best efforts Dennis Wheatley continued to prosper."

★

Another Hutchinson employee of the period, Nigel Fountain, remembers Wheatley would occasionally be seen in the firm's corridors. He regarded him as something of a joke, and "an anachronism, as if Edgar Wallace had turned up." He looked "like a bookie" in his double-breasted brown suit; like "a Thirties chancer", and "an ageing flash Harry." Fountain particularly despised Wheatley for his dated class pretensions: he was "one of those people who tried to pretend the world was still the way it was".

546

Wheatley's agent of the period, Michael Horniman of A.P. Watt, once spotted him crossing Waterloo Station wearing a morning coat and a top hat, "an extraordinary sight." But despite that, for the most part he cut an undistinguished figure, like "a publican who'd been hitting his own stock".

Drink had certainly affected Wheatley's appearance. His face was distinctly florid, with a reddened and enlarged nose. He was, of course, a heavy drinker, although he tried to keep to liqueurs in the week and a bottle of champagne on Saturdays (this was his evening drinking, presumably in addition to wine with dinner). If he felt thirsty in the night, when most of us might have a glass of water, he was quite capable of taking the corkscrew to a bottle of something, probably something white and sweet. He might also nip at a bottle of liqueur while he wrote, in addition to chain smoking.

Inevitably this regime – heavy drinking, heavy smoking, sedentary work, plenty of confectionery, plenty of old-fashioned luxury foods – affected Wheatley's health. He was paunchy, short of breath, impotent, and he had now become diabetic, which must have been a hardship for a man with a craving for sugar. Wheatley equipped himself with several books on the subject, filed together under D, and he also took an interest in an early Sixties fad from America known as 'The Drinking Man's Diet', an unhealthy precursor of the Atkins Diet.

The idea was that you could drink as much alcohol as you liked, while eating all the protein and fat you could manage, as long as you avoided carbohydrates and sugars. It was, in other words, perfectly acceptable and indeed recommended to live on buttered steak with lashings of red wine, but you had to be firm about the chips and have brandy instead of pudding.

In 1965 Justerini's published an updated edition of Wheatley's history, *The Seven Ages of Justerini's*, now entitled *The Eight Ages*. Like its predecessor, this kept a keen eye on world history as well as drink. Wheatley noted that the Russian Revolution had burnt itself out, but foresaw a menace in China.

Meanwhile the British Empire had vanished. "For over a hundred and fifty years we maintained peace, justice and toleration over one-fifth of the world's land surface". Now, with the end of the Pax Britannica, like the end of the Pax Romana before it, the world was fallen into bloodshed. But meanwhile there were staggering scientific advances: hover-craft, nuclear energy, a rocket to the moon, and perhaps even a man on Mars in our lifetime.

On the other hand, there was also the possibility that "some lunatic will set off a matchbox full of anti-matter." It is a particularly period vision that this futuristic substance might be in a matchbox, of all things; one almost wonders that Wheatley didn't postulate a piece no bigger than a conker.

"So", says Wheatley, "let us eat, drink (Justerini's will be happy to advise) and be merry while we may."

★

Wheatley had a less Devil-may-care attitude where the writing business was concerned, and he was becoming annoyed with both his publisher and his agent. For all Wheat-ley's after-dinner good cheer, the firm of Hutchinson had not been what it was for a long time, perhaps not since Walter Hutchinson had killed himself in 1950.

It was a vexation for Wheatley that he never really cracked the American market, for which he blamed his agents. Bill Watt, the founder, had retired, and his son Peter had taken on Wheatley's affairs. Peter was a jolly extrovert and Wheatley got on well with him, but he died. Michael Horniman then took Wheatley over in the mid-Sixties, and although they got on civilly enough – Horniman would take Wheatley to lunch at the Savoy Grill – Horniman found Wheatley to be "a pain in the neck."

"Can't you do something about America?" Wheatley would ask, blaming Horniman for his failure there. Wheatley suffered more disappointment from the American market in 1965, when he and Joan had to abandon their holidays for a proposed television series. Early in 1965 they set off for a second round the world trip, but a contract materialised for twenty-six episodes "in colour" featuring Gregory Sallust, so after only three weeks in Mexico they had to return home. Wheatley sketched out plots for all 26 episodes and the series was budgeted for around £750,000, a great deal of money in those days.

The money was half British and half American, but when the American side saw Wheatley's script for a pilot episode, they backed out. Part of the problem was that the Americans asked Wheatley to modernise Gregory, and this was unsuccessful. A very contrite English colleague writes to Wheatley "It is really heart-breaking . . . Hindsight makes it obvious that we would all have been better to follow Henry's very strong feelings that Gregory Sallust should be presented as written, and the stories set in the war period. I blame myself . . ."

This man was no more to blame than Horniman had been. There was something inherently unsuitable for the American mass-market about Wheatley's pukka, class-conscious, intrinsically English fictions. Anthony Powell, apropos of W.E.Johns, notes in his Journals that

> In middle 1960s the Biggles books were 29th most translated literary works in the world, the top juvenile. The only country where they did not sell was the US. Interesting. The same true of the very widely translated Dennis Wheatley . . .

★

Sales were also beginning to slip in Britain. Wheatley's immense pre-war success as a writer of general thrillers was over, and nondescript thrillers like *Unholy Crusade* (1967) would never match it. Nor would the later Gregory Sallust books match Gregory's wartime popularity. Nothing that Wheatley wrote after *The Satanist* in 1960 really hit the heights of *Toby Jugg*, *To The Devil – A Daughter*, or *The Ka Of Gifford Hillary*, but it is noticeable that Wheatley's most successful postwar books are all occult titles.

When *The Satanist* went into paperback in 1966, it sold over 100,000 copies in ten days. The market for paperbacks increased in the Sixties and it was this, together with a new readership for black magic books, that would save the day for Wheatley. The occult revival was on its way.

CHAPTER FORTY-SIX

Lucifer Rising

Putting the frustrations of American television behind him, Wheatley resumed his travels. He and Joan spent early 1966 in Brazil, Peru, Guatemala and Mexico, before going on to Fiji and the South Seas. "It was a wonderful trip," he said, "we enjoyed it immensely and I collected a lot of material for future books." This was literally the case. "I bring back a mass of material," he told an interviewer:

> Menus, timetables, museum catalogues, plans of cities, postcards. If I want to set a book in Italy I only have to say to my secretary, 'Bring me Italy.' All in cellophane bags in a big trunk. 'Bring me Persia!' Find the names of characters. 'Bring me Portugal!' Ancient monuments. 'Bring me Egypt!' Brings it all back. Stuff you can't get in a library. The dishes, the drinks. The money! 'Bring me Brazil!' Can't get it out of the Encyclopaedia Brittanica.

Wheatley would often say that he had never attended a magical ceremony, which wasn't quite true; we have already seen him watching as Joan Grant's naked body was sprinkled with petals while she went into a trance. In Brazil he attended a voodoo ceremony with friends at the British Embassy, Tony Wellington and his wife Pussy. Knowing his interest in the occult, Wellington had arranged for Wheatley to watch a *macumba* gathering, where the *Loa*, or voodoo gods, come down and possess members of the cult.

Wellington had arranged a discreet police guard for the party in case things went wrong. Wheatley feared that the crowd might turn on them if they discovered they were not real cult members (although plenty of white people were, at least in Wheatley's mind, so ethnicity was not the problem).

Like the Satanists in his books, Wheatley was sure that many "rich, white people" in Brazil, although nominally Catholics, were actually voodoo-worshippers.

Together with Tony and Pussy Wellington, Wheatley and Joan had drinks with the local Chief of Police. Then, together with four police – two men and two women, all in plain clothes – they drove out of Rio into the night, through the dark forest. They were in two cars and they stopped "at a place where there was already a long line of cars at the roadside", some of them Rolls-Royces. Wheatley had been living with this kind of scenario in his head for thirty years, and now he found himself inside it.

They walked into the forest, up a walkway made of planks and ornamented with dead chickens, to the meeting place itself. It was the size of a tennis court and at the end was a voodoo altar, with various offerings and crude pictures of Christian saints adapted to serve as voodoo gods. Wheatley was not impressed by his first sight of this altar:

A Voodoo altar looks like a stall at a cheap jumble sale. One that I saw in Brazil had heaped on it pictures of the Virgin Mary and several saints, bottles of Coca-Cola, little pots of wilted flowers, shredded palm fronds, a dagger, a fly-whisk and flasks of rum.

Jumble sale or not, Wheatley abominated voodoo. It was "one of the vilest, cruelest and most debased forms of worship ever devised by man. It origins lay in darkest Africa, and the Negro has carried its foul practices with him to every part of the world which he inhabits." Now it is seen as a legitimate religion, but for Wheatley it meant bestial cruelty, "compared with which the Black Mass is a civilized proceeding."

It does seem that animals would sometimes have their bones broken, and other cruelties, before being killed, and the recent Mau-Mau troubles in Africa would have been in Wheatley's mind, where new recruits were required to drive a thorn into the eye of a living goat.

"Few people can be so bestial as the Haitian Voodooists," thought Wheatley.

> Moreover, Zora Hurston tells us in her very informative book Voodoo Gods that they are fundamentally dishonest and should never be paid in advance for any service, as they think themselves clever not to perform it, and they cannot be trusted with even a few cents.

Wheatley must have wondered what he was letting himself in for; at the very least, perhaps, a spectacle of topless frenzy, but how far would it go, and what would happen then?

Wheatley grew anxious when he and Joan were separated. The policewomen went with Joan and Pussy to the one side of the arena, while the policemen sat with Wheatley and Tony on the other. They waited as more people arrived, and the place became packed. Then at last the ceremony began.

An elderly black man with white hair, dirty white clothes and a beat-up old straw hat made his way into the central space, walking with the help of a stick. A line of girls followed him, all wearing white dresses with long skirts to the ankle. The line began to dance, swaying to and fro to the beating of the voodoo drums.

It was a hot night, and the air was completely still. Then Wheatley felt a big drop of lukewarm water fall on him, followed by another. People became aware that it was raining, and in moments the rain increased to a torrential downpour. The dancers abandoned their dance and ran for cover. The audience, too, picked itself up and made a near stampede for the exit.

Rain had stopped play.

Wheatley makes a surprisingly fair-minded valediction to the whole business of voodoo in his late non-fiction book, *The Devil and All His Works*, when he writes

> In extenuation of normal voodoo ceremonies, it must be remembered that its votaries are among the most poverty stricken people in the world, and, as Sabbaths were to the

witches in Europe, their excesses are the only thing that makes life worth living. It is a tragedy that they should have been ensnared into such cruel and bestial practices.

★

Wheatley had another memorable experience in Mexico, where he had a sensation of near panic, comparable to his feeling in the First War of being looked at while he had his back to the old German casualty station. He was at the Aztec temple complex of Teotihucan, and he was taken underneath the Pyramid of the Moon to see the treasure chambers (which were more like dungeons; or that was how they struck Wheatley). Suddenly, despite the fact that there was electric lighting and that he was with other people, "I was suddenly seized with such a sense of evil that I could not get out of the place quickly enough".

This was quite unlike his benign experience of the Egyptian pyramids. His impression of Teotihucan must have been influenced by knowing it had been the site of immense sacrificial slaughter, with as many as 20,000 victims regularly killed in a single day; and by the time he published this account he had an interest in playing up all supernatural effects.

The Wheatleys travelled on to the South Seas, where they stayed at Suva, the capital of the Fiji Islands, and were entertained by Sir Derek Jakeway, Governor of the Fijis, and his wife Phyllis. Like the Duke of Edinburgh before him (who is worshipped as a god by one of the cargo cults in the region) Wheatley was honoured to take part in the Kava ceremony, in which he drank an intensely relaxing preparation of *kava kava*.

They were there because Wheatley wanted to see the fire-walking ceremony, which in those days was infrequently performed. Fire walking is no longer regarded as a great mystery, but to Wheatley it was an astonishing phenomenon, like something from the lives of the saints. He went on to assure readers of *The Devil and All His Works* that "there is as yet no scientific explanation. It is achieved by white magic."

★

Still in Fiji, Wheatley was impressed by the paintings of the Fijian artist Semisi Maya. Maya's painting – which is figurative, and typically consists of landscapes, flowers, cyclone scenes and underwater scenes – was remarkable because he had been crippled by leprosy, and his hands were so damaged that he was unable to hold a brush. He would apply paint directly with his deformed knuckles, and use the hair on his forearms to achieve special effects.

Wheatley wanted to meet Maya, and went to St.Elizabeth's leprosy home where Maya was an inmate. Wheatley bought several paintings – which were absurdly cheap by Western standards – and resolved to do something to help him when he returned to England.

★

As usual, when Wheatley got back in March 1966 he was swamped by the accumulated correspondence waiting for him. He also had to correct the proofs of *The Wanton Princess*, revise the typescript of *Unholy Crusade*, and write a new novel for autumn delivery, which would become *The White Witch of the South Seas*.

To the relief of Michael Horniman, Wheatley now had a new handler at A.P.Watt, Hilary Rubinstein. Rubinstein was the nephew of Victor Gollancz, the distinguished publisher who had trounced Wheatley on his 'all men are equal' ticket at the Oxford Union. Lunching an author at the Savoy Grill, with Rubinstein present, Gollancz ordered a cigar for his author. As the cigar waiter was about to leave, the author generously said "What about Hilary?" "What, him?" said Gollancz, full of scorn, then turned to the waiter and said "Give him the smallest you've got."

Somewhat to Rubinstein's surprise he got on reasonably well with Wheatley and found him congenial enough, without altogether liking him. Rubinstein was a man of liberal views, who later served on the board of the Institute for Contemporary Arts, and he couldn't warm to Wheatley's politics.

Wheatley was, says Rubinstein, obviously an arch conservative: he had "rabid" views on the Labour Party, who

555

were then in power under Harold Wilson, and he was "full of vitriol" about the Government. Worse, Rubinstein anticipated when he first dealt with Wheatley that "I might find traces of anti-Semitism", although he adds fairly "but I did not".

★

Wheatley lived up to Rubinstein's image of him when, in 1967, he was asked for his opinions on the Vietnam War for a book entitled *Authors Take Sides On Vietnam*. This was inspired by Nancy Cunard's famous 1937 questionnaire, *Authors Take Sides on The Spanish War*. Cunard's writers had been overwhelmingly against Franco, with Arthur Machen – as if to demonstrate the reactionary tendencies of occult and supernatural writing – being one of the few in favour.

Wheatley had not been asked for his opinion in Cunard's day, but now he was, along with a great spread of writers from Pamela Frankau to William Burroughs. Writing with his strategist's hat on ("ex-Wing Commander . . . member of the Joint Planning Staff of the War Cabinet which prepared the strategic plans for Sir Winston Churchill") Wheatley was in favour of the war. He thought a firm stand in Vietnam was absolutely imperative to stop the spread of communism, on the domino model: if the Vietcong took control of Vietnam, neighbouring countries would soon go down too.

★

Wheatley and Joan set off for more holidays in early 1967; they went to Morocco, Turkey, and Iran. The highlight of the trip for both of them was seeing "wonderful Persian art", and they returned, as usual, with a great stash of ephemera for Wheatley's big trunk.

Wheatley had not forgotten his promise to do something for Semisi Maya. Through a nun at the leper home, Wheatley had been buying Maya's paintings with the intention of getting him a show in a West End gallery. He had so far bought about forty paintings for fifty pounds the lot (about £500 now), and managed to get his friend Sir Danvers Osborn

556

interested: Osborn was a partner in the New Bond Street Art Gallery, near Asprey's.

With the business sense that he had used as a wine merchant – and hardly less as a writer – Wheatley costed the paintings at about 25/– each including air freight (about £15 today). Selling them at Bond Street values therefore promised substantial profits, and the main expense was framing them to a standard in keeping with the prices.

Wheatley wanted about eighty pictures, and he was prepared to commission them on a fully entrepreneurial basis ("For your guidance we do not want any more blue landscapes and prefer landscapes in natural colours. We particularly like his flower paintings and undersea scenes"). Wheatley foresaw that after the publicity gained by the show, American and other dealers would try to buy Maya's work up "at its present absurdly low price" in order to make a profit out of him, and suggested a protective contract, which could be drawn up by his friend Ronald Knox-Mawer, Chief Justice of Fiji, whereby "from May 1967 no more of his paintings should be offered for sale except to me, for a period to be agreed."

The show went ahead in June 1967, with Wheatley making no money from it but sending the profits to the nuns, to be divided between the St. Elizabeth's Home and Maya himself. It may not have sold as well as he hoped, because he originally envisaged another show the following year, which never happened. Wheatley had a strong sense of publicity and human interest journalism, but he was a stranger to the fine art world, and the leprosy angle was not part of it.

The show at least raised Maya's profile, and his work was later featured on Fijian stamps. At the end of his life Wheatley owned more pictures by Maya – possibly unsold stock – than any other artist, his nearest competitor being the English genre painter Birket Foster.

★

Wheatley was now seventy, and the world around him had changed. Even in his fiction, Richard Eaton's little daughter

Fleur, who so narrowly escaped being sacrificed in *The Devil Rides Out*, had grown up to become "a product of her age and the University of London . . . a red-hot Socialist [who] believes passionately in all the 'freedoms' including that of sex."

Young men had long hair, and girls were wearing miniskirts from Mary Quant; these had come in simultaneously with "the Pill", which had become almost as famous an entity as "the Bomb". Posters of Wheatley's old *bête noir* Lord Kitchener were appearing, and the Kings Road was full of young men who might wear sergeant's stripes as patches on their flared jeans, or guardsman's tunics from groovy boutiques like 'I Was Lord Kitchener's Valet'.

It was The Summer of Love. The prime cultural mover was recreational drug-taking by middle-class youth, and the 'psychedelic' aesthetics of the period were shaped by cannabis and particularly LSD. There was a new interest in the irrational, whether in the form of madness or mysticism, and people were reading Herman Hesse and Tolkien, along with the I Ching and the Tibetan Book of the Dead. Eastern religion was big, along with joss sticks, astrology, and tarot cards; and suddenly so was the occult, in a widespread revival that is sometimes referred to as "the occult explosion".

The 'underground' hippy paper, the *International Times*, ran a major feature on Aleister Crowley. By the end of his lifetime Crowley had become something of a joke, but now no one was laughing. The 1967 Beatles' album, *Sergeant Pepper's Lonely Heart Club Band*, featured Crowley on the cover in its Peter Blake collage of 'people we like'. Pink Floyd's equally trippy and lysergic album of the same year, *The Piper at The Gates of Dawn*, took its name from the strange episode with the god Pan in Kenneth Grahame's *The Wind in the Willows*: a bit of belated Edwardian paganism, like Wheatley's bookplate. As for the Rolling Stones, their album for 1967 was *Their Satanic Majesties Request*.

And so it went on for several years: Led Zeppelin's Jimmy Page would become a serious Crowley collector, even buying his old house at Boleskine in Scotland. Another, more downmarket, heavy metal band appeared in 1969 with the name of Black Sabbath, and profiles of the band often claimed this was from a Wheatley novel title (which is not true; it is from a Mario Bava horror film).

There was a darker side to the occult revival, and increasingly to the Sixties themselves, with acid casualties, Altamont, and the Charles Manson killings. Wheatley collector and bibliographer Richard Humphreys was a teenager, reading Wheatley's *The Satanist*, when he heard on his transistor radio that Sharon Tate had been murdered. Asked for his opinion on the mystery slayings by the British press, Wheatley said there was probably an occult angle.

By the standards of the day's youth, Wheatley in person would have been a Churchillian dinosaur, although they might have admired his dragon dressing gown and his smoking jacket. But now his black magic writing took on a new and seemingly contemporary lease of life, as his dated and jingoistic fictions were buoyed up and carried along on the occult wave.

The Devil Redux

Wheatley and Christopher Lee had become friends since that first meeting in Harrods, and it was Lee who urged Wheatley's books on Hammer producer Anthony Hinds. Hinds loathed Wheatley's work, but he saw its potential, and in due course *The Devil Rides Out* became Hammer's greatest film.

It was directed by Terence Fisher, who was completely in tune with Wheatley's vision: Fisher's work has been described as embodying a strictly dualistic universe, split between Good and Evil, Light and Dark, Spirit and Matter, and expressed in images of "bourgeois splendour" versus "decay and death".

Satanism was a taboo subject for the cinema of the time, sailing too close to blasphemy[1]. In the event, no one need have worried; *The Devil Rides Out* is a highly moral tale, where light and darkness battle and the forces of light win. After the film was made, a Catholic bishop came up to Lee on the street near Cadogan Square and told him he and his "flock" had been much impressed, because "in the end . . . Evil is vanquished and Good triumphs."

The first screenplay, by John Hunter, was rejected as too English, and Hinds then commissioned another from Richard Matheson. Matheson stayed close to Wheatley's plot, and his work largely consisted of streamlining. The political and historical situation in the book is lost, with no Talisman of Set and no risk of world war. Simon is no longer Jewish, and it is a cross, not a swastika, that is placed around his neck to protect him before it is removed and he escapes again towards Mocata, making the incident closer to the

---

[1] For that reason the screenplay specifies, with reference to the Satanic chapel, "N.B. The decoration should not contain any inversion or parody of Christianity" [screenplay p.110].

Dracula scene which was probably its inspiration in the first place.

Mocata is no longer half-Irish and half-French; instead he is a menacing pinstriped English gentleman with a carnation in his buttonhole, magnificently played by Charles Gray, who had read Wheatley's books when young. Gray is also well known as the Bond villain Blofeld, and the voice of *The Rocky Horror Show*, but he never did anything better than play the urbanely evil Mocata.

The drama unfolds in a strangely abstracted mid-century England, a dreamlike place where vintage cars chase each other along endless back-projected country roads with not a modern house in sight. Whether we are being shown the astrological observatory at Simon's house, or the occult siege at Cardinal's Folly (a half-timbered house in true Hammer style, with two sphinxes flanking the front door), we are doubly cocooned in the magic of Wheatley and Hammer together. The film has deservedly classic status, not least for "a kind of mythical luminosity, that, with the period styling of the film, makes it distinctly other-worldly."

Wheatley was pleased when he saw the film and sent Terence Fisher a telegram: "Saw film yesterday. Heartiest congratulations, grateful thanks for splendid direction."

Christopher Lee entered thoroughly into the character of the Duke. Just as he says in the film (after they find a magical grimoire, *The Clavicle of Solomon*, in a cupboard) "It is vital that I should go to the British Museum and examine certain occult volumes that are kept under constant lock and key", so in real life Lee claimed to have gone to the British Museum Library and found the supposedly real lines of the Susamma ritual, to be added to the script at the end. "It's a ritual against the forces of darkness", he told an interviewer; "it really exists."

Lee also came up with the "even today . . . in major cities"-style lines familiar from Wheatley blurbs. "Satanism is rampant in London today", he said. "It's generally acknowledged in certain circles that the so-called swinging city is a hotbed of Devil worship and such practices – just ask the police . . ."

And he was right, up to a point: it was more rampant than it had been, although this may not have been saying much. Somehow, a book that had begun life as a Thirties Appeasement novel had bounced back and hit the zeitgeist once again.

★

Simultaneously with *The Devil Rides Out*, Hammer were also filming *The Lost Continent*, an amiably awful adaptation of Wheatley's *Uncharted Seas*, and when Dennis and Joan visited Hammer they looked over both productions on the same day: *The Devil Rides Out* was just winding up six weeks of interior shooting, before two weeks of ritual orgy scenes to be shot on location in Hampshire. As for *The Lost Continent*, the ethnic aspects were happily gone, and the film relied instead on giant crabs, Dana Gillespie's cleavage, and the occasional in-joke, like a passenger reading Wheatley's *Uncharted Seas*.

"One of the great cornball pictures of the decade", said an American review:

> Assortment of typically neurotic Britons on ship destined for . . . where? Hokier by the reel until the splendidly frenetic climax mixing sea of lost ships, degenerate lost race, superbly constructed monster crustaceans, explosions, bosoms, and more, more!

★

Wheatley was concerned with another film around this time, far closer to his heart. A friend's film company had come up with the innovative idea of "living portraits", and Wheatley was making a 'Living Portrait' of himself: a private documentary celebration of his life to be shown to his descendants after he was gone.

Wheatley drafted his own filmscript, which began with a painting of himself at his desk. The camera then dissolves into the same scene, with Wheatley at his desk in his writing clothes. "Here's a health to you all," he says, raising his glass: "May you drink as much fine wine in your lives as I have. My friend Jack de Manio is going to ask me a lot of questions. I'll do my best to answer."

The screenplay then runs through an interview account of Wheatley's life, entirely scripted by Wheatley. Wheatley shows us his brickwork, "the trees which give me the cherries to make my Cherry Brandy", and Joan's needlework ("Joan is a wonderful needle-woman. She worked all the chairs – a million and a quarter stitches").

The magic of cinema whisks us up to Cadogan Square and then to Grove Place again ("Let's go back there"), where Wheatley shows us over his possessions ("Shot of three big stamp albums" says the screenplay; "Open at a page showing G.B."). "You must have made a lot of money," says de Manio. "I have", says Wheatley, "but I contribute up to 18/- in the £ to the Welfare State".

Over at Hutchinson, Bob Lusty and his marketing director confirm just how successful Wheatley is: "Dennis is probably the only living author who has everything he has written still in print. We keep over a million Wheatley books available."

Finally de Manio asks Wheatley if he is afraid of death. "Not in the least", he says, "you see, I believe in Reincarnation." He explains that according to the happiness we give others in this life, so we will be given happiness ourselves in the next. The clincher for Wheatley, the reason why reincarnation must be true, is that if it wasn't (with so many people "born cripples, or brought up in poverty by criminal parents"), then things just wouldn't be *fair*. Old-fashioned Englishman that he was, raised on the *Chums Annual*, it doesn't seem to have occurred to him that perhaps life isn't fair.

So death is no bad thing: it is "the greatest adventure of all", and it means being re-united with old friends. "Here's to it!", says Wheatley, and they drink to death from their goblets of champagne.

*

The finished film, without Jack de Manio, differs from Wheatley's original screenplay, but it is still a spirited performance. The beginning is distinctly 'cinematic,' in a period way: there is an opening shot of a red curtain with 'Dennis Wheatley' on it, and some very dated music; the whole effect is really quite Pearl and Dean.

We see a fine Georgian house with old wisteria, and then under the house we are shown a cellar filled with thousands of bottles of wine, some of them from the nineteenth century or earlier. There are bottles of old Chartreuse, Napoleon brandy, and Imperial Tokay. Some of the bottles are in a wire-doored cabinet, where the camera zooms in slowly and emphatically on the padlock.

Wheatley shows us some favourite possessions including the Chinese Goddess Kwan-Yin ("Queen of Heaven – isn't she lovely?"), and gives us a view of the stars on his bedroom ceiling, in real constellations and correctly orientated. He cut them out of gold paper and stuck them on himself, he tells us, so he could lie on the bed and look at them. In the bathroom we see his fish on the walls ("I cut all these fish out of illustrated books and stuck them on myself").

"Incidentally", Wheatley says at one point, "we have every form of burglar alarm. What is more, I keep a shotgun in my bedroom and I wouldn't hesitate to use it." It sounds oddly like a warning; an unintentionally comic touch, given that the film was primarily made for his family[2].

Wheatley introduces two "friends" to the camera, Blatch and Lusty, and they assure us of his success, with a million books in stock and 25 million copies sold to date. Wheatley explains that if you put a rope between the earth and the moon, you could have a Wheatley book every fifty feet.

Finally Dennis and Joan are seen walking back in through their imposing gates, with which the film ends. Where the first screenplay ended on a toast to death, the finished film seems to close on a celebration of private property.

★

[2] One of Wheatley's grandchildren quoted this scene from memory as "and if any of you watching have been looking at my nice china and nice glass, and you're thinking of coming round to rob me, let me just say that I sleep with a loaded revolver under the pillow and I'm prepared to use it."

Wheatley had finished his last Gregory Sallust, *The White Witch of the South Seas*, and was now slogging away with his new Roger Brook. In an effort to keep up with the permissive modern world, this was entitled 'Enter The Nymphomaniac'.

In December the Wheatleys set off on another world trip, for Rio, Buenos Aires, Santiago de Chile, Mexico City, Fiji, Tonga, Samoa, Noumea, Penang, and Delhi. On the first of March 1968 they returned home, but things were no longer going so smoothly at Grove Place.

The Wheatleys were dependent on their cook-cum-housekeeper, Mrs Betty Pigache, who lived in the servants' quarters at Grove with her husband, Captain Georges Pigache. These were no ordinary servants: Captain Georges had once had a 'set' in Albany, the gentleman's apartment complex on Piccadilly where other residents had included Graham Greene, Lord Byron, and Terence Stamp. His family had owned the Café Royal, his gourmand father Georges having married the founder's daughter. Georges Senior paid a heavy price for his gourmandising, weighing thirty-six stone and dying suddenly at the age of 47.

Despite his extensive knowledge of cooking, Captain Georges did no work for the Wheatleys, spending much of his time in local public houses. In 1968, however, with the pair of them getting old, he decided it was time to retire to a council house, taking Betty with him. This was a blow, because the Wheatleys couldn't find a couple they liked to replace the Pigaches. To make matters worse, their gardener was also coming up for retirement. The writing was now on the wall for Grove Place. The servant problem had done for it.

As a local celebrity and a market gardener (he had a special letterhead for this, with a picture of Grove and the words 'FRUIT, FLOWERS, VEGETABLES & HERBS'), Wheatley was the President of the New Forest Agricultural Show in July 1968, which was to be his last summer at Lymington.

Attractions included showjumping, a dog show, beekeeping displays and competitions, the Women's Institute, rabbits, woodmen's competitions, clay pigeon shooting, stalls from businesses, banks and charities, horticultural and floral displays, rural industries, the New Forest Hounds, and the Band of the Coldstream Guards. The committee had felt that they couldn't afford a band, so Wheatley offered to meet the cost himself. Locally, the show might be felt to represent a fair slice of "everything decent in life".

Wheatley threw himself into being President with characteristic vigour and sense of duty, hosting a large luncheon party in his President's Tent. Dennis and Joan went around on separate schedules of viewings and judgings, then came the presentation of seventy-odd prize cups, and the President's Tea for several hundred people, until around 6.30 Joan drove them both home. Now in their seventies and in indifferent health – Joan's was starting to go first – they must have been tired by the end of it all, if buoyed up by a sense of *noblesse oblige*. The Show Secretary, Air Commodore Geoffrey Le Dieu, wrote to Wheatley to say that despite bad weather, "I felt that this year . . . there was nevertheless a happier and more cheerful atmosphere at the Show among exhibitors, helpers and visitors alike, which extended from the President down."

Already, before the show, the Wheatleys had decided to sell Grove Place. The flat upstairs at Cadogan Square became vacant and Wheatley (or rather 'Dennis Wheatley Ltd.') was able to take on the remainder of the lease and put the two flats together. It was a considerable upheaval, and Wheatley had to superintend the whole move by coming up to London twice a week throughout the autumn, moving four thousand books and three thousand bottles of wine. Wheatley also took the opportunity to sell some of his wine at Christie's, including some seventeenth-century Imperial Tokay.

The Wheatleys auctioned their surplus effects from Grove Place in October 1968, with an auctioneer in a marquee on the lawn. The sale was well publicised, the viewing was thronged, and they took over £11,000 on their discarded items. They were less lucky with the house itself, which was a difficult size to sell in those days. It wasn't quite large enough to be used as a school or hotel, but almost too large to live in as a private house. It was put up for auction with an estimate of £40,000

"Black Magic is Dennis Wheatley": a trade advert from 1969.

"Now — if you dare": the Heron Library advert, early 1970s.

567

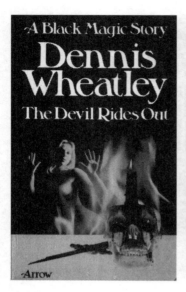

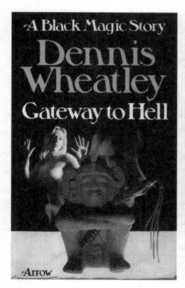
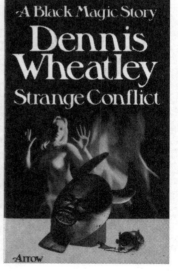

Arrow paperbacks, early 1970s.

and a reserve of £30,000, but failed to sell at £28,000. A few days later Wheatley accepted an offer of £29,000.

Wheatley thought that the new owner intended to live at Grove Place with his family, and hoped that it might be preserved as "a perfect example of a small Georgian Manor House." But this was not the plan, which seems to have included leaving the doors and windows open throughout the winter to hasten the decay of the property.

Grove Place was demolished, and where a Georgian house had once stood, a housing estate in vaguely Georgian style came to replace it. Grove Place is now the name of a road, not a house, comprising twenty-odd terraced dwellings. It is certainly a more utilitarian arrangement. Some of Wheatley's amateur brickwork still survives.

★

Hutchinson had to have a word with Wheatley about the title of 'Enter The Nymphomaniac', and in due course it appeared as *Evil In A Mask* (1969). Meanwhile *The White Witch of the South Seas* appeared in 1968, incorporating an expanded account of Wheatley's voodoo ceremony into its opening. Gregory Sallust and some friends attend a *macumba* gathering outside Rio, in the company of a police officer, who insists the women in the party should leave their jewellery at home. They drive out in two cars, until they meet a long line of parked cars by the forest. They then go up a wooden walkway decorated with chicken heads, and so it continues until the ceremony is rained off.

Things then take a more menacing fictional turn, as the old Macumba priest stares at Gregory. His son then explains "He much opset. He believe yo' an' yo' friends who come with Police enemies of him an' make bad magic that bring rain."

They manage to reassure the old man that this is not so, and the old man goes on to warn Gregory that a "White Witch" will come into his life, and that he must kill her when he has the chance. As for the future, the son translates further: "My father, he say yo' have no vision to tell. Sometimes he have

569

visions. Jus' now, when he come in this room, he have one. He see yo' this time tomorrow night as dead – dead in a ditch."

★

Black people had been an all-too reliable source of menace in Wheatley's work almost from the start, including the "bad black" servant in *The Devil Rides Out*, and the ethnic conflict in *Uncharted Seas*. In *Strange Conflict*, despite some intelligent and kindly black walk-on parts, Haitian Voodoo and the Third Reich were in league, and Chapter V of *Curtain of Fear* is appropriately entitled 'The Persistent Negro', featuring a razor-wielding thug. He does seem to be persistent throughout Wheatley's writing.

The association between black people and evil runs deep in Wheatley's work, ultimately going beyond the obvious 'racism' of the period, and even beyond period ideas of primitive sexuality, to a more radical conflation of ethnic blackness and visual darkness, within Wheatley's Manichaean and Gnostic split between light and dark. Real life, meanwhile, is never as black and white as Wheatley's fictions, but shot through with contradictions and paradoxes, and Wheatley's favourite writer and main model, Alexander Dumas *père*, was black.

Roger Brook is enraged in *Evil In a Mask* when his wife (the incarnate "Evil" and formerly "Nymphomaniac" of the title) gives birth to a black child. His anger, says one academic commentator, "is attributable to the revealed adultery rather than to any horror of miscegenation". Well, *up to a point*. But it is an explanation that might be more appropriate if it was about an event in life, not an event in a fictional narrative, where the author is responsible for all circumstances.

In fact, in the late Sixties, blackness in the ethnic sense seems to have been on Wheatley's mind, and fears of ethnic conflict form the subject of his last great occult novel, *Gateway to Hell*.

570

Rivers of Blood

Wheatley had never been afraid of formula, or even self parody, and *Gateway to Hell* is a late serving of almost classic Wheatley. It opens with Simon Aron having the Duke de Richleau and Richard Eaton round to dinner, where he is giving them smoked cod roe on toast, with a glass of very old Madeira; lobster bisque fortified with sherry, with a 1933 Marco-brunner Kabinett; partridge with *foie gras*, with a 1928 Chateau Latour; and finally a fruit salad of iced oranges laced with *crême de menthe*. Having then refreshed their palates with a small cup of cold China tea, they can move on to a bottle of 1908 Imperial Tokay and some Hoyo de Monterrey cigars.

They have something serious to talk about after dinner, because one of the little band is not present. He is in trouble. In *The Devil Rides Out* it was Simon Aron, and this time it is Rex Van Ryn, who seems to have embezzled a million dollars and fled to South America. The other three will have to help him.

★

As we have seen, most of Wheatley's occult novels had a propagandist engagement with contemporary crises. Now, after World War, Communism, and Trade Unions, Wheatley's new worry was Black Power, and the spectre of worldwide race war.

America's ethnic situation was worsening in the late Sixties. The early advances of the civil rights movement had ended what was effectively American apartheid, but Martin Luther King was shot in 1968. In the same year Julius Lester published *Look Out Whitey, Black Power's Gon' Get Your Mama!* and J.Edgar Hoover – roughly the same age as Wheatley, still going strong from the Thirties – declared the

Black Panthers to be "the greatest threat to the internal security of the country."

The Black Panthers were very different from the old civil rights movement. They were emphatically gun-toting, insisting on firearms as a civil right, they circulated *Quotations from Chairman Mao* in the ghettos, and they appointed each other to ranks such as Minister of Defence and Field Marshal. Their influence probably peaked in 1968 at Berkeley. Shortly afterwards they tortured and murdered one of their own members, and their days were numbered.

The Panthers were lionised by white liberals, as Tom Wolfe records in his essay, *Radical Chic*. In Britain it was none other than Wheatley's own publisher, Hutchinson, who published Bobby Seale's *Seize The Time: The Story of the Black Panther Party and Huey P. Newton* in 1970, with its dedicatory paean to "Huey P. Newton, Minister of Defense of the Black Panther Party, the baddest motherfucker in history."

Wheatley was far from keen on bad motherfuckers, so it was ironic that money he had made should have been pledged to the Panthers in 1972. The Booker Group, sponsors of the Booker Prize, had acquired a profitable share in Wheatley's copyrights, so without particularly wishing to, Wheatley was now helping to fund Booker's prize money and their support of more literary and respectable writers than himself. In 1972, John Berger was given the Booker Prize, and he used the award ceremony as an opportunity to denounce Booker and declare that he was giving the money to the Panthers.

The Panthers were anti-Semitic, and many people felt that despite their naivety they were essentially black fascists. This was what Wheatley felt. The Third Reich was now his touchstone of evil, suitable for smearing everyone from Communists to the Biblical Moses (who Wheatley said would have made a good "SS Gruppenfuhrer", because he killed three thousand pagan worshippers of the Golden Calf). In *Gateway to Hell* he puts Black Power activist Lincoln B. Glasshill in league with old S.S. Gruppenfuhrer Baron Von Thumm.

Gateway to Hell has some nicely characteristic touches. The Duke explains that his beliefs are unshakeable, because they are based on "the Eternal Verities". The travelogue aspect is very strong, with a vivid account of Argentina, where Wheatley had been the previous year. When the friends are besieged inside a magic circle, *Devil Rides Out* style, they are tempted by the apparition of food: it is the old *maitre d'* from the Savoy Grill, no less, who offers them Canard Montmorency, a brace of beccassines, and an Omelette Arnold Bennett. And where Marie-Lou had to endure the apparition of her daughter being menaced by a slug-like Thing in *The Devil Rides Out*, here Richard Eaton has to endure the apparition of Marie-Lou herself being chased by a naked Lincoln B.Glasshill.

Just as Wheatley was at pains to seem fair to ordinary union members in *The Satanist*, in *Gateway to Hell* he is careful to show ordinary black people growing disenchanted with the racial animosity that the Satanists are bringing about. Wheatley had to set *Gateway* back in 1953, because the Duke was getting implausibly old, so the dangers of ethnic conflict are projected forwards:

> By the sixties, there will develop a sort of sporadic civil war in the United States, and by the seventies it will have spread to Europe. There will be bloody street battles, arson, murder, the lot. Nothing could be better calculated to destroy civilisation. Law and order will go by the board. . .

Von Thumm plays the Goat of Mendes at the Satanic orgy, dressed up in goat skin but recognisable by his lopsided walk from an old war wound, and Wheatley manages a contemporary hint with another participant "clad as a black panther".

At the end, the day is saved by the selflessness of former Thirties actress, Silvia Singiest, who jumps into the mouth of Hell and brings divine vengeance on the Satanists. Wheatley gives us a physical gateway to the Underworld located in the

South American jungle, pulsating like a thick membrane and opening after the chief Satanist pronounces the words "Zazas, Zazas, Nasatanada, Zazas!"; a real formula, which traditionally opens the Abyss. The book's occult aspects are gloriously hokey even by Wheatley standards, but the membrane covering a pit full of Hieronymus Bosch creatures is a new innovation.

The Devil has also changed since Wheatley's earlier work: in *The Devil Rides Out*, the Duke is quite clear about the fact that there is no such entity as a personal devil, and Tanith adds that he is just a bogeyman invented by the early Church. In *To The Devil – A Daughter*, however, the Devil arrives in person, although Wheatley wisely refrains from trying to describe him visually: his heroes have their backs turned when he manifests. And in *Gateway to Hell* the Duke now seems closer to believing in a literal Archfiend.

*

Following the success of *The Devil Rides Out*, Wheatley wrote to a Hammer executive whom he had met at one of Christopher Lee's cocktail parties with a proposition. They were already considering *Toby Jugg*, but Wheatley instead urged them to think of *The Forbidden Territory*. He was, in other words, still keen to be associated with something more than the occult, but that was now his identity. It was even helping him to break into the American market at last: Bantam published six titles in 1969, and an American advert promoted Wheatley as coming "from England, the home of witches and black masses."

The occult revival was still going strong, if gradually downmarket; even the New English Library (publishers of Richard Allen's 'Skinhead' series, and other youth exploitation titles) had launched a line of occult books. Montague Summer's edition of the *Malleus Malleficarum*, the turgid witch-hunter's manual from 1486, was improbably re-issued as a popular paperback in 1971, with an introduction by Wheatley.

Historian Ronald Hutton remembers delinquent youths

counterfeiting devil worship, lighting bonfires, stringing up dead animals, and leaving inverted crosses to mystify and frighten, while among his own adolescent peer group, "Dennis Wheatley's novels were eagerly read and despoiled of ideas and images to liven up parties with risqué imagery. For my generation of Essex teenagers, they represented the essential primer in diabolism. . ."

A fifteen-year-old girl, Jacqueline Batters, was even reported in the Press as doing a black magic O level, "swotting up witchcraft, voodoo and naked sacrifices" (less sensationistically, it was her special project in a General Studies GCE). "I got the idea from Dennis Wheatley novels," she said. Wheatley had become Britain's occult uncle.

★

"Wheatley has been grappling with the Devil for over thirty years now," David Blundy told *Observer* readers, "and frankly, the Devil's been pretty decent about it." Noting that Wheatley lived "in some splendour" in Chelsea, Blundy added that although he refused to dabble, "he's invited to all the best orgies and Black Masses in town." He was invited to lecture on black magic to clergymen of the Church of England, a body which had recently begun to take demonic possession seriously again, after its disappearance for a couple of hundred rational years. Wheatley also advised the British Board of Film Censors on witchcraft films, attending a private screening in the company of a psychiatrist, and he was even on the Simon Dee Show – a chat show which began with Dee leaping out of his E-type Jaguar – in the company of witchcraft revivalist Alex Sanders and Vincent Price.

Wheatley's strangest experience with television came in January 1970, when he took part in a programme with a clairvoyant, a palmist, a psychometrist, and an astrologer. Wheatley was masked, and known only as "Mr.Smith", while the four of them were set to discover as much as they could about him by supernatural means.

The palmist got off to a remarkable start: "He is attracted towards the occult and towards psychic subjects", she said.

"In the past I think there may have been some connection with liquids —" there was a momentary hesitation here, perhaps for greater realism — "wines." It is hard not to feel she knew who he was; his wine trade background was mentioned on his book jackets. The psychometrist, working just from a pair of Wheatley's braces, deduced that he was creative in some way, had travelled, and either did live or had lived in the country; all fairly probable for a man of Mr Smith's age and celebrity status.

With the aid of a crystal ball, the clairvoyant deduced that Smith was creative and involved in some way with the occult. He aimed most of his remarks at Smith's future, so unfortunately they were hard to verify. The astrologer, however, deduced that Smith was a "success", as many celebrities are, and then probed deeper with "emotional deprivation as a child, perhaps separated from his parents."

Mr.Smith didn't like the suggestion of emotional deprivation. Separation from his parents, however, was a fairly safe suggestion, because a man of his age and class would probably have been to boarding school, and Smith agreed that at the age of eight he had indeed been sent away. More than that, he volunteered that "I was terrified of my father". What Wheatley was undergoing, in fact, were variations on the 'cold reading' techniques he had experienced all those years ago with Dewhirst.

Wheatley was particularly impressed by the man who suggested he had something wrong with his leg. That was indeed a remarkable finding, unless they divined a slight limp. "The invisible influences are there", Wheatley said dutifully at the end of the show.

There was a postscript to this performance after Quentin Crewe wrote it up in his newspaper column, and asked readers to judge who Smith might be. The overwhelming majority guessed it was Wheatley. Others guessed it might be Ian Fleming, Randolph Churchill, Somerset Maugham, Evelyn Waugh, or Arthur Conan Doyle, all of whom were dead; dead for many years, in Doyle's case. Among living candidates, the most popular wrong answer was the now notorious Lord Boothby, in those days a genial national figure.

There was already a touch of affectionate humour attached to Wheatley's occult image. "I dreamt of this contest months ago and the answer is Dennis Wheatley", wrote one reader, while another declared "Having met Dennis Wheatley often on the Astral Plane I feel certain it is him."

★

Wheatley had done a great deal to create the taste by which he was appreciated, and by this time his expertise on the occult was more than matched by his influence on it. He had infused the idea of occultism with something of his own snobbery and connoisseurship, and the romance of social class. "What really happens 'after the Ball is over' at leading country houses?" asked the blurb of June Johns's 1971 New English Library book, *Black Magic Today*.

Interviewed in *Man Myth and Magic* (available from the newsagent every Thursday in 112 weekly instalments, and itself a remarkable document of the era), a man claims to remember that one evening on the Essex coast, some years earlier, he saw about half a dozen "large and expensive cars" – this suddenly sounds familiar[1] – and traced their destination next day. Rolls-Royces and Bentleys had been driven to the ruins of a house on the edge of town, where traces of incense, black candles, and bloody feathers remained. Before long he and his wife are drawn in, encountering a goat, orgiastic practices, and good financial luck following initiation, followed by a run of bad luck on leaving the group. "I would certainly join Mr Wheatley in his wholesale condemnation of the darker side of black magic", he concludes.

---

[1] *The Devil Rides* Out featured a blue Rolls, a green Daimler, and a silver Hispano-Suiza, and other classic cars figured in the background, notably the convoy parked at the Sabbat. Earlier, when Rex asks the Duke de Richleau if he can borrow his car, the Duke answers offhandedly: "Yes, take any of them". ("One of my favourite lines," says Christopher Lee: "I laugh every time I see that.")

Sandra Shulman's 1970 novel *The Degenerates* ("The sensational novel that exposes the evil of Satanism in Britain today", and another New English Library title) reads almost like the work of the master himself, although it is better written. In the midst of swinging London we meet an evil cult whose members include the rich and influential. Young ingenue Jenny is taken by her boyfriend to an extremely select party ("like one of those exclusive clubs – White's or the Athenaeum"). A butler lets them into a Georgian house, where she is wide-eyed at the carpets, tapestries, silver and china, "even the wall of leather-bound books . . . suggested another unknown world. This, she understood with dismay, was real class."

Incense drifts up from four gilded burners, and there are lobsters, caviar, Veuve Clicquot, and *foie gras*. The thirteen people present, including a bulbous-headed dwarf and a Black Power leader, have *Devil Rides Out*-style occult pseudonyms such as Dame Alice (as in Dame Alice Kyteler, the witch) and Gilles, as in Gilles de Rais. And so it goes on, with obscene murals and young Jenny ritually raped ("they will hold you down until your initiation is accomplished"), while between the horns of a gigantic goat-headed effigy, a black candle is burning.

It is a "rare sideshow of depravity", but these people are not just any old degenerates ("Maxted and Mireille argued about the true value of a Chinese grey jade figurine which had recently been auctioned at Sothebys"). The male protagonist, David, recognises the ambience at once from his reading: "He had whiled away hours . . . in the company of too many Wheatley characters not to recognise the Satanic set-up."

Quite.

★

Anthony Lejeune remembers seeing Wheatley in Pratt's Club with the publisher George Rainbird, when the two of them were in exceptionally high spirits: they had just come up with a name for an occult compendium by Wheatley,

"The Devil and All His Works", and they knew that with such a title it couldn't fail.

It is not altogether clear what the title has to do with the book, which is largely a tour of the world's religions. Satanism only comes in at the end. Wheatley tries to explain the title at the beginning of Part Three, and soon drifts into a spiel about the powers of light and darkness. Occasionally shaky in its scholarship, *The Devil and All His Works* is still an engaging study with plenty of interest and even a certain spiritual dignity, as when Wheatley stresses that serious yoga is good but spiritually pointless fakirism is bad, an instance of "that spirit of negation against which, throughout this book, I speak as clearly as I can."

The Devil and All His Works was attractively illustrated and it hit the mood of the day, selling around 60,000 copies: 'Suddenly the Devil is the new thing' was the very contemporary headline for the *Evening Standard* review of the book. But despite its welcome effect on his sales, Wheatley disliked the occult revival. Asked for his opinion in the final issue of *Man, Myth and Magic*, he said

> There seems no doubt that increasing numbers of people are turning haphazardly to occultism, and I think it's a very bad thing. People tend to become so interested in the subject and get so involved with it that they neglect their families and jobs, and if at all weak-minded are liable to end up in the asylum.

Wheatley produced similar 'lines' whenever the subject arose: risk of blackmail, drugs, possibility of mental illness, neglect of work and family, remote but real possibility of supernatural evil, and so on. He now felt that the Witchcraft laws, the last of which had only been repealed in 1951, should be reintroduced. As *Man Myth and Magic* astutely noted, with his condemnation of occultism and his warnings not to dabble, "Wheatley . . . can almost be said to have taken on the cloak of the late Montague Summers."

"To go out alone at night is to invite a hold-up and a

bashing," Wheatley wrote in *The Devil and All His Works*, and his misgivings about occultism were bound up with a larger cultural pessimism. The late Sixties and early Seventies was not a good time for people of Wheatley's generation and outlook, with the loss of Empire, labour agitation, student revolt, Vietnam protests and race riots in America, and the rise of youth culture as an economic force (records bought by children – "pop music" – were suddenly at the cultural centre stage, taking up prime-time television). There was the permissive society, with drugs, 'free love', hippies, and the rest, and at a more proletarian level there was a massive perceived increase in crime and vandalism, along with a culture of violence ("aggro" and "bovver") and subcultures of skinheads and Hell's Angels, the latter having a Satanic inflection.

American feminists organised themselves into WITCH, The Women's International Terrorist Conspiracy from Hell, while – as if trying to confirm Wheatley's worst fears – an occult groupuscule in New York called Demonic Proletariat circulated a bizarre grimoire consisting of magical diagrams and revolutionary slogans. Arthur Lyons documentary study *Satan Wants You: The Cult of Devil Worship* (1970) had no shortage of contemporary examples, and that autumn – with a band called Black Sabbath topping the British album charts and a record called Voodoo Chile topping the singles charts – Charles Manson was removed from a courtroom after singing the Sinatra song, "That Old Black Magic", at the judge.

The house of the British Home Secretary was bombed by the Angry Brigade, the Schoolkids Issue of *Oz* magazine featured Rupert the Bear having sex with his grandmother, and 100,000 Trade Unionists took to the streets over the Industrial Relations Bill. This was the world Wheatley complained about in a radio interview with William Hardcastle.

"The Power of Darkness is now threatening to come out on top," says Wheatley: "The violence and that sort of thing that's going on today are unbelievable . . . And the government are not controlling it, they've just got to take a line."

Hardcastle challenges Wheatley's discussion of "light and dark, right and left, good and evil" – is it really all so eternally simple? "Warring powers" agrees Wheatley enthusiastically, ignoring Hardcastle's scepticism and responding as if he has just put the whole business in a nutshell.

Wheatley claims there are three hundred covens operating in Britain, and that their numbers are increasing every day. Hardcastle asks if Wheatley isn't actually "stimulating the curiosity that is feeding this evil" and Wheatley denies it: he is warning people. "Aren't you afraid they'll have a go at you?" asks Hardcastle, with ridicule faintly audible in his voice. No, says Wheatley, in a tone of quite dignified sincerity, because they can only harm people who are afraid, and who believe they can be harmed.

> DW: "I don't say that I'm a particularly good person but I believe I'm on the right side, and the Powers of Light will protect me."
> WH: "But you think the Powers of Darkness are taking us over?"
> DW: "I think that civilisation is disintegrating, unless somebody takes a pull, things are getting worse and worse every year . . ."

This was the message at the end of *The Devil and All His Works*. "During the past decade, human behaviour has entered a new phase. It is termed the permissive society." Wheatley was not unsympathetic to this, pointing out that long hair and short skirts didn't mean men were effeminate or women immoral, but he did think – particularly with the disappearance of authority and the shadow of the nuclear threat – that the young had now turned to occultism as a "crutch".

This brought him to its evil side, with reference to the Charles Manson case, and the newly prominent Church of Satan headed by Anton La Vey, which claimed seven thousand members. And this brought him to modern society, which was in danger of returning "to the Dark Ages." Just as the original Dark Ages had come in with the end of the Roman Empire and the Pax Romana, so now the British Empire and the Pax Britannica had ended. "What was the cost of hauling down the Union Jack?" asks Wheatley, pointing to the state of Africa, where the British had built roads and schools. Now it was as if the adults had "locked themselves out of the kindergarten while leaving the children to play with loaded firearms."

Things were not much better in the First World. "Robbery with violence is rife and is increasing all over the United States. In Washington DC, not only white families but also well-to-do coloured ones have been moving out into the suburbs because it is no longer safe to live in the city." Malcontents were smashing embassy windows (Wheatley may have been thinking of the Grosvenor Square riots), ruining sports grounds (a tactic of anti-apartheid campaigners), and altogether committing "outrages which no proper government would tolerate." This was the lesson of the great empires, fulminated Wheatley: "*rulers should rule*, and for the past two decades the governments of the Western world have failed to do so."

Wheatley was not alone in thinking this – we shall encounter some more people with the same opinion in the next chapter – but the particular spin he gave it was his own: "Is it possible that riots, wildcat strikes, anti-apartheid demonstrations and the appalling increase in crime have any connection with magic and Satanism?"

★

Back at the start of the Sixties, a letter had arrived from a fan in Sweden, Iwan Hedman. He wrote again to Wheatley's reply, and Wheatley had to tell him that because he received so many letters, he was unable to enter into protracted correspondence with any one fan. Hedman was not to be put off so easily. He wrote yet again, and eventually succeeded in befriending Wheatley by sheer perseverance.

Hedman had continued to write to Wheatley, and whereas more respectable writers received questions about their work from importunate PhD students and dissertation writers, Wheatley was the object of some close study by his Swedish fans, notably Hedman, Jan Alexandersson and Lars Nylander. Hedman had written a bibliography of Wheatley, and over the years Wheatley had continued to answer questions and bat back correspondence as best he could ("you must forgive me if I don't answer your letters fully and regularly. I have an enormous mail"), and to cope with the mixed blessing of having fans. "While I greatly appreciate your suggestion of forming a fan club for me in Sweden," he wrote in 1968, "I very much fear it might prove a two-edged sword. It would probably mean that quite a number of members of the Club would write to me."

After ten years of exchanging letters, Hedman was coming to England in 1971 and asked if he might meet Wheatley, so Wheatley invited him and his wife Inga to lunch at Cadogan Square. Wheatley and Joan usually lunched at 1.00 and asked Hedman to arrive at 12.30, to allow time for drinks beforehand. Well fortified by these, Wheatley went through lunch in a state of avuncular gusto. Hedman brought a tape recorder, and Wheatley can be heard displaying all the charm he had kept so well concealed from Giles Gordon.

Hedman explains that his name is Iwan as in the Russian Ivan. "Eee-*Van*!" exclaims Wheatley delightedly, as if some complex mystery has suddenly become clear, "Ee-van Ee – *vanovich*!". A few minutes later, Wheatley gives an exposition of *The Devil And All His Works*, solidly grounded in business (25,000 copies already pre-sold in the UK alone) and moving on to a slightly slurred distillation of the central issue. It's not just about witchcraft, he explains, but the two warring powers, "one of light and one of darkness . . . equal in every part of the world . . . twenty-four hours of light . . . twenty-four hours of darkness . . ."

*

Wheatley was working as hard as ever, "utterly overwhelmed" with correspondence and "up to my eyes in work"; he told the writer Anthony Lejeune he was so busy he didn't even have time to mow the lawn. Still, as he said to Hedman, talking about work, "the battle continues."

Joan was already in fragile health and Wheatley's own was increasingly starting to play him up, with bronchial trouble on top of diabetes and cirrhosis. In June 1971 he drew up a will, an extraordinary twenty-three page document. Wheatley was quite adamant that he did not wish to have a public funeral or memorial service. Instead he wanted as many as possible of the people in the will – getting on for a hundred individuals – to meet for an evening party, near the first anniversary of his death, which he would pay for, so that they could speculate about his reincarnation and drink a toast to him, including the hope that "in our future lives we shall meet and become friends with him again."

Wheatley wished his eyes to be used to help another person to see, and that he should have his ashes scattered in the Churchyard of St.Leonard's Church, Streatham. He also wanted his erotic novel, 'The Lusty Youth of Roger Brook', to be published, but not until after Joan's death.

In the event, not one of these things happened

CHAPTER FORTY-NINE

The Music of Time

The 8th of January 1972 was Wheatley's 75th birthday. Hutchinson put out a handsome celebratory booklet, featuring a cake with candles; it looks rather like an album cover of the period. He'd had a family party the night before, with a visit to the theatre, supper for eight at Cadogan Square, and "lots of champagne". Even though it was a Saturday, Wheatley then worked through the day on his next book.

Wheatley's birthday was widely noted in the press, as befitted a national institution. That year he appeared on the radio programme Desert Island Discs, his first choice of record being the 'The Man Who Broke The Bank at Monte Carlo'; a man with whom he could probably identify. The recording is lost, but it is likely that Wheatley talked about his good fortune.

Wheatley's other choices show a mixture of patriotism, sentimentality, and unpretentious musical philistinism. He had the Chelsea Pensioners performing 'It's A Long Way To Tipperary', from the First War, and from the same period 'If You Were The Only Girl in the World (and I were the only boy)', along with Elgar's Pomp and Circumstance, recorded at the Last Night of the Proms. Finally he chose Noel Coward's 'I'll See You Again', from *Bittersweet*, which had been the theme song of his romance with Joan.

Wheatley's books were now widely advertised in the Sunday Colour Supplements and elsewhere, in the 'Heron Library' editions. Heron specialised in sets of classic books bound in luxurious, heirloom quality, leather-look plastic ("like the creamy skin of one of Miss Du Maurier's heroines, these books cry out to be caressed"). Heron's *forte* was extraordinarily sensational advertising copy, which positively *dared* readers to buy the books. "For every real man who has a place in his heart where no women are allowed" was their advert for Darwin's *Origin of the Species*, while "Lose all your illusions about Russian women – for only 75p" was the Heron Dostoyevsky. Those Heron adverts now seem part of the Monty Python era.

Given the genuinely sensational nature of Wheatley's writing, his adverts were less ridiculous than some of the others. They featured a "A solemn warning by Dennis Wheatley" – his old disclaimer from *The Devil Rides Out* – along with a picture of a naked blonde standing before a robed and hooded figure. "Now – if you dare – accept this wickedly handsome volume The Devil Rides Out FREE", ran the offer. Like a box of chocolates, the Heron Wheatley was "a collection of almost sinful luxury", and it was highly contemporary to boot: "witchcraft . . . black magic . . . hardly a week goes by without a sensational headline appearing in our newspapers . . ."

Heron published around fifty volumes of Wheatley, which quite often turn up in charity shops. A few seem to have met a stranger fate, with stories of moral crusaders and born-again Christians throwing expensive leather-bound sets of Dennis Wheatley on to bonfires. Apart from Wheatley's own set of his books, later owned by John Paul Getty, there have been precious few leather-bound Wheatleys. The books in question must be the Heron Library.

*

Wheatley had recently published *The Ravishing of Lady Mary Ware*, the tenth book in the Roger Brook series. He was pressing on with the Brook novels at speed because he was anxious not to die without having completed them, and before long (having knocked off *The Strange Story of Linda Lee* in the meantime) he was at work on another, *The Irish Witch*.

Knowing what his public now wanted, the penultimate Roger Brook story is a tale of black magic. At the climax of the book, with its familiar Wheatley crux of sexual degradation salaciously avoided just in the nick of time, Roger Brook's own daughter is being held down by a large negro named Aboe so that Father Damien, the evil priest, can rape her. The horrified Brook can do nothing except watch, when fortunately a gigantic frog suddenly appears, and gobbles all the Satanists up.

The Irish Witch is not Wheatley's best book. He was particularly mortified when Hedman wrote to point out an error in the opening sentence, which makes Copenhagen the capital of Sweden. He pressed on with the next volume.

★

Wheatley had a number of re-usable 'lines' for journalists, but in 1973 he came up with a new one. Interviewed for the popular paper *Titbits*, he pointed to the wall map he had made of his travels, on which it was apparent that he had been almost everywhere except Russia. And there was a very good reason for that, he said, because he had been so closely involved with secret strategic planning during the War:

> the Russians . . . undoubtedly keep dossiers on people who have been engaged in Intelligence work, and they've probably got one on me. It would be very easy nowadays for somebody to slip something incriminating into my luggage and give the Russians an excuse to pull me in for questioning.

Did he believe it himself? We shall never know, but whether *Titbits* thought it was likely can be judged from their Walter Mitty title, 'The Secret Life of Dennis Wheatley'.

The 1970s were continuing to be anarchic. Following Bloody Sunday in 1972, the IRA stepped up their bombing campaign. Baader-Meinhof and the Red Army Faction were also in the news, along with the Japanese Red Army massacre in Israel, and the Olympic Games murders by the Black September group.

1973 saw immense controversy over the film of *A Clockwork Orange*, with its rape and violence. There was more IRA bombing in London. The young John Paul Getty III was kidnapped and had his ear cut off in the autumn, when things seemed to be reaching rock bottom with the oil crisis, the Three Day Week, and the Miners' Strike. The unions had already been closing one or other of the nation's three TV channels for a night at a time, and now they cut the electricity supply. All over the country, families played board games by candle light. The word "diabolical," which should have been more at home in the work of Montague Summers, could now be heard on television as shop stewards accused the management of taking *diabolical liberties*. "We are having a pretty grim time here but hope for better times in 1974", Wheatley wrote to Hedman in December 1973.

1974 was, if anything, worse. A State of Emergency was declared in January. Wheatley had long been suggesting that someone had to "take a pull", and this was becoming a widespread view among people of his vintage and outlook: things were looking pretty bad from clubland. There were rumours of counter-revolutionary forces being mustered, and 1974 was the year of the so-called "private armies", notably "Civil Assistance", headed by General Sir Walter Walker, and "GB 75", headed by David Stirling, founder of the SAS and a member of White's. These were said to be ready to step in and "keep essential services running". A number of the people involved were friends of Wheatley, including Sir Colin Gubbins and Sir John ("Jack") Slessor, Marshal of the Royal Airforce and now a member of a group called the Resistance and Psychological Operations Committee (RPOC). He had promised practical assistance to Sir Walter Walker.

It has subsequently been suggested by specialist commentators that the private armies never amounted to very much in reality, and that this was less because they represented the fears of a few old men and more because they were a form of PR, their machinations being carefully leaked now and then to the press. They were, it seems, largely a form of 'psy-ops' psychological warfare, or even deception planning.

*

Wheatley's life had become clubbier, largely thanks to Derrick Morley. The Boodles' fiasco was long behind him. In 1968 he had become a member of Pratt's, and in 1969 Morley had put him up for White's. Wheatley had given him a list to help, "Members of Whites Who Are Friends of Dennis Wheatley" with fifteen names and notes on each. He was still on the waiting list for White's, but he was already very much at home in St.James's Street. His favourite restaurant, Prunier's, stood towards the bottom of the slope, with his shoemaker, Lobb, just across the road. Justerini and Brook's had moved once more and now also stood on St.James's Street, just on the corner with Park Place, where Pratt's has its discreet basement premises.

He was also making more use of the St.James's Club on Piccadilly, which Morley had got him into some years earlier. Christopher Lee remembers Wheatley lunching him there, and that on one occasion Wheatley turned up wearing a teddy-bear coat and a white Homburg hat, which Lee said made him look like Al Capone; this made Wheatley laugh.

Wheatley had also become good friends with Anthony Powell, who rather unexpectedly seems to have described himself as "a fan" of Wheatley's books (and whose sinister character Canon Fenneau seems to have something of Copely-Syle about his appearance, although Powell denied any borrowing). They would lunch quite regularly at the St.James's Club. Powell inscribed a number of books to Wheatley, including a copy of *Books Do Furnish A Room*, which he inscribed "from a fellow furnisher". Wheatley brought along his copy of Powell's plays *The Garden God and The Rest I'll Whistle* for Powell to sign, and Powell admired his bookplate with Eric Tombe as Pan: he wrote beside it that it was "eminently appropriate, first, I thought, for the G.G., but really for either play." When it came to *Hearing Secret Harmonies*, a late volume in *The Dance to The Music Of Time* which involves a Crowleyish cult in the late Sixties, Powell wrote "I fear I rather trespass on your own territory here".

Powell sought Wheatley's help with *A Dance To The Music of Time*, not on some point of occult esoterica, but with

589

the plot. Powell was stuck with his plotting, and wrote to Wheatley in January 1972,

> Briefly, the situation is this; the new book opens with Widmerpool involved in trouble with his East/West commercial/cultural activities, in which he has given something serious away to a Communist power . . . Ideally I would like something then to happen that gets him out of the bag. . . it did occur to me that you might have a suggestion . . .

Wheatley wrote back with several suggestions for developing the plot, and Powell ("Tony") in due course wrote back and thanked him for sorting out the situation in the book.

Writing later in his *Journals*, Powell mentions "the Dennis Wheatley category . . . of relatively intelligent men who write more or less conscious drivel." By Powell's standards of condescension, "relatively intelligent" was in fact high praise (compare Henry Green, "not all that intelligent"; Graham Greene, "absurdly overrated"; and Nabokov, "appallingly third rate tinsel stuff".)

A month or so later in the same journal he promotes Wheatley to simply "intelligent". He is now "an intelligent man who writes absurd historical romances", and Powell discloses that the protagonist of his own last novel, Valentine Beals in *The Fisher King*, is "slightly modelled" on Wheatley in that respect, although "not of course in any other."

Not in any other? We shall see. Powell's picture of Beals is worth a closer look for the light it sheds on both of them, and on the reasons why a Wheatley figure should have the strange distinction of being Powell's final protagonist.

Beals is not a very common name, but it was the name of the butler in Wheatley's board game *Alibi*. Valentine Beals has switched from selling drink to writing, and although he is unloved by reviewers, he knows "more than most writers about the ways of business." Beals is not the sort of writer whose acquaintance offered "the smallest intellectual cachet, indeed rather the reverse", although he has his good points.

As for intellectual and critical neglect, he finds compensation in the revenue from his books. In his role of international best-seller (almost everywhere except America, which irks him) he gears any flashes of his imagination "to purely commercial requirements; in practice limiting them severely to the capacities of his regular readership, which he did not overestimate."

He has also been something of a pioneer in putting explicit sex into the historical novel. Another character has never read a Beals book, but he can guess the tone: "I was a great reader of historical novels as a boy. Stanley Weyman, Jeffrey Farnol, Baroness Orczy, Rafael Sabatini. I understand you [Beals] have given them all cause to look to their laurels – anyway, regret their inadequate treatment of life's sexual side." Salacious details aside, his books are educational for the young because of their "easy history"; he has a knack of putting "a lot of information down in a readable form". You could learn a lot about the Lollards, for example, from his book *The Wizard on the Heath*.

The particularly salient point about Beals is that he has "an innate taste for pin-pointing archetypes", and he spots at once that the crippled photographer Saul Henchman is the Fisher King of the Grail myth ("archetypal figures were a hobby of his"). This is precisely Powell's own taste, and what he does in his own work. *The Fisher King* relies on Beals's point of view in this respect, and it is something Powell and Wheatley share, underpinning Powell's much greater novel sequence *A Dance To The Music Of Time*.

In their perception of grand parallels, Powell, Beals and Wheatley all transmute ordinary circumstances into the timeless and reassuring realm of myth, transforming the merely contingent and chaotic into something more Platonic. At the opening of *Dance*, some modern workmen standing around a brazier become firstly Roman soldiers and then the figures in Poussin's painting *A Dance To The Music of Time*. Through the mythological and even astrological patterns that Powell weaves into his work, modern life becomes as harmoniously ordered as the Music of the Spheres, just as Wheatley can subsume a jumble of contemporary problems and anxieties into the timeless struggle between Light and Darkness.

Both writers – the one immensely subtle in this respect, the other notoriously simplistic – share this conservative aesthetic of taking refuge from the slippages of history by turning to the timelessness of myth, something often remarked about reactionary modernists such as Yeats and Eliot. In his final book, Powell assigns this quality to the Wheatley figure, just as he generously gives him the transcendental moment – in this case more Powell than Wheatley – of watching a dancer whose performance seemed to be "taking place on some transcendental plane. The musicians were immediately aware that they were participating in an act of magic."

At the opposite pole from this reassuring magic comes the revealing final line of Powell's last novel, describing the view across a misty Scottish loch. It becomes "the frontiers of Thule: the edge of the known world: man's permitted limits; a green-barriered check point, beyond which the fearful cataract of torrential seas cascaded down into Chaos."

*

P.G. Wodehouse, writing the foreword to Charles Graves's book about London clubs, *Leather Armchairs* (which Wheatley owned, a present from "Don" Donegall) said the subject seemed almost "too sad for my typewriter. I got the impression that all the clubs in London were crying for bread and at a loss to know where their next ten bob was coming from." This was certainly the case with the St. James's Club, which was beset by financial problems. Wheatley was always good at dealing with "the Demon Finance" and "the Boodle Fiend", and he suggested a quarterly members' lottery, to which members could subscribe by Bankers' Order. This idea seems not to have been taken up.

Wheatley liked the St. James's Club, and when he dined there he enjoyed being looked down on by portraits of the original Hell Fire Club, founded by Sir Francis Dashwood; these belonged to the old Dilettanti Club which, having no premises of its own, had loaned them to the St. James's. It was a blow when in 1974 it finally had to close; moving with the times, the building is now a college for teaching English as a foreign language.

In 1975, however, Wheatley at last became a member of White's, a club slightly older than the Bank of England and described by its historian, Percy Colson, as "an oasis of civilisation in a desert of democracy". J.G.Links remembered that Wheatley was so pleased "his first object was to get to the Candidates' Book when no one else was looking and see his own page." He found his candidacy had been supported by thirty-five members, and he couldn't help boasting modestly to Links, "Not bad," he said, "for the Streatham born son of a shopkeeper.".

Wheatley still loved joining things – a 1969 *Times* profile said "He pines, I think, to belong" – and in 1975 he joined a different sort of club, a dining club called the Saintsbury Club. This was founded back in the 1920s in honour of the literary critic and wine buff George Saintsbury, author of *Notes on a Cellar Book*, and it meets twice a year. The club exists by the generosity of its members, who donate the wine that is drunk.

Wheatley's donation included six bottles of Old Brown Sherry, sixty years in the bottle, from the cellars of a marquis, twelve bottles of 1964 Dom Perignon, and four bottles of 1955 Chateau d'Yquem. None of them were drunk in his lifetime. Merlin Holland, Oscar Wilde's grandson and keeper of the Saintsbury Club Archives, describes it as "a very generous gift, especially given his age and the fact that he was only a member for such a short time."

Wheatley had joined both White's and the Saintsbury Club rather late in his life. Writing of the archetypal clubman, back in 1911, Ralph Nevill says how much he loves his club, and how he likes to spend time there.

> So he lunches and dines, dines and lunches, till the sands of the hourglass have run out, and the moment comes for him to enter that great club of which all humanity must perforce become members.

CHAPTER FIFTY

The Hound of Heaven

For some time now, Wheatley had been putting his characters to bed. As we have seen, the elderly Duke de Richleau had died of a heart attack at the end of *Dangerous Inheritance*, exhausted after springing his friends from a foreign jail. Having resurrected Eric as Gregory, and kept up an unusual author–character relationship with him throughout the books, it seems Wheatley couldn't bear to see him die a second time. *The White Witch of the South Seas* ends "So our hero and heroine, once more united, lived happily ever after" – surely one of the few books for adults to close with those words.

In 1974 Wheatley finally killed off Roger Brook, the character with whom he had most identified. In *Desperate Measures* Roger and Georgina, his teenage first love and occasional partner throughout the series, are together at last when a dam bursts. "We are about to die! This is the end!" cries Georgina. Direct speech had never been Wheatley's strong suit, and as a fifty foot wall of water comes roaring down on them Roger answers "Nay, dear heart. 'Tis no more than a passing to a new beginning." Some readers took this as a hint that they might survive, Holmes and Moriarty style, but this was not Wheatley's intention. The new beginning was death.

Hutchinson gave Wheatley a party to celebrate the last of the Roger Brook series. It was held at Locket's, a now vanished restaurant in Marsham Street, Westminster, popular with Members of the nearby Houses of Parliament; it had its own "division bell" to call them in to vote. Locket's was long established (Vanbrugh mentions it in his 1696 play, *The Relapse*), and by the Seventies its theme had come to be Olde Englishnesse. Wheatley drank Imperial Tokay and ate "Sea Bass Lymington", made with herbs grown at Grove Place. It must have had a rather nostalgic flavour.

With Roger dead, Wheatley decided that his career in fiction had come to an end. He knew his time was limited, and he devoted himself to finishing his memoirs in what was left. For some time people had told Wheatley that he looked young for his age, but now his cirrhosis, diabetes and bronchial trouble were really beginning to bite.

Wheatley was shepherding his health as carefully as he could. In what had now become a regular pattern, he was laid up in bed with bronchitis through the autumn and winter, and went to the South of France in the Spring; their days of travelling further afield were over. Life was increasingly curtailed.

Age was taking more of a toll on Joan ("Mentally, she is as brisk as ever, but unfortunately her body is in very bad shape") and she suffered a series of falls. Going out and giving dinner parties were things of the past: Joan found them too exhausting, and entertaining was now limited to having a couple of friends over for a drink in the early evening. They were vexed when a fraudulent Swedish fan arrived and took up their time with a supposed plan to film Wheatley's books.

Hedman had meanwhile completed *Fyra Decennier med Dennis Wheatley* (Four Decades with Dennis Wheatley), and sent Wheatley a copy. He also sent presentation copies for Her Majesty the Queen, and the British Prime Minister of the day, Edward Heath. Wheatley was able to tell him that they had both accepted, the Queen's Secretary writing a gracious acknowledgement: "Her Majesty has asked me to say that she is delighted to accept the book for the Royal Library and much appreciated your kind thought in sending it."

Hedman asked if Wheatley often sent his books to the Queen. No, said Wheatley, because although he had been King George VI's favourite author

> . . . our present Queen is not, I think, much interested in books but mainly in dogs and horses. And although I have been presented to her I have never sent her a book before.

Hedman also wanted know if Wheatley was in line for a knighthood or other honour; in fact, he probably wondered why he didn't have one already. Wheatley pointed out that this was the gift of the Prime Minister and not the Queen, and that "although my sales are said to be larger than any other author in Britain I doubt whether I would receive a Knighthood, as when they are given it is to poets like Betjeman, or someone who qualifies very highly in writing beautiful English."

Wheatley and Hedman had now known each for around fifteen years, but Hedman still had 'more English than the English' qualms about addressing Wheatley as Dennis. In February 1976 Wheatley reassured him: "Please do not hesitate to address me by my Christian name. I appreciate your reasoning but we have known each other for many years and so I am very happy that you should write to me in this way."

*

Arrow books, Hutchinson's paperback subsidiary, had now singled out Wheatley's eight black magic books for special treatment. After numerous cover designs over the years they hit on the covers that many people remember as the definitive Wheatley, each one having the words 'A Black Magic Story' in white across the top of a predominantly black cover. A naked woman, perhaps dancing, raises her hands behind a splurge of flame on each book, while the occult props in the foreground vary: there was a black candle on a skull, a horned goats head, an old leather-bound tome, an incense burner, a strange dagger, a tribal mask, a crystal ball, and so on; all the decor of the arts of darkness. Arrow brought out two boxed sets for Christmas 1974, contemporary with a well-known chocolate advert of the time that asked "Who knows the secret of the Black Magic box?"

These books were ubiquitous in their day, but Wheatley's popularity would barely outlive him (the Sixties had really lasted until around 1974, and around 1977 a very different cultural wave would come in with punk, making the

596

supernatural look about as relevant as flared trousers). Wheatley had enormously influenced the popular image of the occult, but he paid the price in consequent disparagement and ridicule, albeit fairly affectionate.

"I'm damned if I'm memorizing any Black Paternosters backwards or any of that rot," says a character in Kyril Bonfiglioli's novel, *Something Nasty In The Woodshed*.

> "Black Paternosters?" I asked. "Have you been studying the subject a bit, George?"
> "We've all read our Dennis Wheatley at some time or another, Charlie," said Sam.
> "Speak for yourself! " I said sharply.

A humorous column in the occult journal *Aquarian Arrow* purported to be written by one Hugo L'Estrange ("Minister of Moral Decline and grand old man of British Satanism"). Hugo is a port-sodden fogey who lives at Hellgate Hall, in a world of Louis Roederer champagne, Hispano Suiza cars, and Monte Satano cigars from a tobacconist in St.James. Gentlemen in smoking jackets retire to the library with smoked salmon sandwiches and hock, and goats' blood is drunk from 22 carat gold.

An unamused New Age reader wrote in to complain, and accused the column of perpetuating "the very lowest image of Dennis Wheatley type occultism." "– How nice to know that at least one reader fully understood me and what I stood for!" replied L'Estrange. "When occultism dissociated itself from the worst excesses of Dennis Wheatley, it castrated itself; for the worst excesses of Dennis Wheatley are where it's at."

★

Wheatley and George Rainbird, who had produced *The Devil and All His Works*, put together a final scheme for capitalising on Wheatley's name with the 1974 launch of 'The Dennis Wheatley Library of the Occult', an inexpensive series of reprints with short and undemanding introductions by

Wheatley. Rainbird was now the chairman of Sphere, a mass market paperback house. Wheatley lunched with Rainbird in his chambers at Albany, and it was there that Rainbird asked Wheatley to do the Library. Rainbird's apartment, K1, had previously belonged to Wheatley's friend Edward Lydell, and long before that it belonged to the Gothic novelist M.G. "Monk" Lewis, whose novel *The Monk* became part of Wheatley's series.

The Library was launched with a party at Brown's Hotel, hung with nylon cobwebs and lit by black candles. Wheatley was on good form and the *Evening Standard* described him as "the doyen of magic" and "the sprightliest 77-year-old in the book world".

The Dennis Wheatley Library of the Occult was the last Wheatley venture for the mass market, and it ran for the last three years of his life. Originally planned to include hundreds of titles, it finally ran to forty five, with classics like *Dracula* and *Frankenstein* alongside less well known books like Sax Rohmer's *Brood of the Witch Queen*, William Hope Hodgson's *The Ghost Pirates*, R.H.Benson's *The Necromancers*, and A.E.W.Mason's *The Prisoner in the Opal*. Some turn up quite often, but others are so fabulously rare that even in the charity shop of your dreams you might never find them.

★

Horror films had changed after *The Exorcist*, which appeared in Britain in1974, and *To The Devil – A Daughter* appeared from Hammer (it was their last major film) in 1976, with Christopher Lee and Nastassia Kinski. It had been drastically adapted and bore little relation to Wheatley's book, or to the feel of the Hammer *Devil Rides Out*. Where *The Devil Rides Out* had a fruitcake richness, *To The Devil – A Daughter* is an ugly film, verging on medical horror, with a chilly mid-Seventies air blowing through it. Wheatley hated it.

The whole face of horror was changing. James Herbert's first novel *The Rats* appeared in 1974, and represented a downward shift in popular writing. Set in the East End, it

Wheatley's 75th Birthday booklet, 1972.

Britain's occult uncle: Wheatley at his desk in Cadogan Square.

The Devil and All His Works (1971).

included a scene with a baby eaten alive by rodents. Herbert prides himself on having wrested horror from the likes of Wheatley: "Horror novels were written by upper-middle class writers like Dennis Wheatley. I made horror accessible by writing about working class characters".

The liberal media and the BBC were never really out to bait Wheatley in the way that they had baited Evelyn Waugh, but Wheatley had sometimes been written up a little snidely by interviewers during the long years of his success, often on a wavelength he was probably unable to detect.

Shortly before Wheatley's eightieth birthday, Robert Robinson interviewed him for the Book Programme on BBC2, and kicked off by reminding viewers what Wheatley's books were like: they combined "the improbabilities of Batman with the style of Daisy Ashford", Miss Ashford being the Victorian infant prodigy who wrote *The Young Visiters* [sic].

"Some of the critics have said your style isn't so hot . . ." suggested Robinson, and Wheatley agreed cheerfully:

"It isn't, by Jove, it isn't. I think it may be better than it was, but it certainly never has been all that."

Seemingly unruffled, Wheatley explained some tricks of his trade: the chapter ends must break in the middle of a situation, 'cliff-hanger' style; the scenes of crisis must be very long, and the whole thing had to build up to a "smashing end . . . I build the thing up so that when I get to the last chapter it's like going round Tattenham Corner."[1]

And then Robinson stepped up the attack. Weren't Wheatley's heroes "rather snooty and right wingy [sic] and so forth. Is that anything like you?"

It may be, yes, I suppose so. I'm certainly not left-wing, oh no. I worked for years from ten o'clock in the

---

[1] A dangerous bend on Epsom race course, associated with the excitement of the Derby.

morning till midnight and sometimes till two in the morning, and Saturday I treated as an ordinary day. So I consider I've earned my drink and my food, my books and china and so on.

Privately, Wheatley seems to have been hurt by Robinson's attitude, as he told J.G.Links. "I believe you are rather right-wing, Mr Wheatley", was how Links remembered it: "There was a clear hint that [Robinson] had a Bulldog Drummond incarnate before him, if not an out-and-out fascist." Wheatley was "irritated and puzzled," says Links: "You didn't have to be a fascist to know the difference between Good and Evil."

★

January 8th 1977 was Wheatley's eightieth birthday, with a week of public and private celebrations. Foremost among these was the grand party on the night of Tuesday 4th, for which Wheatley hired Vintners' Hall, in Upper Thames Street, with its panelled Court Room and seventeenth-century staircase. Around three hundred guests were treated to a buffet dinner, including Game Pie and "Tartlet Crysta-lysée Dennis." Drink included "Black Velvet a la Bismarck", the champagne and Guinness mixture drunk in Wheatley's books: Hendrik G. Washington, the devil-worshipping U.S. Airforce Colonel, is among those partial to it.

Wheatley wore a powder blue smoking jacket (seemingly the same one he is wearing on the back cover of the early Seventies Arrow paperbacks) with a white orchid pinned to its midnight blue lapel. It has been said that if you only live long enough in England everybody will love you in the end, and the reportage of his birthday was indulgent. Under the heading 'Satanic', the *Times* Diary noted "an appropriate whiff of historical romance, and some suitably Satanic black velvet", with the author himself "stunningly clad" in his blue jacket and orchid.

The 'Living Portrait' film of Wheatley's life was shown three times, and Wheatley exerted himself to make a speech, telling his guests that Vintner's Hall was the only building of its type to have survived both the Great Fire of London and the German Blitz, and that it was on this very same ground that the first Master of Vintners had entertained no less than five kings to dinner in one night.

Joan had to remain seated for the evening, and Wheatley himself was seated while he posed for photographs. Guests queued up to shake his hand, and next day he wrote thank-you letters for all his presents. Wheatley later said he was "utterly exhausted" by the week of partying, and looked forward to going to the South of France, hoping "at last to get a really good rest".

Wheatley and Joan spent three "quiet but pleasant" weeks in the south of France in April, returning on the 26th, and after dinner that evening Wheatley had an attack of breathing difficulties. He had already had several of these over the last few months, but this was the worst yet. He had to be carried to bed. He put a good face on it ("Happily . . . I am in no pain") and in early May wrote to Hedman that he was "well on the mend", but the decline that Mary Lutyens described – "he subsided gently, and quite quickly, into death at the age of eighty" – was now under way.

Wheatley was continuing to deal with an immense post-bag ("You can have no idea of the size of the post with which I have to deal every morning"). The consolidation of his occult image – with the Arrow editions, the Library of the Occult, and *The Devil and All His Works* – was bringing him a higher proportion of young and unstable correspondents. He batted their letters back as best he could, as ever telling them *not to dabble*, and to consult a priest if they were troubled.

Writing to a more mature female fan of his Roger Brook novels in July, Wheatley is polite but firm. First of all, he apologises for taking so long to reply – three weeks – "but I have been ill in bed". Then he gets down to business: "Your bookseller is quite wrong about the Roger Brook series" (he had probably told her that the "new beginning" ending paved the way for more). Wheatley reiterates that *Desperate*

Measures brings Roger's and Georgina's stories to an end, and that he is writing no more fiction, ending "With many thanks for your kind interest". Wheatley ministered carefully to his public, and the tone here is a combination of *noblesse oblige* and first rate after-sales service.

The first volume of Wheatley's autobiography, *The Young Man Said*, had been published in January – the Vintner's Hall birthday party doubled as its launch – and Wheatley continued drafting the others for posthumous publication: he originally intended there would be five. He finally stopped writing on the day before Queen Elizabeth's Jubilee. Wheatley was very aware that he had been born in the year of another Jubilee, Queen Victoria's, and he considered this was a fitting time to end.

Wheatley was a keen monarchist, but there is a further dimension to his royal dates. Although he disliked organised occultism and dabbling ("very bad thing", he told Robinson) he loved the supernatural, and he took an interest in the influence of the planets and the power of numbers.

In *The Devil and All His Works*, for example, he had looked back on the milestones of his life in the light of the number eight, to which his name adds up numerologically. He was sent to boarding school aged eight; he received his commission at the age of seventeen (1+7 = 8); he was sent to the Western Front on the eighth day of eighth month, 1917; and so on. He also says he was first married in June 1924 at the age of 26 (2+6 . . .), although in fact he was married in June 1922 at the age of 25 (he'd have done better to point out that it was the 17th June; numerology is nothing if not adaptable). But the overall drift is clear.

Wheatley wanted to live in a world of pattern and order. Gifford Hillary marvels gratefully at the ways of Providence ("There was, then, a pattern in things after all") and in an interview Wheatley compares the modern world unfavourably with the Regency, complaining "the sense of order has gone". Satanism was a menace to "everything that went to make a well-ordered world", which is why the Powers of Darkness had to be stopped from dragging the world into a new Dark Ages: "It is the duty of every responsible person who values a life of order, stability and decency to do his utmost to prevent this from happening."

As for astrology, Plato said the stars are "the moving image of eternity". Wheatley would have agreed with that. His love of the maps he collected was another aspect of this ideal orderliness (Jonathan Meades, in an essay entitled 'I Like Maps', has written "The covert, non-utile function of a map is to order what is actually very messy, to make a dictionary of the land, to mediate between man and the physical world, to give shape to the strange"). It has been famously said that "the map is not the territory", and that the ideal is not the real. In Platonism and occultism, however, it is.

★

Looking back, there were three books Wheatley felt he would rather have written than any of his own: *The Scarlet Pimpernel*, *The Prisoner of Zenda*, and *The Three Musketeers*. Wheatley particularly admired them because, as he saw it, they had each added a word to the language – Pimpernel, Ruritania, and Musketeers – and each word, "without requiring any context instantly conjures up a complete mental picture." This, thought, Wheatley, was true fame.

Wheatley added no words to the language in this sense, except the words "Dennis Wheatley" themselves; they immediately conjure up a certain ambience, and a place where fine wines, smoking jackets and country-house libraries meet the Powers of Darkness.

Wheatley not only wrote the twentieth-century's great occult novel, but he was arguably twentieth-century Britain's greatest non-literary writer. His rivals are Agatha Christie – a better writer, certainly, but much more limited in genre – and Edgar Wallace. Wallace could knock off a best-seller in a weekend, and he wrote everything from *King Kong* to *Sanders of the River*, along with writing film scripts and a racing column, editing a newspaper, and standing for parliament. But whether his name evokes very much is debatable, unlike the words "Ruritania" or "Dennis Wheatley."

It has been said that to study Wheatley is to study twentieth-century popular taste, and to understand his work is to understand the dreams and nightmares of twentieth-century Britain. But Wheatley was not content just to reflect those dreams; he tried to shape them, and he had ambitions to be more than an entertainer, without wanting to be a fine writer. Like one of Shelley's "unacknowledged legislators", Wheatley was a propaganda artist and a covert Platonic shaper of his people's consciousness. He was what some people today would call a "meme engineer," and he seems to have written his books as a mixture of potboiling and public service, at least according to his own values.

Late in life he wrote that among the thousands of letters he received from readers, "a considerable number have been from patients in hospital who say that while reading my stories they have been able to forget their pain. That is a wonderful thing and for the gift which has enabled me to do this I am truly grateful."

There is an element of pious self-justification here, but it would be unduly suspicious and mean-minded to suggest he didn't receive such letters. In fact his occult books would be a particular comfort in the circumstances, since they were not only escapist page turners but contained a comforting message of mind-over-body and ideal-over-real. For many readers, in fact, Wheatley's books contained an element of spiritual succour (or bad faith and mystic hogwash, depending on your point of view), just as his 1941 *Strange Conflict* was designed to prepare people to withstand wartime bereavement. *The Devil and All His Works* also closes with an assurance that the idea of death should hold no terror: "With this thought I leave my readers."

★

Wheatley spent much of autumn 1977 in bed with bronchial trouble. He had a 'bags packed' attitude to dying, and had stuck typed labels on his possessions and even his drinks, indicating who should have what.

Many years earlier Bobby Eastaugh had given him a copy of Francis Thompson's *The Hound Of Heaven*, a long poem about the pursuit of the poet by God:

> I fled Him, down the nights and down the days;
> I fled Him, down the arches of the years;
> I fled Him, down the labyrinthine ways
> Of my own mind; and in the midst of tears
> I hid from Him, and under running laughter.

And now, in October 1977, Eastaugh himself was at Wheatley's bedside, like the Hound, come to gather him into the fold.

Eastaugh gave Wheatley "Conditional Absolution" for his sins. It was the last time he saw him, but some days later a very scrawly letter arrived:

> My dearest Bobby,
>   This is a very brief line to thank you for the ceremony you performed here the other day. Had it improved my condition physically that would have been more than one could expect and I should have written to you earlier . . .

Steeped in supernaturalism, it looks as if Wheatley still had 'magical', or at the very least 'faith-healing'-type thoughts about his absolution, and to that extent he hadn't quite grasped the point of it. But he continued:

> As it is, it has renewed my faith and courage, at least sufficiently to write in my own hand, which I have not done for many months. I am most truly grateful to you for your interest and cannot thank you for it sufficiently. I do hope that you can read this [illegible] scrawl. Our friendship has been a long one but I am convinced that it will [illegible] continue eternally and that we shall meet many times elsewhere. All my love and thanks, Ever your friend,
>   Dennis

And at the top was scribbled:

> PS by holding this up I hoped to write a more legible
> version, but I find I can't. All love
>   D

He subsequently wrote to Derrick Morley, told him how much he had appreciated what Eastaugh had done, and said he now felt at peace.

Wheatley died alone on the night of the 10th of November 1977. At about half past ten he got into breathing difficulties, and by the time Jack Younger came round to see how he was and sit with him for a while, it was too late. He was gone.

★

Wheatley owned a work by Camille Flammarion, *Death and its Mystery* in three volumes: *Before Death*, *The Moment of Death*, and *After Death*. This had made a particular impression on him, and must have shaped his expectations.

There is now quite an extensive literature of 'near death experiences' in which people who have momentarily 'died' and been revived describe their experiences. These testimonies often feature going towards a light, being met by helping figures, and experiencing a great sense of calm and reassurance. One of the best known examples comes from the philosopher A.J.Ayer. Shortly before his death in 1989, Ayer's heart stopped beating for several minutes, and after doctors managed to revive him he reported having witnessed the presence of a great light which he felt (or indeed 'knew') was responsible for ruling the universe. His atheism was unshaken, although he did say this vision helped him to understand how others could believe in a God.

Writing about this light, the late John Michell comments that "those who have gone further speak of the beauty of that light and the warmth, understanding and forgiveness they find there. On returning to mundanity, they ask nothing more than to help their fellow-creatures to shed their fears and ambitions, urging them to accept that, in Plato's words, 'things are better taken care of than you can possibly imagine.' "

I am not suggesting there is anything supernatural in this phenomenon. Although it is well attested and has spawned a considerable literature, the most respected authority on the subject attributes it to lack of oxygen in the brain. Perhaps the mystery is why the central nervous system should provide such a beneficent illusion as it finally shuts down, since it seems too late to have any evolutionary value.

It would be pleasing to think Wheatley might have had such an experience. Nothing could have been more in tune with his beliefs than to rise up towards the radiance, and be welcomed on board by some really top chaps in the field. Then they could reassure him that the Old Firm of King and Country was going to last for ever, and that all manner of things would be well in the Kingdom, Empire and Commonwealth of Light.

REFERENCES

Dennis Wheatley never threw anything away – not just letters and manuscripts, but brochures, menus, tickets – and instead he filed it for reference.

A quantity of this material was destroyed after his death in 1977, but a good deal survived to be sold at Sotheby's, London, on the 8th December 1983, lot 272: "The personal papers of Dennis Wheatley comprising a huge archive of letters [. . .] photographs, diaries, notebooks, address books, party lists, firm catalogues and Christmas cards [. . .] and many other miscellaneous papers and mementos. Many thousands of items largely bundled up by Wheatley himself according to year in a number of boxes and sacks." This great heap of material ("Sold not subject to return") remained largely intact in the hands of its buyer, Ian Sayer, and was invaluable for this book. It is referenced as 'Archive'.

Central to the archive is Wheatley's account of Eric Gordon Tombe's disappearance, simply entitled DEGT. This is accompanied by Wheatley's scrapbooks about the case, which add up to over two hundred and fifty pages, often with three or four cuttings to a page.

I have anonymised a number of Wheatley's post-war correspondents – none of them remotely public figures – who are all but impossible to trace for permission clearances but can hardly have expected their private letters would appear in a book. I have anonymised individual IRD staff in Chapter 38 for the same reason. Page references to published fiction have been largely omitted when the work itself is clear.

ABBREVIATIONS

Blackwell's: Blackwell's catalogue A1136 *A Catalogue of Books from the Library of Dennis Wheatley*
D&I *Drink and Ink*
DEGT *Disappearance of Eric Gordon Tombe*
DP *The Deception Planners*
GGG *Gunmen, Gallants and Ghosts*
O&TG *Officer and Temporary Gentleman*
STF *Stranger Than Fiction*

SWB *Saturdays With Bricks*
TLS *Times Literary Supplement*
TYMS *The Young Man Said*

INTRODUCTION: THE DEVIL IS A GENTLEMAN

". . . rosy twilight on the skulls of stone demons." Iain Sinclair, *Lights Out For The Territory* (London, Granta, 1997) p.371

Fifty million copies: the largest figure usually quoted in connection with Wheatley's sales, as in D&I p.266.

luxury tradition of cheap fiction: "the luxury traditions of the cheap novel," review of *The Forbidden Territory*, TLS February 9th 1933, p.94.

". . . You're English! You couldn't do it!" *They Found Atlantis* (Hutchinson, 1936) p. 68

To study Wheatley is to study popular taste: J. Randolph Cox, 'Dennis Yates Wheatley,' *Dictionary of Literary Biography* volume 77, p.321.

Maurice Richardson: 'Satan On Our Side' [review of *They Used Dark Forces*], *Observer*, 18th October 1964

"truss-stuffer" Richardson op.cit.; bank manager and lady novelist Graham Lord, 'When Dennis Wheatley Was Scared Stiff of the Devil' [review of O&TG] *Sunday Express*, January 1977.

'Sex, Jingoism and Black Magic: The Weird Fiction of Dennis Wheatley' Jessica Amanda Salmonson, *The Weird Review* [internet] (2000).

". . . how come he is so familiar with their contents?" Robert Irwin, *Satan Wants Me* (Dedalus, 1999) p.195.

". . . Devil's been pretty decent about it." David Blundy, 'That Old Black Magic,' *Observer* 4th July 1971.

CHAPTER ONE: FAMILY ROMANCES

The story of the two boys is in Chapter One of TYMS. Ready Money was less of a country boy than Wheatley suggests: he was not born in St Neots as Wheatley says [TYMS p.15] but Lambeth, South London, in 1849, later living in the St.Neots area with his widowed mother.

"the Great God Respectability" – YMS p.16

"Better to be born lucky than rich" – op.cit p.21

". . . when they were young those '70s were the very devil." – op.cit p.21

"three kings, twenty-one princes [. . .] and many millionaires."
Dennis Wheatley 75 8 January 1972 [Hutchinson 75th birthday brochure, unpaginated, first page]

The John Wheatley story is in Chapter One of YMS; Wheatley's heredity calculation p.15.

"appalling conditions . . . sanctimonious and truly immoral . . ." YMS pp.198–99

"for what it is worth" YMS p.13; "tradesman" YMS p.24; "My mother detested the Wheatleys . . ." YMS p.49

CHAPTER TWO: THE LOST LAND

Wallpaper YMS pp.38–9

Charlie the doll YMS pp.41–2

". . . at any moment they will be shown into his study" Tony Wilmot, 'The Secret Life of Dennis Wheatley', *Titbits* March 15–21 1971 pp.30–31

Wheatley's defence of *Chums* YMS p.45

Kindergarten love of Honor YMS pp.43–4

Aspen house artworks: Auction catalogue for Aspen House by Herring, Son and Daw. Tues 21, Wed 22, Thurs 23, Tues 28, Wed 29, Thurs 30 November 1916. Byron's tea service, Napoleon's smoking outfit, and the piping bullfinch mentioned in contemporary newspaper reports, now in a scrapbook formerly owned by Wheatley.

Knights worth £300 YMS pp.40–41

Olga Franklin on Streatham: *Books and Bookmen*, Vol.8, no.9 (June, 1963) p.9.

Aunt Emily story YMS p.51

Gardener Gunn and "small boy's paradise" YMS p.54

CHAPTER THREE: TELLING TALES

"a healthy mind . . ." George E Clarke, *Historic Margate* p.60.

Skelsmergh: in YMS Chapter Five

The story of the man on the stairs figured in Wheatley's Thirties talks (e.g. Eton Literary Society Feb 22 1939, reported *Eton Chronicle* no.2405, Feb 23 1939) and appears in his novel *The Haunting of Toby Jugg* (1948) pp.24–33; 37–38; TDAAHW (1971) p.264, and finally YMS (1977) pp.62–64.

". . . one swallow really does make a summer" YMS p.64

Little Arthur's History of England, Wheatley's annotation Blackwell's item 322.

". . . knife and revolver are not much in evidence" W.H.Collingridge, *Tricks of Self-Defence* (London, Health and Strength Ltd., n.d.), Introduction

". . . as their young bodies crave" YMS p.84.

Grandmother Sarah and the robin, YMS p.95

CHAPTER FOUR: THE BAD MAN IN EMBRYO

Wheatley discusses his time at Dulwich in YMS, Chapters Seven and Nine.

"Fine innings, Wodehouse . . ." Tom Hiney, *Raymond Chandler* (Chatto, 1997) p.14

"a bad atlas and a damn bad school." Blackwell's item 117

CHAPTER FIVE: JAM TODAY

Wheatley discusses his time on HMS Worcester in YMS chapters 9, 11, 12,

Wheatley's correspondence with Hilda Gosling from 1912 to 1955, the bulk of it covering 1912 to 1921, is held by the Brotherton Library, Leeds.

"Bigger than me . . . Rag-Time Barmy . . . other people existing as well as yourself" DW to Hilda Gosling, Jan 22, 1912 (spelling normalised). "Spicie bits" March 6 1913.

Wheatley's HMS Worcester school reports are in the keeping of The Marine Society, Lambeth Road, SE1

". . . never have expected a prize for Scripture to come in so useful." Blackwell's item 1326.

Contemporary pen portraits of Avery, Ramage, Goldreich et al quoted in YMS Chapter 11

The story of "Blue Hat" is in YMS Chapter 10

Untitled poem of one hundred lines about Douglas, circa 1918. Archive.

". . . we were all like a pack of Monks . . ." Letter to Hilda Gosling 27 November 1913

Wheatley discusses Dieseldorrf in YMS Chapter 12

Escapade of visiting Dieseldorff: YMS 185–87; contemporary account in letter to Hilda Gosling, March 6 1913.

"fine old Pagan god" YMS 187

"ripping sensation" letter to Hilda March 6 1913

"awfly bucked . . . awfly deacent set" letter to Hilda 27 November 1913

CHAPTER SIX: GOOD GERMANS

Wheatley's account of going to Germany is in YMS Chapters 13 and 14. The station master anecdote: YMS 189. Rogniski the sword swallower and Cologne cathedral YMS 190, 191; letter to Hilda 16 May 1913.

"If I believed in JC, I'd be an RC." Annette Wheatley

The German air show, YMS 192–4, contrasted with letter to Hilda 16 May 1913

"awfley deacent and they all like the Englander" letter to Hilda 16 May 1913 "I have found some awfley nice chaps . . . simply topping chaps . . ." 27 November 1913

The Kaysers, little Alfred, "roar their heads off with laughter"; undated letter ("Wednesday") to Hilda, 1913

". . . a sing-song or dance would have been taken as a clear indication that one had sold oneself to the Devil" YMS pp.207–8

Calypso, "Always marry a woman uglier than you!" Anthony Wheatley

Bathing anecdote YMS 210–212 contrasted with undated "Wednesday" letter to Hilda Gosling.

Pia Emert and the cauliflower, YMS 227–8; letter to Hilda 27 November 1913

CHAPTER SEVEN: THE CURTAIN

"cloven hoof" YMS 212.

Letters to Barbara Symonds: there are six draft letters to Barbara in Wheatley's archive, but since all but one are undated no separate references will be given.

Marriage to Barbara as "the dominant decent thought in my existence," undated draft letter to Cecil Cross.

Cousin Laurie on women YMS 245–46

Night at the opera YMS 247–48; OaTG p.14.

". . . nothing about life before 1914 which I didn't like . . . Fools and their wars have spoilt it." Gerald Hamilton in John Symonds, *Conversations with Gerald* (London, Duckworth, 1974) p.163)

Claud Cockburn and Edwardian anxieties *I, Claud* . . . (Penguin, 1967) p.9.

CHAPTER EIGHT: OFFICERS AND MEN

"mob psychology" O&TG p.26

Wheatley on Kitchener O&TG p.29

". . . brother officers who had been at Eton, Harrow, and Winchester." 'Living Portrait' filmscript by Wheatley pp.7–8, circa 1968. Archive.

"Those boots must have cost a small fortune . . ." O&TG pp.61–2

Wheatley's "40 / 70" list of sexual encounters is a sheet of paper inserted into a notebook, now in the possession of the Imperial War Museum, London

Letters to Hilda: "neither God nor the Devil seem to get much forwader" (May 1916); "petticoat . . . the world, the flesh, and the devil" (first letter from France, undated); ". . . the Devil must have had a particularly amusing and gratifying three days at my expense . . ."

(29 January 1918); "petticoat . . . Old Nick his just dues, in oats . . ." (22 May 1918).

CHAPTER NINE: THE RICH WOT GETS THE PLEASURE

". . . night of a lifetime" O&TG pp.92–4

Faked pictures, "Our Boys on the Western Front" O&TG p.95

Watering horses O&TG p.104

"One doesn't fetch horses in the RFC" undated letter to Hilda c. January 1916

"an awfley good stroke of luck . . . [Nobby Clark] . . . one of God's own White Men." Letter to Hilda May 1916.

Forever Amber, Blackwell's item 2222.

Sibilla O&TG 114–16; "Sibyle," diary in Imperial War Museum.

"Well you wouldn't be sittin' 'ere . . ." Untitled poem about Douglas. Archive.

Colonel Clark's report, cited O&TG 129–30.

CHAPTER TEN: ENTER A SATYR

"Made friends in War with curious type of man . . .". With Gosling correspondence, probably by Hilda herself.

"impaired in health and possibly in moral character," unidentifiable press cutting in Wheatley's three scrapbooks about the Tombe murder case. Henceforth Tombe scrapbooks. Archive.

"a very genial young man, clean-shaven . . . walked with a limp"; "a gentlemanly young fellow, well-dressed, and well spoken" Tombe scrapbooks.

Wheatley's notes on Tombe's way of speaking and catchphrases, single sheet c.1922. Archive. Henceforth 'Tombe phrases'.

"Masterly Policy of Inactivity," Tombe phrases, cf *The Devil Rides Out* (Hutchinson, 1934) p.277

Tombe on God: Tombe phrases.

"In mental development I owe more to him . . ." O&TG p.135.

breakfasted "sumptuously" letter to Hilda, January 1916

"conscious hedonist"; "cynical but happy". O&TG p.136

"imitation of gentleman," Tombe phrases.

"bimana," Tombe phrases

Draft letters to Barbara, undated. Archive

Church parade story, Neo-Nestorian O&TG pp.138–9

Praying to the Devil at cards: this story first appears in Wheatley's *Sunday Graphic* articles about *Black Magic* (from June 1956), reprinted in the 1963 revised edition of GGG, p.237. Retold O&TG ("It scared me stiff") pp.139–40.

Lunch anecdote, "Lucullan feast" O&TG pp.142–3.

CHAPTER ELEVEN: THE INCREDIBLE JOURNEY

"a positive menace and had to be got rid of quickly as possible." Michael Howard, 'Haig-bashing' (review of *Haig's Command: A Reassessment* by David Winter) *London Review of Books* 25 April 1991.

"Havre with Colsell" and "Havre Tartoni's" – Wheatley's sex diary sheet, Imperial War Museum.

"extremely interested in sex" and "preventive methods" – note with Gosling correspondence.

VD camps for padres: O&TG p.153

". . . every ounce of food and ammunition . . ." 'Motor Trips' note-book, from the Times Book Club, circa 1939. Archive. Henceforth 'Motor Trips.'

". . . The Overturned Gasometer, The Lunatic Asylum . . ." Motor Trips.

"a German 8in [shell] landed quite near . . ." first letter to Hilda from France, undated. Compare O&TG p.156, SWB p.16.

". . . artillery does go faster than a trot sometimes." ibid.

"long periods of intensive boredom punctuated by moments of acute fear." ibid.

Wheatley's incredible journey is recounted in O&TG pp.157–182, closely adapted from SWB (1961) pp.50–75.

Wheatley's thoughts on officers currying favour O&TG p.54

CHAPTER TWELVE: LAST HOPE OF THE GENERAL STAFF

Allenby had taken Palestine . . . O&TG p.202

Sensation of being watched from the ruins of the chateau: O&TG pp.193–195; TDAAHW pp.265–7

Story of Picquet's sister O&TG pp.195–6 and TDAAHW p.291

Letter to Hilda with "Pickett"; first letter from France, undated.

". . . you can see CAMBRAI plainly . . ." Motor Trips.

". . . no part in the actual fighting . . . But I was there . . ." O&TG p.192

". . . but some madman sent me." First letter to Hilda from France, undated.

"the Gods have been kind to me . . ." ibid.

". . . gunnery course over Christmas . . ." letter to Hilda 29 January 1918

Sergeant Watkins O&TG pp.199; 224

"Pergoda": Motor Trips.

"when father papered the parlour" "quite ancestral" letter to Hilda 29 January 1918

Palmistry, see Blackwell's items 889, 890, 951, 1873, all with annotations about the Western Front; Cheiro's *Book of Numbers*, Blackwell's item 888.

The last German push, O&TG 204ff; Wheatley prays to God and later "Lords of Light" p.205

"Get out! The Germans are coming!"; ". . . and run from the Germans afterwards." O&TG 209; 210.

Brigadier-General Brock and his Jersey cow, SWB p.119; ". . . your men have lost their steel helmets . . ." SWB 120, O&TG 213; ". . . authority over other human beings." SWB p.121.

The girl under bombardment at Amiens, O&TG 216–17

"providing the Hun doesn't send them a special packet . . ." letter to Hilda 29 January 1918

". . . my dear old friend the enemy Bronchitis" letter of 14 May 1918

"I had been badly gassed" SWB p.123

". . . floundering like a man in fire or lime . . ." Wilfred Owen, 'Dulce et Decorum Est'

". . . I am the last hope of the General Staff . . ." letter of 14 May 1918

CHAPTER THIRTEEN: THE ONLY GIRL

"dear old England" O&TG p.226; the ambulance return O&TG pp.227–28.

". . . Chatham House garden . . ."; ". . . your news in re the Devil . . ." letter to Hilda 22 May 1918

Story of Marie at Kettners, O&TG 230–31

Cabinets particuliers: Ann Veronica and Jean Rhys from E.S.Turner *An ABC of Nostalgia* pp.189–90.

"the dominant decent thought of my existence, however remote the possibilities of gaining her affection." – letter to Cecil Cross. Archive.

"Lady Dear . . . with a very large heart . . ." undated draft letter to Barbara. Archive

". . . your (imaginary) wound . . ." O&TG p.234

". . . How dare you?" O&TG pp.235–36.

"I would prefer to say no more about Thursday night . . ." O&TG p.236

"Victory urges me to shout, HOORAY! . . ." O&TG p.239

". . . softly and slowly in the evening when things are quiet and I've got a cigarette on . . ." undated draft letter to Barbara. Archive.

'Rules of Procedure in re B', five page handwritten document. Archive.

". . . if it had not been for your kindness since my return from France . . ." undated draft letter. Archive.

Further quotes from undated draft letters to Barbara, including one written over again in 1922: Archive.

". . . the Captain had a large barrel of oil poured overboard . . ." D&I p.21

"woe betide anyone who dared to lay a hand on a British subject . . . Those were the days." Ibid.

CHAPTER FOURTEEN: ERIC'S CRIMSON NIGHTS

Victory parade: D&I p.27

". . . truly sorry for that nice old man." O&TG p.240

". . . I'm a soldier of fortune now: I'll tackle any proposition." Unidentified press cutting ('Mrs.Dyer's Story / Man Who Was A Mystery to His Wife') in Tombe scrapbooks. Archive.

"Nellie . . . Kittie, Peggy, Beatrice, Desiree, la Belle Americaine, Mrs Hall, and of course Dolly" from 'DEGT' Wheatley's manuscript memoir of Tombe's disappearance. Archive. Henceforth DEGT.

". . . a long discourse on Masochism and Sadism . . ." DEGT

' "Wets" Final Drink', unidentified newspaper cutting. Archive.

". . . Mr Gordon-Tombe will shortly be calling upon you." Undated T.L.S. from Sir Augustus Fitzgeorge, The Anti-Prohibition League. Archive.

". . . but in the suburbs there is a great deal consumed." Wheatley's guide to the London drink trade is enclosed with his letter to Tombe of 14 January 1921. Archive.

Wheatley's draft advert for "BRITISH LIBERTY'S DEFENCE FUND" is enclosed with his letter to Tombe of 14 January 1921. Archive.

"We wish to make known to you Mr D.Y. Wheatley our special representative . . ." T.L.S. from Charles K. Sugden, The Anti-Prohibition League, 16 February 1920. Archive.

Romance with Jean Lester, D&I pp.31–32.

". . . what about calling at the flat, I've got a bottle of the Boy there . . ." Tombe letter to Wheatley quoted at length in Wheatley letter to Hilda Gosling, 19 November 1921.

". . . we drank 6 remaining bottles between the four of us – and – there I draw the curtain —" Letter to Hilda Gosling, 19 November 1921

"... this orgy business is all very well ..." Tombe to Wheatley in DEGT

"... do that sort of thing so very much better at home." Tombe quoted in Wheatley letter to Hilda Gosling 19 November 1921.

Nondescript Players, lamp smashing, police,Louis Newton; D&I pp.33–35.

Monte Carlo: introduction to 'Borrowed Money', *Meditteranean Nights*.

Havelock Ellis's *Studies in the Psychology of Sex*, six volumes, inscribed by Tombe and Wheatley. Wheatley's comments are on his earlier monogrammed bookplates, which have a lined space for notes. In possession of present writer.

"after he had plotted the burning of the Welcomes"; "most wonderful actor he had ever seen" DEGT

"... how wonderful you were on the evening of my famous stunt ..." Tombe letter to Wheatley, 1 May 1921. Archive.

"... when that fainting business began." Tombe letter from RMS Adriatic, 7 September 1920. Archive.

CHAPTER FIFTEEN: SCHEHEREZADE IN STREATHAM

"If I am going to drink ... 'jolly young people' ... but I doubt it." Letter to Hilda 12 November 1921. Brotherton

"a wonderful decade" D&I p.33

praying to Kwan–Yin D&I pp.37–8

Expenses and invoice to Hilda's bridegroom John Gardner enclosed with letter of 3 October 1921. Archive.

"The joy which I derived from seeing you both so happy ..." Letter to Hilda and John Gardner 22 October 1921.

"Will you please forgive an ordinary mortal ..." letter to Hilda and John Gardner 12 November 1921.

"... we do not even see the bubbles ... rising from your helmets." Letter to Hilda and John Gardner 19 December 1921.

"... room of a thousand cushions ... joys that a bachelor can have" letter to Hilda of 12 November 1921.

"... girl in grey who was at the wedding and the Station afterwards ..." ibid.

Orientalist poem to Nancy: D&I p.43

". . . your progress is that of Adonis himself . . ." Tombe to Wheatley 29 November 1921. Archive.

". . . this strange Elixir of Life . . ." ibid.

"Do not . . . neglect your reading . . .", Tombe to Wheatley 31 January 1922. Archive.

". . . you will find epitomised in [Pater's] Conclusion . . ." Tombe to Wheatley, 21 September 1921. Archive.

". . . Major Macsweeney and Major Coode", undated note in Tombe's hand on Wheatley's business notepaper. Archive.

". . . our Russian bookselling friend . . ." Tombe to Wheatley 31 March 1921. Archive.

Krafft-Ebing and Bloch, Ozhol to Wheatley 12 August 1920. Archive. *Book of Strange Loves*, "delightful" Blackwell's item 204.

". . . the hoi polloi [sic] . . ." Tombe to Wheatley 21 September 1921. Archive.

". . . we intellectuals." Ibid.

"penchant for crystallised fruit." Tombe to Wheatley 12 July 1921. Archive

". . . soupcon of 17th century maniere . . ." Tombe to Wheatley 1 August 1921. Archive.

"Our ways of ascending the mount of Olympus may be slightly different . . ." Tombe to Wheatley 17 September 1921. Archive.

"Pagan . . . Eastern point of view . . . How short one's life is . . ." ibid.

". . . the paradise of 'oggins! . . ." Tombe to Wheatley, 29 September 1920. Archive.

". . . the Gallic soul and art." Tombe to Wheatley, 25 May 1921. Archive.

"The excellent kroner . . ." Tombe to Wheatley, 30 September 1921. Archive.

". . . dear boy, a heaven on earth." Tombe to Wheatley, 31 January 1922. Archive.

". . . quite perfect studies (photographic) . . ." Tombe to Wheatley, 11 February 1922. Archive.

"Paradise (complete with houris) . . . lotus eating . . ." Tombe to Wheatley, 2 March 1922. Archive.

Benedict XV: ". . . I do not suppose that my gospel . . . would have appealed to him." Tombe to Wheatley, 31 January 1922. Archive.

Beatrice to Wheatley: "gets about . . . happy as the day is long" 13 July 1921; "Heaven itself" 18 August 1921. Archive.

"Important business . . ." Tombe to Wheatley, 13 June 1920. Archive.

". . . PS will you stamp enclosed letter old man." Tombe to Wheatley, 14 June 1921. Archive.

". . . you have not heard from me." Tombe to Wheatley, 1 May 1921. Archive.

". . . a curious contretemps has taken place in England . . ." Tombe to Wheatley, 2 March 1922. Archive.

". . . the code you suggest is admirable . . ." Tombe to Wheatley, 3 May 1921. Archive.

'X': "will you go to 131 Jermyn St and fix up" Tombe to Wheatley, 30 July 1921. Archive.

"Will you attend to 'X' at once?" Tombe to Wheatley, 8 August 1921. Archive.

". . . destroy (burn) both letters and envelopes . . . a cross at the top of your letter . . ." Tombe to Wheatley, 28 July 1921. Archive.

". . . ring up Mrs BELL, Hammersmith 1447 . . ." Tombe to Wheatley, 17 August 1920. Archive.

"quelle vie" ibid.

Key label "D Key"; scrap of paper with "David Watson . . .". Archive.

Wheatley's letter about Desiree: all quotations, from Bolsheviks and "bimina" down to Burgundy and God, are from this ten sheet letter of 7 September 1920. Archive.

CHAPTER SIXTEEN: DANGEROUS LIAISONS

". . . terrible for you, I truly sympathise . . ." Tombe to Wheatley 26 October 1920. Archive.

". . . shatter some of her illusions regarding your charming self." Wheatley's second letter to Tombe about Desiree, 18 September 1920. All following quotes from this forty page letter. Archive.

". . . unhampered by the constant sex antagonism." Desiree to Wheatley, n.d., envelope postmarked 20 September 1920. Archive.

". . . a masterly letter, the apotheosis of Dennis". Tombe to Wheatley, 29 September 1920. Archive.

". . . thrilling me 6,100 miles away . . . how far she is willing to face comparative poverty with me." Tombe to Wheatley, 17 October 1920. Archive.

". . . this David and Jonathan business . . ." Tombe to Wheatley, 7 September 1920. Archive.

"To have found Sheherezade in Streatham . . ." Tombe to Wheatley, 30 November 1921. Archive.

". . .the more one sees of Nancy . . ." Tombe to Wheatley 21 December 1921. Archive.

"She had always regarded Eric with suspicion and distrust . . ." DEGT. Archive.

". . . a kick from these expeditions, the bizarre and the unusual . . ." Wheatley to Nancy, undated, circa 1921–22. Archive.

Down Street tube station, the flat, Mr Winning, crimes in progress; DEGT.

"nasty little man" D&I p.44.

". . enjoyed so much having one of our little chats together . . ." DEGT.

CHAPTER SEVENTEEN: . . . IN A CLOUD OF BLUE SMOKE

This chapter, including Wheatley's thoughts on his relationship with Nancy, is taken entirely from the DEGT manuscript. Archive.

CHAPTER EIGHTEEN: MR MEYER INVESTIGATES

This chapter continues to be taken almost entirely from the DEGT manuscript. Oddly, Wheatley doesn't mention that Beatrice thought the Tombe telegram was a fake because Tombe would never have used the word "overseas." This is mentioned in several newspaper reports in his scrapbooks, with the same point made by both Tombe's father and mother.

CHAPTER NINETEEN: MARRIAGE – AND A HORROR

The priest and W.H.Mallock D&I pp.45–6

Wheatley's letters to Dr Atkinson [n.d.] and Beatrice, 2 May 1922, Archive.

". . . the Boy who was dearer to me than life itself . . ." Beatrice to Nancy and Wheatley 10 May 1922

Desiree claims to see Tombe in Madrid D&I p.49

". . . valued at more than £800." D&I p.47

"To my darling One with all my love, in memory of June 17th 1922."
Nancy inscription in Blackwell's item 1339.

"Some contrary devil had got into me." D&I p.50

". . . could not have cared less." Ibid.

Pall Mall Gazette on *One Maid Book of Cookery*: quoted on dustjacket
of *My Secret Service* by "The Man Who Dined with the Kaiser"

Hamilton on Maundy Gregory, John Symonds, *Conversations with
Gerald*, "jovial" p.53; hatred of Socialism p.52.

"later became notorious" D&I p.52

". . . good conversation and the finest wines." D&I p.53

"proud to have had such a man as an intimate friend" D&I p.54

Clem Spindler, D&I p.41. The Hutchinson text calls him Gem.

Wheatley on *Ulysses*: from his monogrammed bookplate with space
for comments, which seems to have been steamed out of the book
(possibly to replace it with his later bookplate). Archive.

The Tombe headlines are from Wheatley's scrapbooks of the case,
comprising around 260 pages, often with three or four cuttings
to a page. Many of the papers are unidentifiable, and repetitive
due to syndication. I have drawn on these scrapbooks in the
following account, supplemented by the *Times* 14 September to
26 September 1923.

"Yes, that's my dear boy!' e.g. *Evening News* 13 Sept 1923

"Overseas . . . an expression which my son never used" Rev. Tombe
e.g. *Yorkshire Herald* 14 September 1923.

"BOY" lettered in violets, *Times* 20 September 1923

Wheatley's Tombe Wilde bookplate. Draft on sheet of paper, never
used. Archive.

". . . already caught up with him in a curious way." D&I p.49.

CHAPTER TWENTY: SAVED IN THE NICK OF TIME

Further details of Tombe's case from Wheatley's newspaper
scrapbooks.

". . . bored to tears." D&I p.57

". . . my King who entertains your King . . ." D&I p.55

". . . soulful-eyed Polish Jew." D&I p.57

". . . the vast and mouldy bottle they kept for people of Rex's sort."
Brideshead Revisited (Chapman and Hall, 1945) p.157

". . . the old brandy racket." p.59

"Adjectives fail when one desires to describe Huxley's work . . ." inscription in *Limbo*, one of 48 Huxley items, the whole collection Blackwell's item 1049

Four draft letters to Aldous Huxley, from 10 July to 27 Jly 1926. Archive.

Huxley inscription in Wheatley's copy of *Antic Hay*, Blackwell's item 1049.

Wheatley claims to fire gun during General Strike, D&I p.60

". . . to gratify his lust on their bodies" Vecchi on Rasputin TDAAHW p.281.

". . . his ideas when speaking of marriage . . ." Hilda Gardner on scrap of paper, with Gosling correspondence. Wheatley to her husband, ibid.

". . . getting to know them better" D&I p.73;

". . . desire for one another should gradually wane." Op.cit p.74

". . . anything detrimental about you . . ." Wheatley letter to Gwendoline Liddiard, n.d. from 12 Chepstow Place. Archive.

Account of Liddiard affair from Wheatley's draft 'Account of 1926 and 1927' (runs from 3 August 1928 "Met Gwen" to March 1928 "DW [i.e. Dudley] turns up again". All quotations from this document. Archive.

Proust on jealousy: "The demon jealousy . . ." *Remembrance of Things Past* (London, Chatto, 1982) Vol.III pp.98–99. Love a desire to know, Vol.I pp.298–99.

Private detective reports from Thomas F.Cox, Assistant Vincent, and Assistant Cavell. Archive.

". . . my father died" D&I p.61

Streatham Manor, Leigham Avenue: address recorded on death certificate

CHAPTER TWENTY-ONE: THE SEER

". . . in a big country house . . ." D& I p.65

"Imperial Tokay left Austria only as a gift from the Emperor." D&I p.68; bottle of the 1649 ibid.

Alec Waugh on Tokay, *In Praise of Wine* (Cassell, 1959) pp.180–81

". . . all who are interested in the curious and the rare." Dennis

Wheatley, *At the Sign of the Flagon of Gold* (London, Wheatley and Son, n.d.) p.11

Wilde catalogue inscribed to Wheatley, Blackwells item 2185.

Wheatley's instructions to Pape: 'Particulars for Guidance in Designing Bookplate for Mr Wheatley', typed sheet, together with 'Designe [sic] for Book Plate of D Yates Wheatley', handwritten sheet, and two drawings by Wheatley. Private collection, London.

Gwen D&I pp.75–80; 84.

Wheatley's untitled poem, "The woman, the dog . . ." Handwritten on single sheet. Archive.

Five letters to Gwen, one typed, all undated, circa 1927–8. Archive.

Gwen's *Malleus Malleficarum* Blackwell's item 1279, "Given to me by Gwen Lydywed [sic] in the late 1920s . . ."

"The Lovely Lady of Berkeley Square" D&I pp.80–84

Henry Dewhurst [sic] see D&I pp.84–87; 111–13; TDAAHW pp.66–68; introduction to the Neils Orsen 'Ghost Hunter' stories GGG pp.15–18.

". . . your sex life is over." D&I p.85

". . . unchained from a lunatic." Sophocles, recorded in Plato's *Republic*, Book I. Variantly translated, and since used to great effect by Daniel Farson, the late George Melly and others.

CHAPTER TWENTY-TWO: FALLING IN LOVE AGAIN

". . . Rajahs and millionaires, cabinet ministers and film stars all came to buy those lovely things in which I specialised." *Sunday Graphic* 'Personalities Page' Sunday January 22nd 1939

". . . far exceeds anything ever paid by any other merchant." Ibid.

". . . put my ideas (not more grammatically – dear me no but perhaps more clearly) on paper" letter to Joan 10 November 1929. Archive.

"Am I unreasonable? . . ." letter to Joan 30 September 1929. Archive.

"Alfonso Thirteenth; then finish." D&I p.91

"this farce of married life"; "Miss Craven with her poor blind eyes" Letter to Joan 21 November 1929. Archive.

Mr. Wheatley's "remarkable stocks;" Stambois testimonial, *Flagon of Gold* p.12.

". . . fat, rather tattily dressed, little Polish Jew . . ." p.71

"Oh yes, I've seen life." *Sunday Graphic* 'Personalities Page' January 22nd 1939

". . . Mummy and I are crying." Annette Wheatley

Wheatley's divorce papers: 'Wheatley (N.M.) – v – Wheatley (D.Y)' Petition filed 26 February 1930; Supplemental Petition filed 18 September 1930.

"Come along Dennis, we'll be late for the Duchess" Joan Miller, *One Girl's War* (County Kerry, Brandon, 1986) p.78.

CHAPTER TWENTY-THREE: FIRST BLOOD

"virtual owner"; "personal credit for any reasonable amount" letter to Joan 21 November 1929. Archive.

"Why don't you write a book?" D&I p.110

". . . outsiders coming and upsetting them." Cellarman Lewis, letter of 27 December 1932. Archive.

"the Jews of Asia" Harold Acton, *Memoirs of an Aesthete* (Methuen, 1948) p.270.

"They're Jews! I'm not going to sing . . ." Charlotte Breese, *Hutch* (Bloomsbury 1999) p.77.

". . . but I wanted my party to be a success." *The Diaries of Robert Bernays 1932–1939* ed Nick Smart (Lampeter, Edwin Mellen, 1996) p.219.

'Orchids on Monday' GGG pp.34–47. Doreen Sainsbury p.33

'The Deserving Poor' op.cit pp.178–187

'In the Underground' op.cit. pp.74–82.

"You've written a book!" D&I p.111

'The Snake' op.cit. pp.302–318

"First blood!" ("This is our Christmas card this year – see pages 42 and 116 [. . .]") *Nash's Pall Mall* magazine January 1933, inscribed by Wheatley. Collection of Richard Humphreys.

First book letters: over fifty of these survive in draft. Archive.

Justerini cellars party reported *Daily Sketch* 4 January 1933, and recalled by Wheatley D&I p.114.

"essentially Ruritanian and good of its kind." TLS February 9th 1933, p.94

"Patagonia to Alaska, Iceland, East to Mandalay . . ." reproduced on bookjackets e.g. on the Dossiers

Wrote two books and dovetailed, e.g. lecture to RSA; "boy jumping into bed with girl" e.g. D&I p.251

"People who live in miserable rows of grim little houses . . ." Wheatley interviewed in Popcorn; Anatomy of a Best Seller by Stephanie Nettell, *Books and Bookmen* p.48

"luxury traditions of the cheap novel." TLS 9 February 1933 p.94

"A Tibetan Buddha seated upon the Lotus . . ." *The Devil Rides Out* pp.28–29.

"Entering her palatial music-room . . . Tristan and Isolde." *The Selective Ego: The Diaries of James Agate* ed Tim Beaumont (Harrap, 1976) p.159

". . . sinister potentialities of the cinema and the loudspeaker." Richards cited in T.Eagleton, 'A Good Reason to Murder your Landlady'[rev of Richards's *Selected Works 1919–38*] *London Review of Books* 25 April 2002

Beaverbrook on Christ and propaganda: central idea of *The Divine Propagandist*, his book on Christ begun in 1926 and finally published in 1962.

"hunted like a hare . . . this 'Flight of the King' is the greatest epic of escape in history . . ." GGG p.192

"I do not approve of an author's boosting a previous book of his own . . ." 'A Capital Thriller' [review of *Such Power is Dangerous*] *Daily Mail*, 6 July 1933

The PEN club D&I p.118

"The Nameless Club"; "only important literary club . . . 8,000,000 new books every year" 'Between Ourselves', *Sunday Graphic* 9 April 1939

". . . exactly as described in Hedley Chilver's book . . ." Quoted unsympathetically in review of *The Fabulous Valley*, TLS 30 August 1934.

Driberg escorted by Wheatley: Wheatley's *Sunday Graphic* column, Feb 26 1939

CHAPTER TWENTY-FOUR: LUNCHEON WITH THE BEAST

"One duke, two dukes' daughters, sundry lords, a bishop . . ." Francis Wheen, *Tom Driberg: His Life and Indiscretions*, p.406

Anthony Storr, "evil": Wheen *Driberg* p.347

". . . the presence of a Master" Driberg to Crowley 15 July 1926. Christ Church Library.

". . . I am sorry about the aloes . . ." Driberg to Crowley 7 April 1926. Christ Church Library.

". . . majority could always be led and controlled . . ." Driberg to Crowley 15 July 1926. Christ Church Library.

". . . few and secret . . . rule the many and the known." Crowley, *The Book of the Law* (Weiser, 2004) p.26

". . . will only show them to really promising people." Driberg to Crowley 25 June 1926. Christ Church Library.

". . . really unschooltiesome." Crowley's diary, 30 August 1938. Warburg Institute.

"the Poet", "the Golfer," "the Stenographer" Introduction to Book IV, *Magick* ed. John Symonds and Kenneth Grant (RKP, 1973) p.130.

Powell on Crowley: *Messengers of Day* (Heinemann, 1978): "intensely sinister" p.82, "steady flow of ponderous gags" p.82, "false top to his head like a clown's" p.82 ". . . like . . . a horrible baby." p.83

Maurice Richardson on Crowley: 'Luncheon With Beast 666' in *Fits and Starts* (Michael Joseph, 1979) pp.113–119. Bisque 114; hypnotic eyes 114; sponge-bag trousers 116.

Arthur Calder-Marshall on Crowley: *The Magic of My Youth* (Hart-Davis, 1951): *Who's Who* pp.179–80; ". . . any money of your own?" p.190; ". . . trying to outstare me . . ." p.191; ". . . blacks and whites . . . shadres of grey . . . obsidian monolith of evil" p.177; "Evil was never Pure" p.192

"Recommendations to the Intelligent Reader humbly proffered" etc; Crowley annotations to *Magick in Theory and Practice*. Private collection, Hampshire. This had been Blackwell's Item 433.

"magnificent gift" etc.: Wheatley to Crowley, 12 May 1934. Warburg.

Wheatley's stories about Crowley: The Cambridge Aristophanes story, in e.g. *Sunday Graphic* series article three, reprinted GGG pp.245; D&I pp.132–33; TDAAHW 273. The Paris story: D&I 132; TDAAHW 276; Introduction to Aleister Crowley, *Moonchild* (Sphere, 1974) pp.9–10. Member of Parliament "Z" TDAAHW p.276.

The Paris Working is detailed in John Symonds, *The Great Beast* (Macdonald, 1971) Chapter 13 'The High Magick Art'. Overdrafts, mortgages and Consols p.188.

Orwell and *Gringoire*: in his essay 'W.B. Yeats.'

Crowley, *The Book of The Law* (San Francisco, Weiser / O.T.O, 2004)

[1926; 1938]: "deem not of change" p.47; "The kings of the earth shall be Kings forever . . ." p.47; "We have nothing with the outcast and the unfit . . . the joy of the world." p.41; "on the low men trample . . ." p.42; "Pity not the fallen! . . ." p.45. "I will give you a war-engine . . ." pp.52–3 ". . . worship me with swords . . ." p.53; "Mercy be let off . . . Kill and torture . . ." p.54.

Gerald Yorke's annotated *Mein Kampf* is in the Warburg Institute.

CHAPTER TWENTY-FIVE: TOP CHAPS IN THE FIELD

"top boys": Aleister Crowley, Rollo Ahmed, Harry Price, and Montague Summers, "all of whom were top boys in that line." BBC Radio interview with William Hardcastle 16 September 1971

"a mysterious figure . . . flitting bat-like . . ." cited in *Montague Summers: A Memoir* by 'Joseph Jerome' [Father Brocard Sewell] (London, Cecil and Amelia Woolf, 1971) p.xi

Palazzo Borghese, ". . . an enormous human eye." Summers, *The History of Witchcraft and Demonology* (London, Kegan Paul, Trench, Trubner, 1926) p152. Compare "the well authenticated case . . . an enormous human eye" in *The Devil Rides Out* (Hutchinson, 1934) p.37

". . . January, 1926, at Melun near Paris." TDRO p.34

"Free, Madam, I doubt not, but a thinker, no." Summers, *The Galanty Show* pp.157–58.

"monstrous things . . . our cracking civilisation" *History of Witchcraft and Demonology* p.95

"revolution and red anarchy" HWAD p.23

Summers and Lord Balfour: *The Galanty Show* p.214

H.G.Wells on Summers: 'Communism and Witchcraft,' *Sunday Express* 21 August 1927; reprinted in Wells, *The Way The World Is Going* (London, Benn, 1928) pp.94–102.

"one of the most enigmatical figures of the century" Brocard Sewell, introduction to *The Galanty Show*, p.3.

"chair-croodled" *Galanty Show* p.7

"The Society is a society in London . . ." Timothy d'Arch Smith, 'Montague Summers' in *The Books of the Beast* (Crucible, 1987) p.49;

"Across the the crowded palace . . ." Summers poem 'To a Dead Acolyte' cited d'Arch Smith pp.50–51

"This is Satanism . . ." op.cit p.51

Black Mass with Anatole James op.cit. pp.56–7

"the earliest Black Mass for which there is reliable evidence" Gareth Medway, *Lure of the Sinister* (NY, New York University Press, 2001) p.382.

"aroused only by devout young Catholics . . ." d'Arch Smith pp.56

". . . the god he worshipped and the god who warred against that god . . ." op.cit. p.57

The exorcism, mutton and maggots story is recounted by Wheatley in 'Black Magic is Still A Menace' *Daily Mail* 13 August 1935; his *Sunday Graphic* series, GGG p.243; TDAD Chapter Six; and TDAAHW p.270.

"It has been said that the house was sinister . . . twinkling eyes" Leslie Staples cited in 'Joseph Jerome' [Sewell] *Montague Summers* p.71

"I like spiders" GGG p.243

"positively demoniac" D&I p.133

"Grandma dying come home immediately" Alice Leonie-Moats, *No Nice Girl Swears* (Cassell, 1933) p.106.

"the perhaps not so Reverend gentleman" D&I p.134

This account of Wheatley and Summers is based on twenty three letters from Summers to Wheatley written between 10 February and 9 November 1935. They add up to around 8,000 words, and subjects include suitable stories for Wheatley's *Century of Horror* anthology and Summers's attempt to find a publisher for his now lost manuscript The Black Mass. Private collection, Hampshire.

Wheatley and Summers may have had some prior acquaintance – Blackwell's catalogue lists items 2010 and 2012 inscribed at Christmas 1926 and Christmas 1933 respectively – but these dates could be mistranscribed. On the 14 February 1935 Summers writes ". . . in the near future . . . I trust I may have the pleasure of meeting you" and on the 23 February "I shall very much look forward to meeting you."

"one absentee: Rollo." Crowley's diary, 1 January 1938. Warburg.

Wheatley's Ahmed stories: little black imp hopping about behind Ahmed D&I 134; bungled a ritual and failed to master a demon TDAAHW p.270; hands "warm as toast" D&I 134; TDAAHW p.270; GGG 239

Ahmed's yoga course for Dennis and Joan, undated manuscript of about a thousand words, n.d. (mid-Thirties). Archive.

"... a bit dangerous for you at the present ..." Ahmed letter to Wheatley, accompanying yoga course. Archive.

"the demon finance" Ahmed to Wheatley, 14 November [probably 1936], offered for sale on internet November 2003

"Extraordinary demonstrations ..." flyer for Ahmed talk at Shoreham Town Hall, mid-Thirties, offered for sale on internet November 2003

"a jolly fellow" D&I 134

"... the bunk, and that is what we'll give them'" Harry Price cited in Robert Wood, *The Widow of Borley* (Duckworth, 1992) p.24.

"The devotees are a degraded type.. I have attended a Black Mass in Paris ..." Harry Price in the *Star* newspaper [c.1931] in *Man Bites Man, the Scrapbooks of an Edwardian Eccentric* ed. Paul Sieveking (Penguin, 1981) p.114.

"... as totally English as a man can be ..." Robert Aickman, 'Postscript to Harry Price', *London Mystery Magazine* Aug-Sept 1950 p.88

"cruel tricks ... sexual jealousy and suspicion." Wood, *The Widow of Borley*, p.83

"... never yet met anyone who practised Black, or even Grey, Magic who was not hard up." GGG p.258.

"a new adventure featuring the four friends from The Forbidden Territory"; "Talisman of Evil" Single sheet draft for blurb or similar. Archive.

CHAPTER TWENTY-SIX: THE DEVIL IN HIS DECADE

"the devil's decade". See Collin Brooks, *Devil's Decade: Portraits of the Nineteen-Thirties* (Macdonald, 1948), and Claud Cockburn, *The Devil's Decade* (Sidgwick and Jackson, 1973)

Nazism as a political religion: see Burleigh, *The Third Reich* (Macmillan, 2000)

"... not as an improved economic technique but as a religion." Keynes, 25 October 1925, cited in *Observer Sayings of the Week* ed Valerie Ferguson (David and Charles, 1978)

"... The dark ages are coming again. I wouldn't be surprised ... to see such horrors as people being burnt alive as witches." Wittgenstein cited in Edmonds and Eidinow, *Wittgenstein's Poker* p.94

"We thought that the war would be as depicted in H.G.Wells's film ..." Robert Aickman, *The Attempted Rescue* (Tartarus, 2001) p.219

". . . I could almost hear the bombs bursting." Introduction to 'The Bombing of London', GGG [1942 edition] p.143

". . . wholeheartedly with you from start to finish in your triumphant struggle against the bestial appetites and passions of Leninism." Churchill, cited in Griffiths, *Fellow Travellers of the Right*, pp.14–15

"We cannot act alone as the policemen of the world." Beaverbrook citing Bonar Law: AJP Taylor, *Beaverbrook* p.345

". . . hesitated . . . if they had been told that that the price of destroying Germany would be Soviet domination of Eastern Europe." Taylor, *Beaverbrook* pp.387–88

"Let the people who are misgoverned free themselves of their autocrats." Taylor, *Beaverbrook* p.355

"No war this crisis" Hickey, August 1939, cited Wheen *Driberg* p.287

". . . in that tiny minority, I have since been interested to note, were almost all the autobiographers of the future . . ." Rupert Croft-Cook, *The Sound of Revelry* p.66

"The powers of darkness are gathering," cited Taylor, *Beaverbrook* p.347

". . . sure to be embroiled in war, pestilence and famine," cited Taylor, *Beaverbrook* 348

". . . Europe's guardians against the Communist danger," cited Griffiths p.164

"All this human interest business . . . serves no good purpose and may even do harm." Mosley to Mr WH Britain, editor of the *Sunday Dispatch*, 20 March 1934, collection of Ian Sayer

"tradition of louche goings-on": Anthony Powell, *Infants of the Spring* p.87

"bizarre and dramatic . . ." William Sansom in *London: A Literary Companion* by Peter Vansittart (John Murray, 1992) p.258

". . . Tamerlaine's bad leg . . ." Anthony Powell, *A Writer's Notebook* (Heinemann, 2001) p.81

"Rothschilds, Sassoons, Mocattas, and Goldsmids" [anon., believed to be William Joyce and filed as such by MI5, Public Records Office KV2 / 245] *National Socialist League Monthly* no.2 December 1938 p.6

Nazi swastikas supposedly turn the wrong way: expounded in e.g. *Strange Conflict* (1941), third chapter.

"the might of this Magick burst out and caused a catastrophe to civilisation" cited d'Arch Smith, *The Books of the Beast* (Crucible, 1987) p.23.

Umberto Eco on Manichaean James Bond: 'A Manichaean ideology' pp.161–63 of 'Narrative Structures in Fleming', Eco, *The Role of the Reader* (Hutchinson, 1981)

T.S.Eliot on "pure villainy": Eliot interviewed in a Westminster School paper, *The Grantite Review*, quoted in Tim Jeal *Swimming with my Father* (Faber, 2005 pbk, p.68)

Devil Rides Out questionnaire: page 329 in some copies, excised in others.

Compton Mackenzie review, 'Black Magic', *Daily Mail* 10 January 1935

Wheatley's occult mailbag is first discussed in the *Daily Mail*, 'Black Magic is Still a Menace' 13 August 1935, where he mentions the man who wrote to say the Satanic temple was on the other side of Finchley Road. See also e.g. GGG pp.57 ("the Christ" and the man in Broadmoor); GGG 58–9, 236, TDAAHW p.242 (the woman from Essex).

"I would love another chat, esp. about Magick, as you're on a book; I'd like to hear what you think of mine." Crowley to Wheatley, private collection.

"Most ingenious, but really a little Ely Culbertson . . .". Crowley to Wheatley, note on Claridge's notepaper May 1934, sold at Sotheby's with Wheatley's copy of Crowley's play *Mortadello* 7 December 2007 lot 146, formerly Blackwell's item 534.

"Did you elope with the adorable Tanith? Or did the witches get you Hallowe'en?" Crowley to Wheatley, 1 November 1934. Private collection.

CHAPTER TWENTY-SEVEN: THE RIGHT KIND OF DOPE

'Pills of Honour' unpublished two thousand word manuscript; collection of Richard Humphreys. All quotation, from "should be compulsory reading" to "rapid and quite painless, Sir" from this manuscript.

'Roderick Random', *Time and Tide* 12 January 1935.

Wheatley's reply: Wheatley to Roderick Random Esq., 15 January 1935. Two page typed letter. Archive.

Wheatley on Rome D&I 135–36; more on Mussolini, *Mediterranean Nights* p.73.

'Mussolini: What Europe owes to him.' *Sunday Pictorial* 16 September 1923.

". . . your triumphant struggle against the bestial appetites and passions of Leninism." Churchill to Mussolini, quoted Griffiths, *Fellow Travellers of the Right*, pp.14–15

"a nice Napoleon . . ." J.C.Squire cited Griffiths p.24

Sir Noel Charles, Hoyo de Monterreys and dance in the hall, D&I p.136

Wheatley on Cheney: named Leper D&I 145, "fun" D&I 201

"I knew Tayleur to be in sympathy with the Fascists . . ." D&I 166

"blithering ineptitude" etc. Tayleur to Wheatley, 3 December 1939. Archive

". . . could never come within reach of a pencil and paper without drawing a coronated Devil's head." M15 (Guy Liddell) on Joyce, Public Record Office, Joyce file KV2 / 245

"from Mephistopheles to Faust" Dietze to Joyce PRO KV2 / 253

William Joyce on Goering as Wheatley fan D&I 166

"wittiest man I know" Wheatley on Golding, *Sunday Graphic* column 26 February 1939

"an essentially magical doctrine," cited in DJ Taylor, *Orwell* p.199.

"Author". Paternoster Club card index on Maxwell Knight. Archive.

". . . where I can still keep an eye (or even two) on any undesirables . . ." Maxwell Knight in *The British Lion*, December 1927, reproduced in *Lobster* June 1993

". . . espionage . . . occult . . . clandestine sexual leanings." Joan Miller, *One Girl's War* p.120

"And every propeller is whirring "Red Front" . . ." J.M.Richards, *Memoirs of an Unjust Fella* (Weidenfeld, 1980) p.119

"unmasking the cult of evil of which Aleister Crowley, alias the Beast, was the centre." John Baker White, *True Blue: An Autobiography 1902–1939* (Muller, 1970) pp.129–30. White was a director of the Economic League.

"occult ceremonies"; "novices . . . pupils" Anthony Masters, *The Man Who Was M* (Grafton, 1986) p.90

"If you are going to tell a lie, tell a good one and stick to it." Joan Miller, *One Girl's War* p.34

"Mr Dennis Wheatley is a past-master . . ." *Morning Post*, 23 July 1935

". . . intensity which the sunshine lacked." Beebe *Half Mile Down* p.111

CHAPTER TWENTY-EIGHT: LIKE SPITTING ON AN ALTAR

"Crime Club"; "shilling shocker": Wyndham Lewis in *Left Wings Over Europe*, cited Valentine Cunningham, *British Writers of the Thirties* p.74

"Why can't we just have the facts and the clues?" J.G.Links obituary, *Times* 11 Oct 1997

Times Fourth Leader ('Three Dimensional Fiction') 24 July 1936

Eliot, *Murder in the Cathedral*: Anthony Wheatley

Rupert Croft-Cooke on Peter Cheyney: *The Sound of Revelry* pp.136–37

"its moral character must be designated more than inferior . . ." cited Reg Gadney, 'The Murder Dossiers of Dennis Wheatley and J.G.Links', *London Magazine* March 1969 p.48.

Wheatley to Edward VIII: sold at auction by Trevor Vennet-Smith, Nottingham, February 1995, reported in *Telegraph* 5 January 1995 p.19

"Elspeth Bungle . . . when we only knew the GOOD side of Hitler!" Angus Wilson, *For Whom the Cloche Tolls* (Penguin, 1976) p.44

"We weren't all pro-Abyssinian." Inscription in *The Secret War*, offered for sale by David Bailey Books, London January 2005.

"Budapest . . . civilised mentality" D&I p.146

'We Don't Eat Enough at Christmas!' *Daily Mail* 17 December 1937

". . . absolutely in the clutches of the capitalist." 'Voroshilov and his Campaigns' by Dennis Wheatley, *The Lecture Recorder* June 1938 p.315

"Bino and Lou say I am the grandest drunk they have ever met . . .". Quotes attributed to Diana from Wheatley's diary-letter 'All I Knew Of What Was Going On'. No material directly from Diana seems to have survived in Wheatley's archive.

". . . doctors fear complete breakdown . . ." DW telegram to Cecily Jeppe. Archive.

". . . tragic that I should have left under a cloud . . ." draft letter for Diana to copy. Archive.

"Lou ought to be in an asylum . . ." 'All I Knew of What Was Going On.' Archive.

". . . naked . . ."; ". . . Goat . . ."; ". . . like spitting on an altar . . ." 'All I Knew of What Was Going On'

CHAPTER TWENTY-NINE: THE MYSTERY OF THE BLACK BOX

"definite sense of evil" D&I p.150

"filthy Arab guide" TDAAHW p.125

'Athenian Gold', *Mediterranean Nights* pp.156–65; "more than usually unlikely", introduction p.154.

Franco, "my vote every time" D&I p.166

Churchill on Spain: 'The Spanish Tragedy' *Evening Standard* 10 August 1936, reprinted in *Step by Step* (Macmillan, 1942) pp.50–51.

". . . Duke would be in sympathy with the Spanish Monarchists . . ." *Mediterranean Nights* p. 132

". . . the specialite de la maison . . ." Ralph Partridge on *The Golden Spaniard*, *New Statesman*, 8 October 1938 p.540

'Cookery for Sadists' *New Statesman* 3 December 1938 p.934

Julian Symons on Peter Cheyney: *Bloody Murder* (Penguin, 1974) p.215

Wheatley on Winged Pharaoh, ". . . things of the spirit . . . an inner message . . ." *Current Literature* December 1938; ". . . any sacred book of East or West," Introduction to *Winged Pharaoh* (Sphere, The Dennis Wheatley Library of the Occult, 1974) p.6; ". . . You believe in Winged Pharaoh . . . You won't get such a good deal next time . . ." Wheatley letter to Diana, 29 October 1939. Archive

"the sins of the fathers shall be visited upon the children . . ." *Winged Pharaoh*, Introduction p.5

Joan Grant's Aleister Crowley story: *Time Out of Mind* (London, Arthur Barker, 1956) pp.42–44

'The Ceremony of the Roses' D&I p.216

Barbara Cartland "Lying on her sofa in a darkened room . . ." John Pearson, 'Remembering Barbara' *The Author* Winter 2001 p.178.

". . . only one living saint – Charles Beatty." DW Introduction to Charles Beatty, *Gate of Dreams* (Geoffrey Chapman, 1972) p.xv.

"ruined the natural psychic link . . ." D&I p.216

Beatty besieged: D&I p.153.

". . . earnest appeal not to dabble . . ." *Eton Chronicle* no.2405, 23 February 1939

"Silly of you, Dennis . . . Waste of a pound." Driberg quoted in Wheatley's *Sunday Graphic* column 26 February 1939

'Crime as a Science', *Edinburgh Evening Despatch*

". . . Hitler's ideal girl . . ." *Sunday Graphic* 26 February 1939

". . . greatest force for good or ill in the world today is Propaganda." Wheatley on Bernard Newman, *Current Literature* July 1939. Cited from draft; Archive.

". . . as no country ever makes anything out of a war, the contents of the pool should go into a charity box." *Invasion* [game] (Hutchinson's / Geographia, 1938) p.9, bold print in original.

Wheatley on Sir John Simon, *Sunday Graphic* 29 January 1939

". . . fine dynamic painting of the famous 3.7 anti-aircraft gun . . ." *Sunday Graphic* 26 March 1939

". . . start hoarding . . ." *Sunday Graphic* 22 January 1939

Ermintrude Wraxwell, D&I pp.155–56.

". . . anxious to have unofficial tips . . ." *Sunday Graphic* 12 March 1939

"I do not suggest . . . extremist parties should be suppressed . . ." Wheatley speech, 'The Great Danger'; manuscript of c.4,000 words. Collection of Richard Humphreys.

"characteristically democratic men with dirty hands and small heads . . ." Edward Pease c.1880, cited in Fiona McCarthy, *William Morris* (Faber, 1994) p.466

"excellent book for war time." TLS review of *Sixty Days to Live*

"Witness the anguish of Fred W. Fischer . . ." C.S. Youd, 'Words and Music: Being the Mental Vagaries of a Britisher' *Sardonyx* [American fanzine] Vol.1 no.3 [1941]

". . . all the different skin colours we've got down here"; "I haven't been down there myself . . ."; ". . . remained adamant . . ." *Daily Telegraph Fifth Book of Obituaries* pp.292–93

". . . the simple courtesy with which he defended them." John Michell, *Fortean Times* 83 (Oct–Nov 1995) p.47

"Uncle has taken a turn for the worse and, if you wish to see him before the end, you should return home at once." STF p.17

"large black box, roped and sealed" Receipt from National Provincial Bank Ltd. South Audley Street, 4 May 1937. Archive.

". . . self-supporting until the Government had got things under control." D&I p.161

CHAPTER THIRTY: DEATH OF A FIFTH COLUMNIST

". . . proper dress for any gentleman when Britain is at war" D&I p.160

". . . wouldn't have me as a gift" Garrick speech, 1964

". . . raising a laugh among a few other stupid girls . . ." to ". . . what's happening to Czech and Polish girls" DW letter to Diana, 29 October 1939. Archive

Diana parachuted into France, possibly: D&I p.162

". . . sound him out very gently . . ." Max Knight note to Wheatley, undated. Archive.

"pompous, conceited little creature"; ". . . romantic streak common to all Celts . . ." Max Knight on Joyce cited Peter Martland, *Lord Haw Haw* (National Archives, 2003) pp.120–21

". . . evidence testifying to the couple's abject poverty." Op.cit. p.28

"Oh yes you do . . . He was at one of your parties." D&I p.166. File on Wheatley story, D&I p.167.

Herewith the Clues and MI5 story D&I p.177

". . . so we had a good laugh over it." D&I p.167

". . . more or less throwing her party for MI5". D&I p.173

We don't want to fight, but by Jingo if we do . . . D&I p.176

". . . Phew!" *Daily Mail* 19 January 1940

". . . Major-General Victor Fortune . . ." *Daily Mail* 19 November 1940

"more Gregory" D&I p.183

". . . furiously fascistic books (in nice tweedy covers)". Frederic Raphael, *A Spoilt Boy* (Orion, 2003) p.53

". . . under the aegis of Victor Gollancz." D&I p.169

Paul Dukes: Peter Underwood, *The Ghost Hunters* (Robert Hale, 1985) p.129

Fifth Column broadcast: all quotation, from "with a view to putting the fear of God . . ." to ". . . safety in time of war" from 'Suggestions by Dennis Wheatley for a BBC Broadcast on the Fifth Column as a Postscript to the News'. Manuscript in collection of Richard Humpreys.

'The Man With The Girlish Face:' six stories in the *Daily Sketch*, March – June 1940, reprinted in *Mediterranean Nights*

Captain Ramsay's "Red Book": Wiener Library, London: 1369/1

acc.no.70955. "Le P Trench B" p.2. It is just possible he was infiltrating on behalf of Maxwell Knight.

". . . rather his cup of tea." 'Wheatley's 19 war thrillers were TOP SECRET!' interview with Kenneth Allsopp. Clipping identified by Wheatley as "The Daily Mail, Nov.1957" Archive.

CHAPTER THIRTY-ONE: STRANGE CONFLICT

". . . a rabble, which had to be taken off in its shirts." 'Dunkirk' from the confidential version of 'Total War'; unpublished manuscript in the collection of Richard Humphreys.

"highly successful fuck-up"; Bombardier Kean talking to a young Gunner Milligan in Spike Milligan, *Adolf Hitler: My Part in His Downfall* (Penguin, 1972) p.33.

'Resistance to Invasion' reproduced in STF pp.17–37. All quotes from this version.

". . . a lot of inconvenience and all for no purpose." Wheatley interviewed in the *Guardian*, 12 January 1977.

"delicate, charming man and a real patriot" D&I p.185

'The Invasion and Conquest of Britain' STF pp.38–71.

". . . looking pretty closely at the Nazis for quite a while!" Felix Barker, The War Secrets of Dennis Wheatley, second instalment, *Evening News* 3 February 1959.

". . . but Wheatley thinks like a Nazi." My collation of variants on this quote including STF p.74; Garrick speech; 'The Man Who Can't Help Hitting the Jackpot' interview in *Daily Mail* 30 August 1966; D&I p.190

". . . Britain and France rudely declined . . . Germany's peace proposals . . ." Stalin in *Pravda* 29 October 1939, cited Lashmar p.185

'Further Measures for Resistance to Invasion' STF pp.72–74

'Village Defence' STF pp.78–92

". . . it was that sort of emotional touch which meant so much then . . ." 'This Was My War', Wheatley interviewed in *Reynolds News*, 25 January 1959

". . . we are the champions of Light facing the creeping tide of Darkness which threatens to engulf the world." STF p.92

". . . M's extra-sensory perception . . . projecting one's astral body . . ." Joan Miller, *One Girl's War* pp.114–15

". . . it carries the message that death is not to be feared . . ."

Wheatley on Joan Grant, draft piece for *Current Literature*, winter 1939. Archive.

"everybody is worried about the feeling in the East End, where there is much bitterness." Harold Nicolson, *Diaries and Letters 1939–1945* (Collins, 1967) p.114 [17 September 1940]

INRI ADAM . . . "astral fortress" in *Strange Conflict* Chapter Four, compare de Givry pp.109; 111

Sardinia plans: 'A New Gibraltar' STF pp.110–130; 'The Key to Victory' STF pp.151–61; 'While the Cat's Away' STF pp.182–203.

"I still maintain . . ." Wheatley to Felix Barker, 'The War Secrets of Dennis Wheatley' part 4, *Evening News*, 6 February 1959

". . . long slog up the leg of Italy need never have taken place . . ." Air Marshal Sir Lawrance Darvall, introduction to STF p.13

"150,000,000 Mohammedans are waiting for 'the word' . . ." *Total War* (Hutchinson, 1941) p.31.

Julius Streicher, 'Madagascar' *Der Sturmer* no.1, 1938

Germans should be sterilised: "undoubtedly the one practical way of dealing with the mad dog of Europe" 'After The Battle' STF pp.283ff

Total War as "civil war": TW p.16

". . . decisive sphere of Total War is the Mental Sphere" TW p.18

". . . not Armed Force, but propaganda." Ibid.

Armed force as "the backing for propaganda" TW p.21

"science of influencing ideas" TW p.19

"loses its value if it is recognised as propaganda" ibid.

"If Mr Wheatley had his way . . ." TLS review of *Total War*, 10 January 1942

"Expediency, not morality, is the sole criterion . . ." in both versions of *Total War*, e.g. published version p.17.

". . . if it were calculated that the sinking of a neutral ship . . ." and ". . . steps should be taken for [de Valera's] elimination." From the confidential version of Total War; Wheatley typescript in possession of Richard Humphreys.

". . . select readership of four – King George VI and the Chiefs of Staff." 'The Man Who Can't Help Hitting The Jackpot' *Daily Mail* 30 August 1966

"my most precious souvenir of the war" D&I p.196

Churchill; "magnificent" D&I p.196

"strange adventures in wonderland" Wheatley inscription in Bobby Eastaugh's copy of *Stranger Than Fiction*. Private collection, Hampshire.

"boyish, Biggles-like optimism" *Spectator* review of STF, 6 February 1959.

". . . small hard bench in the draughtiest room of the Joint Planning Staff." STF p.181

CHAPTER THIRTY-TWO: IN THE STRATOSPHERE

"strategic stratosphere" D&I p.225

". . . stories of the poor boy who becomes a millionaire are innumerable . . ." Wheatley's draft note, 'Dennis Wheatley's War Papers Proposal,' to pitch *Stranger Than Fiction* to Hutchinson. Private collection, Hampshire.

". . . not to slap Air Marshals on the back . . ."; ". . . two schoolboys . . ."; ". . . delightful friendship . . ." Wheatley's speech, Garrick dinner 1964. Archive.

"uncanny habit of suddenly appearing in a room . . ." DP p.20

". . . Father of Deception" DP p.19

"cloak-and-dagger"; ". . . everyone involved in any secret activity . . ."; ". . . a good invitation" Garrick speech

"Chanel No.5" DP p.30

'Deception on the Highest Plane' DP p.50

"when things were looking pretty bad for his side at cricket . . ." DP p.58

"The news of our early successes in North Africa is most gratifying. . . ." Churchill cited by Wheatley in draft letter to the *Sunday Times* [1957]. Archive. Published version omits a final dig at Alanbrooke.

"souvenired" Churchill ashtray; mentioned in Wheatley's major but later superceded will of September 1971

"gayest of all my friends" will of 1971

". . . a happy band of brothers" Garrick speech

"Spirits are a very poor return for wine . . ." William Elliott to Wheatley, 23 December 1942. Archive.

"Joan will, I know, love it . . ." Wheatley to William Elliott 26 December 1942. Archive.

"bigger boys" Wheatley interviewed by John Ellison on 'Home This Afternoon,' Home Service 8 December 1966

". . . if you happen to have a day free to lunch with me?" D&I p.62

". . . Eating for Victory" Garrick speech

"Few people can be happy unless they hate . . ." Russell cited in *Scorn*, ed. Matthew Parris (Hamish Hamilton, 1994) p.67

"Dennis, where are the girls?" DP p.129

Denis Capel-Dunn (Widmerpool) DP pp.127–28

"unique," "decisive" Maj-Gen L.C. Hollis, Deputy Chief Staff Officer to the Prime Minister, Minute OS1716(4), reproduced DP p.221

"CBs or, at least, CBEs" DP p.222

"meritorious service to the US army . . .". Bronze Star citation. Archive.

"No one will want to read all this nonsense about the sort of people we are"; "enthusiasm" Bevan to Wheatley cited DP 228; 227.

"great crusade which was to bring light back to Europe"; "a very special bottle of wine" from 'The Opening of the Battle of the Century.' Archive. A later but still unpublished draft surfaced in a chest in 2004, given by Wheatley to an RAF friend (*Stranraer & Wigtownshire Free Press* 8 April 2004). It is adapted as Chapter 18 of DP, pp.196–209.

CHAPTER THIRTY-THREE: GROVE PLACE

"picturesque" D&I p.233

". . . but we are now well on the way to victory." Letter to Mr Downing, 3 January 1946. Richard Humphreys.

"Death to the invaders!" Annette Wheatley

". . . I will do my best before you are invaded". Letter from an earl, 24 January 1949. Archive. From here on I have anonymised many of Wheatley's minor post-war correspondents.

Blackmailer: ". . . I'll have you in the jug" D&I p.234

"Asking for Hunting Kummel and Aurum seems like a breath from the past" Letter from woman at Maurice Meyer Ltd, 7 June 1946. Archive.

Letter re Christopher Lee, 24 December 1946. Archive.

". . . couldn't go and stay while he was working." Annette Wheatley.

"work in the afternoon . . ." D&I p.250

"in purdah"; letter to Joan re Wheatley from Lymington woman friend, 8 July 1968. Archive.

". . . if discovered she would be torn to pieces". D&I p.244

". . . your most wonderful luncheon of yesterday. ." Earl to Wheatley, 28 April 1949. ". . . that delectable hock." Same correspondent, 9 May 1948.

Further social medley of letters largely from 1950s; latest 1961. Archive.

Francois Truchaud on the "the autonomous life of novelistic characters" in 'Vous avez dit Zombie?' introduction to *Etrange Conflit* (Paris, Editions Neo, 1987) p.8; my translation.

CHAPTER THIRTY-FOUR: ROGERING ROGER

"And this is Roger Brook . . ." 'Living Portrait' film of Wheatley (1968)

". . . can't roger that many women, even in your youth." 'That old Black Magic' *Observer* 4 July 1971

". . . like an infant gurgling in his play pen". George Macdonald Fraser, *Glasgow Herald*, widely quoted on later books e.g. *The Irish Witch*

"Talleyrand, tell me what's been happening"; Anthony Lejeune, Foreword to *The Scarlet Impostor* (Hutchinson, 1988 edn.)

Bayley, *George's Lair* pp.16–17

"invaluable" Blackwell's item 572

CHAPTER THIRTY-FIVE: THE MESSAGE IN A BOTTLE

"Botticelli" D&I p.235

'A Letter to Posterity from Dennis Wheatley'; manuscript of approximately 3400 words. Collection of Richard Humphreys. All further quotation from this document.

Diana Eldredge on little simple people: 'To the finder of this note' 5 July 1947

"We'll all end in a concentration camp" Harold Acton, *More Memoirs of an Aesthete* p.314

". . . when your villa and garden are handed over to the proletariat!" op.cit p.293

". . . long sleeves protect one's arms . . ." SWB p.29

"No, it's you!" O&TG p.65

". . . now frequently produced by experts" SWB p.11

CHAPTER THIRTY-SIX: AN INTERNATIONAL SPIDER

"I had heard about a school in Devonshire . . ." D&I p.164

Toby jug on desk at Grove Place: visible in photograph accompanying a feature on Wheatley in *Hampshire Countryside* Vol.2 no.4 (April–June 1950)

". . . this worldwide conspiracy for the overthrow of civilisation . . ." Churchill, 'Zionism versus Bolshevism,' *Illustrated Sunday Herald* 8 February 1920.

CHAPTER THIRTY-SEVEN: INTO THE CAVE OF BATS

Woman's letter about Black Mass at Brighton: GGG p.246

Waldron Smithers's letters 9 January and 28 January 1949. Archive.

Wheatley's draft reply to Smithers, 23 January 1949. Archive.

". . . drugs, alcohol, sexual orgies or Black Mass" Kim Philby, 'The Philby Reports' Appendix II of Nigel West and Oleg Tsarev, *The Crown Jewels* p.317.

My Secret Service by "The Man Who Dined With The Kaiser", Blackwell's item 1493.

Wheatley and Kurt Hahn: D&I pp.252–3

"Wherever the Phoenicians went . . ." TDAAHW p.151

". . . I do not doubt he would have obliged me." TDAAHW p.151

". . . second quarter of the twentieth century", J.Randolph Cox, 'Dennis Yates Wheatley' *Dictionary of Literary Biography* vol.77 (Gale, 1988) p.322.

CHAPTER THIRTY-EIGHT: EASTERN ASSIGNMENT

Aside from Wheatley's draft of his otherwise unseen Islamic novel, this chapter draws on Foreign Office files at the Public Record Office, Kew, cited in the format of e.g. FO 1110 / 383

"a cloak-and-dagger chap with whom I had numerous friendly dealings" D&I p.258

". . . acts of violence, mayhem and murder." Jack Beevor, Assistant to

Sir Charles Hambro (head of S.O.E) cited p.7 of West, *Secret War: The Story of S.O.E.*

"Starting in the Balkans . . ." Paul Lashmar, *Britain's Secret Propaganda War* (Stroud, Sutton, 1998) p.12

". . . the name of this department is intended as a disguise . . ." FO 1110 / 383

". . . about time they got the record right." Celia Kirwan cited Lashmar p.96

'The Life Giving Principles of Islam are a Sound Basis for a New Pattern of Life.' FO 1110 / 413

"earthy press of Persia". FO 1110 / 337

Mein Kampf, 'Minutes of a Meeting of Information Officers, Baghdad 25–28.3.48' FO 1110 / 8

". . . staple diet of the half-educated effendi." 18 February 1950 – FO 1110 / 316

". . . re-written in Arabic by local hacks . . .". 20 March 1950 – FO 1110 / 316

". . . at that level of pornography." 20 June 1950 – FO 1110 / 316

Catalogued as 'Islam' in Wheatley's own 1964 typescript catalogue of his books. Archive.

". . . I do not quite believe in Islam becoming a back number." John Buchan, *Greenmantle*, in *The Four Adventures of Richard Hannay* (Hodder and Stoughton, 1930) [ch.1] p.138

'NOVEL FOR THE MIDDLE EAST' two sheets of anonymous instructions, from a typewriter other than Wheatley's, bound into the front of his own manuscript book. Quotes from "a beautiful Islamic girl" to "see people going into the bedrooms, but should not follow them in" from these instructions. All quotation of Wheatley's novel, from ". . . in the full flower of her beauty" to ". . . ALL WOMEN PROPERTY OF OFFICIALS UNDER COMMUNISM" from the manuscript. This leatherbound manuscript was later owned by Sir John Paul Getty and is now in the Wormsley Library.

Published in Beirut in 1953 as *Ayesha*: Sheridan letter to Wheatley 17 February 1954.

A greenhouse too far: Tayleur to Wheatley 6 June 1956

". . . use of Secret Funds was fully justified, and these would be tax free". D&I p.259

". . . cannot allow any particulars about it to be printed." Wheatley to Iwan Hedman 17 April 1972. Sold at Sotheby's 8 July 2004 Lot 257.

"communism is only a cloak for the most sinister imperialism the world has ever seen", FO 1110 / 327

"Don't back reaction" FO 1110 / 327

" 'We have one foreign policy, IRD has another.' " 'Revival of Political Warfare' Peter Hennessy, *Times* March 1st 1983 p.4

"Is not Dr.Goebbels a magician?" JFC Fuller, 'The Attack by Magic', *The Occult Review* Vol.LXIX no.4 October 1942.

CHAPTER THIRTY-NINE: CLUBLAND HEROES

". . . not so generally awarded as it is to-day." Summers, *The Galanty Show*, p.176

". . . Mr Wheatley needs no recommendation . . ." Gilbert Frankau to RSL ("Gentlemen,"), 24 March 1950. RSL Archives, henceforth 'RSL'.

". . . such very good friends . . ." Frankau to Miss Rudston Brown 12 Novemember 1950. RSL

". . . helping of giant caviar." Douglas Sutherland, *The English Gentleman* (Debretts, 1978) p.14

". . . giving me lunch at Boodle's . . ." Wheatley to Picton Bagge 17 January 1939. Archive.

". . . and numerous thrillers" Candidate form for Wheatley, filled in by Frankau 6 December 1950. RSL.

". . . nor will anyone's feelings be hurt." Secretary of RSL to Frankau 12 december 1950. RSL.

". . . worked himself to death." Letter to Wheatley from friend, Alan. February 1952. Archive.

". . . and other historical adventure novels". Undated proposal from Lord Birkenhead and Eric Gillett. Approved 4 March 1954. RSL.

". . . the great honour they have done me." Wheatley to Mrs J.M. Patterson 11 March 1954. RSL.

"I really will present myself . . ." Wheatley to Mrs J.M.Patterson 25 June 1954. RSL.

". . . and he did not often come to meetings." Mrs J.M.Patterson to Mary Lutyens 31 March 1978. RSL

CHAPTER FORTY: TO THE DEVIL – A DAUGHTER

Gerald Heard, *The Riddle of the Flying Saucers*: "Used by me for my book Star of Ill-Omen" Blackwell's item 919.

". . . whether a writer has produced literature of value" 'Mr Wheatley Keeps the Werewolf from the Door' Philip Oakes, *Evening Standard*, 11 October 1956

". . . wring the factory girl's heart." 'The Novelist's Task' lecture delivered 27 April 1953, reproduced in Journal of the Royal Society of Arts no 4908, 18 September 1953 pp.761–770. All further quotation of lecture from this source.

"what is now called dissociated personality . . . demonic possession" James Atherton, *The Books At the Wake* (Faber, 1959) p.41

A woman at a party: writer in her mid-forties, *Times Literary Supplement* party 2005.

"I'd read and reread Dennis Wheatley's *To The Devil A Daughter* . . ." Lorna Sage, *Bad Blood* (Fourth Estate, 2000) pp.239–40.

"Under this antic [antique] cope I move . . ." Marvell, 'Upon Appleton House', stanza 74.

Somerset Maugham, *The Magician* (Heinemann, 1908) Chapter Seven, pp.113–14; compare *To The Devil – A Daughter* (Hutchinson, 1953) Chapter Fifteen, p.221.

"a spice of wickedness that particularly appealed to adolescents" David Langford, Dennis (Yeats) Wheatley' in *The Encyclopaedia of Fantasy*, ed. John Clute and John Grant

". . . Wheatley could always make me lively around the groin." John Sutherland, 'Bibliofile' *Sunday Times* 7 March 1999 p.11

". . . Wheatley's satanic stuff very exciting." Matthew Parris, 'Bibliofile' *Sunday Times* 27 September 1998 p.11

". . . PS Lynne said it was good . . ." – Wheatley at the very tail end of his popularity with adolescent girls, in an Arrow copy from 1981.

"Wheatley actually did the occult a great disservice . . ." Letter to present writer from Tim D'Arch Smith

1949 book dedication to Mother: in *The Rising Storm*

". . . not turned the clock back a single second." This semi-apocryphal quote seems to be based on "The Conservative Party have never put the clock back a single second," in Frances Donaldson, *Evelyn Waugh: Portrait of a Country Neighbour* (Weidenfeld and Nicolson, 1967) p.15.

". . . the English proletariat has taken over . . ." Letter from friend 10 March 1972. Archive.

". . . what really appreciates a bit of good fish" D&I p.256, spelling normalised.

CHAPTER FORTY-ONE: SIR GIFFORD COMES BACK FROM THE DEAD

Letter to Wheatley from Audrey in Paris, 3 May 1935, refers back to his recommendations re Louvre and Prunier's. Archive.

"Believing me to be poor they will tell me their troubles freely . . ." Unpublished ending to *The Ka Of Gifford Hillary*. Collection of Richard Humphreys.

Oxford Union Debate 17 November 1955, 'That Equality is in Theory a Pestilential Heresy and in Practice a Pitiful Illusion.' Written up in *Isis* 23 November 1955 by Trevor Lloyd and *Cherwell* 22 November 1955 by Nick Hudson.

Wheatley on modern democracy: see e.g. D&I pp.254–55; *Guardian* interview 12 January 1977, 'That Satan Feeling.' Disraeli in *Guardian*, Shute in D&I.

". . . popular assemblies – parliaments & all inventions of Satan." Wheatley's annotation to his copy of Hobhouse, *The Substance of Some Letters, written by an Englishman resident at Paris [. . .]* (Ridgways, 1816). Blackwell's item 977.

". . . tear up the seats of railway carriages." D&I 254

"Hypodermic follows"; confectionery; Joan. Annette Wheatley.

". . . he's a better man than I am, Gunga Din!" Wheatley's Garrick speech, 1964.

' "English," said Frankau.' *The Selective Ego: The Diaries of James Agate* ed Tim Beaumont (Harrap, 1976) 10 April 1938 p.105

CHAPTER FORTY-TWO: THE BEST REVENGE

". . . you can call me a success." To Philip Oakes, *Evening Standard* 11 October 1958.

". . . If the highbrow critics don't like the way it's put . . ." *The Listener*, 13 January 1977

"This is the way to live . . ." *Evening Standard* 11 October 1958

Wheatley's personal effects: I have drawn this list from Wheatley's extraordinarily detailed will of 13 June 1971, later superceded.

"... a collector, obsessive, comprehensive, boyish." Profile by Pooter in the *Times* Saturday Review 9 August 1969.

"... Wells, Kipling, Huxley, Dreiser ..." Wheatley to Martin Fox, *Daily Mail* 30 August 1966

"... catalogue value £715." Philip Oakes, *Evening Standard* 11 October 1958

"rolled gold fountain pen that lights up" Will of 13 June 1971, left to Marqis of Donegall in clause 14.qqq.ii.

"Bright as a rainbow trout", Kenneth Allsopp, 'Wheatley's 19 war thrillers were TOP SECRET!' Clipping identified by Wheatley as 'The Daily Mail, Nov.1957" Archive.

CHAPTER FORTY-THREE: NICE WORK

"... one of those green-glass and deep-carpet wine merchants in Bond St" Account of party principally from 'In London Last Night' *Evening Standard* 30 January 1959; 'Wheatley goes gay' *Daily Express* 30 January 1959; *Daily Sketch* 30 January 1959; *The Wine and Spirit Trade Review* 6 February 1959. All scrapbooked by Wheatley. Archive.

"... just about suits it" Eastaugh to Wheatley on the clothes he would have to wear, 1 January 1959. Archive.

"... a bit foolish" Sunday Despatch 8 February 1959

"Thank you for the party" Eddie Tatham to Wheatley. Archive.

"... first let me fill up your glass ..." Wheatley to Felix Barker, *Evening News*, interview feature to open Stranger Than Fiction serialisation 2 February 1959.

"... a man steeped in espionage"; "I was gassed ..." 'This Was My War' interview with Paul Doncaster, *Reynolds News* 25 January 1959

"The wildness of Mr Wheatley's ideas ..." Ewen Montagu in the *Jewish Chronicle* 23 January 1959

"... poor Ewan!" Wheatley typed note in scrapbook. Archive.

Correspondence with Graucob March–July 1959 and manuscript 'Report on the Nu-Swift Organisation.' Archive.

1959 draft proposal for Dennis Wheatley Ltd., and accompanying correspondence to Robert Lusty. Archive.

"... a few weeks in the Adriatic." Letter to Wheatley from Dennis Wheatley Ltd., 18 May 1962. Archive.

CHAPTER FORTY-FOUR: THE SATANIST

Sunday Pictorial 28 October 1951; 7 November 1954. Cited and discussed in Gareth Medway *Lure of the Sinister* (New York University Press, 2001) pp.143–49.

Robert Fabian, *London After Dark* (The Naldrett Press, 1954) pp.75–6

"Pentagrams and sigils . . ." ibid.

". . . throbbing with jungle drums and chants." Op.cit p.77

Sunday Pictorial 22 May 1955; 29 May 1955; 5 June 1955. ". . . everything decent in life was mocked" cited Medway, *Lure of the Sinister* p.145

'Peers on Yard Black Magic List' . . . "The list reads like pages taken from Debrett! . . ." *Reynolds News* 3 June 1956, cited Medway p.152

Wheatley's *Sunday Graphic* series ran 3–24 June 1956. It is published in its unabridged, unedited form in the six instalments Wheatley originally intended in GGG [1963 edition] pp.233–257. All quotation from this version.

"I'm all right, Jack!"; ". . . boiling resentment . . ." John Calder, *Pursuit* (Calder, 2002) p.148

Byrne and Haxell, Lashmar pp.111–12

"Satanic beanfeast": Wheatley on the Black Mass in his *Sunday Graphic* pieces, GGG [1963] p.247.

The Satanist toned down for the published version: comparison with earlier manuscript in possession of Richard Humphreys.

"several hundred pounds" D&I p.258

"Dear Miss Walker . . .". Letter from Wheatley to fan, 13 May 1963. Possession of present writer.

". . . after reading these pages, the most rational could no longer doubt." Wheatley's annotation to Blackwell's item 634.

CHAPTER FORTY-FIVE: THE REICH REVISITED, AND THE DEATH OF THE DUKE

"Membership of the group entitles the member to about five thousand friends. . . ." Quentin Crewe, 'The First Social Survey of the British Upper Classes' (June 1961) reprinted in *The Sixties in Queen* ed. Nicholas Coleridge and Stephen Quinn (Ebury, 1987) p.72

". . . hard work being entertained straight off the plane by ambassadors and tycoons." Pooter profile, *Times* Saturday Review 9 August 1969

"... British. His hazel eyes moisten at the compliment." Pooter op.cit.

"he used dark forces." Air Marshal Dowding to Michael Bentine, recounted Bentine, *Doors of the Mind* (Granada, 1984) p.91.

"graciousness itself" Christopher Lee. 'Foreword' to *The Devil Rides Out* (Century, 1988 edn.)

"... could have been postdated ... but one wonders." Brocard Sewell, *Like Black Swans* p.169.

"... tried to make the inscriptions as varied as possible." Wheatley to Harold Mortlake, 4 February 1957. Offered for sale on the internet November 2002.

'Contents of Library as at 24th May, 1964.' Typed 84pp foolscap document. Archive.

Draft of Garrick Speech (delivered 20th November 1964). Archive.

Garrick party menu. Archive.

Queen 'In' and 'Out' list; 'Society: The Index' (June, 1965) in *The Sixties in Queen* ed. Nicholas Coleridge and Stephen Quinn (Ebury, 1987) p.128

Giles Gordon and Wheatley, from "middle-brow mediocrity of Hutchinson" to "in spite of my best efforts Dennis Wheatley continued to prosper." *Aren't We Due A Royalty Statement?* (Chatto, 1993) pp.39–43

"... an ageing Flash Harry ..." Nigel Fountain

"... a publican who'd been hitting his own stock" Michael Horniman

Drinking Man's Diet; recommended by Wheatley to friend, Victor Saville, who writes to thank him 17 April, no year given [c.1965]. Archive.

"It is really heart-breaking ..." Letter from an agent or marketing man. 5 November 1965. Archive.

Anthony Powell on Biggles and Wheatley: *Journals 1982–1986* (Heinemann, 1995) p.268

CHAPTER FORTY-SIX: LUCIFER RISING

"It was a wonderful trip ..." Letter to Hedman, 14 March 1966.

"I bring back a mass of material ... Can't get it out of the Encyclopaedia Brittanica." Pooter profile.

Voodoo ceremony D&I pp.245–47. ". . .jumble sale. . . ." TDAAHW p.277; ". . . vilest, cruelest . . ." TDAAHW p.276; "Few people can be so bestial . . ." TDAAHW p.277; "In extenuation of normal voodoo ceremonies . . ." TDAAHW p.278

"I was suddenly seized with such a sense of evil . . . [at Teotihucan] . . ." TDAAHW p.124

". . . It is achieved by white magic." TDAAHW p.261

"Give him the smallest you've got." Gollancz cited in *Aren't We Due A Royalty Statement?* pp.97–8.

"rabid"; "vitriol"; "but I did not" etc. Hilary Rubinstein

Writers Take Sides on Vietnam, ed Cecil Woolf and John Bagguley (Peter Owen, 1967) Wheatley p.139

"wonderful Persian art" letter to Hedman 21 April 1967.

Semisi Maya business details principally from undated [1967] two page letter draft to Phyllis Jakeway, who was acting as intermediary between Wheatley and Maya.

". . . who believes passionately in all the 'freedoms' including that of sex." Blurb of *Dangerous Inheritance*.

Reading *The Satanist* and hearing Sharon Tate had been murdered: Richard Humphreys.

CHAPTER FORTY-SEVEN: THE DEVIL REDUX

"bourgeois splendour" versus "decay and death": David Pirie, *A Heritage of Horror: The English Gothic Cinema 1946–1972* (Gordon Fraser, 1973) p.51.

". . . Evil is vanquished and Good triumphs." Christopher Lee, introduction to *The Devil Rides Out* (Century, 1988 edn.)

". . . mythical luminosity . . . distinctly other-worldly." Graham Skeggs, 'Wheatley and Hammer', formerly on the Net.

". . . congratulations, grateful thanks for splendid direction." *Little Shoppe of Horrors* [Hammer fanzine] no.12, 1994 p.53

"It's a ritual against the forces of darkness, it really exists." Lee on the Sussamma ritual to Bill Kelley, *Little Shoppe of Horrors* no.12 p.45. Lee also talks of his research in the British Museum Library in contemporary interviews and in his autobiography, *Tall, Dark and Gruesome*. What he or someone does seem to have found are the words "Galatim Galata" which are in the film but not the Richard

Matheson screenplay. They are cited in Grillot de Givry's *Witchcraft, Magic and Alchemy*, a Wheatley staple, p.113.

"Satanism is rampant in London today . . . just ask the police . . ." Christopher Lee in 1968 interview, cited Nicholas Schreck, *The Satanic Screen* (Creation Books, 2001) p.130.

"Here's a health to you all" . . . "here's to it." 'Living Portrait', eighteen page typed filmscript by Wheatley. Archive. The finished film is significantly different and is in possession of the Wheatley family.

". . . more cheerful atmosphere at the Show . . ." Geoffrey Le Dieu to Wheatley 15 August 1968. Archive.

"perfect example of a small Georgian Manor House." D&I 263

Leaving doors and windows open. Annette Wheatley.

". . . attributable to the revealed adultery rather than to any horror of miscegenation". Christopher Bentley, 'Fifty Million Copies: The Fiction of Dennis Wheatley', in Bloom (ed.), *Twentieth Century Suspense* p.151

CHAPTER FORTY-EIGHT: RIVERS OF BLOOD

Draft letter to unnamed Hammer executive, possibly Michael Carreras (undated, 1968). Archive.

". . . England, the home of witches and black masses." Flyer from Ballantine publishers, n.d. Author's collection.

"Dennis Wheatley's novels . . . the essential primer in diabolism . . ." Ronald Hutton, *The Triumph of the Moon* (Oxford University Press, 1999) p.268

'Jackie swots for black magic O level' *Daily Mail*, 12 March 1969.

"Wheatley has been grappling with the Devil for over thirty years now . . ." David Blundy, 'That Old Black Magic', *Observer* 4 January 1971

Lecturing to clergymen: 'Secret lesson in black magic for clergy' *Daily Express* Friday 9 June 1972, also reported *Daily Mirror* 17 June 1967 ("Half the drug-pushing in Britain is done by people belonging to the nation's 300 witchcraft covens"). Wheatley lectured to clergymen in Northampton at the request of the Bishop of Peterborough, his friend Bobby Eastaugh, who was announced to be appointing an exorcist for the diocese.

British Board of Film Censors: e.g. invitation from John Trevelyan to screening of unnamed witchcraft picture in company of Stephen Black and psychiatrist William Sargant. 21 November 169. Archive.

Simon Dee show: LWT 8 March 1970.

Programme with a clairvoyant, a palmist, a psychometrist, and an astrologer written up by Quentin Crewe, 'Who Is The Man In the Mask?' *Sunday Mirror* 1 February 1970.

"Having met Dennis Wheatley often on the Astral Plane . . ." Quentin Crewe, 'Mr Wheatley is alive and kicking and nothing like Hughie Green' *Sunday Mirror* 8 February 1970.

"I would certainly join Mr Wheatley in his wholesale condemnation . . ." Kordeiv, 'Dangerous Ritual' *Man Myth and Magic* no.31 [1970]

Wheatley and Rainbird: Anthony Lejeune.

'Suddenly the Devil is the new thing', Nina Bawden, *Evening Standard* 30 November 1971.

". . . liable to end up in the asylum." Wheatley in 'Occultism: The Future' *Man Myth and Magic* no.111 [1971]

". . . taken on the cloak of the late Montague Summers." 'Dangerous Ritual', *Man Myth and Magic* no.31 [1970].

"The Power of Darkness is now threatening to come out on top . . ." BBC radio interview with William Hardcastle 16 December 1971.

". . . riots, wildcat strikes, anti-apartheid demonstrations and the appalling increase in crime . . ." TDAAHW p.290

". . . fear . . . members of the Club would write to me." Wheatley to Hedman 24 March 1968

Headman lunch, ". . . twenty four hours of darkness . . .": tape recording courtesy of Iwan Hedman.

"utterly overwhelmed" 29 October 1970 to Hedman.

Wheatley's will of June 1971: Archive. Not one of these things happened, because this will was superceded by a meaner instruction of 29 July 1977, possibly showing the more practical influence of Joan.

CHAPTER FORTY-NINE: THE MUSIC OF TIME

"lots of champagne" Wheatley to Hedman 8 January 1972.

Desert Island Discs 4 November 1972

'The Secret Life of Dennis Wheatley', *Titbits* 15–21 March 1973

". . . but hope for better times in 1974", Wheatley to Hedman 18 December 1973.

'Members of Whites Who Are Friends of Dennis Wheatley'. Archive.

Teddy-bear coat and white Homburg: remembered by Lee in 'Foreword' to *The Devil Rides Out* (Century, 1988 edn.)

Anthony Powell "a fan" of Wheatley's books: 'He did, however, admit to being "a fan" of Wheatley," Michael Barber, *Anthony Powell: A Life* (Duckworth, 2004) p.233. Powell denied Fenneau was modelled on Copely-Syle in a letter to Tim d'Arch Smith of 29 April 1988.

"from a fellow furnisher" Powell inscription in *Books Do Furnish A Room*, Blackwell's item 1694

"eminently appropriate . . ." Powell inscription in *Two Plays: The Garden God / The Rest I'll Whistle*, Blackwell's item 1704

"I fear I rather trespass . . ." Powell inscription in *Hearing Secret Harmonies*, Blackwell's item 1697

"Briefly, the situation is this . . ." Powell to Wheatley 21 January 1972, letter included with *Books Do Furnish A Room*, Blackwell's item 1694.

". . . relatively intelligent men who write more or less conscious drivel." Powell, *Journals 1982–1986* (Heinemann, 1995) 9 August 1986 p.261.

". . . intelligent man . . . slightly modelled . . ." Powell, *Journals 1982–1986* 5 September 1986 p.268

Wheatley's idea for a lottery: discussed and commended by friend and fellow member Douglas Cox; letter to Wheatley 26 September 1966. Archive.

Enjoyed Hell Fire portraits: mentioned by Wheatley in his introduction to Donald McCormick, *The Hell-Fire Club* (Sphere 'Dennis Wheatley Library of the Occult', 1975)

". . . oasis of civilisation in a desert of democracy" Percy Colson cited in Anthony Lejeune, *The Gentlemen's Clubs of London* (Macdonald and Jane's, 1979) p.295

". . . the Streatham born son of a shopkeeper." Remembered by J.G.Links in his Foreword to the *The Satanist* (Century, 1988 edn)

"He pines, I think, to belong" Pooter profile, *Times* Saturday Review, 9 August 1969.

". . . given his age and the fact that he was only a member for such a short time." Merlin Holland.

". . . great club of which all humanity must perforce become members." Ralph Nevill, *London Clubs: Their History and Treasures* (Chatto, 1919) p.142.

CHAPTER FIFTY: THE HOUND OF HEAVEN

"Sea Bass Lymington" and Lockett's party: 'Goodbye Mr. Brook' *Evening Standard* 3 September 1974]

"Mentally, she is as brisk as ever . . ." DW to Hedman, 27 May 1975

"Her Majesty has asked me to say that she is delighted to accept the book . . ." Queen's Private Secretary to Wheatley, quoted to Hedman in letter of 18 December 1973

". . . but mainly in dogs and horses . . ."; ". . writing beautiful English." DW to Hedman 7 January 1974

"Please do not hesitate to address me by my Christian name . . ." DW to Hedman 27 February 1976

". . . We've all read our Dennis Wheatley at some time or another . . ." Kyril Bonfiglioli, *Something Nasty in the Woodshed*, in *The Mortdecai Trilogy* p.450

"How nice to know that at least one reader fully understood me and what I stood for!" Hugo L'Estrange [Lionel Snell]. 'The Hellgate Chronicles' *Aquarian Arrow* no.9 (Autumn 1980)

". . . the worst excesses of Dennis Wheatley are where it's at." Op.cit no.21 (Summer 1986)

Party at Brown's Hotel: 'An Author Who Met The Wickedest Man', *Evening News*, 3 May 1974

". . . upper-middle class writers like Dennis Wheatley . . ." James Herbert interviewed by Andrew Billen, *Observer* 14 February 1993.

Robert Robinson interview: *The Listener* 13 January 1977

". . . a Bulldog Drummond incarnate . . ." J.G.Links on the Robinson interview: Foreword to *The Satanist* (Century, 1988 edn.)

'MENU: Dennis Wheatley's 80th Birthday Party' Author's collection.

"stunningly clad" 'Satanic' *Times* Diary 6 January 1977

"utterly exhausted" DW to Hedman 18 January 1977

"quiet but pleasant"; "no pain"; "on the mend" DW to Hedman 2 May 1977

". . . subsided gently, and quite quickly . . ." Obituary, Mary Lutyens, *Reports* of the Royal Society of Literature 1977–79

". . . quite wrong about the Roger Brook series . . ." DW letter to Lavinia Collins 11 July 1977. Possession of present writer.

Claims to have married in June 1924 at the age of 26: TDAAHW p.53

657

"the sense of order has gone" Interview with Brendan McCallum 18 March 1969. Cutting from unidentified paper. Archive.

". . . every responsible person who values a life of order, stability and decency . . ." TDAAHW p.286

"The covert, non-utile function of a map . . ." Jonathan Meades, 'I Like Maps,' in *Peter Knows What Dick Likes* (Paladin, 1989) p.579.

"the map is not the territory": Alfred Korzybski, inventor of 'General Semantics'

"without requiring any context instantly conjures up a complete mental picture" TYMS p.81

". . . while reading my stories they have been able to forget their pain . . ." D&I p.266

The Hound Of Heaven given by Eastaugh: Blackwell's item 2041

". . . PS by holding this up I hoped to write a more legible version, but I find I can't. All love D" Wheatley's last letter, collection of Richard Humphreys.

Three volume Flammarion: *Death and its Mystery*, Blackwell's item 634.

". . . the beauty of that light . . ." John Michell, 'Life After Death', *An Orthodox Voice* (Jam Publications, 1995) pp.21–22

BIBLIOGRAPHY

Place of publication London, unless otherwise stated.

[anon.] *My Secret Service* by "The Man Who Dined With The Kaiser" (Herbert Jenkins, 1916)

Acton, Harold, *Memoirs of an Aesthete* (Methuen, 1948)

—— , *More Memoirs of an Aesthete* (Methuen, 1970)

Agate, James, *The Selective Ego: The Diaries of James Agate* ed Tim Beaumont (Harrap, 1976)

Ahmed, Rollo, *The Black Art* (John Long, 1936)

Aickman, Robert, 'Postscript to Harry Price', *London Mystery Magazine* Aug–Sept 1950

—— , *The Attempted Rescue* (Leyburn, Tartarus, 2001)

Atherton, James, *The Books At The Wake* (Faber, 1959)

Barber, Michael, *Anthony Powell: A Life* (Duckworth, 2004)

Barclay, Glen St.John, *Anatomy of Horror* (Weidenfeld and Nicolson, 1978)

Beaverbrook, *The Divine Propagandist* (Heinemann, 1962)

Beebe, William, *Half Mile Down* (John Lane, 1935)

Benson, R. H., *A Mirror of Shalott* (Pitman, 1907)

Bentley, Christopher, 'Fifty Million Copies: The Fiction of Dennis Wheatley', in *Twentieth Century Suspense*, ed. Clive Bloom (Basingstoke, Macmillan, 1990)

Bernays, Robert, *The Diaries of Robert Bernays 1932–1939*, ed. Nick Smart (Lampeter, Edwin Mellen, 1996)

Bonfiglioli, Kyril, *Something Nasty in the Woodshed*, in *The Mortdecai Trilogy* (Black Spring, 1991) [1976]

Bramwell, J. Milne, *Hypnotism: its History, Practice and Theory* (Rider, 1930) [1903]

Breese, Charlotte, *Hutch* (Bloomsbury, 1999)

Brooks, Collin, *Devil's Decade: Portraits of the Nineteen-Thirties* (Macdonald, 1948)

Buchan, John, *Greenmantle*, in *The Four Adventures of Richard Hannay* (Hodder and Stoughton, 1930) [1916]

Burleigh, Michael, *The Third Reich* (Macmillan, 2000)

Calder-Marshall, Arthur, *The Magic of My Youth* (Hart-Davis, 1951)

Cannon, Alexander, *The Invisible Influence* (Rider, 1933)

Catalogue of Books from the Library of Dennis Wheatley: Blackwell's Catalogue A1136 (Oxford, Blackwell's, 1979)

Cavendish, Richard, *The Black Arts* (RKP, 1967)

Churchill, Winston, *Step by Step* (Macmillan, 1942)

Clarke, George E, *Historic Margate* (Margate Public Libraries, 1957)

Cockburn, Claud, *I, Claud . . .* (Penguin, 1967)

—— , *The Devil's Decade* (Sidgwick and Jackson, 1973)

Collingridge, W. H., *Tricks of Self-Defence* (Health and Strength Ltd., n.d. [c.1900])

Cox, J. Randolph, 'Dennis Yates Wheatley,' *Dictionary of Literary Biography* vol. 77 (Detroit, Gale, 1988)

Croft-Cooke, Rupert, *The Sound of Revelry* (W.H.Allen, 1969)

Crowley, Aleister, *The Book of The Law* (San Francisco, Weiser / O.T.O, 2004) [1926; 1938]

—— , *Magick* ed. John Symonds and Kenneth Grant (RKP, 1973)

—— , *Magick in Theory and Practice* ('Published for Subscribers Only', 1929)

Cunningham, Valentine, *British Writers of the Thirties* (OUP, 1988)

Eco, Umberto, 'Narrative Structures in Fleming', in *The Role of the Reader* (Hutchinson, 1981)

Edmonds, David, and John Eidinow, *Wittgenstein's Poker* (Faber, 2001)

Ellis, Havelock, *Studies in the Psychology of Sex* (Philadelphia, F.A.Davies, 1920)

Fabian, Robert, *London After Dark* (The Naldrett Press, 1954)

Flammarion, Camille, *Death and its Mystery*, 3 vols., (Fisher Unwin, 1921–23)

Fuller, Captain JFC, 'The Attack by Magic'. *The Occult Review* Vol.LXIX no.4 (October, 1942)

Gadney, Reg, 'The Murder Dossiers of Dennis Wheatley and J.G.Links', *London Magazine* March 1969

Givry, Grillot de, *Witchcraft, Magic and Alchemy* trans. J. Courtenay Locke (Harrap, 1931)

Gordon, Giles, *Aren't We Due A Royalty Statement?* (Chatto, 1993)

Grant, Joan *Winged Pharaoh* (Arthur Barker, 1937)

Grant, Joan, *Time Out of Mind* (Arthur Barker, 1956)

Griffiths, Richard, *Fellow Travellers of the Right* (Constable, 1980)

Hedman, Iwan, with Jan Alexandersson, *Fyra Decennier med Dennis Wheatley* [Four Decades with Dennis Wheatley, bi-lingual text] (Strangnas, Sweden, Dast Forlag, 1973)

Hiney, Tom, *Raymond Chandler* (Chatto, 1997)

Hodgson, William Hope, *Works* inc. *The House on the Borderland, The*

Ghost Pirates, Carnacki the Ghost Finder (Chapman and Hall, Stanley Paul, Eveleigh Nash, Selwyn and Blount, 1907–21)

Homberger, Eric, 'English Spy Thrillers in the Age of Appeasement', *Intelligence and National Security* vol. 5 no. 4 (October 1990)

Humphreys, Richard, *Dennis Wheatley: A Bibliography* (privately circulated, *c.* 2000)

Hutton, Ronald, *The Triumph of the Moon* (Oxford University Press, 1999)

Huysmans, J-K, *Là-Bas* (Fortune Press, 1930)

Irwin, Robert, *Satan Wants Me* (Sawtry, Dedalus, 1999)

Johns, June, *Black Magic Today* (New English Library, 1971)

Kershaw, Ian, *Making Friends With Hitler* (Allen Lane, 2004)

Knox, Ronald, *The Best Detective Stories of the Year 1928* (Faber and Gwyer, 1929)

Langford, David 'Dennis (Yeats) Wheatley' in John Clute and John Grant (eds.) *The Encyclopaedia of Fantasy* (Orbit, 1977)

Lashmar, Paul, *Britain's Secret Propaganda War* (Stroud, Sutton, 1998)

Lee, Christopher, *Tall, Dark and Gruesome* (W.H.Allen, 1977)

——— , 'Foreword' to *The Devil Rides Out* (Century, 1988)

Lejeune, Anthony, *The Gentlemen's Clubs of London* (Macdonald and Jane's, 1979)

——— , 'Foreword' to Wheatley, *The Scarlet Impostor* (Hutchinson, 1988)

Leonie-Moats, Alice, *No Nice Girl Swears* (Cassell, 1933)

Links, J. G., 'Foreword' to Wheatley, *The Satanist* (Century, 1988)

Levi, Eliphas, *Transcendental Magic* (George Redway, 1896)

Little Shoppe of Horrors [American Hammer fanzine] no.12, 1994

McCarthy, Fiona, *William Morris* (Faber, 1994)

Magré, Maurice, *The Return of the Magi*, trans. Reginald Merton (Philip Alan, 1931)

Man, Myth and Magic, ed. Richard Cavendish (Purnell 1970–72)

Martland, Peter, *Lord Haw Haw* (National Archives, 2003)

Masters, Anthony, *The Man Who Was M* (Grafton, 1986)

Maugham, Somerset, *The Magician* (Heinemann, 1908)

Medway, Gareth, *Lure of the Sinister* (NY, New York University Press, 2001)

Michell, John, *An Orthodox Voice* (Brentford, Jam Publications, 1995)

Miller, Joan, *One Girl's War* (County Kerry, Brandon, 1986)

Nevill, Ralph, *London Clubs: Their History and Treasures* (Chatto, 1919)

Nichols, Stan, 'Whatever Happened to Dennis Wheatley?', *Million* Jan-Feb 1991

Nicolson, Harold, *Diaries and Letters 1939–1945* (Collins, 1967)

Orwell, George, 'W. B. Yeats', *Collected Essays* (Secker and Warburg, 1961) [1943]

Pirie, David, *A Heritage of Horror: The English Gothic Cinema 1946–1972* (Gordon Fraser, 1973)

Powell, Anthony, *Infants of the Spring* (Heinemann, 1976)

—— , *Messengers of Day* (Heinemann, 1978)

—— , *The Fisher King* (Heinemann, 1986)

—— , *Journals 1982–1986* (Heinemann, 1995)

—— , *A Writer's Notebook* (Heinemann, 2001)

Proust, Marcel, *Remembrance of Things Past*, three vols. (London, Chatto, 1982)

[*Queen*] *The Sixties in Queen* ed. Nicholas Coleridge and Stephen Quinn (Ebury, 1987)

Raphael, Frederic, *A Spoilt Boy* (Orion, 2003)

Rees, Philip, *Fascism in Britain* (Hassocks, Harvester, 1979)

Richards, J. M., *Memoirs of an Unjust Fella* (Weidenfeld, 1980)

Richardson, Maurice, *Fits and Starts* (Michael Joseph, 1979)

Sage, Lorna, *Bad Blood* (Fourth Estate, 2000)

Salmondson, Jessica Amanda, 'Sex, Jingoism and Black Magic: The Weird Fiction of Dennis Wheatley' *The Weird Review* [internet] (2000)

Sandell, Roger, 'Behind Right-Wing Conspiracy Theories', *Lobster* no.8 (1985)

Schreck, Nicholas, *The Satanic Screen* (Creation Books, 2001)

Selwyn, Francis, *Hitler's Englishman: The Crime of Lord Haw-Haw* (RKP, 1987)

Sewell, Brocard [as Joseph Jerome] *Montague Summers: A Memoir* (Cecil and Amelia Woolf, 1965)

Sewell, Brocard, *Like Black Swans* (Padstow, Tab House, 1982)

Shulman, Sandra, *The Degenerates* (New English Library, 1970)

Sieveking, Paul, ed. *Man Bites Man, the Scrapbooks of an Edwardian Eccentric* (Penguin, 1981)

Skeggs, Graham, 'Wheatley and Hammer' [internet]

Smith, Timothy d'Arch, *The Books of the Beast* (Wellingborough, Crucible, 1987)

Snell, Lionel [as Hugo L'Estrange] 'The Hellgate Chronicles' in *Aquarian Arrow* nos.9; 21(Autumn 1980; Summer 1986)

Summers, Montague, *The History of Witchcraft and Demonology* (Kegan Paul, Trench, Trubner, 1926)

Summers, Montague, *The Geography of Witchcraft* (Kegan Paul, Trench, Trubner, 1927)

—— , *The Galanty Show* (Cecil Woolf, 1980)

—— , ed. *Malleus Maleficarum* (John Rodker, 1928 [1486])

Symonds, John, *The Great Beast* (Macdonald, 1971)

——— , *Conversations with Gerald* (London, Duckworth, 1974)

Symons, Julian, *Bloody Murder* (Penguin, 1974)

Taylor, A. J. P., *Beaverbrook* (Hamish Hamilton, 1972)

Taylor, D. J., *Orwell* (Chatto, 2003)

Thompson, Francis, *The Hound of Heaven* (Burnes Oates, n.d.)

Truchaud, Francois, 'Vous avez dit Zombie?' introduction to Wheatley, *Etrange Conflit* (Paris, Editions Neo, 1987)

Turner, E. S., *An ABC of Nostalgia* (Michael Joseph, 1984)

Vansittart, Peter, *London: A Literary Companion* (John Murray, 1992)

Waugh, Alec, *In Praise of Wine* (Cassell, 1959)

Waugh, Evelyn, *Brideshead Revisited* (Chapman and Hall, 1945)

Wells, H. G., *The Way The World Is Going* (Benn, 1928)

West, Nigel, and Tsarev, Oleg, *The Crown Jewels* (Harper Collins, 1998)

West, Nigel, *Secret War: The Story of S.O.E.* (Hodder and Stoughton, 1992)

Wheatley, Anthony, 'Foreword' to Wheatley, *The Forbidden Territory* (Century, 1988)

Wheatley, Dennis, *Historic Brandies from the Palaces of the Kings of France* (Wheatley, c.1925)

——— , *At The Sign of the Flagon of Gold* (Wheatley and Son, 1930)

——— , *Old Masters: A Catalogue of Old Brandies and a few Great Wines* (Wheatley and Son, 1930)

——— , *The Forbidden Territory* (Hutchinson, 1933)

——— , *Such Power is Dangerous* (Hutchinson, 1933)

——— , *Old Rowley: A Private Life of Charles II* (Hutchinson, 1933)

——— , *Black August* (Hutchinson, 1934)

——— , *The Fabulous Valley* (Hutchinson, 1934)

——— , *The Devil Rides Out* (Hutchinson, 1934)

——— , *The Eunuch of Stamboul* (Hutchinson, 1935)

——— , *A Century of Horror*, ed. (Hutchinson, 1935)

——— , *They Found Atlantis* (Hutchinson, 1936)

——— , *Murder off Miami*, with J.G. Links (Hutchinson, 1936)

——— , *Contraband* (Hutchinson, 1936)

——— , *The Secret War* (Hutchinson, 1937)

——— , *Who Killed Robert Prentice?* (Hutchinson, 1937)

——— , *Red Eagle* (Hutchinson, 1937)

——— , *Uncharted Seas* (Hutchinson, 1938)

——— , *The Malinsay Massacre* (Hutchinson, 1938)

——— , *A Century of Spy Stories*, ed. (Hutchinson, 1938)

——— , *The Golden Spaniard* (Hutchinson, 1938)

——— , *The Quest of Julian Day* (Hutchinson, 1939)

———, *Herewith the Clues*, with J.G.Links (Hutchinson, 1939)

———, *Sixty Days to Live* (Hutchinson, 1939)

———, *Those Modern Musketeers* [omnibus, first four Duke de Richleau novels including first appearance of *Three Inquisitive People*] (Hutchinson, 1939)

———, *The Scarlet Impostor* (Hutchinson, 1940)

———, *Three Inquisitive People* (Hutchinson, 1940)

———, *Faked Passports* (Hutchinson, 1940)

———, *The Black Baroness* (Hutchinson, 1940)

———, *Strange Conflict* (Hutchinson, 1941)

———, *The Sword of Fate* (Hutchinson, 1941)

———, *Total War* (Hutchinson, 1941)

———, *V for Vengeance* (Hutchinson, 1942)

———, *Mediterranean Nights* (Hutchinson, 1942)

———, *Gunmen, Gallants and Ghosts* (Hutchinson, 1943)

———, *The Man Who Missed The War* (Hutchinson, 1945)

———, *Codeword – Golden Fleece* (Hutchinson, 1946)

———, *Come Into My Parlour* (Hutchinson, 1946)

———, *The Launching of Roger Brook* (Hutchinson, 1947)

———, *The Shadow of Tyburn Tree* (Hutchinson, 1948)

———, *The Haunting of Toby Jugg* (Hutchinson, 1948)

———, *The Rising Storm* (Hutchinson, 1949)

———, *The Seven Ages of Justerini's* (Riddle Books, 1949)

———, *The Second Seal* (Hutchinson, 1950)

———, *The Early Adventures of Roger Brook* [omnibus] (Hutchinson, 1951)

———, *The Man Who Killed the King* (Hutchinson, 1951)

———, *Star of Ill Omen* (Hutchinson, 1952)

———, *Worlds Far From Here* [omnibus] (Hutchinson, 1952)

———, *Ayesha* [written as 'Of Vice and Virtue'] ([I.R.D], Beirut, 1953)

———, *To the Devil – A Daughter* (Hutchinson, 1953)

———, *Curtain of Fear* (Hutchinson, 1953)

———, *These Modern Musketeers* [Duke de Richleau omnibus, but omits TDRO] (Hutchinson, 1954)

———, *The Island Where Time Stands Still* (Hutchinson, 1954)

———, *The Secret Missions of Gregory Sallust* [omnibus] (Hutchinson, 1955)

———, *The Dark Secret of Josephine* (Hutchinson, 1955)

———, *The Ka of Gifford Hillary* (Hutchinson, 1956)

———, *The Black Magic Omnibus* [TDRO; SC; TDAD] (Hutchinson, 1956)

———, *The Prisoner in the Mask* (Hutchinson, 1957)

——, *Roger Brook in the French Revolution* [omnibus] (Hutchinson, 1957)

——, *Traitors' Gate* (Hutchinson, 1958)

——, *Death in the Sunshine* [omnibus] (Hutchinson, 1958)

——, *Stranger Than Fiction* (Hutchinson, 1959)

——, *The Rape of Venice* (Hutchinson, 1959)

——, *Plot and Counterplot* [omnibus] (Hutchinson, 1959)

——, *The Satanist* (Hutchinson, 1960)

——, *Into The Unknown* [omnibus] (Hutchinson, 1960)

——, *Saturdays with Bricks* (Hutchinson, 1961)

——, *Vendetta in Spain* (Hutchinson, 1961)

——, *Mayhem in Greece* (Hutchinson, 1962)

——, *The Sultan's Daughter* (Hutchinson, 1963)

——, *Mediterranean Nights* [different selection from 1942 edition] (Hutchinson, 1963)

——, *Gunmen, Gallants and Ghosts* [variant selection from the 1943 edition, including Wheatley's Black Magic series from the *Sunday Graphic*] (Hutchinson, 1963)

——, *Bill for the Use of a Body* (Hutchinson, 1964)

——, *They Used Dark Forces* (Hutchinson, 1964)

——, *The Eight Ages of Justerini's* (Dolphin Books, 1965)

——, *Dangerous Inheritance* (Hutchinson, 1965)

——, *The Wanton Princess* (Hutchinson, 1966)

——, *Unholy Crusade* (Hutchinson, 1967)

——, *Dennis Wheatley's First Book of Horror Stories*, ed. (Hutchinson, 1968)

——, *Dennis Wheatley's Second Book of Horror Stories*, ed. [re-hashed selections from the 1935 *Century of Horror Stories*] (Hutchinson, 1968)

——, *The White Witch of the South Seas* (Hutchinson, 1968)

——, *Evil in a Mask* (Hutchinson, 1969)

——, *Gateway to Hell* (Hutchinson, 1970)

——, *The Ravishing of Lady Mary Ware* (Hutchinson, 1971)

——, *The Devil and All His Works* (Hutchinson, 1971)

——, *The Strange Story of Linda Lee* (Hutchinson, 1972)

——, *The Irish Witch* (Hutchinson, 1973)

——, *Desperate Measures* (Hutchinson, 1974)

——, *The Young Man Said* [volume one of Wheatley's autobiography, collectively *The Time Has Come*] (Hutchinson, 1977)

——, *Dennis Wheatley* [omnibus, comprising TDRO, Jugg, Gateway to Hell, TDAD] (Heinemann / Octopus, 1977)

——, *Officer and Temporary Gentleman* [vol. two of *The Time Has Come*] (Hutchinson, 1978)

——, *Drink and Ink* [volume three of *The Time Has Come*] (Hutchinson, 1979)

——, *The Deception Planners: My Secret War*, ed. Anthony Lejeune (Hutchinson, 1980)

Wheen, Francis, *Tom Driberg: His Life and Indiscretions* (Chatto, 1990)

White, John Baker, *True Blue: An Autobiography 1902–1939* (Muller, 1970)

Williamson, Philip, *National Crisis and National Government* (Cambridge, C.U.P., 1992)

Wilson, Angus, *For Whom the Cloche Tolls* (Penguin, 1976)

Wood, Robert, *The Widow of Borley* (Duckworth, 1992)

Woolf, Cecil, ed. with John Bagguley, *Writers Take Sides on Vietnam* (Peter Owen, 1967)

Youd, C.S., 'Words and Music: Being the Mental Vagaries of a Britisher' *Sardonyx* Vol.1 no.3 [1941]

Younger, William, *The Hammersmith Maggot* (Eyre and Spottiswoode, 1955)

——, *Gods, Men and Wine* (Michael Joseph, 1966)

THE DENNIS WHEATLEY LIBRARY OF THE OCCULT
(Sphere, 1974–77)

1. Bram Stoker, *Dracula*
2. Guy Endore, *The Werewolf of Paris*
3. Aleister Crowley, *Moonchild*
4. Helena Blavatsky, *Studies in Occultism*
5. William Hope Hodgson, *Carnacki the Ghost Finder*
6. Elliot O'Donnell, *The Sorcery Club*
7. Paul Tabori, *Harry Price: The Biography of a Ghost Hunter*
8. F. Marion Crawford, *The Witch of Prague*
9. Dennis Wheatley [ed.] *Uncanny Tales I* (Sheridan Le Fanu, Wilkie Collins, Walter Scott, Mrs.Oliphant, Washington Irving, Edgar Allan Poe, Theophile Gautier)
10. A. E. W. Mason, *The Prisoner in the Opal*
11. J. W. Brodie-Innes, *The Devil's Mistress*
12. Cheiro, *You and Your Hand*
13. Marjorie Bowen, *Black Magic*
14. Philip Bonewits, *Real Magic*
15. Goethe, *Faust*
16. Dennis Wheatley [ed.], *Uncanny Tales 2* (Arthur Machen, William Seabrook, E. F. Benson, L. P. Hartley, Walter de la Mare, 'Ex-Private X', William Younger, Dennis Wheatley)

17. John Buchan, *The Gap in the Curtain*
18. Zolar, *The Interpretation of Dreams*
19. Alfred Metraux, *Voodoo*
20. R. H. Benson, *The Necromancers*
21. Dennis Wheatley [ed.], *Satanism and Witches* (Benvenuto Cellini, Sax Rohmer, William Godwin, Robert Anthony, Ronald Seth, Margaret Murray, Phineas T. Barnum, Cotton Mather, Nathaniel Hawthorne, Aleister Crowley, Betty May, Elliott O'Donnell, Robert Graves, Wheatley's *Sunday Graphic* articles, various anonymous documents, and a grimoire)
22. Joan Grant, *The Winged Pharaoh*
23. J. K. Huysmans, *Down There*
24. Matthew Lewis, *The Monk*
25. Alexander Dumas, *Horror at Fontenay*
26. Donald McCormick, *The Hell-Fire Club*
27. Marie Corelli, *The Mighty Atom*
28. Frances Mossiker, *The Affair of the Poisons*
29. Hilda Lewis, *The Witch and the Priest*
30. Julian Franklyn, *Death by Enchantment*
31. Ida B. Prangley, *Fortune Telling by Cards*
32. Peter Saxon, *Dark Ways to Death*
33. William Hope Hodgson, *The Ghost Pirates*
34. Gaston Leroux, *The Phantom of the Opera*
35. Charles Williams, *The Greater Trumps*
36. Maurice Magre, *The Return of the Magi*
37. Dennis Wheatley [ed] *Uncanny Tales 3* (Conan Doyle, F. Tennyson Jesse, Theodore Dreiser, Louis Golding, Hugh Walpole, H.R. Wakefield, Edith Wharton, W. W. Jacobs, Dennis Wheatley, Frank Harris, Algernon Blackwood)
38. Evelyn Eaton, *The King is a Witch*
39. Mary Shelley, *Frankenstein*
40. Lord Dunsany, *The Curse of the Wise Woman*
41. Sax Rohmer, *Brood of the Witch Queen*
42. Pedro McGregor, *Brazilian Magic: Is It The Answer?*
43. Jack Williamson, *Darker Than You Think*
44. Charles Williams, *War In Heaven*
45. John Cowper Powys, *Morwyn*

ACKNOWLEDGMENTS

"Writing a book is a horrible, exhausting struggle, like a long bout of some painful illness," wrote George Orwell. "One would never undertake such a thing if one were not driven on by some demon . . ."

One of the rewards of this struggle is meeting some excellent people, and I must particularly thank Charles Beck, Roger Dobson, Richard Humphreys, Anthony Lejeune, Ian Sayer, and Timothy d'Arch Smith for their invaluable help.

I am also very grateful in various ways to Bob Anderson, Michael Barber, Louis Barfe, Derek Bradley, Bill Breeze, Bryan Clough, Nicholas Culpeper, Linda Donald, Jeremy Duns, Geoffrey Elborn, Mari Evans, Giles Foden, Nigel Fountain, Keith Hargreaves, Tamsen Harward, Iwan Hedman-Morelius, Michael Horniman, Andrew Jefford, Steve Kandell, Jane Lewis (née Tombe), Patrick Matthews, Benedicte Page, Liz Parratt, Mark Pilkington, Ian Pindar, Robert Potts, Jon Preece, Isabel Quigly, Sandy Robertson, the late Bob Rothwell, Hilary Rubinstein, David Rule, Helmut Schwarzer, Derek Slavin, Jamie Sturgeon, Stephen Whatley, Paul Willetts, Derek Witty, Lizzie Wright, Cheryl Younson and, of course, Sheena.

Philip Brown of Blackwell Rare Books very kindly presented me with a copy of Catalogue A1136 from 1979 – an essential item for anyone interested in Wheatley – and helped with the questions it raised. Robert Hardy and Oliver Irvine of Maggs Bros showed me Wheatley's manuscript of 'Of Vice and Virtue' (*Ayesha*), courtesy of the Wormsley Library.

Research is one of the more enjoyable parts of writing, and I am indebted to the following people and institutions, visited or corresponded with: Sara Land of the Brotherton Library; Janet McMullin of Christ Church Library; Jan

Piggot of Dulwich College Archives; Penelope Hatfield of Eton College Archives; Imperial War Museum Library; C. J. Roberts of the Marine Society; Sheila Knight and other staff at the Public Record Office; Jean Rose of Random House Archives; Pamela Clark of The Royal Archives; Malcolm Brown of the St John's Wood Society; Professor William Ryan at the Warburg Institute; Westminster Local Studies Library; the Wiener Library; Geoffrey Dunster of the Old Worcesters; and the Wormsley (Getty) Library. I also used the British Library, and above all the irreplaceable London Library (in the words of Borges, "I have always imagined that paradise will be a kind of library.")

Wheatley always liked to belong, and in pursuit of this strand of the story I want to thank R. T. Smith of Boodle's; Graham Snell of Brooks's; Betty Beesley of the Garrick; Peter Bond of the Savage; David Anderson of White's; Christopher Denvir of the Royal Society of Arts; Maggie Ferguson and Julia Abel Smith of the Royal Society of Literature; Ilene Wilson of the Royal Society of St George; and particularly Merlin Holland of the Saintsbury Club.

I was helped financially during the long haul of this book by the Authors' Fund, the Royal Literary Fund, and the Wingate Foundation. It is very encouraging to receive awards from such bodies, and their role in keeping writers from despondency as well as financial ruin is probably under-recognised. I am doubly grateful to them.

Last – but, in fact, foremost – I should like to thank Dennis Wheatley's family, particularly Anthony, Annette, and Dominic, for their hospitality and generosity with their time.

★

Unpublished material from Aleister Crowley, Tom Driberg, Eric Gordon Tombe and Dennis Wheatley is quoted by gracious permission of Hymenaeus Beta of the Ordo Templi Orientis, David Higham Associates, Jane Lewis, and the Wheatley family, respectively. The author and publishers would be glad to hear from any other copyright holders that they have been unable to trace.

List of Illustrations

Photographs of Wheatley by courtesy of the Wheatley
    family unless credited otherwise.

Wheatley admiring the stars he cut out and stuck on his bedroom ceiling at Grove Place. He liked to look at them by candlelight: "One feels away from it all. It is enchanting."

A NOTE TO THE SECOND EDITION

When I was writing this book I used to tell people that I intended to be the Richard Ellman of Satanic pulp. I wasn't, however, thinking of Ellman's reputation for mistakes. A Joyce enthusiast once subjected me to a litany of errors in Ellman's definitive James Joyce biography, later to be dwarfed by the number of slips in his magisterial book on Oscar Wilde. Horst Schroeder has published a list of these, which has itself now run to an enlarged second edition of 311 pages (*Additions and Corrections to Richard Ellman's Oscar Wilde*, Braunschweig, 2002).

Inevitably a few errors crept into *The Devil is a Gentleman*. It is irritating to have first and second editions which differ in unknown ways, leaving unspecified errors in the first, so I'd like to identify them here. This will also serve as an errata list for the earlier book, to which page references are given:

* Guildford Street [p.97] should be Guilford Street.
* Dr. X. Jacobus [p.111] should be Dr. Jacobus X.
* J.G. Flecker [p.175] should be J.E. Flecker.
* Baron Von Gloedel [p.180] should be Baron von Gloeden.
* Aleister Crowley's dictum should be "Do what thou wilt shall be the whole of the Law", not "name of the Law" [p.299], and there is another misquotation from Crowley's *Book of the Law*: "Mercy be let off" [p.305] should be "Mercy let be off".
* Montague Summers's secretary-companion should be Hector Stuart-Forbes, not Forbes-Stuart [p.318]

* Two and sixpence should be a half crown, not "a florin" or two shillings [p.320].
* Reticent widows [p.327] should be reticent windows.
* Gerald Gardner's "Grand Rite" [p.525] should be "Great Rite".
* *To The Devil – A Daughter* was not quite Hammer's last film [p.598]; that was their remake of *The Lady Vanishes* in 1978.
* Nine words of text ("where the Talisman is hidden. Here,'the perverted maniac'") were missing around the pictures on pp.332–335.

Anthony Powell is said by his biographer to have described himself as "a fan" of Wheatley's work, and I have quoted this on p.589. Having now seen the letter that this is based on (to Timothy d'Arch Smith, 29th April 1988) I'm sure that when Powell says he knew Wheatley "as a fan," he meant Wheatley was a fan of his.

The absurd thing with errors is that they tend to be things one actually knows – what was I thinking of with "Do what thou wilt. . ."? – but something I didn't know was who Charles Morgan was, and I over-enthusiastically confused him with Charles Williams on p.484. Morgan was on the Royal Society of Literature panel, but he was not an esoteric Christian writer and he never appeared in The Dennis Wheatley Library of the Occult.

Phil Baker
Saint Walburga's Eve 2011

Index

679

British Russia Club 365
British Union of Fascists 272, 344, 351
Brixton 18, 19, 30, 32, 64, 149, 183
Brock, Brigadier-General Henry 142–3
Brood of the Witch Queen (Rohmer) 598
Brooks, Brigadier Sir Dallas 411, 413
Brooks, Collin 323
Brooks's Club 483
Brothers of the Shadow, The 529
Brown, James 535
Brown, Miss Rudston 481
Brown's Hotel 274, 535, 598
Brueghel, Pieter 515
Buchan, John 9, 60, 104, 350, 373, 392, 418, 470, 481
Buchan, Mr., bank manager 91, 94
Buchman, Frank 291
Buddha 111, 112, 287, 329
Budge, Wallis 111
Bulldog Drummond (Sapper) 282, 290, 602
Burbidge, Ruby 112
Burn, Captain Hubert Pelham 267
Burn, Colin Pelham (step-son) 267, 317, 386
Burroughs, William 556
Buszards, cake shop 32
Butler, R.A. 'Rab' 324
Butler, Samuel 490
Butlin, Sir William 374
Byron, Lord 30, 506, 565

Cabell, James Branch 255
Cadbury and Pratt 13–14
Cadogan Square 90, 535, 560, 563, 566, 583, 585, 600
Café de Paris 280, 404
Café Royal 565
Cairo (Asche) 168
Calder, John 529

Calder-Marshall, Arthur, on Crowley 300
Callcott, Lady 40
Cambrai, Battle of 134, 137
Cambyses 371
Camel Corps 371
Campaign for Nuclear Disarmament (CND) 507
Cannon, Alexander 332
Capel-Dunn, Lieutenant-Colonel Dennis ('Widmerpool') 422
Cardinal's Folly 252, 335, 561
Carnacki the Ghost Finder (Hodgson) 282, 320, 492
Carol, King of Romania 240
Cartland, Barbara 376, 429, 544
Casanova, Giacomo 11, 543
Castlereagh, Viscount 506
Cave of Bats (Nice) 464, 494
Cavell, E.G., private detective 249
Chamberlain, Neville 325, 343, 386
Charles I, King 76, 253, 512
Charles II, King 289, 301, 485
Charles, Sir Noel 343
Charlie (doll) 22, 23, 437
Chatsworth Court 408
Chaucer, Eve (see Wheatley, Joan)
Chekhov, Anton 111
Cheshire Cheese, public house 292
Chesterfield, Lord 179
Cheyney, Peter 344, 345, 358, 359, 372, 377, 511; as Mosleyite 344; Wheatley writes introduction for 345; as "good fellow" 345
china figurines 30, 327, 512
Chinese people 24, 139, 280, 282, 475, 498–9, 512
Choronzon 331
Christ 111, 115, 138, 336, 375, 418, 490
Christ, The (madman) 336
Christianity, DW's dislike of 47, 48, 49, 60, 119, 139, 140, 227
Christie, Agatha 11, 336, 448, 605
Chu Chin Chow (Asche) 168

682

status in DW's work 574
Dewhirst, Henry, seer or psychologist 264, 265, 266, 267, 282, 576; and 'cold reading' 264
Diary of a Drug Fiend (Crowley) 297
Dickens, Charles 40, 61, 287, 461
Dickson, Group Captain Sir William "Dickie" 414
Dictionary of National Biography 439
Dieseldorff, Mrs. 67
Dieseldorff, Ralph 66–69
Dietz, mentor of Lord Haw-Haw 347
Dilettanti Club 592
Disraeli, Benjamin 451, 506
Dissociation of a Personality, The (Prince) 491
Doctor Faustus (Marlowe) 437
Doctrine and Doctrinal Disruption (Mallock) 227
Don't Send Your Son to the Shambles of a Jew-Made War (Seton-Hutchison) 348
Donegall, Lord 292, 358, 378, 402, 535, 592
Dostoevsky, Fyodor 586
Douglas, George 490
Douglas, Norman 342, 490
Dowding, Lord, Air Marshal 487, 540
Doyle, Conan 42, 355, 576
Dracula (Stoker) 341, 561, 598
Drake, Sir Francis 142
Dream, The (Churchill story) 446
Driberg, Tom 292, 325, 352, 377, 378, 531; and Crowley 297–303, 493
Drinking Man's Diet, The 547
Du Maurier, Daphne 585
Du Maurier, Gerald 290, 291
Dukes, Sir Paul 393
Dulau, book dealers 243, 254, 273
Dulwich College 49–52, 57

Dumas, Alexander 40, 42, 43, 46, 50, 57, 60, 61, 169, 372, 509, 512, 520, 570
Dunkirk 398, 400, 417
Dutch, Dr 89, 90
Dyer, Ernest 161–2, 170–71, 199, 200, 203–15, 219–24, 234–39

Eagle, boys' paper 25
Eastaugh, Cyril "Bobby" (worldly clergyman) 231–2, 344, 384, 414, 518, 607, 608, 642, 650, 654
Eastbourne 19, 73
Eaton Hall 433
Eco, Umberto, on Manichaeanism 331
Economic League, The 351, 427
Edward VII 67
Edward VIII 360–61
Edwardian era, Edwardianism 10, 32, 85, 86
Egypt 104, 111, 255, 267, 304, 318, 330, 370, 373, 374, 376, 442, 468, 501, 542, 551, 554; DW visits 370–71
Eight Ages of Justerini's, The (DW) 547
Eldredge, Wentworth 'Went' 384, 440
Elgar, Sir Edward 585
Eliot, T.S. 358; on evil 332; on crime fiction 357
Elizabeth I, Queen 19, 32
Elizabeth II, Queen 293, 366, 440, 470, 484, 604
Elizabeth, Queen, on bombing of Buckingham Palace 407
Elliott, Air Chief Marshal Sir William 420, 543
Ellis, Havelock 111, 170, 233, 256, 373
Elmhirst, Leonard 450
Emert-Kohl, Pia von 78–80
Empire, DW on benefits of 342, 362, 363, 365, 448, 515, 548, 582

683

685

694

revolution 86, 186, 244, 289, 293,
   309, 388, 461, 473; French 86,
   275, 281, 438, 461, 462;
   Russian 245, 365, 547
Richards, Grant, publisher 463
Richards, John, hairdresser 236
Richardson, Freddy 292, 392
Richardson, Maurice, on DW 10;
   on Crowley 299–300
Richelieu (Lytton) 40
Richmond Hill 95
Richmond, Freddy, Duke of 416,
   434, 487, 543
Riddle of the Flying Saucers, The
   (Heard) 487
Riefenstahl, Leni 304
Right Book Club 393
Right Club 348, 351
Rip Kirby (comic strip) 544
Rising Storm, The (DW) 462
Robertson, Admiral Sir
   Brear 413
Robey, George 154
robins 45
Robinson, Robert 601–2
Roedean 18
Rogniski, sword swallower 70
Rohmer, Sax 9, 541
Rokesley School 18
Romeike and Curtis, cuttings
   agency 234
Romeo and Juliet 41
Rommel, Erwin 371
Rothermere, Lord 323, 324, 326,
   343
Rothschild, Baron 84, 93
Roupell Park 32
Roussel, Raymond 489
Royal (story paper) 60
Royal Flying Corps 100, 252
Royal Society of Arts 489
Royal Society of Literature 480–86
Rubaiyat of Omar Khayyam
   (Fitzgerald) 112, 175, 186,
   470

Rubinstein, Hilary 555–56
Rules of Procedure in re B
   (DW) 154–55
Rules, restaurant 418
Rupert of Hentzau (Hope) 42
Ruritania 42, 70, 285, 605
Russell, Bertrand, on need for
   hatred 421
Russia 84, 85, 86, 163, 245, 280,
   284, 285, 286, 287, 323, 324, 330,
   353, 357, 365, 393, 407, 429, 439,
   443, 450, 468, 470, 472, 478, 488,
   499, 587

Sade, Marquis de 111, 275
Sadler, Mr. 46
Sage, Lorna, on *To The Devil – A*
   Daughter 491
Sainsbury, Alan 281
Sainsbury, Doreen 281
Saintsbury Club, The 593
Saintsbury, George 593
Saklatvala, Shapurji 244, 346
Salisbury Plain 102, 105, 107, 113;
   and *The Devil Rides Out* 103
Sampson, Mr, bank
   manager 208–10
Sanders of the River (Wallace) 605
Sanders, Alex 575
Sands, Richard 248
Sanger's Circus 44
Sangorski and Sutcliffe,
   bookbinders 477, 542
Sapper 282, 373
Sarajevo 84, 85, 339
Sardinia 409, 413, 520, 521
Sardonyx fanzine 381
Satan Wants You: The Cult of Devil
   Worship (Lyons) 580
Satanism, historical scarcity of 306,
   312, 460; allegedly in Paris 331,
   329, 332; and Communism 452,
   453, 479; as a materialism 453;
   taboo subject for cinema 560;
   Wheatley style of 9, 12, 302, 303,

697